R25.00

D0260623

THE OXFORD HISTORY
OF ENGLAND

Edited by SIR GEORGE CLARK

THE OXFORD HISTORY OF ENGLAND
Edited by Sir George Clark

THE
AGE OF REFORM
1815–1870

BY

SIR LLEWELLYN WOODWARD, F.B.A.

SECOND EDITION

OXFORD
AT THE CLARENDON PRESS

Oxford University Press, Walton Street, Oxford OX2 6DP

Oxford New York Toronto
Delhi Bombay Calcutta Madras Karachi
Petaling Jaya Singapore Hong Kong Tokyo
Nairobi Dar es Salaam Cape Town
Melbourne Auckland

and associated companies in
Beirut Berlin Ibadan Nicosia

Oxford is a trade mark of Oxford University Press

Published in the United States
by Oxford University Press, New York

ISBN 0 19 821711 0

First published 1938
Second edition 1962
Reprinted 1964, 1967, 1971, 1979, 1985 (three times), 1987

Printed in Great Britain by
Thetford Press Limited
Thetford, Norfolk

PREFACE

I SHOULD like to give particular thanks to four of my friends for their help. Professor G. N. Clark has been a kind and wise guide at every stage. Mr. B. H. Sumner and Mr. R. Pares have read my proofs, to my very great advantage, and Professor E. A. Milne has given me the benefit of his learning and insight in my chapter on 'Movements in the Sciences'.

E. L. W.

July 1938

PREFACE TO SECOND EDITION

IN this second edition I have tried to take account of the work done on nineteenth-century English history by scholars in Great Britain and elsewhere since my volume was published in 1938. The new material listed in the bibliography or mentioned in footnotes shows the emphasis and direction of this recent scholarship. I have therefore made many detailed changes in my text. I have also treated certain subjects, e.g. Anglo-American relations, more fully, but I have not found it necessary to recast the book as a whole or to alter the arrangement of the chapters.

I want to thank Mr. M. G. Brock, Fellow of Corpus Christi College, Oxford, for his great kindness in reading my proofs, correcting a number of errors, and giving me the benefit of his wide knowledge of English history between 1815 and 1870.

LLEWELLYN WOODWARD

Princeton—Oxford 1961

CONTENTS

II. MONARCHY, MINISTERS, AND PARTIES, 1832–46
THE AGE OF MELBOURNE AND PEEL

Book II. ENGLAND AND EUROPE

I. FOREIGN POLICY, 1815–29; CASTLEREAGH, CANNING, AND WELLINGTON

II. THE FOREIGN POLICY OF PALMERSTON, 1830–41; THE *ENTENTE* WITH FRANCE, 1841–6; PALMERSTON AND THE CROWN, 1848–52

III. THE EASTERN QUESTION, 1841–54, AND THE CRIMEAN WAR

II. THE COLONIES

III. INDIA

Book IV. THE AGE OF REFORM

I. THE ORGANIZATION OF A CIVILIZED SOCIAL LIFE

II. EDUCATION, 1815–70

III. RELIGION AND THE CHURCHES

IV. ENGLISH LITERATURE AND THE DEVELOPMENT OF IDEAS

V. MOVEMENTS IN THE SCIENCES AND ARTS

VI. THE CONDITION OF THE PEOPLE, 1850–70

LIST OF MAPS

(at end)

1. The canals of England and Wales, from Smith's Map of Inland Navigation corrected to June 1810.

2. The British railway system, from Cheffins's Map of the English and Scotch Railways, 1847.

3. Crimea, 1855. After Sir John Fortescue's *History of the British Army*, volume xiii (maps and plans), by permission of Macmillan & Co., Ltd.

4. British North America, 1849. From the Atlas of the Society for the Diffusion of Useful Knowledge.

5. South Africa, 1849. From the Atlas of the Society for the Diffusion of Useful Knowledge.

6. India, 1857.

ENGLAND IN 1815

Early on a September morning, in the second year of the nineteenth century, William Wordsworth saw the 'mighty heart' of London from Westminster Bridge,

> silent, bare,
> Ships, towers, domes, theatres, and temples lie,
> Open unto the fields, and to the sky;
> All bright and glittering in the smokeless air.

Although for many years to come it was still possible to begin a walk through parkland and open country from the north end of Portland Place, London at the time of Wordsworth's death in 1850 had taken in field after field on the northern and southern slopes, and had more than doubled its population.[1] This increase in population was general. The census figures were 12,000,000 in 1811, over 14,000,000 in 1821, 16,500,000 in 1831, and, in 1851, over 21,000,000. The causes of the increase were not clear to contemporaries and indeed are still in doubt.[2] Many people thought that the employment of children in cotton mills, and subsidies paid out of the rates to agricultural labourers, encouraged improvident marriages and large families. These guesses were not altogether wrong, but they did not account for more than a fraction of the increase. Subsidies in aid of wages were unknown in Scotland, and never universal in England. Even in 1830 only about one-eightieth of the people of Great Britain worked in cotton factories. In any case, the number of births per thousand of the population, though greater than in the first half of the eighteenth century, appears to have fallen a little after the decade 1780–90; it then remained fairly stable until another fall took place after 1830.

One reason for the rise in numbers after 1760 appears certain. In comparison with the fearful infant mortality rates of earlier centuries a smaller proportion of children now died at birth or before their sixth year. The saving of life also explains why the

---

[1] The figures are: 1801, 960,000, and 1851, 2,400,000.

[2] For a summary of recent hypotheses, see E. F. Habbakuk, 'The economic history of modern Britain', *Journal of Economic History*, vol. xviii (Dec. 1958).

population increased in those decades when there was a fall in
the birth-rate. At the same time the birth-rate fell because the
economic checks on family increase operated more strongly
when more children survived, and the survival of a larger
number of children brought more competition in the labour
market, and hence delayed the age of marriage.[1] There were
fewer deaths in childhood or early youth and middle age
because people were better fed, better clothed, more temperate
in their habits than in the days of cheap gin, and less likely to
catch diseases like smallpox which had been endemic in earlier
times. These changes affected the towns, bad as they were, as
well as the country. The rise in the death-rate after 1820 was
probably due to the larger numbers suffering from the bad
urban conditions, but the expectation of life continued to be
greater than at any time in the eighteenth century. The average
length of life in London was longer than in Paris, or than in
rural Prussia.

The growth of the towns must not be exaggerated, though it
was one of the most important features of the age. Sixteen years
after Waterloo one-quarter of the families of Great Britain
lived by work on the land, and another quarter by the trades
and industries which served countrymen. If a worker in a rural
area might be employed in a coal-mine or a cotton mill, many
of the urban areas still possessed that *summa rusticitas* which
Erasmus had noticed centuries earlier as one of the features
of English towns. Liverpool had grown from 82,000 in 1801 to
202,000 in 1831, and Leeds from 53,000 to 123,000. Sheffield
and Birmingham doubled in size during the same period;
Manchester and Salford increased from 95,000 to 238,000 and
Glasgow from 77,000 to 193,000. The new population of these
cities, including London, came largely from neighbouring counties,[2] but there was also an important movement of population
from Ireland, and the absorption of the Irish immigrants,
with their low standard of life, became one of the social and
economic problems of the early nineteenth century.[3] Within
twenty years after 1815 there were 100,000 Irish in Lancashire

----

[1] Methods of birth-control as a deliberate means of checking population were
widely advertised after about 1823; Francis Place (see below, p. 73) was among
those responsible for propaganda on the subject, but for a long time the general
effect of this propaganda was very small.

[2] See A. Redford, *Labour Migration in England, 1800–50*.

[3] The problem was not solved in 1870. See below, p. 601.

alone. The Irish did not go only to the cotton districts and the west of England or Scotland. They found their way to agricultural work in Essex; one-third of 2,000 beggars counted in London in 1815 were Irish. They were an important element in the population of Edinburgh as well as of Glasgow, where they competed with immigrants from the highlands of Scotland.

Most townsmen were following trades or occupations with which Englishmen had been long familiar. In 1829 there were more tailors and bootmakers in London than there were men and boys in Northumberland and Durham mining one-quarter of the English and Welsh coal-supply. The number of women and girls in domestic service at the accession of Queen Victoria was far greater than the number employed in cotton mills. The building trades were the largest single group in the country, and for many years after 1815 Barclay's brewery was one of the sights of London for those who wanted to look at a large-scale, power-driven industry. The old English words 'master' and 'servant' were still in common use to describe the relation between employer and employed; Robert Owen spoke of the 'working-class' in 1813, but Brougham was the first to bring the term into ordinary speech. As late as 1825 a writer in *Blackwood's Magazine* protested against the newfangled word 'operatives, as if they were so many doses of glauber salts'.[1] Nevertheless, if the 'typical town worker of the decade 1820–30 was very far indeed from being a person who performed for a self-made employer in steaming air, with the aid of recently devised mechanism, operations which would have made his grandfather gape',[2] and if he were not normally attached to a large business, the tendency of the time was for businesses to increase in size, and for mechanical power to provide rapidly increasing means of large-scale production. This transformation has been described as an industrial revolution, lasting, roughly, from 1750 to 1850. It was not concerned merely with industry, and the 'revolution' in productive technique is not

---

[1] Coleridge used the term in 1809–10 to describe 'operatives in science, literature, and the learned professions'; Southey wrote, in 1824, of the 'active . . . or the operative clergy'. The older term 'hand' was more commonly used on ships. The term 'factory' also took on a new meaning. Until the latter part of the eighteenth century it meant, primarily, a warehouse or depot established for merchants and traders—'factors'—in a foreign country, e.g. the English 'factories' in India. The early 'factories' in the modern sense were called mills because their most prominent feature was a great water-wheel.

[2] Sir J. Clapham, *Economic History of Modern Britain*, i. 74.

yet over,[1] while the changes could not have taken place on a large scale if there had not been corresponding progress in agriculture, in methods of transport, in the organization of trade and the diffusion of credit. In 1815 French or Swedish roads and Dutch waterways were as good as those of Great Britain; in the combined development of means of transport England was pre-eminent even before the building of railways. The English, Welsh, and Scottish main roads were being re-made by McAdam[2] and Telford;[3] there were 'flying' coaches on the roads before the days of 'express' trains. The canal system was nearly complete, and the canals had lowered the cost of inland transport by about 75 per cent.; machinery, minerals, or heavy goods could not have been carried in bulk without them.[4] Similarly, the capital expenditure upon the new machines, and upon the manufacture of goods for distant markets, would have been impossible without a highly developed system of banking. The migration of inventors from Scotland to England was due largely to the greater ease of getting capital in England.

The new inventions worked, as it were, cumulatively to speed up the rate of change. The use of coal increased the output of iron; a larger output of iron cheapened the cost of machinery, and cheaper machines lessened the expense of coal-mining. The cotton industry made the greatest use of the new inventions. This industry had been early organized on a capitalistic basis owing to the need for large quantities of raw material. The first steam-loom in Manchester was set up in 1806, and within

[1] See Sir G. N. Clark, *The Idea of the Industrial Revolution* (1953). See also below, p. 5, note 3.

[2] John Loudon McAdam (1756–1836), s. of a banker, b. Ayr; brought up by an uncle in New York; came back to Scotland, 1785; magistrate, road trustee, and D.L. for Ayrshire, agent for revictualling the navy in the western ports, 1798; surveyor-general of the Bristol roads, 1815; published works on road-making, 1819–20; surveyor-general of roads, 1827; between 1798 and 1814 he had travelled over 30,000 miles of roads, in 2,000 days, and spent large sums of money on experiments in road-making.

[3] Thomas Telford (1757–1834), s. of a Dumfriesshire shepherd; apprenticed as a mason, 1772, moved to Edinburgh, 1780, and London, 1782; engineer of the Ellesmere and Caledonian canals, and director of road and bridge building and harbour improvement in Scotland, 1803; built the Shrewsbury–Holyhead road, with the Menai suspension bridge, 1814–25; one of the founders of the Institute of Civil Engineers, 1818. Telford was much interested in literature, wrote poems, and became a friend of Southey. He cared so little for money, and charged so little for his professional advice, that a representative body of engineers is said to have expostulated with him on the subject. [4] See also below, p. 47.

twelve years there were about 2,000 steam-driven looms; five years later the number in Great Britain had increased about fivefold, and in 1835 there were about 85,000 power-looms in England, and 15,000 in Scotland. The woollen industry was less centralized, and changed less quickly; steam-power was not much employed until 1830. In the metal industries the demand for munitions during the Revolutionary and Napoleonic wars led to the general adoption of coke in blast furnaces; there were uses enough for iron when the demand for guns ceased. The machine-making industry developed during the twenty-five years before 1815, and with the inventions of Bramah,[1] Maudslay,[2] and Roberts the modern engineer and the engineering firm came into existence, though the invention of machine tools tended ultimately to diminish the advantages of English manufacturers over their continental rivals.[3] These new engineering firms worked on a small scale; in 1824–5 Bramah's employed about a hundred men, and there were not many firms with a larger business. Shipbuilding was more advanced; even so in 1832, 389 out of 708 ships built in Great Britain were less than 100 tons, and only 40 were above 300 tons; the largest shipyard on the Thames in 1825 employed no more than 700 workmen when at full pressure of work. Few of the cutlery or hardware firms used steam-power in 1815, and the steam-driven printing-press was an innovation in 1814.

The changes in technique, though slow until the coming of the railway, were fast enough to cause distress among workmen thrown out of employment by the new machines. The distress among the handloom weavers was soon to be one of the grimmest features of English working-class life, or rather, of working-

[1] Joseph Bramah (1748–1814), s. of a farmer, b. nr. Barnsley; apprenticed to a village carpenter; set up for himself after working for a London cabinet-maker; patented the modern form of water-closet, 1778; invented a lock which was not picked until 1851; devised a planing machine, and, with Maudslay, a hydraulic press. One of Bramah's inventions was the 'pull-over' tap used in public houses.

[2] Henry Maudslay (1771–1831), s. of a Yorkshireman who became an artificer at Woolwich Arsenal, b. Woolwich; in Bramah's employment, 1789; started his own business in Marylebone, 1798; invented a screw-cutting lathe, a measuring machine, and the slide-rest. His pupils included Joseph Whitworth and James Nasmyth; two of his sons developed the marine-engineering side of their father's business, and built in 1841–2 the first screw-steamer used in the British navy.

[3] The automatic reproduction of these tools was, in fact, a 'revolution'. There had been very little increase in the variety or accuracy of machine tools from the end of the middle ages until the last quarter of the eighteenth century. Between that time and 1850 practically all the more important modern tools were invented.

class life in England, since a large number of the handloom workers were Irish immigrants;[1] yet in 1815 there was still an overwhelming majority of handloom weavers. Twenty years later the number of handloom cotton workers was still about 200,000; their wages had fallen during this period by about a half or two-thirds.

New methods of selling were coming in with the increase in the size and output of firms. Once again the rate of change must not be exaggerated. In retail trade the small shops of the nation of shopkeepers had taken the place of the pedlar and of the fair, at least as a centre for buying and selling non-perishable goods. The shop was supplied by the commercial traveller, with his samples and printed catalogue. These printed or engraved lists were not entirely new; before the French Revolution Wedgwood published lists with engraved examples of his wares. Even in foodstuffs large-scale organizations were developing. The new roads and the increasing size of the towns led to the establishment of capitalistic dairies. The potato business had grown up in the eighteenth century; there was a long-standing wholesale trade in salted butter, and the sale of coal, beer, and corn, among the staple necessities of life, had already made the fortunes of a good many English families.

The coal-trade in coastal ships was greater in tonnage in 1815 than the whole foreign trade of the country. This foreign trade was mainly, though not entirely, in valuable goods of comparatively small bulk. Timber was the most important exception. The demands of the navy, and of house-builders, had caused a shortage of English wood; between 1820 and 1830 almost a third of the tonnage discharging at the harbours of the United Kingdom from foreign ports brought loads of American or Baltic timber. There was also a growing import of raw cotton. The quantity rose from about 50,000 tons in 1815 to 100,000 tons in 1825, when the American crop had begun to dominate the market. During the reign of George IV about 220,000 tons of sugar were imported annually; a third of it was re-exported. In 1825 the average annual consumption of coffee was under a

---

[1] The English weavers, therefore, had to meet the double competition of the power-looms and of the immigrants. The weavers' children were 'caught up' in the industry, since their parents put them to it early in order to increase the family earnings. For the misery of the handloom weavers see the reports of commissioners in *Parliamentary Papers*, 1839, vol. xlii, 1840, vols. xxiii and xxiv, 1841, vol. x, and 1845, vol. xv, *Report on the Condition of the Framework Knitters*.

pound per head, and of tea about a pound and a quarter per head of the British population. On the other hand, though the imports of wine showed that the people as a whole were not wine-drinking, the import of spirits, mainly West Indian rum and French brandy, was very large; 2,000,000 gallons of rum and 1,300,000 gallons of brandy paid duty in 1825, and about another 500,000 gallons of brandy were smuggled into the country.[1] Flax, hemp, wool, tobacco, and, in some years, grain and flour were the other notable imports. Few manufactures, other than French silks and a certain amount of fancy fabrics, gloves, and mirrors, came into British ports.

These commodities were exchanged for manufactured goods or re-exported 'colonial' products, or paid out of the foreign earnings of British merchant shipping, the services to foreigners rendered by British banks or technicians, and increasingly, though not as yet to a very large extent, by the interest on British investments abroad.[2] Ships were too small in 1815 to make the export of coal to distant ports a profitable undertaking, and until the coming of the railway there was no great demand in foreign countries. Five years after Waterloo, when the export of produce of the United Kingdom was valued at £36,000,000,[3] nearly one-half of the exports were cotton goods and yarn. Woollen fabrics, the main export of the eighteenth century, were now far less important; the figures for 1820 were £5,500,000; throughout the third decade of the century they did not rise above £6,500,000. In 1820 the value of the iron and steel exports was about one-sixteenth that of cotton goods and yarn; in 1840 the fraction was about a tenth. The export of machinery except under licence was forbidden until 1843, but evasion was easy, and models, drawings, or machine-tools, owing to the conservatism of customs officials, did not count as machinery.

The United States was still the largest single customer of

[1] The French authorities did not assist British revenue officers in the prevention of smuggling. Public opinion in the early years of the nineteenth century still considered smugglers, in Charles Lamb's words, as 'honest thieves', who robbed 'nothing but the revenue, an abstraction I never greatly cared about' (*The Old Margate Hoy*).

[2] Estimates of the British balance of trade and investments abroad during the first half of the nineteenth century are difficult and intricate. For a recent statement, and a criticism of earlier estimates, see A. H. Imlah, *Economic Elements in the Pax Britannica: Studies in British Foreign Trade in the Nineteenth Century* (1958).

[3] These figures must be taken as approximate; see ibid., ch. ii.

Great Britain outside the British Empire, though after about 1835 the Germanic Confederation, Holland, and Belgium took the first place for some ten years, when the United States once more outdistanced them. This trade was carried on mainly by private merchants. The East India Company, a magnificent survivor of the old trading companies, still kept a monopoly of the trade with China; on the renewal of the charter in 1813 the Company had been compelled to open their ports and stations east of the Cape of Good Hope and west of the straits of Magellan. A complicated system of licences remained in force for Indian ports, but these restrictions did not hinder well-established private merchants. The navigation laws, which belonged to an older policy of state, and to a period when America was merely the colonial territory of European Powers, still limited freedom of shipping. The chief products of British colonies and of non-European countries except the United States could be shipped only in British ships;[1] the goods of European countries could be imported only in British ships or in ships of the country of origin. The laws excluded foreign ships from the coastal trade, and, in order to give British shipping the advantage of long-distance traffic, restricted the number of non-European commodities which could be brought from European ports even in British ships. There were also differential dues on the 'legal' cargoes of foreign ships; in 1815 the principle of reciprocity was conceded only to the United States.

The people of Great Britain, chiefly engaged in the cultivation of the soil, in small industries, or in the business of retail trade and domestic craftsmanship, lived in a country ditched, inclosed, and drained to an extent which would have astonished their great-grandfathers. There was little inclosure of waste land after 1820 outside Wales, the West and North Ridings, Cumberland, and Westmorland. In the English lowlands the commons were, roughly, as they are to-day. Inclosure of the open fields had also been carried out before 1815 over most of the country. There were in 1820 only six English counties— three of them in the Midlands—with more than 3 per cent. of inclosures to be completed; in Oxfordshire and Cambridgeshire alone the old common fields formed a considerable part of the

---

[1] This term included ships of British colonies.

cultivated land. There had been similar, and even more rapid, inclosures in Scotland. The inclosure movement had increased the amount of land in the hands of the upper and wealthy classes; the more enterprising small freeholders became large farmers, the weaker and poorer men sank into the status of labourers at a time when, owing to the increase in the rural population, there was already a drift of the labouring class into the towns.[1] The dislocation had not been universal, even where inclosures were most widespread; about 1830 roughly one-fifth of English land was cultivated by its owners. On the other hand, Arthur Young pointed out, rightly, that in nineteen out of twenty inclosure acts the poor were injured, 'in some cases grossly injured'. The compensation for a small holding was only a few pounds, or a piece of land costly to fence and too small for grazing. The labouring families, in areas of recent and considerable inclosure, lost their customary privileges of stubbling on open fields or putting a beast on the commons. The loss of fuel was also a hardship at a time when timber was scarce.[2] In any case, high prices and bad harvests during some of the war years made the period before 1815 dismal for the poor. The diet of most labouring families was bread[3] and cheese for six out of seven days of the week, though some labourers kept a pig, and many had small gardens. It is difficult enough, on these low standards, to make any comparison with earlier times. On the whole, taking into account all sources of income, the average labourer was probably not worse off in the ten or twenty years after 1815 than he had been in 1790, and certainly better off than in the terrible years at the beginning of the century; yet, if in some counties the labourer's humble fortune improved, there were others in which his wages had fallen, and subsidies from the poor rate just kept him from starvation. These subsidized areas included the East and North Ridings of Yorkshire, East Anglia, the home counties, and southern England as far west as Wiltshire; relief was also given in most parishes elsewhere, in cases of large families, sickness, or temporary misfortune. Foreign observers generally noticed a higher standard than that of the peasantry in most European countries, and a difference

[1] For the inclosure movement before 1815, see vol. xii of this *History*, pp. 520–1.
[2] For the timber shortage generally, see also vol. xii of this *History*, p. 522.
[3] Wheaten bread; barley, oats, and rye had almost ceased to be used for bread before 1815.

particularly in favour of the south and east of England, where
the poor rate was used most freely to supplement wages.

It is as difficult to generalize about housing as about other
conditions of living. South of the Thames the labourers' cottages were mainly brick-built or half-timbered; about half of
them were three-roomed. The north of England had lower
housing standards. In Scotland turf hovels were still common
in the north-west, and the one-room cottage was general in
the lowlands. Owing to the shortage of fuel, the labourers in
districts away from the coalfields probably suffered more from
damp floors and walls and the lack of hot food and drink than
from overcrowding. On the other hand, improvements in land
drainage had begun to remove the agues and fevers which had
been endemic in low-lying regions. The town labourer was no
better housed than the countryman. Every old city had its
slums, and the new houses run up by jerry-builders[1] were as
unhealthy as they were drab. The housing problem was not a
new one, though rapid increase and greater mobility of the
population made it more serious. Dirt and stench had always
been the normal features of towns, and, in spite of the improvements which had begun in the latter half of the eighteenth century, until cheap pipes and mains were devised to bring water
to the newly invented water-closets and to carry away sewage,
and traps and gullies were invented by the sanitary engineers,
the condition of the poorer quarters of cities remained bad.[2]
There was, in Mill's words, 'a certain order of possible progress'. Moreover the relation between dirt and disease was not
fully understood before the discovery of the transmission of infection by germs.[3] It would be unfair to judge the houses of all
by the cellar dwellings which existed in almost every town;
there were 20,000 of them in Manchester as late as 1832, the
last refuges of Irish immigrants and the victims of declining
industries. A working man of good standing lived in a house
with three or four rooms and a kitchen, and on the whole the
standard was rising with the extension of the skilled trades.

[1] The term belongs to the second half of the century. The distinction between
good and bad building, as far as the houses of the poor were concerned, is perhaps
a sign of rising standards.

[2] Doulton's manufacture of cheap glazed earthenware pipes began in 1846.

[3] The theory of the transmission of disease by minute living organisms was not
new, but until the improvement in the microscope it could be little more than a
lucky guess or a rough deduction from facts observed in the large.

This variation between the well-paid and the starved makes it almost impossible to strike an average wage which is not misleading. The middle figure hides the miserable and the prosperous. Statistical attempts to find an average of wages, based mainly upon thirty industries distributed over twenty-four towns and coal-fields, show that, if the year 1790 be taken as 100, there was a rise to 169·4 in the latter years of the war, followed by a gradual fall over a period of years from 160 in 1816 to 137·4 in 1845, broken by a slight rise between 1820 and 1824. To a certain extent wages suffered from the employers' habit of putting a large proportion of profits back into their businesses; in other words, the workers bore too much of the burden of providing capital for industrialization, but, if they were paid lower money wages in order to provide for an expanding trade, they gained from the fall in prices and increase in employment resulting from this expansion. The gain was slow. Food prices fell from 1814 to about 1821–2, when it is probable that the cost of the standard diet of a working-class family was much what it had been in 1790. After 1821–2 food prices rose again by rather more than 10 per cent., though, from 1815 onwards, taking all in all, there was some improvement in housing, and textiles, that is to say clothes, were cheaper. Here again the statistical evidence is incomplete and doubtful, since, apart from sharp rises or falls according to the condition of trade and the character of the harvests, local variations—both of wages and prices—were much greater than in later years.[1] After 1840 there was another fall in the cost of living: from 1842, except in the bad years 1846–7, prices were below the levels of 1790. Thus from about 1820 wage-earners in employment are likely to have lived in most years as well as, or better than, their fathers or grandfathers in the last years of peace. Even this conclusion is uncertain, and, if it be correct, does not give reason for complacency. Furthermore, although in the long run factories brought greater regu-

---

[1] The work of economic historians and statisticians in this field during the last twenty years has been remarkable for its originality and thoroughness, but, as in other branches of English history, the result of greater precision in method has been for the time at least to cast doubt upon earlier conclusions rather than to substitute 'firm generalizations'. 'Optimistic' and 'pessimistic' views (in each case, only relative) of working-class standards of living are well set out, respectively, by T. S. Ashton, 'The Standard of Life of the Workers in England, 1790–1830' (Supplement IX to the *Journal of Economic History*, 1949, pp. 19–38) and E. J. Hobsbawm, 'The British Standard of Living, 1790–1850' (*Economic History Review*, 2nd ser., vol. x, No. 1, 1957, pp. 46–68).

larity of work, the new industries were subject to periods of unemployment against which the worker had no protection. There were also large numbers of unskilled or partially skilled labourers who had gained nothing from the general rise, if rise there were, in prosperity; the fate of the thousands of handloom weavers, and of others whose humble skills lost their economic value, was harsh beyond tears.

For those who had been disinherited of their skill by the new machines life was a long and losing fight against starvation; the more fortunate working men who had enough to eat did not often live in conditions which made for happiness. Country people worked, according to their tasks, while daylight lasted— only at curfew, in the words of Gray's *Elegy*, 'the plowman homeward plods his weary way'—but the work was done under conditions which gave some scope at least to the practical imagination, even if its endless repetitions, its total lack of diversion or chance of betterment through education, must have been deeply depressing to a minority above the general intellectual level. The town worker also had to endure very long hours of labour; in most cases his employer shared them. Craftsmen in their homes had always worked a full day, and so had their children,[1] often in conditions worse than the overcharged air of cotton mills. Factories were not adding to the burden of occupied time, but their discipline and regularity were a greater strain on the workers; the Belfast weavers called factories 'lockups'.[2] Moreover the night shift, which became more common after the introduction of better artificial light, was an innovation. The first limitations of this tyranny of the machine were made in the case of children. An act of 1802 safeguarding the interests of poor-law apprentices in factories limited the daily work of these children to twelve hours. With the development of steam-power, the mills were moved from remote watercourses to the neighbourhood of towns where there was a supply of 'free' children, and pauper apprentices were no longer needed.

[1] Child labour was universal in agriculture, and remained so until the enforcement of elementary education in 1870. Some of the work done by children was too hard, but much of it—such as bird-scaring or cattle-watching—was not in itself arduous. The work was mainly out of doors, though its open-air healthiness was less than it might have been owing to the poor diet and clothing of most children.

[2] R. B. McDowell, in *The Great Famine*, ed. R. Dudley Edwards and T. Desmond Williams, p. 15. Discipline rather than monotony was the hated feature of factory work. Not all machine work was uninteresting, and in some industries it lessened the amount of severe physical exertion.

In 1815 the elder Sir Robert Peel proposed the extension of the act of 1802 to 'free' children. After long discussion about the number of hours which a child of nine or ten could be expected to spend at work in the bad atmosphere of a cotton mill, the house of commons agreed in 1818 to fix a limit of eleven hours a day. Robert Owen[1] had shown that it was possible to make a fortune out of cotton-spinning without employing any child under ten, but the house of lords thought otherwise, and postponed the bill. It was reintroduced in 1819, and passed with a limit of twelve hours a day, exclusive of meal-times, for children between the ages of nine and sixteen; the employment of children under nine was forbidden. The act applied only to cotton mills, and did not provide for supervision by inspectors, although it was clear that haphazard inspection by the justices had been useless in the case of the act of 1802. Hence the act was largely evaded. There was no attempt to regulate the hours of adults, or the conditions of child labour elsewhere than in cotton mills.[2]

The act of 1819, for all its shortcomings, was a reform of great importance. The innovation lay not in the employment of children for eleven and twelve hours a day, but in the recognition of the principle that any limit need be laid down or that parliament had a right to interfere with the discretion of parents. Moreover the general view was not that the working poor needed leisure, but that leisure was a snare and a danger. When Robert Owen told a parliamentary commission that he thought it unnecessary for children under ten to work in the mills, he was asked: 'Would there not be a danger of their acquiring vicious habits for want of a regular occupation?' This idea was vaguely prevalent for another thirty years. It had indeed some grim justification. If the townspeople of Great Britain had been given more leisure, there would have been little chance of enjoying it in the larger cities. As late as 1844 Preston was the only town in Lancashire with a public park. Sheffield, in 1833, was 'singularly destitute' of open spaces. A committee appointed in 1833 to consider the lack of 'public walks and places of exercise' in towns reported that 'as respects those employed in the three great Manufactures of the Kingdom, Cotton, Woollen, and Hardware, creating annually an immense Property, no provision has been made to afford them the means of healthy

[1] See below, p. 131.
[2] There is a good engraving of a child at work in a cotton mill in E. Baines, *History of the Cotton Manufacture* (1835), p. 182.

exercise or cheerful amusement with their families on their Holidays, or days of rest'. Accidie, and the *dégoût de la vie*, are not often killing diseases, but lives may be dragged on as well as cut short; the 'loss of common enjoyment'[1] must have been particularly irksome, as well as physically unhealthy, to a population drawn largely from the country, and with a tradition of rough field sports. Religion offered no way of escape for the majority. The established church and the protestant sects were afraid of ritual and ceremonial. The Methodists were fortunate in the musical talent of the Wesleys; elsewhere church music was almost at its lowest ebb. In any case the very poor had not good enough clothes for attendance at church or chapel. There was no more chance of recreation for the mind than for the body. Few cities had public libraries, and the serious theatre, in the towns where it existed,[2] was out of reach of the labouring poor. Public picture-galleries were rare; the great patrons and collectors kept their works of art in their private houses. Music was more popular, but there were no chances of hearing good concerts at cheap prices. The houses of the poor in large cities did not often have gardens, and the provision of allotments was difficult in crowded areas. Education gave few ways of escape from the drabness of life. The technique of elementary education was almost unknown, and there was not much to choose between the education of the rich and of the poor, if one judged by modern standards; but the rich and the well-to-do at least sent their sons to school, and kept them at school, while Sunday schools, dames' schools, and the education provided for the poor by the two anglican and nonconformist religious societies did not touch more than a small number of children.[3] As late as 1839 33·7 per cent. of the men and 49·5 per cent. of the women married in church could not sign their names in the marriage register. After 1824 there was a considerable movement for the foundation of Mechanics' Institutes, where adult working men could obtain some form of instruction. Here again, the methods of teaching were unsuitable. The pioneers of working-class education too often 'confounded a knowledge of useful things with useful knowledge',[4] and the ordinary working man had

---

[1] The term is used by J. L. and B. Hammond.
[2] See below, pp. 559–60.   [3] See below, p. 478.
[4] W. Bagehot, *Biographical Studies*, p. 81 (quoting Hazlitt). See also below, pp. 494–5.

neither the background nor the leisure to gain much from lectures on subjects mainly out of his reach.

The town and country labourers who made up the majority of the English people had little political organization of their own, and no means of stating their case, except by the cumbersome method of petition to parliament, even if they had known any remedy for their misfortunes. In a few open boroughs[1] they could give a clouded opinion by their votes, but the time of party programmes and election pledges had not yet come, and from a working-class point of view there was little to choose between whigs and tories. Before the development of statistical and parliamentary inquiry, the middle and upper classes did not even know the extent of social evils; otherwise good men like Wilberforce would have been more impressed by the misery at their doors. Public opinion, even the opinion of the poor, did not expect government to cure poverty. No one had the idea of public expenditure on a large scale for purposes of social betterment. The expenditure of money meant jobbery, and might give too much power to the executive. Castlereagh described the refusal of parliament in 1816 to continue the property tax (in modern terms, the income tax) as 'an ignorant impatience' of taxation, but Castlereagh himself would not have spent a penny of the tax on public purposes outside the old-established functions of government. The whigs were even more timid. Lord John Russell said that there could be 'no more dreadful calamity for this country' than the continuance of a tax which would allow the Crown, with the help of a standing army, 'to erase even the vestiges . . . of departing liberty'.[2]

A French observer wrote in 1810 that Englishmen 'seem to think that liberty consists full as much in having made, or assisted to make, the laws as in enjoying their protection'.[3] At the same time it is possible to exaggerate the opposition to the interference of the state in economic questions other than those connected with the revenue or the protection of national interests. The expenditure of a large sum of public money in compensating slave-owners might have been explained as consistent with *laisser faire* on the ground that slaves were not free agents, but at all

---

[1] See below, p. 25.　　　　　　　　　　[2] Hansard, xxxii, 33 and 843.
[3] *Journal of a Tour and Residence in Great Britain during 1810 and 1811 by a French Traveller*, L. Simond, 1815. Quoted in W. Smart, *Economic Annals of the Nineteenth Century*, i. 308–9.

events the money was spent on carrying out a measure of social improvement. A distinction was drawn early in the nineteenth century between interference with industry as a matter of general policy and special action to prevent particular evils. Howick[1] put this point clearly in the debates on the factory act of 1844. 'There is an important distinction between restrictions imposed upon industry with the visionary hope of increasing the nation's wealth, or with the unjust design of taxing one class for the benefit of another, and those of which the aim is to guard against evils, moral or physical, which it is apprehended that the absence of such precautions might entail upon the people.'[2] A great deal of the talk about *laisser faire* must be discounted, or at least put into its proper context. In many cases the argument concealed an admission that a problem was insoluble, or that it must be endured because no one could think of any method of solving it. From this point of view, the policy of *laisser faire* was not the result of a new and optimistic belief in the progress of society through private enterprise. It was rather an acknowledgement that the fund of skill and experience at the service of society was limited, and that in the management of their common affairs men would not be able to find the elasticity and adaptiveness which individuals showed in devising schemes for their own self-interest. The treatment of social and economic questions was more haphazard and empirical than Englishmen were ready to acknowledge. If a practical solution suggested itself, if a tentative experiment could be made, the doctrine of *laisser faire* would be thrust aside, only to be used again after another failure to discover the way out of a difficulty.[3]

These failures were common. The governing class was not altogether to blame for them. If the magnitude of social evil and the weight of misery had been generally realized, and the grievances of the poor tabulated and examined in a clear and orderly way, the governments of the early years of the nineteenth century would have had no effective means of dealing with them.

---

[1] For Viscount Howick (later 3rd Earl Grey), see below, p. 270, note 3.

[2] Hansard, 3rd ser. lxxiv. 643. For the attitude of political economists towards *laisser faire*, see also below, pp. 445–6.

[3] Lord Morpeth, in proposing railway construction at government expense in Ireland, told the house of commons in March 1839 that 'the course which is perfectly consistent with true political economy' might not be the same in Ireland as in England. R. B. McDowell, op. cit., p. 18. See also below, p. 348.

Material progress had long outrun administrative order. The simple legislative barriers against economic oppression and the earlier safeguards of the standard of life of the poor had broken down. There were no properly constituted bodies to provide a substitute for the older mechanism of state regulation.[1] The civil service was small in numbers, limited in function to the executive work of the great departments, and recruited entirely by patronage. It is a curious fact that the first attempt to secure a choice of men properly qualified for administrative work was made in connexion with the government of India, as an indirect result of public feeling over the trial of Warren Hastings. In 1800 Lord Wellesley suggested the establishment of a college in India for training the servants of the Company. Six years later a college at Hertford, moved in 1809 to Haileybury, was founded for this purpose. When the charter of the Company came up for renewal in 1813 Grenville suggested that candidates should be chosen after public examination. The idea was too new for acceptance, but the Company agreed to lay down a rule that all candidates for administrative appointments should spend not less than four years at Haileybury.[2] No arrangements of this kind were tried on a large scale in the English civil service for forty years after 1815, though between 1834 and 1841 a few departments instituted easy qualifying examinations. As early as 1833 the lord-lieutenant of Ireland ordered that county surveyors should be chosen by competitive examination; Ireland was not England, and surveying was a technical subject. The easy ways of the English service may be seen from Trollope's account of his own work in the post office after his nomination to a clerkship in 1834, while the amount of leisure time enjoyed, for two generations, by the family of Mill in the service of the East India Company shows the slow pace of the administrative machine.[3]

The development of a higher standard of professional competence was one of the greatest needs of the age. Outside the

---

[1] See below, pp. 444–73.

[2] An act of 1833 laid down that the directors should nominate candidates in a proportion of not less than four to every vacancy. The directors disliked any diminution in their rights of patronage, and in 1834 persuaded the president of the board of control to allow them to postpone the operation of these rules.

[3] The Company, which allowed its clerks free tea, found it necessary in 1757 to forbid the use of it after 10 a.m. C. R. Fay, *Great Britain from Adam Smith to the Present Day*, p. 133.

service of the Crown, the law, the church, and medicine offered
the only professional careers which carried a good social status.
Of these three professions, the church did not require much
technical knowledge; the more important and lucrative posts
in its hierarchy were generally given to persons of family or
to their friends and clients, and the standard of duty in the
performance of the customary ecclesiastical work, though not
scandalously low, was none too high. The legal profession was
caught, like the law itself, in a net of vested interests, formalism,
and pedantry. During the eighteenth century the decline in
intellectual level of the inns of court had been more serious
even than the decline of higher study in the universities. The
legal corporations did not reform themselves until the middle
years of the nineteenth century, and the lawyers, as a body,
were perhaps the greatest obstacle to the reform of the law.

The doctors were hardly less conservative. The Royal College
of Physicians, one of the creations of the English renaissance,
recruited its members almost entirely from Oxford and Cambridge, and did little or nothing for medical education. In
1834 there were only 113 fellows and 274 licentiates of the
college. The raising of professional standards came from the
lower ranks. Surgery had broken away from its association
with barbers largely through the work of a number of able
surgeons in the eighteenth century. The Royal College of Surgeons, founded in 1800, had in 1834 a membership of about
200 fellows and 8,000 licentiates. Most of the licentiates were
apothecaries who had taken the examinations of the college.
The status of apothecaries was low; they charged for their
drugs and not for their services, and tended to rank as small
traders. They tried to improve the standard of their occupation
by excluding unqualified persons. They persuaded parliament
in 1815 to pass a bill giving power to the Society of Apothecaries
to examine all apothecaries in England and Wales. The act
was carefully enforced, and led indirectly to the modern system
of medical education. The society required five years' apprenticeship before examination; the custom of 'walking the hospitals', as a supplement to apprenticeship, had already begun,
and the act of 1815 gave an opening for private medical schools.
The hospitals now organized schools of their own, beginning
with the school attached to University College, London, soon
after its foundation. These schools took the place of appren-

ticeship, and sent out a number of 'practitioners' who were relatively well educated and well trained, though inferior in social rank to the physicians and surgeons. Fifteen years after the passing of the act the term 'general practitioner' came into use. Many of the improvements in public health were due to these efforts of the apothecaries to justify their claim to a higher professional standing by offering services of greater value.

The architects had already freed themselves from dependence upon aristocratic patrons, and were developing a more careful system of training.[1] Civil engineering was recognized as a profession, and the foundation of the Institution of Civil Engineers in 1818 (incorporated in 1828) was an important stage in the development of new occupations based upon applied science. The Institution included within its scope 'roads, bridges, aqueducts, canals, docks, harbours, lighthouses, marine engines, machinery, and drainage': in other words, the technical foundations of modern industrial society. Yet an engineer could be described as 'a mediator between the philosopher and the working mechanic', and public opinion still took almost a fatalistic attitude towards questions for which, a few decades later, 'expert' knowledge and advice found a solution. Even Bentham, for all his belief in the possibility of a better organization of social life, failed to realize the full significance of this growing body of technical knowledge. The public at large, in 1815, may well have felt that the machinery of state was powerless to deal with problems which private enterprise had raised.

The attitude of the upper to the lower class in Great Britain was not merely negative. There was indeed a certain callousness, an indifference to suffering, and, in some respects, an invincible blindness. On the whole this indifference was passing away, and the humanitarian movement which had begun during the eighteenth century had lost little of its force. Similarly, the principle of toleration, hitherto limited to matters where it was considered unlikely to have violent effects, was making rapid progress before 1790. It was a misfortune that the French Revolution diverted these movements from their proper channels, and checked their political expansion. The French Revolution produced among most propertied Englishmen a peculiar fear of mob violence. The intensity of this fear was

[1] See below, p. 578.

something new in English history. It accounts for phrases like 'the swinish multitude' which earlier statesmen rarely used of the commons of the realm. It was aggravated by the powerlessness of authority before large assemblies collected together with riotous intent. There was no regular police force, and the morale of the troops suffered if they were scattered about the country in small detachments to put down civil disturbances. The Gordon riots of 1780 had shown what an angry mob could do in the centre of London. It was therefore easy to object to any reform on the ground that, as in France, it would lead to further demands or that it was a surrender to jacobin extortion. Every minor riot reminded orderly citizens of the excesses of the French. In 1818 a Westminster mob became out of hand at an election; Greville noted in his diary that it 'displayed the savage ferocity which marked the mobs of Paris in the worst times'.[1] Sir Samuel Romilly, who was very far from being a militant jacobin, put the case from an opposite point of view: 'If any person be desirous of having an adequate idea of the mischievous effects which have been produced in this country by the French Revolution and all its attendant horrors, he should attempt some reforms on humane and liberal principles. He will then find not only what a stupid spirit of conservation, but what a savage spirit, it has infused into the minds of his country-men.'[2]

This 'stupid conservation' did not prevail in an extreme form for much more than nine years after 1815, though there was a revival of panic after the agrarian troubles of 1830. In 1815 the tone of the democratic writers who were read by the people, and claimed to speak for them, gave some colour to the fears of the propertied classes. These orators and pamphleteers were also under the influence of the French Revolution; they attacked not merely the measures of the government, but the constitution of the country. They aimed at political and social upheaval,

---

[1] Charles Cavendish Fulke Greville (1794–1865), educ. Eton and Christ Church, Oxford; obtained the sinecure secretaryship of Jamaica, through the influence of his relative, the duke of Portland; clerk to the privy council, 1821–59; on close terms of friendship with most of the leading statesmen of his time, especially with Wellington, Palmerston, and Clarendon; one of the earliest members of the Jockey Club, manager of the duke of York's racing stable, and, for some time, racing partner with his cousin, Lord George Bentinck; kept a political diary, published after his death (see pp. 639–40).

[2] W. Bagehot, op. cit., pp. 291–2. For the life of Romilly (1757–1818), see vol. xii of this *History*.

they used language deliberately reminiscent of jacobinism, and made a flourish of revolutionary emblems in their meetings and processions. Their anti-clerical and atheistic propaganda was largely borrowed from French revolutionary pamphlets, and seemed to have other motives than a desire for liberty of thought. None of these men of whom the government was afraid showed much constructive leadership or power of organization, but it was not easy for the authorities to obtain full information about the state of opinion among the 'lower orders of society', and the confidence and violence of the attacks misled superficial observers into exaggerating their effects. Cobbett and Hunt were the most prominent speakers and writers on the radical side. Hunt[1] was a good speaker before large audiences, but too vain and self-centred to work well with any party. Cobbett[2] was a free-lance journalist, and, like most people who 'hate nonsense', full of nonsensical prejudices. He was never a revolutionary; he knew rural England as few men knew it, and his sound, if over-pugnacious, love of justice was that of a hearty countryman. His sharp question, 'What is a

[1] Henry Hunt (1773–1835), s. of a well-to-do farmer, b. Upavon, Wilts.; ran away from school owing to ill treatment; quarrelled with his father, and thought of taking a post as clerk on a slave-ship; married the daughter of an innkeeper, 1796; left her in 1802 and eloped with a friend's wife; joined the Wiltshire yeomanry, but was indicted for challenging his colonel to a duel, and imprisoned because he would not apologize, 1800; adopted advanced political views after meeting Horne Tooke and others; imprisoned for assaulting a gamekeeper, and shared rooms in prison with Cobbett, 1810; opposed Romilly's candidature at Bristol, 1813; took part in Spa Fields meetings, 1816; contested Westminster, but obtained only 84 votes, 1818; arrested after 'Peterloo', and sentenced to two years' imprisonment, 1820; wrote his memoirs while in prison; M.P., 1830; quarrelled with Cobbett and opposed the reform bill; gave up politics, 1833.

[2] William Cobbett (1763–1835), s. of a small farmer and innkeeper, b. Farnham; found work with a copying clerk in London, 1783; enlisted in the army a few months later, and served in Canada; went to France, 1792; emigrated to the United States in 1793, where he taught English to French refugees, and translated French books; wrote in defence of English policy, and attacked Paine; published a daily newspaper, *Porcupine's Gazette*, 1797–9; fined 5,000 dollars for libel; came back to England, 1800; began the *Weekly Regis er*, 1802, and the *Parliamentary Debates*, 1804; became a reformer; fined £1,000, and imprisoned for two years, owing to his attack upon flogging in the army, 1810; returned to the United States through fear of imprisonment for debt, and further prosecution for seditious libel, 1817; came back to England, 1819, bringing with him the bones of Paine; opened a seed-farm in Kensington, 1821, and began the series of journeys through England described in *Rural Rides* (1830); M.P. for Oldham, 1832. In his sixty-first year Cobbett was present at a meeting of Sussex farmers who passed a motion that he should be thrown out. He rose in his seat 'so that they might see the man they had to put out'.

pauper?', and the answer, 'Only a very poor man', might well have occurred to a good many administrative reformers who thought that they knew the needs of labouring men. Cobbett's tory democracy anticipated in some respects the Young England movement of the next generation, and his plain, vigorous style, based upon a study of the English classics, stood out in healthy contrast with the bloated newspaper writing of the time; but his fine gifts and energy were largely wasted because they were not directed to a single end. He was out of his depth in political and economic theory, though he stirred up opinion recklessly on the currency question. In spite of his respect for knowledge he never admitted his own limitations, and, although he made a great stir, he never founded a school of thought or initiated reforms of the first order. His cantankerous abuse and his readiness to excite the passions of the people did harm to the cause of parliamentary reform and other movements which he took up.

On the other hand, Cobbett and Hunt, with their supporters and imitators[1] who outdid them in abuse and indifference to public order, were right to insist that from the point of view of working men, and of the country in general, the reform of parliament was the first condition of reform in other spheres. Even if there had been facilities for carrying out a well-planned administrative policy, the central authorities were unlikely to do anything unless parliament called upon them to act, and parliament would remain unresponsive to public opinion of a moderate kind as long as the house of commons did not properly represent the people of England. In any case the past history and traditions of Englishmen concentrated attention upon parliament, and a demand for the reform of the system of election and representation took precedence over other necessary reforms. It is curious to notice that those who wanted sweeping changes no less than those who were content with things as they were failed to see how much the custom of the constitution was being modified by the facts and needs of the time. Reformers and anti-reformers believed that the constitution had reached a position of stability, whereas in fact the outward forms remained, but the relations between the Crown and parliament, between ministers and the Crown, and between the executive and the two houses of parliament were

[1] For the pamphleteers, see below, pp. 30–31.

very different from the condition of affairs at the accession of George III.[1]

In 1815 George III was an old man of seventy-seven, and mad beyond hope of recovery. His son George, Prince Regent, was a good target for republican attack. George was a clever, versatile, lazy man, of some taste in architecture and painting, attractive and rude by turns, but always a liar, always selfish, bad in his private and public conduct, and without the least understanding of his age. He was a fair judge of character, and could turn a pleasant phrase,[2] but he never used his judgement for the good of the state, and never concerned himself with anything which did not, ultimately, affect his own pleasure. He shared to the full the practical views of the counter-revolutionaries, though he had no notion of their philosophy. He defended the institution of monarchy because, like the 'little kings who came out into the sun again' after the fall of Napoleon, he belonged to the class of monarchs. He was a poor argument for his own cause, and the English monarchy could hardly have survived a successor of his kind. It may be said that he showed in his private life signs of his father's madness,[3] and that, in his selfishness and low behaviour, he was no worse than four of his six brothers. It is difficult to find other arguments in his favour.

Fortunately for the country, the centre of power was in parliament, although the eccentricities and moral insignificance of the members of the royal house were not without effect upon constitutional development. The king's support still counted for a great deal in the parliamentary life of a ministry. The stubborn protestantism of George IV did much to prevent a settlement, or at least an alleviation, of Anglo-Irish difficulties; a speech by the duke of York turned the scale in 1821 against catholic emancipation in the house of lords.[4] George IV sent out whips from Carlton House during the discussion of the catholic question, though in each case the king and his brother

---

[1] Since the year 1815 was not a turning-point in English constitutional history, these relations can be understood only by reference to the developments of the previous fifty years. See vol. xii of this *History*.

[2] It would be difficult to find a better nickname for Leopold of Coburg than 'Marquis Peu-à-Peu'.

[3] George had a mania for hoarding hardly less strong than his love of extravagant spending. He kept all his coats, boots, and pantaloons over a period of fifty years. After his death bundles of love-letters, women's gloves and locks of hair were found among his papers. He also left about £10,000 scattered in some five hundred pocket-books or loose in his boxes. [4] See below, p. 342.

were taking a dangerously old-fashioned view of the constitution. The personal likes and dislikes of George and of his brother
William IV affected the formation of ministries, took up the
time of ministers, and created an atmosphere of petty intrigue.
The effect upon public policy might have been more serious
if the duke of Wellington had not exercised some kind of
personal authority over his sovereigns.

The history of the relation of ministers to parliament in
modern times is the history of the cabinet. In 1815 the authority
of the cabinet was of recent growth.[1] Montesquieu had not
mentioned it in his analysis of the British constitution. At the
beginning of the twentieth century a writer on the government
of England could point out that the cabinet had 'no regular
time of assembly, no fixed place of meeting, no office, no staff,
no secretary, no rules, no corporate funds, no permanent loca-
tion. It could not receive a letter or answer it, except through
the first lord of the treasury, for it has no notepaper, and no
seal, and no petty cash to buy stationery or pay messengers'.[2]
Opinion in 1815 was not even clear about the collective responsibility of the cabinet. No one, since 1801, had challenged the
view that office-holders alone had the right to attend cabinet
meetings, but the responsibility of the cabinet as a whole was
difficult to establish. On the traditional theory, the responsibility of ministers was well established in law, and carried with
it the sanction of impeachment; but it was scarcely possible to
impeach a whole cabinet. Furthermore the collective responsibility of the cabinet implies responsibility to a prime minister.
Twice in 1827—in February, owing to Liverpool's paralytic
stroke, and in August, owing to the death of Canning—a
cabinet was left without a prime minister. It was not clear for
some time that Liverpool was permanently incapacitated. A
modern cabinet would have resigned at once; each of these
cabinets of 1827 held meetings when they were without a chief
to assume responsibility for their decisions. In any case, the
prime minister was still overshadowed by the king's majesty.
Peel, in 1850, did not go beyond the view that the task of
choosing a government was left 'almost exclusively' to the
prime minister. On the other hand, if the authority of the

---

[1] See vol. xii of this *History*, and A. Aspinall, 'The Cabinet Council, 1783–1815',
in *Proceedings of the British Academy*, xxxviii (1952), pp. 145–252.
[2] S. Lowe, *The Governance of England*, p. 37.

cabinet and of the prime minister had not yet taken their now familiar shape, the position of ministers in relation to parliament was in some respects stronger than it became in the later years of the nineteenth century. No ministry between 1783 and 1830 resigned as a result of defeat in the house of commons; no ministry before 1830 ever resigned on a question of legislation or taxation. In 1841 Macaulay was defending ordinary practice when he said that a cabinet need not resign owing to a failure to pass legislation unless the measures in question were necessary 'for carrying on the public service'.[1]

The changes in the position of the executive did not attract general notice because opinion within and without parliament concentrated upon the question of the composition of the house of commons and the electorate. Here matters were much too stable. There had been only minor change in the representation of England and Wales since the reign of Charles II. The acts of union settled the representation of Scotland and Ireland. The representation of the counties of England, Wales, and Scotland was largely in the control of the great landed families. If the representation of the boroughs had been adjusted to meet the changes in the distribution of wealth, interests, and population since the seventeenth century, the demand for parliamentary reform would have been less urgent; but the grouping of the English boroughs was predominantly in favour of the maritime counties of the east, south, and south-west. More than half of the 204 English boroughs were concentrated in Wiltshire and the seaboard counties from Norfolk to Gloucestershire. Wiltshire and Cornwall had more boroughs than the eight northern counties. The franchise in these boroughs varied in a haphazard way. In some cases, not necessarily in the largest towns, there was almost household suffrage. Elsewhere only the holders of certain tenements could vote. In many places the freemen of the city or borough or the members of the corporation were the electors. In boroughs with a small electorate a patron could use money or territorial power to secure the return of candidates according to his wishes; Croker estimated in 1827 that 276 out of 658 seats in parliament were at the disposal of landed patrons and that 203 of these seats were under tory control; eight peers alone controlled fifty-seven seats.[2] In some cases, where an

---

[1] Hansard, 3rd ser. lviii. 885.
[2] *The Croker Papers*, ed. L. J. Jennings, i. 368–72. John Wilson Croker (see below,

ancient town had declined in importance, the votes of a handful of dependent electors returned two members. Old Sarum, the most notorious of these rotten boroughs, was not even a village. On the other hand, many of the new manufacturing towns of the midlands and the north were unrepresented. These towns included Manchester, Birmingham, Leeds, and Sheffield.

The position in Scotland was even more absurd. In 1831 about 4,000 electors returned all the members for the Scottish counties and burghs; there were only 128 county voters in Sutherland. The majority of the burgh electors were drawn from the municipal corporations, and in nearly every case the retiring members of these bodies nominated their successors. Thus 33 voters returned a member for Edinburgh. The Irish counties and boroughs were in the hands of protestant landlords and patrons. In Scotland the general discontent was at least mitigated by the reservation of Scottish places for Scotsmen alone, but in the greater part of Ireland the catholic population could expect nothing good from its protestant rulers, and the vote was as much an instrument of the English ascendancy as the military garrison.

The existence of the nomination borough and of the patron gave a peculiar character to English politics. Since political power had become centred in the house of commons, and power in the house of commons depended on votes, parties or men who wanted power had to buy votes, as it were, in the open market; the 'pocket boroughs' thus became 'the instrument by which the Government of the day maintained its majority.[1] The price paid to the patron was sometimes in money, but more often in political advancement and in jobs in the public services for the patron's relations and dependents. When George III attempted to build up a party of his own, he too was forced to become 'the first of the borough-mongering, electioneering gentlemen of England'.[2] As new interests grew up, their representatives also sought out the control of boroughs. West and East Indian interests were represented, and indeed

p. 640) was a strong party man, and a harsh controversialist, but the picture of him as Rigby in Disraeli's *Coningsby* is unfair.

[1] C. R. Fay, *Huskisson and his Age*, pp. 46–47. Fay summed up the system as it worked before 1832: 'As with the slave trade and slavery, it was a case of property where there should have been no property, an immoral way of getting things done —of governing the country on parliamentary lines. The Reform Bill of 1832 was in a sense the abolition of Electoral Slavery.'

[2] L. B. Namier, *England in the Age of the American Revolution*, p. 4.

over-represented, in this way. The manufacturers and merchants of Manchester thought of combining to buy a borough for the representation of the cotton industry in parliament. A political theory, invented to justify the taxation of American colonists, defended this curious system. It was held that variations in the franchise allowed the representation of different sections of the community: that the opinion of the towns could be declared in the open boroughs; that the county members represented agriculture; that the great manufacturing interests were 'virtually' represented in the boroughs controlled by rich manufacturers and merchants, and a member for Old Sarum might be the representative of 'millions in India';[1] that patrons used their boroughs to introduce young men of talent into parliament. Arguments were found in English history to show that the bill of rights was drawn up mainly by representatives of rotten boroughs, and that the house of Brunswick owed the throne to the votes of these boroughs. It was said that representation was, and should be, based, not on numbers but on wealth, 'as constituting the real effective strength of the country'. Finally, the alarm caused by the French Revolution made reform appear dangerous. Parliamentary reform meant 'copying the unhappy French constitution-mongers', the transformation of members into delegates. Russell told the house of commons in 1819 that, although he wanted gradual reform, he would not support an inquiry into the general state of the representation 'because such an inquiry was calculated to throw a slur upon the representation of the country, and to fill the minds of the people with vague and indefinite alarms'.[2]

The whigs realized in time that the refusal of parliamentary reform might cause the revolution of which the propertied classes were afraid; meanwhile a parliament of landowners, rich manufacturers, and merchants was unlikely to look at industry, trade, and agriculture from the point of view of the labouring classes. This bias on the side of wealth and property was not the only evil. An unreformed parliament was disinclined to reform the municipal corporations, but the reform of these corporations was essential to any general improvement in the conditions of the great towns. Until parliamentary

---

[1] *Observations on the British Constitution* (anonymous pamphlet, 1831), p. 112. The manufacturing interests tended to have less free capital for the purchase of seats.
[2] Hansard, xl. 1496.

elections ceased to be a form of jobbery, there was no chance of breaking away from the tradition which gave official posts, active and sinecure, to the party in power as a means of rewarding followers and maintaining a majority. As late as 1820 Castlereagh summoned the office-holders to a meeting at which he warned them that the fate of the government might depend upon their votes on the following day.[1] The 'spoils system' was indeed at its worst in the last years of the unreformed parliament; patronage was no longer fully controlled by the government, but was subject, as in France, to the increasing demands of private members. Wellington, who was no reformer of the constitution, complained of this loss of control. 'Certain members claim a right to dispose of everything that falls vacant within the town or county which they represent, and this is so much a matter of right that they now claim the patronage whether they support upon every occasion, or now and then, or when not required, or actively oppose; and in fact the only question about local patronage is whether it shall be given to the disposal of one gentleman or another.'[2] Finally, reform in the other great institutions of the country, the church, the universities, the courts of law, was improbable until parliament, instead of providing specious arguments for the maintenance of abuses, set a standard by which laxity and corruption in other spheres could be judged and condemned.[3]

Within the house of commons the need of reform was urgent. The level of intelligence and instruction among the rank and file of members was low. The argument that the rotten boroughs gave a chance to clever young men without means does not bear statistical investigation. A number of able men entered parliament in this way; they generally took the first opportunity to escape from the control of a patron and to be the representatives of a wider public opinion. Furthermore a system which gave the landed aristocracy too great a predominance in the house of commons weakened the position of this house in

[1] A. Aspinall, 'English Party Organization in the early nineteenth century', *E.H.R.* July 1926, p. 395, n. 2.
[2] C. S. Parker, *Sir Robert Peel*, ii. 140. The administrative reforms of Pitt and his successors had cut down the number of sinecures available to the government.
[3] An amusing, though not very reliable account of jobbery and corruption may be read in the *Black Book* (1820) and its successor, *The Extraordinary Black Book: an exposition of abuses in Church and State, Courts of Law, Representation, Municipal and Corporate Bodies* (1831).

relation to the house of lords. In any case the authority of the commons required confirmation from a larger and more powerful electorate. The record of the house of lords in the nineteenth century is a sorry one. This record must not be judged by the number of eminent peers—a small and a decreasing number— or by the few occasions when the upper house showed a wiser understanding and a cooler judgement in important questions of national policy; it rests upon the attitude of the house over many years to the reforms passed in the house of commons. From the relief of little boys tortured by chimney-sweeps to the relief of millions of catholics, from dislike of the factory acts to the defence of the monopoly of a few theatres, the house of lords was an obstacle to changes reasonable in themselves and demanded by the country as a whole. The lords spiritual were hardly less narrow-minded than the lords temporal; in matters affecting the established church they were out of touch with the opinions of Englishmen, and still more with the opinions of Irishmen.[1] The house of lords remained a drag upon the social progress of the country after the reform of the commons, but its power for harm was limited by the extension of the franchise, the redistribution of seats, and the greater authority and prestige of the reformed parliament.

In spite of faults and shortcomings, the parliamentary system of Great Britain was still the best government in Europe, and the most responsive to popular demand. The stability of the country and its institutions impressed foreign travellers.

'If I were asked at this moment [1811] for a summary opinion of what I have seen in England, I might probably say that its political institutions present a detail of corrupt practices, of profusion, and of personal ambition, under the mask of public spirit very carelessly put on, more disgusting than I should have expected; the workings of the selfish passions are exhibited in all their nakedness and deformity. On the other hand, I should admit very readily that I have found the great mass of the people richer, happier, and more respectable than any other with which I am acquainted. I have seen prevailing among all ranks of people that emulation of industry and independence which characterise a state of advancing civilisation properly directed. The manners and the whole deportment of superiors to inferiors are marked with that just regard and

---

[1] The relative, or at all events the numerical importance of the bishops had diminished with the increase in the numbers of the peerage since 1783. See below, p. 622.

circumspection which announce the presence of laws equal for all. By such signs, I know this to be the best government that ever existed.'[1]

There was considerable truth in the view put forward by the opponents of reform that parliament was subject to real democratic pressure. This pressure showed itself in the number of petitions to the house of commons, in the interest taken by the country as a whole in parliamentary debates, and in the increasing number of organs of public opinion. The press was better informed, if not more important, in Great Britain than in any other country, although the status of journalism was low; in 1808 the benchers of Lincoln's Inn considered that writers to the press were unfit to be called to the bar. In 1815 there were 252 newspapers circulating in the United Kingdom. Most of these journals were merely of local importance, but the larger newspapers had gained during the French wars an independence and a standing which they were never to lose. The demand for reliable news gave a wider circulation to the newspapers of London and of the great northern cities; they became rich enough to stand without government subsidies. The revenue from advertisements was increasing; the introduction of steam printing after 1814 lowered costs and multiplied nearly threefold the number of copies which could be printed in a short time, while distribution was easier owing to improvements in the road and coaching services.[2] The publication of parliamentary debates was of great significance because political meetings, except at election times, were almost unknown. The stamp duties were raised in 1815 to 4d. a copy, and the price of newspapers rose to 7d. These duties were opposed, especially by the radicals who wanted cheap newspapers as means of propaganda; they had a very considerable effect upon sales, but not enough to counterbalance the factors making for a wider circulation of newspapers in general. Below the 'respectable' newspapers, and, in many cases, evading stamp duty, there was a mass of periodical and pamphlet literature, of which Cobbett's *Political Register*, Wooler's *Black Dwarf*, and Hone's satires were the outstanding examples.[3] Few of these flysheets contained much

---

[1] L. Simond, in Smart, i. 320–1.

[2] The daily circulation of *The Times* in 1817 was about 6,000–7,000 copies. *The Courier*, an evening paper, sold about 5,000 copies. Carrier pigeons were used to carry news quickly; even prize fights were reported in this way.

[3] Thomas Jonathan Wooler, a Yorkshire printer, took up Cobbett's work after

news; they attracted readers mainly by the virulence of their language. It has been claimed that these pamphleteers and newswriters secured for Englishmen a free press. They certainly aimed at this freedom; Carlile,[1] in particular, showed great courage and devotion to liberty of thought, but to some extent the most provocative writers caused themselves unnecessary hardship by 'trailing their coats' and inviting persecution. There was no preventive censorship, and action could take place only after publication. It has been estimated that between 1816 and 1834 there were 183 prosecutions in Great Britain for seditious or blasphemous libel, or defamation of the king and his ministers. Of these prosecutions 131 took place in 1817 and 1819–21;[2] after 1824 the number was very small. The authorities realized that prosecution merely advertised an author, and that it was difficult to secure convictions, especially in cases brought by associations formed for the purpose. For these reasons a regime of toleration, or at all events of forbearance, came almost silently into effect.

The newspapers were not the only channels for the expression of public opinion. The foundation of the *Edinburgh Review and Critical Journal* in 1802 began a new era in public criticism. The *Edinburgh* was a whig journal, conservative in literary standards, but not afraid of innovations in politics. Under the editorship of Francis Jeffrey, and with the help of contributors like Sydney Smith and Brougham, the circulation soon rose above 10,000 copies; 14,000 copies of one number were sold in 1815, and there was a steady demand for bound volumes. The *Quarterly Review* was founded in 1809 largely through the

Cobbett left for America in 1817. William Hone, a London bookseller, sold about 100,000 copies of a parody of the anglican liturgy.

[1] Richard Carlile (1790–1843), s. of a shoemaker, b. Ashburton; a tinman until the depression of 1817, when he began to sell periodicals; reprinted Paine's *Age of Reason* and other works of a radical kind. Between 1818 and 1843 Carlile spent over nine years in prison, mainly owing to his persistence in defying the law. His wife and sister were also imprisoned for assisting in his work.

[2] For the prosecutions see W. H. Wickwar, *The Struggle for the Freedom of the Press, 1819–32*. Two bodies, the Constitutional Association and the Society for the Suppression of Vice and the Encouragement of Religion and Virtue throughout the United Kingdom, considered it their duty to secure convictions for press offences. The former of these societies was of an undesirable kind, and its enemies accused it of making profits for its members by giving information about libels; the latter society, which was strongly supported by Wilberforce, was meddlesome and priggish, but did some good in raising standards of decency; its activities were directed only incidentally against press offences.

influence of Sir Walter Scott, as a tory answer to the *Edinburgh*, and in 1824 the radicals began the *Westminster Review* as a challenge to whigs and tories alike. The *Edinburgh* and *Quarterly* paid contributors at rates hitherto unknown; their articles were longer, more serious, and more directly polemical than those of the journals of the Augustan age. They brought public questions before a wide audience, and gave openings to writers who could not afford the risk of printing and publishing their work.

The political critics of the government, the 'literature of doctrine', civil and ecclesiastical, took little account of the humbler needs of labouring men. The greater part of the literature of imagination was equally remote from these needs. This literature of imagination was in 1815 at one of its most remarkable periods of development. Wordsworth, Coleridge, Keats, Byron, Shelley, Southey, Lamb, Jane Austen, Hazlitt, Landor, Blake, Scott were the great figures,[1] thought there were others who would have stood out in a less brilliant time. The best work of this age, as of all ages, had more to do with the interpretation of life than with the organization and mechanism of government, but most writers concerned themselves directly or indirectly with politics, even if their interests were mainly in government in the older sense of the term, and not in economic or social functions connected, for example, with housing, public health, or wages. Blake's flowing vision of beauty and goodness, his revolt against the militant 'reason' of the eighteenth century, led him far beyond his time.[2] On his own contemporaries he had little direct influence. His criticism of society went much deeper than talk about politics. He included 'the dark, satanic mills' in the sweep of his condemnation, and warned the age that

> 'the harlot's cry from street to street
> shall weave old England's winding sheet.'

Yet he was not thinking in terms of political economy, or of evils which could be reformed or removed either by legislation or by societies for the suppression of vice. Landor was equally remote from practical politics; he was in some respects a revolu-

---

[1] For the early history of these writers, and of the romantic movement, see vol. xii of this *History*.

[2] For example, in the *Marriage of Heaven and Hell*: 'Improvement makes us straight roads; but the crooked roads, without improvement, are roads of genius.

tionary, but a revolutionary of the classical, aristocratic type. Scott was a romantic tory, with an easy, open mind, and little care for doctrine; his broad and generous sympathy, which gave him an interest in the 'romantic past', did not take him into social inquiry about present evils. Scott made use of the history of the past as a subject for the novel; his influence spread over Europe and did much to widen the scope of imaginative writing and to bring about the second phase of the romantic movement—the phase of which Victor Hugo's *Les Misérables* may be taken as the masterpiece, but his own political activities were not on the side of reform. If Keats had lived beyond his twenty-sixth year, he might have written political poetry, even though he had not the background of his great contemporaries. He was born too late for the excitement of the French Revolution, and his few years of creative work were dominated by his direct and almost overwhelming love of external beauty. Shelley and Byron, unlike Keats, belonged to an aristocratic class which took politics and talk about politicians as its central interest of a serious kind. Shelley wrote a great deal of political satire, but he was too lyrical a poet to be satisfied with political subjects. He was concerned mainly with the larger questions arising out of current politics: the relation between political and moral issues, the ideas of freedom and liberty, the tyranny of law. Shelley disliked didactic verse and explained that his own poetry was not dedicated 'solely to the direct enforcement of reform'[1] *Hellas*, the only one of his great poems directly concerned with detailed political fact, gives an idealized view of the Greek insurrection of 1821. *The Mask of Anarchy*, suggested by Peterloo, is nearer, in its flashes of intuition, to the poetry of Blake than to a political pamphlet. *Oedipus Tyrannus, or Swellfoot the Tyrant*, is an attack on George IV, but it is not a great poem.[2]

Byron was at the height of his creative power in 1815. He gave his life for a political cause. It was not an English cause, but Byron himself was typically English in his attitude towards politics. The prose-poetry of his satires is more splendid and even more full-blooded than the current talk of men of his class

[1] 'Didactic poetry is my abhorrence; nothing can be equally well expressed in prose that is not tedious and supererogatory in verse.' Preface to *Prometheus Unbound*.

[2] *Men of England*, the best of Shelley's political poems, was not published until 1839.

and country on political affairs; it is no less personal. A great
deal of it indeed is an open and sustained attack upon the
hypocrisy of those who pretended to be shocked by his immorality. Moreover, the satire of Byron is satire without
remedy, savage as in *Don Juan*, good-natured as in *The Vision
of Judgment*, but never directed towards a practical, concrete
purpose which might issue in legislation; he cared no more than
George IV for the sufferings of the English poor.[1] His immense
influence upon European literature was due largely to the
peculiarly English character of his work: a broad, biting common sense based upon the tradition of the only country with a
living, political experience of a liberal kind.

The liberalism of Byron and Shelley was not the only political
expression of the romantic movement. The romantic revival
in its earlier stages had been a reaction against formalism of
idea and method. The romantics had broken through the set
themes and shallow jargon of the successors of Addison and
Pope; they had insisted upon freedom of choice in subject and
diction and restored to poetry the emotion of wonder, a sense
of the past, and a type of realism which was not afraid of violent
passion. Before 1820 the romantic movement, as a liberating
force, had done its work in literature. Its political implications
were still to be worked out in prose. Romanticism was a return
to men and women, living, like the characters in Scott's novels,
in a world of passion, excitement, and memory. On this side
the movement was a release from the staleness of custom and the
restraint of authority, and might easily become an attack upon
authority itself in the interest of personal freedom. For this
reason Shelley and Byron were romantics in their attack upon
the political reaction which followed the defeat of Napoleon
and the restoration of monarchical authority in Europe. It
was possible for the romantic movement to develop in a different direction. Liberalism might be considered a form of
jacobinism, and jacobinism a product of the superficial rationalism against which the earliest romantic protests had been made.
The appeal to instinct might well be an appeal against reason
and even against liberty; a sense of the significance of the past
might lead to a belief in the principle of continuity, and a better
understanding of those ancient institutions which the early
rationalists had discarded because they were unsymmetrical

[1] He spoke once in the lords (1812) about the grievances of frame-work knitters.

and incapable of explanation in general terms. The study of history was unlikely to confirm the optimism of revolutionaries. Thus Coleridge was led to political opinions entirely different from those of Byron.

Coleridge was less masterful than Byron, less violent in expression, deeper but less clear in thought. His philosophy was always trying to shine through a cloud of German metaphysics. He wrote nearly all his best poetry before 1800, and, after this creative period, his dream-like arrangement of beauty showed itself only in a rich, vivid, and often disordered prose. This prose was practical, or, at all events, didactic in intention. Charles Lamb said that he had never heard Coleridge 'do anything else but preach'. There was a subtlety about this preaching which Sara Coleridge noticed in her remark that her father's talk was to Wordsworth's as Greek to Latin. Coleridge saw that the foundations of society were instinctive as well as intellectual. This insistence upon growth and development in time was not merely learned from Burke and the German romantic writers; it was a form of imaginative intuition which enabled Coleridge, like Blake, to see far ahead of his age. For this reason Coleridge had little direct and immediate influence upon English political development. Moreover he lacked the practical *flair*—Byron's common sense—necessary for deciding between rival political issues in ordinary life. His justification of anglicanism was as remote from the facts of the relation between church and state as Shelley's *Hellas* was remote from the realities of the Greek rebellion.

From this point of view Coleridge is the opposite of Bentham.[1] His imagination, his power of dreaming, saved him from Bentham's superficiality, but it deprived him of Bentham's ceaseless cleverness and concentration upon limited but positive ends. J. S. Mill described Bentham in terms which bring out this contrast with Coleridge: 'He had neither internal experience nor external. . . . He never knew prosperity and adversity, passion nor satiety; he never had even the experiences which sickness gives. . . . He knew no dejection, no heaviness of heart. He never felt life a sore and a weary burthen. He was a boy to the last.'[2] In other words, Bentham, like Goethe, failed to

---

[1] For Bentham (1748–1832) see also vol. xii of this *History*, pp. 330–1.
[2] J. S. Mill, *Dissertations* (1859), i. 354–5. The description hardly applies to Bentham's schooldays, or to his years at Oxford; it also ignores his sensitiveness and

understand either a Christian or a hero and, as he lived in a world which contained both these types, his philosophy was unsatisfactory. Bentham was interested, not in the problems of life, but in the mechanism of living; his reforms were a series of political gadgets. Even his legal reforms were concerned for the most part with procedure. His principle of 'utility' and his judgement that actions tending to pleasure are as necessarily good as actions tending to pain are necessarily bad will not stand an investigation into the nature of 'good'; the test of pleasure indeed broke down in the case of Bentham's disciple, James Mill, who, in his son's words, 'had scarcely any belief in pleasure'. Yet, for practical achievement in the early nineteenth century, and for the removal of patent abuse and injustice, there could have been few better standards than 'the greatest happiness of the greatest number', and until the evils in the way of happiness had been removed, there was no need to look very far beyond this test. Bentham's standard of utility was indeed so very simple that it convinced men who suspected any other method of reform with a claim to theoretical justification of an absolute kind. There might be disagreement about a final definition of happiness; it was obvious that peace and public order, and a system of laws plainly and logically worded and arranged, tended more to happiness than to pain. Thus Bentham was one of the few great reformers to be appreciated in his own lifetime, though he had to wait a good many years for this appreciation. His long life, perfect health, and sufficient private fortune gave him every chance of developing his ideas. He was not a revolutionary; he believed in action through parliament. He attacked abuses, such as the confusion of the law, and the cost and delays of legal procedure, which only lawyers defended. He did not threaten private property, but tried merely to prevent the 'sinister interests' of any one class from encroaching upon the general convenience. He believed that security of possession was more important than equality of distribution.[1] He had no wish to increase the powers of the state, and no feeling that the

diffidence in practical life. Bentham cared for music, flowers, and animals, but thought that poetry was misrepresentation.

[1] 'In consulting the grand principle of security, what ought the legislator to decree respecting the mass of property already existing? He ought to maintain the distribution as it is actually established. . . . When security and equality are in conflict, it will not do to hesitate a moment. Equality must yield.' Bentham, *Principles of Legislation* (1876 ed.), pp. 119–20.

state had any claims, beyond those of convenience, upon the loyalty of its citizens. His belief in the freedom of contract fitted well with the economic views of Adam Smith and the practical desires of manufacturers. He wanted reasonable government, but not too much of it; he thought that the business of public authority was, as it were, to hold the ring, and to inspect rather than to undertake the conduct of affairs which could be left in private hands. Some legislative restrictions were necessary, not only for convenience of arrangement, but also because the principle of the 'natural identity of interests' (i.e. that in working for himself, an individual was working for society as a whole) was not always valid, yet Bentham argued that 'it is with government as with medicine, its only business is the choice of evils. Every law is an evil, for every law is an infraction of liberty.'[1] He was ready to hand over the administration of the poor law to a private company, and his scheme of prison reform allowed a contractor to feed the prisoners at a fixed sum per head in return for the profits on their labour.

Bentham's ideas and suggestions affected many of the ablest men of the younger generation, without distinction of party. Peel, Brougham, and Francis Place learned much from him; the reform of the penal code by the tories, the reform of the poor law by the whigs were measures which Bentham had supported. The reform act of 1832 was a direct, though an incomplete, application of his principles, since it transferred political power, in some measure, to the class which, on Bentham's view, was most likely to identify itself with the greatest happiness of the greatest number. Bentham's favourite principle was, however, little more than an assaying machine for judging good or bad coin: a valuable mechanical device in a society troubled with counterfeit money. There could be nothing creative about it; it did not satisfy the imagination. It could not take the place of a religion;[2] Bentham's solution of the problem of pain was merely to avoid it.

Wordsworth, like Coleridge, was concerned far more with life itself than with any of these contrivances which might

---

[1] Ibid., p. 48.
[2] Bentham's view of religion entirely missed the point. 'The clergy are a body of inspectors and moral instructors who form, so to speak, the advance-guard of the law. The expense of their support ought to be referred to the same branch of the administration with justice and the police, viz. the support of internal security.' Ibid. p. 133.

smooth the business of the day. The influence of Wordsworth is thus difficult to estimate because it was, and is, an influence on persons and not on things. Wordsworth himself had no doubt that he was destined to have an influence of some kind. Long before 1815 he had lost his belief in political progress through violent or rapid change, but he still had a strong, perhaps too strong, sense of his mission to the world. He was indeed the very opposite of an 'idle singer of an empty day'. Carlyle described him as 'essentially a cold, hard, silent, practical man . . . a man of an immense head, and great jaws like a crocodile's, cast in a mould designed for prodigious work'.[1] Wordsworth's power over ordinary serious-minded men was far greater than that of Shelley, far more enduring than the tumult of Byron. Wordsworth has been described as 'the only poet who will bear reading in times of distress'.[2] He belonged to the tradition of English puritanism, and if, in his later years. he was, like Coleridge, on the side of political reaction, his poems and the example of his 'august, innocent life' were among the few positive and steadying intellectual forces of an age which was soon to lose the certainty of religion. Wordsworth's poetry did not provide a body of doctrine. It fortified and strengthened the mind; it did not assist, directly, in the solution of any political or administrative problem, but the solution of such problems is not the province of poetry.

The lesser men illustrated, though they did not begin or direct, movements of political and social importance. Southey's conservatism was more practical than the conservatism of Coleridge; it was also less profound, and had no lasting effect. Moore's attacks upon Castlereagh and the Regent were fashionable pieces written for the amusement of whig society. Lamb was not interested in making converts or in advocating policies, though his gentle, friendly prose was one of the influences working for greater kindliness and toleration. Hazlitt was primarily a literary critic; his radicalism has no more significance in the history of the time than his admiration for Napoleon.

The shapes and colours of English life in 1815, the dress, the street scenes, the landscapes, are familiar through paintings

---

[1] Quoted in O. Elton, *A Survey of English Literature, 1780–1830*, ii. 55.

[2] Ibid., p. 94. J. S. Mill had said almost the same thing. Mill, *Autobiography* (1873 ed.), pp. 146–51.

and etchings, prints and caricatures, through discussions in letters, debates, novels, newspapers. It would be idle to call the age a period of transition; every age of English history has been a period of transition. On the other hand, there was, about the year 1815, an increase in the rate of change, a greater stir and movement in every sphere of public activity. The causes of this more rapid *tempo* of change can be summed up, roughly, in the term 'rational and purposive control', based upon measuring, counting, and observing. The extent of this application of reason is sometimes overlooked because the plans were made and carried out, especially in the production and distribution of things, largely by individuals working for private gain. Something like an anarchy of individual profit-seeking was the first stage in the development of a planned order of society. It was necessary for men to apply reason to the management of their own enterprises before they learned how to use the new instruments of production, the new methods of administration and government, on a larger scale. Thus one of the most important facts of the age is the emergence of a class of manufacturers and business men who

knew nothing of the cult of tradition, custom, and inherited beliefs which Burke described as characteristic of the whig landed aristocracy. . . . They had acquired through their own activities a very different mental outlook. They regarded the cult of tradition as bound up with the old régime of guilds, of government regulation, and an uninventive technique. . . . These industrial leaders were rationalists . . . who had learned to weigh every act, to secure that these acts were mutually consistent and in harmony with a desired end. They made in this way a complete break with the modes of their predecessors who were content merely to imitate their fathers. Modern industry, like everything else modern, is the child of rationalism.[1]

The pursuit of rational ends by rational means did not begin in the year 1815; it was not universal after 1815. Nevertheless it is possible to notice so great an increase in these methods of measuring, counting, and observing that they may be taken as the most distinctive and original feature of the age. Outside the comparatively new fields of scientific study they were not

---

[1] G. de Ruggiero, *Storia del liberalismo europeo*, p. 104. [Eng. trans. R. G. Collingwood, 1927.]

formulated and defined by more than a few of the large number
who applied them; the Benthamites indeed devised a formula,
but most men, especially men of business, were content to act
without any clear knowledge of the principles underlying their
actions. They felt themselves doing something which the state
could not do for them, and could not by any means do well.

How far did observers realize in 1815 that their country was
entering upon an 'age of reform'? A few chemists, physicists,
and engineers, again, recognized the immense potentialities of
applied science.[1] Ordinary opinion did not make this inference,
and, in politics, even the most active reformers tended to think
in terms of past issues, or, at all events, of reform within the
limits of society as it was known to their ancestors. Demands
for reform were more for the redress of grievances, or for a
return to standards enjoyed in the past, than for the improvement of conditions of life. To the propertied class, afraid of
revolutionary violence, to manufacturers and merchants, landowners and farmers meeting the fall of prices after the end of the
war, to the great mass of labourers in town and country barely
maintaining the struggle against want, to ministers of state faced
with an immense burden of public debt, there would have been
something almost absurd in the idea that the year 1815 was the
beginning of a long period of social betterment. Even the
Benthamites hardly wanted to do more than make the best of
things, and to apply methods which would allow the machinery
of society to run more smoothly. Many of the signs of improvement were regarded with alarm. The rise in the numbers of the
population might have been interpreted as a sign of increasing
control over material conditions; it appeared to contemporaries
as a problem of the most serious kind, leading to the pessimistic
conclusion that with the physical pressure of numbers upon the
means of subsistence there must always be a starving fringe of
losers in the struggle for life.

There was a change of opinion within a generation after
1815: a vague popular belief that immense material improvements were possible, and that the good things of the world were
being kept from the poor only by the greed of the rich. This
belief was expressed in chartism and other attempts at organiz-
ing the less well-paid majority of the working class. The change
of opinion was equally noticeable in other classes. The de-

[1] See below, p. 564.

fenders of privilege and tradition, of things as they were, fought a losing battle in their respective political parties; agitation over the reform of parliament showed the strength of feeling in favour of administrative reform, and after 1832 whigs and tories adapted themselves to the new conditions. The new party names, liberal and conservative, represented a far-reaching change of outlook. The coming of railways did much to bring about a general belief in the possibilities of improvement, and, incidentally, to produce for the first time, on a large scale, a familiarity with power-driven machines, and a sense that these machines were something more than socially embarrassing instruments of industrial competition. The consumer, and not merely the producer, made use of the railway; middle-aged Englishmen, travelling from place to place at speeds thought impossible in their youth, found it easier to assume a quickened rate of change, and of change for the better, in other matters.

The history of the railways shows in a remarkable way the temper of mind of the English people in the generation after Waterloo. The building of railways was the greatest physical achievement carried out by the human race within a comparatively short space of time. A work of this kind was likely to touch almost every aspect of the national life. The railways were one of the results of progress in the iron industry and of the increased consumption of coal brought about by the use of steam-power. They were in turn, the cause of a vast expansion in the metal trades and of a much greater demand for coal. Directly or indirectly they influenced the development of most industries in the country. Lower costs of transport facilitated the division of labour, increased the volume of internal demand, and enabled British manufacturers to offer goods at prices which found an increasing number of purchasers in foreign countries. The railway itself was an article of export; British contractors built lines in every continent and organized companies to buy them. Agriculture was affected hardly less than manufacturers. There were more opportunities of marketing perishable goods, bringing animals to large centres, and getting manure to the soil. The movement of capital into railways modified the structure of credit and the attitude of opinion towards joint stock companies, provided a new form of investment outside government securities, and was one of the first instances, on a large scale, of the separation of ownership from control in industry. Socially the railways did much to break down the isolation and caste system of rural England; they brought thousands of children within the range of secondary schools in the towns, and enabled the middle and poorer classes to see places beyond their market or county towns. Migration to a large city no longer meant exile from friends and relations. This movement of travellers, rich and poor, was far greater than the promoters of railways had ever imagined.[1] In 1839 the Great Western railway had not decided how to transport 'the very lowest order of persons'; a year later, the company allowed contractors dealing with goods to take 'persons in the lower stations of life'. In 1844 parliament, under the influence of Gladstone's early work at the board of trade, required railways to run at least one train a day carrying passengers at the rate of a penny a mile.

The attitude of public opinion towards this sudden change in the economic and social environment is perhaps the best example of the conflict between the older, irrational dislike of innovation and the newer and more confident application of means to ends without regard to prejudice or habit.[2] The development of railways shows the good as well as the bad effects upon society of what may be called collective private enterprise. Parliament never initiated a railway scheme; the engineers found the best route, and the promoters took the financial risk, though before they obtained legislative sanction for their projected lines they had to prove that they were satisfying a public demand. There was an outburst of specula-tion in railways when it was found that the first enterprises returned a good profit, but the earliest lines were to some extent works of public utility, supported by public committees of

[1] Before the building of the railway it was estimated that the coaches between Liverpool and Manchester did not take more than about 500 passengers a day. The railway carried an average of 1,200 passengers a day in its first year, at half the rate charged by the coaches and in less than half the time.

[2] The displacement of older methods of transport on land was more immediate than the change introduced by the use of steam-power in ships. Steamboats ran with success in 1790 and 1803 on the Forth–Clyde canal, but the idea of steam-towing was given up because the canal company was afraid of damage to the banks from the wash of paddle-wheels. There were five steamboats on the Thames in 1815—two of them had come by sea from the Clyde. The channel was crossed from Brighton to Havre in 1816 and the Atlantic from Savannah to Liverpool in 1819 in 25 days. In 1825 the voyage from Falmouth to Calcutta was made in 103 days, 64 of which were under steam. Steam-power thus came in gradually as an auxiliary to sail, and although the time taken in voyages was greatly reduced, the average speed in 1838 was only 10–11 miles per hour. See also below, p. 595, note 3.

influential citizens. At Bristol the corporation of the city, the Society of Merchant Venturers, the dock company, and the chamber of commerce supported the project of a railway to London. The dividend of the Liverpool and Manchester company was limited to 10 per cent.; no shareholder could hold more than ten shares.

This picture of private enterprise at its best must not be over-drawn. There was a great deal of waste and confusion result-ing from the lack of planning by public authority. Parliament did not lose the old suspicions that monopoly meant abuse, and that state control could not be dissociated from corruption. Public opinion favoured a number of small, and even of com-peting, lines owing to the fear that a railway without competi-tors would misuse its powers. In 1844 Gladstone persuaded the house of commons to reserve for the state the right of purchasing any new lines after an interval of twenty-one years. Gladstone was safeguarding the future, but he did not think that the state would find it expedient to exercise this right, or that railways under state control would be as well managed as lines owned by private companies. Moreover, the control exercised by parlia-ment over railway projects was itself a source of jobbery. For many years the procedure in railway legislation was cumber-some, and very costly. The London and Birmingham company spent over £72,000 before it could get an act through parlia-ment. The owners of property whose land was acquired by compulsory purchase had too great an influence over parlia-mentary committees, and soon found that they could hold the companies to ransom.

It is equally necessary to avoid exaggerating the foresight of the new industrial entrepreneurs in the development of rail-ways. In many respects the railway promoters showed a curious lack of foresight. Each stage in their success came as a surprise to them. It is even remarkable that railways did not come earlier into general use. They were not new in Great Britain in 1815. Trucks had been drawn along wooden lines in the sixteenth century. In 1789, when cast-iron rails were already laid down, Smeaton[1] suggested that the flange which kept the wheels in position should be removed from the rail to the inner side of the wheels. These early railways transported coal over

[1] John Smeaton (1728–92), civil engineer, built the third Eddystone Lighthouse, 1756–9.

short distances, but as early as 1799 there was a proposal to build a line from London to Portsmouth for the transport of every kind of commodity; in 1801 the Surrey Iron Railway Company obtained an act of parliament for the construction of part of this line between Croydon and Wandsworth, and the line was opened in 1804. Nineteen railway acts were passed between 1801 and 1821, and there were 150 miles of lines in operation in South Wales before 1812. Trevithick designed a steam-engine in 1804 for the railway serving the Merthyr Tydvil coal-mines. The engine did not work well, but Trevithick went on with his experiments. William Murdoch designed a locomotive engine while in the employment of Boulton and Watt of Soho; his firm did not want to lose him, and would not take up his invention. George Stephenson built his first locomotive for the Killingworth colliery in 1814. The malleable iron rail, even before the steam-engine, caused the first important extensions of the railway, but engineers were still slow to consider the possibility of transporting passengers and, in Dr. Clapham's words, 'the railways of 1820–5 remained substantially what railways had been for a century and a half on Tyneside—a means of moving bulky goods over short distances at moderate speeds to or from navigable water. Occasionally they formed links in a through route, and the idea of using them further in this way was familiar in technical circles; but, apart from the very imperfect locomotive, the technique of the permanent way up to and even after 1820', supported the view that railways would not be much else.[1]

The act authorizing the Stockton and Darlington railway was passed in 1821. The promoters did not adopt steam-power until half the line was built; even then they decided to use stationary engines for certain gradients. They opened the railway for traffic in 1825; two years later, it was in full working order for mineral traffic. They thought of their business as similar to that of the turnpike trusts and canal proprietors. They were toll-collectors, ready to let their rails to any merchant or contractor who would pay their charges. When the locomotive took the place of the horse, the railway companies charged for locomotive-hire as well as for the use of the line, but the proprietors who had acquired the right to put their own

---

[1] Clapham, i. 90. In 1819 Rees's *Cyclopedia* discussed railways under the heading 'canals'. Ibid.

horse-drawn carriages on the Stockton and Darlington railway were not bought out until 1833–4, and as late as 1837–8 a committee of the house of commons suggested that the right of private persons to run their own engines and trains might be extended to the post office.[1]

The earliest project of a railway from Bristol to London, suggested in 1824, shows the same lack of foresight and optimism about the future of steam-driven engines. The project took the form of a combined railway for goods traffic and turnpike road for passengers. The Liverpool and Manchester railway[2] was planned before the opening of the Stockton and Darlington line. The directors obtained their act of parliament in 1826; they could not decide between the merits of stationary or locomotive engines, and offered a prize for the best locomotive. In 1829 Stephenson's *Rocket* won the prize, and its performance settled the question for the future, though the directors of the Newcastle and Carlisle line waited until 1834 before asking parliament to rescind the clause in their act which forbade the use of locomotives.

The success of the two northern lines hurried on other plans. There was little co-ordination between the different proposals. Few people supported a comprehensive scheme of trunk lines,[3] though in many cases amalgamation took place before lines were completed or even laid down. A line from Liverpool to Birmingham was projected in 1824; two companies were formed in order that the work might be put in hand at each end. Peel was chairman of one of the companies, but there were long delays in settling financial and other arrangements. In 1832 the two companies were merged to form the Grand Junction Railway Company, and, a year later, the line received parliamentary sanction. The London and Birmingham company secured an act in 1833, after three years of parliamentary negotiation.

[1] In 1839–40 another committee realized that, with the increase in the amount of traffic, the system was unworkable. The committee also suggested that the companies should be allowed a monopoly.

[2] The purpose of the line was not so much to transport goods at a higher speed as to relieve the congestion of traffic on the waterways; merchants complained that cotton imports and textile exports were delayed for weeks. When the bill was under discussion Sir John Barrow, of the Admiralty, recommended the promoters to point out that there was not water available for another canal. Barrow did not expect many passengers and advised a speed limit of five miles an hour.

[3] Even the advocates of a planned development of trunk lines underrated the volume of traffic on the railways. One scheme assumed that six lines of rails would be enough for all traffic coming in and out of London.

They opened their line to Tring in 1837, and to Birmingham in 1838. The Great Western railway developed out of the London and Bristol project in 1835. A year earlier the house of lords threw out the bill authorizing the line on the ground that there was no security for the completion of the railway. It was also said that the noise of the trains in the Box tunnel would be so nerve-shaking that 'no passenger would be induced to go twice'. The Great Western act included a provision which illustrates the lack of any general scheme for the whole country. Stephenson had taken, almost at haphazard, the 4 ft. 8½ in. gauge suitable for horse-drawn trucks on the colliery line with which he was familiar; other engineers copied this gauge. Brunel, the engineer-in-chief of the Great Western, arranged that the act of 1835 should not define the gauge of the line. He was therefore free to choose a broader gauge than Stephenson's, and, though from a technical point of view his choice was probably a better one, the railways were not even uniform in one of the most essential features.

The objections to railways, and particularly to steam loco-motives, came chiefly from landowners and others whose property was being 'invaded'.[1] They complained of smoke, of noise, of the effect upon hunting, and of the bad characters whom the railways would bring to the countryside. They feared that the permanent way would affect the drainage of farm lands and the flow of water, and that it would divide fields and closes. Some towns were mistaken enough to keep the railway from their neighbourhood; Northampton refused to take the carriage works of the London and Birmingham line. The university of Oxford and the provost and fellows of Eton were among the strongest opponents of the Great Western.[2] There was also

---

[1] The objections of the duke of Cleveland to the Stockton and Darlington line and of Lords Sefton and Derby to the Liverpool and Manchester line may be summed up in Creevey's phrase: 'The loco-motive Monster, carrying *eighty* tons of goods, and navigated by a tail of smoke and sulphur, coming thro' every man's grounds between Manchester and Liverpool.' *The Creevey Papers*, ed. Sir H. Maxwell, ii. 87–88.

[2] The authorities at Eton wanted to screen the railway by a ten-foot wall over a distance of four miles near Slough. They obtained a clause in the Great Western act preventing the company from opening a station at Slough. The company stopped its trains there, and used two rooms in a public house as its offices. When a branch line from Slough to Windsor was sanctioned in 1848, the provost and fellows compelled the company to police the line in case the boys trespassed on it. A man was kept on this work until 1886, and then withdrawn on condition that he would be replaced if it were found necessary.

opposition from vested interests. Farmers and others with a local monopoly did not want towns in the neighbourhood to draw their supplies from a wider area; thus the farmers of Middlesex, Buckinghamshire, and Berkshire realized that the Great Western would bring Irish produce into competition with the produce of the home counties. Rival transport interests had good reason for their opposition. The railways brought so great an increase in traffic that there were, ultimately, more horses and wagons on the roads and more ships and barges on the most important canals, but the first effect of railway-building was to ruin many turnpike trusts and all the great coaching establishments, and to reduce the profits of the canals. The canals in the south of England had not provided much return to their owners: a number of the northern canals, however, made enormous profits. The Bridgewater canal cost about £220,000 and returned an annual profit not far short of £100,000; the thirty-nine original proprietors of the Mersey and Irwell navigation company received their full capital in the form of interest every two years for nearly half a century. There had been no attempt to build canals on a standard plan, and differences in depth or in the size of locks meant a great deal of reshipping. The companies had few arrangements for through booking at reasonable rates, and no regular time-tables. They often wasted on parliamentary opposition to railway bills money which might have been spent on improving the service and management of their waterways.

The canal companies could not maintain their opposition, and the railways established themselves beyond any question. Within fifteen years of the opening of the Stockton and Darlington line most of the main trunk roads had been laid down. There were lines from London to Bristol (with an extension to Exeter under construction), Southampton, Portsmouth, Dover, Brighton, Colchester (with an extension planned to Norwich), Cambridge, Lincoln and York (under construction), Birmingham, Lancaster, and the great provincial towns of the north-west. Lines were also in operation from Carlisle to Newcastle, Darlington to York and Rugby, Liverpool to Manchester, Leeds, and Hull, and Derby to Bristol.[1] By 1850 these main lines had been extended, especially in the west of England, South Wales, and the Midlands; the total mileage was round about 5,000.

The results of cheap postage were hardly less important than

[1] For the later history of the canals and railways, see below, pp. 595-7.

those of cheap travel in impressing upon the public the idea of a continuous improvement of the ordinary conditions of life. The introduction of the penny post in 1840 is another example of the conflict between reason and prejudice, and also of the way in which the initiative in reform came from private enter-prise, and often met blind opposition and timidity in the civil service. Rowland Hill,[1] whose suggestions convinced parlia-ment and the public, worked out his plans without any help from the postal officials. Hill's ideas were based on a few simple sums. It was common knowledge, twenty years after Waterloo, that few poor people ever sent letters by post, and that there were towns of 12,000 people without a post office or a postman; the cost of sending a letter from London to Ireland, and getting an answer, was about one-fifth of the weekly wage of a poor labourer.[2] The upper class used the privilege of franking letters which belonged to members of parliament and high officials; they took advantage of this free postage to such an extent that Stephen[3] at the colonial office once complained that the time which he gave every year to addressing envelopes was equal to six hours' work a day for a month. The postal charges were high, for those who paid them, because the system of postage was extremely wasteful. Letters were charged by weight and on delivery; hence every letter had to be weighed and charged on an elaborate scale, and the postman had to wait at every house to receive payment. Hill found by comparatively easy calculations, which no one in the post office had troubled to make, that the cost of carrying a letter from London to Edin-burgh was about one thirty-sixth of a penny; the postal charge was 1s. 4½d. Hill suggested that all letters should be prepaid, and that there should be a uniform set of charges, beginning at a penny, for all distances. He also suggested the postage

[1] Sir Rowland Hill (1795–1879), s. of a schoolmaster, b. Kidderminster; after teaching in his father's school, started a school of his own (see below, p. 485); secretary to the South Australian commission, 1835; considered question of reduc-tion of postage rates, and published a pamphlet on *Post Office Reform: its importance and practicability*, 1837, after Melbourne's government had refused to act on his suggestions; given an appointment in the post office, but dismissed after two years; director, and chairman of the Brighton railway, 1843–6; introduced express and excursion trains on the line; received a public testimonial, 1846; secretary to the postmaster-general, 1846–54; permanent secretary of the post office, 1854–64; member of railway commission, 1865, and published a separate report in favour of state purchase.

[2] There were cheaper local rates. Manchester and other towns had a penny postage.   [3] See below, p. 367.

stamp. In spite of resistance from the post office Hill's plan was put into effect. Within twenty-five years the number of letters and packages carried by post rose from 76 to 642 millions; the social and economic results of the change are beyond calculation.[1]

Gas-lighting was another invention of far-reaching importance. The demand for a new source of illumination came first from mill-owners who wanted something safer and cheaper than lamp-oil for lighting their factories at night. The French wars had interfered with the supply of whale-oil and Russian tallow. Hence the incentive to get over the difficulties of storing and distributing, as well as generating gas. It was soon clear that the only practical method of distribution was to provide gas-mains from a central generating plant. Capital was thus needed on the scale of joint stock companies. A 'National Light and Heat Company', later renamed 'The Gas Light and Coke Company', was formed in 1812. Part of Pall Mall opposite Carlton House had been lit by gas for exhibition purposes in 1807. In 1814 the oil lamps in the parish of St. Margaret's, Westminster, were discontinued. Next year Westminster Bridge was lit by gas. Insurance companies were already offering lower premiums for gas-lit mills, and the improvement in lighting made the streets safer against robbery. If gas-lighting added to the labour of the working class by facilitating night work, it also made possible more of the amenities of social life; Mechanics' Institutes, large concert and meeting halls as well as factories could be lit by gas.[2]

The Great Exhibition of 1851 thus summed up, for a nation which had already become 'machine-minded' and accustomed to 'railway speed', the immense possibilities of the future as well as the material advances made during the first half of the century. On the other hand the Exhibition, like the Diamond Jubilee forty-six years later, was in some respects the pageant of an epoch already passing away. Even before the Exhibition took

---

[1] One comment on the measure—from an aristocratic whig—is an interesting example of contemporary manners: 'The aristocracy are very furious at it, and think it beneath their dignity to understand anything about a *penny*.' Earl of Ilchester, *Chronicles of Holland House, 1820–1900*, p. 269.

[2] There was no gas at the Great Exhibition (which closed at sundown), but the gas industry organized an exhibition of their own at the Polytechnic Institution in London.

place political liberalism had been defeated in central Europe; the children born in the decade after 1851 were to see in their later middle age the sinister consequences of this defeat.

It is possible to treat the history of the years 1815–70 from the point of view of the technical progress and scientific discovery recorded in the immense glass house set up in Hyde Park. A history written from this angle would give a larger place to Faraday and Darwin than to Peel or Gladstone. A student of the progress of science or technology, however, would soon find that this progress was not uniform, and that it was determined by a number of circumstances outside its particular field; the history of science would become a history of politics, if it were to attempt explanation as well as narrative. Again, administrative developments might well be considered the most important features of the period. If any one field of administration were chosen as determining the rate and character of change in other spheres of English life, a history of England after 1815 would begin with a chapter on the growth of public education. Once more it would be found that the solution of administrative problems, including the treatment of education, depended upon political issues; each step was affected, every advance made or delayed, by a 'yes' or 'no' in parliament, after decisions taken by political parties and their leaders.

Great Britain was an island within sight of the coast of Europe, and an island possessing sovereignty over a widespread empire; these facts were of the greatest importance in determining the character of English policy, and, to an extent not always realized, the nature of English institutions and their development in the nineteenth century; here also the decisions taken in matters of foreign and imperial policy depended upon party leaders and party politics. Thus, whatever one's starting-point, one is brought back to the history of English politics, centred in Westminster, and even if this political history is to be explained as an economic conflict of classes, it is necessary, as a preliminary to analysis, to see what there is to be analysed. Therefore the clearest method of study, and the method suggested by the subject-matter, is to begin with an account of the rise and fall of parties, the character of the leaders chosen by these parties, the relations between ministers, parliament, and the country, and the political movements and events which affected the English people and their elected representatives.

With these guiding facts in mind, it is possible to extend the survey to the position of Great Britain in the world, and to consider the relations of the government and people of the country with other sovereign states (in other words, foreign policy) and the treatment of problems created by the existence of the empire (in other words, colonial and Indian policy). The relations of England and Ireland, though they were technically the relations between two parts of a United Kingdom, belong, from a realist standpoint, to a category of their own.

If these general and determining facts are known, it is easier to set in their right place a number of internal questions which can be studied in a certain isolation, but must always carry with them a reference back to the main political situation. These matters include the improvement in the facilities of local government, that is to say, the organization of a civilized social life, and the measures taken to raise the standard of knowledge and trained intelligence of every class through primary and secondary education. With this background it is possible to consider aspects of English life which do not draw their living force from politics, however much they affect and are affected by political change. Religion, literature, science, and art take a particular shape in society according to the conditions of the time, though they may respond to needs more enduring than any manifestation of temporal power in the kingdoms of this world.

It is important to remember the interdependence of the different subjects treated in this order of narrative and analysis. The method is one of convenience for the purpose in view: a history of England during a period of fifty-five years. A history of the world during this same period would require a different method; so too would a chapter on these years introductory to a history of England since 1870. Moreover, it should be possible for every chapter to throw light on every other chapter, and yet to be read as a story with a theme of its own.

BOOK I

POLITICS AND PARTIES

I

THE POLITICS OF THE UPPER CLASS AND THE REFORM OF PARLIAMENT, 1815–32

THE tories, who were in office in 1815, kept their parliamentary majority until 1830. The leaders of the party were able men; they had the support of the church, the universities, the services, the unreformed municipal corporations in the towns, most of the great landed families, and nearly all the country gentry. These supporters were likely to be content with things as they found them, and to oppose reforms which threatened their monopoly of place and power. On the other hand they were not fools; they had practical experience of government, since the administration of local affairs was largely in their control. They wanted to keep their authority and their privileges, but they were ready to use their common sense and to accept changes which did not affect their own position in the state. Thus, within a few years after Waterloo, and as soon as the immediate fears of revolution had passed, toryism began to change into conservatism. This transition from a blind defence of the existing order to a policy of cautious improvement could not be complete until after the reform of parliament. The reform of parliament was a difficult matter for the tories; it implied an attack upon vested interests, and, particularly, upon the vested interests of tory members in tory seats. The break-up of the tory majority, however, occurred before parliamentary reform became a dominant issue.

Sooner or later, a breach was inevitable between the 'pigtail' tories of the old school and the younger generation which was less afraid of change. This breach was unlikely while Lord

Liverpool[1] remained prime minister. In some respects, and especially in his views on economic questions, Liverpool was in advance of the rank and file of his party, but he lacked originality and breadth of mind. A French critic once said of him that, if he had been present on the first day of creation, he would have called out in panic, 'Mon Dieu, conservons nous le chaos!' He had been a minister almost continuously since 1793, and had seen the work of the board of control, the home, foreign, war, and colonial offices without making any suggestions for the improvement of these departments. On the other hand he had learned how to deal with men; his tact and patience, his own modesty and common sense kept his party together. Liverpool 'looked at party divisions almost with the eyes of a permanent official who can work loyally with chiefs of either party'.[2] Moreover, in the house of lords Eldon and Wellington were more commanding figures than the prime minister. Wellington's position was unique in England and in Europe. In spite of his high tory sympathies, he was regarded as 'a kind of fourth estate' above and beyond political rivalries.[3] Wellington's interpretation of politics was simple: he was a servant of the Crown, and, in this capacity, bound to do his duty. He had no political ambitions; his reputation was already so great that he had no need to concern himself with his popularity, even if he had cared to be popular. His opinions were narrow and unimaginative. He never understood economic problems; he was unaware of the new field of activities opened up by Bentham and his followers. He believed that the institutions of the country were perfect, and that change must be for the worse; his forecast of the results of parliamentary reform was absurdly wrong. Yet he never lost his nerve, and in times of party confusion his readiness to collaborate with any party or group in

[1] Robert Banks Jenkinson, 2nd earl of Liverpool (1770–1828), educ. Charterhouse and Christ Church, Oxford; saw the capture of the Bastille, 1789; M.P., 1790; held office, except for a short break in 1806–7, from 1793 until 1827; foreign secretary, 1801–4; cr. Baron Hawkesbury, 1803; home secretary, 1804–6 and 1807–9; refused to form an administration on the death of Pitt; succeeded his father, 1808; foreign secretary, and, later, secretary for war and the colonies, 1809–12; prime minister, 1812–27.

[2] G. C. Brodrick, *History of England, 1801–37* (1906), p. 209.

[3] Mrs. Arbuthnot (second wife of Charles Arbuthnot, see below, p. 107) wrote in March 1821 that Liverpool and Castlereagh thought that Wellington 'belonged too much to the country generally to be put into any situation which might render him an object for party violence to attack'. *Journal of Mrs. Arbuthnot*, ed. F. Bamford and the duke of Wellington, i. 83.

carrying on the king's government was of great value to his country.

Eldon,[1] owing to his intellectual power and force of character, drew attention to himself as the leader of the 'ultra-tories'.[2] He was a curious example of a man spoiled by his profession in an age when this profession made for harshness of character. Eldon was tolerant by disposition, and at the same time an obstinate opponent of relief for catholics or nonconformists. He was kind and affectionate in his private relationships, and ruthless in maintaining the death penalty for minor offences against the criminal law. Outside the courts he knew his own mind and spoke with decision; as chancellor he balanced legal niceties until his court was encumbered with immense arrears of business. Sidmouth,[3] as home secretary, also sat in the house of lords. He was to some extent a lightning conductor for the unpopularity of the domestic policy of the government. His administrative blunders brought him into contempt with the opposition; he was never rated highly enough to take the blame for decisions of policy.

Castlereagh,[4] as leader of the house of commons, had to bear the burden of parliamentary attack, and to accept responsibility for the unpopular legislation which he introduced. Castlereagh agreed with this repressive legislation, but his main

---

[1] John Scott, 1st earl of Eldon (1751–1838), s. of a coal-factor, b. Newcastle-upon-Tyne, educ. Newcastle grammar school and University College, Oxford; eloped with Elizabeth Surtees, d. of a rich banker, 1772; called to the bar, 1776; took silk, 1783; M.P., 1783; solicitor-general, 1788; attorney-general, 1793; lord chief justice of the common pleas, 1799; lord chancellor, 1801–6 and 1807–27. Eldon's eldest brother, Lord Stowell (1745–1836), was also a noted judge.

[2] The term 'ultra' was taken from the name of the extreme royalist party in France.

[3] Henry Addington, 1st Viscount Sidmouth (1757–1844), s. of a doctor; educ. Winchester and Brasenose College, Oxford; gave up the bar for politics owing to his friendship with Pitt; M.P., 1783; speaker of the house of commons, 1789–1801; prime minister, 1801–4; cr. Viscount Sidmouth, 1805; joined Perceval's ministry, 1812; home secretary, 1812–21; resigned from the cabinet owing to his disapproval of the recognition of the Latin American republics, 1824; his last speech in the house of lords was against catholic emancipation in 1829, and his last vote against the reform bill of 1832.

[4] Robert Stewart, Viscount Castlereagh, and 2nd marquis of Londonderry (1769–1822), b. Mountstewart, co. Down; educ. Armagh and St. John's College, Cambridge; travelled abroad, 1788–9; M.P., 1790; married Lady Emily Anne Hobart, d. of the earl of Buckinghamshire, 1794; chief secretary for Ireland, 1799–1801; resigned on refusal of George III to accept catholic emancipation; president of the board of control, 1802; secretary for war and the colonies, 1805, and again in 1807–9; foreign secretary, 1812–22. See also vol. xii of this *History*.

interests lay elsewhere, and his work in foreign policy was misunderstood because he had neither the wish nor the ability
to explain it to the country at large. In 1816 Canning,[1] the
ablest and most effective speaker on the tory side, held only a
minor post as president of the board of control. For this failure
to reach a position equal to his talents Canning was himself to
blame, though men of high rank who expected office almost
as of right were in no position to blame him for pushing his
claims. It is also true that Canning made enemies by a wit so
good that it deserved to be forgiven. On the other hand he
was a little too ambitious, and, at times, too unscrupulous. Sir
Walter Scott, who liked him, said that 'he wanted prudence
and patience, and in his eager desire to scramble to the highest,
was not sufficiently select as to his assistants'. Canning's unpopularity with the magnates of the party was one of the causes
of the break-up of the tories after the death of Liverpool.

Nevertheless, if the tories were soon to lose their unity as a
party, the whigs were also divided. For some years after 1815
they consisted of three groups. There was no leader strong
enough to unite these groups, or even to prevent one of them
from joining the tories. The secession of the Grenvillites[2] shows
the importance of family groups in the unreformed parliament.
Liverpool bought in 1822 the twelve votes controlled by Lord
Grenville as the easiest means of strengthening his majority.[3]
The loss of these minor place-hunters made no difference to the

---

[1] George Canning (1770–1827), b. London, s. of a barrister, whose widow went
on the stage after her husband's death in 1771; brought up by an uncle; educ.
Eton and Christ Church, Oxford; M.P., 1794; under-secretary for foreign affairs,
1796–9; paymaster-general, 1800–1; treasurer of the navy, 1804–6; foreign
secretary, 1807–9; resigned, and fought a duel with Castlereagh, 1809; refused
office under Perceval and under Liverpool in 1812; president of the board of control, 1816. See also vol. xii of this *History*.

[2] For the Grenvillites see vol. xii of this *History*.

[3] Grenville did not seek office for himself, but his nephew inherited his claims,
and was satisfied with nothing less than a dukedom. The group included three
cousins of the Grenvilles, and two clients who sat for the marquis (now duke) of
Buckingham's boroughs. One of the cousins, Charles Wynn, became president of
the board of control. Charles Wynn, whom Canning called the worst man of business he had known, held the post until 1828; he was then turned out owing to the
jealousy of Buckingham, who wanted office for himself. Wynn joined the opposition, and was secretary at war in Grey's administration. He held a minor post under
Peel, and is said to have refused the governor-generalship of India three times.
Owing to their peculiar voices Wynn and his brother were known as 'bubble and
squeak'. Charles Wynn was once a candidate for the speakership, and Canning's
remark that every one would address him as 'Mr. Squeaker' is a good example of
the way in which Canning made himself disliked.

intellectual strength of the whigs, but the remaining groups
did not form any closer union. Grey was the nominal head of
the party after Grenville left it; there was no recognized chief
in the commons.[1] The great whig families had thought Whitbread beneath them, because he was a brewer and therefore
a tradesman. Brougham[2] had many of the qualities of a leader.
He was quick, versatile, sharp in debate, but too rash in temper
and judgement. In any case the whig magnates distrusted
Brougham, as the tory magnates distrusted Canning. They were
jealous of his parliamentary reputation; they disliked his novel
habit of introducing subjects like education into the business
of the house. They could not deny his cleverness, but they
agreed with Greville's estimate of his character: 'Brougham
is...a...very remarkable instance of the inefficacy of the most
splendid talents, unless they are accompanied with other qualities, which scarcely admit of definition, but which must serve
the same purpose that ballast does for a ship.'[3] On the whole,
the whig magnates were right; yet they could not find anyone
whose ballast was also accompanied by splendid talents. They
accepted Tierney as leader with some reluctance, because he
too was not of good birth; they recognized in whig language,
that he was 'as much inferior to Brougham as the Regent to
Bonaparte'.[4] Tierney withdrew from the leadership in 1821
owing to disputes in the party. For the next nine years the whig
opposition had not even a nominal head. Althorp[5] was asked
to take the post in 1827; he refused it. He gave way to the
pressure of his friends in 1830, and members of the house

[1] For the history of the whig leadership, see M. Roberts, 'The leadership of the
whig party in the house of commons', *E.H.R.*, Oct. 1935, and A. Aspinall, ibid.,
July 1926.

[2] Henry Peter Brougham, 1st Baron Brougham and Vaux (1778–1868), s. of
Henry Brougham; educ. Edinburgh high school and university; passed advocate,
1800; took part in founding the *Edinburgh Review*; admitted Lincoln's Inn, 1803;
M.P., 1810; lord rector of Glasgow University, 1825; lord chancellor, 1830–4; lived
mainly at Cannes after 1840 when parliament was not sitting.

[3] Greville, *Journal of the reigns of King George IV and King William IV*, 2 Jan. 1828.

[4] The earl of Sefton to J. G. Lambton, quoted in Aspinall, op. cit. p. 391.

[5] John Charles Spencer, Viscount Althorp, and 3rd Earl Spencer (1782–1845);
educ. Harrow and Trinity College, Cambridge; M.P., 1804; began as a tory but
joined the whigs largely owing to the influence of his friends; supported parliamentary reform after 1815; brought forward measures for establishing local courts for
the recovery of small debts, 1821–4; chancellor of the exchequer, 1830–4; retired
from politics after 1834 and refused the lord-lieutenancy of Ireland and the
governor-generalship of Canada. Althorp was interested in farming and cattle-
breeding, and was a member of the Society for the Diffusion of Useful Knowledge.

noticed that Peel started when, for the first time for many years, a whig speaker used the term 'we' in describing his party. Althorp owed his reputation to his honesty and plain common sense; Melbourne described him as 'the tortoise upon whom the world rests'. His mind worked slowly, and he was sensitive enough to dislike the 'pain and puzzle in his brain'. He described his entry into politics as the 'great fault of his life'. When he took office under Grey, he wrote to Russell: 'I have not been able to escape, and have been obliged to sacrifice myself, for to me it is an entire sacrifice.' He shared the burden of the debates on the reform bill; on the resignation of the ministry his first thought was not for the measure which was exciting the whole country, but for the happy chance which would allow him to go back to his shooting.[1]

Lord John Russell[2] was twenty-three in 1815. He was not strong, and for some years came rarely to the house of commons. He spoke only once between 1816 and 1818, and even thought of giving up politics. In 1819 he took up the question of parliamentary reform. He wanted large towns to be given the seats of boroughs found guilty of corruption. He suggested a moderate widening of the franchise, but described himself as 'an enemy to extensive reform because he found that every principle of that sort led to a remodelling of all our political institutions which he was far from wishing'.[3] He believed it necessary to keep, and even to increase, the county constituencies where the landed interest was predominant.

The whigs might have gained in popularity by bringing forward a comprehensive scheme of reform. They were not agreed about any scheme. The magnates of the party did not wish to lose their 'pocket' boroughs; in 1830 Lord Holland wrote that he was 'never a very keen reformer'. Grey gave so little heed to the matter that he asked in 1820 what the ordinary members of the party thought about it, and whether it was likely to be

[1] A few days later the news was brought to Althorp that Wellington had failed to form a ministry. Althorp was ound 'in a closet with a groom, busy oiling the locks of his fowling-pieces, and lamenting the decay into which they had fallen during his ministry'. Lord Cockburn, *Life of Lord Jeffrey*, i. 332.

[2] Lord John Russell, 1st Earl Russell (1792–1878), 3rd s. of 6th duke of Bedford; educ. mainly with tutors, and at Edinburgh University; M.P., 1813; paymaster-general, 1830; home secretary and leader in the house of commons in Melbourne's second administration, 1835; prime minister, 1846–52, and in 1865–6. Russell was a short man, with a small and thin voice.

[3] Hansard, N.S. i. 520.

'the *sine qua non*' of a whig ministry. Four years later Tierney said that it could 'never be a bond of party', because even among those who supported reform there were 'a thousand different shades of opinion'.[1] The whigs were united on the subject of catholic emancipation. They were more interested than the tories in advocating economy; they were also more careful, largely because they were out of office, in scrutinizing the abuses of the pensions list. Their defence of constitutional liberty had narrow limits. They approved of the suppression of revolutionary literature, and accepted what they called the legitimate influence of the Crown. They were hardly less alarmed than the tories at the popular disturbances which affected the country after the war, and equally disgusted at the small group of radicals who voted with them against the government. There was a good deal to be said for Hazlitt's remark that the two parties were like rival stage-coaches which splashed each other with mud, but went by the same road to the same place.

The parliamentary radicals[2] counted for little in the unreformed house of commons, though their following in the country must be judged by the steady growth of opinion in favour of electoral reform. Until this reform had taken place, the radicals could not hope to increase their numbers in the house. They were associated, not always wrongly, with reckless support of agitation; they did not produce any leader of high talent or personal weight before 1832. Ricardo[3] indeed voted with them during his four years in parliament, but he represented the twelve electors of the Irish rotten borough of Portarlington, took no part in English election contests, and spoke in the commons mainly on economic questions. No other radical member had much authority, or was heard with much respect.

The main problems of government, after the war, may be expressed in terms of the defence of property. Without a stable currency, and a reduction of the heavy expenditure of the war period, the property of fundholders, merchants, and all creditors

---

[1] Hansard, N.S. xi. 721.

[2] The term 'radical' or 'radical reformer' came into use towards the end of the eighteenth century, but was not generally employed until about 1819.

[3] David Ricardo (1772–1823), s. of a Dutch Jew; went into business, 1786; wrote on economic questions from 1809; published his *Principles of Political Economy and Taxation* in 1817.

was unsafe. Without the protection of agriculture the landed interest would have to meet a catastrophic fall in rent-rolls. Without public order, no property was safe. The first of these problems was a technical one, and never a clear-cut party question; Peel[1] and Ricardo held the same views about the restoration of the currency, and a parliamentary committee of inquiry (1819) into the expediency of a return to cash payments included Tierney as well as Castlereagh, Canning, Huskisson, and Peel. The committee recommended a return to payments on a gold basis in four stages between February 1820 and May 1823. There was little opposition to their report, but too sharp a contraction of the note-issue brought a fall in commodity prices, and widespread unemployment. Public opinion began to accuse the government of undue favour to the fundholders, and another parliamentary committee, dealing with agricultural distress, blamed the return to gold;[2] the whig leaders supported the ministry and, in spite of criticism from the landed interest in each party, no change of policy was adopted.

The question of a stable currency was thus settled; the regulation of credit was equally important for all business transactions and for the security of those who put their money into banks. There was no limit to the amount of notes which a bank might issue; many small country banks had failed in the general collapse of prices after the war, but as soon as trade recovered from the effects of deflation there was a wave of speculation, particularly in the newly recognized states of South America. The small notes of the country banks financed much of this increase in credit. The greater part of the South American ventures were bound to fail, and Liverpool warned speculators as early as March 1825 that they were running grave risks. The crisis came in November 1825; a number of London bankers were called out of church on a Sunday by demands for gold from their country customers. Over sixty country banks and six London houses failed. The lesson was obvious. The country

[1] Sir Robert Peel, 2nd bart. (1788–1850), b. near Bury; educ. Harrow and Christ Church, Oxford; M.P., 1809; under-secretary for war and the colonies, 1810; chief secretary for Ireland, 1812; home secretary, 1822–7 and 1828–30; prime minister, 1834–5 and 1841–6.

[2] In 1817 the mint issued new gold coins. These coins were $\frac{20}{21}$ of the weight of the old guineas, and were known as 'sovereigns'—a name given to gold pieces in Tudor and Stuart times. The country had lost the habit of gold coins, and the 'sovereigns' were little used in internal trade. The act of 1819 allowed free export of gold; many of the coins were exported for reminting into French gold pieces.

banks were too small; they had remained small because the
monopoly of the Bank of England prevented the establishment
of banks on a joint-stock basis. Hence in 1826 an act, supported
by both parties in the commons, permitted the opening of joint-
stock banks for the issue of notes (of not less than £5 in denomination) outside a radius of sixty-five miles from London.[1] In
1833 the bank charter act allowed joint-stock banks to come
within the sixty-five-mile radius.[2]

Currency and credit affected every interest, and a division
of opinion was unlikely in parliament; most of the agitation in
the country was carried on by cranks who did not understand
what they were talking about. The protection of agriculture
was hardly less important, but it was more difficult to find a
solution likely to be accepted outside as well as inside parliament, because agricultural protection meant taxes on corn, and
taxes on corn might well appear to be taxes imposed upon the
community by whig and tory landlords acting in their own selfish
interests. The country labourers gained nothing from the high
price of bread, and the landlords represented no one save themselves and their tenant farmers. Thus after 1815 the attack
upon the corn laws, which had once been directed against corn
dealers and millers, became an attack upon a comparatively
small class accused of taking excessive profit from the ownership
of land. The analysis of rent expounded by Ricardo and others
added to the unpopularity of the landed interest. Ricardo
limited the application of this analysis to rent from land, and
English revolutionary thought, for obvious reasons, concerned
itself by tradition more with land than with capital.

The landowners held a majority in parliament, and the corn
law of 1804 has been described as the first attempt by a parliament of landlords to legislate purely in their own interest as
owners of arable soil, and to secure for themselves and their
tenants the high prices resulting from war and bad harvests
between 1793 and 1801. The details of the act of 1804 matter
little; the renewal of the war, the continental system, and the
bad harvests of 1811 and 1812 kept the price of corn far above
the figure at which a protective duty came into effect.

There was a change in 1814. The defeat of Napoleon, the

---

[1] The act did not apply to Scotland, where the banking situation was more
stable. Sir Walter Scott's *Letters of Malachi Malagrowther* were written to defend
the Scottish system.   [2] For the history of banking after 1833, see p. 112.

end of the blockade, and an excellent harvest in 1813 brought a rapid fall in the price of corn. In 1814 a committee appointed by the house of commons estimated that, although the cost of growing corn at a fair profit varied according to place, time, and season, the average price for an equitable return was about 80s. a quarter. The committee recommended the exclusion of foreign corn until the price of home-grown wheat reached this figure. These recommendations were discussed in the press and in a number of pamphlets. The arguments of Malthus[1] and Ricardo represent the most balanced statements of the case for and against protection. The evidence laid before the committee convinced Malthus that 80s. was a fair price; he thought it dangerous to depend upon foreign corn, since the supply might be cut off by legislation in foreign countries at times of scarcity. Anyhow he feared that if foreign corn were admitted at a price below 80s. farmers would be unable to pay their way, labourers would have their wages lowered, and manufacturers would suffer from a fall in the purchasing-power of landlords and farmers. Ricardo wanted free trade in corn in order that Great Britain might use her wealth and population to the greatest advantage. There was no risk of a sudden closing of the supply, since no foreign country could resist the pressure of those who lived by meeting the British demand. Parliament accepted the committee's figure, and passed an act in 1815 allowing foreign corn to be imported, or taken out of bond, free of duty when the price of wheat was 80s. The act of 1815 did not satisfy the landowners because it did not keep the price of corn up to 80s. At the beginning of 1820 wheat fell to 64s., and in November 1822 to 38s. 10d. These figures caused an outcry among farmers and landlords. The ministers would not increase the amount of protection, but, as matters grew worse from the point of view of the landed interest, they substituted a sliding scale for the sharp distinction between absolute prohibition and absolute freedom of entry for foreign corn. The price of corn began to rise in 1823, and there was now an agitation against the landlords, although war rents and prices had disappeared. The pamphleteers made use of the Ricardian theory of rent; Thompson's *Catechism on the Corn Laws* spoke of measures 'which enact that the labourer shall not exchange his produce for food, except at certain shops, namely, the shops of

---

[1] For the Rev. T. R. Malthus (1766–1834), see vol. xii of this *History*.

the landowners'. The effect of the corn laws was 'the same in kind, as would arise from limiting the food consumed in the United Kingdom to what could be produced in the Isle of Wight'.[1]

These attacks gained in force after Huskisson had begun to reduce the duties on raw materials and manufactured goods. Creevey thought that the government was ready 'to hold out the landed grandees as the enemies of the manufacturing population' if they resisted a change in the law.[2] One of the landed grandees asked the house of commons 'to put down with all their might and force the abominable theories of political economists',[3] but the government listened to the views of the experts that the British market could not be flooded by cheap corn from the Baltic, and, in 1828, fixed a new sliding scale with a nominal duty of 1s. when the price of corn reached 73s. Large quantities of corn were imported after the bad harvests of 1828-9. The harvests between 1830 and 1835 were good; the price of corn was low, and the demand for repeal of the laws did not revive until the succession of bad harvests and bad years of trade after 1839.[4]

The protection of agriculture, supported by whigs and tories, was a difficult matter because it could be interpreted as a class measure, but there is much to be said for the view that the corn laws were of little use to the landed interest and did little harm to the consumer, and that most of the arguments brought forward on either side of the question were economically unsound or exaggerated. The third problem connected with the defence of property was equally exaggerated. The maintenance of public order was not easy, but the chances of revolutionary disturbance on a large scale were never as serious as they appeared to the governing class. A few desperate men aimed at a complete overthrow of society; their plans, foolish in themselves, were always betrayed, and public opinion was never behind them. The real cause of disturbance was the misery of the poor, and the poor asked for little more than local and immediate remedies which would maintain their standard of life within the framework of the existing scheme of things.

A sudden fall in the demand, at home and abroad, for British

[1] Quoted in D. G. Barnes, *History of the English Corn Laws*, pp. 210-11.
[2] *The Creevey Papers*, ii. 100.
[3] Smart, op. cit. ii. 117. Tom Moore once said, 'When you tread on a nobleman's corn, how he winces!'
[4] For the later history of the corn laws see below, pp. 118-25.

manufactures was the main cause of unemployment immediately after the war. The reduction in the numbers of the army and navy added to the distress; the strength of the navy fell from 100,000 in 1815 to 35,000 in 1816. The labourers, on the verge of starvation, began desultory rioting, particularly in the eastern counties. There was a certain amount of destruction of machinery in Nottinghamshire; elsewhere most of the strikers were orderly. The colliers in the Wolverhampton district started the novel method of sending deputations round the country, but they travelled in a law-abiding way. About the same time there was a revival of the Hampden Club, which had been founded in support of parliamentary reform by Major Cartwright[1] on a basis excluding all working men. Branches were set up throughout the country, and membership was now extended to every one who cared to pay a contribution of a penny a week.[2] The middle-class movement thus came into contact with the less cautious propaganda carried on by Cobbett, and, in a more violent form, by Hunt and his associates. These agitators took up the idea of large petitions to the Regent. They held a great meeting in Spa Fields on 15 November 1816, at which Hunt appeared with an escort carrying the tricolour flag and a revolutionary cap on top of a pike. The meeting was adjourned until 2 December. Hunt was again billed to appear, but deliberately arrived late. The less reputable leaders preceded him, and took away part of the crowd in procession to Clerkenwell. They broke into a gunsmith's shop, wounded a bystander, and marched towards the City, where a force collected by the lord mayor dispersed them.

In the following month some one threw a stone, or aimed an air-gun, at the Regent on his way to parliament. These disorders, and the dangerous excitement produced by the great meetings in favour of reform alarmed the government. A year earlier the cabinet had refused Sidmouth's demand for a general prohibition of meetings; they now called secret committees of the two houses, and produced evidence of a revolutionary plot to seize the Bank and the Tower. Their evidence was not very reliable, since it was necessarily based upon stories

[1] For Major Cartwright, see vol. xii of this *History*, p. 571.
[2] Halévy has pointed out (*Histoire du peuple anglais au xixme siècle* (Eng. trans.), ii. 13–14) that the idea of a small weekly subscription was borrowed from the wesleyan and other evangelical organizations.

told by informers.[1] Most of the meetings had been peaceful, and the Spa Fields riot was an isolated case. Nevertheless memories of the French Revolution were too near for ministers or parliament to take lightly these invocations of violence. The cabinet decided to suspend the Habeas Corpus act, and to pass measures against the holding of seditious meetings, or attempts to weaken the loyalty of the troops. The bills passed the two houses within a week. There were protests in the country; a band of petitioners started out from Manchester on a march to London. They carried blankets for their night shelter, and became known as the Blanketeers. There were alarmist rumours about them, but the leaders were arrested before the day of the march, and most of the rank and file who were not held up at Stockport fell out at Macclesfield. Two months later an outbreak in Derbyshire was a complete failure.

Sidmouth, again relying upon evidence from spies and informers, secured another commission of inquiry, and the government began to take measures against the authors and printers of seditious and blasphemous pamphlets. Their most important prosecutions broke down. Public opinion thought that the ministers were interfering unnecessarily with the rights of citizens, and Sidmouth himself was discredited when it was found that some of his information came from *agents provocateurs*. In any case the good harvest of 1817 and the revival of trade put an end both to the disturbances and to the panic. There was another cycle of disturbance in 1819. In July a meeting at Birmingham elected an attorney to represent the city at a self-styled parliamentary convention; Leeds and Manchester would have taken similar steps if Sidmouth had not declared the proceeding illegal, but there was nothing to prevent the holding of meetings for the lawful purpose of drawing up petitions. The Manchester reformers invited Hunt to speak at a meeting on 16 August, and chose an open space, known as St. Peter's Field, as their meeting-place. They drilled large numbers of men, according to their own statement, in order that they might march without confusion to the Field: according to their opponents, in order that they might be prepared for resistance in arms. On 16 August some 50,000–60,000 people assembled at the meeting-

---

[1] There was no other term for a detective in 1817, and 'informers' were generally hated owing to their connexion with revenue cases. The staff of the home office at this time did not include more than twenty clerks.

place, carrying banners with revolutionary inscriptions. There was no disorder; unfortunately, the magistrates, who had brought special constables and detachments of the Lancashire and Cheshire Yeomanry, lost their nerve, and ordered Hunt's arrest. The soldiers who tried to reach him were pressed by the mob and drew their sabres. A troop of hussars came to their rescue and caused a general panic, in which eleven people were killed (including two women) and about four hundred wounded.

This 'massacre of Peterloo' caused great indignation in the country. The common council of London, using their right to approach the sovereign, sent a protest to the Regent, who had congratulated the magistrates on their action. In Yorkshire, Earl Fitzwilliam, the lord lieutenant of the West Riding, attended a meeting of protest. On the other hand the government decided that the meeting had been an illegal assembly; they acted upon the opinion of their law officers, but the position was uncertain and even Eldon was not entirely convinced. Hence the cabinet decided to clear up the law about public meetings, and to take steps to prevent any revolutionary outbreak. They brought forward six bills, three of which were not unreasonable. These three measures dealt with the procedure of bringing cases to trial, the prohibition of meetings for military exercises, and the issue of warrants for the search of arms. A fourth, regulating public meetings, was much more open to dispute. The existing freedom of public meeting was not a recognition of the right of agitators of avowedly revolutionary opinions to collect thousands of people at open-air assemblies; on the other hand the government went too far in limiting meetings for the drawing up of petitions to residents of the parish in which the meeting was held.[1] Liverpool admitted that these parish meetings 'would generally be flat'. The fifth and sixth acts allowed magistrates to seize blasphemous and seditious literature, and extended the stamp act to all papers and periodical pamphlets of a certain size.

It may be said on the tory side that these laws were passed at a time of general unrest in Europe. In October 1819 Grey wrote to a friend who supported reform that 'the leaders of the popular party, or rather of the Mob' wanted 'not Reform but

---

[1] Meetings called by the mayors of corporate towns were exempt from the prohibition, but many large towns, such as Birmingham, Manchester, and Sheffield, were not incorporated. Two of the six acts survive to this day in an emended form.

Revolution', and that 'if a convulsion follows their attempts to work upon the minds of the people, inflamed as they are by distress, for which your Reform would afford a very inadequate remedy, I shall not precede you many months on the scaffold'.[1] A wild but dangerous conspiracy was detected in London within two months after the passing of the six acts. A certain Arthur Thistlewood, who had been imprisoned after the Spa Fields riot, had finished his term in the autumn of 1819. On his re-lease he revived an absurd plan for the seizure of London, and, with a few associates of no political importance, arranged a plot to murder the cabinet. The conspirators had vague ideas of a general insurrection; it is doubtful whether they intended to do more than make something for themselves out of the con-fusion. The plot was given away, and the conspirators arrested in Cato St. (off the Edgware Road). Before their trial proclama-tions were posted in Glasgow, on behalf of a committee for the organization of a provisional government, inviting the work-men of the city to begin a general strike. There were minor disturbances, but a troop of horse was enough to put them down. Once again, an improvement in the economic situation brought a period of quiet, and took the edge off the demand for reform. Although another depression might bring a renewal of agitation, James Mill was probably right in thinking that there was no hope of any steady popular support for a progressive policy until the people were better educated.

The affair of Queen Caroline justified such a view. This sordid incident had a long history behind it. In 1795, nearly ten years after his illegal marriage with Mrs. Fitzherbert, the Regent married Princess Caroline of Brunswick-Wolfenbüttel. He treated her badly, and wanted to be rid of her. In 1806 he forced the government to accept an inquiry into her conduct. The princess's reputation was damaged, but the serious charges against her were not proved. After 1815 there was a new factor in the case. George III might die at any time; the Regent's health was not good, and his daughter Princess Charlotte might therefore succeed to the throne. Meanwhile the queen was wandering about Italy, and reports of her entourage were well known in England; on the other hand, her cause offered prospects, in view of her daughter's chances of succession. Brougham observed these possibilities, and became the queen's

[1] Quoted in J. R. M. Butler, *The Passing of the Great Reform Bill*, pp. 34-35.

chief adviser. Princess Charlotte died in 1817; henceforward the queen's business was something of an embarrassment. In 1819 Brougham made an offer on Caroline's behalf, but without her knowledge, which looked as though he wanted the matter to be taken out of his hands. He proposed that, in return for an increase in her allowance from £35,000 to £50,000 a year, and a grant of this sum for life, she should give up her title and agree never to come back to England.

A few months later George III died. The new king at once asked his ministers to begin divorce proceedings on his behalf. Liverpool doubted whether the evidence would be convincing, and hinted that the queen's counter-charges might discredit her husband and the monarchy. He suggested a settlement providing the queen with a large allowance on condition that she lived abroad. After a good deal of petulance, and threats to change his ministers or to retire to Hanover, the king gave way. The next move rested with the queen, and, to some extent, with Brougham. If Brougham wanted to wreck the ministry, he might persuade the queen to come back and to claim her rights. For a time Brougham hesitated. In March 1820 he let it be known that if he were given a silk gown[1] he would do his best to keep the queen out of the country. The ministers considered Brougham's terms without enthusiasm. While they hesitated, Brougham's ambition increased. He seems to have thought that he might turn out the government, and become prime minister in a new administration. Liverpool now asked him to tell the queen about the offer of money. Brougham kept the offer to himself for some time, and then advised the queen to reject the terms.

Meanwhile the queen's cause was taken up by others, notably by Alderman Wood, a radical politician whom George IV described as 'that beast Wood'.[2] The queen trusted Wood more than she trusted Brougham. Wood saw her in France, and advised her to come at once to London. She took his advice, and, under his escort, entered London in triumph on 6 June 1820; even the sentries at Carlton House saluted as she passed. To the popular mind the queen was a wronged and courageous

[1] i.e. if he were appointed King's Counsel: this appointment would be of great financial use because it would give him precedence over barristers other than K.C.s. There is still some obscurity about Brougham's attitude.

[2] Queen Victoria made him a baronet.

woman, pursued by ministers who had suppressed the liberties of the nation. Wilberforce himself felt the excitement, and wrote: 'One can't help admiring [the queen's] spirit, though I fear she has been very profligate.'[1] The tumult lasted throughout the proceedings in parliament against the queen. The cabinet introduced a bill to dissolve the king's marriage, and thereby to deprive the queen of her title; a public inquiry into the queen's conduct thus became a necessary stage in passing the bill. The inquiry lasted from 17 August until the early part of November, and the bill was passed in the house of lords by a small majority. It was clear that the peers thought the queen guilty, but doubted the expediency of the divorce. The cabinet decided that there was little chance of getting their bill through the commons, and dropped it.

Although the town was illuminated when the news became known, the queen's popularity did not last much longer. In January she accepted an offer of £50,000 a year and a house. She was no longer a symbol of resistance to oppression; she had passed over to the side of the pensioners. The king's coronation in July gave her a chance of regaining popular sympathy. She claimed the right to be crowned. Her claim was not technically valid, but the crowd was on her side as she drove to the abbey with Lord Hood and asked to be admitted. Lord Hood had only one ticket of admission, and the doorkeeper would not allow him to enter the abbey with the queen. Thereupon the queen gave up the attempt, and at once the crowd turned against her. She died in the following month.

The popular disturbances of 1817 and 1819 and the affair of the queen were outside the range of whig politics. The whigs had not suggested plans for the relief of distress; they agreed with the tories that parliament could do nothing to cure commercial depression. Their demands for financial reform and economy in administration did not go far enough to win popularity. The Grenvillites had voted for the six acts; Russell had taken care to dissociate himself from the democratic reformers by a statement that he disliked 'the cry of new lamps for old. ... Small as the remaining treasure of the constitution is, I cannot consent to throw it into the wheel for obtaining a prize in the lottery of constitutions.'[2] Brougham, who had wanted

---

[1] R. I. and S. Wilberforce, *Life of W. Wilberforce*, v 55.
[2] Hansard, xli. 1105.

co-operation between the whigs and moderate radicals, described the radical group in 1827 as 'a set of drivellers, who
call themselves a kind of *doctrinaires*, and hold opinions subversive of all liberty. . . . These men have much of the press in
their hands, which makes them look bigger than they are. They
are in their religion intolerable atheists, in their politics bloody-
minded republicans, and in morals somewhat gross, and most
selfish latitudinarians.'[1]

It was equally characteristic of the whigs that, as a party,
they made little use of the affair of the queen. They voted
against the bill of divorce. They realized that the king's folly
had put the tories in a difficult position. Russell hoped for a
revival of the old alliance between the whigs and the people,
but few whigs believed that the outburst of feeling for the
queen would be lasting, or that it would destroy the ministry.
Grey and his friends thought the business vulgar and discreditable. Lord Holland, in a letter to J. G. Lambton, pointed out
the contrast between the indifference of the public to the death
of Grattan on 4 June and the excitement about the landing of
the queen at Dover. 'Such is the happy effect of that beautiful
institution called monarchy, and such the disposition of that
enlightened nation called England.'[2]

The suicide of Castlereagh in 1822 did not break up the tory
government; it marked the end of the old toryism because the
leadership of the house of commons passed to Canning. Canning resigned his office at the time of the queen's trial, and
thought so badly of his political future at home that he accepted
the governor-generalship of India. He was still in England at
the time of Castlereagh's death. Liverpool and Wellington
thought his support necessary to the ministry and were prepared
to take him at his own terms; Canning therefore became foreign
secretary and leader in the commons.

Within a short time Canning gave a new tone to the administration. He maintained tory principles; he had agreed
with the repressive domestic policy of the cabinet, and did not
support parliamentary reform. On the other hand he favoured
catholic emancipation and realized that the tory party could
check the reform movement only by showing that they could
pass 'improving' measures of an administrative kind, and were not

[1] A. Aspinall, *Lord Brougham and the Whig Party*, p. 145.   [2] Ibid., p. 111.

occupied merely with the maintenance of abuses. He took care
to explain his foreign policy in terms which Englishmen understood, and of which they approved.[1] He supported Huskisson at
the board of trade. The general effect of this progressive policy
may be seen in the temporary decline of interest in parliamentary reform. In 1822 Russell obtained 164 votes for the transfer of a hundred seats from the smallest boroughs to the counties
and the great towns; four years later only 123 members voted
for the disfranchisement of boroughs found guilty of corruption.

Huskisson[2] was more important than Canning in bringing life
and new ideas into the commercial and fiscal policy of the
government. He knew how to win the support of business men;
he did not conceal his opinion that the commercial interest of
every country was 'most effectually consulted by leaving [sic] to
every part of the world to raise those productions for which soil
and climate are best adapted'.[3] There was a considerable movement of opinion in favour of free, or, at all events, less protected,
trade as a remedy for commercial depression. In 1820 the merchants of London drew up a petition against restraint of trade.[4]
The petitioners used the classic arguments against tariffs. They
held that 'a declaration against the anti-commercial principles
of our restrictive system' was necessary because foreign manufacturers regarded the British tariff as a reason for protecting
themselves against British goods. These foreign competitors
insisted 'upon our superiority in capital and machinery, as we
do upon their comparative exemption from taxation'. Even if
the removal of British protective duties did not result in concessions from other countries, 'our restrictions would not be less
prejudicial to our capital and industry because other governments persisted in preserving impolitic regulations'. This

---

[1] Mrs. Arbuthnot wrote in Nov. 1823 that 'Mr. Canning has been making himself more ridiculous than ever by going round the country *speechifying* and discussing
the acts and intentions of the Government. This is quite a new system *among us* and
excites great indignation.' *Journal of Mrs. Arbuthnot*, i. 275.

[2] William Huskisson (1770–1830), b. near Wolverhampton; lived in France,
1783–92; saw the capture of the Bastille, and, in Aug. 1792, helped the governor
of the Tuileries to escape from the mob; M.P., 1796; under-secretary at war,
1795–1801; secretary to the treasury, 1804–5, and 1807–9; colonial agent for
Ceylon, 1811–23; run down and killed at the opening of the Liverpool and Manchester railway.

[3] Huskisson's pamphlet on *The Depreciation of the Currency* (1810, reissued in
1819), quoted in S. Buxton, *Finance and Politics*, p. 17 n.

[4] The petition, drawn up by Thomas Tooke, author of the *History of Prices*, is
printed in Smart, op. cit. i. 744-7.

petition, and others presented by the merchants of Glasgow and Manchester, had an effect upon parliament; a committee of the commons reported that all restriction on trade, of whatsoever nature, was an evil, 'to be justified only by some adequate political expediency'.

Most supporters of this view would have held that 'political expediency' justified the protection of agriculture and shipping, and indeed that complete free trade was unpractical. It was not easy to transfer capital and labour to new industries, and the demand for British manufactures, especially in less civilized countries, was limited. Hence 'open trade', the substitution of protective for prohibitive duties, might be taken as a general aim. In any case, owing to the refusal of parliament to accept an income tax, import duties of some kind were necessary for revenue purposes; the receipts from taxation did not reach £60,000,000; about half of this sum was used for the service of the debt (apart from the sinking fund), and a quarter was spent on the army and navy. The margin of possible economy was therefore limited.

In 1822 Robinson[1] and Thomas Wallace, as president and vice-president of the board of trade, persuaded parliament to relax the navigation laws in order to attract the commerce of the former Spanish colonies, and to give British colonists in North America or the West Indies direct access to European ports for their own produce or manufactures. In 1823 Robinson became chancellor of the exchequer and Huskisson succeeded him at the board of trade. Wallace resigned because he thought, not unreasonably, that he had a claim to the latter post, but Robinson supported Huskisson on the financial side, while leaving him to bring forward proposals for the improvement of trade. Huskisson's great ability soon made him the dominant partner in their collaboration. In 1824 the duties on rum, silk, and wool were reduced; the duties on raw silk fell from 4s. 0d. to 6d., and on wool from 6d. to a 1d. a pound.[2] An *ad valorem* duty of 25 per cent. on silk goods took the place of prohibition. In 1825 there was a reduction in the high duties on cotton, linen, and woollen goods, on coffee, glass, books, paper, porcelain

---

[1] Frederick John Robinson, cr. Viscount Goderich, 1827, and earl of Ripon, 1833 (1782–1859); s. of 2nd Baron Grantham; b. London; educ. Harrow and St. John's College, Cambridge; M.P., 1806. His two nicknames, 'Prosperity Robinson' and 'Goody Goderich' were given him by Cobbett.

[2] The reduction came into force in 1826.

and china, copper, zinc, lead, and iron. Huskisson found a general duty of 50 per cent. on manufactured goods other than those specially taxed, and lowered it to 20 per cent. He also increased the freedom of colonial trade, modified the navigation laws in the interest of the British re-export trade, by excluding from their application European goods put into bond, and offered equality of shipping dues to all countries ready to make similar concessions. Foreign and British ships now entered British harbours on the same terms.[1]

Public opinion recognized the change in the attitude of ministers towards domestic questions. Hitherto the leaders of the popular movement had not taken much interest in minor reforms such as the repeal of the combination laws of 1799 and 1800. There seemed little hope of persuading the tory majority to allow liberty of association to working men. The new move in the party encouraged a direct attack upon the restrictive laws. After the repeal of the statute of apprentices in 1814,[2] nothing remained of the old paternal supervision of the conditions of labour. If working men could no longer appeal to authority, they might well claim the right to protect themselves by combining with their fellow tradesmen. A combination of working men was, however, illegal, although it was no longer directed against decisions given by magistrates and equally binding upon employers and employed. On the other hand, with the greater concentration of industry, combination might interfere with freedom of contract, or be diverted to political ends. For this reason, although the combination act of 1800 applied to masters as well as to workmen, the combinations of masters were tolerated more easily because they were not politically dangerous. The laws were not always enforced against workmen, but they could be used for strike-breaking. During the

---

[1] Threats of retaliation from the Prussian government had made this step inevitable, and Huskisson's measure, which put an end to a system which had been one of the mainstays of British policy for a century and a half, passed in a house containing only ninety members. Since 1816 there had been reciprocity of treatment between British shipping in U.S. ports and U.S. shipping in ports of the United Kingdom. This reciprocity was extended to the West Indies in 1822, but, owing to mutual discriminatory duties, was not effective until 1830. See R. L. Schuyler, *The Fall of the Old Colonial System*, ch. iii. The navigation laws were finally repealed in 1849, though the reservations on coastwise shipping remained in force for another four years.

[2] For the combination laws, and the statute of apprentices, see vols. xii and ix of this *History*.

disturbed years there was some reason for the distrust of the associations of working men. Many of their leaders held extravagant political opinions, and the men had little experience of collective bargaining. The violence of opinion and of method was greatest in the larger and less well-paid industries, and in trades threatened by new machinery where domestic labour was fighting a losing battle. As late as 1834 a committee of the London Compositors' Society pointed out that

unfortunately almost all trades unions hitherto formed have relied for success upon extorted oaths and physical force. The fault and destruction of all trades unions has [sic] hitherto been that they have copied the vices which they professed to condemn. While disunited and powerless they have stigmatised their employers as grasping taskmasters; but as soon as they were united and powerful, then they become tyrants in their turn, and unreasonably endeavoured to exact more than the nature of their employment demanded, or than their employers could afford to give. Hence their failure was inevitable.[1]

The London compositors were better paid than the cotton operatives of Lancashire; their livelihood was not threatened by new machinery, and their trade was less subject to extreme fluctuations of demand. In any case the best solution was the removal of the need for 'extorted oaths'. The initiative came from the radical side, and from a politician who never sat in parliament. Francis Place[2] was in advance of his time in the technique of managing committees and carrying reforms by clever manipulation. Place belonged to the steady, intelligent upper class of London artisans. There was nothing academic or doctrinaire about his opinions; he was a cocksure radical individualist, accepting most of the orthodox economic views of his time, sympathetic towards working-class ambitions, yet satisfied with the structure of society as he found it: at all events, he worked, not for revolution, but for social betterment.

[1] S. and B. Webb, *History of Trade Unionism* (1920 ed., p. 198).

[2] Francis Place (1771–1854), s. of a bailiff to the Marshalsea court; apprenticed to a leather-breeches maker; set up as an independent journeyman, 1789; organized a strike and was subsequently refused work by the masters, 1793; opened a tailor's shop, 1799; gave a great deal of his time to reading and politics, but made his business pay for the upkeep of his family (fifteen children were born to him between 1792 and 1817; five died in infancy); carried on a campaign against the sinking fund, 1816–23. Place's influence declined soon after the passing of the reform bill, but in his years of greatest activity the library behind his shop in Charing Cross Road was the centre of moderate radicalism in London.

He was always willing to collaborate with men of a different class, because he realized that, without this collaboration, working men's demands would get little support. In the repeal of the combination laws he was helped by the economist J. R. McCulloch, and by Joseph Hume, a radical politician.[1] Hume, at Place's suggestion, packed a parliamentary committee appointed to inquire into the combination laws. The committee reported in 1824 in favour of repeal; the report was accepted almost too easily, and the laws repealed. Hume and Place seem to have thought that working men would find that they could not defeat economic laws and that their combinations would cease to be a regular feature of the relations between capital and labour. The working men were less convinced that trade unions could not raise wages. There was an outburst of strikes, accompanied in some places by violence and intimidation, and even by murder. A second parliamentary committee was set up. Hume could not pack it, and, if Place had been less skilled in 'wire-pulling', the freedom gained in 1824 might have been lost. Place produced evidence to stop a panic, and the committee merely recommended the re-establishment of the common-law prohibition of combinations, with a special exception in the case of associations for the regulation of wages and hours of labour.[2]

Canning's methods, and Canning himself, were less popular with the old tories than with the country. In February 1827 Liverpool had a paralytic stroke; at once the unity of the tory party was broken. Canning had every right to claim Liverpool's place. The leading tories in the commons, with the exception of Peel, wanted him; the members of the cabinet in the lords and the rank and file of the party, distrusting Canning's views on catholic emancipation, or thinking his foreign policy too liberal, refused to have him. The king, as usual, acted from motives of astute but unenlightened selfishness; he knew that a tory cabinet without Canning and his friends was impossible. Canning therefore became prime minister, and

---

[1] Joseph Hume (1777-1855), s. of a shipmaster, b. Montrose; surgeon in India, 1800-7; M.P., 1812. Hume added 'retrenchment' to the radical programme of 'peace and reform'.

[2] It is of some interest for the history of the cabinet control of legislation, and the attitude of ministers towards social questions, that the prime minister said in parliament that the act of 1824 had been hastily passed, and that 'he had not been aware of its extent, and did not, until it came into operation, know its provisions'. Hansard, N.S. xiii. 1478. Huskisson made almost the same admission, though in more guarded language.

Wellington, Peel, Eldon, and four others resigned from the cabinet.[1] The whigs also held different views about Canning. Grey would not support him. Tierney, Holland, Lansdowne, and Brougham were on his side. Althorp and Russell, after some hesitation, decided that they would give him their votes. Four whigs accepted places in his government and agreed not to raise the question of catholic emancipation.

Canning died in August 1827. The coalition rested upon his ability, and after his death there was no one strong enough to keep a majority in the commons. The collapse came within a few months because Goderich, the new prime minister, was 'as firm as a bullrush', and unable either to settle disputes in his cabinet or to deal with the wayward and unscrupulous king. George IV could not forgive Wellington and Peel for leaving the cabinet earlier in the year. He would not consider a tory ministry, and approached Goderich as a friend of Canning and as a weak man whom he could dominate. At the same time he would not allow any more whigs in the ministry, and, on the refusal of Sturges Bourne, who hated office, insisted that Herries should be chancellor of the exchequer. Herries was a tory, but each party suspected him. There were rumours (not, in fact, true) that he had made a fortune during the war by selling official information to the Rothschilds; it was also believed that the king wanted him at the treasury in order that he might be free to carry out his large building schemes. Herries soon quarrelled with Huskisson over the appointment of Althorp to the chairmanship of a finance committee. Huskisson would not give up Althorp; Goderich could not do without Huskisson or Herries, and, as he was certain to lose one of them, settled the matter in January 1828 by his own resignation.

Whigs and tories were alike so much divided that no party leader would take office. Wellington had little sense of the significance of party, and a strong conviction that it was his duty to carry on the king's government. He made no difficulty about forming an administration; for a time, until his friends gave him better advice, he thought of combining the office of prime minister with that of commander-in-chief. The whigs

[1] One withdrew his resignation. For the history of the political groups after the resignation of Liverpool, see A. Aspinall, 'The coalition ministries of 1827' (*E.H.R.*, Apr. and Oct. 1927), 'The last of the Canningites' (ibid., Oct. 1935), 'The Canningite party' (*Trans. R. Hist. S.* 4th ser. xvii, 1934), and 'The formation of Canning's Ministry' (*Camden Soc.* 3rd ser. lix, 1937).

would not serve under him, but he kept Huskisson and some of the Canningites. Peel came back to the home office, and his father wrote, in terms which throw light upon the views of the governing class, that, 'due consideration having been paid to talent, family connexions, and the circumstances of the Empire', the new government would give general satisfaction.[1]

The satisfaction was not lasting. At the first meeting of the cabinet one of its members thought that the relations between ministers showed 'the courtesy of men who had just fought a duel'. Wellington complained that he was in arrears with business because his time was spent 'in assuaging what gentlemen call their feelings'. There was no Liverpool to keep together the different sections in the cabinet; there was no Canning to persuade the country, by a *tour de force*, that parliamentary reform was unnecessary because the unreformed parliament was responsive to public opinion and ready to support a 'progressive' policy. The ministry indeed accepted the abolition of the test and corporation acts.[2] The proposal came from Russell; Peel, Huskisson, and Palmerston opposed it until they saw that the commons favoured the measure. The importance of repeal, as the tories realized, lay in its effect upon the question of catholic emancipation; it did not remedy any grievance of fact, since annual acts of indemnity had long exempted the dissenters from the penalties of the existing statutes.

The divisions in the cabinet soon came to an open quarrel over the fate of East Retford and Penryn, two boroughs found guilty of corruption. Huskisson and his friends proposed to transfer the seats to unenfranchised towns; the high tories wanted to throw the boroughs into the adjoining county constituencies. A compromise was arranged: East Retford was to be dissolved into the county, and the representation of Penryn was to be transferred to Manchester. The house of lords refused to create a new seat for Manchester; Huskisson then declared himself free to reject the proposal about East Retford. In May 1828 he voted against the government, and offered to resign. To his surprise, Wellington took him at his word.

The tories were not displeased to see the Canningites out of the cabinet, but the changes in the ministry had an unexpected result. Wellington chose an Irish landlord, Vesey Fitzgerald, member for Clare, to succeed a Canningite at the board of

---

[1] C. S. Parker, *Sir R. Peel*, ii. 33.   [2] See below, p. 509.

trade. Vesey Fitzgerald had to stand for re-election, and O'Connell defeated him.[1] Wellington and Peel knew that the revolt of the freeholders of Clare against the protestant ascendancy would be followed by similar action in most of the constituencies of Ireland; they realized that if they did not give way on catholic emancipation they would be faced with an Irish war. Peel would have resigned if Wellington had not thought his support as a minister essential to the government. In April 1829 a catholic emancipation bill passed both houses, but the tory party was again broken, and now consisted of the ultra-tories, who had voted against emancipation,[2] the Canningites, who had left the ministry and were not in agreement among themselves, and the centre group who followed Wellington and Peel. The whigs were still divided between those who had opposed and those who had supported Canning. The confusion was greater because a section of the tories began to favour parliamentary reform, on the grounds that a more representative house of commons would not have passed catholic emancipation, and that the increasing cost of elections and the rise in the price of boroughs were favouring rich financiers at the expense of the landed aristocracy. Wellington might have kept the whigs out of office for some years, if he had brought forward a moderate measure of reform; but he did nothing.

The French Revolution of 1830 affected the situation; the fall of Charles X caused considerable excitement in England and brought a revival of interest in parliamentary reform. If Frenchmen could turn out their reactionary government after a short and almost bloodless contest, why could not Englishmen do the same? George IV died on 26 June 1830 and was succeeded by his brother William;[3] the news from France came

---

[1] See below, pp. 339–44, for the history of catholic emancipation in Ireland.

[2] In the election of 1826 two members of the government (Copley and Goulburn) had opposed a third (Palmerston) at Cambridge University on the catholic question.

[3] William IV (1765–1837) went to sea in his fourteenth year, and continued, with a few intervals, until 1790 the career of a young naval officer. He then lived until about 1811 mainly in retirement at Bushey with an actress, Mrs. Jordan, by whom he had nine children (who took the name of FitzClarence). On the death of George IV this family asked for 'something to be done for them'. Wellington told William IV that 'with time and patience, much might be done, but that it would not do to run any risks when H.M.'s Civil List was still unsettled'. *Journal of Mrs. Arbuthnot*, ii. 368. William was an eccentric, simple, kindly man, less troublesome—in spite of occasional outbursts of temper—to his ministers than was George IV. He was nicknamed 'Silly Billy' from his rambling and incongruent speeches, but he

too late to have much influence upon the general election which, according to custom, followed the death of the sovereign.[1] There was no 'united front'; the division of each of the great parties into groups made it difficult to calculate the strength of the ministry even after the election results were known, but the trend of opinion was clearly against the old 'system'.[2] In most contested elections the reform of parliament and the destruction of aristocratic privilege had been the questions at issue. Two societies, the London Radical Reform Association and the Birmingham Political Union, had used the occasion to stir up popular feeling. Tories and whigs alike saw that the problem of electoral reform could not safely be postponed, but in November Wellington went out of his way to give his opinion that the state of the representation was perfect. This paradox destroyed the government within a fortnight. Brougham proposed a motion in favour of reform. The cabinet would probably have been defeated: they took the chance of resigning after an earlier defeat on a motion affecting the civil list.

A *Quarterly* writer now thought that the 'appellations of whig and tory' should be dropped; the struggle was no longer 'between two political parties for the ministry, but between the mob and the government . . . the conservative and subversive principles'.[3] The term 'conservatism'[4] had a future; the present was in the hands of the whigs. Most of the Canningites joined them, but Canning's friends had ceased to be a united group after the fall of Goderich's ministry, and Huskisson's death in September 1830 had lost them their ablest member. Grey,[5]

had a good deal of common sense. Like most princes of his time, he was greatly interested in military uniforms. Within ten days of his accession he ordered all military moustachios to be cut off.

[1] For the election see N. Gash, 'English Reform and French Revolution in the General Election of 1830' in *Essays presented to Sir L. Namier* (1956), pp. 258–88. Professor Gash points out that anyhow only about a quarter of the seats in England and Wales were contested.

[2] The treasury analysis of the returns listed the members as friends 311, moderate ultras 37, doubtful favourable 37, very doubtful 24, foes 188, violent ultras 25, doubtful unfavourable 23, the Huskisson party 11. A. Aspinall, *Three Early Nineteenth Century Diaries*, pp. xxi–xxii.

[3] *Quarterly Review*, Jan. 1831.

[4] Canning had used the term 'conservative' in 1824.

[5] Charles Grey, 2nd Earl Grey (1764–1845), b. Fallodon; educ. Eton and King's College, Cambridge; M.P., 1786; one of the managers of Warren Hastings's impoachment; took up parliamentary reform, 1793; first lord of the admiralty, 1806; foreign secretary, 1806–7; succeeded his father, 1807; acted with Grenville as joint adviser to the prince regent, 1811; see also vol. xii of this *History*.

the whig prime minister, belonged to the right wing of the party. He described himself as 'aristocratic both by position and by nature', and 'with a predilection for old institutions'.[1] The revolution of July had revived his interest in reform; he made the acceptance of a reform bill a condition of forming his ministry, but he thought in terms of a necessary concession to popular demand, and of a measure which should be a final reckoning between the nation and the aristocracy, and not the first stage in a movement towards democratic government. He believed in a large settlement which would 'afford sure ground of resistance to further innovation'.[2] The support of the radicals embarrassed him. His cabinet was the most aristocratic of the century; all its members except four were in the house of lords, and, of these four, Althorp was heir to an English earldom, Palmerston was an Irish peer, Graham an English baronet with large estates, and Grant a Scottish landowner who was later raised to the peerage.[3] One of the first acts of Grey's government after the passing of the reform bill was the creation of two dukes.

The attitude of the whigs towards popular disturbances hardly differed from that of the tories. During the autumn of 1830 troubles broke out once again in the agricultural districts of southern England.[4] Rumours of events in France excited the labourers, but they were asking only for a living wage; there was no organized plot, and no co-ordination between the various outbreaks. The country districts of the north were quiet, though many of the towns were disturbed by strikes. The government sent out special commissions to try the labourers. Nine men or boys were hanged,[5] and about 450 others were sentenced to transportation (in nearly 200 cases, for life) though the only casualty had been one man killed by the yeomanry. In many cases the farmers agreed to a rise in wages, and Grey himself suggested a private subscription, with a grant from parliament, to increase the sum available for the relief of distress. Yet the whigs had no proposals for the redress of the labourers' grievances, and the commons defeated, by a large majority, a motion for a general pardon. The ministers noticed

[1] *Correspondence of Earl Grey with Princess Lieven*, ii. 392.

[2] C. S. Parker, *Life and Letters of Sir J. Graham*, i. 120.

[3] A duke's son and an earl's grandson were added in 1831. The ministry included a son, a son-in-law, a brother-in-law, and a cousin of the prime minister.

[4] For the effect of these disturbances upon the reform of the poor law, see below, p. 450.   [5] Six of them for arson. Another 400 were imprisoned.

that the outbreaks followed the appearance of Cobbett and other radical speakers in the country districts. They decided to make an example of the 'journalists'[1] Cobbett and Carlile. Carlile was fined £200, sentenced to two years' imprisonment, and ordered to find security for £1,000. It is fair to add that he neither paid the fine nor found the security, and that he served only eight months of his sentence. Cobbett's trial did not take place until the country was agitated over the reform bill. He defended himself with great skill, and after the jury had discussed the matter for fifteen hours the case was dismissed.

The reform bill must be seen in the light of these disturbances and their repression. The whigs had no doubt about their intentions, but they were out of touch, at the moment of their triumph, with the opinion of Englishmen. Cobbett once used a striking phrase about the wretchedness of the common man in the 'little, hard parishes'. The poor in these little parishes, and the submerged masses in the industrial towns, were below the horizon of the whig magnates, who had no more understanding than the tories that the greatest changes resulting from the reform bill would take place outside parliament and in the sphere of administration. The strength of the whigs and their services to the country lay rather in their view that concession to a sustained popular demand was the wisest policy for a governing aristocracy. In this frame of mind they brought forward a measure which had consequences beyond their cold and narrow vision.

The first reform bill was drawn up by a cabinet committee,[2] and introduced to the commons on 1 March 1831. The bill disfranchised sixty boroughs of less than 2,000 inhabitants, and returning 119 members;[3] it took one member from forty-seven boroughs with a population between 2,000 and 4,000, and cut down the representation of the combined boroughs of Weymouth and Melcombe Regis from four to two members. Thus 168 seats disappeared, and in their place 97 new seats were given to English constituencies, one to Wales, five to Scotland, and three to Ireland. Seven large English towns, including

[1] The common English use of the words 'journal' and 'journalism' date from this time. See Halévy, iii. 18.

[2] Lord John Russell was largely responsible for framing the bill, although he was not a member of the cabinet until June 1831.

[3] The list of boroughs was known as Schedule A. The second category was listed in Schedule B.

Manchester and Birmingham, and four districts in London were given two members each; twenty towns were given one member each. Twenty-six counties had their representation doubled; Yorkshire, which already elected four members, obtained two more seats and the Isle of Wight one seat. The franchise in boroughs was to be uniform, and to include occupants of buildings of £10 annual value; in the counties votes were given to £10 copyholders and £50 leaseholders for a term of years, while the long-established forty-shilling freeholder kept his rights. The fact that the bill did not redistribute all the available seats showed the care taken to maintain the balance of power in parliament. Russell, in introducing the bill, said more about ending the abuses of the electoral system than about enfranchising new towns. Althorp explained to the commons that the government 'felt the necessity, while they were adding to the democratic share of the Representation . . . of preserving . . . the aristocratic share by increasing the influence of the great landed proprietors in the counties'. The representation of the counties should be confined, as far as possible, 'to the gentlemen of property resident in them'. He regarded it as an 'evil' that 'mere popularity' should result in the return of members, 'oftentimes even of . . . strangers, to the exclusion of gentlemen of retiring habits, holding large property in the county, and well qualified to represent its interests'.[1] The whigs, whose definition of 'the people' did not go beyond the middle class, looked by habit at redistribution at least as much in terms of 'interests' as in those of population; Frome, for example, was given the status of a parliamentary borough because it could be taken to represent the woollen industry in the west of England.

Nevertheless whigs and tories alike in the house of commons were surprised at the far-reaching character of the bill. Russell was interrupted by ironical laughter while he was reading out the list of condemned boroughs. At first the radicals were inclined to think that the bill did not go far enough; the whig scheme of reform was 'a damnable delusion, giving us as many tyrants as there are shopkeepers. . . . To keep the whigs in power the lion must give place to the rat, and the tiger to the leech.' A small group of extremists continued to use violent language about 'the liberty-undermining Whigs'.[2] On the

[1] Hansard, 3rd ser. v. 1227.
[2] Quoted in C. Seymour, *Electoral Reform in England and Wales* (1915), pp. 40–41.

whole, however, Grey's calculation had been right. The bill went so far beyond general expectation that it satisfied most people, though Grey was wrong in believing that the working class would take it as a final settlement. The tory opposition did Grey's work for him in the country; a bill which frightened the tories could not be merely an example of whig hypocrisy. As the tory attack developed, the nation came out in defence of the whigs. Carlile himself had begun to think that he might become 'what is commonly termed a ministerial man'.[1]

Even in the early stages the excitement was great. The tories blamed the whigs for stirring up the people at a dangerous time; the whigs blamed the tories for refusing to see that property could be defended only by wise concession. Peel stated his objections in moderate terms. He did not deny the need for reform. He objected to the 'levelling' character of the bill and the uniformity of the suffrage. He pointed out that the bill was unlikely to be final, since it set for the first time a clear line between the voting and voteless classes. Peel thought that, if the bill were rejected, there was a risk of civil war, though he put the responsibility upon the whigs. Macaulay appealed to the house to save the country from revolution: 'Save property, divided against itself. Save the multitude, endangered by their own ungovernable passions. Save the aristocracy, endangered by its own unpopular power. . . . The danger is terrible. The time is short.' On 23 March at 3 a.m. the bill passed its second reading by a majority of one vote in the largest house within living memory; the balance of votes in England and Scotland was on the tory side, and the decision was due to the Irish members. In April the tories defeated the government in committee, and the king, after a first refusal, agreed to dissolve parliament. He came in person, and in some haste, before the house of lords could pass a resolution against the expediency of his action.

The general election gave the reformers a larger majority. They brought forward a second bill in June. The terms were substantially those of the first bill, though in the course of the debates the government made one important concession. They accepted an amendment proposed by Lord Chandos extending the franchise to £50 tenants-at-will in the counties. This proposal was intended to strengthen the position of landlords by

[1] Butler, op. cit., p. 201.

enabling them to control more votes on their estates;[1] the radicals accepted it on the principle that every extension of the suffrage ought to be welcomed. The bill passed the commons in September 1831, after a session of three months; the lords rejected it on 8 October after a debate of five days.[2] Twenty-one of the bishops in the house voted against the bill; if they had voted for it the result would have been a majority of one in favour of reform.

There had been excitement, and occasional rioting, during and after the elections in the spring. At that time the mood of the people was not dangerous because the success of the bill seemed fairly certain. The position was different in the autumn. Two London papers appeared in mourning, and, when the news reached Birmingham,[3] the bells were muffled and tolled. Throughout the country meetings took place in support of the government, and riots broke out almost at once in Nottingham and Derby. Within three weeks of the vote in the lords there was trouble in Bristol on a scale which alarmed men of property. Sir Charles Wetherell, who had been attorney-general in Wellington's government, was recorder of Bristol. Wetherell had opposed the first and second bills in the commons. He came to Bristol on 29 October for the ordinary gaol delivery. A body of special constables escorted him into the city, and three troops of horse were sent to assist in keeping order. A few hours after Wetherell's arrival, a mob attacked the Mansion House. On the following morning they made another attack upon the House, and sacked it. An eyewitness thought that fifty of the new London police could have settled the affair, but the magistrates and the officer in command of the troops lost their nerve; they allowed the mob to break into the old and new prisons and to burn the bishop's palace and a number of other buildings. Next day a cavalry charge restored order. The reformers dissociated themselves from the riots; there was, however, a danger that similar disturbances might break out in a score of towns. The monster meetings in London and elsewhere

[1] The government had fixed seven years as the minimum term of tenancy for a £50 leaseholder. An 'occupier' tenant-at-will might hold for one year only.

[2] 111 of the peers (excluding representative peers) voting in this division had titles anterior to 1760. 60 of these 111 voted in favour of the bill.

[3] Birmingham—not Manchester—was the most important provincial centre of the reform agitation.

might get out of hand, and the language used by the extreme radicals came very near to threats of revolution.[1]

Meanwhile parliament was prorogued, and the ministers announced that they would persevere with their bill. Their own friends did not help them. The political unions, formed in many large cities at the suggestion of the radicals, gave some colour to the tory fears. The council of the Birmingham Union discussed the formation of a national guard, and the ministers had to use great tact in dissuading them. The majority in the house of lords was so large that the cabinet as well as the king thought a creation of peers out of the question. An attempt to coerce the lords might drive a good many supporters of the bill to the opposite side. The third reform bill, introduced in December 1831, contained a few concessions in order to win over those peers who did not want to fight to the end in a conflict likely to produce civil war. The government would not give way on the number of boroughs to be disfranchised. Minor changes were made in the list, but 56 boroughs, returning 111 members, remained under sentence. On the other hand the boroughs condemned to partial disfranchisement were cut down to thirty. This concession was made possible by giving up the proposal, already somewhat eroded, to reduce the numbers of the house of commons. Each of 22 new parliamentary boroughs was now to return 2 members, and each of 20 one member.

The government had already approached 'doubtful' peers; the king now tried to persuade the bishops to change their views. When the negotiations seemed to have failed, the cabinet was in danger because Althorp, Durham, and Graham wanted Grey to make sure that the king would create enough peers to pass the bill through the lords. Brougham persuaded his colleagues to ask William IV to create a dozen or more peers as a sign that, if necessary, he would add to their numbers. The king agreed, though at first he insisted that most of the new peers should be heirs to existing peerages. These facts became known and were enough to persuade the 'waverers'. In April the bill passed its second reading in the upper house by a majority of nine votes. If the lords had accepted the principle of reform, they could still discuss details. After the Easter recess Lynd-

---

[1] Sydney Smith did something to relieve the general tension by the speech in which he compared the resistance of the lords to Mrs. Partington's efforts to keep the Atlantic out of her cottage with a mop.

hurst carried by 151 votes to 116 a motion postponing the disfranchisement clauses until the rest of the bill had been settled.
He pointed out that the house ought to know how many seats
were to be transferred before they accepted schedules A and B.
The question was one of procedure, but the government took it
as a challenge that the lords claimed the right to treat the bill
on what they considered to be its merits. Grey asked the king
to make fifty—or more—peers; William IV refused to go beyond
twenty. Thereupon, on 9 May, the ministers resigned. Few
men have ever resigned with greater pleasure. They were
tired of the strain. Some of them were glad to be rid of the
bill; others were sure that public opinion would force the lords
to give way. In any case the burden now fell upon the tories.

Within a week Grey was back in office. The king had sent
for Lyndhurst; Lyndhurst advised him to ask Wellington to
form an administration which would carry through a moderate
reform bill. Wellington's view of the general situation and of
his duty to the king led him to agree, but Peel refused to join
him in bringing forward a measure which the tory party had
opposed to the point of civil war. Peel's attitude mattered little
because the country would not have the tories, or anything less
than the whole reform bill. The commons passed a vote of
confidence in Grey's government, and, outside the house, petitions from the court of common council of the City, from Manchester, and elsewhere asked that supplies should be stopped.
The length of the crisis had unnerved the public as much as it
had tired the ministers. The first of the cholera outbreaks of the
nineteenth century had come to the ports of the north-east coast
in October 1831, and to London three months later. The news
of Grey's resignation, at the end of months of unrest and disquiet, upset business and ordinary life. For the moment there
was no disorder. The Rothschilds and Barings did their utmost
to prevent a heavy fall in the funds. The middle-class leaders,
notably Francis Place, suggested a run on the banks, and put out
placards 'To stop the duke, go for gold'. There was a refusal to pay taxes, and, although the leaders believed that they
had the popular movement well in hand, others were less sure.

Wellington was not afraid of civilian agitators; he gave way
because he found that the tory party agreed with Peel. The
whigs could now make their own terms. They would not resume office unless they could pass their bill 'unimpaired in its

principles and its essential provisions'. If the tories would not surrender, the king must create peers enough to provide a majority. William IV tried to persuade the tories to give way. Wellington, as usual, obeyed his sovereign's orders. Lyndhurst and a number of peers also promised to withdraw from the debate, but no public statement was made, and the violent language used by the seceders gave the impression that they might come back. The cabinet insisted that the king should pledge himself to create as many peers as might be necessary, and the king at last submitted.

The whigs did not use their powers. The tories were disorganized by the withdrawal of their chiefs, and the king's promise was soon known. On 4 June the bill passed its third reading in the lords. Grey and his colleagues thought that the king might regain a little popularity if he came in person to announce the royal assent to the bill. The king would not come, and his assent was declared by commission.

Historians have not ceased to ask how near the country was to revolution during the period of confusion after Grey's resignation. Wellington knew the danger, but was not afraid of it. He believed that 'the people of England are very quiet, if they are let alone'; if they were not 'let alone', 'there was a way to make them' quiet. He thought the position less serious than it had been in the years immediately after the war.[1] Place, on the other hand, was sure that a movement like the French Revolution of 1830 would have succeeded after two or three days of 'commotion'. Wellington knew more than Place about the use of force; Place knew more than Wellington about the temper of the English people in 1832. Place underrated the reaction of the well-to-do and middle classes against mob violence. The political unions were too certain of controlling the crowds whom they were ready to incite to illegal action; Wellington was wrong in supposing that the temper of England in 1831 and 1832 was similar to that of the desultory insurrections caused by misery after the war.

At all events the bill became law, and after the excitement had died down, and the banquets, illuminations, bell-ringing, and

[1] Wellington was, however, concerned at the small number of troops—most of them concentrated in and around London—available for the defence of public order.

speeches were over, neither side found the result as dramatic as it had expected. Yet the change was real, and the act of 1832 was a turning-point in modern English history. A fly-sheet, illustrating 'The Grey Horse and the Union Coach', showed a bystander asking the question: 'Pray, who drives the coach, neighbour?' The neighbour answers: 'Why, friend, she runs by steam now, but old Bill King, a sailor chap, drove her first.'[1] As a rough summary of English political history during the next forty years, the neighbour's answer may serve.[2]

Note on the Scottish and Irish reform acts

Reform bills for Scotland and Ireland were passed in 1832. They were less discussed since the main questions in dispute had already been decided, but the changes in Scotland were greater in the matter of enfranchisement than in England. There were less changes in Ireland because the act of Union had already altered Irish parliamentary representation, and in 1829 the county franchise had been modified. The Scottish act raised the representation of Scotland from 45 to 53 seats, of which 30 were for the counties, and applied the £10 household vote to the burghs. While the bill was in the house of lords a proposal was made for the representation of Scottish universities. The proposal was defeated. The representation of Ireland was increased from 100 to 105 members; the disfranchisement of the 40s. freeholder was maintained, but a £10 franchise was introduced in the boroughs.

[1] Quoted in Butler, p. 415.
[2] For the text of the main clauses of the act, see W. C. Costin and J. S. Watson, *The Law and Working of the Constitution*: *Documents 1660–1914*, ii. 55–68.

II

MONARCHY, MINISTERS, AND
PARTIES, 1832–46

THE AGE OF MELBOURNE AND PEEL

THE extension of the franchise and the redistribution of seats in 1832 added 217,000 voters to an electorate of 435,000 in England and Wales. Whigs and tories alike had expected a larger figure. The rise in the population and wealth of the country brought a further increase of about 400,000 before 1867. The number would have been greater, especially during the early part of the period, if the register of voters had included all who were qualified to vote. Before 1832 there were no official lists of voters; the electorate was small in most boroughs, and impostors would have been detected, while in the counties most voters could prove their qualifications by producing receipts for the payment of land tax. The larger franchise made a list necessary, if only to avoid delays at the polling-booths while the electors established their identity. The employment of registration officers would have been the simplest method of drawing up a list, but, apart from the expense of this method there was a fear that the party in power would make appointments in their own interest; hence the duty of keeping the lists was given to the overseers of the poor, who compiled the rate-books. Claims and objections were settled in court through special 'revising barristers'. The system worked badly for some time. The voters took little trouble to find whether their names were on the list; many people did not think it worth while to pay the registration fee of a shilling. The overseers were slack and, as a voter had to appear in person to defend his claim, the party organizations could raise frivolous or unfair objections. These organizations gained in importance after 1832; hitherto the tories had taken less trouble than the whigs to keep in touch with the constituencies, but the foundation of the Carlton Club, as a centre of tory interests, and the efforts of the party to build up local associations soon put the tories ahead of their rivals.[1] In any case the Tadpoles and Tapers whom Disraeli described in *Coningsby* were quick to see the importance of registration. They used every chance of increasing their voting strength; they multiplied leaseholders and created small freeholders who gave a lease to the original owner; thus £1,000 worth of land could produce five hundred votes. They used dead men's names, produced fictitious receipts for rent, and did their best to disfranchise hostile voters.[2] Many voters lost their rights owing to delay in the payment of rates. The period of grace was extended in 1843[3] from two weeks to three months and to six months in 1848, but the numbers affected were still large. A great many occupiers, particularly in London, paid their rates through their landlord; these 'compounders' could make a special claim for registration, but until 1851 the claim had to be renewed after every payment. Compounders made little use of their right; probably one-tenth of the £10 householders of England and Wales were not on the register.

Under the act the borough members fell from 465 to 399, and the county members rose from 188 to 253. As the whigs had intended, the direct territorial influence of the landed aristocracy was thereby increased; the increase, for a time, was greater because the extension of borough constituencies (about half the English boroughs were enlarged) often meant the inclusion of villages under the control of some territorial magnate. Many small boroughs, however, remained; even the 'pocket' borough did not altogether disappear. About forty peers after 1832 were able to nominate members of the house of commons, though only a few of them controlled more than one seat; the tories lost far more safe seats than the whigs. The extent of influence

[1] Peel supported, but did not take much active part in this work of organization. His own contribution was made chiefly in the house of commons.

[2] The anti-corn law league used similar tactics. The league announced in its journal that it would find money for the purchase of freeholds: 2,000 voters were created in Yorkshire by these methods in 1846. The league also sent out solicitors to raise objections against voters known to oppose repeal of the corn laws. The Walsall branch of the league once polled nine dead men, three of whom had been strong protectionists.

[3] Until 1843 the fiscal year ended on 6 July. In 1843 the year was fixed from April to April, but the last day for payment of rates was left unchanged. This regulation led to bribery; party agents often paid electors' rates for them. Disraeli complained in 1832 that he was defeated at High Wycombe because his agent had not attended 'to our registration . . . [and] the rates of many of my old supporters were not paid up'. W. F. Monypenny, *Life of Disraeli*, i. 220.

may be seen from the number of uncontested elections. In the five general elections between 1832 and 1847 the average of contested seats was only just over a half.[1]

An immediate change was not to be expected either in the habits of the landed magnates or in the demands of the electors. In 1841 the marquis of Westminster thought that Gladstone's canvass of the electors of Flintshire was 'an interference between a landlord... and his tenants... not justifiable according to those laws of delicacy and propriety... considered binding in such cases'.[2] Similarly in the boroughs a great landlord still felt justified in enforcing his electoral will upon his tenants. Contested elections remained rough and rowdy affairs, whose 'chartered license' was accepted as in the nature of things. The habit of bribery was deep-rooted, and the preservation in 1832 of the rights of existing voters (if resident) maintained a bad tradition.[3] Politics, especially in the smaller boroughs, were concerned primarily with local interests, and until party organization was more strongly developed at the centre it was unlikely to be a dominant feature in the constituencies.[4] On the other hand it would be a mistake to concentrate too much upon the exigencies and parochialism of voters and the assumptions of landlords. The reform act released and gave opportunities to the more active forces in English political life. These forces were already obvious in the newly enfranchised constituencies; within a generation they were to spread throughout the country.[5]

---

[1] Uncontested elections, on the other hand, were often the result of a careful calculation of forces or, in two-member constituencies, of bargaining.

[2] Morley, *Life of Gladstone*, i. 239.

[3] Placards were shown at Bristol in 1832 with the words: 'Vote for Blue. Money no object.' Pamphlets issued at Yarmouth in 1841 described bribery as 'an ancient custom' and a 'privilege'. There was a good deal of indirect bribery in the form of payment for services rendered during elections. When Gladstone was elected at Newark in 1832 a band played during the poll at 15s. a day for each bandsman, and after the election the inns of the town sent in bills for meat and drink 'to the tune of a couple of thousand pounds' (ibid. i. 93).

[4] The question of the electorate after 1832 is treated in N. Gash, *Politics in the Age of Peel* (1953). See also G. S. R. Kitson Clark, 'The Electorate and the Repeal of the Corn Laws', *Trans. R. Hist. S.* 5th ser. (1951) i. 108-126. Gladstone told his friend Thomas Acland in July 1858 that 'few people could expect to be returned to Parliament unless they had overwhelming personal claims or position, or else attach themselves decidedly to one of the local parties and share its fortunes'. A. H. D. Acland, *Memoir and Letters of Sir Thomas Acland*, p. 212.

[5] Disraeli gave party agents (whom he used) a bad name. Recent research (e.g. Gash, op. cit.) has been kinder to organizers such as F. R. Bonham for the conservatives, Joseph Parkes and James Coppock for the liberals. These men did a

In addition to cutting away much rottenness, the act did something to redress the over-representation of the agricultural south and the under-representation of London and the industrial areas. The 'something' was not enough. Ten southern counties, with Oxfordshire and Buckinghamshire, had 174 seats; Lancashire, the West Riding of Yorkshire, and the urban and industrial districts of Middlesex, with almost as large a population, had only 58 seats.[1] There was, however, no doubt that, in spite of whig ideas of 'finality', further changes would work in favour of the newer England.

Moreover, although attempts to get rid of corruption, that is to say, to change by law the habits of the nation, were at first slow, the act did mark a turning-point. A few flagrant cases were dealt with—more willingly than before 1832—by disfranchisement, and acts passed in 1841 and 1842 made proof of bribery less difficult. In 1848 the house of lords, which was lenient in these matters, threw out a bill authorizing a local investigation of charges of corruption; the bill was accepted in 1852. The Corrupt Practices Act of 1854 required an audit of accounts payable by a candidate, and defined the various forms of corrupt practice, including, for the first time, the intimidation of voters. The act did not put an end to direct bribery, still less to indirect bribery such as the payment of election expenses; but public opinion had changed, and the new generation of voters did not know the methods common before 1832. The cost of fighting an election fell from the fantastic figures of the early days of the nineteenth century to little more than £200–£400 (in 1857) for an ordinary borough, and at least £1,000, in most cases a larger sum, for a metropolitan or a county constituency. The adoption of the ballot would have lessened chances of corruption. Grey had refused to introduce it in 1832 because he did not want to deprive the landed interest of an important means of controlling votes. Voting by ballot was one of the points in the radical programme, but the chartist agitation discredited the movement in its favour. Moreover the supporters of open voting were not arguing merely in favour of safeguarding the influence of landlords, and the division of

good deal, in the name of party, to bring larger issues before an electorate which included so many 'backward' constituencies.

[1] London and Middlesex were not treated as well as Lancashire and Yorkshire owing to the view that 'interests' rather than mere aggregations of people should determine representation.

opinion did not run altogether on party lines. Gladstone for a long time opposed the ballot though he finally gave way to the pressure of his party. It was held that secret voting was 'un-English'; that it was unconstitutional because the franchise was a trust, and the public had a right to know how the trust was used. Stanley and Russell thought that secret voting might lead to increased bribery because there would be no means, after the election, of proving an offence.[1]

The act of 1832 did not have much immediate effect upon the composition of parliament.[2] The new parliament which met in 1833 contained 217 sons of peers or baronets; in 1865 the number was 180;[3] the landed interest which was nearly 500 strong in 1833 had about 400 representatives in 1865. The number of dissenters was less than the tories had feared when they foretold that the new type of town voter would elect 'presbyterians of the lowest class'. On the other hand the radicals won a good many seats; Grote, Roebuck, and Sir William Molesworth entered parliament for the first time.[4] Although Sir James Mackintosh once described the course of business in the unreformed parliament as a 'continuous, animated, after-dinner discussion' a change had begun before the reform bill. Lord Egremont, a friend and contemporary of Fox, wrote in 1827: 'The business and eloquence of parliament have undergone a total change within the short period of my remembrance. . . . In parliamentary eloquence the change does not come from taste but from necessity, for the flights of Demosthenes

---

[1] In 1832 Hunt presented a petition from a woman in Yorkshire who claimed that, as she paid taxes, she had a right to vote. A clause in the first draft of the 'People's Charter' (see below, p. 134) advocated votes for women, but the first proposal laid before parliament was made by Mill in 1867, on the ground that taxation and representation could not be separated. Mill's proposal had little support. The agitation for women's rights which began about 1840 was concerned with civil rights, and not with the parliamentary vote.

[2] For the composition of the house of commons between 1832 and 1867, see J. A. Thomas, 'The House of Commons, 1832-67' (*Economica*, Mar. 1925), and 'The Repeal of the Corn Laws' (ibid., Apr. 1929), H. R. G. Greaves, 'Personal Origins and Interrelations of the Houses of Parliament since 1832' (ibid., June 1929), S. F. Woolley, 'The Personnel of the Parliament of 1833' (*E.H.R.*, Apr. 1938), and W. O. Aydelotte, 'The House of Commons in the 1840's' (*History*, vol. 39, 1954).

[3] There were only ten less in 1880. The property qualification for members of parliament was modified in 1838 to include personal as well as real property, and abolished in 1858. It was largely evaded; there were only six exclusions between 1832 and 1858.

[4] The freak choices by the new electorate included Gully, a well-known prize-fighter. Cobbett was elected for Oldham, but had little success in the house.

are as little suited to Sinking Funds and paper money, and corn and fir timber and cotton, as a trumpet would be to a Quakers' meeting.'[1] The character and conduct of the proceedings of the house became even more prosaic after 1832 because public opinion expected reforms in many other spheres unsuited to the display of eloquence. The new parliament set about collecting information on a scale hitherto unknown.[2] The sessions were longer, and the number of papers printed by order of the commons increased. The petitions presented to the house multiplied about fourfold, and their number brought about a change in parliamentary procedure. Hitherto any member presenting a petition had been allowed to introduce a debate on it. After 1832 this practice was discouraged; ten years later the right was abolished, except in cases where immediate action was necessary.[3] Hence the number of petitions fell rapidly. Members were still jealous of their right to introduce subjects of debate, and allowed the government only two nights a week for its own business; in 1838 and 1840 Russell failed to secure a third night. A reporters' gallery was provided in the temporary house of commons in 1834 (after the old house had been destroyed by fire), and parliamentary speeches were recorded with greater accuracy. From 1836 division lists were regularly published, and the large committees appointed to consider private bills were cut down in number; after 1864 all private bills were referred to committees of five members.

The new conditions had some effect upon the character of parties. The tories at first exaggerated the consequences of their defeat. They could not hope to get the confidence of the

---

[1] Earl of Ilchester, *Chronicles of Holland House*, ii. 229–30.

[2] The employment of royal commissions rather than select committees of inquiry made it easier to get expert opinion from outside. Many of the reports were very widely read; hence there was often a tendency to 'pack' committees and to choose evidence for propagandist purposes. See H. D. Clokie and J. W. Robinson, *Royal Commissions of Enquiry*, 1937. This demand for information was one of the features of the age. The Manchester Statistical Society was founded in 1833, and the London Statistical Society in 1834. The statistical department of the board of trade was not set up until 1833, but its establishment had been discussed earlier. 'Statistics' at this time included what would now be called general social surveys. See L. Brown, *The Board of Trade and the Free Trade Movement, 1830–1842*, 1958, pp. 76–93.

[3] The Speaker told Gladstone in 1838 that the restriction of discussion upon petitions did not merely save the time of the house. 'There was a more important advantage . . . [The] discussions very greatly increased the influence of popular feeling on the deliberations of the house; . . . by stopping them . . . a wall was erected against such influence' (Morley, i. 150).

electorate for some time to come. There was, however, a good
chance of their revival under a new programme. They represented solid interests. They were not hampered, like the whigs,
by a radical wing which had little sense of party loyalty. Their
predominance in the house of lords gave them tactical advantages, though it made them, at times, unpopular in the country.
The strength of the whigs lay in their wide tolerance, their
belief in government by discussion, and their readiness to
adapt themselves to facts. If the tories had the church on their
side, the whigs had the dissenters. The whig ministers were
harrassed by O'Connell and the radicals, and by the house of
lords, but to a certain extent they could rely upon the support
of Peel. The whigs knew that Peel and his friends would resist
radical measures which, on a whig view, went beyond the limits
of ordered progress and that they would support the lords in
opposing whig measures only if they thought that the country
would bear with the opposition. The weakness of the whigs lay
in the curious fact that they never produced a good chancellor
of the exchequer, though it is fair to remember that they had to
meet a number of years of bad harvests and commercial depression. Moreover, every reform which the whigs introduced
brought them enemies. The clergy disliked their attitude towards the church, the lawyers their reform of the law, the business classes their taxes. The manufacturers objected to the
factory act of 1833 and the working class hated the new poor law.

The radicals saved the whigs under Melbourne from resting
upon their achievement in passing the reform bill. They suggested many of the measures which the whigs passed into law.
They brought the whigs to the limit of whig principles; they
were never strong enough, or sufficiently united, to form a large
party. Their numbers had increased under the new franchise
law, but the electorate was unlikely to return a radical majority.
Hence the radicals were forced to appeal to a wider public
and to speak on behalf of this public in the house. Their use
of such a form of appeal meant that, as earlier, the other parties
associated great political meetings and propaganda with radicalism, and the radicals were left almost alone in the field, until
the founders of the anti-corn law league followed the methods
used by O'Connell in Ireland. The exploitation of local influence
through the newly formed party organizations, election addresses,
a few speeches at ceremonial occasions, a few addresses to

deputations were enough for Peel or Melbourne. For the rest they relied upon the publication of the debates in the houses, and shared William IV's objection to 'itinerant speechifying, particularly by individuals holding high offices'.[1] Peel's manifesto of 1834,[2] though it was discussed in the cabinet, and was intended for the whole electorate, took the form of an address to his constituents at Tamworth. It was not a party programme in the modern sense of the term. It did not mention the name of a political party; it did not include any legislative plan, though it referred in a general way to measures already under consideration. Moreover it was issued in special circumstances. Peel was taking office against his own judgement, at a time when he scarcely expected to have a majority in the house of commons, and something out of the ordinary was necessary to justify his position.

If the parliamentary radicals represented the opinions of the unenfranchised majority, they had the weakness of men defending the interests of a class to which they did not belong. Their political views were too often a revolt against a society to which they could not adapt themselves. Molesworth[3] challenged his Cambridge tutor to a duel; Wakefield[4] twice abducted an heiress. Durham[5] was absurdly vain, and his radicalism did not prevent him from intriguing for an earldom. Moreover radical electors tended to regard their members as delegates. In Marylebone, for example, the radical candidates were asked not merely to support a detailed set of measures, but to promise that they would resign, if called upon to do so by a majority

---

[1] L. C. Sanders, *Lord Melbourne's Papers*, p. 217. [2] See below, p. 102.

[3] Sir William Molesworth, bt. (1810–55); studied at Edinburgh, 1824–7; sent down from Cambridge, 1828; travelled in Germany and Italy, 1828–31; M.P., 1832; first comissioner of the board of works, 1853–5; secretary for the colonies, July–October 1855; made a special study of colonial policy, and, after 1837, attacked the system of transportation; a regular contributor to the journals of the philosophical radicals; edited, with an assistant, the works of Thomas Hobbes.

[4] Edward Gibbon Wakefield (1796–1862), s. of a land agent; attaché in diplomatic service, 1814–26; sentenced to three years' imprisonment for eloping with an heiress under false pretences, 1826; studied the problems of colonization while in prison, and published (from Newgate prison) *A Letter from Sydney*, which led to the foundation of the National Colonization Society; went with Durham to Canada in 1838; from 1837 to 1846 mainly interested in the colonization of New Zealand.

[5] John George Lambton, 1st earl of Durham (1792–1840), served in 10th dragoons, 1809–11; M.P., 1813; married, as his second wife, the eldest d. of the 2nd Earl Grey; created Baron Durham, 1828; lord privy seal, 1830; ambassador-extraordinary to Russia, 1835–7; high commissioner and governor-general of the British provinces in North America, 1838.

of their constituents. Many radical members were afraid of the extension of the franchise for which the working-class leaders were asking. Others believed too strongly in *laisser faire* principles to accept the policy of state interference implied in the demands of the trade unions. Within the house the radicals were too erratic, too self-willed, to follow any leader. If the ablest members of the party had lived beyond middle age, they might have become rivals of the 'elder statesmen' who dominated parliament in the decade after the Crimean war, but Molesworth died at 45, Durham at 48, Charles Buller[1] at 42, and Wakefield never recovered from an attack of paralysis of the brain in his fifty-first year. The 'intellectuals' who maintained the tradition of Benthamism had a deeper influence, but less popular appeal. They believed in the type of administrative reform represented by the poor-law amendment act of 1834, against which the working class was united. Thus the government could play one section of radicals against another. The 'intellectuals' were, in their way, hardly less petulant and erratic than other members of the party. Their contempt for orthodox whiggism was a political mistake which destroyed any chance of the younger men getting into parliament early through the small boroughs under whig control or obtaining posts in whig administrations. The whigs, who were in possession, paid the radicals in their own kind. Grey and Russell thought of them in the lowest terms. The duke of Bedford was more cautious, but no more friendly. 'You may act in co-operation with these men for a great public good without trusting them, or placing implicit confidence in them.'[2] Melbourne, who thought the Benthamites 'all fools', and hated Durham's arrogance, was unlikely to get on well with men who were always asking him to undertake reforms. Melbourne weighed his words with Queen Victoria, but he told her in 1839 that the radicals had 'neither ability, honesty, nor numbers'.[3]

The whigs bought the support of O'Connell between 1834 and 1840; neither side gained much from the bargain.[4]

---

[1] Charles Buller (1806-48), a pupil of Thomas Carlyle, 1822-5; M.P., 1830; voted for the extinction of his own constituency; proposed the establishment of the record commission; went with Durham to Canada, 1838; secretary to the board of control, 1841; judge-advocate-general, 1846; chief poor law commissioner, 1847.

[2] S. Walpole, *Life of Lord John Russell*, i. 219.   [3] *Q.V.L.* 1st ser. i. 195.

[4] See below, pp. 344-8, for the history of Anglo-Irish relations during this period.

O'Connell did not expect the whigs to repeal the Union, but he required the consideration of Irish grievances. The tithe question was the most immediate of these grievances. It was impossible to deal with the payment of tithes without raising the larger problem of the position and revenues of the anglican establishment in Ireland, and on this problem the views of Irish catholics and English protestants could not be reconciled. Thus the whig ministers were bound to bring forward proposals affecting Ireland which were unpopular in Great Britain and not sufficient to remedy Irish discontent. As long as this discontent remained, it was difficult to govern Ireland by ordinary means of law, but the whigs, to their credit, disliked coercion bills, and the radicals never made allowances for the difficulties of the position. On the other side, the house of lords could afford to be less cautious about rejecting Irish measures of reform than about matters affecting England. O'Connell was hated by the tories, and disliked by upper-class and middle-class opinion in England. The lower classes, jealous of the competition of Irish labour, were not inclined to sympathize with Irish grievances, though O'Connell generally voted with the radicals on social and economic questions.

Peel dominated English politics between 1833 and 1846. Except for a few months, he was out of office until 1841, but his importance went beyond the division lists in the house of commons. He considered measures on their merits, and disliked pledging himself in advance. At the height of the agitation over the reform bill he had written: 'No one can feel more strongly than I do the absurdity of the doctrine that because a certain course was taken one session, it must necessarily be taken the next, with reference to the same measure.'[1] On these grounds he had justified his change of view about catholic emancipation, and on similar grounds he was to justify the repeal of the corn laws. In the years between 1832 and 1840 he argued that the whigs and their radical supporters had asked for innovation. It was their business to bring forward a programme; the opposition was entitled to suspend judgement. Peel summed up his policy in 1833: 'I presume the chief object of that party which is called Conservative . . . will be to resist Radicalism, to prevent those further encroachments of democratic influence which will be attempted (probably successfully attempted) as the natural

[1] Parker, ii. 199.

consequence of the triumph already achieved.'[1] From Peel's own point of view there was everything to be said for caution. He wanted to convince the country that the 'party which is called Conservative' was ready to make sound administrative changes. He knew that he would not find it easy to persuade the high tories to accept many of the changes which he thought necessary. The less he committed himself to a detailed programme, the better for his party.

Grey retired in the summer of 1834, when he failed to get Althorp's support for an Irish coercion bill.[2] Althorp was leader in the commons, and without him the prime minister could not pass a measure opposed by the radicals and the Irish, but the loss of Althorp was more the occasion than the cause of Grey's withdrawal. Grey was an old man; he had returned to politics against his will, and carried a measure which, in his opinion, would preserve the type of government best suited to the country. The strain had been great, and Grey wanted to go back to his country house in Northumberland.

The king, with his usual blindness to the facts, wanted a coalition. He was told that the tories could not join a ministry which they had opposed with such bitterness. If he could not have the tories as his safeguard, William IV accepted the most conservative of the whigs. Lord Melbourne[3] was a sensitive, impressionable man, distinguished yet indolent, fastidious and at the same time unable to resist the social corruption of the class into which he was born. Private happiness meant more to him than to many public men, but his own marriage had been unhappy, and his only son, for whom he showed the most delicate affection, was mentally defective. Melbourne once said of his own mother: 'She was the most sagacious woman I ever knew. She kept me right as long as she lived.' She died in 1818. After 1830 Canning and Huskisson, whom Melbourne admired, were also dead, and Melbourne was alone in a new age. He did not care overmuch to be prime minister. It is said that he told his secretary that 'he thought it a damned bore', and that 'he was in many minds what he should do—be Minister or no'. The secretary

---

[1] Parker, ii. 212.   [2] See below, p. 346.
[3] William Lamb, 2nd Viscount Melbourne (1779–1848); gt.-grandson of an attorney of Southwell and legal adviser to the Cokes of Norfolk; educ. Eton and Trinity College, Cambridge; studied at Glasgow, 1799; called to the bar, 1804; M.P., 1806; chief secretary for Ireland, 1827–8; home secretary, 1830–4.

answered: 'Why, damn it, such a position never was occupied by
any Greek or Roman, and if it only lasts two months, it is well
worth while to have been Prime Minister of England.'[1] Once
he had taken the office, his own pride and intellectual interests
made him want to hold it, and after his defeat in 1841 he felt
hurt at his isolation from affairs. Such a party leader, with his
disdain of vulgar aims and methods, his disillusion about men
and things, was not likely to be an active reformer. His kindness and quick sympathy were limited to his own class, and were,
in a last analysis, selfish, or at least too much self-regarding. His
contemptuous dismissal of Benthamism showed the narrowness
as well as the sharpness of his mind. Throughout his administration he gave the impression that he was enjoying, or accepting,
an intellectual experience, rather than directing a government
upon whose activities millions of poor men had set their hopes.
He believed in letting things alone at a time when there was
every reason for not letting them alone. Towards the end of his
ministry he could still tell the house of lords that the making of
laws was 'only a subsidiary and incidental duty of Parliament;
the principal duty of Parliament is to consider the estimates
for the public service, to retrench what is superfluous, to correct
what is amiss, and to assist the Crown with those supplies and
subsidies which it thinks right and necessary to afford'.[2] He
could be content with his own work because he had never
looked forward to an elaborate programme. In 1834 he took
over a ministry formed by Grey. In 1835, when he was likely to
have a cabinet of his own making, he spoke of himself in the
eighteenth-century manner as 'entirely free to choose both the
principles upon which, and the men with whom, I will consent
to engage either in government or in opposition. Now the difficulties with respect to the government of the country, with respect to further measures, seem to me to be little or nothing. . . . In
an empire like ours there will always be . . . peril or apprehensions
in some quarter or another, but there appears to me at present
to exist as little of this nature as can reasonably be expected.
Not so the difficulties with respect to men.'[3] Thus the Irish
question, the 'condition of England', the hungry labourers with
whose troubles Melbourne had come into contact, if only
through the sentences of the courts, and the reorganization of

[1] Greville, 4 Sept. 1834.   [2] Hansard, 3rd ser. l. 518.
[3] Sanders, p. 237 (Melbourne to Grey, 23 Jan. 1835).

the English administrative system were of less importance than
the 'difficulties with respect to men', in other words, the task of
obtaining the cooperation of the party described by the duke
of Bedford as 'a noisy and turbulent pack of hounds . . . Whigs,
Moderates, Ultra-Whigs, Radicals, Ultra-Radicals, etc., etc.'[1]

Russell was of little use to Melbourne, since he rarely understood the needs of the country. His politics, like his books,
tended to be didactic and wire-drawn, and his manner was unlikely to get him personal support. Russell, even more than
Grey, was the arch-whig of the nineteenth century, and the
nearest approach to the heaven-born oligarchs whom Disraeli
attacked in his novels. He was more concerned with the removal
of obstacles to civil liberty than with the creation of a more
reasonable and civilized society. His political theory centred
in the revolution of 1688, and in the clique of aristocratic
families to whom the country owed loyalty in return for something like the *charte octroyée* of the reform bill. On this theory a
parliamentary election was a plebiscite in favour of the whig
magnates, and the rank and file of the party were of little
importance. The party leaders on each side were on better
terms with one another than with their own followers.[2] Russell's impetuosity was another difficulty. He had a habit of
stating his own opinion without reference to its effect upon the
position of the government. There were times when he expressed a view which had general support. He described political economy as 'an awful thing'; he added later, 'without going
the length of the Venetian proverb "Primo Veneziani, poi Cri-
stiani", I am disposed to say, Let us first be Englishmen, and
then economists'.[3] Most working men would have agreed with
this opinion; yet Russell himself, as well as his colleagues in
the cabinet, accepted nearly every line of orthodox economic
theory. His outbursts were not always on 'open' questions.
In 1834 Graham, Stanley, Ripon, and Richmond resigned
because Russell insisted on raising in the commons the ques-

[1] Walpole, i. 214.

[2]   'Like or dislike, he does not care a jot:
                   He wants your vote, but your affections not,
                   Yet human hearts need sun as well as oats,
                   So cold a climate plays the deuce with votes.'

These lines were written of Russell. They might equally well have been written
of Peel. See Walpole, i. 305.

[3] Walpole, i. 366.

tion of the appropriation of surplus revenues of the Irish church to secular purposes.[1] Russell was not the only headstrong member of the cabinet. Palmerston was no less masterful, and no less blunt about having his own way, but he was not leader of the house of commons. It is also true that considerable latitude was necessary for an administration supported by so many shades of opinion. In 1839 Melbourne described a proposal for the repeal of the corn laws as 'the wildest and maddest scheme that had ever entered into the imagination of man'; Russell and a number of other ministers voted for a committee on the subject. Disagreement of this kind was still not enough to destroy a government, but the spectacle of ministers differing in public did the ministry little good.

In November 1834 Lord Althorp, the most reliable member of the cabinet, succeeded his father and therefore withdrew to the lords. Melbourne had made his support a condition of taking office; he might well doubt whether, in view of the pressure from O'Connell and the radicals, the ministry could survive without Althorp to defend it in the commons. He put the case to William IV, and offered to resign, though he suggested that Russell might take Althorp's place as leader. The king, who disliked and distrusted Russell, accepted Melbourne's offer of resignation. It is not unlikely that Melbourne wanted the king to come to this decision. Peel was in Rome at the time, but Wellington agreed to look after the king's government. Peel was sent for at once, and in the meanwhile Wellington drove round from ministry to ministry doing the work in hand.

The 'dismissal' of Melbourne at his own suggestion was already an anachronism in constitutional practice. No prime minister since 1834 has allowed his sovereign to decide whether an administration should or could be continued, or to reject his choice of a leader in the house of commons. No modern leader of the opposition would accept office without testing the opinion of the house of commons. Peel's interpretation of the constitutional issue was a little fanciful; he assumed that in taking office he made himself responsible for the king's action, whereas the responsibility rested partly with Melbourne. William IV had been delighted to get rid of the whigs, and the queen was believed to share his views. The king's brother, the duke of

[1] See below, p. 346. This was the occasion of Stanley's note to Graham: 'John Russell has upset the coach.'

Cumberland, a stupid and savage tory, was wild enough to consider the possibility of a military *coup d'état*. The king told Peel that if the whigs came back to office he could not treat them as his confidential servants.[1] Here, rather than in the circumstances of Melbourne's dismissal, was the danger of a constitutional dispute of the first order; but Melbourne knew his sovereign's eccentricities, and Peel advised the king's secretary to warn William IV against the risks of using violent language about his ministers. On 20 June 1837 William IV died. The duke of Cumberland was shipped off to Hanover, where the rule of succession did not allow a woman to take the throne. Henceforward Cumberland and Hanover pass out of English history.

The king's action in 1834 made a general election necessary. Peel took the chance of explaining his policy to the country and of showing that the conservatives accepted the reform act of 1832 as 'a final and irrevocable settlement'. In spite of the novelty of the Tamworth manifesto, the election did not raise much interest, and fewer seats were contested than in 1832. Peel was unable to secure a majority, though his party won about a hundred seats; Melbourne was disappointed at the increase in the radical vote. The old traditions and habits were still strong enough for a prime minister to ask that the king's government should be given a fair trial, and Peel did not resign until he had been beaten six times in six weeks. When he gave up office he let the English electors understand that he was being turned out by an alliance between the whigs and O'Connell.

After the return of Melbourne Peel continued the same tactics. He treated questions on their merits, and aimed at conciliating, in his own words, 'the sober-minded and well-disposed portion of the community'. He accepted the principles of the municipal corporations bill introduced by the government in 1835, and refused to support some of the amendments proposed by the lords. Peel's contemptuous support or damaging criticism were equally humiliating to the ministry. Melbourne again failed to see that the only way of escape from his 'difficulties with respect to men' lay through a bold programme boldly carried through. Without a programme which would

[1] The king's language was so absurd that no one could take him seriously. In 1835 he said in a moment of temper: 'Mind me, . . . the cabinet is not my cabinet; they had better take care, or, by God, I will have them impeached.'

have satisfied at least one section of his supporters, and put the opposition once more in the position of negative critics, the whig administration began to break up. It survived the general election of 1837, but early in May 1839 Melbourne carried only by five votes a proposal to suspend the constitution of Jamaica.[1] He refused to stay in office. The resignation of the cabinet brought another constitutional crisis, though the good sense of the leaders on each side prevented any serious consequences.

The accession of Queen Victoria[2] in 1837 affected the relations between ministers and the Crown. The sovereign was now a young girl of eighteen, without experience of public affairs, but self-possessed, tenacious, and honestly wishing to do her duty by the country. Her own training had been little more than the conventional education of a young girl of the upper class. Her father, the duke of Kent, died in 1820. Her mother, Princess Victoria of Saxe-Coburg, and widow of Prince Charles of Leiningen before her second marriage, had quarrelled with William IV; she had fallen entirely, and, as rumour had it, scandalously, under the direction of her secretary, Sir John Conroy, but she guarded her daughter against any influence outside her own. The princess's only friend was her governess, Fräulein Lehzen, to whom George IV gave a Hanoverian title. Lehzen was safe, and a little dull; hence the princess

[1] See below, p. 374.

[2] The queen was born on 24 May 1819: she was named Victoria after her mother, and received the first name of Alexandrina owing to her father's gratitude to Alexander I of Russia, who had supplied him with money when, after Princess Charlotte's death in 1817, the duke of Kent and two of his brothers married in order to secure the succession. In 1831 there was a proposal that, as the names Alexandrina Victoria were not well known in England, the princess should take the additional names Elizabeth or Charlotte. At her first privy council meeting the queen signed the register as 'Victoria', but the documents prepared for publication described her as 'Alexandrina Victoria'. The first name was withdrawn at her own wish. For the circumstances of the queen's accession see C. K. Webster, 'The accession of Queen Victoria' (*History*, June 1937).
Queen Victoria was under five feet in height, not beautiful, or even handsome, but she carried herself with grace and dignity, and her voice was clear and musical. The queen was physically a strong woman; she bore nine children, and never had a serious illness, though in her later years she was almost nervously careful of her health. She was a good horsewoman, a good dancer, fond of indoor and outdoor games and of fresh air, often to the discomfort of her court. The queen's letters (see p. 637) give an excellent picture of her character and tastes, though too much stress should not be put upon her language and style of writing; here, as in many other respects, the queen was not very different from other women of high rank and station in the Victorian age.

kept her own counsel. Her mother—and Conroy—expected an important position when the princess became queen. Fortunately William IV lived long enough for the queen to reach her nineteenth year before she came to the throne. The risks of a regency were avoided, and the queen at once asserted her independence. Conroy was sent away from London, and the queen's mother given to understand that her authority was at an end. Leopold of Belgium[1] was discouraged from offering his niece too much advice.[2] It was rumoured that Baron Stock-mar,[3] who was in England at Leopold's orders during the illness of William IV, might become the queen's private secretary. Melbourne saw the danger of allowing a foreigner to hold a posi-tion which was as important as it was new,[4] and, as there was no suitable candidate, undertook the duties himself.

Nothing in Melbourne's career was of greater value to his country, but his delicate and loyal service had one inevitable result. The queen, surrounded by whigs, and treated by them with tact and consideration, thought of the whigs as her friends, while the tories, remembering past history, assumed that they had a whig sovereign. For some years the queen herself held this view. In 1840 she wrote to Prince Albert: 'The Whigs are the only safe and loyal people, and the Radicals will also rally round their Queen to protect her from the Tories.'[5] The queen's experience of a tory ministry and her marriage with Prince Albert soon taught her other views, but in 1839 there was no doubt about her opinion. Peel, therefore, on taking office

---

[1] Leopold had married Princess Charlotte, daughter of George IV; he lived mainly in England, on his marriage grant of £50,000 a year from the British government, after the death of the princess. On Stockmar's urgent advice, Leopold gave up this pension (with reservations) after he became king of the Belgians. See also below, p. 228.

[2] The queen wrote in Dec. 1839: 'dear Uncle is given to believe that he must rule the roast everywhere. However that is not a necessity.' Q.V.L. 1st ser. i. 254. Leopold continued his advice, mainly, though not always, to the good of the monarchy.

[3] Baron Christian Friedrich von Stockmar (1787–1863), b. Coburg; entered the service of Prince Leopold as private physician, 1816; lived mainly in England until 1831 as the prince's private secretary and controller of his household; returned to Coburg, 1834, but remained the family adviser of the Coburgs.

[4] The office had come into existence owing to the blindness of George III, when the need of a private secretary was obvious. George IV's ministers were too suspi-cious of his intrigues to allow him an official private secretary, though he employed one unofficially throughout his reign. William IV's use of Sir Herbert Taylor was officially accepted. Taylor was too old to continue the work after the king's death.

[5] Q.V.L. 1st ser. i. 268.

wanted some mark of confidence from the sovereign. He had in mind that the queen might make some changes in the disposition of her household. He did not want to touch the minor posts, but expected the resignation of those ladies in the higher offices who were related to whig ministers.

Peel had not Melbourne's grace and ease of manner. Lady de Grey warned him that she thought his bearing 'too reserved and too cautious' to gain the queen's confidence.[1] The queen herself, after her first meeting with Peel on 8 May 1839, noted that he was 'such a cold odd man she [the queen] can't make out what he means'.[2] Peel told Ashley,[3] whom he asked to take over the household, that it was a great responsibility to 'provide the attendants and companions of this young woman, on whose moral and religious character depends the welfare of millions of human beings'.[4] On 9 May, at a second interview with Peel, the queen herself suggested Ashley. Peel then proposed changes in the higher appointments, but the queen answered that she would make no change. Peel asked Wellington to see her; Wellington could not persuade her to give way. The queen then wrote to Melbourne, and Melbourne put the question to Grey and Russell. The whig leaders did not understand that Peel wanted only a few changes. They thought that he was pressing his case too strongly, and early on 10 May Melbourne wrote to the queen on behalf of his cabinet that they would stand by her. Peel therefore resigned his commission. In his letter of resignation he used the phrase 'some changes' in the household. Melbourne pointed to the words 'some changes', but the queen explained that, from her point of view, there was no difference between 'some' and 'all'. Grey thought the phrase important, but not decisive.

It is difficult to assign responsibility for this absurd business. Peel had a good case, even if his manner had been stiff. The queen was unreasonable, a little angry with Peel, and not clear in her letter to Melbourne. The whigs ought not to have advised the queen until Peel had refused to form a ministry. On the other hand, the queen was not yet twenty, and might well claim to choose her closest companions.[5] The whigs were misled

[1] Parker, ii, 389.   [2] Q.V.L. 1st ser. i. 200.

[3] For Lord Ashley (later Lord Shaftesbury), see below, p. 151.

[4] Parker, ii. 393.

[5] According to the duchess of Bedford the queen did not talk politics with her ladies. Parker, ii. 459.

by the queen's statement of her case, but the ministers, and, above all, Melbourne, would have found it difficult to refuse her appeal. They may have been afraid of driving the queen to the radicals. From a political point of view, the whigs had little to gain, and the conservatives little to lose. Peel had no wish to lead another minority government; if his position had been stronger, he would not have insisted upon the changes in the household. Melbourne did not look forward with pleasure at all events to the parliamentary side of office. The question was settled in a friendly way between the two parties before Melbourne's final resignation in 1841, and the queen's marriage put the affair into the background.

The marriage of Queen Victoria to her cousin Prince Albert of Saxe-Coburg-Gotha[1] took place on 10 February 1840. Prince Albert was no genius, and something of a prig. His education, under Stockmar's guidance, had been superficial: Roman law; political economy; history; philosophy; modern languages; natural science; music—all in a year and a half at the University of Bonn, with travel throughout the vacations. Stockmar, who made the most of his pupil, spoke of the prince's habit 'of not dwelling long upon a subject'! The prince shared the ambition and the financial acuteness of his family. His uncle Leopold had marked him out as the future husband of the queen of England, and Albert himself, after his marriage, was no less anxious to provide for his own brother out of the bountiful pocket of the British taxpayer. It is typical of him that he described the reduction of his own allowance from the £50,000 proposed by Melbourne to £30,000 as 'a truly unseemly vote'. Stockmar, with his devotion to the Coburg house and his earnest, commonplace mind, was not a good tutor. The prince was awkward and tactless; the English magnates were quick to notice the awkwardness, and to take offence at the lack of tact. A letter written by Arbuthnot, a friend of the duke of Wellington, to Peel shows the first reaction to this new phenomenon at the English court. 'Prince Albert says that no tailor in England can make a coat, and that the right time to dine is three o'clock.

[1] Albert Francis Charles Augustus Emmanuel, Prince Consort of England (1819–61), 2nd s. of Ernest, duke of Saxe-Coburg-Gotha, and Louise, d. of the duke of Saxe-Gotha-Altenburg, b. Rosenau, nr. Coburg. Prince Albert was delicate as a child, but grew up into a healthy young man, of good looks and bearing. He took his public duties very seriously, and overwork was one of the causes of his failure to resist typhoid fever in 1861.

He is a metaphysician. At least such reading is his favourite study.'[1] The queen herself did not wish to share with the prince the responsibilities of constitutional monarchy, though she wanted him to be given a precedence which the house of lords refused to allow. The queen first met the prince in 1836. She seems to have liked him, and to have made it clear that she would not object to him as a husband. William IV wished her to choose a prince of the house of Orange, and Melbourne favoured the queen's cousin, Prince George of Cambridge, but the Coburgs took the matter for granted. In 1839 the prince and his brother came on a visit to Windsor; before their arrival the queen wrote to Leopold that she considered the project at an end, at least for the present.[2]

The queen soon changed her mind, and within a short time after her marriage gave the prince almost too much confidence. She found that his advice was good, and that he lightened the burden of her work. On the other hand he never fully understood his position, and throughout his life there were traces of those 'stirring and ambitious views' which the duchess of Cambridge noticed in his youth. It is also difficult to estimate the degree of influence exercised by Stockmar after his pupil's knowledge and experience were greater than his own. Stockmar came and went as he pleased; his service in a princely house was more German than English, and his treasury of political maxims was at all events richer than the intellectual endowments of the Coburg family. He was upright, intelligent, and self-reliant. Palmerston, who had no reason to like him, thought that he was 'the one absolutely disinterested man' whom he had met in politics. Gladstone described Stockmar's view of the British constitution as 'only an English top-dressing on a German soil',[3] and Stockmar himself wrote, in 1858, of the 'absurd, usurping house of commons'.[4] Stockmar's confidence in his own opinions, and his exasperation over Palmerston's refusal to give weight to these opinions when they were expressed by the queen or the prince, brought the Crown dangerously near to

---

[1] Parker, op. cit. ii. 414. Charles Arbuthnot (1767–1850), diplomatist and politician, lived in Wellington's house during his latter years.

[2] There are many rumours about the causes of the queen's hesitation. Most of these, and a good many other stories about the queen, the prince, and the court, are based upon unreliable gossip, and it is unsafe to give them much, or any, historical value. [3] Gladstone, *Gleanings*, i. 84.

[4] E. von Stockmar, *Memoirs of Baron Stockmar*, ed. F. Max Müller, ii. 546–7.

unconstitutional action, but, on the whole, his advice was sensible and moderate. In minor matters such as the extravagance and mismanagement of the royal household his suggestions were much to the point.

There is little doubt that the prince was a steadying influence upon the queen.[1] His seriousness of mind was not a disadvantage. The queen might well have developed in a different way, if the prince's influence had not been felt at court. After the sons of George III an improvement of tone was necessary, and, although the mere facts that the sovereign was young, and a woman, brought a change for the better, the prince could make his wishes felt in quarters inaccessible to the queen herself. From this point of view the respectability of the royal *entourage* under the queen and her husband corresponded with the wishes of their subjects. The queen's standards of moral behaviour for her court and her subjects were formal and severe. She even objected to the remarriage of widows, but she was neither prudish nor sentimental; the only touch of morbidity in her character was an excessive cult of memorials of the dead, particularly after the death of her husband; in this respect it is necessary to take into account the queen's isolation as a widow, even in a friendly and sympathetic court, and the effect of a palace environment in leading royal persons to externalize and dramatize their private feelings. In many directions the prince's own tastes taught the queen a good deal. The queen's general intelligence was not above the average, though she had an excellent memory. She knew nothing, and could hardly learn much, about the social questions of the age. She had a natural vivacity and wide interests, but little artistic sense, and of her own accord could not have encouraged the patronage of art, science, and letters; George IV's extravagant habits in architecture hardly formed a good precedent, and the prince introduced quieter and better methods of encouraging talent and education in craftsmanship. The prince was more popular among the people at large than among the aristocracy; this popularity was to a great extent earned by his lively interest in the problems of his time.

The last two years of Melbourne's administration were increasingly unsatisfactory to the whigs. They were embarrassed

[1] The prince himself owed much to Peel's friendship and counsel.

by chartism. In the early part of 1841 they lost four successive by-elections; they were beaten on a fiscal motion in May, and on 4 June Peel obtained a majority of one on a vote of no-confidence. The whigs had no programme likely to attract supporters; Russell might have taken up the corn laws, but Melbourne's attitude towards them was as unchangeable as Wellington's belief in the perfection of the unreformed parliament.[1]

The conservative cabinet of 1841, formed after the whig defeat, was particularly strong. It included three out of the four ministers who had left the whig government in 1834 on the Irish question; five of Peel's colleagues had held, or were to hold, the office of prime minister, and four were to be governors-general of India. Peel himself was at the height of his powers.[2] Gladstone, who thought Peel, 'taken all round', the greatest man he had ever known, described him as the 'best man of business who was ever Prime Minister'.[3] Peel was a little frigid outside his own very happy family life. Palmerston believed that the 'reserved and apparently cold manner' was due to 'proud shyness', and also that it was 'purposely assumed to assist him in that self-control which he feels to be constantly necessary'.[4] Peel was a quick-tempered man, 'peppery', in Gladstone's words, but his own justification for this coldness of manner was that he had assumed it in Ireland out of self-defence against claimants for patronage. 'I had early experience in that country of the danger of saying a civil word.' A feeling of social isolation in Dublin society may have had a good deal to do with Peel's reserve. Before he went to Dublin he was known for his openness of manner, and in later life he impressed Carlyle with his 'warm sense of fun, really of broad, genuine drollery'. Peel was oddly sensitive about his social position. He spoke with a slight Lancashire accent, and was a little over-aware that he was the son of a rich cotton-spinner. There is an element of hidden conflict in his political career; this tall, blue-eyed, auburn-haired man, conscious of his great abilities, matched himself against the older, privileged, high-born tory society, and asserted the rights and energies of a new social class. One may notice a

---

[1] See above, p. 101.

[2] Peel was a very strong man. On one day in Jan. 1835 he went to bed at 2 a.m., got up at 4 a.m., drove to Drayton, and attended a ball in the evening. Next day he was out shooting.

[3] Peel himself regarded his cabinet of fourteen members as too large.

[4] Ashley, *Life of Palmerston*, i. 119.

similar motive in the elder Sir Robert Peel's insistence that his
son should take up a political career. At the end of Peel's
ministry his breach with the old landed aristocracy over the corn
laws revealed this latent antagonism. Peel turned sharply against
the rank and file of his party, and the protectionist leaders.

To have your own way, and to be for five years the Minister of
this country in the House of Commons is quite enough for any man's
strength. . . . But to have to incur the deepest responsibility, to bear
the heaviest toil, to reconcile colleagues with conflicting opinions
to a common course of action, to keep together in harmony the
Sovereign, the Lords, and the Commons . . . and to be at the same
time the tool of a party—that is to say, to adopt the opinions of men
who have not access to your knowledge, and could not profit by it
if they had, who spend their time in eating and drinking, and hunting, shooting, gambling, horse-racing, and so forth—would be an
odious servitude, to which I never will submit.[1]

It has been said that Peel chose the wrong party.[2] This view
does not take account of the change in the whigs between the
beginning and end of Peel's career. The whig party at the
beginning of the nineteenth century was the party of high family
and of general ideas. Peel's memory was almost as astonishing
as Macaulay's, but his weak point was his slow response to
general ideas. In Bagehot's words, he was converted to an idea
only when the average man was converted; he would have
nothing to do with new ideas 'as long as they remained the
property of first-class intellects, as long as they were confined
to philanthropists or speculators'.[3] Moreover it was not until
the close of Peel's career that whiggery became liberalism. The
term 'liberal' was not applied to the party as a whole until
1847, though it was used nearly thirty years earlier as a term

---

[1] Parker, iii. 473–4. Lord Ellenborough noted in his diary on 29 Jan. 1831 that
it was 'advisable to conciliate Peel to the Aristocracy, and this the Duke may
manage by asking him to meet peers, who will ask him to dinner'. A. Aspinall,
Three Early Nineteenth Century Diaries, p. 43. Such dinners might have been a little
frosty. Mrs. Arbuthnot (who disliked Peel as she had disliked Canning) wrote in
Mar. 1830 that Peel 'asks immense parties of the House of Commons to dinner every
week and treats them so *de haut en bas* and is so haughty and silent that they come
away swearing they will never go to his house again; so that his civilities do him
harm rather than otherwise.' *Journal of Mrs. Arbuthnot*, ii. 345.

[2] There is a story that the elder Sir Robert Peel warned the tories that his son
might go over to the whigs if he were not given office.

[3] W. Bagehot, *Biographical Studies*, pp. 6–7. Bagehot's judgement is not wholly
fair, e.g. it takes no account of Peel's attitude towards legal reform.

of reproach.[1] Gladstone, the greatest of Peel's followers, became the leader of this liberal party; but if Peel had had his way, the conservative party would not have become, in contrast with the liberals, the party of the landed aristocracy and the rich manufacturers. Peel brought the tories a certain distance with him. Their failure to go the whole distance was responsible ultimately for the rise of a compact liberal party out of the confused and quarrelling groups led by Melbourne. With these groups as they existed between 1832 and 1846 Peel had not much more in common than with the whigs of Grey's generation. The Peel family had little fault to find with the general conditions of industrial England; they were unlikely to take up reform for reform's sake. They were neither ungenerous nor blind to abuses. The elder Peel had been one of the most prominent supporters of the first factory act for the protection of children. His son carried out reform after reform of a practical and limited kind; but his measures were never part of a widely envisaged plan of great social change. They were always set against the larger mass of English institutions and habits which Peel did not want to alter.

As prime minister Peel continued the policy which he had adopted with success years earlier as home secretary. He had the confidence of his cabinet. Gladstone said to Peel after his defeat in 1846: 'Your government has not been carried on by a cabinet but by the heads of departments each in communication with you.' Peel answered that Melbourne's administration had been 'a mere government of departments without a centre of unity'.[2] Peel introduced his own budgets in 1842 and 1845, although he had an able chancellor of the exchequer. He drew up drafts for the cabinet on important questions, read 'the whole foreign correspondence', prepared himself 'for every debate, including the most trumpery concerns', and wrote in his own hand 'to every person of note' who chose to send him a letter.[3]

Apart from the unending difficulties of Ireland, Peel's main work was concerned with finance. One aspect of this work was more a matter of controversy between experts than a party

---

[1] For the history of the term 'liberal' (which was used by the Spanish opponents of absolute monarchy) in English politics, see Halévy, ii. 81 n. and iii. 180 n. After the retirement of Huskisson in 1828, an article in *Blackwood's Magazine* noted that 'we have, at last, thank God, got rid of the Liberals, and once more have the happiness to live under a pure Tory government'.

[2] Morley, i. 298.   [3] Parker, iii. 219.

question. After the bank charter act of 1833,[1] it was hoped that there would be no financial crises due to the imprudent extension of credit by small banks. Unfortunately a rapid increase in the number of joint-stock banks brought about an expansion of credit just at the time when the railway boom was encouraging speculation; three hundred companies, with a subscribed capital of £135,000,000 were formed between 1834 and 1836. There was a similar wave of speculation in the United States, followed by the collapse of many American banks. English houses provided a great deal of the credit which financed Anglo-American trade, and the English public, distrusting 'political loans' used in Europe to maintain autocratic governments and in South America to support dishonest politicians, had turned more readily to invest in the United States. The crisis which resulted from this rash expansion of credit and over-confident investment lasted for several years. A bad harvest in 1838 led to the export of gold for the purchase of foreign corn. The whigs appointed a committee, including Peel, to look for remedies against these recurrent crises. Peel accepted the view that commercial crises would not take place if the issue of paper notes, together with the coin in circulation, never exceeded the amount of money which would circulate if the currency were wholly metallic. This statement of the problem was too simple because it ignored the importance of other forms of paper, such as cheques,[2] but it enabled Peel, when he came into office, to modify the charter of the bank of England. He asked parliament in 1844 to put further restrictions upon the issue of notes by other banks, to limit the fiduciary note issue of the bank of England to £14,000,000, and to insist that coin or bullion should cover all notes issued above this sum. Peel realized that in an emergency it might be necessary to suspend the act of 1844; he thought that, with these precautionary controls, an emergency was less likely to occur.[3]

The regulation of the note-issue was a mode of protecting property upon which all parties were agreed. The whigs left Peel a more difficult and controversial problem. Melbourne's administration had not been extravagant, but for five years the income from the revenue had not been enough to balance

[1] See above, p. 60.
[2] This omission was probably fortunate; otherwise Peel's policy might have hampered the normal expansion of the national economy.
[3] The act was suspended three times between 1844 and 1866.

the budget. Peel therefore had to find new sources of income. Four-fifths of the revenue came from the customs and excise. An increase in the duties might check consumption and diminish the returns; if the duties were lowered, there might be an increase in consumption, but, at all events for a time, there would be a fall in the returns. Peel decided to encourage consumption by lowering the duties, and to tide over the interval by means of an income tax which would also give him a surplus. He could apply this surplus to further reductions of indirect taxation. He found that 1,046 articles were subject to duty. In 1842 he cut down the duties on 769 articles, and chose, as far as possible, raw materials. Within three years the increase in consumption almost balanced the loss to the revenue. Peel then persuaded the commons to renew the income tax for another three years. Before his defeat in 1846 he had abolished the duties on 605 articles, and reduced the rate of taxation on most of those which remained dutiable. He had thus remitted taxation at the rate of £2,500,000 a year, and yet provided a surplus. He also repaid about £14,000,000 of the national debt, lowered the rate of interest on £250,000,000 of stock, and thereby cut down the annual debt charge by £1,500,000.

During these experiments in the direction of free trade, Peel maintained that the duties on sugar and corn required special treatment. On this point, at the end of 1845, he broke with his party. Nearly twenty years earlier Creevey noticed that, on the question of the corn laws, unhappily for toryism, 'that prig Peel seems as deeply bitten by "liberality" . . . as any of his fellows'.[1] It was likely that the strain upon the loyalty of the old tories to the new conservatism would come in this division of interest between town and country, but the opposition to Peel within his own party had been growing stronger before his attacks upon vested protectionist interests reached the grand concern of the landlords. This opposition was not merely in defence of landed wealth. Peel based his conservatism upon the view that government must take account of fixed and steady interests, wherever in the state these interests might be found. Such a policy did not attract young men without experience of the difficulties of government or the unexpected results of violent change. Above all, it was not a policy likely to satisfy a generation influenced by the ideas of the romantic revival.

[1] *The Creevey Papers*, ii. 100.

It happened that, owing to the ease with which the sons of great houses could find seats in parliament, owing to the looseness of party ties and the tradition of an assembly which took more account of ability than of age, the criticism of Peel's classical and cautious leadership expressed itself more freely, and obtained a wider publicity, than any similar criticism in later times. From this point of view the movement known as 'Young England' had a parliamentary importance out of proportion to its influence in the country. It was in one respect a revolt against Peel's attempt to strengthen and enforce party discipline through the whips, but the revolt against this discipline came from a deeper discontent. The movement was begun by a small group of young men whose social and economic position enabled them to oppose changes in the structure of society without fully understanding what they were attacking. The leaders of this last attempt to assert the ideal significance of a territorial aristocracy were a group of Cambridge friends, of whom George Smythe[1] and Lord John Manners[2] were the most prominent figures. Cambridge had little to do with the movement except to provide an early meeting-place for its members. Smythe and John Manners were more affected by the views of F. W. Faber,[3] a product of the Oxford movement, though Faber himself, in his political interests and in his opposition to liberalism and the school of *laisser faire*, was nearer to the theocratic writers of the Continent than to the tractarians. Faber thought that revolution in England was both imminent and necessary; Smythe and John Manners believed that there was a chance of avoiding revolution if the upper and lower classes came together to resist the radicals and the manufacturers. The upper class would thus be the leaders in a new feudalism of a paternal kind, based upon the romantic toryism of Southey and a humourless book, *The Broadstone of Honour*,[4] written in 1822 by Kenelm

---

[1] George Smythe, 7th Viscount Strangford (1818–57); b. Stockholm; educ. Eton and St. John's College, Cambridge; M.P., 1841; under-secretary for foreign affairs, 1845–6; wrote for the *Morning Chronicle*, 1847–52; fought in the last duel on English soil, 1852.

[2] John James Robert Manners, 7th duke of Rutland (1818–1906); educ. Eton and Trinity College, Cambridge; M.P., 1841; succeeded his brother, 1888.

[3] Frederick William Faber (1814–63), educ. Harrow and Oxford; Fellow of University College, Oxford, 1837; joined Roman Catholic Church, 1845; superior of the London Oratory, 1849.

[4] The first two editions of this work had a sub-title, *Rules for the Gentlemen of England*.

Digby. Digby's work was a pale imitation of Scott, and the revival of medieval notions, in an age when the scientific study of medieval institutions had only just begun, was little more than play-acting and pageantry. This pageantry was carried to an absurdity in the revival of a medieval tournament at Eglinton in the summer of 1839; it is oddly characteristic of the movement that the tournament was spoiled by rain.

George Smythe was a brilliant dilettante. Manners was in deadly earnest about politics and religion; his criticism of the 'greasiness' of the free-traders was not mere snobbery, and there was some reason in his judgement that 'nothing but monastic institutions can Christianise Manchester', or that 'there never was so complete a feudal system as that of the mills'. His solution of the problems of industrial England has been described as 'a curious mixture of public baths, public open spaces, and Church festivals'; yet it was no bad thing to insist upon the responsibilities of wealth, and, at a time when the emphasis of religion lay upon the duties of the poor, to point out that poor men had a right to the external conditions of happiness.[1]

In 1842 the leaders of the Young England Movement found an odd supporter in Disraeli.[2] Disraeli was nearly fifteen years older than Smythe and John Manners. He had sat in parliament since 1837, and voted on the conservative side. His debating powers were already well known, and, if Stanley had not objected to 'that scoundrel', Peel might have given him a place in his administration. Disraeli wrote that he had been compelled 'to struggle against a storm of political hate and malice which few men ever experienced'.[3] This statement is partly true, but it is not the whole truth. Disraeli's father was a distinguished

---

[1] It is a little hard on Lord John Manners that two unfortunate lines from one of his early poems should have been tied to him for a lifetime. If the lines

'Let wealth and commerce, laws and learning die,
But give us back our old Nobility'

are considered in relation to the coal-mining industry, the law under Eldon, and learning at Oxford and Cambridge in the reign of William IV, their meaning is not altogether ridiculous.

[2] Benjamin Disraeli, 1st earl of Beaconsfield (1804–81), s. of Isaac D'Israeli, a Spanish Jew whose family had settled in Venice and migrated to England in 1748; b. London; educ. privately; articled to a solicitor, 1822, and began to read for the bar; published his first novel, *Vivian Grey*, 1826–7; travelled abroad, 1828–31; M.P., 1837, after three unsuccessful attempts, 1832–5; published *Coningsby*, 1844; married Mrs. Wyndham Lewis, 1839. See also vol. xiv of this *History*.

[3] W. F. Monypenny, ii. 118.

man of letters, long naturalized in England, and 'an acceptable guest in the best society'.[1] The 'hate and malice' against which Disraeli struggled were in some measure the result of his provocative and wounding speeches; the distrust, which was more dangerous, was felt by many of his own friends, and caused not merely by the strangeness and originality of his opinions but also by doubts of his sincerity. Smythe wrote of Disraeli's support of the church: 'Dizzy's conversion to moderate Oxfordism is something like Bonaparte's to moderate Mohamedanism.'[2] Even Manners, who was a loyal friend, was a little doubtful: 'Could I only satisfy myself that D'Israeli believed all that he said, I should be more happy.'[3] Disraeli may have chosen extravagance of dress and manner as the easiest way of getting over the obvious handicaps to a political career in the party of the 'gentlemen of England'. It was better to be ridiculed as an eccentric than to be ignored as an outsider; but he could play the part too easily because it was not merely a part. Disraeli's intellectual powers could not hide the vulgarity of his taste, though, in his speeches and his books, a certain rococo imagination saved him from mere flatness.[4] He was sincere enough to be the victim of his own undisciplined fancy; it was not easy for his contemporaries to discover his sincerity and too easy for them to notice his ambition or to feel his disdain. To the last he never had a high opinion of his colleagues, and it is never certain whether his political career was not as cynical as Gladstone or, on the tory side, Shaftesbury believed it to be:[5] the amusement of vanity, a game in which Disraeli could beat the serene and highly placed leaders of England on their own

---

[1] Duke of Argyll, *Autobiography*, i. 279-80. This judgement would apply to the town rather than the country. Disraeli took a long time to establish his position in Buckinghamshire. As late as 1858 he wrote to Stanley that one of the Drakes of Amersham had asked him for an eastern cadetship. He added: 'For [them] to ask a service from me is the Hapsburgs soliciting something from a parvenu Napoleon. After thirty years of scorn and sullenness they have melted before time and events.' G. E. Buckle, *Life of Disraeli*, iv. 173-4.

[2] C. Whibley, *Life of Lord John Manners and his Friends*, i. 153.

[3] Ibid., i. 149.

[4] Only Disraeli could have described a present of prawns from Torquay as 'the rosy-coloured tribute of Torbay' (Buckle, iv. 355).

[5] Gladstone described Disraeli's opposition as 'malignant'. Shaftesbury regarded him as 'without principle, without feeling, without regard to anything, human or divine, beyond his own personal ambition. He has dragged, and will continue to drag everything that is good, safe, venerable, and solid through the dust and dirt of his own objects' (Hodder, *Life of Lord Shaftesbury*, iii. 234).

ground. In 1868, when the game had been won, Disraeli wrote to Cairns about his election to 'The Club':

Entre nous, I greatly dislike our feeble mimicry of 'the feast of reason and the flow of soul' of the eighteenth century. Lord Stanhope's list of *the* Club seems our friends, the Grillionites,[1] under another name. I have not dined with these gentry for three years; but my recollection of them is extreme dulness; no genuine and general conversation, but a dozen prigs and bores . . . over a bad dinner in a dingy room. . . . Nevertheless, as you and I are both candidates for the Consulship, we must not run counter to the social traditions of the country any more than against any other traditions; so you can tell Lord Salisbury that I shall feel honoured in belonging to so classical and renowned a society as the Club.[2]

Disraeli's political ideas have not stood the test of time. His novels are pieces of extravaganza, interspersed with disquisitions on history, race, religion, economics, and the future of England and the world. His doctrine of race is as unscientific as the anti-Semitism which he attacked; Sidonia, the Jewish sage of the novels, is a trumpery figure, a cosmopolitan snob dealing in commonplaces. The reading of English history as an aristocratic conspiracy against monarchy, church, and people, is a *tour de force*, based, like the whiggism of John Russell, upon an exaggerated view of the revolution of 1688. Disraeli's description of the 'two Englands' in *Sybil* offers neither an analysis nor a solution of the social problem; he did not always support attacks, even from his own party, on grave social abuses. His detachment from English prejudices did not give him any insight into foreign affairs; as a young man he accepted the platitudes of Metternich and failed to understand the meaning of the nationalist movements in Europe. The imperialism of his later years was superficial: an interpretation of politics without economics. Although Disraeli liked to think of himself in terms of pure intellect, his politics were more personal than intellectual in character. He had far-reaching schemes but little administrative ability, and there was some foundation for Napoleon III's judgement that he was 'like all literary men, . . . from Chateaubriand to Guizot, ignorant of the world'.

[1] The Club was, and is, a continuation of the dining circle founded in the time of Dr. Johnson. Grillion's Club was, and is, a dining club of members of parliament and others.   [2] Buckle, iv. 414.

[3] Malmesbury, *Memoirs of an ex-Minister*, ii. 66.

In spite of these faults, for which opponents and *frondeurs* in his own party never forgave him, Disraeli's courage, quickness of wit, capacity for affection, and freedom from sordid motives earned him his position. His ambition was of the nobler sort. He brought politics nearer to poetry, or, at all events, to poetical prose, than any English politician since Burke. Peel paid heavily for his refusal to give him office. Disraeli gave the 'Young England' idealists the help of his debating powers. He was not likely to support them for long. He did not want to spend many more years out of office; these young men who had time in front of them could afford to wait. Meanwhile they were useful to him; they might win him the support of the great territorial families, whose toryism was not of Peel's type.[1] They provided him with a platform from which he could make his attacks upon Peel, and their assistance saved him from isolation in disloyalty. The 'Young England' group broke up in 1845 over the question of an increased grant to Maynooth.[2] Manners voted for it, Smythe took a middle line, and Disraeli opposed it. A few months later Smythe joined Peel on the repeal of the corn laws, and Manners stayed with Disraeli. Disraeli had already said that, in their proposals for the relief of agriculture, the conservative government was an 'organized hypocrisy'. He discovered in the fact and circumstances of Peel's change of view over the corn laws a more extended field of attack, and the chance of a wider following than that of 'Young England'.

The revival of the demand for the repeal of the corn laws took place during the succession of bad harvests and the industrial depression after the summer of 1836.[3] An anti-corn law association had been formed in London in 1836, but the initiative in a larger movement came from Manchester. An association was started there in the autumn of 1838 when corn prices were rising. Other cities followed the example: a conference of delegates of these associations was held in Manchester early in 1839 and adjourned to London. Here, in March, the anti-corn law league was established. This league owed its success to a number

[1] In 1844 the duke of Rutland did not know Disraeli by sight, though he believed him to have a bad influence upon his son.
[2] See p. 351.
[3] For the history of the corn laws, 1815-38, see above, pp. 60-62.

of different factors. Its purpose was simple, easily understood, and negative; there could be no disagreement about it. The league appealed to the desire for equality because it attacked privilege and monopoly; it appealed to the self-interest of the middle and working classes because it offered cheaper food. It made full use of the economic argument that imports of foreign corn would be paid for by an increased export of textile and other goods. The supporters of the league quoted biblical and other precedents against those who became rich on the hunger of the poor; they addressed audiences who knew little about agriculture, and took no account of the capital spent in draining or fertilizing land. The league had the advantage of the new cheap rates of postage, and quick and cheap means of transport. Peel's budgets were in the direction of free trade; the protectionists could no longer say that all manufacturers wanted protection for themselves and free trade for other people.

On the other hand enthusiasm declined after 1842. The harvests of 1842, 1843, and 1844 were good. In 1842 Peel reduced the duties at the lower end of the sliding scale, and therefore took away any temptation to keep foreign wheat from the market when the price was about 66s.[1] This measure, and a fall of 14s. in the price of corn during the years 1842–3, did much to satisfy the manufacturers. Moreover the league ceased to have the field to itself. The protectionists began to answer the mass of pamphlets and oratory. They replied to phrases about 'titled felons', 'foot-pad aristocrats', 'bread-stealers', 'chawbacon, bullfrog, and clodplate farmers' by counter-charges against the 'mean rapacity and monopolizing spirit of merchants and manufacturers'. They pointed out that the manufacturers wanted cheap bread in order to save money on wages: 'the party from which the Anti-Corn Law League has been formed, instead of being remarkable for their humane and liberal conduct to the labouring poor, have uniformly been distinguished for their rapacious and brutal cruelty toward them'.[2] This attack was not wholly unfair; it impressed working men who were already a little suspicious of the middle-class character of the movement.

[1] i.e. in the sliding scale fixed in 1828 there was a steep fall in the duty on imported corn after the price of corn in England had risen above 66s.; at 66s. the duty was 20s. 8d., at 73s. only 1s. Hence speculators tended to push prices up to 73s. in the hope of importing corn at this low rate of duty.

[2] D. G. Barnes, p. 258, quoting Almack, *The Character, Motives, and Proceedings of the Anti-Corn Law League*, 1843.

The chartists were unfriendly to the league, and inclined to protection in agriculture. They believed that a fall in prices would benefit only those who lived on fixed incomes, and that the competition of foreign corn would drive thousands of agricultural workers to join the overcrowded labour markets of the towns. In any case they looked upon the league as an attempt to divert the working class from the struggle to obtain political rights. At the first large open-air meeting addressed by Bright the chartists in the audience amended a motion against the corn laws to a motion in favour of franchise reform.

The support of Cobden and Bright was of immense value. These two men gave life and energy to the movement, and never allowed lack of immediate success to depress their public attitude. They were manufacturers, but they convinced their hearers that their motives were not selfish. They wanted to raise the standard of life of the labouring class, and not merely to lower the cost of producing cotton goods, or to extend British markets into the corn-growing countries of Europe. Their collaboration was particularly useful because they differed in temperament. Cobden[1] was of southern English yeoman stock; his tastes and character inclined him towards the older, agricultural England. Like Peel, he did not want cotton-mills. Cotton-mills existed, and Cobden thought it necessary 'to mitigate, as far as possible, the evils that are perhaps not inseparably connected with this novel social element'.[2] He believed that there was one great advantage to be gained from the change. The economic interests of the manufacturing and business classes were directly opposed to war and in favour of free trade. Cobden took the view that aristocracies were naturally bellicose. 'The sooner the power in this country is transferred from the landed oligarchy, which has so misused it, and is placed absolutely—mind I say absolutely—in the hands of the intelligent middle and industrious classes, the better for the condition and destinies of this country.'[3] The campaign against the corn laws was there-

[1] Richard Cobden (1804–65), b. Midhurst, Sussex; s. of a small farmer; educ. at a bad private school in Yorkshire; clerk, and commercial traveller, in a London warehouse, 1819; set up in business on borrowed capital, 1828; took part in Manchester municipal politics, and was one of the first aldermen of the city; M.P., 1841; nearly ruined in 1845; a public subscription of £80,000 collected for him, and a second collection made in 1860; offered the presidency of the board of trade by Palmerston in 1859.   [2] An Advertisement to Russia: Morley, i. 96–97.
[3] 15 Jan. 1845. Cobden's Speeches: ed. J. Bright and Thorold Rogers, i. 256.

fore part of a wider plan for the extension of free trade as an instrument of peace. Cobden was a quick-minded, sensitive man; he was neither the first nor the last opponent of aristocracy to feel the charm of good breeding; he wrote, in 1846: 'I am afraid that if I associate too much with the aristocracy, they will spoil me. I am already half-seduced by the fascinating ease of their parties.'[1] He disliked the speeches which he had to make at public meetings, and 'constantly regretted the necessity of violating good taste and kind feeling' in his 'public harangues', but he felt that he could not 'keep the ear of the public for seven years upon one question, without studying to amuse as well as instruct. People do not attend public meetings to be taught, but to be excited, flattered, and pleased.'[2]

It is doubtful whether Cobden could have given the anti-corn law league its wide extension without the help of Bright.[3] Bright was a north countryman, the son of a self-made manufacturer who had neither the political ambitions nor the social rank of the Peels and the Gladstones. The family moved in quaker circles, and Bright did not escape the self-righteousness and unction of the later evangelicals. In other respects he was a typical Englishman of his time. He was an active member of the Rochdale cricket club and a founder of the Rochdale literary and philosophical society, a good fisherman and a good billiards-player. He gave much time and energy to the agitation against church-rates; he disbelieved in state subsidies to education and in state interference with the conditions of work of adults.[4] He shared Cobden's optimism about the beneficent moral results of free trade, and was as strongly convinced that wars were the amusement of an aristocracy. He was one of the greatest orators of his age. He read widely, and based his style upon the Bible and Milton; when he was speaking, he forgot the seriousness and even the charity, of his quakerism, and allowed himself a sarcasm and irony entirely lacking in the prosy and, at times, repellent religiosity of his letters and diaries.

[1] Morley, *Life of Cobden*, i. 383.　　　　　[2] Ibid., p. 207.

[3] John Bright (1811–89), s. of a textile manufacturer; b. Rochdale; entered his father's business after leaving school; met Cobden in 1835, and, after his wife's death in 1841, gave most of his time to the anti-corn law league; M.P., 1843; took a prominent part in supporting the northern states during the American civil war; refused the secretaryship of state for India, but accepted the board of trade in Gladstone's administration, 1868. See also vol. xiv of this *History*.

[4] Bright opposed the manufacture of munitions by the state as contrary to the principles of individualism.

Cobden and Bright were in many respects absurdly wrong in a reading of past history which left out the economic motive in war, and in their forecast of the future development of industrial civilization; they spoke to audiences who knew little of the past and had no ideas about the future, while their arguments about the present were difficult to answer. These arguments ultimately convinced Peel.

Peel's decision to modify the corn laws was made before he knew of the failure of the potato crop in Ireland in the late autumn of 1845.[1] He had intended to bring the matter before the cabinet in his own time, but he felt that, with famine in Ireland and a bad harvest in England, the question could not be postponed. He tried to persuade the cabinet to agree to an order in council suspending the duties on grain; he also made it clear that, if the duties were suspended, they would not be reimposed. Finally, on 2 December, he said that he was willing to bring in a bill 'involving the ultimate repeal' of the duties. An open letter sent by Russell on 22 November from Edinburgh to his constituents in the City of London strengthened Peel's case. Russell announced his conversion to repeal in language typical of the whigs. He agreed to repeal, as he had agreed to parliamentary reform, because he wanted to avoid 'a struggle deeply injurious to an aristocracy which (this quarrel once removed) is strong in property, . . . strong in opinion, strong in ancient associations, and the memory of immortal services'.[2]

Russell spoke for the country, but he did not speak for the conservative majority in the commons. Peel doubted whether he could carry a temporary suspension, and ultimate repeal, through the house unless he had the full support of his cabinet. Stanley and the duke of Buccleuch refused to support him, and others only agreed after much hesitation. On 5 December Peel therefore resigned. Within fifteen days he was back in office. His return was due to the *grands amours-propres* of the whig party, and possibly to Russell's uncertainty whether he could persuade parliament to accept a measure upon which he also had changed his mind suddenly. Peel gave only a general promise of support. Russell said that he could not do without Grey[3] and Palmerston. Grey would not join a ministry in which Palmer-

---

[1] For the Irish famine, see below, pp. 352-5.   [2] Walpole, i. 406-8.
[3] Lord Howick had succeeded his father as Earl Grey three months earlier. See p. 270, n. 3.

ston was foreign secretary; Palmerston refused to take any other post. In Peel's words, 'One intemperate and headstrong man objected to another gentleman having one particular office.'[1]

The protectionists soon showed that they intended to take their revenge on Peel. Gladstone, who had resigned earlier on the question of the increased grant to Maynooth, now agreed to come back into the ministry. The duke of Newcastle would not let him sit for his borough of Newark; the duke of Marlborough took the same line at Woodstock with Sir F. Thesiger, and the dukes of Buckingham and Richmond ordered the resignation of Peel's supporters from their family seats. Peel's position was very difficult. The protectionists refused to admit that the emergency required even a temporary suspension of the corn duties. They held that Peel had betrayed them and broken his pledges. They believed that he had taken unfair advantage of Russell's refusal to form a government, and that he might have acquiesced in repeal without going out of his way to assume responsibility for it. They argued that loyalty to party was essential to consistent and honest government. Peel might have replied that, even if Russell had taken office, the conservative party would have been broken; Peel himself and some of his party would have felt bound to support repeal, but a majority would have voted against it. Moreover, Peel himself agreed with the economic arguments against the corn laws, and therefore assumed that a conservative party which refused to accept these arguments would be ruined in the country. If he were to save the party, he must think of its future in the constituencies. He may have been too anxious to keep power because he liked power; it is also possible to say that he acted in an unselfish spirit of patriotism. He over-rated his influence upon the party on a question which affected the interests and not merely the political opinions of the landowners, but the response of the country showed that, even on tactical considerations, Peel was right. Within a few years the protectionist leaders had given up protection.

When parliament met in January 1846, Disraeli and Lord George Bentinck attacked Peel. Bentinck[2] had once been private

---

[1] Parker, iii. 289.
[2] Lord George Cavendish-Bentinck (1802–48), s. of the 4th duke of Portland; b. Welbeck; educ. privately; joined 10th hussars, 1819, and 2nd life guards, 1825–8; M.P., 1828; offered office by Peel, 1841, but would not spare time from racing.

secretary to Canning; he had sat in the commons for eighteen
years without taking much part in debate. He was honest,
vigorous, popular, and of high social position. He knew his own
limitations, and admitted that he was a better judge of race-
horses than of politics: he joined in the attack upon Peel as
though Peel were a dishonest jockey. He summed up his views
in two sentences: 'I keep horses in three counties, and they tell
me that I shall save £1,500 a year by free trade. I don't care for
that; what I cannot bear is being sold.'[1] On this single issue
Bentinck did not hesitate to take part with the whigs, the Irish,
and the radicals in an alliance described by Wellington as
'a blackguard combination'. The third reading of Peel's bill
for the reduction of all duties on wheat, oats, and barley to
the nominal sum of 1s. a quarter was carried on 25 June 1846,
after five months' debate.[2] On the same evening the 'combination' defeated Peel by 73 votes. The defeat took place over a
coercion bill for Ireland. The protectionists had never opposed
coercion for Ireland before Peel had supported free trade; the
whigs in the upper house had voted for the coercion bill. Peel
resigned on 29 June; his last speech as prime minister included
a deliberate and magnificent eulogy of Cobden which offended
Gladstone and Aberdeen[3] because Cobden had argued for the
repeal of the corn laws 'on the principle of holding up the landlords of England to the people as plunderers and as knaves'.

The controversy over the repeal of the corn laws is curiously
out of proportion to the results obtained by repeal. Throughout
the years in which the league attacked the landlords, and the
landlords accused the Manchester school of endangering the
safety and prosperity of England, each side was exaggerating
its case. The country could nearly feed itself in years of good
harvests, and the high duty on imported corn mattered little.
In years of bad harvests foreign crops generally suffered, and the

---

[1] Morley, *Life of Cobden*, i. 358.

[2] Peel did not intend the full effect of repeal to come into operation until 1849.
Before this date he proposed to admit grain from British colonies, at a nominal
duty, and foreign wheat at a duty of 10s. a quarter when the price was under
48s. The duty would decrease with a rise in prices; at 53s. it fell to 4s. Owing to
the conditions of 1847–8 Peel's measure was suspended from 26 Jan. 1847 until
1 Sept. The suspension was continued until 1 Mar. 1848.

[3] George Hamilton-Gordon, 4th earl of Aberdeen (1784–1860); b. Edinburgh;
educ. Harrow and St. John's College, Cambridge; took part in diplomatic negotiations, 1813–4; foreign secretary, 1828–30 and 1841–6; secretary for war and
colonies, 1834–5; prime minister, 1852–5.

price of imported corn would hardly have been lower, even if there had been no duty. Moreover, the foreign supply was never unlimited. A steady British market might have encouraged European producers, or hastened the development of American corn lands, but the increase in supply would not have been very considerable before 1846. The rapid growth of new facilities of transport after 1846 was of great importance, yet for two decades after 1850 prices remained, on an average, about 52s. On the other hand, if prices did not fall, they did not rise, whereas under the old sliding scale they would probably have risen in a good many years to 73s. Other factors affected the price of corn. The discovery of gold in California and Australia raised world prices[1] and for a long time the population of Great Britain increased at a greater rate than the increase of production in continental and American wheatfields. The real threat to English agriculture came about a quarter of a century after the repeal of the corn laws, when the fall in the cost of transport on sea and land brought American corn into severe competition with the British harvest.[2]

[1] The fact that, at a time of rising world prices, there was no rise in the price of corn in England, is in favour of the argument that the effect of repeal was to lower the price of corn in the English market.

[2] See vol. xiv of this *History*, pp. 115–18.

III

THE POLITICS OF THE PEOPLE, 1830–50

CHARTISM: FACTORY LEGISLATION

THE agitation in favour of the reform bill, the political and party conflicts which followed the passing of the bill, the disintegration of the whigs, the rise of conservatism, and the movement which ended in the repeal of the corn laws had profound effects upon the working men of Great Britain who were still almost entirely without direct representation in parliament. At the same time, throughout these years there were other movements, coming directly from the working class, and developing outside parliament, and often in opposition to parliament, or to the social and economic system of which parliament was the guardian. These movements were influenced by currents of opinion and emotions hardly understood by the older governing classes or by the newly enfranchised middle class; they were directed by men whom the ministers regarded as interlopers and dangerous agitators. The radicals attempted, a little uneasily, to keep in touch with the politics of the poor, but they too thought of themselves as leaders, or at all events as the official interpreters, of the people before parliament and public opinion. In many ways the tories were nearer to the working class by temperament than were the radicals: nearer in their dislike of change, their suspicion of 'progress', their unsystematic, unintellectual support of familiar standards and habits of life. Yet attempts to correlate working-class movements with toryism broke down. The tories, like the radicals, wanted to lead the movements; working men, who now insisted upon choosing their own leaders, had good reason for suspecting the leaders presented to them from above. The 'Young England' party offered them the landed aristocracy, transformed and idealized; to the working class the landed aristocracy, unidealized and untransformed, was the oldest and most conspicuous branch of their oppressors. The free traders of the Manchester school also suggested themselves as leaders; to the working class they represented the hated factory system. As for the whigs, they were, after 1832, responsible for the new poor law.[1] This law, with its threat of refusal of outdoor relief to the able-bodied in distress, outraged the feelings of the poor. The philosophy of natural right, expressed in simple terms, appealed to hungry and wretched men; there was a widespread popular belief that the whigs were robbing the poor of their legal as well as their moral rights. Cobbett's *History of the Protestant Reformation* was only one example of the view that, in return for the seizure of church lands by the state, the old poor law had guaranteed to the people of England an aid which was their lawful patrimony.

Poor men, without education, reason in and around their own humble interests and needs. They are often at the mercy of words; they cannot see even the immediate consequences of their acts. They give their confidence too easily, and make heroes out of those who themselves take up their cause as they would have it upheld. The leadership of popular movements therefore falls too often to outcasts or adventurers from other parties and classes, to jealous or unsuccessful men with a grudge against the existing order. The leaders are soon drawn into exaggeration; they speak to large audiences, untrained in argument, unfamiliar with compromise, and ready to take half-measures for cowardice, or moderation for treason to the cause. In any case, it is not easy to advise patience to those who are suffering from immediate grievances and have no resources to carry them over periods of delay.

It is necessary to keep these facts in mind while considering the different movements which arose out of the aspirations and hopes of the labourers of England during the period between 1832 and 1848, and also to remember that the separation between movements of the working class and those of other classes was never complete. There was no single agitation including all manual labourers; the better-paid artisans distrusted the violence of the chartist leaders, though they agreed with their aims. On the other hand, there is hardly a point in the chartist political programme which did not find some support among the middle-class political parties. This programme itself was fluid, although it was based upon a document embodying a number of political demands. The charter was to some of its supporters almost an end in itself, or, at all events, there was a finality about the establishment of a political democracy. To

[1] See below, pp. 451-3.

others, the attainment of political power was the first stage in the establishment of a new economic order of society. The rank and file thought of the charter as a symbol, an instrument for the removal of hard, local grievances. Thus the enthusiasm behind the chartist movement was not constant. It died down in years of good harvests, full employment, and better conditions of life; it took new force with the return of bad times. It was diverted in its later stages from a political programme to an agrarian programme of the crudest kind.

The chartist movement came into existence after the breakdown of earlier attempts by the labouring poor to improve their condition. In the months of trade depression after the repeal of the combination laws local associations of working men had little chance of carrying through successful strikes. The collapse of many of these smaller unions led to attempts at organization on a larger scale, with greater resources and bargaining power. The idea was sound, but failure was almost certain. If a larger union could exercise a stronger bargaining power, it also had more liabilities, and required a higher standard of managing ability. An early move towards amalgamation came from the cotton-spinners of Lancashire. In 1829 they formed a Grand General Union of All the Operative Spinners of the United Kingdom.[1] The Union did not last much longer than a year, but John Doherty, an Ulster catholic who had settled in Manchester and taken a leading part in the Grand General Union, suggested a combination including all the work-people of the country. In 1830 Doherty founded at Manchester a National Association for the Protection of Labour which gained considerable support in the north and midlands during the months following the July revolution in France. Doherty soon quarrelled with the executive committee. The funds of the society were never large, and its members were jealous of expenditure outside their own districts. Hence in 1832 this association also broke down. A builders' union—sometimes known as the General Trades Union—was also founded about 1830; it united the seven main branches of the trade, joiners, masons, bricklayers, plasterers, plumbers, painters, and builders' labourers, and spread rapidly over the country. It published a journal, and held 'parliaments' in which its more revolutionary

---

[1] See S. J. Chapman, *The Lancashire Cotton Industry*, pp. 201–5. Place described Doherty as 'a very extraordinary, rigid, intolerant, wrong-headed, persevering man'.

members made threatening speeches against their employers and capitalists in general.

The most important of these attempts to organize the power of the working class was the Grand National Consolidated Trades Union, founded in 1834 under the influence of Robert Owen. The purpose of the Union went beyond the defence or improvement of the standard of life of its members; it was a direct answer to the Reform Act of 1832 which had left five out of six working men without votes. Owen himself sums up in his remarkable career the main elements of anti-capitalist thought in the early nineteenth century. The arguments used in this attack upon capitalism came from different sources. The English revolutionary school, of which Thomas Spence (1750–1814) was the most outstanding figure, concentrated upon the nationalization of land, and, in the jacobin terms of the age, denounced the landed aristocracy, whose 'emblazoned arms and escutcheons' were 'audacious Gothic emblems of rapine'. Other writers had begun an attack upon capital; in *The Effects of Civilisation on the People in European States*[1] Charles Hall had seen the significant features of capitalism and suggested the restriction of manufactures to articles of luxury, but Hall, like William Ogilvie[2] and other writers, still assumed as his ideal a society of small landowners; in any case Hall's book never had a large circulation.

The political economists provided the anti-capitalist writers with a new weapon. Ricardo's theories were not put forward as an attack upon capitalism, but as a scientific analysis of economic phenomena. Ricardo believed that a system of private property, including property in land, secured better results for all concerned than any other mode of ownership; on the other hand he gave his high authority to the view that the value of commodities was determined 'almost exclusively' by the 'relative quantity of labour' employed in their production. Ricardo qualified his statement by reference to the rewards of management and risk. To the labouring class the bare assertion of fact was sufficient to raise the question: What reward does labour receive for the commodities which it has produced?

[1] Little is known of Hall's life. He seems to have practised as a doctor in the west of England, where he observed the bad effects of factory work upon the labouring class.

[2] William Ogilvie (1736–1819) was a professor at the university of Aberdeen and a Scottish landowner.

Patrick Colquhoun's *Treatise on the Population, Wealth, Power, and Resources of the British Empire in every quarter of the world* (1814) supplied an answer of a rough but convincing kind: the share of the labouring class, including the pay of soldiers and sailors and the sums given in poor relief, amounted to one-quarter of the whole.[1]

The interests of capital and labour were thus opposed; Ricardo's theory of rent provided another argument to show the exploitation of the labourers. Thomas Hodgskin,[2] in his *Labour Defended against the Claims of Capital, or the Unproductiveness of Capital proved* (1825) and *Popular Political Economy* (1827), argued that in the distribution of wealth the landlord claimed a share based upon the difference in the fertility of different soils; the labourer received enough to provide him with a bare living, and the capitalist took the rest. How could this injustice be remedied? The remedy was as simple as the diagnosis of the disease. Substitute co-operative production and the capitalist would not be needed; take the 'relative quantity of labour' employed in the production of goods as the standard of measurement, and difficulties of exchange and distribution would disappear. There were two ways of bringing about this change: a political way, which implied revolution, and an economic way. The economic method also meant a revolutionary change, but the power of organized labour could bring about the transformation without bloodshed. Robert Owen[3] insisted upon this peaceful method and for a time carried the new unions with him. He was among the first English thinkers to realize that the evils of industrialism were not incurable, and that the new machinery might be used to abolish poverty, and not merely to extend its range. He based his conclusion upon his experience as a manufacturer, and reinforced it by a view of human nature taken from the philosophy, or rather the *philosophes*, of the eighteenth century. At the age of nineteen Owen became the manager of one of the largest factories in Manchester and in 1800 a partner in one of the largest mills in Scotland. He

---

[1] Colquhoun was a magistrate whose interests were primarily statistical and scientific, but his figures could be used to attack the existing order.

[2] Thomas Hodgskin (1783-1869) was one of the founders of the London Mechanics' Institute. See below, p. 495.

[3] Robert Owen (1771-1858), s. of a tradesman; b. Newtown, Montgomeryshire; apprenticed to a draper at Stamford, 1781; moved to London, and thence to Manchester, where he set up a workshop on borrowed money.

set up factories of his own at New Lanark, and made them a
model for the world. His success seemed to prove the truth of
his opinion that human character depended upon environment.
Apply the right method, and the right form of organization,
and social evil must disappear. Owen was a masterful man,
stubborn in his convictions; no evidence of fact ever made
him change his mind. His sincerity was beyond doubt, and his
criticism of orthodox political economy was reasonable when
he pointed to the neglect of the problem of under-consumption.
He refused to associate his ideas with attacks upon the rich or
with the encouragement of class hatred. He believed that the
rich themselves would realize that the age of private property
had passed, and that the new order of society would take the
form of groups of producers owning the means of production
and organized into small, self-directing communities. He wanted
the working class to set up these communities instead of wasting
their time and resources in strikes. He planned his ideal society
to the last detail, and went to America in 1824 to establish it on
a small scale. While he was away his friends in Great Britain
founded societies in support of co-operation, with co-operative
shops and 'labour exchanges' for the marketing of goods, and
proclaimed their views under the new term 'socialism'.[1]

Owen's model villages, arranged in squares, were not a success; their failure suggested to him another plan. The Grand
National Consolidated Trades Union (1834) was this larger
experiment, which would allow the workers, organized in their
respective crafts and industries, to control the economic
machinery, and therefore the political government, of the
country. Owen took no account of the obvious difficulties of
management; he did not see that, in creating a number of
monopolist bodies, he was merely shifting the burden of competition from individuals to communities. He did not consider
that he was asking the employers to commit economic suicide.
He was convinced that he could organize every trade or occupation, skilled or unskilled, from agriculture to bonnet-making,
into units of co-operative producers exchanging their products
on the basis of the labour-value employed in their production.

[1] Robert Owen made use of this term about 1817. According to Beer, *History of
British Socialism*, i. 185–7, the term was used in the *Co-operative Magazine* in 1827
to denote as 'Communionists or Socialists' those who believed that capital should
not be held in private hands.

A movement of this kind, brought forward by a rich business man, and promising immediate relief from the misery of the times, won very wide support. Within a few weeks the Union numbered, by direct membership or affiliation, half a million supporters. It was soon involved in a large number of sectional and local strikes. Most of the strikes failed before any attempt was made to put Owen's co-operative ideas into practice. The whigs were not responsible for the collapse. They were afraid of the movement; they exaggerated its dangers to such an extent that they would not act upon the recommendation of a parliamentary committee in favour of strong measures against picketing or attempts to threaten men or masters. To their credit the whigs thought as much of safeguarding the liberties of the constitution as of the effect of their proposals upon working-class opinion. To their discredit they imposed harsh penalties upon poor men. The most notorious of these acts of local tyranny was the transportation of six labourers, of Tolpuddle in Dorset, in March 1834, for seven years because they had administered illegal oaths to fellow members of a union. Melbourne's cabinet upheld the sentence. Public opinion was less panic-stricken, and the case brought to parliament the first of those monster petitions which were part of the tactics of working-class movements during the next fourteen years. In 1836 the men were pardoned, and brought home, after some delay, at public expense.[1]

The collapse of the Grand National Union disappointed thousands of the poorest-paid labourers in the country, though it had little effect upon the skilled tradesmen who had never supported Owen's immense schemes. For the time there was no further attempt to bring together the working people of the country into one union; the number of trade-unionists during the militant years of the chartist movement was probably less than 100,000. The failure of direct economic action by the working class had two results. The highly skilled trades, particularly those centred in London, opposed the hazarding of their funds in large schemes, and concentrated upon the improvement of their own conditions of labour. At the same time the working-class leaders saw that they could not hope to carry important measures of social change until their supporters had

---

[1] Subscriptions collected by working men provided five of them with farms in Essex; the sixth went back to Dorset.

votes. Thus they decided to apply to the middle class and the reformed parliament the pressure which had carried the bill of 1832 against the upper class.

The centre of this political group was also in London, and the leading members were Lovett, Hetherington, Watson, and Benbow. Hetherington and Watson were Yorkshiremen whose revolutionary language brought them sentences of imprisonment. Lovett[1] was a man of different physical and mental type: less robust and violent, more sensitive and embittered. He was not a leader of men; he could not save the movements which he began from falling into the hands of demagogues. He was clear-sighted and fastidious enough to break with these political adventurers, but he left them in possession of the field. Lovett accepted the economic arguments of Hodgskin, the anti-clerical views of Carlile, and the co-operative schemes of Owen, though he did not think that Owen's direct economic programme could take the place of an agitation for the extension of political rights.

The reduction of the stamp duty on newspapers in 1836 encouraged Lovett and his friends to found the London Working Men's Association. They wanted 'to draw into one bond of unity the intelligent and influential portion of the working classes in town and country, and to seek by every legal means to place all classes of society in possession of equal political and social rights'; they hoped to create a favourable public opinion by 'collecting every kind of information appertaining to the interests of the working classes in particular and to society in general, especially statistics regarding the wages of labour, the habits and condition of the labourer, and all those causes that mainly contribute to the present state of things'. They limited ordinary membership to working men, though sympathizers from other classes, including radical members of parliament, could become honorary members. Francis Place, as an honorary member, took part, with Lovett, in drawing up a list of the political demands of the working class in the form of a parliamentary bill. These demands were the basis of the 'People's Charter',

[1] William Lovett (1800–77), b. Newlyn; his father, captain of a small trading ship, died before his son's birth; apprenticed to a ropemaker, disliked the trade, and went to London in 1821, where he found work as a cabinet-maker; married in 1826, and set up a pastrycook's shop which did not pay; became a storekeeper in the first London co-operative trading society, and, in 1829, secretary of the British Association for Promoting Co-operative Knowledge. His autobiography, *The Life and Struggles of William Lovett*, was written in his old age.

which was published in May 1838. The six points of the charter were annual parliaments, universal male suffrage,[1] equal electoral districts, the removal of the property qualification for membership of parliament, secret ballot, and payment of members.

From the point of view of the more cautious members of the Working Men's Association the charter was too much of a success with their working-class supporters. The radicals in parliament knew that the commons would reject every one of the six points; many of them distrusted the use which the working class would make of political power. The idea of a national petition in support of the charter came from the Birmingham Political Union. This Union, which had been active in the agitation for reform in 1830-2, was revived under the direction of its founder Thomas Attwood, a banker, who wanted support for his confused views on the currency question.[2] The movement soon went beyond the control of the London and Birmingham associations. It was more than doubtful whether its supporters would keep within the bounds of legality laid down in the constitution of the London Association; the mass of working men outside the better-paid and fairly stable trades were not in a mood for a peaceful agitation which would have no effect upon Melbourne and his cabinet.

The People's Charter and the National Petition appeared at a time when the labouring class was full of resentment over the new poor law. For two years the effects of the law were not much noticed in the manufacturing areas. The depression which began at the end of 1836 brought home the significance of the prohibition of outdoor relief. The attack on the poor law was supported by men who had nothing to do with the London and Birmingham associations. Of the leaders, John Fielden, of Todmorden (1784-1849), M.P. for Oldham, was a rich manufacturer of radical views who ruled his factories as a benevolent despot. Owing to the strength of local feeling and the weakness of the central administrative authorities Fielden was able to prevent the introduction of the Registration of Births, Mar-

---

[1] Lovett wanted to include the enfranchisement of women, but his friends thought that the suggestion would not be taken seriously.

[2] Attwood (1783-1856) believed that depreciation of the currency would of itself put an end to commercial depression. He made no distinction between a rise in prices brought about by increased demand, and a rise caused by measures of deliberate inflation.

riages, and Deaths act of 1836 into Todmorden;[1] for a generation there was no union workhouse in the place. Fielden's
influence was widespread in Lancashire; Richard Oastler and
J. R. Stephens raised excitement throughout the country.
Oastler was steward to the family of Thornhill, whose estates
were near Huddersfield; he had already come into prominence
as a supporter of factory laws for the protection of children.
Stephens was a Wesleyan minister who had resigned his ministry
as a protest against his suspension for attending meetings in support of disestablishment. These two men had no new social
theory; they believed in the old-established union of religion
and the people, and used in their speeches biblical denuncia-
tions of those who oppressed the poor. Stephens was absurdly
violent, and preached fire and civil war against the 'hell-hounds
of commissioners'.

These speeches were made to wretched and hungry men who
felt that they had been cheated of their rights. It was inevitable
that, if such audiences accepted the political demands of the
People's Charter, they would set aside the limitation to moral
force advocated by Lovett. Thus the charter became something
more than a document of educational propaganda; it was a
battle-cry for those who had lost by the failure of Owen's large
schemes, and were suffering from the increasing competition
of machinery, the long months of a trade depression, and the
hardship of the poor law. Moreover, although the popularity
of the charter alarmed Lovett, other members of the London
Association were satisfied by the growth of popular excitement.
Among the honorary members of the association was James
Bronterre O'Brien.[2] O'Brien is an example of the spoiled child,
the clever boy overpraised at school, the sensitive, ambitious
man warped by a sense of social inferiority. He came to London
in 1830 to read for the bar; he met a number of radical and
working-class reformers, and took up their ideas. He was an
easy and convincing speaker, with little originality or critical
judgement, strongly in favour of political action, and ready to
use class hatred as a political instrument. His constructive
plans were a mixture of other people's ideas. He borrowed from

[1] This act was associated with the poor law because its administration was given
to the boards of guardians.
[2] James Bronterre O'Brien (1805–64), s. of an Irish wine and tobacco merchant;
educ. Edgeworthstown and Trinity College, Dublin.

the writers of the eighteenth century the view that land was the ultimate source of wealth, and from Owen the view that labour should be the standard of value, though he varied this opinion by proposing corn as his standard. He wanted the nationalization of land, and, through the resources thus secured to the state, the extension of credit to the working class. The charter gave him his opportunity; he also reached a wider public through his association with Feargus O'Connor. O'Connor was the ruin of the chartist movement. It would be unfair to say that he did not believe the ideas which he, like O'Brien, borrowed from others, but he acted as though he did not believe them.

O'Connor's history reads like a debased and exaggerated version of the life of Daniel O'Connell. He came of a protestant family; his father was an Irish revolutionary of doubtful character; an uncle, more respectable but not less revolutionary, settled in France, where he was given the rank of general in Napoleon's service, and married a daughter of Condorcet. Feargus entered English politics in 1832 as member for County Cork. He was one of O'Connell's followers, but quarrelled with him. From this time O'Connor supported the working-class movement. He became an honorary member of the London Working Men's Association, and left it to found a rival body, the London Democratic Association, where he could use his powers of violent invective to greater advantage. In the latter part of 1837 he took over from a committee in Leeds the project of a new radical newspaper, the *Northern Star*. Place believed that the *Northern Star* lowered the tone of the whole radical press; it established O'Connor's position as a political boss, and brought him a good deal of money. O'Connor had the qualities of the successful demagogue; he was a big, heavily built man, with a tremendous voice, a rough humour, and a quick power of epigram and repartee. He knew how to flatter his audiences, and never minded attack or interruption. Lovett, with his passionate, nervous sincerity, was no match for a self-advertiser of this kind. Moreover O'Connor gathered round him a band of supporters. He gave O'Brien a platform in the *Northern Star*; he flattered the conceit and rancour of orators like G. J. Harney, who thought himself an English Marat, and soothed the resentment of those who had turned to revolution out of sheer wretchedness.

Throughout the year 1838 these different elements in the

chartist movement encouraged the hopes of the poor. O'Connor set the pace in denunciation, though he was careful to keep within the law. The moderates could not control him without wrecking the agitation to which they were now committed. They had no newspaper as important as the *Northern Star*; their scrupulousness hindered them in dealing with O'Connor and his followers, while their own principles would not allow them to accept middle-class help even if they could have secured it. Ideas of violent revolution gained ground, especially in the north, at meetings of workmen, tired, under-nourished, and full of resentment. Towards the end of the year these meetings and processions were held by torchlight. Hitherto the government had left the speakers alone, but the torchlight meetings and incitements to physical violence became so very alarming that they were forbidden. In December 1838 Stephens was arrested for using seditious language.

It was impossible for Lovett and his friends to draw back. Attwood and the Birmingham Union committed them to the plan of a Convention of the Industrious Classes at which representatives of the people would accept and acclaim the charter and national petition. They had to consider what they would do in the likely case of the rejection of their demands. Here again Attwood took up Benbow's proposal for a general strike.[1] The Convention met in London on 4 February 1839. The moderates, middle-aged and 'respectable' working men, were in a majority, and, with their help, Lovett hoped to bring back the movement to his 'moral force' views. The delegates had been chosen by enthusiastic supporters as mandatories of the popular will; they were worried by their own importance. Many of them wrote 'M.C.' after their names, in self-conscious imitation of the 'M.P.s' against whom they proposed to assert the authority of the people. They had assembled on the day of the meeting of parliament and of the first large conference of the anti-corn law league. Few of them intended to go as far as armed insurrection, but they felt that a threat of physical force might prevent the whigs from tricking the people a second time. O'Connor used his influence against moderation, and did his best to get rid of Lovett and his friends. The Convention recognized the right of the people to arm themselves, and accepted

---

[1] Benbow did not invent the idea of a general strike or 'national holiday', or 'sacred month', but his pamphlet in support of the idea had a wide circulation.

the plan of a general strike if parliament rejected the petition and charter. On 6 May the petition was ready for presentation to the House. It contained 1,200,000 signatures—less than half of the three million names announced earlier in the year. On 7 May the government resigned on a question unconnected with the charter,[1] and the delegates had to face a long postponement. They decided to move from London to Birmingham; the extremists, who could reckon on more popular support outside London, argued that Birmingham, half-way between south Wales and the north of England, was a better centre, and that the Convention would be less exposed than in London to the threats of a tory government.

The whigs continued to treat the movement with good sense, if not with sympathy. They could not ignore the talk about violence, the drilling of men, the circulation of handbooks on the use of the pike, and other signs of danger. They received alarming reports, and demands for troops, from every part of the country. They appointed Sir Charles Napier[2] to the command of the northern district. Napier was a good soldier, and in sympathy with many of the radical demands. He concentrated his men at important points—Nottingham, Leeds, York, Newcastle, and Manchester. He invited a number of the chartist leaders to a demonstration of artillery fire, and pointed out to them that they could not move, feed, or keep under control a large force. Napier explained that he could fall on them if they dispersed to collect food, 'maul them with cannon and musquetry'[3] if they tried to march, and, if they ventured upon an attack with pikes, scatter them before they reached him, or countercharge with his own cavalry.

The Convention reassembled in Birmingham on 13 May. They realized that the bluff of armed insurrection was not deceiving the authorities, and that a general strike might fail, or lead to an insurrection. They tried to leave the responsibility of decision to their supporters. They published a manifesto to be read at every chartist meeting; their measures of resistance included a general strike, a boycott of non-chartist shopkeepers, a run on the banks, a refusal to pay rent, rates, and taxes, an armed defence of their rights, and a refusal to 'read hostile newspapers'. Lovett favoured this surrender of leadership on

---

[1] See above, p. 103.   [2] See below, pp. 421-2.
[3] Sir W. Napier. *Life and Opinions of Sir C. J. Napier*, ii. 43.

the view that it was honest to let the people understand that they might be asked to make sacrifices; he was on surer ground when he moved for a committee to study the question of the general strike. The delegates decided that, as soon as the petition was rejected by parliament, they would fix the date of the 'sacred month'. On 4 July there were riots in Birmingham. Two members of the Convention who had hitherto supported 'physical force' tried to quiet their followers, and were arrested by the police. The Convention protested against their arrest, and Lovett, with great courage, took responsibility for the protest by publishing it under his signature alone. He too was arrested, and released nine days later on bail. A crowd gathered in Birmingham to cheer him on the evening of his release. After a certain amount of disturbance someone suggested turning out the lamps to hamper the movements of the police. In the confusion a few shops were sacked and set on fire.

On 12 July the commons refused by 235 to 46 votes to consider the national petition, and on the day of the second Birmingham riot the Convention, reduced by resignation to less than half its numbers, fixed 12 August as the first day of the general strike. There was not the least chance that the workers in the country would come out on strike. O'Connor now denied that he had ever agreed with the plan, and O'Brien, who had been one of the most reckless supporters of violence, began to protest against imprudent action. A few days later the Convention gave up the 'sacred month', suggested a 'holiday' of two or three days for processions and solemn meetings, and then dissolved.

In November there was an attempt at armed rebellion in Monmouthshire. The history of this outbreak was obscure even at the time. The facts seem to have been that John Frost, a draper of Newport and a justice of the peace, honest and brave as he was fanatical, believed that an outbreak in Wales would be supported by revolution in Lancashire and Yorkshire. O'Connor was asked to lead the northern movement. He did all he could to stop the plan, and then decided that he must pay a visit to Ireland—his 'unfortunate country'. Frost heard too late that the northern men were not coming out. He would not desert his followers. He led them in a hopeless move on Newport where they met a small force of troops. Fourteen chartists were killed, and ten died of wounds. Frost and two other leaders were sentenced to death, but the sentence was commuted to one of transportation for life. They were pardoned in 1854; Frost died in England twenty-three years later.

The first great political movement of the labouring class had been as tragic a failure as the attempt at economic liberation under Owen's influence. Lovett was given twelve months' imprisonment for his Birmingham manifesto. O'Connor went to prison for libel and used his time in making a reputation for himself as a martyr in the popular cause. On the other hand Lovett and the moderates began to ask whether they were prudent in refusing middle-class help. The growth of the anti-corn law league forced the chartist leaders to define their attitude; hitherto they had looked upon the league as an indirect move on the part of the manufacturers to reduce wages. There was, however, a simple test: would the anti-corn law league support universal suffrage?

O'Connor did not want anything which might destroy his position as a political boss. He was a protectionist, and his political judgement enabled him to see that the middle class would not show much zeal for the points of the charter. His own prestige was scarcely shaken; the *Northern Star* was still a source of income and power. He was ready to give his name to another working-class movement. A meeting of chartists at Manchester, including only three of the members of the Convention, decided to start a National Charter Association. O'Connor hoped to dominate the Association, while Lovett refused to join it. Lovett had already come to the conclusion that associations of poor, uneducated men were of no use. He spent his time in Warwick jail in writing a long pamphlet on *Chartism: a new Organization of the People.*[1] He appealed to 'persons of all creeds, classes, and opinions'. He did not expect immediate success; his plan included a scheme of voluntary education which would enable the working class to present their demands to the governing classes with an irresistible 'moral force'. Towards the end of the year 1841 Lovett found a new supporter. Joseph Sturge (1793–1859), a Birmingham quaker and corn-miller, believed that the middle class was under an obligation to help the political movement of the working class in return for their help in 1832. In 1841 Sturge published a series of articles on the 'Reconciliation

[1] John Collins, a Birmingham shoemaker, collaborated in the work, but Lovett seems to have written the greater part of it.

between the Middle and Working Classes'. Lovett and his friends took up the idea; O'Brien, who was drifting away from O'Connor, joined the Complete Suffrage Union, and the 'New Move', as it was called, made considerable progress. Once again a breakdown was certain. O'Connor attacked Lovett and O'Brien, denounced the New Move, as a plan to 'domesticate the charter', and went on with his agitation for a second great national petition. On 2 May 1842 the petition was brought to the house. O'Connor had played on the hopes of his supporters. He offered them an immediate remedy, while Lovett had postponed the day of deliverance. He made no preparations for failure, and his optimism was easily caught by many thousands of wretched and half-starved men. The petition, signed by 3,317,752 persons, began with a preamble against the poor law, and a list of grievances; the main feature was the demand for universal suffrage. There was a debate on the subject in the commons; the leaders on either side of the house spoke against any change in the franchise. Macaulay regarded universal suffrage, unless preceded by universal education, as 'fatal to all purposes for which government exists and . . . utterly incompatible with the very existence of civilization'. The radicals supported the petition, but Roebuck described O'Connor as a 'foolish, malignant, cowardly demagogue', and the house rejected by 287 to 49 votes a motion that the petitioners should be heard.

O'Connor could not blame others for this second failure. He still refused to take up 'physical force', but to a certain extent the movement broke away from his control. In August 1842 strikes against a reduction of wages began in Lancashire and spread to Glasgow and the midlands.[1] The executive council of the National Charter Association had already arranged a meeting in Manchester; it could hardly avoid asking the strikers to include the charter in their demands. The connexion of the political movement with these outbreaks of desperate working men was dangerous. The strikes were unlikely to succeed; industrial conditions in the late summer of 1842 were at their worst, and the manufacturers were not trying to increase profits, but merely to avoid bankruptcy. There was rioting in many districts; O'Connor himself had done his best to keep the peace; many of his supporters were less cautious. The strikes failed,

[1] The Lancashire strikes were known as the 'Plug Plot' because the strikers drew the plugs from boilers in the factories.

and the authorities turned against the chartist leaders. O'Connor was arrested, and escaped imprisonment only by a technical point in his indictment. In Staffordshire alone, where the judges were most severe, fifty-four men were sentenced to long periods of transportation. Public opinion made no move to save them. The radicals in the commons brought forward a motion censuring the language used by the presiding judge of the special commission trying cases in Lancashire and Cheshire; they were defeated by 228 to 73.[1]

Lovett's 'New Move' also failed. Already in April 1842 there were threatening signs. At a conference of the Complete Suffrage Union in Birmingham the chartist members carried motions embodying the terms of their charter, but Sturge and his friends were afraid that direct and complete acceptance of the charter would frighten the middle class. The next conference took place in December 1842. The disturbances in the north stiffened the resistance of the middle-class members to a policy which looked like surrender to chartism, and the conference ended in a breach between Lovett and Sturge. Sturge and his party would not take the chartist name or give up control of the movement. They were willing to put forward the six points; they insisted on giving them another form, and came to the conference with the draft of a new Bill of Rights. The working-class leaders felt that they were being asked to surrender a name associated with working-class struggles merely 'to suit the whim, to please the caprice, or to serve the selfish ends of mouthing priests, political traffickers, sugar-weighing, tape-measuring shopocrats'.[2] The supporters of Sturge answered that they would accept the chartist principles, but not the chartist leaders. Lovett carried the conference with him; Sturge withdrew, and the movement collapsed.

O'Connor was now left in possession of the field. The goodwill of chartism was not worth much, and O'Connor's flair for journalism would have given him a standing in any other political party. He chose to remain the leader of a scattered and broken force and, although he led his supporters into another and more discreditable defeat, the last stage of his political career was the most remarkable of his adventures. Moreover, although he

---

[1] A second motion, on the conduct of the magistrates, was also defeated.
[2] *Northern Star*, 14 Jan. 1843, quoted in M. Hovell, *The Chartist Movement*, p. 264. The 'mouthing priest' was an uncle of Herbert Spencer. Herbert Spencer took part in the Complete Suffrage movement, and attended the second conference.

wasted the money of men who could ill afford to lose even small sums, he was more sincere in these latter years than at any other time. O'Connor's opposition to the anti-corn law league was not mere jealousy of a rival organization. He disliked factories and industrialism; his own tradition was that of an Irish landlord interested in the establishment of a stable and prosperous peasantry. He believed that the remedy for the social evils of industrialism was the creation of a body of small landholders in England. He thought that a scheme of this kind would prevent the overcrowding of the labour market in the towns, and lead to a rise in wages and an increased demand for manufactures. Here again O'Connor, like most of the chartists, was on the right lines in realizing that the problem of industrial depression was one of under-consumption, and that orthodox political economy neglected this aspect of the question. He knew also that, in the *malaise* of the new towns, thousands of labouring men looked back upon the country life of their fathers and grandfathers. The long popularity of Spence and the agrarian reformers was due to this land-hunger of the English proletariat.

Unfortunately O'Connor was reckless in money matters, and selfishly eager for popularity. His scheme was financially unsound and entirely unpractical. He proposed to collect subscriptions for the purchase of land, and to lease this land to smallholders. With their rent and the mortgage money from their holdings he would buy more land. He would repeat the process until he had provided four acres of land for every one who wanted a holding. O'Brien called the scheme a land lottery, and other chartist leaders warned the working class against it. Moreover O'Connor's plan would divert interest from political demands; the smallholders were likely to turn conservative, or at all events to side with capitalism. O'Connor knew that his own New Move would be more popular than Lovett's educational projects. Parliament was indifferent to petitions, strikes, and threats of violence as well as to the arguments based upon 'moral force'; the labourers despaired of betterment through political agitation. O'Connor's land-purchase had something of the self-help belonging to the temper of the time. After 1842 the misery of the poor was less keen; a reduction in wages did not follow the fall in the price of corn with the return of good harvests. Peel's tariff policy favoured business and prosperity. The administration of the poor law was less harsh, and emigration was offering a way of escape to men who might otherwise have turned to political agitation.

The Chartist Co-operative Land Society, founded in May 1845, bought an estate near Watford in 1846; a year later the society changed its name to the National Land Company and added other estates to the list. Meanwhile the run of good harvests and brisk trade came to an end, and a new economic depression affected the working class. The repeal of the corn laws brought no immediate relief, in spite of the optimistic forecasts of the anti-corn law league. On the other hand the land scheme was working: its success did not depend upon the goodwill of the upper and middle classes in parliament. O'Connor was at the height of his popularity; in July 1847 he was elected at Nottingham as the first chartist member of parliament.

Within two years the last phase of chartism ended in ludicrous failure. For a third time O'Connor tried at once to arouse and to control a great political agitation. There was nothing new about his methods, but the working-class movement was more difficult to manage because the apparent success of revolution in Europe affected public opinion. O'Connor himself was now a European figure. He had always taken an interest in France; his chief supporter in the land campaign was a young man, Ernest Jones, whose father had been equerry to the duke of Cumberland and had followed him to Hanover. Jones was a poor creature, excitable, immensely proud of his mediocre literary talents, and full of German romanticism.[1] He was in touch with the leaders of the German revolutionary party, and brought them into contact with chartism. In 1845 O'Connor went to Belgium to study Flemish methods of small farming; the German exiles in Brussels welcomed him, and Marx and Engels signed a letter of congratulation upon his work. The news of the fall of Louis Philippe in February 1848 greatly excited the chartist leaders. They were already considering another national petition; they now called a general convention for 3 April. The new petition repeated the points of the People's Charter, though, under O'Connor's influence, the ballot was dropped from the demands. The convention opened with speeches from the less cautious members announcing that the country was ready for revolution. O'Connor would not commit himself to any declara-

[1] His diary is full of humourless exhibitions of *Weltschmerz*, e.g. '10 September 1839. Bought a pair of boots. Mein Herz bricht.' See Hovell, p. 280, n. 2.

tion in favour of physical force, and O'Brien warned the delegates that the chartists were not prepared for insurrection. The convention decided, if the petition were rejected, to present an address to the queen asking for the removal of ministers, and to call a national assembly for the enforcement of the charter.

The government acted at once. The police would not allow a great procession to escort the petition to the house of commons; the law officers of the Crown made use of a seventeenth-century law forbidding the presentation of a petition by more than ten persons, and parliament accepted a bill punishing seditious language with transportation for life. Wellington, now in his seventy-ninth year, was still commander-in-chief. He brought troops to London, and concentrated them at important points, though, as far as possible, he used the police for ordinary patrol work. A large number of special constables were enrolled; the authorities at Manchester and other centres of chartism in the north took similar precautions.

The chartists had arranged that on 10 April deputations from different quarters should meet on Kennington Common and march to Westminster. O'Connor kept up his bluff to the last. He appeared in state on Kennington Common, though the crowds were much smaller than he had expected, and included more spectators than active chartists. The police warned the leaders that the procession would not be allowed to cross the bridges to the north side of the river; O'Connor asked the crowd to obey the order. After a number of speeches, which came to an end in heavy rain, the petition was taken in three cabs to the house, while the demonstrators went back to their homes.

The provinces were as quiet as London, and the movement suddenly collapsed, though there were a few local disturbances between April and July. The petition was found to contain a great number of bogus signatures, including those of 'Victoria Rex', Sir Robert Peel, the duke of Wellington, and 'Mr. Punch'; O'Connor tried to bluster about it, but found no support. The convention, summoned to deliberate upon further measures, broke up through lack of funds. O'Connor did not attend its meetings; he was occupied elsewhere. The National Land Company was already in distress; the smallholders could not pay their way, and O'Connor himself was accused of dishonest management. In August a parliamentary committee found that the company was bankrupt, and without proper accounts.

O'Connor had not taken the subscriptions for his own use; money was actually due to him, but the affair discredited him for good and all. Four years later he went out of his mind; he died in 1855. Ernest Jones tried to revive the movement and, to his discredit, attacked the defeated and broken O'Connor. After some years of failure, Jones gave up his efforts and turned radical. He made a stir in 1867 when he defended the Fenians charged with the murder of a police sergeant at Manchester; but he was never much more than a provincial barrister, with a taste for letters.

Chartism deserved better leaders than O'Connor, O'Brien, Jones, and the host of lesser agitators. Lovett, in a pathetic way, realized the weakness of any movement among the disinherited masses and the sufferers from industrial change. These men had neither the leisure nor the education to develop a political technique and a convincing background of theory. Their political philosophy, such as it was, came mainly from their reading of the bible; their enthusiasm from a sense of present injustice and a conviction that, for reasons which they could not understand, the changes and 'progress' of the time worked cumulatively to their undoing. The people of England were, in Wellington's words, a 'very quiet' people, respectful of authority and obedient to the law. The wonder is that the distress of the early industrial age did not bring more disturbance; to the credit of the commons of England, the refusal to disturb the public peace was not due merely to fear of the physical force under the control of authority. Most of the political demands of the chartists have been accepted by public opinion, and voted by parliament. On the other hand the refusal of the middle and upper classes to grant the demands put forward in the national petitions was not entirely a selfish refusal. There were elements of selfishness, and, on the strict interpretation of class antagonism suggested by later revolutionary theory, the epithets used by chartist speakers in hours of bitterness exactly describe the facts of capitalist and bourgeois exploitation. It may, however, be argued that the later revolutionary theory does not give more than a partial explanation of these facts. The unwillingness of the prosperous classes and, for that matter, of the better-paid members of the working class to recognize the chartist demand for immediate social equality (to be attained through control of the political machinery of state) was in some measure a recognition of the complexity of social problems, of the need of time, inquiry, and scientific examination, and, finally, of the difficulty of changing institutions without wrecking them.

The chartists were divided by personal rivalries and by disagreement about the measures they would introduce after the attainment of political power. Many of them rejected industrialism and machinery and thought in terms of a nation of small landowners; others, like Lovett, followed Robert Owen in believing that the new inventions might solve the problems of poverty. Thus chartism included supporters of extreme individualism and of complete collectivism. All agreed that the existing order of society was unjust; the individualists wanted greater freedom and equality of opportunity for the common man, and the Owenites a more sensible arrangement of production and distribution. This agitation of the poor compelled other classes to think about the 'condition of England'. The chartist demands came upon a society which had already begun to take this question seriously; the great parliamentary inquiries into industrial conditions were signs that this society was finding its way towards a better organization of its resources and a better interpretation of liberty. The attitude of the governing class towards the chartist movement was itself the sign of a new age. Only in the general alarm of 1848, when most of western and central Europe was disturbed by revolution, was there any exceptional legislative measure against freedom of speech. Most of the chartist leaders were imprisoned at some time or other for breach of the peace or language inciting to violence. It would be hard to maintain that, from the point of view of public authority, the majority of the sentences were vindictive. No chartist newspaper was ever suppressed; no pamphlet or book was confiscated. During the two critical periods when the government used troops in large numbers for the maintenance of order, the commanding officers showed wise discretion, and avoided threats or provocation. There was something more than common sense in Russell's view that, if the chartists had real grievances, they had a right to express them, and that, if they had no real grievances, they would not keep their following. It is mere speculation to ask how near England was to revolution during these years; the credit for keeping the peace may well be divided between different classes of Englishmen, though the sympathy of later generations will lie with those thousands of over-worked and under-nourished labourers to whose unlettered minds chartism brought at least hopes of redress and betterment.

Among the different motives which had led working men to support the chartist movement was the desire for shorter hours of labour. This demand was particularly strong in Yorkshire and Lancashire. As early as 1818 the cotton-operatives of Manchester asked for a ten and a half hours' day, but the textile workers did not take up the question on a large scale until after 1830. This sudden prominence of the ten hours' agitation was due to the enthusiasm of two men: John Wood, a rich Yorkshire manufacturer, and Richard Oastler.[1] Oastler's violence of language ultimately did his cause harm, but in the early days nothing short of sensational and even denunciatory statements would have served to excite opinion. Oastler wrote a number of letters to the Leeds press headed 'Slavery in Yorkshire', and giving particulars of the long hours worked by children. The first result was a bill, introduced by Hobhouse[2] in 1831, extending from sixteen to eighteen the age-limit under which the working day in cotton mills was limited to twelve hours.

Hobhouse's bill, and the support given to it by Oastler and others, showed two features which recur throughout the many years of agitation for a ten hours' day. The movement cut across political parties. Hobhouse was a radical, Oastler a tory. Sadler, whose prominence in the debates on the bill gave him the parliamentary leadership of the movement at a critical time, was also a tory, and a strong opponent of catholic emancipation. Ashley, who succeeded Sadler, had been anti-catholic until 1829. On the other hand Hume, and for many years Roebuck, two prominent radicals, fought every measure of restrictive legislation. Bright opposed Ashley with great harshness, and voted against the ten hours' bill in 1847; Brougham, whose best work was done in support of working-class education, made long and sarcastic speeches against the enforcement of a maxi-

---

[1] See above, p. 135.
[2] Sir John Cam Hobhouse, cr. Baron Broughton (1786–1869); b. Bristol; educ. Westminster and Trinity College, Cambridge; radical politician, and friend of Byron; M.P., 1820; pres. of bd. of control, 1835–41 and 1846–52. Hobhouse invented the phrase 'His Majesty's Opposition'. See Costin and Watson, op. cit., ii. 166.

mum number of hours for the work of grown men. The cross-
divisions were multiplied during the years after 1840 because
the landowning class found in the support of factory laws a
convenient way of answering the manufacturers' attacks upon
the corn laws, but there were always a number of enlightened
manufacturers among the leaders of the movement for shorter
hours. Fielden in Lancashire was a larger employer of labour
than Wood in Yorkshire. The dividing line was less one of
party than of temperament; Ashley's phrase that Peel was always
thinking about imports and exports shows this difference in temperament. The motive force of the supporters of limitation of
hours was humanitarian; the motive force of their opponents—
leaving out in each case those who were acting merely out of
spite or self-interest—was a conviction, upheld by the economic
theories of the time, that a shortening of hours must bring
higher costs of production, and therefore a falling-off in demand
and a decrease in employment. Here, as in many other historical issues, judgements coloured by the emotions were wiser
than calculations based upon an intellectual survey of the facts
as they appeared in the light of current theory.

At the same time, it is necessary to remember that neither the
supporters nor the opponents of the ten hours' movement were
fighting only for a limitation of the hours of children or young
persons. Cobbett remarked that the opponents of the act of
1833 seemed to base the industrial welfare of England upon
'30,000 little girls. If these little girls worked two hours a day
less, our manufacturing supremacy would depart from us'.
Nassau Senior's demonstration—in itself a *tour de force*—that
the profits of industry were made in the last hour of the day's
work would have been less impressive if the argument had
affected only the labour of children.[1] Owing to the conditions
of work in cotton-mills, a ten hours' day for children and young
persons would also mean a restriction of the hours of adults.
The operatives knew this simple fact; most of the children were
employed directly by the spinners, not by the manufacturer.
The operatives would have agreed to a modification of the act

[1] Nassau Senior himself was not opposed to a limitation of children's hours of
work. On the contrary he wrote: 'No facts have been proved . . . and I do not believe that any exist, which show that it is proper to keep a child of 11 years old for
12 hours a day, in attendance on the employment, however light, of a factory.' See
L. R. Sorenson, 'Laissez faire and the Factory Acts', *Journal of Econ. Hist.* xii (1952),
pp. 247–62.

of 1833 and an increase in the children's hours from eight to ten, if they could have secured a ten hours' day for adults. When they found that there was no hope of persuading parliament or public opinion to accept a compromise of this kind, the rank and file of the movement tried to obtain a ten hours' limitation for themselves by cutting down the number of hours worked by women.

This attitude was not simply callous. The operatives believed that the legislation in favour of children would not be enforced until a general rule prevented chances of evasion and the machinery in every factory was stopped after ten hours. They also knew that public opinion was ready to accept legislation on behalf of women and children; the regulation of the hours worked by men conflicted with the belief, or rather with the fallacy, that adult men were free to choose for themselves the number of hours they worked for their employers. As late as 1855, after the textile workers had won, indirectly, a sixty hours' week, Palmerston could declare that a limitation of the freedom of adult men to make their own bargains was based upon a 'vicious and wrong principle'.[1] It is little wonder that the men should have used the best tactical weapons. These weapons were very powerful. A parliamentary committee of inquiry in 1832 produced evidence which shocked public opinion. The evidence was not altogether fair; Engels described the report as 'emphatically partisan, composed by strong enemies of the factory system, for party ends';[2] but, if the exaggerations are disregarded, the main facts were grim enough to justify interference. It was a poor argument to say that children were better employed in factories than in running about the streets, or that the standard of life was probably higher in homes where children went out to work. The manufacturers asked for a further investigation. A body of commissioners, including Chadwick, made local inquiries. The operatives believed that the commissioners were prejudiced in favour of the manufacturers, and gave them a bad reception. In return the commissioners protested against the 'hired agitators' who were deluding the working classes; on the other hand they too realized the need for legislation and their report confirmed the existence of the evils reported by the

[1] Hansard, 3rd. ser. cxxxvii. 615–16.

[2] F. Engels, *The Condition of the Working Class in England in 1844* (Eng. tr., 1920 ed.), p. 170. Engels thought that the second commission came 'somewhat nearer the truth, but its deviations therefrom' were 'in the opposite direction'. For a criticism of the 1832 report, see W. H. Hutt, *Economica*, Mar. 1926.

first inquiry. At this point Sadler, who lost his seat in the first election after the reform bill, handed over the parliamentary leadership of the movement to Ashley.[1]

Ashley's place in English political life for the next twenty years appears, at first sight, a paradox. He was an aristocrat in manner, bearing, and opinions. He disliked trade unions; he would not hear of any final opposition between capital and labour. He was more of a tory than Peel, more rigid than Wellington in his conception of authority and duty. His religious views were narrow; he was not an easy colleague. He had few constructive ideas, and, though he was a shrewd judge of men, he was never able to inspire them. The secret of his power and influence lay in his disinterestedness and in his hatred of cruelty and unmerited suffering. His own childhood had been bleak and unhappy; he described his first school as a 'Dotheboys Hall' in harsh reality. He entered parliament as member for the pocket borough of Woodstock, and stood in 1831 as an anti-reform candidate at a county by-election which cost him £16,000. He decided as a schoolboy to give his life to the interests of the poor, but hitherto he had shown little sign of undertaking parliamentary work on their behalf. He paid no attention to the discussions on the limitation of hours, and did not even know that Sadler had obtained a committee of inquiry in 1832. The report of this committee changed his attitude. He offered his services to Sadler and, a few months later, accepted the suggestion that he should take up Sadler's work in the commons. Henceforward, until 1850, he was the leader of the working men's cause. The act of 1833, which followed the outburst of just indignation over the facts made public by the parliamentary inquiries, disappointed Ashley and his supporters. They did not secure a ten hours' day for all persons under eighteen and, thereby, a ten hours' day for adult workers. On the other hand the bill was a better measure than Ashley and the operatives believed it to be. It applied to all textile factories with special exceptions in the case of the silk industry. It secured the exclusion of children under nine from factories, and limited the

---

[1] Anthony Ashley Cooper, 7th earl of Shaftesbury (1801–85); b. London; educ. Harrow and Christ Church, Oxford; M.P., 1826; succeeded his father, 1851; commissioner of the board of control, 1828; lord of the admiralty, 1834; chairman of the sanitary commission for the Crimea, 1855. In addition to his parliamentary support of social reform Shaftesbury also took part in philanthropic and religious work, and was chairman of the Ragged School Union for thirty-nine years.

work of children under thirteen to forty-eight hours a week, or nine hours in any one day. No person under eighteen could be employed for more than twelve hours a day, or sixty-nine hours a week. These hours were to be fixed between 5.30 a.m. and 8.30 p.m. Children under thirteen were to attend school for not less than two hours a day.

The most important feature of the act was the provision of inspectors to enforce the regulations. The factory hands thought that the inspectors would always take the side of the employers. They might well feel these suspicions, because the appointment of experts, responsible to a government department, was an administrative measure of a new and remarkable kind. In fact the inspectors soon proved their value. They protected the good employer against the bad employer; their reports also did much to instruct public opinion, and to give parliament an insight into the working of the industrial system, but for some time the commons would go no farther in the regulation of hours. In any case, during the next few years, the political demands of the chartists, and the agitation against the new poor law, which affected far more people than the ten hours' movement, diverted attention to other matters. Ashley himself refused to have any-thing to do with the proposals to give up an eight hours' day for young children in return for a general ten hours' day. In 1840 he asked for an inquiry into the working of the act of 1833, and also for a wider investigation of the conditions of child labour in factories and trades outside the textile industry. The report of the first committee of inquiry showed that there were evils in silk and lace mills as bad as those in cotton factories. Ashley prepared a bill extending the act of 1833 to the lace and silk trades, but the change of ministry upset his plans.

Peel's government came into office at a time of bad trade. Peel himself had bold schemes for lowering the tariff; he knew that his ideas would be opposed, and did not want to strengthen the opposition by undertaking other measures likely to be un-popular with the manufacturers. On the other hand the larger commission of 1840 issued in 1842 the first of two reports. The report dealt with conditions of employment in coal-mines. Once more the facts stirred public opinion. In nearly every district children were employed underground at the age of six, in some cases at five, or even younger. These child workers drew trucks along passages too narrow for grown men, or looked after the ventilating doors under conditions which were very like solitary confinement in darkness. In Scotland, South Wales, the West Riding, and parts of Lancashire women and girls took part in the heavy work of drawing and carrying coal. The fact that these women, children, and girls were employed, like the children in cotton mills, by small sub-contractors, or by the workmen themselves, made no difference to the issue, or indeed to the ultimate responsibility of the mine-owners.

There was no difficulty in persuading the commons to take action on this report. The mines act of 1842 prohibited the employment of women and girls underground, set an age-limit of ten to the employment of boys, and provided inspectors to enforce the law and report to the central authority. The treatment of the act by the peers is an interesting comment upon Ashley's view that the members of the house of lords had 'few sparks of generosity and no sentiment'. Lord Londonderry, a great colliery proprietor, defended the mine-owners. Only three bishops were present at the most critical time in the debates, though the archbishop of Canterbury and the bishops of London and Norwich spoke for the bill.

Early in 1843, when the scandals of the coal-mines were still in people's minds, the commission of inquiry published a second report dealing with the employment of children in the potteries, in calico-printing works, nail-making, and other industries. The report showed that these children needed protection even more than the children in cotton mills. As a first stage the government introduced a new bill, limited in scope to textile factories, which lowered the age-limit of employment from nine to eight, and at the same time cut down the number of hours of work from eight to six and a half. The bill came to grief over the rules for supervising the education of children in factory schools. Nearly two million nonconformists signed petitions against a measure which might extend the influence of the church, and the concessions made to satisfy the nonconformists only alienated churchmen. The bill was withdrawn, and a new measure introduced in 1844. Owing to the rivalry of church and chapel the act of 1844 did nothing to improve the scandalous conditions of factory schools, but it secured a day of six and a half hours for children between eight and thirteen, and a twelve hours' day for all women above as well as under eighteen. Evasion of the act by intermittent employment throughout the day was checked by a rule that the hours of all workers should begin at the same time. Regulations for the fencing of machinery were inserted mainly in the interests of women and girls, whose clothes were liable to be caught up in shafts or gearing, but this provision was the first instance of factory laws explicitly affecting adult men. In 1845 Ashley was able to bring calico-printing among protected industries. He wanted to add dye-works and bleaching-works, but the argument that these trades were subject to great fluctuations of demand was too strong for him.

From the point of view of the supporters of a ten hours' day the act of 1844 was a failure. The debates had shown that parliament was fully aware of the issue; the hours of work of women and young persons had been fixed at twelve because every one knew that 'to enact that no young persons or women of any age should work more than ten hours was, in point of fact, to enact that no factory engines should be kept in operation more than ten hours'.[1]

Within three years the commons passed a ten hours' bill. It was clear that a majority wanted to limit the hours of women and young persons. The whig leaders, Palmerston, Macaulay, and Russell—a late convert—had voted in favour of ten hours, and the fact was noted in the country. Ashley brought forward a bill in January 1846. It was postponed owing to the political crisis over the corn laws, and Ashley himself lost his seat because he took the side of repeal. Fielden succeeded him as leader of the movement in parliament, and the ten hours' day, or week of fifty-eight hours, went through without much opposition in May 1847. Two facts, apart from the general conviction of the majority in the commons, worked in favour of the bill. Peel had opposed it, and the protectionists were ready to vote for anything which Peel disliked. At the same time the trade depression weakened the argument that the cotton industry could not stand a reduction in the hours of work; most mills were open for a shorter period than ten hours.

Once again the working men were disappointed. They had expected that a ten hours' day for women and young persons would secure a similar working day for themselves. Owing to faulty drafting the act did not prevent the employment of women and young persons on a relay system. As the factories

[1] Hansard, 3rd ser. lxxiii, 1111. The lowering of the age-limit for child workers was not criticized during the debate.

could remain open between 5.30 a.m. and 8.30 p.m., employers using this relay system worked their machinery, and therefore kept their men, for more than ten hours. The law officers of the Crown agreed with the inspectors that the system was against the intention of parliament; the home secretary, alarmed by the number of petitions from manufacturers in favour of the plan, told the inspectors not to start prosecutions. The inspectors showed their social use and independence of mind by refusing to accept dictation from the home secretary against the opinion of the law officers. Finally, on a test case in 1850, the court of exchequer declared that the wording of the acts of 1844 and 1847 was not strict enough to carry into effect the apparent decision of parliament.

Ashley, who was now back in the house, proposed to introduce a bill prohibiting the relay system. At this point a compromise was suggested. The employers would give up their right to keep their factories open for women and young persons at any time between 5.30 a.m. and 8.30 p.m., if the weekly limit for the 'protected workers' were extended from fifty-eight to sixty hours. The hours of opening would range from 6 a.m. to 6 p.m. or 7 a.m. to 7 p.m., with an hour and a half for meals, and a closing time at 2 p.m. on Saturdays. Thus the working day for women and young persons would be ten and a half hours on week-days, and seven and a half (allowing a half-hour's interval) on Saturdays. Ashley agreed to this compromise, though it cost him his popularity with the operatives. The gain was undoubtedly on the side of the workmen. They had established a 'normal day', with a Saturday half-holiday for women and young persons, and in most cases for themselves. Evasion of the law was hardly possible on a large scale, though by a curious loophole, not closed until 1853, children could be employed before or after the period laid down for women and young persons. The results of shortening the hours of labour justified those who foretold that there would be little or no falling off in production. The fall was slight even when the machinery was run at the old speeds, and in most cases the operatives were so much healthier in mind and body that they could stand the strain of working with the machines set at higher speeds.

Although there was no further reduction of hours until 1874, conditions of work improved in the important and dangerous occupation of coal-mining. The act of 1842 had not dealt with the safety of mines, and the one inspector appointed to enforce the terms of the law had powers only to prevent the employment of women or of young persons under the prohibited age. There was a belief in 1842 that the miners would object to inspection, but the movement in favour of state interference came from the men themselves. It was opposed by some coal-owners, including Lord Londonderry, who described the coal mines inspection act of 1850 as 'infernal'; on the other hand a number of bad colliery disasters aroused public opinion and, although Disraeli described the bill as 'a piece of hasty and ill-considered legislation',[1] there was no serious opposition. The Royal School of Mines was founded in 1851 in order to provide qualified inspectors. The work of the school, the reports of the inspectors, and the lessons of mining accidents led to a number of improvements during the next twenty years, while the prosecution of a mine-manager and two of his staff after an explosion in 1856 showed that the government intended to enforce the law of 1850. In 1860 boys under eighteen were forbidden to act as enginemen; two years later, after another accident, an act of parliament laid down that every mine should have at least two entrance shafts. The coal mines act of 1872 introduced a new set of regulations, and required managers of mines to have a certificate of competency. Meanwhile the invention of large fan ventilators, wire ropes, improved winding machinery, and better safety lamps contributed to the ease as well as to the safety of work underground.

The improvement in trade after 1842 brought a revival and extension of trade unionism. The cotton-spinners and the potters revived their associations; other trades, printers, glass-makers, tailors, shoemakers, curriers, either linked up different branches of their crafts in a single union, or extended their separate associations throughout the country. The Miners' Association of Great Britain and Ireland was founded in 1841; within a few years it had sufficient resources to pay a solicitor £1,000 a year for the conduct of its legal business and to resist oppression by fighting cases in local courts. The miners also organized, with the help of other unions, a successful protest against a government bill of 1844 for increasing the powers of the justices in disputes between masters and men. On the other hand they

[1] Monypenny and Buckle, iii. 255.

were too weak to resist their employers in a long strike; their association did not survive the depression in the coal industry in 1847 and 1848. Attempts to bring about a general association of trades also broke down, though they were made on more prudent lines than those of the earlier national unions. The National Association of United Trades for the Protection of Labour, founded in 1845, did not aim at taking the place of the craft unions; its purpose was to watch over the interests of workmen, and to promote measures which might be to their advantage, including the establishment of co-operative workshops. The lessons of earlier failures were not lost; the association took care 'to keep trade matters and politics as distinct as circumstances will justify', and to point out the desirability of maintaining good relations between masters and men. It did a certain amount of conciliatory work, but the large unions preferred to trust to their own strength; the association was of little importance after 1856 and disappeared a few years later.

The revolutionary outbreaks in Europe during 1848 did not have much effect upon English trade unions. The unions continued to avoid far-reaching political plans, and to concentrate upon improvement within their own organizations. The increase in the size of the larger associations led to the appointment of permanent officers giving their whole time to the work. These appointments resulted in further amalgamations, and in a more consistent and careful policy. As their resources grew, the unions were able to afford meeting-rooms of their own; this break with the old habit of doing business in public houses, where the members were expected to give the publican a good return for the use of a room, produced more orderly discussions and more cautious resolutions. In 1851 nearly all the branches of the engineering trade were united in the Amalgamated Society of Engineers. This step was mainly due to the work of two men, William Allan[1] and William Newton,[2] and to the steady policy

---

[1] William Allan (1813-74), b. Carrickfergus, of Scottish parentage; worked in a cotton mill, 1825-8; apprenticed to an engineering firm in Glasgow, 1828; married the niece of a partner in the firm, 1832; worked as a journeyman engineer at the Liverpool railway works and, later, at Crewe; general secretary of the Journeymen Steam-engine and Machine Makers' Society, 1847, and of the Amalgamated Society of Engineers, 1851-74.

[2] William Newton (1822-76), b. Congleton; worked in an engineering shop, 1836-48; dismissed from the post of foreman owing to activity in the trade union movement, 1848; took a public house at Ratcliffe, and worked for the amalgamation of the engineering unions; became the proprietor of a local newspaper, chairman

of the Journeymen Steam-engine and Machine Makers' Society, which had absorbed a number of smaller unions. The Amalgamated Society began with more than 11,000 members; each of the two unions nearest in strength—the ironfounders' and stonemasons' unions—had only 4,000 to 5,000 members. The income and the constitution of the amalgamated society were also new features in trade unionism. No other union had an income of £500 a week; these sums and the large balance accumulated in the course of time gave the society's rules a new importance. The union had a common purse, but the branches administered benefit funds according to strictly framed regulations. The executive committee settled disputes about the interpretation of the rules, and took care to prevent hasty or ill-considered change. The power of granting or withholding strike pay enabled the committee to secure uniformity of policy in trade disputes, and checked local agitation. The society abolished the traditions of secrecy which clung to the unions from the early days when they were treated as conspiracies against the law; every report and most of the circulars were published.

The engineers soon tried their strength by asking for the abolition of piecework and regular overtime. The employers, who had formed an association of their own, refused arbitration and locked out their workmen on 10 January 1852. After three months the masters won, and insisted that the men should sign a promise to give up the union.[1] The promise, given under compulsion, was not kept; the men suffered little from the defeat, while their society became an example for other amalgamations, though the rules of each union varied according to the requirements of the trade and the specialized skill of the operatives. The builders were the next body of workmen to organize a long strike. During and after the Crimean war the different branches of the trade in the provinces had been carrying on strikes with some success, and had reached the stage of negotiating working agreements with the masters. In 1858 the London carpenters, masons, and bricklayers asked for a nine hours' day. Messrs. Trollope's firm dismissed a man who had presented a manifesto to his employers, and his fellow workmen

of Stepney vestry, and representative of the vestry on the metropolitan board of works; served on the board of works, 1862-76; contested parliamentary seats 1852, 1868, and 1875.

[1] This promise to give up membership of trade unions was known to workmen as 'the document'.

went on strike in his defence. The employers tried to break the union by refusing negotiations and locking out their men, but other unions paid £23,000 towards the strike funds; the Amalgamated Society of Engineers contributed £1,000 a week for three weeks. Although the strikers did not get all their demands, they were strong enough to resist a boycott of members of trade unions, and their strike showed the advantages of a large, national association. The stonemasons already had a strong society; the carpenters had only local organizations, and decided to follow the example of the engineers. Within two years of the strike, the Amalgamated Society of Carpenters and Joiners became one of the four most important unions.[1]

Thus sixty years after the passing of the combination laws, and a generation after their repeal, the skilled workmen of the country laid the foundations of those societies which were, ultimately, to do far more than defend a received standard of life against encroachment. The trade-unionist movement was a sign of the vitality of the age. Chartism had been an attempt to secure social justice. The attempt was based upon a sound instinct as well as upon a consciousness of sufferings which were less endurable than in the past because there was now a remedy for them. Chartism had failed to provide working men with the right leaders from their own class. Factory legislation came, as it could only come, through parliament, and therefore largely through the agency of men outside the working class. The trade-unionist movement between 1850 and 1860 was thus the first example of a constructive political achievement carried out almost entirely by working men for working men; to this extent at least their wish to choose their own leaders had been fulfilled. Upon Mill's view of 'a certain order of possible progress', the next step was the enfranchisement of working men for which the chartists had agitated. The first stage in this enfranchisement was reached in 1867.

[1] For the history of trade unions between 1860 and 1870, see below, pp. 612–16.

IV

PARTY POLITICS AND POLITICAL
LEADERS 1846–70

THE CONFUSION OF PARTIES: THE REFORM ACT
OF 1867

PEEL was thrown from his horse on 29 June 1850, and died three days later. He had refused to organize his followers as a party, but had continued to sit in parliament. It is impossible to say what political course he would have taken if he had lived for another ten years. As things were, a long period of confusion and instability followed the break-up of the conservative party. From July 1846 until the passing of the reform bill of 1867 there were eight administrations; between 1846 and 1852, from 1858 to 1859, and from 1866 to 1868 no ministry had a stable majority in the commons. In 1852 Russell was beaten by eleven votes, and Derby by nineteen. After a parliamentary defeat of sixteen votes in 1857 Palmerston obtained a majority of 70–80 at a general election, and lost a critical motion in the following year by nineteen votes. The reform bill of 1866 passed its second reading by five votes, and the government was defeated soon afterwards by eleven votes. Party discipline was still very loose; it was impossible, after a general election, to know the exact state of parties until the first division had been taken in a new parliament. In 1852 the estimates of conservative strength varied between 320 and 290. Gladstone put the strength of the coalition government at the beginning of 1853 at about 310, 'liable on occasions, which frequently arise, to heavy deductions'; the government was defeated three times in one week even before the budget. The very names of parties were unstable for a time. The terms 'conservative-liberal' and 'liberal-conservative' came into use, though Russell thought whiggism a simpler term than 'conservative progress', and the protectionists were inclined to give up the name 'conservative party' owing to the 'odious associations' with Peel. Lord John Manners spoke of his dislike of 'wearing dirty men's dirty linen'. The allegiance of party leaders was as uncertain as that of their followers. Palmerston was offered a place in Derby's administration of 1852; a few months later he served with Aberdeen in the coalition, although the two men had quarrelled over foreign policy. Russell was reconciled with Palmerston after no less bitter personal opposition. Disraeli, after attacking Peel for giving up protection, led the way in accepting free trade as an accomplished fact. Gladstone, who distrusted Palmerston almost as much as he distrusted Disraeli, joined Palmerston's administration in 1859 after voting against the motion which overthrew Derby's government.

These facts merely reflect the hesitancy and quick changes of opinion inevitable at a time when the issues were so much confused and in many cases so new that the old party distinctions did not apply to them. In foreign politics, the face of Europe was changed between 1859 and 1871 by the action of large armies outside the range of interference by Great Britain. In domestic affairs the greatest changes also took place outside the routine of parliamentary conflict. They resulted from administrative measures voted and discussed in the commons; but few members realized the cumulative significance of these administrative reforms passed session after session. The popularity of Lord Palmerston with the middle-class electorate and the fact that most of the middle-class electors continued to choose upper-class representatives contributed to this 'time-lag'. Government was still a grand business, the exercise of sovereignty; Palmerston and most of his social equals would have agreed with the view (expressed in the debates on the reform bill of 1860) that, if working men came to the house of commons, they would waste time in discussions upon wages, the relation between capital and labour, 'the grievances of journeymen bakers, who disliked night work', and other matters 'which did not lie within the province of legislation'. Thus Gladstone's first administration shows the liberation of forces and currents of opinion held up almost by parliamentary accident.

Until 1867 few working men had votes, and working-class opinion could influence parliamentary action only by indirect pressure. In any case this opinion still hesitated between the two parties. The conservatives might support movements against the manufacturers, but an alliance with the conservative party tended to break down over the franchise question and the treatment of the landed interest. On the other hand, the working class distrusted the middle-class free-traders, and found little to attract them in the programme of the Manchester reformers. The working-class leaders warned their followers against 'the millocracy', the 'free-traders in labour', the 'mill-owning evaders of the factory relief bill, the money lords, the comfortable atheists on 'Change'. The radicals formed only a small wing of the liberal party, and the Crimean war widened the gap between middle-class radicalism and the working class. Working men were curiously unresponsive to the peace party, and readier to support the language and policy of Palmerston. The mismanagement of the war discredited aristocratic government, while the rise in prices due to the war, and the consequent check to the improvement of conditions of living, led to a renewal of the agitation for a wider franchise; this agitation died down with the return of prosperity. It revived after the death of Palmerston; the reform act of 1867 was the result of exigencies within the house of commons, and of the accidents of debate, but it was none the less wanted by the country.

Russell's administration in 1846 lasted until a general election; although the whigs, radicals, and Irish were in a minority, neither wing of the conservatives would allow the other a chance of taking office. The whigs came back with slightly increased numbers after the general election of 1847. The supporters of the ministry were about 325; the conservatives 330, but of this number about 100 were Peelites. The constituencies accepted free trade; few protectionists had ventured to go beyond saying that free trade might be given a chance, but would certainly prove a disaster. Moreover, after the end of 1847 the protectionists were without a leader in the commons. Bentinck offended the old tories, and the country gentlemen who formed the bulk of his supporters, by voting in favour of the removal of Jewish disabilities.[1] Bentinck's withdrawal showed the weakness of the

---

[1] The oath which every member of parliament was required to swear contained the words 'on the true faith of a Christian'. In 1833-4 the lords rejected proposals from the commons for removing these words, which excluded practising Jews from parliament. In 1847 Baron de Rothschild was elected for the City of London; the lords again refused a motion to change the wording of the oath, and Rothschild could not take his seat. For some time the lords held out against the commons; in 1858 a compromise allowed each house to determine the form of oath to be taken by its members. In 1866, after Roman catholic pressure for the removal of words pledging catholics to abjure any intention of subverting the established

party; Graham, Gladstone, Goulburn, Sidney Herbert had followed Peel. Disraeli was the ablest of the protectionists, but a party which had driven out Bentinck because he supported the claims of Jews was unlikely to look with enthusiasm upon Disraeli as their leader. Yet after Bentinck's sudden death, in September 1848, the choice of Disraeli seemed inevitable. The party tried to avoid this painful necessity by appointing a committee of three, but within a few weeks Disraeli's opponents, if not his own side, regarded him as leader.[1] He tried to persuade the party to 'abandon the narrow defile of protection' and to compensate the landed interest by removing inequality of taxation between landed and other property. At the end of 1850 Disraeli hoped that Graham might join a reunited conservative party, but Graham's refusal was one of the long list of Disraeli's failures to win back the Peelites. Two months later the government was defeated on a private member's motion for a uniform county and borough franchise. The conservatives did not want this uniformity, but they and a number of liberals refused to support Russell.[2] Russell resigned, and the negotiations which followed his defeat illustrate the confusion of parties. The queen sent for Stanley.[3] The protectionists pointed out that they were not responsible for the fall of the government, and suggested a coalition of whigs and Peelites. The Peelites would not serve with Russell or Stanley. Russell refused to form an administration without Peelite support; Stanley was approached a second time, but his followers decided that they could not get enough support in the house; Russell therefore came back to office because there was no one to take his place. Disraeli noticed one conclusion which could be drawn from the negotiations: 'Every public man of experience and influence, however slight, had declined to act under Lord Derby unless the principle of Protection were unequivocally renounced.[4]

church, a new oath was drawn up; this oath did not contain the words 'on the true faith of a Christian'.

[1] Guizot wrote to Disraeli: 'I think that your being the leader of the Tory party is the greatest triumph that Liberalism has ever achieved.' M. and B., iii. 137.

[2] The ecclesiastical titles bill had already lost Russell the Irish catholic vote. See below, p. 522.

[3] Edward George Geoffrey Smith Stanley, 14th earl of Derby (1799–1869); b. Knowsley; educ. Eton and Christ Church, Oxford; M.P., 1820; succeeded to earldom, 1851; under-secretary for the colonies, 1827–8; chief secretary for Ireland, 1830–3; secretary for war and the colonies, 1833–4 and 1841–5.

[4] Disraeli took every chance of dissociating the party from protection. The

Russell's government did not survive more than a year. It was weakened by the dismissal of Palmerston owing to his premature approval of the *coup d'état* of Louis Napoleon Bonaparte.[1] It fell when Palmerston took his revenge. The *coup d'état* led to the first of several panics over the danger of a French invasion. Russell proposed to meet any possible danger by means of a local militia. Palmerston wanted a national militia; this plan would provide a more mobile but also a more expensive force. The protectionists voted with Palmerston, and on 20 February 1852 Russell was beaten.[2]

The conservatives now had their chance, but they were still divided upon the question of protection. Disraeli offered to give up the leadership of the commons to Palmerston in a conservative ministry, but Palmerston would not join any ministry which was not committed to free trade. Derby therefore had to limit himself to his own party. He offered Disraeli the chancellorship of the exchequer. Disraeli said that he knew nothing of financial questions, but Derby answered: 'You know as much as Mr. Canning did. They give you the figures.' The new ministry included only three men who had held office; not one of the others was even a privy councillor.[3] Before the general election Derby had come round to Disraeli's view that the party must give up protection. His followers were not equally convinced, and as, according to the habit of the time, a peer, even if he were prime minister, did not make public speeches at elections, the country did not know Derby's attitude. It was held that a Derbyite was 'a protectionist in a county, neutral in a small town, and a free-trader in a large one'.[4] Thus the conservatives increased their strength, but still returned without a majority. They were faced, at the opening of parliament, with a resolution in favour of the

protectionists spoke disparagingly of the Great Exhibition as an encouragement to the entry of foreign products. One of them called the Exhibition 'an unwieldy, ill-devised, unwholesome castle of glass'. Disraeli described it as 'that enchanted pile which the sagacious taste and the prescient philanthropy of an accomplished and enlightened Prince have raised for the glory of England and the delight and instruction of two hemispheres'. M. and B., iii. 303.

[1] See below, p. 249.

[2] This vote was Palmerston's 'tit-for-tat with John Russell'.

[3] Wellington, on hearing the list of ministers, thought that, owing to his deafness, he must have mistaken the names. His questions 'Who? Who?' were overheard, and gave the ministry a nickname.

[4] Derby always found it difficult to speak on economic questions for the simple reason that he did not understand them. He told the house of lords in March 1852 that he 'elected to be tried by God and his country'.

principle of free trade. Palmerston saved them from a motion commending the repeal of the corn laws by saying that gentlemen in the house of commons should not be asked to make public recantation of their opinions. Disraeli indeed made it clear that he was prepared to accept free trade; his attacks upon Peel were too recent for his acceptance to bring him much credit. In any case he did not conceal the fact that his budget was a measure of 'compensation instead of protection' for the three great interests affected by free trade. The reduction of the malt tax was a benefit given to the landed interest; the shipping interest was relieved of the payment of various dues, and the sugar interest allowed to refine in bond. Disraeli invited the small income-tax payer and the small householder to pay for this 'compensation'. The extension of income tax to 'precarious', i.e. earned, incomes of £100 a year, and unearned incomes of £50 a year, and of the house tax to houses of £10 rateable value was too much for the opposition.

Gladstone's attack on this budget destroyed the government in December 1852. There were difficulties about finding a successor, until the Peelites agreed to serve in a coalition ministry.[1] The Peelites took the largest slice of a cake which was too small to satisfy everyone claiming a share. The cabinet contained six whigs, six Peelites, and one radical, though the combined strength of whigs, liberals, radicals, and the 'Irish brigade' was about ten times that of the Peelites. A cabinet with Aberdeen as prime minister, Russell as foreign secretary, Palmerston at the home office, and Gladstone as chancellor of the exchequer[2] included, in Palmerston's words, 'almost all the men of talent and

---

[1] For an account of the manœuvres leading to this coalition (of which Madame Lieven wrote 'qui est le fou qui eût osé prédire cette trinité'), see C. H. Stuart, 'The Formation of the Coalition Cabinet of 1852', in *Trans. R. Hist. S.* 5th ser. vol. iv (1954), pp. 45–68.

[2] Disraeli and Gladstone had a stiff exchange of letters over the payment for furniture at the official residence of the chancellor in Downing St., and the transfer of the official robes, which had belonged to Mr. Pitt. Gladstone wrote, finally: 'It is highly unpleasant to Mr. W. E. Gladstone to address Mr. Disraeli without the usual terms of courtesy, but he abstains from them only because he perceives that they are unwelcome.' In Oct. 1853 Aberdeen wanted to resign the prime ministership in favour of Russell but his colleagues would not agree to the change. Russell himself had given up the foreign secretaryship to Clarendon in Feb. 1853. In Dec. he brought forward a reform bill, but was persuaded to withdraw it; meanwhile Palmerston had resigned (though he took back his resignation) out of protest against it.

experience in the house of commons except Disraeli', but there was a certain feeling that the 'old stagers' and the 'mandarins' were keeping office to themselves. The unequal representation of different sections was likely to lead to discontent in the house, and the leaders did not agree upon important matters of policy. As one member of the government said plainly: 'We shall all look strangely at each other when we first meet in cabinet.'[1]

These differences of view had serious results during the months before the Crimean war, but for the time the conservatives could not break up the coalition. Disraeli saw that his party needed a programme to attract the urban voters. He founded a newspaper, the *Press*, to spread criticism of the government, and tried to stir Derby into more vigorous action. Disraeli complained that his chief, and the magnates of the party, did not even use their social influence in rallying their followers. Derby was 'always at Newmarket or Doncaster'. His house was 'always closed'. He subscribed to nothing, 'though his fortune is very large, and [he] expects . . . everything to be done'.[2] During the autumn of 1853, at the height of the eastern crisis, Derby and Disraeli hardly exchanged letters. Disraeli paid his first visit to Knowsley, Derby's country house, in December 1853. Malmesbury thought that the visit bored Derby, because he had to leave off translating Homer and talk politics.

Gladstone's budgets formed the main domestic interest of the coalition government. Public opinion in 1853 wanted to get rid of the income tax. Gladstone agreed that the tax was a temptation to fraud, and inequitable because its demands pressed 'upon the whole too hard upon intelligence or skill, and not hard enough upon property as compared with intelligence or skill'. He thought that a distinction between earned and unearned incomes would break down, and that it would be better to reach indisputably unearned income by extending the legacy duty to real property. With this extension, Gladstone hoped that the income tax might be lowered by instalments, and come to an end in 1859. He chose this year because £2,000,000 of 'long annuities' ceased in 1859; he did not suggest an earlier date because he wanted to continue Peel's experiments in reducing customs duties. He therefore had to provide for a temporary fall in the revenue. He abolished most of the duties on partially

---

[1] Morley, i. 449.
[2] M. and B., iii. 546-7. Derby later subscribed £20,000 to the party.

manufactured goods and on foodstuffs and halved nearly all duties on manufactured goods. There was a certain irony in Gladstone's forecast about the income tax. He considered this tax 'an engine of gigantic power for great national purposes': in other words, an instrument to be kept in reserve for an emergency, and particularly for war expenditure. Between 1817 and 1850 there was extraordinary military or naval expenditure only in nine years; from 1851 to 1870 there were only four years without such expenditure, and in three out of these four years, 1862, 1863, and 1864, expenses of a military type were met out of savings on the army and navy votes, while in 1866 a supplementary estimate was necessary to pay for the conversion of the Enfield rifle from a muzzle loader to a breech loader. Furthermore Gladstone's estimate of the return from the legacy duty was wrong because he allowed assessment to be made on the life interest of a holder, and did not take into account the extent to which real property was encumbered. On the other hand Gladstone tried to meet the cost of the Crimean war by an increase in taxation rather than in increase in the debt. He brought the 'engine of gigantic power' into operation, and raised income tax to 1s. 2d. in the summer of 1854. Gladstone reckoned on a short war; he was out of office before the budget of 1855, but his successor, Sir George Cornewall Lewis, could not do without a loan.

Aberdeen's leadership of the coalition ministry did not survive the anger of the public at the mismanagement of the Crimean expedition during the first winter of the war.[1] The cabinet refused to accept a motion for a committee of inquiry. Russell resigned as a protest against this decision, and on 29 January 1855, the motion was passed by 305 to 148 votes. The conservatives were the largest numerical group in the opposition, and the queen asked Derby to form a ministry. Disraeli was again ready to give up the leadership of the commons to Palmerston. Palmerston would not join Derby, and Derby would not go on without him. The queen then turned to Russell, but Russell could not get any support. Palmerston therefore became prime minister, to Disraeli's disappointment and disgust. 'He is really an impostor, utterly exhausted, and at the best only ginger-beer, and not champagne, and now an old painted pantaloon.'[2]

[1] See below, p. 286.
[2] M. and B., iii. 567.

For a time Palmerston had the Peelites with him, but Gladstone, Graham, and Herbert[1] would not agree to the committee of inquiry. Palmerston realized that the country wanted an inquiry, and the Peelites resigned. This withdrawal made it easier for Russell to come back to the cabinet,[2] and left the seceders in isolation. The prime minister was at the height of his popularity. Herbert wrote that he was 'the only public man in England who has a name. Many criticize, many disapprove, but all, more or less, like him and look upon him as the only man.'[3] In March 1857 Palmerston was defeated on a motion condemning his treatment of the second war with China.[4] He used his popularity to fight a general election. He won a majority; about 370 members were elected to support him, but these supporters were bound very loosely to his government. The election had turned upon Palmerston's name; Shaftesbury noted that there was 'no measure, no principle, no cry . . . simply, were you, or were you not . . . for Palmerston'.[5] Disraeli pointed out that 'a man returned pledged to support Palmerston really means nothing, for there is always the proper mental reservation, "when Palmerston, in his, the pledger's, opinion, is not wrong" '.

A prime minister of greater moral authority, or a younger man, more open to new ideas, might have founded a strong progressive party in a parliament which contained 189 new men. The Peelites were numerically unimportant, but strong in talent. If they distrusted Palmerston, they disliked Disraeli even more vehemently. Palmerston, however, had neither the initiative nor the desire to draw up a programme. His interests were still in foreign affairs. The issue of electoral reform was coming to the front. Palmerston considered the franchise 'a trust reposed in the elector for the public good', not a right which every citizen might claim. For this reason he opposed the ballot. He told his constituents at Tiverton in 1852 that 'to go sneaking to the ballot-box, and, poking in a piece of paper, looking round to see that no one could read it, is a course which is unconstitutional and unworthy of the character of straightforward and honest Englishmen'.[6] He did not object on principle to a wider franchise, though he believed that the demand came from

---

[1] Sidney Herbert, 1st baron Herbert of Lea (1810–61), s. of 11th earl of Pembroke; secretary at war, 1845–6 and 1852–5; secretary for war, 1859–61.

[2] He soon resigned. See p. 290, n. 1.

[3] Lord Stanmore, *Memoir of Sidney Herbert*, ii. 68.

[4] See below, pp. 297–8.   [5] Hodder, iii. 43.   [6] Ashley, i. 362.

'those who cannot sway the intelligent and the possessors of property, and who think that they could wield for their own advantage the lower classes whom they want to . . . let in to vote.'[1] Palmerston told the queen that he 'would give much to discover some qualification which would admit some of the best and most intelligent of the working classes'. He considered franchises based upon savings-bank deposits or rates of wages. His failure to make any definite proposal irritated his more radical supporters without satisfying the conservatives. He might have diverted attention by bringing forward a programme of administrative reform. Here again he was not troubled by doctrine. He was ready to consider matters submitted to him; admission to the civil service by examination, cheaper divorce, improved facilities for trying testamentary cases. Yet he had no notion of the immense range of activity open to his party. Seven years later, before the opening of parliament in 1864, Palmerston was asked what reference should be made in the queen's speech to 'domestic affairs and legislation'. He answered, 'rubbing his hands with an air of comfortable satisfaction, "Oh, there is really nothing to be done. We cannot go on adding to the Statute Book *ad infinitum*. Perhaps we may have a little law reform, or bankruptcy reform; but we cannot go on legislating for ever." '[2] Disraeli might have taken advantage of the situation if he had been at the head of an obedient party. He had long thought of important changes in the machinery of government; a ministry of education, a ministry of trade, navigation, and public works. The conservative party as a whole was on Palmerston's side in thinking that there was 'really nothing to be done', and Disraeli was only the leader in the commons. A large, though miscellaneous, section of the conservatives disliked him, and the official chief was difficult to move. A conservative who spent a week as Derby's fellow-guest wrote that 'as a leader of a party he is more hopeless than ever—devoted to whist, billiards, racing, betting. . . . Bulwer Lytton came . . . for three days, and was in despair. Not one word could he extract from Derby about public affairs; nothing but the odds and tricks.'[3]

Palmerston's government, apparently so strong because opposition to it was so weak, fell in a curious way. The prime minister, who had used in his time the most high-handed

[1] P. Guedalla, *Palmerston*, p. 394.
[2] A. D. Elliot, *Life of Lord Goschen*, i. 65.   [3] Buckle, iv. 59.

language to foreign Powers, was accused of unpatriotic deference to French public opinion. In January 1858 an Italian revolutionary, Felice Orsini, nearly succeeded in killing Napoleon III. Orsini had arranged his plot in London and obtained his bombs from Birmingham. There was an outburst of feeling in France when these facts became known, and a number of army officers presented an address to Napoleon in which they delivered a severe and almost threatening lecture to the British government. Napoleon also sent an official protest, but at the same time let it be known privately that he was taking this step against his will. Palmerston introduced a bill amending the law of conspiracy in order to prevent the misuse of English hospitality by foreign refugees plotting assassination. Palmerston and Napoleon behaved with good sense; the parliamentary opposition took a line which, at other times, they could not denounce too strongly. Bright and others spoke of England as an oasis in a desert of tyranny, and of the 'disgrace' of 'truckling to France'. The government was beaten by 234 votes to 215. Palmerston might well have held out against resignation, but he refused to try a vote of confidence.

Once more Derby, as the leader of the largest section of the opposition, was asked to form a government. He could not refuse a second time, though he had not the personal following which Palmerston could command. His cabinet was less obscure than the ministry of 1852; Greville thought it, on the whole, 'a more decent-looking affair than anybody expected'.[1] In any case, the country was tired of the 'old worn-out materials'; but the change of government did not bring with it any clearer alignment of parties or announcement of policy. Gladstone, who was again offered a place in the conservative cabinet, wrote explicitly: 'Perhaps I differed more from Lord Palmerston than from almost any one, and this was more on account of his temper and views of public conduct, than of any political opinions. Nay more, it would be hard to show broad differences of public principle between the government and the bench opposite.'[2] A general agreement on matters of principle did not lessen the violence of personal feeling. An observer of one of the debates wrote, many years later: 'I have never seen anything approaching the ... resentment which was shewn ... not only in the House, but

---

[1] Greville, *Journal of the reign of Queen Victoria*, 27 Feb., 1858.
[2] Morley, i. 584-5.

in society. Wherever you went, nothing else was spoken of. Language almost transgressing the bounds of decency was used, and it seemed at one time as if men would have come to blows.'[1] The government made tempers worse by threatening a dissolution which would have given members the expense of a second general election within some twelve months.

The opposition was also divided. Russell and Palmerston were on terms of polite disagreement. The radicals would not accept the leadership of Palmerston. The high whigs still believed in their own divine right to govern the country. Sidney Herbert wrote that Russell and the whigs were 'incurable in their superstitions about ducal houses. I see no prospect of the formation of an efficient party, let alone Government, out of the chaos on the Opposition benches. No one reigns over or in it, but discord and antipathy. The aristocratic Whigs seem to be nearly used up, and the party produces no new men, but at the same time complains of the old ones. Middle-aged merchants, shrewd men of business, feel their vanity hurt that they have not the refusal of office.'[2] Disraeli wanted his party to take up the question of electoral reform. There was much to be said for refusing to let the opposition gain the credit for a measure which seemed inevitable. On the other hand the conservatives were afraid that they might be forced to go too far in concessions. It was difficult to find any line of demarcation short of household suffrage to which the term 'finality' could be applied. Some members of the cabinet thought that, if the qualification for the franchise were lowered, there would soon be an 'ugly rush' to cross the boundary separating voters from non-voters. Disraeli at last persuaded his colleagues to accept a reduction of the county occupation franchise from £50 to the borough figure of £10, the creation of special franchises which would give votes to the 'upper working class', and a redistribution of fifteen seats in favour of large unrepresented towns and in thickly populated county areas (the West Riding, South Lancashire, and Middlesex). At the same time the measure deprived certain freeholders in boroughs of their right to vote in the county constituences.

Gladstone supported the bill; radicals opposed it because it

[1] Buckle, iv. 145–6, quoting Sir W. Fraser, *Disraeli and his Day*, pp. 252–4. Fraser adds: 'The Derby intervened: this breathing-space gave a little time to cool; but the fury was renewed afterwards.' One of Lord Derby's horses was the favourite, but did not win the race.

[2] Stanmore, ii. 165.

did not touch the boroughs and therefore included few working men. The special qualifications, though they were borrowed by Disraeli from earlier whig proposals, were ridiculed as 'fancy franchises'. Palmerston agreed with the main principles of the bill, but he joined Russell in turning out the ministry on a motion to lower the borough qualification. On 31 March 1859 the government was beaten by thirty-nine votes. The house of commons had now overthrown two ministries, and a dissolution was not unreasonable. The general election increased the conservative strength by some thirty votes—ten less than they needed for an absolute majority. Disraeli made another approach to Palmerston, but Palmerston had the game in his hands. On 10 June the ministers were defeated by thirteen votes on a motion of confidence. The new government, without much enthusiasm, introduced a bill establishing a £10 (rating) occupation franchise for the counties, and lowering the borough franchise to £6 (rental value). The bill was withdrawn on 11 June 1860. Bright almost alone among the party leaders made any serious complaint later about broken pledges.

The last administration of Lord Palmerston was an interlude before the resumption of clear-cut party divisions. The reconciliation of Palmerston and Russell settled the composition of the cabinet. After Derby's resignation the queen, who did not want either of the elder statesmen, and distrusted, or rather detested, their foreign policy, sent for Granville. Granville could do nothing because he found that Palmerston implicitly, and Russell explicitly, claimed the leadership of the commons; neither would take a third place. Palmerston therefore became prime minister, and offered Russell his choice of offices. Russell chose the foreign secretaryship, and, at the first cabinet meeting, Palmerston showed his usual flair. Russell took a seat at the far end of the table. Palmerston called to him, 'Johnnie, you will find that place very cold. You had better come up here.' Palmerston was still popular in the country. His great physical vigour concealed from the public the drawbacks of failing sight and hearing; his good humour and common sense were untouched by age, and his freedom from the moral torments which affected Gladstone made it easier for him to endure the strain of public business. The conservatives were ready to give him the tolerance and even the support which they would never give to Russell.

His cabinet reassured high conservative opinion. It contained three dukes, and the brother of a fourth, five other peers or sons of peers, three baronets of respectable standing and landed property, and only three men without titles.

Gladstone[1] was one of the commoners in this ministry which depended partly upon radical support. Gladstone's acceptance of office in 1859 was the decisive moment in his public career. Hitherto this career had been remarkable, but, from a parliamentary standpoint, dangerously near to failure. Herbert feared in 1857 that Gladstone was 'a *lost man* . . . he has no judgement, and does not seem to understand the purport or value of his own acts'. Gladstone later spoke of himself as having been 'outside the regular party organization' and 'mischievous in an isolated position'. He was now in his fiftieth year. He had sat in parliament since 1833, and had held office of cabinet rank as early as 1843. His first speech of importance in the house had been a defence of the treatment of slaves on his father's Demerara plantations. In 1834 he opposed Hume's proposal for the admission of dissenters to the universities. In 1838 he published a work on *The State in its relations with the Church,* in which he argued in favour of maintaining the Irish church establishment, and upheld the view that the English state recognized as among its duties the support of religious truth, as embodied in a particular church, against religious error. In the following year he opposed an increase in the parliamentary grant for education because the grant was distributed to all religious denominations. It has been said that Gladstone's life was spent in unlearning the prejudices in which he was educated. The judgement is only half true. His education was of the conventional kind which a rich merchant was likely to choose for his son: Eton, under Keate, and Christ Church. The classical discipline of Oxford shaped his mind, though he also gained from his mathematical studies, and was affected as much by Dante as by Homer. He told Sir Francis Doyle in 1880 that his four teachers had been Aristotle, St. Augustine, Dante, and Butler. Neither at Eton nor at Oxford was there much encouragement to study the second and third of these masters. Gladstone, however, read more widely than

[1] William Ewart Gladstone (1809–98); b. Liverpool, of Scottish descent; under-secretary for war and the colonies, 1835; vice-president of the board of trade, 1841; president, 1843; secretary for war and the colonies 1845; chancellor of the exchequer, 1852–5 and 1859–66; high commissioner in the Ionian islands, 1858–9: prime minister, 1868–74, 1880–5, 1886, and 1892–4.

most undergraduates of today. At school, in a single year, this reading included Molière and Racine, Fielding, Ben Jonson, Locke, Massinger, Milton, Burke, and Clarendon. His religious development at Oxford was due more to his own reading than to his surroundings. Eton under Keate, and Christ Church in 1829, were not ideal places for the cultivation of personal religion. Gladstone wanted at one time to take holy orders, but his 'first conception of unity in the church' came to him on a visit to Rome.

From first to last Gladstone combined in a curious but not illogical way a deep conservatism with an equally fundamental desire for improvement. He respected antiquity and old usages, and, like his political master, Peel, did not wish for change unless change were the only alternative to mischief or injustice. He could always find reasons for maintaining anomalies; as late as 1859 he defended rotten boroughs as 'nurseries of statesmen'. He disliked Disraeli because he thought that Disraeli had no respect for authority in secular or spiritual matters. On the other hand, he belonged, like Peel, to the new conservatism. He came from the mercantile class which had attained its position by a struggle, and had not the easy traditions of the landed aristocracy.[1] He took politics as seriously as the manufacturers and merchants applied themselves to business; he felt the responsibilities of political life more keenly because a political career was not, as with Palmerston or Melbourne, the accepted consequence of the station into which he was born. This sense of responsibility and passion for improvement appear in his most illiberal period. Thus, after a defence of the West Indian interest in 1838, he noted in his diary: 'Now is the time to turn this attack into measures of benefit for the negroes.'[2] His views about the church must be looked at from the same point of view. Gladstone himself considered, more than fifty years afterwards, that he had written his book on church and state 'in total disregard, or rather ignorance, of the conditions under which alone political action was possible in matters of religion', and that 'Oxford had not taught me, nor had any other place or person, the value of liberty as an essential condition of excellence in human things'.

[1] About this time Clarendon told Lady Burghclere that Palmerston had said that Gladstone 'might be called one of the people; he wished to identify himself with them; he possessed religious enthusiasm, and made it powerful over others from the force of his own intellect'. Lady Burghclere, *A Great Man's Friendships*, p. 33.

[2] Morley, i. 147.

He added that he had published his book because he had noted 'the many symptoms of revival and reform' within the church of England, and 'dreamed that she was capable of recovering lost ground, and of bringing back the nation to unity in her communion'.[1] He learned from experience; in 1843 he had already discovered that 'the idea of Christian politics cannot be realized in the State according to its present conditions of existence'.

If Gladstone came to realize that his theory of society, and the political consequences which he drew from this theory, differed from the facts of English society and English politics, the condition of England also changed to a remarkable degree during his long parliamentary life. The anti-religious liberalism which he opposed in his early career was very far removed from the liberalism which he adopted in later years. Gladstone, like Bismarck, was fortunate in the circumstances which delayed his rise to power, and gave him time to test his own ideas. Gladstone's financial work was perhaps greater than that of any other minister in the nineteenth century; yet he had not wanted the vice-presidency of the board of trade in 1841. 'I was totally ignorant both of political economy and of the commerce of the country. . . . In a spirit of ignorant mortification I said to myself at the moment: the science of politics deals with the government of men, but I am set to govern packages.'[2] Nothing could have been better as a training for a financial reformer. Similarly, the business of setting his brother-in-law's Staffordshire property in order during the years 1847–9 gave him experience of value in understanding the working of a large industrial concern. The split in the conservative party over the repeal of the corn laws was another advantage to Gladstone. He broke with the party on a question of major importance. Henceforward the problem was not one of leaving conservatism but of returning to it. The uncertain position of the Peelites was an inconvenience in public affairs, since it was largely responsible for the disarray of parties, but, from Gladstone's point of view, this freedom from close allegiance gave him the liberty of decision which he needed.

Thus Gladstone's decision in 1859 was an honest expression of his convictions. Palmerston, in his careless, untheoretical way, represented fairly closely the views which Gladstone had reached after long and subtle consideration of principles. A

[1] Ibid. i. 179–80.   [2] Ibid. i. 244.

cynic might notice that in June 1859, Palmerston was 74 and
Russell 67, while Disraeli was only 54. The highest place would
be vacant in the liberal party sooner than on the other side. A
Yorkshire member, W. E. Forster, who sat in parliament for the
first time in 1861, noted in 1863 that 'the want of the liberal
party of a new man is great, and felt to be great; the old whig
leaders are worn out; there are no new whigs; Cobden and
Bright are impracticable and un-English, and there are hardly
any hopeful radicals. There is a great prize of power and
influence to be aimed at.'[1] Yet, apart from the fact that if
Gladstone had joined the conservatives he might well have
expected that he, rather than Disraeli, would succeed Derby,
there is no reason to doubt his sincerity in supporting Palmerston. Once again circumstances were in his favour. Although
he distrusted Palmerston's general conduct of foreign policy he
was sure in 1859 that Palmerston and Russell would assist the
cause of Italy, which he had long upheld, while Derby and
Disraeli were more likely to take the other side.

At the same time it would be idle to pretend that Gladstone
had no wish for office. He might put the case impersonally:
'I felt sure that in finance there was still much useful work to be
done', but he knew his own powers. This belief in his providen-
tial mission led him to misjudge other men, particularly Disraeli,
and to assume that those who did not possess his convictions
were adventurers whose opposition could be described as 'malignant'. Nevertheless he was right in thinking that his support
was of the greatest value to Palmerston's government. The
prime minister's best years of work were now over. Gladstone
had the physical as well as the mental strength necessary for
carrying on public business. From his tenth to his forty-fifth year
he was only once ill in bed for more than eight or nine days; he
could work for fourteen hours a day over long periods of time,
and compress into an hour business which took most men twice
or three times as long to complete. His marriage was intensely
happy, and the peace of his domestic life was an ideal counterpart to his incessant public activity. The conditions of English
parliamentary life suited his genius. As a speaker he was un-
surpassed. His fine physical presence, his leonine head and
eyes, put him above all his contemporaries. Even in old age he

[1] Sir T. W. Reid, *Life of W. E. Forster*, i. 362. Forster was writing two years
after the death of Sidney Herbert.

did not mind whether he was addressing an audience of four hundred or four thousand people. His control of long, inter-locked sentences and periods saved him, in moments of passion, from losing himself in unwary or disconnected thought. This power over words was responsible for his worst failing: a tor-tuous mode of expression which at times conveyed nothing to his hearers. His habit of theological disputation and his Oxford training gave him something of the tractarian fallacy that words must be taken, not in their plain meaning or current associa-tions, but in their subtlest implications; that the listener must apply the principle of *caveat emptor*, and be on his guard lest he miss these implications. It would be unfair to accuse Gladstone of deliberate mental reservation; from the point of view of the ordinary man, the reservations were there, hidden behind a cloud of qualifying phrases. In May 1864 Gladstone was speak-ing on the second reading of a private member's bill, opposed by the government, for the extension of the borough franchise to £6 occupiers. Palmerston had warned Gladstone not to make any promise on behalf of the cabinet; Gladstone spoke, accord-ing to instructions, against any 'sudden and sweeping measure'. Then he explained that the present condition of the franchise was unsatisfactory, and concluded: 'I call upon the adversary to shew cause, and I venture to say that every man who is not presumably incapacitated by some consideration of personal unfitness or of political danger, is morally entitled to come with-in the pale of the constitution.[1] Of course, in giving utterance to such a proposition, I do not recede from the protest I have ... made against sudden, or violent, or excessive, or intoxicating change.' Gladstone's conclusion outweighed his qualifications; opinion at large took him to mean that he supported household suffrage. Tories and radicals understood the speech in this sense. Disraeli described it as a revival of the doctrine of Tom Paine. The speech gave Gladstone the succession to the leader-ship of the liberal party after Palmerston and Russell, and ulti-mately won him Lancashire. The prime minister sent him a friendly remonstrance, pointing out that every man was already 'within the pale of the constitution'. Gladstone was 'at a loss'

[1] Oddly enough, almost the same phrase had been used by Stanley in an article in the *Press* (Nov. 1853) suggesting that the government should bring 'within the pale of the constitution everyone whose admission cannot be proved danger-ous'. Disraeli had not seen the phrase before it appeared in print, and dropped it at once. Buckle, iv. 403.

to understand the excitement. His words required 'to be construed'.[1] He wrote to his brother: 'It would have been quite as intelligible to me had people said, "Under the exceptions of personal unfitness and political danger you exclude or may exclude almost everybody, and you reduce your declaration to a shadow".'[2]

The duration of the ministry thus depended largely upon Palmerston's skill in handling men. He judged them with his old verve. Russell was 'a strange compound of talent and foolishness'.[3] Gladstone was more difficult. He spoke of Palmerston's weakness in the cabinet, and of his 'low standard for all public conduct'. The two men agreed, broadly, on the Italian question. They disagreed in their attitude towards questions of national defence. Palmerston had taken office at one of the many periods of alarm in England over the plans of Napoleon III. The volunteer movement of 1859, to which Palmerston supplied rifles and Tennyson a patriotic poem,[4] was an effort to strengthen the force available for home defence. The interest of the French people in the building of ironclads[5] and construction of the Suez canal seemed to show a revival of anti-English designs. Napoleon's acquisition of Nice and Savoy added to these fears. Palmerston had opposed the project of a Suez canal. At first he thought it impracticable; when the facts showed that the opinions of earlier engineers were wrong, Palmerston's view was that the canal would set 'a French colony in the heart of Egypt', threaten India, and cut off the sultan's armies from access to the Nile. Palmerston assumed that the scheme was a cunning French plot. He believed that 'we have on the other side of the channel a people who, say what they may, hate us as a nation from the bottom of their hearts, and would make any sacrifice to inflict a deep humiliation upon England. . . . At the head of this nation we see an able, active, wary, counsel-keeping, but ever-planning sovereign.'[6] The

---

[1] Morley, ii. 129.
[2] Id., ii. 130.   [3] Bell, ii. 233.
[4] 'Riflemen, form!' The defence movement, in which the queen and the prince consort were greatly interested, led to a change in social habit noticed by Bright: 'The Court seems now to find its chief occupation in connexion with military affairs—Reviews in Hyde Park—Reviews at Aldershot—Shooting matches at Wimbledon—occupations which for a long time have been foreign to the English Court.' S. Buxton, *Finance and Politics*, i. 177.   [5] See below, p. 293.
[6] Guedalla, pp. 207-8. One of the plans was the extension of the fortified naval base at Cherbourg.

dockyards and arsenals of England were unprotected from attack; a royal commission on national defence, appointed in 1859, recommended the expenditure of £11,000,000 on coastal fortifications. Palmerston favoured the plan, and wanted also to build more wooden ships. Gladstone distrusted Napoleon, but did not reckon upon any immediate danger; hence there was time for experiments in armour-plated ships. Palmerston suggested a loan for the fortifications; Gladstone said that the figure was too high, and that, in any case, the cost should be met out of revenue. Gladstone agreed with Cobden that an Anglo-French commercial treaty would be the best means of ending the panic about Napoleon's intentions; Palmerston thought that the terms of the treaty negotiated by Cobden in 1860 were unfavourable to England,[1] and that the conclusion of any treaty weakened the case for the armaments which he believed necessary.

Gladstone's budget of 1860 aggravated the dispute. The budget reduced the tariff to such an extent that only sixteen articles continued to make an important contribution to the revenue. There was little disagreement about this reduction, but Gladstone also proposed to abolish the excise duty on paper, at a cost of £1,250,000, or the equivalent of a penny in income tax. Palmerston held that Gladstone was sacrificing money needed for national defence to the demands of advanced liberals and radicals for cheap newspapers.[2] The house of lords threw out the proposals on the dangerous ground that they could oppose the repeal of a tax. Gladstone wanted to fight the lords on the question; Palmerston, with the support of the cabinet, refused to begin a troublesome dispute between the two houses over a question in which he agreed with the lords. He told the queen that the peers would 'perform a good public service' if they rejected the bill.[3] Gladstone had to accept a compromise

[1] The French manufacturers took an opposite view. Cobden described the iron-masters as 'the landed interest of France. . . the praetorian guards of monopoly' (Morley, *Cobden*, ii. 294). The treaty reduced French duties on coal and most English manufactured goods to rates not exceeding 30 per cent.: Great Britain lowered the duties upon French wines and brandy. The value of British exports to France more than doubled between 1859 and 1869, and the increase was mainly in manufactured goods. The imports of French wines also doubled. The treaty survived the protectionist views of the Third Republic for ten years. See A. L. Dunham, *The Anglo-French Treaty of Commerce of 1860.*

[2] Palmerston could argue that concessions had already been made. Thus the tax on newspaper advertisements had been abolished in 1853, and the stamp duty in 1855. Gladstone was concerned as much with lowering the price of books. See also p. 623.   [3] Martin, *Life of the Prince Consort*, v. 100.

over the fortifications, but the left wing of Palmerston's supporters also disliked spending large sums on armaments. Before the meeting of parliament in 1861 sixty members of parliament signed a petition for a reduction in this expenditure; Cobden and Bright even offered their support to the conservatives at the price of a franchise reform bill.

Palmerston and Gladstone continued to quarrel about fortifications. Three times Gladstone threatened to resign, while Palmerston made it clear that if the commons rejected the budget the responsibility lay not with the cabinet but with the chancellor of the exchequer; he disapproved of Gladstone's new plan of putting all his financial proposals into one bill in order to prevent the lords from interfering with the repeal of the paper duty. Palmerston now began to negotiate for the support of the conservatives, but the budget resolutions were passed by fifteen votes, and the prime minister persuaded the house to agree to his programme of naval construction and the completion of his forts.[1]

After the budget of 1861 there was less reason for differences of opinion in the cabinet about taxation. The public was less nervous about French aggression, and the most dangerous gaps in the national defences had been filled. National expenditure had risen from £55,800,000 in 1853 to £72,840,000 in 1860, excluding the fortifications loan, but the increase was due mainly to the greater cost of the naval and military services. In 1862 expenditure fell to £69,250,000; the estimates for 1863 were £67,750,000. Civil expenditure remained almost constant during Palmerston's administration, and the revenue responded favourably to the free-trade measures of 1860. Each year gave a surplus, and allowed new remissions of taxation.

Gladstone now had to decide what to do with the income tax.

[1] Gladstone's insistence upon economy and precision in war office finance could lead to unfortunate results. Herbert, as secretary for war, wanted to carry out the recommendations of the sanitary committee (appointed after the Crimean war) with regard to defective and unhealthy barracks. He proposed to sell these barracks and apply the proceeds of the sale to supplement grants made for new barracks. Gladstone argued that the money should be paid into the consolidated fund. Thus the whole cost of new barracks would have to be met by new grants. It was less easy to obtain new grants from parliament than to secure an appropriation from sums already voted. Under Gladstone's chancellorship every grant for barracks meant a fight with the treasury and, as it was hard enough to find money for defence works, the improvements in barracks were postponed and soldiers were still housed in barracks—including those at Windsor—where there was a high death-rate from typhoid fever. See also below, pp. 266 and 292.

He had changed his views about this tax since 1853. Although he still disliked it, he had come to see that there was little chance of getting rid of it. He said in his budget speech of 1861 that 'if the country is content to be governed at a cost of between £60,000,000 and £62,000,000 a year, there is not any reason why it should not be so governed without the income tax. . . . If, on the other hand, it is the pleasure of the country to be governed at a cost of between £70,000,000 and £75,000,000 a year, it must . . . be so governed with the aid of a considerable income tax.' Gladstone's estimate was midway between these figures; he could not do without an income tax; at the same time he believed that the rate of the tax need not be high. In 1863 he reduced it from 9d. to 7d. In 1853 he had brought the limit of total exemption, fixed by Peel at £150, to £100, on the ground that tax-payers of small incomes had already gained from the remission of indirect taxation; incomes between £100 and £150 were charged at a lower rate. Gladstone now raised the limit of abatement to £200. In 1864 he felt safe in laying down, for the second time, a future policy in relation to income tax, though he was too cautious to give any pledge. He suggested that 5d. might be a reasonable rate; on this basis the tax would bring in about £6,000,000. In 1865 it was possible to take off another penny, and to continue the reduction of customs duties. In 1863 Gladstone lowered the duty on tea, and in 1864 the duty on sugar;[1] in 1865 he cut down the tea duty from 1s. to 6d. a pound.

A chancellor of the exchequer who could show annual reductions in direct and indirect taxation for three successive years was a valuable source of strength to a government which was being attacked for the mistakes of its foreign policy.[2] Palmerston was still uneasy about Gladstone's impulsiveness, and doubtful about the results of his increasing popularity, but Gladstone's finance as well as Palmerston's hold on the middle class secured the return of the last Palmerstonian majority in the general election of 1865.

Within three months of the election, Palmerston died (18 October 1865). Some time before his death he had said to Shaftesbury: 'Gladstone will soon have it all his own way, and,

[1] The average consumption of sugar per head, after remaining fairly constant during the years 1816–42, had more than doubled by 1862, and was nearly double again by 1882. For tea, see below, p. 623, n. 1.   [2] See below, p. 323.

whenever he gets my place, we shall have strange doings.'[1] It is significant that in the general election, after defeat at Oxford, Gladstone turned to South Lancashire; his first words in his new constituency were: 'At last, my friends, I am come among you, and I am come among you "unmuzzled".'

After the death of Palmerston it was assumed that the cabinet would try to settle the question of electoral reform. Russell, who became prime minister, wanted to give his name to a second reform bill. He was in his seventy-fourth year, and could not wait for another general election. Moreover, although reform was not the main issue at the election of 1865, the question had been before the country for many years. There was general agreement that an extension of the franchise, and a considerable redistribution of seats, had been postponed too long. The facts were striking. In 1865 the adult male population of England and Wales was over five millions; the number of voters was under one million. The distribution of the population had changed since 1832, but there had been no change in the distribution of seats.[2] Cornwall returned as many members as Middlesex and the metropolitan boroughs north of the Thames. One half of the borough population of England and Wales had 34 and the other half 300 seats.

Russell's cabinet decided to deal with the franchise before they touched the question of redistribution. It had been suggested that every municipal voter, in other words every ratepaying householder, should have a parliamentary vote. Some members of the cabinet thought this extension too wide; others thought it too narrow, owing to the character of the residential qualification for municipal voting. There was also the technical difficulty about householders who compounded with their landlords for the payment of rates. The practice of compounding was not uniform throughout the country. If the 'compound householder' were excluded, there would be little change in Sheffield, while the working class in Birmingham, where compounding was general, would be shut out from the provisions of the new bill. The cabinet considered other proposals. An

[1] Hodder, iii. 187.
[2] Sudbury had been disfranchised for corruption in 1844, and St. Albans in 1852; one of the four seats was given in 1861 to Birkenhead, two to the West Riding of Yorkshire, and one to South Lancashire.

extension of the borough franchise to householders of £6 rental would add about 240,000 working-class electors, and give the working-class voters an overall majority in the urban constituencies. If the line were drawn at the £7 householder, the increase would be about 145,000. The abolition of a rate-paying qualification, and a franchise for lodgers, would add 60,000 more working men. An extension of the county franchise to householders, or householders with land, rented from £14 to £50, would add another 170,000 voters, mainly from the middle class.

A £7 line in the towns and the £14 occupier in the counties formed the basis of the franchise bill. There was little support for the proposals in the house. The conservatives opposed them; Cranborne[1] thought that the American civil war had shown the incapacity of a democratic government to deal justly with the claims of minorities.[2] He disbelieved in the right of every man to an equal share of political power, and drew an analogy from the procedure of joint-stock companies. 'The wildest dreamer never suggested that all the shareholders should each have a single vote, without reference to the number of shares they might hold.'[3] Disraeli was more cautious; he criticized the arrangements of the bill, and spoke in clouded language of the place of the working-class voter in the constitution. The strongest opposition came from dissentient liberals. Horsman, who had been chief secretary for Ireland in Palmerston's first

[1] Robert Arthur Talbot Gascoyne-Cecil (1830–1903), 2nd s. of the 2nd marquess of Salisbury, became Lord Cranborne on the death of his elder brother in 1865; succeeded his father, 1868; b. Hatfield; educ. Eton and Christ Church, Oxford; M.P., 1853; secretary for India, 1866–7 and 1874–8; foreign secretary, 1878–80; prime minister, 1885–6, 1886–92, 1895–1902.

[2] *Quarterly Review*, July 1861. The reformers, however, took the victory of the north over the 'aristocratic' south as an encouragement. Some of them also regarded the willingness of the Lancashire cotton operatives to make sacrifices for the anti-slavery cause as evidence that the working class was more open than other classes to 'great disinterested ideas'. R. H. Hutton, editor of *The Spectator*, in a curious inversion of the theory of a class war, wrote that the enfranchisement of trade unionists might be a 'diversion of some of (their) high *esprit de corps* from the narrow organisation of the Trade Society into the wider organisation of the nation ... only the working class have got a clear conception of how much individuals owe, by way of self-sacrifice, to the larger social organisation to which they belong' (*Essays on Reform* (1867), pp. 37–38).

[3] Lady Gwendolen Cecil, *Life of Salisbury*, i. 152–3. Salisbury realized that the state was not a joint-stock company, but he argued that the Manchester school and the radicals thought of it in these terms. 'They are estopped by their own philosophy from appealing to the loftier views of it which have descended from less business-like times.'

administration, Lowe,[1] whose residence in Australia had made him distrust democracy, and Lord Grosvenor (later duke of Westminster) refused to follow the government.[2] In June the opposition carried an amendment that the rateable value and not the annual rent of a house should be taken as the basis of the borough franchise. As the rateable value was generally lower than the rent, the change would have lessened the number of new voters.[3] The ministers had decided not to consider the amendment as a vital question, but the debate ranged over the whole of their proposals. A general election would bring to light the divisions within their ranks; hence they resigned, and once more Derby took office without a conservative majority in the house.[4]

Meanwhile the meetings held by the reformers and the debates in the house had produced a good deal of excitement. The attack on the legal position of trade unions[5] made the leaders of the working class realize the importance of direct representation in parliament, and the economic crisis of 1866[6] revived the almost forgotten agitation against aristocratic misgovernment. A large meeting was organized for 23 July in Hyde Park. The law officers of the Crown told the new ministers that if they wished to prohibit the holding of a meeting in the park they must post notices to this effect, and deal with offenders as trespassers. The cabinet decided to close the park on the day of the meeting. The leaders of the demonstration brought their processions to the gates, and withdrew after asserting the right of public meeting, but the crowd pushed against the railings. The railings collapsed at one point, and were knocked down over the length of some 1,400 yards. This disturbance near the houses of the wealthier classes convinced conservative opinion that electoral reform could not be delayed.

The conservatives adopted a rating and not a rental qualification for the franchise. During their discussions Derby suggested, a little vaguely, that 'of all possible hares to start' he did not 'know a better than the extension to household suffrage, coupled

---

[1] See below, p. 481.

[2] Bright described their defection as a retirement into a 'political "cave of Adullum"'. Lincoln had used the analogy two years earlier.

[3] i.e. most occupiers rated at £7 paid at least £8 in rent.

[4] The cabinet resigned during the week of the outbreak of the Austro-Prussian war. The queen, who wanted a reform bill to be carried by agreement between the two parties, was at first unwilling to accept Russell's resignation.

[5] See below, p. 615.

[6] See below, pp. 605-6.

with plurality of voting'.[1] From this time the ministers made rapid changes in their position. They were not putting into effect a plan which they had thought out before taking office. Disraeli, who was the leader of his party in the commons, cared little for consistency in detail. He wanted a lasting settlement, and thought that household suffrage, based upon rating, and balanced by suitable safeguards, would be popular, logical, and final. Derby and Disraeli assumed that the plural voters, a number of special franchises and the exclusion of the 'compound householder' would limit the effects of household suffrage. Once, however, they had declared in favour of household suffrage in any form, they could not go back upon their declaration. Their safeguards disappeared, and left them with a measure far more radical than the bill which they had thrown out.

The ministers were not agreed about details before the meeting of parliament in February 1867, but the queen's speech referred in general terms to the state of the representation of the people. General Peel, secretary for war, threatened to resign if his colleagues accepted household suffrage, even with plural voting and a rating basis. Disraeli announced, six days later, that the government intended to increase the representation of the labouring class without giving them a majority; it would be contrary to the constitution to allow any class a predominance. 'The principle of plurality of votes, if adopted by parliament, would facilitate the settlement of the borough franchise.'

The opposition asked for more information. Disraeli could not tell them anything more because the matter was still under discussion in the cabinet. Meanwhile Peel again talked of resigning, although Disraeli suggested a £5 rating basis for the

---

[1] Buckle, iv. 484. In Jan. 1853 Edward Stanley wrote to Disraeli that Malmesbury had said to him that, if the conservatives adopted a franchise reform programme, they ought not to stop at a £5 qualification; the five-pounders were democratic, but the labourers conservative; therefore 'if we must go as low as £5, he (Malmesbury) would rather go on to universal suffrage' (W. D. Jones, *Lord Derby and Victorian Conservatism*, p. 193). An article in the *Quarterly Review* of 1869 summed up this judgement: 'The phantom of a Conservative democracy was a reality to many men of undoubted independence and vigour of mind. A vague idea that the poorer men are the more they are influenced by the rich: a notion that those whose vocation it was to bargain and battle with the middle class must on that account love the gentry: an impression . . . that the ruder class of minds would be more sensitive to traditional emotions . . . all these arguments . . . went to make up the clear conviction of the mass of the Conservative party that in a Reform Bill more radical than that of the Whigs they had discovered the secret of a sure and signal triumph' (quoted, ibid., p. 300).

borough franchise. The queen wrote to Peel. He gave way, and with his surrender the £5 limit also vanished. The cabinet had reached household suffrage, based upon residence and personal payment of rates. They proposed to enfranchise persons with certain educational qualifications, or owning £50 in the savings bank. Householders paying £1 a year in direct taxation would get a second vote. At a cabinet meeting on 23 February Disraeli convinced his colleagues that these safeguards were enough. Cranborne and Carnarvon, studying the figures over the week-end, came to the conclusion that the statistics told a different story if they were examined in detail; the safeguards were illusory, and the working class would be in a majority in three-fifths of the boroughs. Cranborne pointed out 'the error of attempting to frame a Reform Bill during the week previous to its production',[1] and made it clear that he intended to resign. His letter, written on Sunday evening, reached Derby on Monday morning. Derby sent it at once to Disraeli. The cabinet could not be called together until half-past one. There was a party meeting at half-past two; at half-past four Disraeli had to explain the proposals to the house.[2] After ten minutes' deliberation[3] the cabinet decided to go back to a modified form of the plan which had been brought forward to satisfy Peel. Disraeli therefore announced to the house that the borough franchise would extend to householders of £6 rating, and the county franchise to householders of £20 rating. The 'fancy franchises' were maintained; plural voting was given up.

The conservatives themselves brought about the next stage in the surrender. A majority of conservative members favoured the scheme which Disraeli had abandoned to satisfy Cranborne, Carnarvon, and Peel. On 1 March Malmesbury wrote to Derby that he had 'always preferred household suffrage (properly counterpoised) to any halfway resting-place'.[4] He thought that the country was of the same opinion. Next day the cabinet took the decisive step; Cranborne, Carnarvon, and Peel resigned, and the ministers who remained, believing that at last they had reached 'finality', sat down to draft their bill. Their 'counter-

[1] Cecil, i. 232.

[2] It is interesting to speculate whether the course of the bill would have been different if ministers had been able to hold telephone conversations.

[3] Sir John Pakington revealed the circumstances of the change of plan in a speech a few days later. Hence the name 'the ten minutes' bill'.

[4] Buckle iv. 511.

poises' to general household suffrage in the boroughs were the 'fancy franchises', including the second vote for householders paying £1 a year in direct taxation, the personal payment of rates, and two years' residential qualification. They reduced the county occupation franchise to a £15 rating limit. Their redistribution clauses gave fifteen seats to counties, fourteen to boroughs, and one to the university of London. Gladstone at once attacked the dual vote and the redistribution clauses. He thought that the bill would enfranchise only 140,000 people, and pointed out the difficulty of dealing with the compound householder. He proposed a limit of £5 rating in boroughs.[1] Disraeli gave up the dual vote, and, after the Easter recess, surrendered on the question of the compound householder. His plan had allowed these householders special facilities for putting their names on the rate-book.[2] When it was proposed to make all occupiers responsible for the payment of rates, Disraeli had either to abandon the principle of rating as the qualification for the franchise or to accept nearly 500,000 more working-class voters. He accepted the new voters. After this concession the 'fancy franchises' were of less importance. They were struck out. The county occupation franchise was lowered to a £12 limit; the redistribution clauses were expanded to meet the situation created by the increase in the number of voters. One member was taken from boroughs of less than 10,000 inhabitants; forty-five seats were thus at the disposal of parliament. After a debate, magnified by Disraeli, in a letter to the queen, as 'an affair of Inkermann',[3] twenty-five seats were allotted to the counties, fifteen to the towns (mostly new boroughs), a third member to Liverpool, Manchester, Birmingham and Leeds, and a member to the university of London. In this form, with minor amendments, the bill became law on 15 August 1867.

The act of 1867 added 938,000 voters to an electorate of 1,057,000 in England and Wales. In towns working-class voters were in a majority, but most of the new county voters came from the middle class, and the general result was slightly in

---

[1] Some 50 whigs and radicals who disliked Gladstone's plan met in the tea-room of the house of commons; hence the name of 'the tea-room party'.

[2] Disraeli had assured the queen that, in his opinion, not 50,000 compound householders would avail themselves of the facilities. *Q.V.L.* 2nd ser. i. 408. The surrender on the question of the compound householder was told to the queen in a single sentence. Ibid. i. 424.   [3] Ibid. i. 431.

favour of the conservatives. The industrial towns were already on the liberal side, while the middle-class voters in the smaller boroughs and the counties were becoming suspicious of the radical tendencies of the liberal party. The introduction of the ballot in 1872 weakened the power of the landlords, but in spite of the redistribution of seats the small boroughs were still over-represented. Most conservatives were afraid of the increase in the electorate. Carlyle described it, in a pamphlet, as 'Shooting Niagara'; Derby, in a phrase invented by Disraeli, called it 'a leap in the dark'. Even Bright was doubtful about the measure. Between 1867 and 1880 there was little change in the composition of parliament; the working-class voters returned very few working men. The act lessened resistance to popular demands, increased the importance of party organization, and thereby weakened the power of local committees and affected the relations between members and their constituencies.[1] One of the amendments carried by the lords indirectly furthered the development of party organization. This amendment gave voters in three-member constituencies only two votes; the managers of the Birmingham liberal association soon realized that, by careful distribution of votes, three seats could be carried by one party.[2]

From the passing of the reform bill until the spring of 1868 there was a short political interlude. Derby resigned in February 1868 owing to ill health. Disraeli took his place as prime minister.[3] Two months earlier Russell let Gladstone know that he intended to give up his leadership of the liberal party. Gladstone succeeded him, and, for the first time in the nineteenth century, the leaders of the two great parties were men born

---

[1] The act brought to an end the long period of small majorities, though, owing to the absence of strong traditions, or regular political interests, in the new electorate there were quicker changes of opinion. This 'swing of the pendulum' was particularly noticeable in the elections of 1868, 1874, and 1880. During the debates on the bill J. S. Mill suggested the adoption of proportional representation and brought forward a motion for the enfranchisement of women. He was beaten on the latter motion by 196 to 73. Disraeli did not vote.

[2] This manœuvre required a three-fifths majority for one party; every voter on the majority side thus had to be told how to vote. See Lowell, i. 469–71.

[3] Bright wrote of Disraeli's appointment: 'a great triumph of intellect and courage and patience and unscrupulousness employed in the service of a party full of prejudices and selfishness and wanting in brains.' Disraeli himself used different language: 'Yes, I have climbed to the top of the greasy pole.' Buckle, iv. 597 and 600.

after 1800. The personal antagonism of these leaders did much, after long years of confusion, to fix the two-party division which survived the secession of the liberal unionists in 1886.[1]

Disraeli announced that his government proposed to follow a 'truly liberal policy'; these words showed that the confusion of parties had not altogether cleared. Disraeli had to face a parliament, elected to support Palmerston, which had thrown out one reform bill and accepted another of a more drastic kind. A general election could not be long postponed, but the initiative came from Gladstone. Gladstone approached the question of Ireland, which was to become the dominant pre-occupation of his later political career, in a characteristic manner. He told his brother-in-law, Lord Lyttelton, in April 1865 that since the Maynooth grant of 1845 he had seen that 'resistance *in principle* was gone'. The disappearance of 'resistance in principle' did not mean, for Gladstone, the disappearance of resistance in practice. He added: 'I held this embryo opinion in my mind as there was no cause to precipitate it into life, and waited to fortify or alter or invalidate it by the teachings of experience.' In 1865 'the teachings of experience', which a cynic might have called the chance of getting a parliamentary majority, still opposed precipitation. In this year Gladstone voted against a radical motion that the Irish church 'called for the early attention of the government'. In 1866 he agreed with Russell in meeting a similar proposal with a direct negative. 'In meeting a question with a negative, we may always put it on the ground of time, as well as on the merits.' Nevertheless, Gladstone's mind was made up even before Fenianism[2] showed the danger of delay; in 1868 he told Granville that, for years past, he had been 'watching the sky with a strong sense of the obligation to act with the first streak of dawn'.[3]

In March 1868 Gladstone declared that the time had come when the church of Ireland must cease to exist as a church in

---

[1] Before 1868 and after 1886 Gilbert and his collaborator Sullivan could not have introduced into *Iolanthe* (1882) the chorus

> That every boy and every gal
> That's born into the world alive
> Is either a little Liberal
> Or else a little Conservative.

[2] For the Fenian movement, see below, pp. 359–61.

[3] For the change in Gladstone's opinions see Morley, ii. 237–43. For the Irish church bill, see below, pp. 361–2.

alliance with the state. A few weeks later he carried resolutions to this effect through the house. The issue was now clear. Disraeli announced that his government would dissolve in the autumn, when the elections could take place under the new register. The result of the elections disappointed the conservatives. They expected to be given credit for their reform bill; if they had known more of working-class opinion, they would have realized that the working class summed up fairly well the reasons why the conservative party had passed the bill. They hoped for greater support from the church party on the question of the disestablishment of the Irish church, but opinion in the great towns and among the nonconformist middle class was not anglican in sympathy. In any case the liberals, with Gladstone and Bright as the chief orators, undertook a great campaign in the country, while Disraeli, in accordance with older traditions, merely wrote an address to the electors of Buckinghamshire and made one speech after the borough elections were over.

The liberals had a majority of 112 seats. Disraeli resigned without waiting to meet parliament, and Gladstone included in his cabinet representatives of the groups which made up the liberal party: whigs and radicals, reformers and anti-reformers, men as different in opinion as Clarendon, Bright, and Lowe. The first measure brought before the house showed the change in the position of the lords since the days when the peers wrecked Melbourne's legislation. The Irish church bill passed the commons by a majority which Disraeli could reasonably call 'mechanical'. The lords might reject the bill, or introduce changes in its financial provisions which the cabinet would refuse to accept. Gladstone thought that the result of a conflict with the upper house would be unfortunate from a constitutional point of view, and trusted 'the sagacity of the peers themselves with reference to the security and stability of their position in the legislature'. The peers gave way;[1] their surrender was the first conservative defeat in the lords, on a major question of domestic policy and legislation, for twenty years. The Irish church bill took up the greater part of the session of 1869; it was followed by an Irish land bill in the early part of the session of 1870,[2] and an education bill which occupied

___

[1] The queen let Lord Derby and the archbishop of Canterbury know that she was strongly opposed to a collision between the two houses over the bill.
[2] See below, pp. 362-3.

public attention at the time of the outbreak of the Franco-Prussian war.[1]

Gladstone's measures gave the opposition a chance to attack him on issues more important than those of the party warfare of the previous decade. The opportunity was taken, and the conservatives had their reward in the election of 1874. Meanwhile the conservative party was setting its affairs in order. The personal opposition to Disraeli grew weaker, though it never disappeared. The younger generation had not known Disraeli's flamboyant youth; he was now among the elder statesmen, a former prime minister, and a leader in high favour with the queen. Salisbury continued his attacks to such an extent that Disraeli could doubt whether 'Lord Salisbury and myself are on speaking terms', but even this hostility died down. The leadership of the conservative party in the house of lords might have been a difficulty, but, on Derby's death in October 1869, Stanley[2] took his seat in the upper house, and the problem was solved. Disraeli, in the comparative leisure of opposition, returned to novel-writing, after an interval of twenty years, and finished the last chapters of *Lothair* while Gladstone was fighting for the details of his Irish land bill. Disraeli liked to think of himself as standing apart from politics, a detached and at the same time an intimate observer of English ways and English thought. *Lothair*, with its undercurrent of irony and subtle exaggeration,[3] described the last chapter in the reign of the English territorial magnates. The book was written shortly after the appearance of the first volume of Marx's *Capital*; this conjunction of two worlds, the older and more familiar world of caste, and the distant yet more brightly burning vision of a classless society, may be taken as a significant date in the political history of England. Castlereagh and Liverpool, Cobbett and Orator Hunt lived under a different sky, and in the years between

---

[1] See below, pp. 482–3.

[2] Edward Henry Stanley, 15th earl of Derby (1826–93), ed. Rugby and Trinity College, Cambridge; M.P., 1848; offered colonial secretaryship by Palmerston, 1855; colonial secretary, 1858; president of the board of control, 1858, and secretary of state for India, 1858–9; foreign secretary, 1866–8 and 1874–8; joined the liberal party, 1880; colonial secretary, 1882–5; became a liberal unionist, 1886. In 1862–3 the Greeks considered offering Stanley the throne of Greece.

[3] Disraeli wrote of the duke who is the magnate if not the hero of the book: 'Every day when he looked into the glass, and gave the last touch to his consummate toilette, he offered his grateful thanks to Providence that his family were not unworthy of him.'

1815 and 1870 'pig-tail' and 'cannon-ball' tories, Spencean philanthropists, philosophic radicals, radical reformers, Canningites, Peelites, chartists, liberals, and conservatives had fought their political battles, some to gain and others to lose, but none to win a complete victory or to disappear nameless in defeat.

Note on the Scottish and Irish Reform Bills

Supplementary bills were brought forward in 1868 for Scotland and Ireland. The Scottish bill applied the principles adopted in England. The borough franchise was extended to rate-paying householders and to lodgers, and the county vote to £5 owners and £12 occupiers. The house raised the occupation franchise in the counties to £14, and refused to apply the rate-paying clause to the boroughs. The government suggested an increase in the numbers of the house of commons by giving two seats to the Scottish universities, an additional member to Glasgow, three to large counties, and a new member to a group of towns in the south-west. The house would not agree to this increase, and seven seats were found by disfranchising small English boroughs with less than 5,000 inhabitants.

The house of commons also modified the terms of the Irish bill. The government proposed to enfranchise £4 householders in boroughs, and £12 householders in counties, to include certain boroughs in county constituencies, and to give to Dublin the seat belonging to Portarlington. The house threw out the redistribution clauses, but accepted the enfranchisement proposals.

BOOK II

ENGLAND AND EUROPE

I

FOREIGN POLICY, 1815–29

CASTLEREAGH, CANNING, AND WELLINGTON

ON 29 June 1815 Castlereagh proposed in the house of commons that a public monument should be set up in London to commemorate the victory of Waterloo. At the beginning of the session of 1816 he made a similar proposal for a monument in honour of Nelson and the victory of Trafalgar. Trafalgar gave Great Britain control of the sea; Waterloo secured her against the domination of the continent of Europe by one nation. The maintenance of naval supremacy and of a European balance of power were the governing principles of British foreign policy throughout the nineteenth century. The safeguarding of British naval supremacy was primarily a domestic affair, a matter of men and ships and money; the preservation of the balance of power implied diplomatic action, and, at times, the threat or use of force. The balance of power was not a fact, but an ideal towards which reasonable men worked. To the statesmen of the nineteenth century the balance of power meant an equilibrium or ratio between states or groups of states, a ratio established in due form by treaty settlement, affirmed by public declaration, and giving to each state, or group of states, a position based upon a rough assessment of its material and moral strength. Europe never attained this equilibrium because the relative force and ambitions of each state were continually changing, and required a continual adjustment of claims and interests. Towards this adjustment Great Britain could make an important and even a decisive contribution. Great Britain could not dictate to the Powers of Europe the policy which seemed most favourable to the peace of the Continent; she could always throw her wealth and influence into the scale against any Power or combination of Powers likely to disturb the existing equipoise. It is thus misleading to speak of the isolation of Great Britain from continental affairs. British statesmen interfered very often in these affairs. The first principle of British security, the maintenance of naval supremacy, had its continental aspect. If France held Belgium, if Russia controlled the Turkish Empire, British sea-power would be challenged in home waters and in the Mediterranean; the 'overland' route to India through Mesopotamia would be in Russian hands. The eastern question therefore was enough to entangle Great Britain in the international rivalries of the continental powers. The only continental war between 1815 and 1870 in which Great Britain took part was a war between Russia and Turkey.

The allies of Great Britain in 1815 accepted the fact of British naval supremacy. The events of the war had shown both the measure and the significance of this supremacy. Great Britain had destroyed or captured the fleets of her enemies, and had saved herself from any risk of invasion by French armies. At the height of the peninsular war, the British fleets were blockading the ports of France in the Channel, the Atlantic, and the Mediterranean, and also preventing a French army from crossing the two thousand yards of river estuary between the south and north banks of the Tagus at Lisbon. This maritime dominion was equally important at the peace settlement. The allies did not discuss at Vienna questions of maritime law affecting the exercise of British naval supremacy. They accepted the British decision to retain Heligoland, Malta, Mauritius, Trinidad, St. Lucia, Tobago, Demerara, Essequibo, and the Cape of Good Hope, and to set up a protectorate over the Ionian islands, a vantage-point for the control of the eastern Mediterranean. No single continental Power could hope to challenge the navy of Great Britain. A combination of Powers would have been difficult, and was in any case unlikely, unless Great Britain attempted to use her control of the seas against the interest of other trading and manufacturing countries.

British statesmen were unlikely to disturb the peace of the world by a policy of territorial acquisition. They had no wish to acquire more colonies. They wanted nothing in Europe except markets in which British merchants could buy and sell. The public at large, as well as the small governing class, knew that

British interests required peace, and that the maintenance of peace depended upon the general stability of the European state system. Great Britain had taken part in the continental settlement. She was a member of the alliance constituted at Chaumont in 1814, and continued in 1815, to protect Europe against attack from France. As a member of this quadruple alliance she was pledged, with Russia, Austria, and Prussia, to employ against France the whole of her forces. The British representatives in Paris and at Vienna did their best to bring about a settlement under which the danger of French or any other aggression would be small. With the help of Russia, they prevented Prussia from enforcing a vindictive and humiliating peace upon France. With the help of France and Austria, they prevented Prussia from becoming too strong. They assisted in the construction of the Germanic Confederation as a bulwark against France in the west and Russia in the east of Europe. They supported the union of the Austrian and the Dutch Netherlands as a barrier on the road from France to the north European plain, and the enlargement of Piedmont as a barrier against France on the road through the plain of Lombardy to central Europe. They shared the views of Metternich that French jacobinism, to which Napoleon had given an untimely encouragement during the Hundred Days, was an unstable and bellicose factor; they believed that any revival of revolutionary ideas would be a threat to European peace.[1]

For seven years after 1815 British foreign policy was directed by Castlereagh. Castlereagh's rank and bearing, his fine address, good manners, self-control, courage, and power of work served him well. His position in the cabinet was extremely strong. He knew most of the sovereigns and leading ministers of Europe. He had carried British policy through a period of great danger. During this time he had followed carefully the guiding lines laid down by Pitt. As a result he obtained for Great Britain nearly everything she had wished to obtain after the fall of Napoleon. He was on intimate terms with the prime minister and with Wellington, the greatest figure in Europe after the fall of Napoleon. No member of the tory party could object to a policy approved by these three men. The whigs might oppose Castlereagh; but their opposition was often factious and illogical. They put 'honour' before peace, and wanted

[1] For the negotiations of 1814-15, see vol. xii of this *History*.

more interference abroad to resist the plans of autocratic monarchs; they asked for a reduction in naval and military expenditure, and made it difficult for the government to provide the means for an 'active' policy. The tory country gentlemen, 'the finest brute votes in Europe', knew little about foreign affairs, and were not inclined to discuss them at length. Castlereagh did not provide them with much material for criticism. The prince regent was the best-placed and the most dangerous critic of his ministers. George was shrewd and well-informed, at least on personal questions. He talked freely, and even intrigued with foreign ambassadors at his court; he was able to use the diplomatic service and state machinery of Hanover to obtain information which was not within the reach of his British ministers. He believed, naturally enough, in the monarchical principle and in the solidarity of interests of the European monarchs. He was ready to support every repressive measure undertaken by continental statesmen. On the whole, though he wasted a great deal of his ministers' time, and caused them embarrassment, his prejudices tended to coincide with the policy of state. Thus he was anti-Russian, not out of principle, but because he never forgave Alexander I for his rudeness during a visit to England in 1814. In spite of his high conservative and monarchical views, he came to realize, after Castlereagh's death, that, however much he might dislike Canning's measures, these measures were popular, and resistance to them might endanger his throne. He treated Wellington with respect; Wellington spoke plainly to him when this respect was not forthcoming.

The rudimentary character and training of the official staff and the lack of really competent men threw too great a strain upon the foreign secretary. Castlereagh and Canning broke down under the strain. Palmerston was of a different type, but he too found the work very severe, and his clerks found him a hard taskmaster. In the year 1821 the staff of the foreign office consisted of twenty-eight persons, including the two under-secretaries and a Turkish interpreter; the cost of the diplomatic service abroad was under £300,000. There were at this time twenty-one unpaid and seven paid attachés in the service. Appointments were made by favour and patronage. There was no test of the general abilities of a candidate. George I had the interests of the diplomatic service in mind when he founded professorships of modern history at Oxford and Cambridge. In 1815 these chairs were held by nonentities.[1] The usual method of training was unconnected with any organized course of studies. A young man was attached to a minister, lived in his family, and acted as one of his clerks. The higher posts were given for political or personal reasons. They were held by men of good birth, with considerable knowledge of the world, but there was no rule that this knowledge should include familiarity with diplomatic business. During the long period of continental war, British relations with foreign courts had been intermittent and incomplete, and the habit of the grand tour had been broken. Of Castlereagh's ambassadors, Earl Cathcart was a soldier; he was kept at St. Petersburg because the emperor liked him. Castlereagh's half-brother, Lord Stewart, ambassador at Vienna, was also a soldier; he was selfish and unbalanced, without *finesse*, and no match for Metternich. The ambassador at Madrid (until 1822) was a younger brother of the duke of Wellington. Lord Strangford, who went to Constantinople in 1821, was the only ambassador of more than moderate ability. He served Castlereagh well, but Canning enforced his resignation because he did not carry out his instructions, and intrigued against the official policy of his country. Castlereagh's belief in diplomacy by conference was to some extent an unrealized reaction against the confusion caused by defective machinery, though he also found positive justification for his ideas. He had been impressed by the improvement in the collaboration of the Powers against Napoleon after the allied sovereigns and their ministers had met together and talked over possible lines of action. He knew from his own experience how much he had gained from this personal contact. He wanted to continue these meetings, in which his own strength of character and influence counted for a great deal. The draft of the treaty of Chaumont allowed for periodical meetings to supervise the execution of the treaty. Castlereagh persuaded the Powers to give a more general purpose to the meetings. The sixth article of the treaty of alliance of 20 November 1815 laid down that, in order to carry out the Vienna settlement and 'to consolidate the connections which at the present moment so closely unite the Four Sovereigns [of Great Britain, Austria, Prussia, and Russia] for the happiness of

---

[1] Henry Beeke, professor at Oxford from 1801 to 1813, and afterwards dean of Bristol, was an economist of some note. Vansittart often consulted him on financial questions.

the world, the High Contracting Parties have agreed to renew their meetings at fixed periods, either under the immediate auspices of the Sovereigns themselves or by their respective Ministers, for the purpose of consulting upon their common interests, and for the consideration of the measures which at each of those periods shall be considered the most salutary for the repose and prosperity of Nations, and for the maintenance of the Peace of Europe'. Castlereagh's plan was unlikely to succeed. The High Contracting Parties to the Alliance were the Great Powers. The distinction between greater and smaller Powers had been emphasized at Vienna, to the dissatisfaction of the lesser Powers. There was no place for these Powers in Castlereagh's scheme. Moreover the Great Powers were not likely to be unanimous in their view of the dangers which might threaten Europe. There were old rivalries which made it difficult to speak of the common interests of the Powers. There was also something new. The statesmen at Vienna could hardly be expected to show much sympathy for the principles of national self-determination and popular government as these principles had manifested themselves since 1789. When revolutionary principles took a constitutional form, and were neither militant nor jacobin, the attitude of Great Britain would differ from the attitude of Austria and Prussia. Alexander of Russia showed signs of benevolence towards constitutional ideas; his mood soon changed, and his enthusiasm was unable to stand against disappointments of fact. Castlereagh thought that there might be a revival of French revolutionary aggression. He did not foresee that revolution might break out, not in the great states, but in the smaller states, and against misgovernment for which the British public had no sympathy.

British public opinion would not consider that these revolutionary movements threatened the tranquillity of Europe; they might threaten 'the monarchical principle', as this principle was interpreted by absolute monarchs. A parliamentary state like Great Britain could not make common cause with absolute monarchs in the suppression of constitutional movements. Castlereagh's position therefore became illogical and a little absurd. He saw the diversion of the alliance from its original purpose and the meetings of the Powers used for declaring the unlimited right of interference in the affairs of small states. He objected to this misuse of the instrument which he had devised as a means to secure Europe against general war. In 1820 he put his objections in his clumsy and involved style: 'What is intended to be combated, as forming any part of their duty as Allies, is the notion, but too perceptibly prevalent, that whenever any great political event shall occur, as in Spain, pregnant perhaps with future danger, it is to be regarded almost as a matter of course, that it belongs to the Allies to charge themselves collectively with the responsibility of exercising some jurisdiction concerning such possible eventual danger.'[1]

A plain declaration in favour of moderate constitutional principles would have been simpler and more in harmony with British public opinion. The truth was that Castlereagh was not in favour of the spread of constitutional principles. British public opinion was an obstacle to be surmounted rather than a guide to his policy. Castlereagh could not risk open support of the autocratic monarchs; he did not believe in any general right of interference. He summed up his policy in one inglorious sentence: 'We are always pleased to see evil germs destroyed, without the power to give our approbation openly.' Castlereagh ought to have realized as early as 1815 that the union between Great Britain and the continental Powers would not outlast the removal of the immediate danger from France. The Holy Alliance should have been a greater warning to him, as it was a warning to English opinion, of the difference of outlook between constitutional and autocratic states. The treaty of the Holy Alliance, proposed by Alexander, and signed on 26 September 1815, was a rival scheme to Castlereagh's matter-of-fact proposal that the Powers should talk over questions of common interest. Alexander's treaty bound its members to act on Christian principles. The alliance was open to all Christian sovereigns. The constitutional position of the prince regent forbade his accession to a personal union of sovereigns. The pope could not be one among equals. The sultan of Turkey did not profess Christian principles. Metternich was no less cynical than Castlereagh about the wording of the emperor's treaty, but Metternich had more reason to be satisfied with a document which emphasized the divine right of monarchs and said not a word about the rights of subjects. An inner union of this kind

[1] Castlereagh's memorandum of 5 May 1820, from which this quotation is taken, was partially printed in 1823. For the full text, see the *Cambridge History of British Foreign Policy*, ii. 622–33.

between Russia, Austria, and Prussia was not likely to help the discussions to which Castlereagh looked forward.

Even if there had been no inner alliance of the monarchical Powers, and if the revolution had not reappeared in unexpected quarters, Castlereagh's proposals were not very practicable. He had suggested periodic meetings; he did not suggest any permanent organization. No one had the duty of collecting material for the objective study of any European question. There were no arrangements for the preparation of agenda, no rules of procedure. The common presence of absolute monarchs and of ministers bound to take account of the wishes and the criticism of parliament would hardly make for easy decision. The failure of Castlereagh's honest improvisation—one can scarcely use a more favourable term—did not come at once. The first problems were solved in congress by the allies, because these problems were the legacy of the war with France. The settlement of 1815 imposed upon France an army of occupation 150,000 strong, an indemnity of seven hundred million francs, and unassessed liabilities for war damages. Fortunately for Europe, Wellington was in command of the army of occupation. He enforced a discipline which had distinguished the British forces alone among the invaders of France, and kept the cost of maintaining the troops as low as possible; in January 1817, after some hesitation, he recommended that the army should be reduced by 30,000 men. Wellington soon realized that the army of occupation was a danger to the French monarchy, since French public opinion was becoming restive at the presence of foreign troops. In March 1818 the British cabinet suggested that the troops should be taken away from France, and that a special force should be kept in the Low Countries. The allies agreed to meet for a discussion of the question.

The congress of Aix-la-Chapelle opened at the end of September 1818. The financial questions affecting France had already been discussed. Once again Wellington stood for moderation. The greatest trouble came from Prussia, who refused to give up any of her very large claims until her allies forced her to accept a drastic reduction. The withdrawal of the troops of occupation caused little difficulty. The four allies agreed to invite France publicly to take part in the general deliberations. The cabinet, under Canning's influence, began to be afraid of committing

Great Britain to fixed meetings of the Powers. These meetings might involve the country in common action with despotic Powers against their rebellious subjects. Such rebellions might not always be unreasonable, according to British standards; their success or failure might not concern British interests, and the smaller Powers would object to the discussion and settlement of their affairs by the great Powers. Castlereagh was able to meet these criticisms largely because Alexander wanted to go to the other extreme. Alexander proposed a general league of the Powers guaranteeing to every sovereign his throne and his territory. Castlereagh explained that Great Britain would never accept commitments of this kind, and that the plan was impracticable until every state had a government which was beyond criticism. The emperor gave way, and the British cabinet accepted a compromise. France was invited to join the Concert of the Powers; the five Powers signed a declaration of their good and just intentions. The declaration included a reference to periodic meetings for the discussion of matters of common interest.

Castlereagh thought that he had saved his plan of diplomacy by conference; but already there were signs of the differences of view which were to wreck the system. The Russian plan was as vague as the terms of the Holy Alliance, but the root of the matter lay in the question of mutual guarantee. The monarchs wanted to be roped together.

Within fourteen months of the congress of Aix-la-Chapelle, Great Britain began to part company from her allies. Ferdinand VII of Spain was a low character judged even by the standards of the Spanish and Italian Bourbons. After his restoration his private and public vices soon brought him into disrepute with his subjects. In January 1820 a wild plan to reconquer his rebellious American colonies caused a military revolt at Cadiz. The king was forced to accept the ultra-democratic constitution of 1812. This constitution had been set up by one party in Spain after the fall of the Napoleonic régime, and before the return of Ferdinand. It was unsuited to Spanish conditions; Ferdinand had lost no time in over-throwing it. He now appealed to his brother sovereigns to help him to regain absolute power. The insurrection in Spain brought up the problem which Castlereagh believed he had settled at Aix-la-Chapelle. Wellington and Castlereagh summarized the views of the British government. Wellington looked at the matter from a military point of view. The army was the only real power in Spain, and had made the revolution; interference would add to the confusion, while the history of the French armies in the Peninsula showed the danger of invading a difficult country against the wishes of the inhabitants. Castlereagh dealt with the question on its political side. He thought that joint action by the Powers was unnecessary. The Spanish revolution might be a bad example, but it did not threaten the safety of the Great Powers. Advice, unsupported by military action, would be useless, and the advisers would not be unanimous. The rulers of autocratic states were free to ignore public opinion, but British public opinion was hostile to Ferdinand, and would not accept any general interpretation of the European alliance as an agreement justifying interference in the internal affairs of another state 'in order to enforce obedience to the governing authority'.

Henceforward Castlereagh withdrew step by step from the collaboration upon which he had set his fine hope of a better European order. The stages of his withdrawal were marked by further revolutions. Revolution in Portugal had followed revolution in Spain. In July 1820 there was an outbreak in the kingdom of the Two Sicilies. Castlereagh had no sympathy with Italian revolutionaries. He recognized the danger to Austrian interests in Italy if the revolution were not suppressed, but he wanted the movement to be put down by Austria alone, without any declaration of principles or open support from Great Britain. Alexander, on the other hand, found an excellent opportunity for insisting upon a meeting of monarchs. Austria had to choose between the British and the Russian views. Great Britain offered nothing more than a secret understanding; Russia at least gave a promise of support. Castlereagh was back again at the conflict of views and interests which he had tried to settle at Aix-la-Chapelle. He was afraid of the emperor's suggestion of a general guarantee. 'The more Russia wishes to transport us to the heights, the further we must descend into the plain.'[1] Once again Castlereagh maintained that the Neapolitan, Spanish, and Portuguese revolutions were merely 'domestic upsets' which did not threaten the security of Europe.

[1] See C. K. Webster, *The Foreign Policy of Castlereagh, 1815–1822*, p. 279.

Castlereagh could not prevent the summoning of another European congress. His plans were now turned against him. He would not allow Great Britain to make a public declaration of the kind proposed by Alexander. He did not want a complete break with the monarchical Powers. He took the middle course of sending Stewart to the congress at Troppau in October 1820. Stewart went not as a plenipotentiary but as an observer; he was completely surprised when the monarchical Powers of Austria, Prussia, and Russia presented to him a protocol announcing that they based their right of interference upon the treaties of alliance. Stewart protested against the protocol, and Castlereagh sent a dispatch declaring that its terms were incompatible with the system of international law. A doctrine of general interference would 'tend to destroy all wholesome national energy and all independent action, more especially within the Smaller States'. The British government would not 'charge itself as a member of the Alliance with the moral responsibility of administering a general European Police'.[1]

The protests had little direct effect. The Neapolitans threw away the chance of a compromise by rejecting the offer of a moderate constitution. In January 1821 the congress reassembled at Laibach. Stewart was again present in his capacity as observer,[2] but the breach was almost beyond repair. Castlereagh's own position was not strong. The other Powers knew that he sympathized with the suppression of revolution. They thought that his arguments were put forward to satisfy his colleagues and British public opinion. The Austrian ambassador in London said that Castlereagh was 'like a great lover of music who is at Church; he wishes to applaud, but he dare not'.[3] The three Powers assembled at Laibach agreed to hold another meeting in the autumn of 1822. Metternich hoped to bring Castlereagh back into the alliance. The outbreak of the Greek

---

[1] For Castlereagh's protest of 16 Dec. 1820, see Webster, op. cit., pp. 303–5. Austria, Prussia, and Russia followed up the preliminary protocol by a circular dispatch to their diplomatic representatives at foreign courts (8 Dec. 1820). The wording of this dispatch implied that Great Britain and France agreed with its terms. Castlereagh therefore issued a statement of British policy (19 Jan. 1821). This statement repeated in strong language the argument that any general rule of intervention would be contrary to international law and to the terms of the Alliance, and would have bad practical results.

[2] He arrived late, and after three weeks went back to Vienna, where his young wife was expecting a child. He had twice left Troppau to see his wife.

[3] Webster, op. cit., p. 326.

revolt changed the British position.[1] Castlereagh was now afraid
that Russia might intervene on the side of the rebels; Great
Britain did not want any further weakening of Turkey. The
best way of holding back the tsar was to bring him into another
meeting of the Powers. Castlereagh himself therefore had to
return to these meetings. He went with George IV on a visit to
Hanover in the late autumn of 1821; here he agreed with
Metternich—to the latter's comfort—on joint action. For the
time Alexander made no military move, and the main business
of the next congress of the Powers was the question of Spain.
Before the congress opened at Verona in October 1822 Castlereagh was dead. His mind became deranged owing to overwork;
bad medical treatment only aggravated his weakness, and, on
12 August, he killed himself.

Castlereagh's diplomacy after 1815 had been concerned primarily with Europe; it had also included some far-reaching
arrangements with the United States. The Anglo-American war
which ended with the treaty of Ghent in 1814 had been unnecessary and was inconclusive; the peace settlement left over
most of the important issues between the two countries.[2] Both
sides, however, agreed tacitly that such a war must not recur.
Two things made easier a policy of restraint, which did not
exclude a good deal of trumpet-blowing and coat-trailing—
largely, though by no means only, on the American side. Most
Anglo-American disputes were about boundaries, and were due
to imperfect maps and vague definitions going back in some
instances to the years before 1783. In spite of mutual recrimina-
tion and much higgling these boundary questions could be
determined without damage to the vital interests of either party.
The United States, especially after the Louisiana purchase, held
vast unsettled lands; although the addition of other areas might
be sought for strategic, economic, or sentimental reasons, there
was room enough for adjustment. In any case the main interest
of American policy lay in completing the acquisition of territory
formerly belonging to the Spanish Empire. The British govern-

---

[1] See below, p. 214.

[2] See vol. xii of this *History*, p. 555. One matter which had caused great anger in
the United States had been the impressment of British seamen who—on the British
view—had been evading their duty by engaging on American ships or even taking
out American nationalization papers. This grievance faded out at the end of the
European war.

ment might try, as in the case of Texas (where the question of slavery introduced a complication), to hinder the absorption of this territory into the United States: they would not go to war to prevent it. American claims on the Canadian border did not excite much public feeling in Great Britain because they were concerned with colonial lands at a time when the colonies seemed to be more of a financial and military embarrassment than an advantage. Canadian opinion was an important factor, but in the last resort the burden and cost of another American war would fall on Great Britain. British statesmen, whatever their views about the future status of colonies in general and Canada in particular, never hesitated about fulfilling their duty to defend Canada or any other part of the Empire against aggression. They also realized the strategic importance of the great harbours on the Pacific coast and of the land route from Montreal and Quebec to Halifax; they had no wish to fight for claims based on ancient markings drawn across inaccurate maps.

British and American interests were more complementary than conflicting. The political treaty of Ghent had been followed by a treaty of commerce between the two countries. Great Britain was the best customer of the United States, and between 1815 and the American Civil War supplied over a third of American imports. The trade in raw cotton was a dominant feature of the economy of both countries. The credit provided through British merchants was as essential as it had been before the American revolution; British capital was employed in canal and, later, in railway building in the United States. There were also close political ties. The English regarded Americans and Americans regarded Englishmen as arrogant; each side had reasonable grounds for such a view. Irish emigrants, especially during and after the terrible years of the famine, brought with them unhappy memories of British government. On the other hand very many emigrants came from Great Britain; they were, on the whole, more skilled than those from other countries, and, while they were easily assimilated, they maintained friendly relations, below the level of high politics, with the circles which they had left. There was also much common action as well as community of ideas between British non-conformists and the protestant denominations in the United States. American political developments, seen from a long way off,[1] and often misunderstood, were taken by Englishmen as a warning against the dangers of a levelling democracy, but, at least until after the Civil War, the traditions and background of American thinking were predominantly English.

One of the first matters to be settled after the treaty of Ghent was ultimately of great importance. In 1817 Charles Bagot, British minister at Washington, exchanged notes with Richard Rush, American secretary of state, to the effect that neither country would continue to maintain armed naval forces on the Great Lakes except for the prevention of smuggling. The Rush–Bagot agreement did not lead at once to the so-called 'unguarded frontier' between Canada and the United States. Even on the Great Lakes the two parties, though they stopped naval construction, did not get rid of large ships already on the stocks.[2] A good deal of money was spent by each government in building forts, not necessarily on the frontier.[3] In any case the British government realized that they could not defend Canada on land except at enormous cost, and that the real protection was the British fleet based on the dockyards of Halifax and Bermuda.

The land frontier itself was not delimited throughout its length for many years after 1815. In 1818, during the discussion of various claims, mainly about fishing rights, the American negotiators would have agreed to carry the frontier line westwards along the 49th parallel from the Lake of the Woods (almost half-way across the North American continent) to the Pacific Ocean. The British government, however, was unwilling to give up claims to sovereignty over the portion of the so-called Oregon territory[4] south of the 49th parallel. There was no immediate demand for frontier delimitation; neither the United States nor Canada could colonize the territory for some time to come; the trappers, fur-traders, and a few missionaries in the area were left to the general control—such as it was—of the Hudson's Bay

[1] And, as in the case of J. S. Mill, seen largely through the eyes of A. de Tocqueville.

[2] The largest of the American ships—the *New Orleans*— was not taken off the strength of the United States navy until 1882. See C. P. Stacey, 'The Myth of the Unguarded Frontier, 1815-71', in *American Historical Review*, lvi. 1 (1950).

[3] One of the more expensive American forts was nearly completed when it was discovered that, owing to a defective map, the site chosen was several miles inside Canadian territory.

[4] This territory covered, vaguely, the whole area west of the Rocky (or, as they were earlier called, the Stony) Mountains and north of San Francisco Bay as far as the equally ill-defined area of Russian expansion.

Company. Hence an Anglo-American Convention of 1818 laid down that the country west of the 'Stony Mountains' should be 'free and open' for ten years to the vessels, citizens, and subjects of the two powers. The arrangement was renewed in 1827—two days before Canning's death—subject to termination after a year's notice from either party.

Canning took over the direction of British foreign policy at a difficult moment. He was not new to the work, or afraid of quick decisions. As foreign secretary in 1807–9 he had suggested the seizure of the Danish and Portuguese fleets. He was mainly responsible for the expedition to the Peninsula, and the choice of Wellington as commander. Between 1816 and 1822, both in and out of office, he had been a careful critic of foreign policy. He agreed more with Castlereagh's decisions than with his methods. He distrusted the plan of diplomacy by conference, and wished to keep clear of European intervention. Canning had not shared Castlereagh's practical experience of the value of these conferences in the months before and after the fall of Napoleon. In any case he could not apply Castlereagh's methods; few European rulers or statesmen knew him, and still fewer trusted him. His mind was sharper, more brilliant than the mind of Castlereagh. He saw the weakness of a policy which did not allow ministers to take parliament or the people into their confidence. The collaboration between Great Britain and the Powers of the Holy Alliance had already broken down; Canning was willing to emphasize the breakdown. On the other hand, as a conservative, and a pupil of Pitt, he was not inclined to interfere on the side of revolution. 'Let us not, in the foolish spirit of romance, suppose that we alone could regenerate Europe.'[1] Before his death Castlereagh had drawn up for the approval of the cabinet, his own instructions for the preliminary conferences at Vienna which were to precede the grand meeting at Verona. Wellington took Castlereagh's place as British representative, and left London scarcely more than forty-eight hours after Canning had taken office. Castlereagh had raised the question of the Spanish colonies; Canning brought this question into the forefront of British policy. The situation changed before the meeting of the Powers. The Spanish liberals had shown little administrative or political competence;

[1] Hansard, N.S. iv. 1374.

Ferdinand VII was still asking for armed help against them. When Castlereagh was writing his instructions there was no immediate danger of intervention. Alexander wanted to march a Russian army across Germany and France. Metternich and Louis XVIII had no wish to see Russian armies outside Russia. The French had brought troops to the Spanish frontier under the pretext of policing the border to prevent an outbreak of yellow fever in Spain from spreading into France. In September 1822 Wellington found that these troops were shortly to be moved into Spain in support of Ferdinand. Canning refused to agree to any such interference. Wellington protested at Verona against the 'moral support' which the continental Powers were ready to give to France. He would not sign a *procès-verbal* defining the conditions of this support; he left Verona on the day before the end of the congress, saying—so Metternich told his colleagues—that 'all of us were wrong'. For a time it appeared that nothing more than 'moral pressure' would be put on Spain, but in January 1823 the king's speech at the opening of the French chamber included a statement that Ferdinand VII should be free to give to the Spaniards the institutions which 'they cannot hold but from him'.

This assertion of divine right was too much for British opinion. Canning told the French that Great Britain would recommend the Spaniards to modify their constitution, but not on lines opposed to British constitutional principles. He made a public speech in which he warned France of the danger of war with Great Britain. He asked parliament to assent to an increase in the personnel of the navy from 21,000 to 25,000 men. Although Canning had public opinion behind him, he had not obtained the unanimous support of his cabinet. The king and the duke of York were on the side of the monarchical principle. In spite of this opposition Canning announced that Great Britain could not allow a permanent military occupation of Spain, the violation of Portuguese territory, or the appropriation of any part of the Spanish colonies. When the French armies entered Spain, Canning told the house of commons that he hoped Spain would come 'triumphantly out of the struggle'. His hope was not fulfilled. The French armies met with practically no resistance. The constitutional party withdrew to Cadiz and surrendered (30 September 1823).

From the British point of view, the importance of the affair

lay not in Europe but in the American colonies of Spain. Since
the breakdown of the Spanish monopoly, the trade between
Great Britain and Latin America had increased about fourteen-
fold. The central and south American markets became so much
more valuable during the French wars that British merchants
were nervous about any reversion to the old Spanish colonial
system. In 1823 the Manchester chamber of commerce declared
the textile trade with South America to be 'of the first magnitude'. Castlereagh had announced as early as 1817 that Great
Britain would not allow any Power to make a bargain with Spain
over the reduction of the colonies. He hoped for the establishment of monarchical government in the Latin American
countries. Before his death he had recognized the commercial
flags of the colonies, and stated that full political recognition
was rather 'a matter of time than of principle'. Canning did
not want to embarrass the constitutional party in Spain by an
immediate recognition of the independent status of the colonies;
he had no love for republics, whether in the new or in the old
world; but he left no doubt that Great Britain would oppose any
action taken by France to help Ferdinand to recover the colonies.
In August 1823 he suggested to Rush, at this time United States
minister in London, a joint Anglo-American declaration that
neither Power would acquire for itself, or allow any other Power
to acquire, any portion of the colonies. The United States had
already recognized the independence of the revolted colonies.
Rush would not agree on his own responsibility to Canning's
proposal for a joint declaration unless the British government
would also announce recognition. Canning therefore turned to
negotiate with the French. He acted immediately after the fall
of Cadiz since he was afraid that the French might send an
expedition to South America. On 3 October, 1823 he invited
the Prince de Polignac, French ambassador in London, to state
his government's intentions. The ambassador, in an agreed
memorandum, disclaimed on behalf of the French government
any design of using force against the colonies or appropriating
colonial territory in America. Canning took care that this memorandum—a French acknowledgement of British sea-power—
was soon known to the other European Powers. It put an end to
projects of interference.

Canning's approach to Rush led to a momentous declaration
from the United States. Canning had shown that Great Britain

was prepared to fight France or Russia if either Power attempted to interfere in South America. The United States had no wish to go to war for South America, but, with their knowledge of British intentions, President Monroe and his advisers could safely declare that they would not allow European interference. Moreover they could make this declaration in language which dissociated them from any suggestion of subservience to Great Britain. On 2 December, 1823, therefore, in a message to Congress, the President asserted that the United States would regard any attempt on the part of the Allied Powers to extend their 'political system' to any portion of the western hemisphere as 'dangerous to our peace and safety'. The message went on to explain that any interposition in the affairs of the governments whose independence the United States had acknowledged would be considered as 'the manifestation of an unfriendly disposition towards the United States'.

The President's message had begun by dealing with a Russian ukase of 1821 which excluded non-Russian subjects from navigation, fishing or trade within a hundred Italian miles[1] of the west coast of North America from the Bering sea to a latitude of 51 degrees and along the coast of Siberia to a latitude of 45 degrees. Castlereagh had protested against this absurd claim, but neither he nor Canning had been inclined to take it seriously. Monroe now stated, with explicit reference to it, the 'principle' that 'the American Continents . . . are henceforth not to be considered as subjects for future colonisation by any European Power', though the United States would not interfere with 'the existing colonies or dependencies' of such Powers. Canning refused to accept this statement of 'principle' since it might be interpreted as meaning that the United States would not allow British colonization in the Oregon territory where the boundaries were still unsettled.[2] For the rest the President's

[1] Italian (Roman) miles were commonly used as units of measurement by geographers and navigators in the sixteenth and seventeenth centuries. Their use outside Italy was rare in the nineteenth century.

[2] Canning used the term 'new Doctrine' in describing Monroe's declaration, but this term did not come into general use for another thirty years. The Monroe declaration, as a unilateral statement, was not legally binding on any Power (including the United States, since it was not embodied in an act or resolution of Congress). The United States government came to an agreement with Russia in 1824 defining the southern limit of Russian claims on the Pacific coast as latitude 54.40. Great Britain made a similar agreement with Russia in 1825. Spain had already (1819) renounced all claims north of latitude 42.

declaration was useful in following up the initiative which Great Britain had already taken.

Canning had delayed official British recognition of the new Latin American republics in the hope that after all they might come to some arrangement with Spain, or that they might accept monarchical forms of government. These hopes disappeared in 1824; on the other hand there seemed some risk that Monroe's message might leave the United States free to assume rights of interference denied to others. Hence, in the last months of 1824, Canning decided to recognize those colonies which had duly established their governments. The merchants of London, in a petition signed by Baring, Ricardo, and Benjamin Shaw,[1] had asked for recognition; this pressure was useful to Canning in persuading his tory colleagues in the cabinet. On 31 December Great Britain recognized the republics of Buenos Aires, Mexico, and Colombia[2] as independent states. At the opening of parliament the king refused to read the royal speech announcing this step; Eldon, who had opposed the measure, read the words without enthusiasm.[3]

The recognition of the independence of Brazil was an easier matter. In 1807 the regent of Portugal took refuge in Brazil after the French armies had marched into Lisbon. The regent became King John VI in 1816, but he and other members of the royal family stayed in Brazil until 1821. In this year the king sailed for Europe, and left his son Dom Pedro as regent of Brazil. At the end of 1822, Dom Pedro proclaimed himself 'constitutional emperor' of an independent Brazil. For another two years King John refused to accept the fact of Brazilian independence; in 1825 a settlement, reached through British mediation, established a Brazilian empire which lasted for sixty years. The settlement had a curious result in Portugal. King John died in 1826. Dom Pedro was now king of Portugal. His younger brother, Dom Miguel, who had already tried to overthrow King John, claimed the succession. Dom Pedro tried to meet these claims by renouncing the throne of Portugal in favour of his daughter, Donna Maria, a child of eight. He

---

[1] Shaw was chairman of Lloyd's Coffee House; Baring was one of the leading bankers of the City.

[2] Canning argued for the recognition of Mexico on economic grounds, owing to the amount of British capital invested in the country, and on political grounds, since Mexico would form a barrier against the ambitions of the United States.

[3] The king said that he had an attack of gout, and that he had lost his false teeth.

proposed to get a papal dispensation allowing Donna Maria to marry Dom Miguel. The scheme was not popular, and Dom Pedro tried to improve it. Dom Miguel was known to be absolutist in sympathy. Dom Pedro therefore said that, with his daughter, he would give Portugal a constitution. Canning did not think that Pedro had acted wisely, but he refused to interfere, and held that the monarchical Powers had no right to oppose the free grant of a constitution by a legitimate sovereign to his subjects. The Spanish government gave arms and equipment to Portuguese deserters in order that they might attack the constitutionalist party in Portugal. The constitutionalists appealed to Great Britain for help according to treaty obligations. Canning sent a fleet and 4,000 troops to Lisbon, and the Spaniards gave way. The deserters were disarmed, and Miguel's following broken up. The constitution remained to give trouble to Canning's successors as well as to Portugal. Canning had no difficulty in justifying his action in a speech which included his most famous words. He defended his policy of tolerating a French occupation of Spain, on condition that this occupation did not extend to the Spanish colonies. 'Contemplating Spain, such as our ancestors had known her, I resolved that if France had Spain, it should not be Spain "with the Indies". I called the New World into existence to redress the balance of the Old.'

Canning could not use such brave words about the Eastern question. British interests in the new world were limited and well defined; the British fleet could be used to enforce recognition of these interests. The king and the high tories might dislike Canning's support of rebels against their legitimate sovereigns; public opinion was on Canning's side. The chronicler of the *Annual Register* summed up the general view: 'The spirit with which [Mr. Canning] broke loose from any suspicious connexion with the Holy Alliance, the recognition of the South American republics, and, above all, the energy and manliness with which, in maintenance of the national faith, he stretched forth the national arm to the defence of Portugal, had completely fallen in with the feelings of the public, and had identified him, in some measure, with the dignity and character of the empire.' There was no such unanimity about the attitude and policy of Great Britain towards the Greek revolt. Great Britain could not use her maritime supremacy to enforce a settlement against the wishes of the monarchical Powers; the initiative lay as much in Russian as in British hands. Until the last years of the eighteenth century the Near East had mattered little in British policy. Great Britain was more concerned with keeping on friendly terms with Russia than with the protection of Turkey. There were two main reasons for the change of view: the growth of British interests in India, and the advance of Russia towards the centres of Turkish power. The expedition of Napoleon to Egypt in 1798 had shown the importance of the southern over-land route to India. A nearer and easier route lay through Asia Minor to the great rivers of Mesopotamia, and the posses-sion of Constantinople might give to a strong military Power control of either way to the East. The Turkish empire had never been more than a settlement of military nomads, without poli-tical originality or civilized traditions, in the ruins of the fallen power of Byzantium. During the eighteenth century the empire showed signs of collapse. The Russians established themselves on the Black Sea, and obtained in the treaty of Kuchuk Kainardji (1774) certain ill-defined rights of interference in favour of the Christian subjects of the sultan.[1] Russia was likely to use these rights to the full when the occasion arose. The Greek rebellion of 1821 might well provide this occasion.

Turkish rule in the mainland of Greece had taken the line of least resistance. In the mountainous districts the Turks had done little more than enforce tribute. For the rest the Greeks lived in an isolation which amounted almost to independence. Each village stronghold—'city state' would be too dignified a term—formed a little republic, and had its own band or bands of armed men. During the later years of the eighteenth century the Turks tried to break the power of these armed bands. They set companies of Moslems to fight companies of Greeks; the Greek rebellion was a continuation and a generalization of these local conflicts. Such a generalization was made possible by the career of Ali Pasha of Janina and Trikkala.[2] Ali was an Albanian brigand, who had fought his way to recognition by attacking Greek bands. He taught the Greeks whom he

---

[1] This imprecision was more to the advantage of Russia than of Turkey.

[2] The family of Ali Pasha were hereditary beys of Tepeleni. Ali's grandfather was a captain of brigands; his father, a mild man, was dispossessed of his office and put to death. Ali's mother then took over the captaincy and educated her son in the profession. Ali was an apt and curious pupil. Among his many murders was the drowning of eighteen Greek women because they were living loose lives.

subjected regular modes of fighting, and organized them as units of a small army. In 1820 he quarrelled with the sultan. The sultan declared him an outlaw, and Ali was forced to defend himself. He appealed to the Greeks. He drank to the health of the Virgin, and promised an assembly of captains that he would give religious liberty and political independence. The Greeks paid little attention to his offers, but for a time the Turkish troops were engaged in dealing with him.

The Greek islanders also had grievances of their own. During the French wars they had grown rich. They had taken a good deal of the French carrying trade when the French dared not sail in the Mediterranean. Many of the shipowners had agencies at Odessa, Marseilles, and other ports. Thither the agents brought their families. On their return many of them started schools for their fellow countrymen. After the suppression of these schools the movement became revolutionary. Secret societies were formed with headquarters outside the Turkish empire; the most important of these societies, the *Philike Hetaireia*, or Friendly Association, established in 1814 at Odessa, had branches in Moscow, Trieste, Bucharest, and other cities. The leaders of the Greek bands on the mainland were affiliated to the society and given arms for themselves and their men.

Ali's rebellion encouraged the members of the *Philike Hetaireia* to take their chance. They organized an outbreak in the Danubian Principalities. Prince Alexander Hypselantes, the leader, was the son of one and the grandson of another of the hospodars, or governors, of the Principalities. He had fought in the Russian army, but he offended the emperor by issuing a manifesto which assumed that Russia would attack the Turks, and by starting a revolution at the moment when Alexander was assisting 'morally' in the suppression of revolutionaries elsewhere. The Rumanian peasants in the Principalities had no interest in the liberation of Greeks; the nobles wanted to keep on good terms with the Turks. Although Hypselantes ran away to Austria when the movement failed, he had given the signal for a rising in the Morea. Ali Pasha was keeping Turkish soldiers busy in the north; the islanders provided money and arms, and the rebels won success after success. In January 1822 they proclaimed a constitution for an independent Greece. At this point the tide turned against them.

The Greeks had to deal with the Sultan Mahmud II. Mahmud, the son of a French Creole brought to Constantinople by the Barbary pirates, succeeded to the sultanate in 1808 after a palace revolution. He was then twenty-three years old. For nearly thirty years, until his splendid body and active mind went to ruin, he carried out reforms. Change without violence was almost unknown in Turkey, and life counted for little among people who resisted disinfection and quarantine on the ground that such measures were in blasphemous opposition to the wrath of God. Mahmud did away with feudalism in Asia Minor, restored Turkish authority in Iraq, and, during the height of the Greek rebellion, massacred the janissaries who stood in the way of military reform. He was not a man to be frightened by rebels. He localized the rebellion by terrorizing the Greeks in Constantinople and Asia Minor. On Easter Day 1821 the patriarch and three Greek archbishops were murdered in the Greek cathedral.[1] A year later more than three-quarters of the inhabitants of the rich island of Chios were killed or taken away into slavery. European opinion was shocked, but no further danger was to be feared from the Greeks of the dispersion. Before the massacre at Chios Mahmud had settled with Ali Pasha, and moved his troops southwards into the Morea. Although the Greeks defeated Mahmud's forces they had already begun to quarrel among themselves. They had made little or no attempt to organize a government or to collect a revenue. When Byron came to Greece in the autumn of 1823 he found civil war among the factions; after Byron's death no one had sufficient authority to reconcile the different parties. The proceeds of two English loans, which had already passed through a number of hands before reaching the Greeks, were spent upon these faction fights.

Mahmud II took the decisive step of inviting the help of Mehemet Ali, pasha of Egypt. Mehemet Ali, like Ali Pasha, was an Albanian. He began his career in Macedonia as a small trader. He had the good fortune to become second in command of a regiment of Albanian irregulars in the service of Turkey at the time of Napoleon's expedition to Egypt.[2] He settled in

[1] It is fair to remember that the Greeks had put to death a Sheikh-ul-Islam whom they had found in a ship on his way to Mecca, and that there was little to choose on either side between the treatment of prisoners.

[2] Mehemet Ali (1769–1849) was nearly drowned at the siege of Acre. He was picked out of the sea by a boat's crew from Admiral Sir Sidney Smith's ship.

Egypt in 1801. Four years later the sheikhs of Cairo made him their Pasha. He spent the next twenty years in consolidating his power in Egypt. He rebuilt Alexandria, constructed the Mahmudieh canal between Alexandria and the Nile, introduced new crops into Egypt, founded a school of medicine under French direction, borrowed French officers to organize his army, and built a navy and an arsenal. Bentham wrote him a letter of congratulation and advice, which he could neither read nor answer. His reforms were not carried out on Benthamite lines. The canal cost the lives of 20,000 fellaheen. Mehemet confiscated the title-deeds of those who objected to his taxes. He massacred the mamelukes, as Mahmud massacred the janissaries; there was no other way of getting rid of a turbulent, privileged body of praetorians. He used Sudanese troops to put down mutinies among his ill-disciplined levies; with these mixed forces he broke the resistance of the Wahabis[1] in the Arabian peninsula and reconquered the cities of Mecca and Medina. He advanced into the Sudan and founded Khartum. At this point Mahmud asked him to lend troops and ships for the suppression of the Greeks. Mehemet Ali was the vassal of the sultan, but he had given little attention to the sultan's interests. Mehemet had allowed a number of his Albanian troops to go back to Europe in order to fight on the side of Ali Pasha. He had tolerated the *Philike Hetaireia* in Egypt; he had put no obstacles in the way of Greek volunteers wishing to join their fellow countrymen. He now accepted the sultan's invitation because acceptance seemed more advantageous than refusal. The sultan offered him the Morea as the price of his help. Mehemet Ali's fleet was better manned and better supplied than the Greek ships. In February 1825 Ibrahim Pasha, son of Mehemet Ali, landed an army in the Morea. Thenceforward, unless the Powers intervened, the end of the rebellion was only a matter of time.

Before the summer of 1827 the sultan, or rather Ibrahim, had won back almost the whole of the mainland. Ibrahim proposed to turn out the Greeks and to colonize the Morea with Turks and Egyptians. The Greek rebellion had now lasted six years. Combined action by the Powers would have forced the Turks to give way in as many months or weeks. Liberal opinion in Europe supported the Greeks; the sympathies of

[1] The Wahabis were a body of militant Moslems with strongly ascetic views.

scholars and poets in an age of classical education were on their side. Even Lord Eldon subscribed £100 to the Greek committee in London. On the other hand the European governments were more than embarrassed by the rebellion. Castlereagh had seen that the situation was particularly dangerous, and that Russia must be compelled to work with the other Powers. In March 1823 the British government recognized the Greeks as belligerents. This action was due to economic reasons as well as to philhellene pressure. British commerce in the Levant was carried on by Greeks and by Turks. Until Ibrahim's fleet came on the scene, the fleet of the Greek islanders was more formidable than that of the Turks, and British commerce suffered accordingly. Canning argued that Great Britain must treat Greeks and Turks alike, and that recognition of belligerency was not recognition of anything more than a fact. Canning would not go beyond neutrality. He refused to join the continental Powers in a conference; he was afraid that Alexander would use the conference to get 'moral' support for interference in Turkey.

Canning might protest that England would not go to war for 'Aristides or St. Paul'; he could not overlook the effect upon public opinion of Byron's death at Missolonghi and Ibrahim's victories, or allow Russia to overthrow the Turkish empire. Canning, like Castlereagh, realized that the only way to control Alexander was to act with him. Alexander had broken off diplomatic relations with Turkey; in 1824 he suggested the establishment of three separate semi-independent Greek principalities. This plan would have given Russia pretexts for interfering between the sultan and his subjects; it was therefore unwelcome to Great Britain and Austria. It was detestable to the Greeks themselves, since they would have been governed by the Greeks of Constantinople who would continue to be subservient to the Turks.[1] In September 1825 a deputation of Greeks asked Canning for British help. Canning answered that he was prepared to mediate between the sultan and the rebels, but that his proposals would not give the Greeks complete independence.

Alexander died on 1 December 1825.[2] His brother Nicholas,

---

[1] The 'Phanariote' Greeks of Constantinople (who took their name from the Phanar, or 'lighthouse', quarter of the city) had been compelled by their situation and their interests to come to terms with the Turks. The Turks cared little about the details of administration and employed Phanariotes and Armenians in their service.

[2] Alexander had been preparing for war against Turkey in 1826.

who succeeded him, was nineteen years younger. He had been brought up in retirement until Alexander gave him a military command, which occupied his attention and interests to such an extent that for the rest of his life he would never wear civilian dress. Nicholas was a brave man—hard-working, gloomy, and unrestful, a military pedant, with dark moods of hatred and un-reasoning prejudice. He believed in the divine mission of all legitimate sovereigns, including himself. A prince who saw the vengeance of God in the burning of the houses of parliament after the passing of the reform act of 1832 was not likely to feel much sympathy for rebels; but Nicholas was a Russian, a soldier, and an Orthodox Christian. Canning approached the emperor at once. Wellington went on a special mission to St. Petersburg with a proposal that Great Britain and Russia should interfere, if necessary by force, between Turkey and the Greeks. Nicholas was ready to accept an agreement which would lead Great Britain a good way towards the recognition of complete independence for Greece, and prevent a combina-tion of the European Powers in the Turkish interest. A proto-col, signed by Wellington on 4 April 1826, laid down the terms of the agreement and the conditions of mediation. Greece would become a tributary dependency of Turkey, with liberty of conscience and the right to manage her own affairs, though the sultan would have a share in the nomination of officials. Austria, France, and Prussia were asked to join Russia in guaranteeing the settlement. Charles X of France had no wish to see an Anglo-Russian agreement which excluded France; he insisted for reasons of national dignity, upon a formal treaty to which France would be one of the signatories. The treaty was signed in London on 6 July 1827. Austria and Prussia still held out against interference.

The three allies pledged themselves to interfere if the Turks did not accept an armistice within fourteen days; they sent a fleet to enforce these terms. The British and French squadrons were nearer to the scene, and arrived before the Russian ships. Vice-Admiral Edward Codrington, the senior officer, and one of Nelson's captains, had taken a French ship at Trafalgar with a single broadside. He was strongly philhellene, and unlikely to hesitate before a fleet of Egyptians. His instructions were not clear. He was told to enforce his orders 'if necessary, by cannon-shot'. The Turks refused an armistice, and the period of grace expired on 7 September.

On 12 September Admirals Codrington and de Rigny found the Turkish and Egyptian fleets in the bay of Navarino, at the south-west corner of the Morea. They invited Ibrahim to go back under convoy to Egypt. Ibrahim sent no reply. The admirals warned him that resistance, even a single gun-shot from one of his ships, would mean the destruction of his fleet. At the beginning of October Ibrahim tried to leave the bay of Navarino, but Codrington four times forced him back, although on the third attempt the enemy had more than five times as many guns. On 14 October a Russian squadron joined the allies. Ibrahim's fleet had brought reinforcements from Egypt, and his soldiers were devastating crops, cutting down olive-trees, and killing or enslaving the Greeks on land. The admirals therefore decided that they would compel Ibrahim to go home. There is little doubt that they intended to fight if they were provoked, and that they hoped to be provoked. On 20 October the allied fleets sailed into the bay. The ships were cleared for action, but did not advance in battle formation against the Turkish and Egyptian ships, drawn up in a crescent.[1] The allies had 24 ships, of which 10 were line-of-battle, and 9 frigates, the Turks and Egyptians had 3 line-of-battle ships, 17 frigates, and 69 smaller craft. The admirals sent a boat, under flag of truce, to order the removal of a Turkish fire-ship on which some sailors were working at the entrance of the harbour. Ibrahim fired at the boat. A general battle followed in which the Turkish and Egyptian fleets were destroyed; more than fifty of their ships were sunk.[2]

The news of Navarino caused a certain alarm in England. The tories feared that the destruction of the Turkish fleet would

[1] The classical answer to the crescent formation was to sail, as Nelson sailed at Aboukir Bay, between the upper end of one of the horns of the crescent and the shore, in addition to taking up positions on the seaward side. Codrington was so sure of victory, in spite of an inferiority in gun-power, that he put his ships at a disadvantage by sailing towards the head of the crescent.

[2] Codrington had four bullets in his hat and his clothing, and a fifth in his watch. He was nearly killed by the fall of a mizen-mast. His official dispatch announcing the result of the battle shows the effect upon the admirals of Ibrahim's devastation of the Morea. 'When I found that the boasted Ottoman word of honour was made a sacrifice to wanton, savage devastation, and that a base advantage was taken of our reliance upon Ibrahim's good faith, I own I felt a desire to punish the offenders —But it was my duty to refrain, and refrain I did; and I can assure His Royal Highness that I would still have avoided this disastrous extremity, if other means had been open to me.'

increase the danger of Russian action against Turkey, though from the Russian point of view the disorganization of the Turkish land forces after the massacre of the janissaries was of more importance. Canning had died two months before the battle. Wellington, who succeeded Goderich in January 1828,[1] could not decide upon a policy; Lord Dudley, the foreign secretary, had nothing to suggest. The king's speech at the opening of parliament on 29 January deeply lamented the 'conflict . . . with the naval force of an ancient ally', and hoped that 'this untoward event' would not prevent a settlement of the differences between the Porte and the Greeks. Wellington still hoped that he might arrange the matter by diplomacy, but the obstinate blunders of the Sultan brought about a Russo-Turkish war six months after the battle of Navarino. The direct cause of the war was not the Greek question, but the failure of the sultan to fulfil the terms of the Convention of Akkerman (6 October 1826), which had settled Russo-Turkish differences about the government of the Danubian principalities. The Turks held up the Russians north of the Balkans until the appointment of General Diebitsch as commander-in-chief; but no Turkish troops could be spared for Greece, and in the summer of 1828 the French drove the Egyptians out of the Morea. Diebitsch, who had fought at Austerlitz, Eylau, Friedland, Dresden, and Leipzig, did not have much trouble with the generals of Turkey. He crossed the Balkans and took Adrianople. The Turks could get no help from Great Britain. Wellington and his colleagues affirmed that 'the existence of Turkey as a European Power was essential to the preservation of [the] balance of power'; but war at this stage on behalf of the Turks was out of the question. Rumour magnified the size of Diebitsch's army; no one on the Turkish side seems to have known that the Russians were suffering from disease. The sultan understood that a force of 40,000 Albanians was moving to cut the Russian line of march; he was hardly less afraid of the Albanians and their commander than of Diebitsch and the Russians. He agreed to unfavourable terms, and, in the treaty of Adrianople (14 September 1829), gave up to Russia the delta of the Danube, and also the fortresses which dominated the road into Circassia. A Russian garrison remained for five years in the Danubian principalities.

[1] See above, p. 75.

It was clear to the British cabinet that Greece could not be left under Turkish suzerainty. Wellington, after Navarino, had failed to save the Turks from disaster by close collaboration with Russia; but he knew how to carry out a strategic retreat. The earlier proposal to create a tributary Greek state was recast in favour of complete independence. For the rest, the settlement, which took the form of protocols signed in February 1830 under the guarantee of Great Britain, Russia, and France, did not satisfy the Greeks. The frontier of the kingdom was drawn along a line south of the gulfs of Volo and Arta. It excluded the western strategic pass into Greece, the rich plain of Thessaly, and centres of Greek life such as Janina. Thousands of Greeks who had taken part in the rebellion were left under Turkish rule. Crete was also excluded from the kingdom. The western Powers assumed that the new state would come under Russian influence; therefore they made it as small as possible. In 1827 the Greeks had chosen Count Capo d'Istria as their president. Count Capo d'Istria was a Greek of Corfu. He had been born a subject of Venice, and lived as a Russian minister and diplomat. He could not even write Greek correctly. He made himself unpopular in Greece by attempting to introduce Russian bureaucratic methods, and by putting his relations into offices of state. In October 1831 two of his enemies assassinated him. The throne of Greece had already been offered to Leopold of Saxe-Coburg-Gotha, who found Belgium a more desirable kingdom. Six months later the Greeks chose the candidate recommended to them by the Powers: Prince Otho of Bavaria. Great Britain advised him to become a constitutional ruler; his father warned him that the grant of a constitution would be his ruin, and would lose him the support of Austria and Russia. Otho brought with him a staff of Bavarian officials who attempted to apply western ideas to the conditions and ways of life of Greek peasants. The Powers might have made a wiser choice, but they were occupied with matters of greater importance, and, in particular, with the settlement of Belgium.

II

THE FOREIGN POLICY OF PALMERSTON, 1830–41; THE *ENTENTE* WITH FRANCE, 1841–6; PALMERSTON AND THE CROWN, 1848–52

PALMERSTON became foreign secretary in November 1830.[1] He was only forty-six, but he had served as a lord of the admiralty from 1807 to 1809 and as secretary at war from 1809 to 1828. Palmerston held his post from 1830 until 1841, except for the four months of Peel's administration of 1834–5. He was foreign secretary from 1846 to 1851, home secretary from 1852 to 1855, prime minister from 1855 to 1858 and from 1859 until his death in 1865. During this time he sat for five different constituencies and was elected to sixteen parliaments; there were only two administrations between 1807 and 1852 in which he took no part. This record gives some measure of his energy and power of work. In an age when there were few figures to dispute with leading politicians the foremost place in public attention, Palmerston was marked out by temperament, by place, almost by continuity of tenure, for popularity among the English people. His gaiety, his love of horses,[2] his easy-going courage, good temper, and fine bearing stood in his favour with a high-spirited and over-confident nation. This popularity came to him later in life than to many of his contemporaries. During his earlier years at the war office he was more of a social figure; his work was concerned mainly with finance, and did not bring him into prominence, though, in spite of Canning's remark that he reached almost the summit of mediocrity, he did this work extremely well, and was never an idler.[3] In his later years he was the personification of England. His patriotism, his prejudices,

[1] Henry John Temple (1784–1865), 3rd Viscount Palmerston in the peerage of Ireland; spent most of his childhood abroad; educ. Harrow, Edinburgh, and St. John's College, Cambridge; M.P., 1807.

[2] Sir John Tenniel's cartoons show Palmerston with a straw in his mouth.

[3] When Sir W. Hamilton was publishing Dugald Stewart's lectures from the notes taken by pupils at Edinburgh, he found Palmerston's notes more full and more reliable than any others.

his language summarized the opinions of the ordinary man. Palmerston distrusted France and Russia; he called Austria 'an old woman', 'a European China'; he had a low opinion of Spanish politicians and of Italian absolutists, and considered that all foreigners, at some time or other, might benefit by English advice and English examples.[1] He saw no reason for concealing his opinions. Palmerston was never ungenerous,[2] and rarely tactless in his talk; but his dispatches were no less incisive than his conversation.[3] There was a bluntness about them hitherto almost unknown in diplomatic circumlocution. Bulwer, who admired him, noticed that 'the organ of veneration was not broadly pronounced in Lord Palmerston', and that 'generally when Lord Palmerston talks of diplomacy, he talks also of ships of war'. This sharpness of tone appeared mere bluster when applied to the great military Powers of the Continent, and mere bullying in the case of minor Powers. Palmerston was too ready to give advice without considering whether this advice might be resented. He was too often 'Lord Pumicestone'; he had not the caution of a trained diplomat, and his dislike of pedantry sometimes led him too far. Thus he allowed material from Woolwich Arsenal to be sent to the Sicilian rebels in 1848 because he was disgusted at the action of King Ferdinand ('Bomba') of Naples. He defended his action in a 'slashing, impudent speech'. His colleagues became increasingly restive at these speeches and

---

[1] Others who were less complacent about the institutions of their country also took this high view of English examples. An explanatory statement put out by the Council of the University of London immediately before its foundation, and revised by J. S. Mill, mentioned that 'at the desire of some persons high in authority in one of the liberated governments of South America, inquiry has been made whether an arrangement could be entered into for the reception of about 100 young men at the University of London from that country. . . . Were those who are to be the future legislators, governors, and leading men in the various classes of society of those countries, educated under the liberal and enlightened system of England, and accustomed, during the early years of life, to see around them the happiness and security which flow from our free institutions, it would be difficult to estimate too highly the extension that might thus be given to the moral influence of this country over the destinies of the New World.' Quoted in A. Aspinall and E. A. Smith, *English Historical Documents, 1783–1832*, p. 698.

[2] It is characteristic of Palmerston that he should have paid counsel to conduct the defence of a mad lieutenant who tried to kill him while he was leaving the war office in 1818.

[3] There were times when Palmerston could turn a fine phrase; thus he described the Polish question as 'that sad inheritance of triumphant wrong' (Duke of Argyll, i. 446).

foreign statesmen found them intolerable; Louis Philippe des-cribed Palmerston as *l'ennemi de ma maison*. Queen Victoria and the prince consort accused him of taking decisions without consulting the Crown. Palmerston made a spirited defence; but the complaints were not altogether ill founded.

It would be unfair to judge Palmerston by his rasping words and his high-handed ways. He decided questions on his own responsibility because he was not afraid of responsibility, and had taken the trouble to master the facts. He told the queen, in 1838, that 'in England the Ministers who are at the heads of the several departments of the State are liable any day and every day to defend themselves in Parliament; in order to do this they must be minutely acquainted with all the details of the business of their offices, and the only way of being constantly armed with such information is to conduct and direct those details themselves'.[1] He kept his ambassadors well informed, and expected to be well informed by them. He went as far beyond Canning in instructing the public as Canning had gone beyond Castlereagh. The business of the foreign office increased during his tenure of office. In 1830–1 there were only 11,546 dispatches; in 1849 the number had risen to 30,725. About twice as many dispatches were received. In spite of this mass of material Palmerston was never overwhelmed by detail. He had a policy of his own. He did not work on a 'system'; he might well have pointed to the failure of European statesmen like Metternich or Guizot, who had attempted to work by con-tinual reference to first principles. It is true that certain pre-suppositions or axioms governed Palmerston's policy. In 1832 he told the house of commons that 'the independence of con-stitutional States. . . . never can be a matter of indifference to the British parliament, or, I should hope, to the British public. Constitutional states I consider to be the natural allies of this country; and . . . no English Ministry will perform its duty if it be inattentive to the interests of such States'. He believed that the British government should act upon the principle of 'non-interference by force of arms in the affairs of any other country'. He did not think that 'we should be precluded, where it was expedient for us to do so, from interfering by friendly counsel and advice'.[2] In 1859 he put forward the same view in a letter to the queen. 'England is one of the greatest powers of the

[1] *Q.V.L.* 1st ser. i. 136.   [2] Hansard, 3rd ser. xiv. 1045 and 1067.

world ... and her right to have and to express opinions on matters ... bearing on her interests is unquestionable; and she is equally entitled to give upon such matters any advice which she may think useful, or to suggest any arrangements which she may deem conducive to the general good.'[1] The 'meddling' of which foreign ministers complained was thus a deliberate attempt to secure the creation of satisfied, peaceably inclined states under intelligent rule throughout the world. Palmerston was too clear-sighted to believe that this reconciliation of interests was within immediate reach. He accepted the judgement that *les nations n'ont pas de cousins*. His view that constitutional states were the 'natural allies' of England did not mean a rigid adherence to any single line of policy. He said in 1848 that 'it is a narrow policy to suppose that this country or that is to be marked out as the eternal ally or the perpetual enemy of England. We have no eternal allies, and we have no perpetual enemies. Our interests are eternal, and those interests it is our duty to follow.'[2]

Thus in matters of execution Palmerston, like Bismarck, was a master of improvisation. He was not unlike Bismarck in his attitude towards political parties. Although he sat in parliament for more than half a century he was never a party man. Party men could not 'place' him. He supported parliamentary reform in 1832, and resisted it twenty years later. He was a free-trader, yet he believed in a fixed duty on corn. Finally it would be a mistake to judge Palmerston by the angry criticisms of foreign statesmen. Englishmen have a right to judge their leaders by their devotion to English interests. The abuse of Palmerston came mainly from reactionary statesmen and reactionary Powers. Liberals throughout Europe told a different story. In any case, foreign statesmen who had dealings with Palmerston did not merely dislike and abuse him. Talleyrand thought him well fitted for his post, though he criticized his readiness to score a personal success at the expense of his general policy. Guizot wrote that he was 'without largeness of imagination', and that he concentrated too much upon the question of the moment; but Guizot admired Palmerston's directness. 'Sa manière de traiter, quoiqu'un peu étroite et taquine ... est nette, prompte, ferme.'[3]

---

[1] *Q.V.L.* 1st ser. iii. 463. [2] Hansard, 3rd ser. xcvii. 122.
[3] Guizot, *Mémoires*, vi. 131.

Palmerston, like Canning, began his work at the foreign office at a difficult moment. Until the year 1830 the revolutions which had disturbed the monarchs of the Holy Alliance had taken place in the less important countries of Europe. In 1830, and for the rest of Palmerston's career, the attacks upon the established political order came from the greater as well as from the smaller states. The French Revolution of July 1830 was welcomed in Great Britain as an imitation of the revolution of 1688. British interests were not harmed by the removal of Charles X of France. The accession of Louis Philippe broke the unity of the continental sovereigns. Henceforward France was a liberal power, and the two western constitutional states might well form a common front against the absolute monarchies of Russia, Prussia, and Austria. On the other hand, in every crisis between 1830 and 1841 French and British interests were dissimilar. Public opinion in each country was suspicious of the other; there might be common action, but there was little mutual confidence. The outbreak of revolution in Belgium put a severe test upon Anglo-French collaboration.[1] The union of the southern, or Austrian provinces with the northern, or Dutch Netherlands in a new kingdom had been due largely to English pressure at the Congress of Vienna. This union offered a reasonable solution of an awkward problem: the protection of Europe against the revival of militant jacobinism in France. The Belgians differed from the Dutch in language and religion; but there were three languages and two religions in Switzerland, and, for that matter, two languages in Belgium. The economic interests of Belgium and Holland were not irreconcilable and the union might have been lasting. It was neither satisfactory nor lasting because Belgians and Dutch were unwilling to merge their separate interests. Even so the Belgians, who complained that the Dutch kept a monopoly of public and private interest, did not suggest complete separation; the success of the revolution of July in France changed their views. In August 1830 the people of Brussels rose against the Dutch. At first the Belgians asked merely for administrative autonomy, but the Dutch king decided to reoccupy Brussels before making any concessions. The result was a general rising.

The Belgian revolution affected Great Britain in her most

---

[1] For Palmerston's diplomacy during these years, see Sir C. K. Webster, *The Foreign Policy of Palmerston, 1830–1841* (1951).

vital and long-standing interests. In the months before his fall, Charles X had caused suspicion in England by his expedition to Algeria and his plans for a vast exchange of territory in Europe which would give the Rhineland to France. Charles X was now an exile; his successor might try to win popularity by bringing forward one of his sons as a candidate for the throne of an independent Belgium. He might even propose the annexation of Belgium. The Belgians would certainly ask for French help, and French sentiment could hardly allow the defeat of Francophil Belgian revolutionaries by Dutch troops. Prussia and the Germanic states, Russia, and Austria, would be on the side of the Dutch. Therefore the Belgian question might involve Europe in a general war. Great Britain was too much concerned with the fate of the Low Countries to keep out of such a war. On the other hand Louis Philippe did not want Europe or his own countrymen to consider him a jacobin king; the liberal bankers and moderate politicians who had supported him against Charles X did not want a revolutionary crusade or a European coalition against France. Louis Philippe took the wisest possible step. He sent Talleyrand as ambassador to London. Talleyrand saw that the interests of France required an *entente* with Great Britain, and that this *entente* could be obtained only if France took account of the traditional British views about Belgium. If Great Britain and France worked together, the other Powers would accept their decisions.

A conference of the five great Powers, Great Britain, France, Russia, Austria, and Prussia, met in London at the beginning of November 1830. The Powers invited the Belgians and the Dutch to withdraw their troops to the respective territories which they had occupied before the Union in 1815. At this point Palmerston succeeded Aberdeen as foreign secretary. Palmerston had the advantage of the prime minister's wise, if hesitating, judgement.[1] This advice was necessary because the Belgians, to the anger of Prussia, Austria, and Russia, wanted complete independence and made large territorial demands. They asked for Luxemburg, Limburg, and Dutch Flanders as well as for the old provinces of the Austrian Netherlands and the bishopric of Liége.[2] The Powers settled otherwise. The conference of

---

[1] Palmerston wrote a full and generous account of the value of Grey's advice and help at the time of Grey's retirement in 1834.

[2] Luxemburg had been created a grand duchy at the Vienna settlement, and

London drew up a protocol on 20 January 1831, assigning to Holland Dutch Flanders and Limburg, and leaving Luxemburg in possession of King William. The new Belgian state would be established under guarantees of perpetual neutrality and the 'integrity and inviolability of its territory'. The Dutch accepted the decision with bad grace; the Belgians rejected it, and looked to France for help. Talleyrand had already alarmed Palmerston by suggesting that France should receive Luxemburg, or the fortresses of Philippeville and Marienbourg which she had lost after the Hundred Days. Palmerston told Lord Granville, British ambassador in Paris, that English friendship with France rested upon 'the supposition that she contents herself with the finest territory in Europe, and does not mean to open a new chapter of encroachment and conquest'.[1] The suggestions were not renewed, but there was a further problem. The Belgians would not take any member of the house of Orange as their king. They put forward two other candidates: the duke of Nemours, a son of Louis Philippe, and the duke of Leuchtenberg, a grandson of the Empress Josephine. Great Britain would not accept Nemours,[2] Louis Philippe would not accept a close connexion of the Bonapartes. The Belgians voted for Nemours, but Louis Philippe, after some wavering and a good deal of intrigue, wisely declined the offer. In April 1831 the Powers advised the choice of Leopold of Saxe-Coburg-Gotha.[3] The Belgians themselves had talked of Leopold, and were ready to elect him; but they still held out for more territory. The Powers gave them until 1 June 1831 to accept the award of January, and threatened that an attack on the Dutch would be regarded as an act of war against the European Concert. Finally the Belgians sent a delegation to London. The delegates took back with them an agreement of eighteen articles (25 June 1831). The Powers had their way over Dutch Flanders, and left the question of Luxemburg for negotiation. The proposals had a stormy time in Belgium, but were accepted.

given to the Orange family in compensation for their estates in Nassau, which were handed over to Prussia. Dutch Flanders, the country on the left bank of the Scheldt below Antwerp, had been taken from Holland by France in 1795.

[1] H. L. Bulwer (Lord Dalling), *Life of Viscount Palmerston*, ii. 29.

[2] Palmerston wrote to the British ambassador in Paris: 'If the choice falls upon Nemours, and if the king of the French accepts, it will be a proof that the policy of France is like an infection clinging to the walls of the dwelling, and breaking out in every successive occupant who comes within their influence.' Bulwer, ii. 96.

[3] See above, p. 104.

It was now the turn of the Dutch. They protested against the election of Leopold, and refused to recognize the eighteen articles. They marched into Belgium at the beginning of August 1831, and in ten days defeated the Belgian levies. Meanwhile a British fleet sailed to the Belgian coast, and a French army advanced to keep the Dutch out of Brussels. The Dutch attack had thus changed the situation. British public opinion was alarmed at the presence of a French army in Belgium, and still more alarmed when the French did not retire after the Dutch had gone back to Holland. Palmerston might well write: 'So here is a pretty fly out of the King of the Netherlands! Who has bit him I cannot guess; we have some suspicion of France.'[1] Talleyrand did not improve matters by suggesting to the Prussian representative at the London Conference that Belgium might be partitioned. On 13 August 1831 Palmerston wrote to the British ambassador in Paris that he would shortly have to answer a parliamentary question about the French intentions. 'The Yes or No which I shall have to utter will imply events of most extensive consequences to the two countries, and to all Europe.'[2] The French had already raised the question of the demolition of some or all of the barrier fortresses set up in the Belgian part of the united Netherlands after the fall of Napoleon.[3] The British minister in Brussels discovered that Leopold was beginning secret negotiations with France over these fortresses. Palmerston had agreed that the number of fortresses might be cut down; he insisted that the Belgians must have some defensive works on their exposed frontier with France. Otherwise Holland and the German states would be open to French invasion. The matter did not concern Great Britain alone. Prussia was preparing to move against the French; Nicholas of Russia, whose hands had been tied by rebellion in Poland, was now free to support Prussia. The French gave way and withdrew their troops. Palmerston then agreed to the dismantling of five fortresses.

[1] Bulwer, ii. 96–97.
[2] Ibid. 105.
[3] See also vol. xi of this *History*. By 1830 about 25 fortresses had been built or rebuilt at a cost of £7,000,000, but the Dutch and Belgians had not kept them in good condition. It was unlikely that Belgium would have the men or money to maintain them adequately. The neutralization of Belgium provided, on the French view, a strong argument for doing away with a military threat to France on Belgian territory.

Henceforward Great Britain and France worked together with less mutual suspicion. The Belgians and the Dutch were still quarrelling over the terms of separation. The twenty-four articles of October 1831, drawn up in London, gave the Belgians a share of Luxemburg and Limburg, and at the same time charged them with a larger amount of the public debt of the former united kingdom of the Netherlands. Again the Dutch refused to agree. For some months there was a deadlock. The Dutch would not give up the citadel of Antwerp; hence the Belgians would not hand over any part of Luxemburg or Limburg. The king of Holland and the absolutist Powers were waiting for a change of government in England. They believed that the reform bill would be defeated, and that a tory government would be more favourable to the Dutch. Meanwhile Leopold of Belgium married a daughter of Louis Philippe, and the Belgians once more set their hopes on France.

The British cabinet was tired of the affair. Grey disliked the 'princelings' Leopold and William. He wrote early in September to Lord Holland: 'What is to be done with these damned Dutch and Belgians?' Palmerston wisely followed the policy laid down by Castlereagh, and continued by Canning, in relation to Russia. If Great Britain acted with France, the French would do no more than help the Belgians, while the other Powers could not object to the coercion of the Dutch by combined Anglo-French action. A French army besieged the citadel of Antwerp; a Franco-British squadron blockaded the Dutch ports. Antwerp surrendered on 23 December 1832, and the French troops went back to France. The danger was past, although the Luxemburg question was not settled until 1839.[1] Palmerston's first negotiation on a grand scale had been a success. He had avoided war and kept the French out of Belgium.

Meanwhile two other states, with the 'limited interests' of minor Powers, threatened to disturb Anglo-French relations. In 1829 Ferdinand VII of Spain lost his third wife. Ferdinand was childless; he disappointed his brother Don Carlos and his party by marrying a fourth wife, Maria Christina of Naples. In October 1830 the queen gave birth to a daughter. There was some doubt whether the law of succession excluded women

---

[1] The final treaty which defined the frontiers and the neutrality of Belgium was signed under the guarantee of the five Great Powers in 1839.

from the throne.[1] At all events, after the death of Ferdinand in September 1833, the Carlist faction refused to recognize the regency of Maria Christina for her daughter.

There were similar troubles in Portugal. Soon after Wellington had withdrawn the British troops sent by Canning in 1827,[2] Dom Miguel, the absolutist uncle of a constitutional queen, was offered the crown. The queen went to Brazil; in 1832 Dom Pedro landed at Oporto with a force brought from Brazil to enforce his daughter's rights. Here he was blockaded until, in the summer of 1833, his fleet, commanded by Captain Charles Napier,[3] defeated Miguel's ships off Cape St. Vincent. Pedro entered Lisbon. British interests were not directly involved in these Spanish and Portuguese quarrels, but Palmerston was afraid of French interference in Spain. French public opinion disliked English pressure in the Belgian question, and Louis Philippe, realizing that he could not regain the Rhine frontier, might consider that a close connexion with Spain was in French interests. Once again Palmerston thought it prudent to work with France: a quadruple alliance of the constitutional states of the west, Great Britain, France, Spain, and Portugal, would serve 'as a powerful counterpoise' to the three absolutist monarchies of eastern Europe,[4] Palmerston knew that Talleyrand wanted an Anglo-French military alliance. British opinion would not have supported an alliance of this kind; the tories were already restive at the 'desertion' of Holland in favour of Belgium. Palmerston's idea of an alliance including Spain and Portugal was therefore a clever move. If it was not worth much as a counterpoise against the eastern Powers it prevented separate action by France in Spain. Palmerston carried the plan through the cabinet 'by a *coup de main*, taking them by surprise, and not leaving them time to make objections'. He described his work as 'a capital hit, and all my own doing'.[5] He won the assent of the Spanish and Portuguese constitutional parties before he explained his plan to Talleyrand. The French

[1] The changes in the law of succession went back to the eighteenth century. Ferdinand excluded his daughter in 1832, and restored her rights three months later. These rights were recognized by the cortes in June 1833.

[2] See above, pp. 211–12.

[3] Napier took no notice of the foreign enlistment act of 1819. He served in tne Portuguese navy as Admiral Carlos de Ponza. For his later career, see below, p. 274.

[4] Bulwer, op. cit. ii. 180–1. Palmerston added that he would 'like to see Metternich's face when he reads our treaty'. [5] Ibid. ii. 186.

accepted the offer; they could hardly refuse. The terms of the treaty (22 April 1834) bound the regents of Spain and Portugal to compel Carlos and Miguel to leave their respective countries. Great Britain promised a naval force to co-operate in this work of compulsion, and the French agreed, in a supplementary treaty (August 1834), to prevent help from reaching the Carlists through France.

The troubles of Portugal were soon settled. Dom Miguel left Portugal for ever; the Miguelists remained quiet, and in 1836 Queen Maria married a Coburg husband. In Spain the Carlists were beyond the range of the British navy; the cabinet suspended the foreign enlistment act, and allowed a British legion to serve with the Spanish constitutionalist troops.[1] Wellington, who disapproved of the plan, put every obstacle in the way of recruiting; the Spanish authorities never gave the legion enough supplies or ammunition, and in spite of British protests the Carlists put to death the legionaries whom they captured. The war dragged on until 1839, and might have lasted longer if Don Carlos's commander had not deserted to the constitutionalist side.

The French were jealous of the friendship between Great Britain and the Spanish and Portuguese leaders. In 1836 they withdrew their soldiers from Spain. Palmerston wrote in January 1837 that 'the spirit of the treaty was to expel Carlos from Spain; and I should like to know what [the French] have done, which could be in the slightest degree calculated to produce that effect—absolutely nothing'.[2] 'Not one word' was said about France or the French alliance in the king's speech at the opening of parliament in 1837. Palmerston wrote: 'We can say nothing in their praise, and therefore silence is the most complimentary thing we can bestow upon them.'

Although Anglo-French co-operation was necessary in the Near East, if the absolutist Powers were not to have their way,

[1] Colonel George de Lacy Evans (1787–1870) commanded the British legion. He had seen active service in India and in the Peninsular war. In the war against the United States, he occupied Washington with a small force of light infantry and burned the Capitol. He took part in the Waterloo campaign, and, in 1830, entered parliament as a radical. He commanded a division in the Crimean war; he was severely wounded at the battle of Alma, but fought again at the Russian sortie from Sebastopol. He was then invalided, only to leave his bed on board ship at Balaclava when he heard the sound of firing. Evans was knighted in 1837 for his services in Spain.   [2] Bulwer, ii. 242–3.

the eastern question brought France and Great Britain to the verge of war at the end of Palmerston's first period at the foreign office, and led the way to the final break between Palmerston and Louis Philippe in 1846. In 1828–9 Great Britain, for all her words about Turkish integrity, did nothing to prevent Russia from obtaining more concessions and the sultan from losing territory and prestige. At this time Palmerston believed that Turkey was rapidly falling to pieces. Mehemet Ali complained that Mahmud had not given him anything in return for his help in suppressing the Greek rebellion. Mahmud held that Mehemet Ali had no claim because he had not reconquered the Morea; Mehemet answered that he had lost his fleet in the sultan's service. In October 1831 Mehemet sent his son Ibrahim into Palestine, proclaimed the sultan a heretical reformer, and declared war on him. Ibrahim defeated two Turkish armies, and occupied Syria. In November 1832 Mahmud appealed to Great Britain; in December Ibrahim won another victory at Konieh. The way to Constantinople was now open. Mahmud could get no help from Great Britain. France was inclined to support Mehemet Ali. The sultan therefore turned, as a last hope, to Russia. In February 1833 a Russian fleet anchored off Constantinople, and Russian troops encamped on the eastern side of the Bosphorus.

Russian policy had changed since the war of 1828–9. In September 1829 Nicholas had considered whether the breakup of Turkey would really serve Russian interests. Russia could not take the whole of the Turkish empire, unless she were prepared to fight Great Britain, Austria, and France. If Turkey were partitioned, Austria would ask for Bosnia, Albania, and Montenegro. France would want Egypt, Great Britain the Aegean Islands and Crete. The Powers would insist upon leaving Constantinople a free port. Thus Russia would have strong neighbours instead of a weak Turkey, and the Black Sea would be open to the British and French fleets. Therefore Russia might find it more expedient to keep Turkey alive, and to extend her control over the Turkish Empire.[1] This plan would not exclude an advance in Asia, and the steady growth of Russian influence in Greece, the Danubian principalities, and Servia; if the sultan

---

[1] One of the Russian experts consulted by Nicholas pointed out that a Turkey confined, or practically confined, to Asia Minor might well become much stronger than a loosely ruled Turkish Empire with a large number of non-Moslem subjects.

were in danger, Russia would interfere in his favour. Hence the Russian action in 1833. Palmerston did not know Nicholas's decision. If he had known it, he would not have been reassured. He seems to have been taken by surprise at the Russian promptness in answering the sultan, but he had wanted to intervene on the Turkish side, and had failed to get the cabinet to agree to immediate action. The British fleet was occupied in the North Sea and off the coast of Portugal; a large squadron could be sent to the eastern Mediterranean only at the cost of mobilizing more ships.

Turkey was saved, at a price, from Mehemet Ali. Mahmud surrendered Adana to Ibrahim and the pashaliks of Syria and Tarsus for the lifetime of Mehemet. Mehemet accepted the terms, and the Russian expedition went home. Russia then asked for her reward. The methods of her agents were simple. They bribed the ministers in power; they bribed the ministers out of power. Nesselrode, the Russian minister of foreign affairs, wrote: 'Le Sérail resta pour un moment sans rivalité et sans intrigues. Car les favoris et les ministres rivaux également compromis les uns vers les autres se voyaient tous à la fois complices de la même entreprise.'[1] The Russians now asked for too much. The treaty of Unkiar Skelessi, signed on 8 July 1833, was an agreement of mutual alliance and assistance. In a secret annexe Russia resigned all claim to material help from Turkey in return for a promise that the Dardanelles should be closed to foreign warships at the demand of the Russian government. This annexe repeated the old rule about the closing of the Dardanelles, but Palmerston suspected that Russia intended to use the treaty to secure a kind of protectorate over the Turkish empire, and to establish a right of passing through the straits, nominally to defend the European coasts of Turkey.[2]

The Powers soon heard of the secret annexe. Although Great Britain and France protested to the sultan the treaty was ratified. In September 1833 the Austrian and Russian emperors met

---

[1] Schiemann, *Geschichte Russlands unter Nikolaus I*, iii. 221.

[2] The Anglo-Turkish treaty of 1809 affirmed the 'ancient regulation of the Ottoman Empire', in other words, the opening of the straits to merchantmen, and the closing of the straits, in time of peace, to ships of war. In time of war the sultan would open the straits to his friends and close them to his enemies. The Russo-Turkish treaty of Bucharest (1812) did not mention the straits. The question was not discussed at Vienna. The treaty of Adrianople (1829) said nothing about warships. The Russian fleet which fought at Navarino came from the Baltic.

at Münchengrätz in Bohemia for a general discussion. They agreed upon common action to protect the sovereignty of the sultan. Their interests were so very different that a promise to act together was little more than a form of words; Metternich suggested a joint pact among the four great Powers directly interested in Turkey. Palmerston could not believe that Nicholas was sincere. The emperor explained that the treaty of Unkiar Skelessi was merely a 'moral guarantee' of the independence of Turkey, and that he did not intend to obtain exclusive privileges for Russia. Palmerston gave in March 1834 his own interpretation of Nicholas's disinterestedness; 'Russia . . . perhaps thinks it better to take the place by sap than by storm' —a good summary of Russian intentions. He thought that Russia was 'pursuing a system of universal aggression on all sides, partly from the personal character of the Emperor, partly from the permanent system of her Government'. He pointed to the fortification of the Åland islands and the line of the Vistula, and to Russian intrigues in Persia.[1]

For five years there was peace in the Near East. During this period Palmerston began to think that the reform of Turkey was not impossible. He wrote in 1838: 'I am inclined to suspect that those who say that the Turkish Empire is rapidly going from bad to worse ought rather to say that the other countries of Europe are year by year becoming better acquainted with the manifest and manifold defects of the organization of Turkey.' A year later (September 1839), in one of his few references to political philosophy, Palmerston was even more confident.

As to the Turkish empire, if we can procure for it ten years of peace under the joint protection of the five Powers, and if those years are profitably employed in reorganizing the internal system of the empire, there is no reason whatever why it should not become again a respectable Power. Half the wrong conclusions at which mankind arrive are reached by the abuse of metaphors, and by mistaking general resemblance or imaginary similarity for real identity. Thus people compare an ancient monarchy with an old building, an old

---

[1] Bulwer, ii. 175 and 179. In Feb. 1834 the king's speech included a direct warning to Russia. 'The peace of Turkey since the settlement made with Mehemet Ali has not been interrupted. . . . It will be my object to prevent any change in the relations of that Empire with other Powers, which might affect its stability and independence.' King William IV shared Palmerston's distrust of Russia. In Aug. 1833 his speech contained a reference to the preservation of the Turkish empire. He 'spoke the passage. . . with emphasis and looked round at [the Russian ambassador] to see how he took it'.

tree, or an old man ... they imagine that ... the same laws which
govern inanimate matter, or vegetable and animal life, govern also
nations and states. Than which there cannot be a greater or more
utterly unphilosophical mistake. ... Therefore all that we hear every
day of the week about the decay of the Turkish empire, and its
being a dead body or a sapless trunk, and so forth, is pure and un-
adulterated nonsense.[1]

These hopes for the future of Turkey seemed paradoxical at
the time when they were written. The Turkish empire was
again in danger from Mehemet Ali. Mehemet had never been
satisfied with the concessions made to him in 1833. He was an
old man; he wanted to secure his dominions for his house. The
Syrian provinces were necessary to him for the protection of
Egypt and Arabia; they were rich in men for his armies, timber for his ships, and money for his treasury. Mehemet thought
that he could rely upon the diplomatic help of France, and that
Great Britain was more interested in a strong Turkey than in
the rule of any particular sultan. Mahmud II was no longer
young. He too wanted to secure his dominions. He was afraid
of the spread of disaffection from Syria to Asia Minor. He
believed that he could take the risk of military defeat because
he knew that Great Britain would not allow the break-up of his
empire. In 1839 Mahmud advanced his armies to meet those
of Mehemet Ali. The Turks took with them Moltke, who was
at this time on the Turkish staff; but at the decisive battle
of Nezib (June 1839) they refused to listen to Moltke's advice
and chose dispositions suggested by their mullahs, who ranked
as generals, while Moltke was only a captain. They were utterly
defeated; the question of the fate of Turkey was reopened.

Palmerston warned Mahmud not to attack the Egyptians;
but his own policy had shown that, in the last resort, he would
support the Turks. In 1838 he signed a commercial treaty with
Turkey on terms which assisted British merchants, and incidentally affected the finances of Mehemet Ali. The sultan
agreed to abolish monopolies throughout his dominions. These
monopolies had been an obstacle to British trade; they were the
basis of the Egyptian fiscal system. In 1838-9 the sultan of Aden,
threatened by Mehemet and bribed by the English, was forced
to accept a British protectorate.[2] Palmerston intended that

[1] Bulwer, ii. pp. 287 and 298.
[2] Aden was the best coaling-station on the new steamship route from Egypt to

Mehemet should be kept within his own dominions, and that Ibrahim should not succeed to his father's conquests beyond Egypt. He was not afraid of Mehemet himself, even if the Egyptians took Constantinople; the danger to British interests lay in a possible alliance between Mehemet, as ruler of Asia Minor, and Russia. There was a further risk. France and Russia might arrange a settlement, at the expense of Great Britain, giving France a predominance in Egypt and Syria, and Russia the control of Persia. A Franco-Russian agreement was unlikely: if Palmerston distrusted France, Nicholas hated Louis Philippe. Moreover the Russian decision of 1829 still held good. Any change of policy might bring a coalition of the Powers against Russia. Nicholas also thought that, by joining the concert of the Powers, he might separate France from Great Britain.

In July 1839 Great Britain, France, Russia, Austria, and Prussia agreed to settle the eastern question in concert. Mahmud was on his death-bed, and unconscious, when the news of Nezib reached his ministers. The Turkish fleet deserted to the Egyptians, and sailed for Alexandria, as soon as the result of the battle was known in Constantinople. French opinion disliked the agreement of the five Powers. Thiers, who took office in March 1840, spoke of Mehemet Ali as a *nouvel Alexandre*, and thought that England and Russia would not easily dislodge him from Asia Minor and Syria. Thiers seems to have tried secretly to bring about a settlement between the new sultan, Abdul Mejid, and Mehemet. Palmerston was sure that the power of Mehemet, 'an ignorant barbarian', was 'the arrantest humbug, built upon delusion and fancy', and that France would not risk a war with the rest of Europe.[1] In July 1840 he made a new agreement between the four Powers without consulting the French.

India. This route, though dangerous, was already important, and its importance was likely to increase with the rapid improvement in the ocean-going capacities of steamships. Attempts to survey the 'overland' route through Mesopotamia had been disappointing, and had caused jealousy in France. The French consul at Basra tried to persuade the Arabs to block the passage of the British ships of exploration by putting a boom across the river.

[1] Palmerston's estimate of the military weakness of Mehemet Ali was based partly upon the long British experience of eastern despotisms. He was also influenced by reports from Generals Chrzanowski, a Pole, and Jochmus, a Hanoverian who had served with the British legion in Spain. The British admiral commanding the Mediterranean squadron, and Colonel Campbell, British consul-general at Alexandria, thought that it would be difficult to drive the Egyptians out of Syria. Wellington believed that the Egyptian communications could be cut.

Nicholas's hopes were fulfilled; France and Great Britain would no longer work together against Russia. Mehemet Ali was promised the southern part of Syria, including Acre, for his own lifetime, and the whole of Egypt for his house if he accepted these terms within ten days. Thiers was indignant at the exclusion of France, and talked of war. His talk alarmed the Germans,[1] but left Palmerston, though not his colleagues, untroubled. Mehemet Ali was already embarrassed by a revolt of the Christian tribes in the Lebanon, where the rebels were supported by British and Austrian marines and Turkish soldiers. Acre was bombarded and taken, and Mehemet gave way. Palmerston wanted to punish him for his obstinacy, but the British cabinet was glad to see the end of a dangerous crisis. Thiers resigned, and France came back into the concert of the Powers. Mehemet Ali restored Syria, Crete, and Arabia to Turkey; he was confirmed in the hereditary possession of Egypt on condition of the payment of an annual tribute to the sultan. In July 1841 the Powers, in the first international agreement on the subject, agreed to respect the 'ancient rule' about the closing of the straits, while Turkey was at peace, to the warships of all nations.

Throughout the eastern crisis Palmerston had shown great coolness of mind. Many of his party thought his policy dangerous. Melbourne himself had serious doubts about it. In July 1840 Palmerston talked of resignation, and complained that his colleagues criticized him in conversation with the ministers of foreign states. He was right in thinking that co-operation with Russia was of the first importance. If he followed the tradition of working with the Power whose independent action he most feared, he would run the least risk. Palmerston did not trust Louis Philippe: 'The truth is that Louis Philippe is the prime mover of the foreign relations of France, and one must admit in one's own mind that if he had been a very straightforward, scrupulous and high-minded man, he would not now have been sitting on the French throne.'[2] Yet he knew that the French king was 'not a man to run amuck'. He could indeed not be sure that French opinion would not force Louis Philippe's hand. In October 1840 he advised the British ambassador in

---

[1] Thiers began the fortification of Paris. This plan had been talked of for ten years. The German alarm may be seen in the popularity of Becker's 'Die Wacht am Rhein', which was published in a newspaper at Trier. The term 'armed peace' was first applied at this time to describe the condition of Europe.

[2] Bulwer, ii. 311.

Paris what he should do about his house and archives 'in the event of [his] coming away'. He believed that 'all Frenchmen want to encroach and extend their territorial possessions at the expense of other nations. Their vanity prompts them to be the first nation in the world. . . It is a misfortune to Europe that the national character of a great and powerful people, placed in the centre [*sic*] of Europe, should be such as it is.'[1]

The settlement of 1841 was chiefly to the advantage of Great Britain, but there was a reverse side to it. Nicholas had not obtained much from defending the integrity of Turkey in the hope that Turkey might fall slowly but more surely under Russian influence. After some years the emperor began to think of a more drastic solution: the partition of Turkey. His failure to obtain the closing of the straits in time of war showed him that the Powers would not give up their right to enter the Black Sea at the sultan's request. Nicholas took his own precautions. The construction of new docks and fortifications at Sebastopol would make a Russian attack upon Constantinople easier, even if France or Great Britain occupied strong points in the Aegean islands within reach of the Dardanelles.[2]

Moreover Palmerston's methods had been too drastic. He may have been right in thinking that 'firm and stout language to the French Government and to Frenchmen' was the best way of 'usefully supporting the interests of peace'; but he might have remembered his own words that 'of all mistakes, in public affairs as well as in private, the greatest is to truckle to swagger and bully, or even to unjustifiable violence'.[3] Greville wrote of Palmerston during the eastern crisis: 'Everything may possibly turn out according to his expectations. He is a man blessed with extraordinary good fortune, and his motto seems to be that of Danton, "De l'audace. . .". But there is a flippancy in his tone, an undoubting self-sufficiency, and a levity in discussing interests of such tremendous magnitude, which satisfies me that he is a very dangerous man to be entrusted with the uncontrolled management of our foreign relations.' Greville admitted that 'events have so befriended Palmerston that he is now in the right, and has got his colleagues with

---

[1] Bulwer, ii. 349.

[2] Barante, the French ambassador at St. Petersburg, who saw the fortress in construction, wrote in 1838 that it would be the cause of a European war (Barante, *Mémoires*, vi. 131–6).   [3] Bulwer, ii. 318–19.

him; but where he is and always has been wrong is in his neglect
of forms; the more *fortiter* he is in *re*, the more *suaviter* he ought
to be in *modo*. . . this is the reason he is so detested by all
the *Corps Diplomatique*, and has made such enemies all over
Europe.'[1]

Palmerston paid heavily in later years for his faults of manner
and method; the immediate burden of improving Anglo-
French relations fell upon his tory successor. Fortunately the
policies of Great Britain and France were directed between
1841 and 1846 by men whose general outlook was similar.
Guizot found in Peel and Aberdeen statesmen of the *juste milieu*,
and in the British constitution the balance between democracy
and aristocracy which was wanting in France. He realized that
with English support the monarchy of July was safe in Europe.
The friendship of England would allow France a free hand in
Algeria, and a personal *rapprochement* with the English monarchy
would more than counterbalance the coldness of the imperial
houses of Austria and Russia.

Aberdeen and Peel also knew the advantages of an Anglo-
French understanding, though Peel was never hopeful of success.
The *entente* would not be popular in either country; there would
be attacks in parliament and in the French chamber. Time
alone could efface the memory of Palmerston's 'capital hits';
meanwhile every minor point of difference would become a
question of prestige. The first of these problems arose out of
the methods used to put down the African slave trade. There
was only one way of suppressing this trade. If no slave-ships
crossed the Atlantic, there would be no slaves to sell. The passage of slave-ships could be prevented if the warships of those
nations which patrolled the west coast of Africa had the right
to examine all vessels, whatever their flag and nationality, under
suspicion of carrying slaves. An effective police measure of
this kind required international agreement. Great Britain had
more ships on patrol work than any other nation; she had
made agreements about the right of search with other Powers,
notably, in 1831 and 1833, with France and, in 1835, with

[1] Greville, op. cit., 24 Aug. and 13 Nov. 1840. Guizot had Palmerston's aims
and methods in mind when he described the characteristic faults of English foreign
policy as 'l'orgueil ambitieux, la préoccupation constante et passionnée de soi-
même, le besoin ardent et exclusif de se faire partout sa part et sa place, la plus
grande place possible, n'importe aux dépens de quoi et de qui'. Guizot, vii. 309.

Spain.[1] Palmerston, who worked with determination to suppress the trade, had prepared a treaty allowing the cruisers of Great Britain, France, Prussia, Russia, and Austria a general right of search. The United States alone of the great Powers refused to join in this common arrangement. Great Britain and France were indeed the only Powers likely to exercise the right; no other European Power sent regular patrols to the African coast.

The signature of the treaty was delayed by the eastern crisis, but Guizot agreed to sign it after Palmerston had left office.[2] The French Chamber protested against the treaty; Guizot attacked the view taken by the deputies[3] but did not venture to resist them. The matter was settled in 1845 by an arrangement allowing naval officers of each nation to assure themselves of the nationality of any vessels under suspicion; the right of search was not reciprocal.

The second question at issue between France and Great Britain was a little absurd, though it raised large issues. In the year 1825 a protestant missionary named Pritchard settled in the island of Tahiti. Eleven years later two French catholic missionaries were not allowed to land on the island. They appealed to the nearest French naval officer, Dupetit-Thouars, who insisted upon an apology and an indemnity. The indemnity was paid in 1838 and the queen of Tahiti signed a treaty of friendship with France. In 1826 Pritchard had persuaded her to ask for the protection of Great Britain and for permission to use the British flag; Canning would not allow anything more than a promise of general friendliness. In 1838 the queen, as soon as she was free from the presence of a French ship, appealed to Queen Victoria. Once again the British government refused to bring the island under British protection. In 1842 Dupetit-Thouars reappeared with a suggestion that Tahiti might gain much from the protection of France. In 1843 the admiral took

[1] Between 1835 and 1840 British cruisers captured over a hundred ships equipped for the slave trade and claiming Spanish nationality. Eighteen of these ships were carrying slaves. See also below, p. 370, and C. Lloyd, *The Navy and the Slave Trade*, 1949.

[2] Guizot refused to sign the treaty during the last months of Palmerston's tenure of office because Palmerston made an ill-informed and incautious criticism of the French treatment of the native population of Algeria.

[3] The opposition was led by a deputy from Nantes. The main reason for the support given to him in the chamber was jealousy of English sea-power; but it was suggested that some representatives of the shipping interests in the west of France were not unconnected with the transport of slaves across the Altantic.

the law into his own hands, and formerly annexed the island to France. Early in 1844 he arrested Pritchard.

Guizot was once more in a difficult position. If he disavowed the admiral, French opinion would hold that he was being subservient to Great Britain.[1] He settled the matter by refusing annexation, and assuming a protectorate over the island. Louis Philippe gave Pritchard a thousand pounds in compensation out of his private fortune, and the affair was over.[2]

Other matters might have led to friction. The plan of a customs union between France and Belgium was disliked by French manufacturers, and did not outlast the fear that Belgium might be attracted into the German Zollverein. There were local disputes over the question of the government of Greece; but these disputes caused little interest in France or Great Britain, and were kept for the most part within the limits of diplomatic correspondence. On the other hand the affairs of Spain became a major issue. The defeat of the Carlists left Queen Isabella established on the Spanish throne. In 1840 the queen was ten years old; within a few years she would marry, or, rather, a husband would be found for her. Louis Philippe wanted one of his sons to be the queen's husband. The British government objected to any form of union between the crowns of France and Spain. Guizot described this policy as 'obstinately retrospective,' but the French occupation of Algeria had given the old maxims of British foreign policy a new significance. On the other hand Louis Philippe would not agree to the queen's marriage with a prince of the house of Coburg. The French suggested a Bourbon, though they were ready to accept a Bourbon of the second rank from Naples. The Neapolitan Bourbons thought that, however insecure they might be at Naples, they would be even more unpopular in Spain. A marriage with the son of Don Carlos was impossible owing to the violence of

---

[1] Anglo-French rivalry over the occupation of New Zealand was partly responsible for the strength of French feeling about Tahiti. See below, p. 392.

[2] Tahiti was annexed to France in 1883. The violence of French opinion over the affair may be seen from a single instance. When Guizot told the chamber that English and protestant missionaries could be as devoted as French and catholic missionaries, he was interrupted by cries of '*commerçants*'. Guizot himself used language which belongs more to the imperialism of the latter half of the nineteenth century, 'Partout où la civilisation européenne et chrétienne se porte et se déploie, la France doit prendre sa place et déployer son propre génie. . . . Ce qui lui est indispensable, c'est de posséder dans tous les grands foyers d'activité commerciale et internationale, des stations maritimes sûres et fortes'. Guizot, vi. 275.

Spanish factions. There remained two other cousins of the queen. Unfortunately Don Henry, the younger cousin, was too wild in morals and too liberal in politics,[1] and Don Francis, the elder, too effeminate, while their mother had quarrelled with Maria Christina, the mother of the queen.

The Spanish marriage was discussed between Aberdeen and Guizot, and between Queen Victoria and Louis Philippe at meetings of these two monarchs in 1843[2] and 1845. Guizot promised not to work for an Orleanist prince; Aberdeen would not bring forward a Coburg. Aberdeen was ready to agree that the queen should marry one of her Spanish cousins; and that, after the queen had had children, her sister might marry a son of Louis Philippe. There was no written compact between France and Great Britain: Guizot thought that the Coburg candidature was out of the way. Aberdeen felt that the question must be decided by the Spaniards and that the 'exclusions' were not of equal value. A marriage with a prince of the reigning house of France would revive an international question of the first order; a Coburg marriage would not affect the balance of power. Aberdeen would not encourage the Coburg marriage. He did not consider himself pledged to prevent it. The affair was complicated by personal rivalry between the British and French ambassadors at Madrid,[3] by the intrigues of the Coburg family, with Stockmar as their man of affairs, and by the anxiety of the queen mother to obtain a better match for her daughter than was offered by any of the Bourbon princes.

In the early months of 1846 Guizot sent a formal memorandum to Aberdeen that France would not accept a Coburg. Aberdeen made no direct answer, but warned the British ambassador at Madrid not to work for the Coburgs. The French ambassador suggested to his government that the marriage between the son of Louis Philippe and the queen's sister might take place simultaneously with the marriage of the queen to Don Francis. Don Francis was believed to be impotent. If, therefore,

[1] Greville's brother thought him 'a hideous little monster'. Bell, i. 374.
[2] The meeting at Eu in 1843 was the first visit of a reigning sovereign of England to France since the time of Henry VIII. See below, p. 254.
[3] Sir Henry Lytton Bulwer, the British minister at Madrid, was known to the French to be 'de l'école et de la clientèle de lord Palmerston', of whom he was in later years the biographer. Bresson, the French ambassador, according to Guizot, was 'très préoccupé de lui-même et de sa fortune'. Twenty years afterwards a writer in the *Quarterly Review* revealed the dreadful secret of Bresson's past; 'his early years had been passed in a counting-house'.

the French marriage were delayed until children were born to the queen, it might never take place. On the other hand, if the two marriages were simultaneous, the children of the Orleanist prince might inherit the crown of Spain. Louis Philippe thought the plan dishonourable, and would not listen to it. At this point (June 1846) Peel went out of office, and Palmerston succeeded Aberdeen. Immediately the French became suspicious. Palmerston found no agreement in the foreign office defining the position either of the British government or of the different candidates. He acted with his usual directness. He wrote a dispatch (19 July) for Bulwer, and showed a copy to the French ambassador. His dispatch could hardly have been more tactless. He made no reference to the conversations between Guizot and Aberdeen. He discussed the candidates with a terrible impartiality. He reduced the list to three: the Coburg, and the two Spanish cousins. He said that the British government was not prepared either 'to give any active support to the pretensions of any of the Princes ... or to make any objection to any of them'. The exclusion of the Orleanist prince was taken for granted. Palmerston lectured the Spanish ministers upon their behaviour, and hinted that they might well be dismissed. The latter part of his dispatch offended the Spaniards; the former part offended Louis Philippe. Moreover, if Palmerston insisted upon the Coburg candidature, the French might feel themselves released from any promise to delay the marriage of a French prince with the queen's sister. A month later (after delays for which Palmerston was not responsible) the French were told that, on the whole, the British cabinet favoured the claims of Don Henry, the younger Spanish cousin, though they did not consider that the French had any right to rule out the Coburg prince.[1] This was too much for Louis Philippe. At the end of August 1846 he announced the betrothal of his son to the queen's sister, and of Don Francis to the queen. The two marriages would take place at the same time.

Louis Philippe might have remembered his own belief in the

[1] The final decision may have been due to the influence of Lord Clarendon. Clarendon had been ambassador in Madrid from 1833 to 1839, and was regarded as an authority on Spanish affairs. He had supported the *progresista* party in Spain. Most of the leaders of this party were exiles in London in 1846; Don Henry was their candidate. Clarendon may also have been responsible for the lecture to the Spanish politicians in office. For the whole affair, see E. Jones-Parry, *The Spanish Marriages*, 1841-6.

importance of an *entente* with Great Britain. He might have remembered that Palmerston, for all his truculence of manner, was not a man who broke his word. He might have realized also that he had gained nothing; Great Britain, and the Powers in general, would never allow his family to inherit the throne of Spain.[1] He knew that Palmerston would not accept a *fait accompli* of this kind without resentment, and that British public opinion would have one fact only upon which to base a judgement: the fact that a French king had not kept his promise. Public opinion in England was on Palmerston's side. Queen Victoria wrote, in Palmerston's words, 'a tickler' to Louis Philippe.[2] The absolutist governments of Austria and Russia were more satisfied. The collaboration of the two constitutional states of western Europe was at an end; in November 1846 Russia, Austria, and Prussia were free to suppress the republic of Cracow, and thus to destroy all that was left of Polish independence. Guizot could do no more than protest in dignified language. He found it necessary to come to terms with Metternich, and Palmerston was free to support the revolutionary parties throughout Europe. Palmerston sent Lord Minto on a special mission to give 'moral support' and advice to the liberals in Italy. British encouragement was enough to start open revolution in Sicily in January 1848; two months later Guizot and Louis Philippe were exiles in England.

The European revolutions of 1848, which overthrew Louis Philippe in France and Metternich in Austria, and led to a general movement against Austrian domination in Italy, were not a surprise to Palmerston. He was afraid only that a conflict of doctrines in Europe might lead to a European war in which Great Britain would be involved. The republic which took the place of the Orleanist monarchy in France might offer active support to the Italians. Palmerston did not understand the full significance of the nationalist movements in Italy or elsewhere. He did not expect the movement for German unification to succeed; the doctrinaire views of the liberals did not attract him, and his policy in the Schleswig-Holstein[3] question was

---

[1] The queen of Spain had children, though it was said that Don Francis was not their father.

[2] The French ambassador in London told Clarendon that Louis Philippe had acted only *en bon père de famille* in order to secure the dowry of the queen's sister for his son! [3] See below, pp. 317–23.

directed to the maintenance of peace and of the balance of power; but he thought that Austria would be wise to give up her Italian possessions, and, in their place, to develop the non-Italian lands east of Venice. He was pleasantly surprised to find that the leaders of the French republic were not inclined to fight a 'war of principles'; on the other hand he reckoned without the recovery of Austria, and, when this unexpected recovery took place, it was not remarkable that the ministers of Francis Joseph should regard Palmerston as their enemy. Palmerston thought that the existence of Austria as a great Power was necessary to check Russia in the Near East. For this reason he did not encourage the Hungarian rebels. He was indignant over the Austrian treatment of prisoners in Italy and in Hungary, and used violent language in his private letters. 'The Austrians are really the greatest brutes that ever called themselves by the undeserved name of civilized men.'[1] He supported the Turks in their refusal to surrender Kossuth and other refugees who had escaped into Turkish territory,[2] and added to the discontent both of Russia and of Austria by his own high-handed action in Greece.

The immediate circumstances of this action were a little ridiculous. One Don Pacifico, a Portuguese money-lender who claimed British citizenship on the ground that he had been born in Gibraltar, asked for a large sum in compensation for the pillaging of his house at Athens. Palmerston took Pacifico's exaggerated complaints at their face-value and treated the affair as the last count against the Greek government in a long record of dishonesty, incompetence, and hostility to Great Britain. In January 1850, after the Greeks had failed to pay all outstanding debts owed to British subjects, Palmerston ordered a blockade of the Greek coasts. He did not consult France and

[1] Ashley, op. cit. ii. 105.
[2] Palmerston's opponents thought that his support of the refugees brought a risk of war. Palmerston did not hold this view. He wrote to Russell: 'With a little manly firmness we shall successfully get through this matter'. G. P. Gooch, *Later Correspondence of Lord J. Russell*, ii. 9.
The queen objected to Palmerston's interference in the question. His answer was written to the prime minister, but appears to have been shown to the queen. It sums up the old whig attitude towards the Crown. 'The Hungarian leaders may certainly be called revolutionists, but they are revolutionists in the same sense as the men to whose measures and acts at the close of the seventeenth century it is owing that the present Royal Family of England, happily for the nation, are seated on the throne of these realms'. Bell, ii. 20.

Russia, who shared with Great Britain the guarantee of Greek independence, because he believed that these two Powers would put difficulties in the way of a settlement. He made matters worse by coming to an arrangement with France and failing to notify the British minister at Athens of the terms. The British minister enforced harsher conditions upon the Greeks, and, until the cabinet forced him to give way, Palmerston wanted to support the local settlement instead of the milder terms of the Anglo-French agreement. The French government withdrew their ambassador from London, and, although Palmerston tried to conceal the reason for this withdrawal, the facts were generally known.

Palmerston had thus given his political enemies a good occasion for an attack upon his methods of conducting foreign policy. He defended himself, on 25 June 1850, in a long statement of the principles of British policy since the death of Canning.[1] His victory was complete. He added to his popularity in the country by refusing more than a perfunctory apology for the rough treatment given to General Haynau. Haynau—nicknamed 'Hyena' in England—was hated by the British public because he had ordered the flogging of women in Italy. He came to England on a visit, and was mobbed by the workmen in Barclay's brewery.[2] Palmerston sympathized with the workmen, and would not listen to the remonstrances of the queen over the indirect insult to a foreign sovereign. The queen insisted upon the withdrawal of the first letter sent to the Austrian ambassador, but Palmerston angered her the more by writing to her of the 'want of propriety' in Haynau's visit to a country where he was regarded as 'a moral criminal'.

The queen and the prince had long disliked Palmerston's attitude towards Austria. Palmerston thought, with some reason, that they were too much under the influence of Leopold of Belgium, and of Louis Philippe, Guizot, and Metternich. Aberdeen was in close touch with this foreign group and in agreement with

[1] Palmerston took immense trouble over the preparation of this speech, but one need not accept the story that over 2,000 volumes of foreign papers were searched for material. The speech ended with the peroration: 'As the Roman, in days of old, held himself free from indignity, when he could say "Civis Romanus sum", so also a British subject, in whatever land he may be, shall feel confident that the watchful eye and the strong arm of England will protect him against injustice and wrong.'

[2] Barclay's brewery was one of the 'sights' of London for foreign visitors.

the reactionary government of Austria as well as with the exiled Orleanists in England. Disraeli believed that Aberdeen had planned the grand attack over the Greek question 'under the inspiration of Mme Lieven and Guizot', with the support of the court.[1] If Palmerston had been more cautious in his language he would have been in a stronger position. His failure to understand the recuperative powers of Austria had given the court an argument against him. He weakened his position by a certain carelessness in sending off dispatches without showing them to the queen, though he complained that the queen often kept drafts too long, and 'when events are going at a hand-gallop, one's instructions become rather stale before they reach their destination'.[2] He also pointed out that it was impossible for the responsible minister to accept the queen's advice if the queen gave her confidence to the enemies of the ministry, and, in Palmerston's view, to the enemies of the country.

Every move in Palmerston's policy increased the queen's anger. The queen and the prince complained in 1850 that Palmerston was so very difficult that they had not spoken to him for a year. They put pressure upon Russell, and, in spite of Russell's defence of Palmerston's policy, obtained a promise that at the end of the session of 1850 Palmerston should exchange the foreign office for the home office and the leadership of the commons. They wanted his dismissal from the cabinet, but Russell pointed out that, if Palmerston were driven into opposition, he might come back as prime minister. The result of the Pacifico debate was a disappointment to the queen; the prince wrote to his brother of 'the unhappy combination of circumstances' that allowed 'the immoral Palmerston such a triumph'. The queen almost overstepped her constitutional position, but she could claim that, when the foreign secretary sent dispatches for her approval, he should explain his policy 'distinctly', in order that she might 'know as distinctly to *what* she has given her Royal sanction', and that 'having *once given* her sanction to a measure... it be not arbitrarily altered or modified by the Minister'.[3]

Palmerston was shown this statement in August 1850; he agreed with it, but soon afterwards dealt with the Haynau incident without consulting the queen. The defeat of Russell's

[1] Buckle, iii. 259.   [2] Gooch, ii. 5.
[3] Q.V.L. 1st ser. ii. 315. See also Martin, ii. 299–310. The queen believed that she had a right to dismiss Palmerston if he broke these rules.

administration in February 1851 brought no relief; Russell came back to office, and could not do without Palmerston's support. Before the year was out Palmerston gave the queen and the prince a chance which they were quick to take. On 2 December 1851 Louis Napoleon Bonaparte carried out a successful *coup d'état* against the second French republic. A day later Palmerston, without asking the opinion of the cabinet, mentioned to the French ambassador his 'entire approbation' of Louis Napoleon's act. Palmerston had long been an embarrassment to Russell, and not merely in matters affecting the court. The two men had been carrying on a barbed correspondence about the reception of Kossuth in England. Russell asked Palmerston not to entertain Kossuth; Palmerston answered that he could not allow the prime minister to dictate to him the guests he might receive at his own house. The limit had now been reached; Russell wrote to Cowley that he could not 'stand any more of these tracasseries',[1] and asked Palmerston to resign.

Palmerston maintained that he had a right to give an 'unofficial' approval of the *coup d'état*, and that he was doing no more than Russell himself had done. He knew that Normanby, the British ambassador at Paris, was intriguing against him, and that Lady Normanby, a friend of the queen, wrote long letters of complaint to her brother-in-law, Colonel Phipps, who was the prince's secretary. Palmerston behaved with greater propriety towards the queen than the queen or the prince showed to him: he did not attempt to raise a constitutional issue. On the other hand his dismissal was not regretted by his own colleagues or by well-informed judges outside the prejudiced circle of the court. Macaulay was sorry that Palmerston was 'out', but thought it 'high time'. Lansdowne, who was Palmerston's closest friend in the cabinet, did not support him. Nonetheless the queen's attempt to obtain a firmer control on foreign policy was quietly checked. Clarendon,[2] whom the queen wanted as

---

[1] Gooch, ii. 92. In his old age Russell thought that he had been too 'hasty and precipitate'. Walpole, ii. 142. Schwarzenberg, the leader of the Austrian reaction, gave a ball in Vienna in honour of Palmerston's dismissal.

[2] George William Frederick Villiers, 4th earl of Clarendon and Baron Hyde (1800–70); b. London; attaché at St. Petersburg, 1820; commissioner of customs, 1823; negotiated commercial treaty with France, 1831; ambassador at Madrid, 1833–9; succeeded his uncle in the peerage, 1838; lord privy seal, 1839–41; president of the board of trade, 1846; lord-lieutenant of Ireland, 1847–52; foreign secretary, 1853–8, 1865–6, and 1868–70. Clarendon twice refused a marquisate and the governor-generalship of India.

Palmerston's successor, refused the office; Granville[1] accepted it, and, with his smooth and easy manners, soon brought a settlement. The queen asked for a general statement of the principles governing the foreign policy of her ministers; the answer was given in vague platitudes, and the matter ended.

The dispute was little more than a personal one and should not be given too much importance. Clarendon believed that the queen and the prince 'laboured under the curious mistake that the Foreign Office is their peculiar department, and that they have a right to control, if not to direct, the foreign policy of England'.[2] Clarendon was not altogether wrong, but the queen and her husband were prudent enough not to push their views too far, though they were in some danger of risking a conflict with the ministry and public opinion. In any case the tact of their ministers, and Palmerston's forbearance, saved them from the consequences of their mistakes. It should also be remembered that, apart from Palmerston's own responsibility for the misunderstanding, the position of the Crown in relation to foreign affairs was not yet stabilized. The foreign exiles, and Palmerston's political opponents, were older and more experienced than the queen; many of them remembered the traditions of thirty years earlier. The important point is that Victoria and Albert were more conscientious than George IV. Madame Lieven, the arch-busybody of Europe, and her friends had far less influence upon the court of Victoria than upon the court of George IV, and this difference may be taken as a rough measure of the constitutional advance between 1820 and 1850.

The ministers did not want to commit themselves to royal interference; furthermore they did not in fact disagree with the general views of Palmerston. They had dismissed Palmerston owing to his premature approval of the *coup d'état*. They could not refuse their own approval. Within two months Derby's administration was in office. Malmesbury[3] became foreign secretary

[1] Granville George Leveson-Gower, 2nd Earl Granville (1815–91); educ. Eton and Christ Church, Oxford; attaché in Paris, 1835; M.P., 1836; under-secretary of state for foreign affairs, 1840–1; succeeded to peerage, 1846; vice-president of the board of trade, 1848; foreign secretary, 1851–2, 1870–4, and 1880–5; leader of the liberal party in the house of lords from 1855; colonial secretary, 1868–70 and 1886; chancellor of the university of London, 1856–91.

[2] Sir H. Maxwell, *Life of Clarendon*, i. 341.

[3] James Howard Harris, 3rd earl of Malmesbury (1807–89); educ. Eton and Oriel College, Oxford, where Newman was his tutor; travelled abroad and met

largely because he had long been a friend of Louis Napoleon. Malmesbury was not a clever man, and had never held office. He had learnt a good deal from reading his grandfather's letters and papers; he admitted that 'without this accidental education I should have been as great a novice in political business as were most of my colleagues'.[1] He was generous enough to acknowledge that when he took office 'Palmerston . . . kindly offered to . . . give me some advice upon the main principles of our English policy with foreign countries. Of course, I gratefully accepted.' The advice was typical of Palmerston's good sense and vigour. Malmesbury would be wise 'to keep well with France', though, on the eastern question, France and England were 'like two men in love with the same woman'. He would soon discover 'what a power of prestige England possesses abroad'; it would be his 'first duty to see that it does not wane'. Palmerston warned him that other foreign countries would try to get from him concessions which they had hitherto failed to secure; that the work of his office would take a great deal of time; that, although he had the advantage of 'young eyes', he must insist on legible handwriting, and 'intervals between the lines', and that, in the matter of diplomatic appointments, he would be 'struck with a very curious circumstance —namely that no climate agrees with an English diplomatist excepting that of Paris, Florence, or Naples'.[2]

Malmesbury took the advice to heart; he kept on good terms with France at a time when English public opinion was suspicious of Louis Napoleon, but his period of office lasted less than a year. In the coalition government of 1852 Russell went to the foreign office; he soon found that he could not combine the work with the leadership of the commons. Clarendon succeeded him; for the first time in the nineteenth century the foreign secretary was a man who had served for some six years as an ambassador. The cabinet which drifted into the Crimean war thus included, apart from Clarendon himself, four men—Aberdeen, Palmerston, Russell, and Granville— who had held or were to hold the foreign secretaryship.

Louis Napoleon, 1827–9, and remained on friendly terms with him; M.P., 1841; succeeded his father in the same year; supported protection in 1846; attempted in 1863 and 1866 to secure from the French government the statues of Henry II and Richard I in the abbey of Fontevrault.

[1] Malmesbury, *Memoirs of an ex-Minister*, i. 41.
[2] Ibid. i. 317–18.

III

THE EASTERN QUESTION, 1841–54
AND THE CRIMEAN WAR

THE Straits Convention of 1841 had given Turkey a chance of survival. For a time it appeared that the reforms of Mahmud would be continued under his successor. Abdul Medjid was an amiable, weak boy of sixteen, but in November 1839, when Mehemet Ali was threatening the existence of the Turkish Empire, even the reactionary party saw the need of impressing the Powers. The sultan published a decree promising all manner of administrative improvements. The decree was obsolete even before it had been translated into the languages of many of the sultan's Christian subjects. Reschid Pasha, a reforming minister of the previous reign, was dismissed in 1841, and his plans were quickly set aside. Nevertheless some attempt was made to increase the efficiency of the army, and close observers of Turkish methods did not despair of the future. The return of Stratford Canning[1] as British ambassador in 1841 encouraged the reformers. Stratford had first seen Constantinople in the year 1808. In 1810, although he was only twenty-three, he was left in charge of the Embassy, with few instructions from home; he remained in charge during the important period of the negotiation of the treaty of Bucharest. Stratford went from Turkey to Switzerland in 1814 and from Switzerland to Washington in 1820. In 1824 he was appointed to Constantinople, but at this time he wanted to leave diplomacy for English politics. He disagreed with Aberdeen on the Greek question, and gave up his post in 1829.[2] For the next twelve years he sat in parliament. In 1833 Palmerston offered him the post of ambassador at St. Petersburg, but the emperor refused to receive him. It seems clear that Nicholas did not want as British

---

[1] Stratford Canning, 1st Viscount Stratford de Redcliffe (1786–1880), cousin of George Canning; b. London; educ. Eton and King's College, Cambridge; appointed précis-writer at the foreign office while an undergraduate; published, in youth and old age, a number of poems, including a poem on Bonaparte, which was praised by Byron, and a play in blank verse about Alfred the Great.

[2] He went back to Turkey on a special mission in 1831–2.

minister the greatest English authority on Russian policy at
Constantinople. In 1835 and 1841 Peel proposed Stratford
as governor-general of Canada, and finally pressed him to
go back to Constantinople. Again he went 'with no small
reluctance'.

In 1809 Stratford believed that Turkey was 'rotten at the
heart; the seat of corruption is in the government itself'.[1]
Twelve years later, at the outbreak of the Greek revolt, he
wrote to his cousin that he wished 'as a matter of humanity ..
that the Greeks were put in possession of their whole patrimony
and that the Sultan were driven, bag and baggage, into the
heart of Asia, or, as a provisional measure, that the divided
empire which existed four centuries ago could be restored'.[2]
After the suppression of the janissaries Stratford was more hopeful about the immediate future of Turkey, though in 1832 he
thought that reform might postpone, but could not prevent,
the inevitable collapse. 'The Turkish Empire is evidently
hastening to its dissolution, and an approach to the civilization
of Christendom affords the only chance of keeping it together
for any length of time.'[3] He did what he could to 'retard the
evil hour' when the final collapse of Turkey might bring a
general war over the disposal of the wreckage. No one was
better fitted for directing the Turks towards sensible and honest
methods of rule. Stratford was a man of fine presence, proud,
serious, even majestic; quick-tempered and yet infinitely patient.
He dominated the sultan and his advisers by his force of character, knowledge of the world, and imperious will. His authority
was immense. He once noticed, at a time of financial stringency,
that workmen were laying the foundations of a new summer
palace on the Bosphorus; he drove to the palace, and in a few
minutes obtained an order that the work should be stopped.
Nevertheless he could not change the ways of Turkish officials.
The Turks had an endless capacity for going back upon their
promises and acquiescing in measures which they had no intention of carrying out. In 1845 Stratford persuaded the sultan to
dismiss the corrupt minister of finance and to give his confidence
to Reschid. Stratford left Constantinople for two years, and came
back to find that Reschid had been driven out once more. Again
Stratford restored him to power. Reschid's attempts at reform
were real, though incomplete; they could do little to cure the

[1] S. Lane-Poole, *Life of Stratford Canning*, i. 51.   [2] Ibid. i. 307.   [3] Ibid. ii. 78.

corruption, indifference, and carelessness which were destroy-
ing the empire. Reschid himself lost heart, and the sultan became frightened of losing his throne. From one point of view
Stratford's prestige worked against reform. The Turks believed
that, in the last resort, Great Britain would save them from
destruction. Stratford gave up his post in 1852, convinced that
he was leaving Turkey for the last time, and without much
hope that 'the evil hour' could be long retarded.

Nicholas of Russia held the same view. The policy of under-
mining Turkey had not been profitable to Russia; the Turkish
Empire might collapse, and the emperor wanted to be ready
to meet the situation. He was uneasy at the improvement of
Anglo-French relations. Queen Victoria met Louis Philippe at
Eu in 1843, and a return visit was arranged. In June 1844,
Nicholas came uninvited to Windsor to undo the mischief. He
explained his views. He suggested Anglo-Russian collaboration.
Turkey was a 'dying man'. If Turkey should 'collapse', there
was danger to be feared from France. Great Britain, Austria,
and Russia ought to make their 'arrangements'. The emperor
assumed that Constantinople would not be given to any single
Power. Aberdeen left Nicholas with the impression that the
views of Russia and Great Britain were similar, and that this
agreement would be kept in mind. He was too prudent to
accept the offer of an alliance which would break the Anglo-
French *entente*. He still believed that there was in Turkey 'a
principle of vitality, an occult force, which sets at naught all
calculations based upon the analogy of other states'.[1]

Thus the question remained in suspense until a new and un-
expected danger threatened ancient Russian claims in Turkey.
Louis Napoleon wanted to secure the catholic vote in France.
He had restored the temporal power of the popes in the city of
Rome. He now came forward to assert French and catholic
rights over the Holy Places in Palestine.[2] Orthodox and catholic
Christians alike claimed superior rights over these buildings.
To the French the Capitulations of 1740,[3] to the Russians the
treaty of Kuchuk Kainardji and earlier *firmans* of the Porte ap-
peared to justify exclusive privileges. Nicholas and his ministers

---

[1] Aberdeen to Stratford, 20 Jan. 1844. See H. W. V. Temperley, *England and the
Near East. i. The Crimea*, p. 255.

[2] The Holy Places included the churches of the Holy Sepulchre and the Virgin
in Jerusalem, the church of the Nativity at Bethlehem, and the place Golgotha.

[3] See Temperley, i. 463-9.

took little trouble to examine the terms of the treaty of Kuchuk
Kainardji; they seem to have thought that they had far more
rights than they really possessed.

The Holy Sepulchre was the most important of the sites.
Until 1808 the Latins had a share in the church. After a fire
in this year the sultan handed the church over to the Greeks,
who repaired and redecorated it after the eastern fashion with
icons and other emblems. The French protested against the
change; a *firman* was issued in their favour in 1812, but the
Greeks kept their control, and the Turks did not turn them out.
The Greeks began to enlarge their buildings and to buy more
land; they received grants from Russia, and Russian pilgrims
were far more numerous than pilgrims from France. French
interest in the Holy Places began to revive, for political reasons,
after the fall of Mehemet Ali.[1] Louis Napoleon was not therefore initiating an entirely new policy when he told the French
ambassador at Constantinople to ask on behalf of the Latins
for keys of the gates of the church at Bethlehem and of the
grotto of the Holy Manger. In February 1852 these keys were
assigned to the French; the French government was also given
the right to place in the Holy Grotto a silver star with the arms
of France. About the same time the sultan told the Greeks that
the *status quo* would be maintained. Russia protested against the
privileges allowed to the Latins, France against the reassurance
given to the Greeks.

Nicholas thought that Russia had a right to ask for guarantees.
Early in 1853 he revived the claims to a general protectorate
over the Christians in the Turkish Empire, and sent Prince
Menschikoff on a special mission to secure recognition of these
claims.[2] Napoleon's action had produced results far beyond his
intentions. Great Britain was indifferent to the rights of Greeks
and Latins over the Holy Places, and equally suspicious of
Russia and of France.[3] In January 1853 the emperor had renewed the familar talk about the sickness of Turkey and the
need for Anglo-Russian collaboration. Nicholas was afraid that

[1] At this time (1842) the great dome of the church of the Holy Sepulchre was
said to be in danger of collapse. Greeks and Latins claimed the right to carry
out repairs; at Stratford's suggestion, the work was left to the Turks.

[2] Nicholas was influenced by the success of an Austrian mission on behalf of
the Montenegrins and Bosnians. See Temperley, i. pp. 301–3.

[3] The new French steamships were causing alarm. It was feared that Napoleon
might use them for a sudden attack on the British navy. See above, p. 164.

the patient might even die before the 'necessary arrangements' had been made.[1] The arrangements included vivisection to avoid the risk of sudden death. Great Britain was invited to take Egypt and Crete; Russia would act as protector of the Danubian Principalities, Servia, and, probably, Bulgaria, and would occupy Constantinople during the crisis of dissolution. Ultimately Constantinople would become a free city.

Russell, who was foreign secretary at the time of these overtures, gave no encouragement. Turkey was not yet dead;[2] the emperor's proposals could not be kept secret from France, and in any case his suggestion about Constantinople was not satisfactory. The British government was not far wrong in thinking that Nicholas really wanted to separate Great Britain from France and that he had not told the whole truth about his plans. The Menschikoff mission showed the measure of the Russian terms. Menschikoff asked for an acceptance of the Russian claims in treaty form. If France opposed these terms, Russia would offer the sultan a secret defensive alliance. If, after three days, the sultan refused to give way, Menschikoff, at his discretion, could leave Constantinople. The emperor expected that the Turks would be frightened. He believed that he had reassured Great Britain, and that he could now deal with France. He did not expect, and did not want, a European war.

Menschikoff was not a tactful man; Madame Lieven described him as *parfaitement mal élevé*. He began by insulting the grand vizier and the Turkish foreign minister. Then he became conciliatory, and waited. He waited too long. Aberdeen and Russell had asked Stratford to go back once again to Constantinople; they were not sorry to be rid of a dangerous critic of their eastern policy, but they put their critic in a dominant position. Stratford did not want war. He had not expected that the war over the partition of Turkey would take place in his lifetime. He went to Constantinople with the knowledge that the cabinet intended to defend the place; his instructions did not allow him

---

[1] The emperor's words were modified in the account of the conversations published by the British government. Nicholas did not talk of a 'sick man' but of a 'sick bear'. 'The bear dies . . . the bear is dying . . . you may give him musk, but even musk will not long keep him alive.' Temperley, i. 272.

[2] Palmerston thought that the Turkish Empire was superior to the Russian 'in many points of civilization', and that the Christian subjects of the sultan enjoyed greater 'security for person and property' than the Christian subjects of the emperor of Russia. Bell, ii. 83.

to call the British fleet into the Dardanelles without reference to London.[1] Stratford himself was largely responsible for drawing up these instructions, and it is more than probable that this limitation upon his powers was his own suggestion.

On 5 May Menschikoff was given guarantees about the Holy Places. He repeated his demand for a convention assuring to Russia her ancient rights of protection over the Christian subjects of Turkey; again he offered a secret alliance. Nesselrode had told Clarendon that there were no ulterior demands. Menschikoff hesitated to let Stratford know the extent of the Russian claims, but the Turks were so much alarmed that they told almost the whole truth, and Stratford guessed the details which were kept from him. He recommended the Turks not to break off negotiations. He would not promise British naval aid even if Russia invaded the Principalities; the British fleet would interfere only to protect Constantinople. Menschikoff insisted upon the acceptance of all his terms; Turkish opinion, strong and united as ever on religious and anti-Russian questions, refused to surrender. On 21 May Menschikoff left Constantinople.

Stratford now thought that everything depended 'upon our Cabinet at home. . . . Will they look the crisis in the face?' Aberdeen had not been alarmed by Nicholas's proposals of partition. He told the queen in February 1853 that there was 'nothing very new in this demonstration by the Emperor. It is essentially the same language he has held for some years, although, perhaps, the present difficulties of Turkey may have rendered him more anxious.' He believed that Menschikoff's instructions related 'exclusively to the claims of the Greek Church at Jerusalem'. The queen and the prince consort were more suspicious. The queen wrote that Menschikoff's 'mode of proceeding is not such as would be resorted to towards a sick friend for whose life there exists much solicitude'.[2] Russell was the first of the ministers to doubt the emperor's sincerity. As early as 20 March he thought that the emperor was 'clearly bent on accomplishing the destruction of Turkey, and he must

[1] For the first time during an international crisis British ministers were able to use the electric telegraph (as far east as Belgrade). Clarendon wrote (on 18 October 1853) to Russell: 'These telegraphic dispatches are the very devil. Formerly Cabinets used to deliberate on a fact and a proposition from foreign governments; now, we have only a fact.' Maxwell, ii. 27. Russell had already written of 'the fatal facility of the electric telegraph'.

[2] Q.V.L. 1st ser. ii. 532, 537, 538.

be resisted'.[1] When the extent of Menschikoff's demands became known, Palmerston wanted 'a bold, firm course, based on right'[2] . . . 'the policy and practice of the Russian Government has always been to push forward its encroachments as fast and as far as the apathy or want of firmness of other Governments would allow it to go, but always to stop and retire when it was met with decided resistance. . . . In furtherance of this policy, the Russian Government has always had two strings to its bow —moderate language and disinterested professions at Petersburg and at London; active aggression by its agents on the scene of operations.'[3] Clarendon was anxious to keep a divided cabinet together, while Russell was more interested in parliamentary reform than in foreign affairs. The hesitation of the cabinet, and the opposition of Cobden, Bright, and the radicals to any policy which might lead to war, encouraged the Russians to take a dangerous step. They decided to invade the Danubian Principalities if the Turks did not accept their demands. On 2 June the cabinet sent the fleet to Besika Bay, outside the Dardanelles. Napoleon III agreed to support the British ships with a French squadron.

Napoleon was more headstrong than Aberdeen, and no less vacillating. He welcomed an alliance with Great Britain; he needed British consent to the changes which he hoped to make in the European settlement of 1815. He did not want a war with Russia. He knew that French opinion would be suspicious of a war in which British interests seemed more at stake than any interests of France. Thus Napoleon did not intrigue to bring about war, but his suggestions for the maintenance of peace were never very prudent. The French ambassador at Constantinople sent home excited and exaggerated dispatches; Napoleon and his advisers in Paris were unfamiliar with the conduct of large affairs of state. French influence, therefore, was unlikely to correct the tactical mistakes of Aberdeen and his colleagues.

The British fleet reached Besika Bay on 13 June; on 3 July the Russian troops crossed the Pruth and entered Moldavia. The division of opinion in the cabinet was still too great to allow decided action. The Turks were given no promise; the Russians were given no warning. Meanwhile Stratford worked for delay and conciliation. He advised the sultan to send a special mission

---

[1] Walpole, ii. 181.   [2] Temperley, i. 337.   [3] Ashley, ii. 25.

to Russia; the Russians at all events would have time to see
the results of their policy. Stratford persuaded the Turks to
draw up a note that 'the ancient privileges of the religion professed by H.M. the Emperor of Russia, and by the greater
part of his subjects, have been fully confirmed in perpetuity'.
The note was never sent.[1] A conference of the ambassadors of
the great Powers met in Vienna in July. The ambassadors set
aside Stratford's plan, and accepted a form of words suggested
by Napoleon III and Clarendon. Negotiations broke down
upon the modifications proposed to this note. The points at
issue may be narrowed to one sentence. The sultan was asked
to promise 'to remain faithful to the letter and to the spirit of
the treaties of Kainardji and Adrianople relative to the protection of the Christian religion'. No modification in the existing rules would be allowed without the consent of France and
Russia. This stipulation offended Turkish sentiment because it
put the sultan under French and Russian supervision, while,
in the note drawn up by Stratford at Constantinople, the sultan's guarantee was, technically, spontaneous, though it was
witnessed by the ambassadors of Great Britain, Austria, and
France. The Vienna Note was shown privately to Russia;
naturally, the Russians accepted it when it was sent to them
officially. The sultan had no opportunity for criticism; the note
was presented to him for his signature.[2]

The Turkish promise of guarantee was the final concession
which the sultan was prepared to make. Turkish resistance was
stiffened by the belief that, in the last resort, Constantinople
was safe because Great Britain and France would not allow the
Russians to take it. The British cabinet told Stratford that the
sultan must sign the Vienna note. Stratford disapproved of
the note, but advised the Turks to give way (12 August). There
is no evidence that he failed to carry out his instructions, or

[1] There was delay at Constantinople owing to the difficulty of conducting business during the months of Ramadan and Bairam.

[2] The note was shown to the Turkish ambassador at Vienna. The ambassador
approved of it; he could hardly take upon himself the risk of rejecting it. Reschid
denied that the Turkish ministers at Constantinople knew the contents of the note.
It is possible that the Turkish ambassador may have been afraid to admit that he
had seen the note. In any case the sultan could complain with some reason that
he was asked to sign a document affecting his sovereign rights without the chance
of stating his case. Clarendon admitted that 'the Turks who are about to contract
an engagement have a right to look closely at its terms, and we should not be
justified in cramming down their throats what they declare they can't digest'.
Maxwell, ii. 20.

that, while carrying out these instructions with formal correctness, he suggested that the Turks should refuse their signature. On the other hand, the Turks knew Stratford's every mood; his honesty and seriousness told against him. He had framed a note of a different kind; the Turkish ministers knew that he had not changed his own opinion. In any case feeling at Constantinople ran dangerously high; the sultan could not neglect this opinion.[1] Therefore the Turks rejected the terms of the note sent to them, or rather they proposed an addition to the central clause. The sultan would 'remain faithful to the stipulations of the treaty of Kainardji, confirmed by that of Adrianople, relative to the protection *by the Sublime Porte* of the Christian religion'.[2] The Russians refused the Turkish addition. They went beyond mere refusal. Nesselrode interpreted the Vienna note as granting the whole of the Russian claims, and allowing Russia a right to interfere in the interest of the twelve million Christian subjects of Turkey.[3] When this interpretation became known Great Britain and France could no longer support the note; Russia could hardly recede from the attitude she had taken up. The Turks claimed that they had been justified in their action, and the war party threatened revolution if the sultan would not fight Russia.

Public opinion was as much excited in Russia as in Turkey. Nicholas knew that he had so little support in other matters from the mass of his subjects that he could not afford a public humiliation over the one question upon which Russian patriots were almost unanimous. There was in Great Britain a strong

---

[1] One of Stratford's own staff wrote to Lady Stratford on 20 Aug.: 'The Turks have resolved to reject the Austrian Note in spite of everything the United Elchis could say. Whatever Lord S.'s private opinion may be, you may rest assured that this has in no way added to their exultation by influencing them either one way or another. Considering the dogged attitude they have assumed, it is lucky that H.E. has a chance of preserving his well-earned influence.' Lane-Poole, ii. 296.

[2] There were other points of difference between the ambassadors' and the Turkish notes. The ambassadors asked the sultan to promise that the Greek Church should 'share in the advantages granted to the other Christian rites by convention or special arrangement'. The treaties of Carlowitz, Belgrade, and Sistova had given Austria the right of protecting all Roman Catholics in the empire, whether they were Ottoman subjects or not. The Turkish note read: '... advantages granted or which might be granted to the other Christian communities, *being subjects of the Porte.*'

[3] Nesselrode's interpretation was sent to the Russian minister at Vienna. It found its way into a Prussian newspaper. Clarendon wrote: 'How an old fox like [Nesselrode] could have committed such a *niaiserie* as writing that dispatch passes my comprehension.' Maxwell, ii. 26.

antipathy towards Russia, not merely because Russian designs on Turkey threatened British political and economic interests. Russia had been the main support of reaction in 1848; Nicholas was an enemy of liberty abroad, and an upholder of serfdom at home. Thus the arguments of Cobden and Bright seemed to ignore the justice of the anti-Russian case, and to put considerations of trade before considerations of honour.[1] The arguments of the Manchester school appeared even to show that the years of peace had weakened the sense of right in the English people.[2] A generation earlier considerations of honour had brought opinion on the side of the Greeks. Russia, not Turkey, was now the villain; the Turks were the victims. Aberdeen, like most irresolute men, depended upon the advice of others. He wasted Clarendon's time by spending hours in talk at the foreign office. He took steps hardly compatible with his peaceful intentions. On 23 September Aberdeen and Clarendon were so much affected by exaggerated news of disturbances at Constantinople, and by the demand of the French that the fleets should be sent to protect the city, that they ordered the movement of the ships without even calling the cabinet to a meeting.

War was not yet certain; the emperor was alarmed to find that he might be faced with fanatical Turkish resistance, and that Aberdeen and his cabinet had set a limit to their concessions. At the end of September Nicholas met the Austrian emperor at Olmütz. He was ready to retract the extravagant interpretation of the Vienna note. Buol, the Austrian foreign minister, suggested the repetition of the original note, with a statement

[1] Bright's hatred of war was not based on self-interest, but some of the entries in his diary during the Crimean war explain why his arguments did not appeal to an over-excited popular opinion. 'Panic in the Funds, and great fluctuations. War disturbs everything. It has disturbed the session, and will greatly injure, if not destroy the country. . . . Our carpet trade grievously injured by war raising the price of tow'. *Diaries of John Bright*, ed. R. A. J. Walling, 11 and 18 April 1854. For the state of public opinion, see B. Kingsley Martin, *The Triumph of Lord Palmerston*.

[2] Tennyson's *Maud* is a curious example of this view of the Crimean war as a purging of the baser emotions, and an escape from the pursuit of private gain:

> 'And many a darkness into the light shall leap,
> And shine in the sudden making of splendid names,
> And noble thought be freer under the sun,
> And the heart of a people beat with one desire;
> For the peace, that I deem'd no peace, is over and done,
> And now by the side of the Black and the Baltic deep,
> And deathful-grinning mouths of the fortress, flames
> The blood-red blossom of war, with a heart of fire.'

recognizing that the duty of protecting the Christian religion in Turkey had devolved on the sultan; Russia only reserved to herself the task of watching that the engagements of the treaty of Kuchuk Kainardji were carried out. The British cabinet thought that this proposal was a trick arranged by Russia and Austria. Aberdeen wished, after the war, that he had accepted the proposal; at the time he believed that it did not wholly cancel the Russian interpretation of the Vienna note. The cabinet agreed with him, rejected the wording of Buol's compromise, and again ordered Stratford to call up the fleet (8 October).

On 4 October the sultan declared war on Russia. In spite of the excitement of the Turks, Stratford still worked for peace. He disobeyed the order of 23 September about the fleet,[1] because he thought that the presence of British and French ships would encourage the Turks. He received the second order; again he waited. On 20 October he persuaded the ambassadors of France, Austria, and Prussia to ask the Turks to suspend hostilities for ten or twelve days. He might have obtained this suspension earlier if the Austrian ambassador had been willing to act without authority from Vienna. This delay wrecked the plan. On 23 October Omar Pasha attacked the Russians in the Principalities. The British cabinet made one final effort for peace.[2] Stratford was told to ask for delay. He had already done all that he could do; he persuaded the Turks not to send their fleet into the Black Sea, but he could not prevent the dispatch of a light flotilla to Sinope. The Russians could not be expected to make war on land and keep the peace at sea. They did not know the Turkish naval plans, and suspected, wrongly, that the ships were being sent to stir up rebellion in the Caucasus. On 30 November they destroyed the Turkish ships.[3]

[1] This order reached Stratford on 4 October.

[2] Aberdeen suggested a declaration that the four Powers would not 'permit themselves, in consequence of unfounded objections or by the declaration of war, which they have already condemned, to be drawn into a policy inconsistent with the peace of Europe, as well as with the interests of Turkey itself'. The cabinet would not accept this half-hearted and ambiguous statement, but Aberdeen wrote to Madame Lieven of his 'strong feeling that war, under present circumstances, would not only be an act of insanity, but would be utterly disgraceful to all of us concerned'. Lady Frances Balfour, *Life of Aberdeen*, ii. 180. It is difficult to think of anything more imprudent than a letter of this kind, at a time when it was necessary to convince Russia that the cabinet was resolved not to allow further encroachment upon Turkey.

[3] It was said that after the battle the Russians had cleared the wounded off the Turkish ships with grapeshot. Lane-Poole, ii. 334.

The effect upon British opinion was remarkable. The action was called a 'massacre'; Aberdeen was accused of cowardice, and of betraying his country to Russia. On 14 December Palmerston resigned from the cabinet. His resignation was due to differences of opinion over the proposed reform bill,[1] but it was interpreted as the result of differences about the eastern question. Aberdeen himself was shaken, and, even before the news of Sinope had reached London, Russell wanted the emperor to know that, if Russian troops crossed the Danube, British ships would interrupt Russian transports and supply-ships sailing from one Russian port to another. The cabinet believed, wrongly, that the French would act alone if they could not get British support. Aberdeen took yet another step on the road to war. On 22 December he agreed to co-operate with the French in keeping the Russian fleet at Sebastopol, if the French would join in making new peace proposals. Meanwhile the allied fleets would protect Turkey from aggression.

The order to send the fleets into the Black Sea reached Stratford on 3 January 1854. Stratford had compelled the Turkish ministers, in spite of popular clamour, to make another proposal for a peaceful settlement. The dispatch of the fleets into the Black Sea might not have led to war, but the order to concentrate their warships at Sebastopol was too much for Russian pride. Early in February Nicholas withdrew his ambassadors from London and Paris. War did not follow at once. Austria and Prussia asked for delay while Russia was invited to leave the Principalities. Finally, without waiting for any definite promise of Austrian support, though Austria was more interested than Great Britain and France in the Principalities, the British and French governments sent an ultimatum to Russia. Nicholas made no answer. On 12 March Great Britain and France became allies of Turkey; a fortnight later the Crimean war began. To the last Aberdeen refused to face facts. He wrote to Clarendon on 12 February: 'I still say that war is *not* inevitable; unless, indeed, we are determined to have it; which, for all I know, may be the case.'[2]

Thus England 'drifted' into war with Russia. If Stratford had been in control, he might have secured concessions from Turkey which would have satisfied Russia. If Aberdeen had been master of his cabinet, he would have made almost any

---

[1] He withdrew his resignation on 24 Dec.   [2] Maxwell, ii. 40.

concessions to avoid war. If Palmerston had been in Aberdeen's place, he might have obtained a Russian withdrawal from the Principalities. If Nicholas had not assumed too long that Aberdeen would keep his country out of war, the Russians might not have committed themselves to a course from which retreat was almost impossible. If the British cabinet had not suspected the Austro-Russian negotiations at Olmütz, a settlement might have been reached. If the Russians had not destroyed the Turkish ships at Sinope, public opinion in Great Britain would have been less warlike. Finally, the clumsy plan of threatening Russia at the moment when Great Britain and France were making their last offer of peace destroyed any chance of escape.

On the other hand Russia had never abandoned the aim of controlling Turkey. The success of the Menschikoff mission would have given her the control for which she had been working. Stratford, who did his best to avoid war, believed that, sooner or later, war was inevitable. Aberdeen, who had seen the battlefield of Leipzig in 1813, hated war; in his last years, remembering the words of David to Solomon, he refused to rebuild a church on his estate because he had 'shed blood abundantly' and 'made great war'. Nevertheless he thought that the Crimean war was a 'just war', even if it might have been avoided. Gladstone, to the end of his days, held the same view.

The Crimean war was fought by a British army which had seen little active service outside India for forty years. There were no commanders of first-rate ability; probably the ablest soldier who took a prominent part in the direction of the war was Todleben, the defender of Sebastopol.[1] The blunders of the staff, the breakdown of the system of supply in the first stages of the war, may be paralleled in other British expeditions. The allies at least avoided the worst error of the first Napoleon: they did not attempt to march into the interior of Russia.

There was, however, one new feature about the Crimean war; for the first time in British history public opinion was deeply stirred by the sufferings of the troops. The lives of British soldiers had been cheap enough in the past, but their fellow citizens had been indignant only by fits and starts over the waste of men. The anger felt during the first Crimean winter

---

[1] Todleben's work was good, but it is much exaggerated in his own and other Russian accounts of the siege.

was due to several causes. The British public knew more about the horrors of the Crimea than they had known about previous wars. For the first time newspaper correspondents followed the campaign. The high command had not yet discovered the advantages of close censorship. The newspapers were larger; their circulation had increased, and the technique of modern journalism had been invented. The postal service was far better than that of the Revolutionary and Napoleonic wars. Englishmen at home could see photographs of the camps and trenches. Moreover, public opinion was less prepared to condone mistakes. During the years of peace the standard of administrative efficiency in Great Britain had risen to an extent not realized at the time. The public expected more of its civil servants and departments of state, and was even too ready to criticize the failure of the army supply services.

There was another reason for disquiet and indignation. The attitude of educated men towards war and fighting was changing. The mood of truculence and anger which preceded the outbreak of the Crimean war was not lasting, and did not represent the state of public feeling over a long period of time; the reaction was likely to be as sudden and as extravagant. For forty years there had been no great war in Europe; hence, after hostilities had begun, and the significance of the Crimean campaign, in terms of death and misery, could no longer be evaded, the speeches of those who had denounced war, apparently for sordid reasons, took on a different and more sombre aspect. It would be a mistake to read into the speeches and writings of a small minority in the middle years of the nineteenth century an attitude towards war which is the result of the experience of a later generation; but there was a greater sense of the value of human life, and of the rights of the individual, than in the wars of earlier times. The decline of religious belief had a similar effect; death on the battlefield was even more terrible, if death were not the prelude to immortality.[1]

The high command of the army and the civilian heads of the supply departments deserved much of the blame thrust upon them. The professional soldiers had done little to develop the scientific side of their profession; they had made few protests

---

[1] John Ruskin and Bismarck did not often agree; but each of them said that a man's attitude towards war must be affected by belief or disbelief in human immortality.

against inadequate conditions of training. They had forgotten most of the lessons of the Peninsular war. They had not applied to the auxiliary services the lessons of fighting in India. On the other hand, parliament must take some share in the responsibility for the discredit which the Crimean war brought upon the military reputation of Great Britain.[1] It was difficult to persuade parties, and particularly the supporters of economy, to look at military questions from any angle except that of finance. Joseph Hume, who opposed flogging in the army, never seems to have given much thought to other questions affecting the well-being of the private soldier. In 1822 Hume objected to the building of new barracks, though existing barracks were dangerously overcrowded. As late as 1856 Sir Joseph Paxton pointed out that the cost of housing a convict in the new prisons was greater than the sum allowed for housing a soldier. The average allowance of air for a convict in a cell was 1,000 cubic feet and for a soldier in barracks 400 cubic feet; in many barracks and in five military hospitals the figure was less than 300 cubic feet. Lord Ebrington told the commons in 1858 that the rate of mortality in the foot guards was 20·4 per 1,000, in line regiments 18 per 1,000, in cavalry regiments 11 per 1,000, while the average for the civilian population of military age was about 9 per 1,000, and 7¾ in healthy districts. The death-rate from tuberculosis among soldiers was five times as great as the death-rate among civilians; many were invalided out of the service only to die soon after their discharge. The water-supply was generally impure; the clothing worn by the troops was too tight at all times and not warm enough in winter.[2] The food

---

[1] In 1815 the military prestige of the British army was very high. Tocqueville wrote to Nassau Senior in Feb. 1855 that the conduct of the Crimean war had 'sensibly diminished' the moral force of England in Europe. 'The heroic courage of your soldiers was everywhere and unreservedly praised, but I found also a general belief that the importance of England as a military Power had been greatly exaggerated, that she is utterly devoid of military talent, which is shown as much in administration as in fighting, and that even in the most pressing circumstances she cannot raise a large army.' *Memoir of A. de Tocqueville*, Eng. trans. ii. 288. European opinion changed during the course of 1855, and the suppression of the Indian Mutiny restored British military prestige.

[2] For the accumulated absurdities of military costume during the long period of peace, see J. Laver, *British Military Uniforms* (1948). As an example of the lack of elementary decency in the arrangements provided for the troops, it may be mentioned that the urinal tubs, which stood in the rooms during the night, were emptied out in the morning and used for washing. Married quarters, as far as they existed, were bad, and almost without privacy. It is no credit to Wellington that he should never have used his immense authority to insist upon an improvement of the condi-

rations were 1 lb. of bread and ¾ lb. of meat daily. The only cooking-utensils were two coppers, one for meat, the other for potatoes. The meat was always boiled beef; there were two meals a day—breakfast at 7.30, dinner at 12.30. A third meal was provided only a few years before the Crimean war, and at the men's expense. The pay of a private of the line was nominally seven shillings a week, but half this sum was taken for messing, 1s. 10½d. for general maintenance and washing, and the soldier was thus left with 2¾d. a day for himself. No amusements were provided for him; the state made a profit of £50,000 a year out of canteens where contractors sold bad drink at high prices. The men were never in proper health, and the bad conditions led to bickering and quarrels, and, above all, to drunkenness and venereal disease. Discipline under these conditions was maintained by severe and brutal punishments.[1]

If conditions at home were bad, conditions abroad were worse. A soldier enlisted for life or for a term of years. He was required to serve ten years abroad for every five years at home; but the period of foreign service was often longer, especially in the artillery.[2] The rates of mortality in the years of peace after 1815 were terribly high: 28 per 1,000 at Bermuda, 71 in the Windward Islands, 121 at Jamaica.[3] At Sierra Leone the figures reached the fearful total of 75–80 per cent. Few British soldiers survived ten years' service in India. These conditions would have been worse but for the care taken by numbers of regimental officers to provide amenities—supper, coffee, and the like.

The efficiency of the officers was hampered by the survival of the practice of purchasing commissions. This practice was never applied to the artillery and engineers; but it was the common rule in the cavalry and infantry. The prices were high;

tions under which soldiers lived. He abolished the rule under which two soldiers shared a bed, but he did little else to make barrack life tolerable. It is also obvious why few young men of ambition and ability wanted to join the army.

[1] Flogging by order of regimental courts martial was restricted in 1812 to 300 lashes, though a district or general court martial could still order an unlimited number of lashes. This punishment was not merely uncivilized and inhumane, but was open to grave abuse. In 1832 the sentences of district courts martial were limited to 300 lashes, and of regimental courts to 100 lashes. Four years later further restrictions were imposed; in 1850 the punishment was limited to 50 lashes. In 1867 flogging was forbidden except for offences in war time; the order was shortly afterwards extended to the navy.

[2] See below, pp. 269–70.

[3] For the plight of the soldier returned from the tropics at the end of his service, see Wordsworth, *The Prelude*, Bk. iv, 387–467.

hence, if the interest on the capital spent in buying a first commission and subsequent promotions is deducted, the average
rate of pay was low, and excluded likely candidates of small
means. The system was supported by Wellington, Raglan, and
Panmure as late as 1850, and by military opinion as a whole
even twenty years later. Palmerston accepted it, and Russell
opposed its abolition in 1871.[1] It gave little scope for enterprising men to make a study of their profession. The officers of
the army were drawn from a social class educated in the literary
tradition of the public schools. Few of them were fitted by
temperament for this type of education, and the unchanging
round of Greek, Latin, and formal mathematics left the majority
with a distaste for any effort or discipline of the mind. They
were content to be gentlemen, and to leave the technical questions to those who were not gentlemen.[2] Even if they had shown
more professional interest in their work, they had little chance
of training their men or themselves under suitable conditions.
Until the establishment of county and borough constabularies
the army in Great Britain and Ireland was dispersed in small
units on police duty; but these difficulties did not excuse the
failure of the high command to attempt field training on a large
scale. Even musketry was neglected. Until 1852 the Guards
fired only thirty rounds of ball once in three years. It is characteristic of the military authorities and of public opinion that
during the Crimean war the war office complained of 'the great
difficulties about [establishing] ranges in this free country'. The
rise of Napoleon III caused alarm about the defencelessness of
England. Money was spent on fortifications of little value, but
at last the military authorities formed a camp of exercise. They
assembled from 8,000 to 10,000 men of all arms at Chobham,
and bought land at Aldershot for use in future years. Although
from the officers' point of view the work was much interrupted
by social distractions, Lord Panmure acknowledged in 1856 that,

[1] Wellington drew up a memorandum in favour of the system in 1833. The
argument that the system avoided the 'block' in promotion from which the navy
suffered after 1815 is hardly borne out by the facts.

[2] A guards officer who knew the Prussian and Russian armies 'lamented' to Sir
T. Acland in 1866 'the want of scientific knowledge in our officers'. They would
often 'fight bravely and sacrifice a lot of men for simple want of knowledge of
principles to know when and how to retire. . . . We suffer from the fact that military
men are not held in such high honour as abroad, so that a man tries to sink his
military character, and only to be an agreeable gentleman'. A. H. D. Acland, op. cit.,
p. 262.

without this experience at Chobham, the Royal Artillery in 1854 could hardly have produced six batteries fit for service in the field.[1]

If the senior officers had not been content for forty years with the routine of the parade-ground, the faults of the cumbrous administrative machinery might have been disclosed under less tragic conditions. The division of responsibility was incredible. The secretary of state for war held his office with the secretary-ship for the colonies. He decided important questions of military policy; his financial work was done by the secretary at war, but the functions of the secretary at war were never clearly defined. Palmerston, who held the office from 1809 to 1828, was always quarrelling with the commander-in-chief. The commander-in-chief at the Horse Guards had control over the forces in matters of discipline, appointments, and promotion; the militia, yeomanry, and volunteers were under the adminis-tration of the home office, the artillery and engineers under the master-general of the ordnance. The master-general sup-plied fire-arms, ammunition, and greatcoats to the army; the treasury provided supplies and transport. There were other authorities: an army medical department, an audit office, a paymaster-general's department, and a board of general officers for the inspection of clothing. The commissioners of Chelsea Hospital were an independent body. Two commissions, in 1833 and in 1837, had reported in favour of placing the ordnance under the direct supervision of the commander-in-chief and of consolidating the work of the most important departments under the direction of a board, with a civilian minister as chair-man. Wellington opposed these reforms; therefore nothing was done.

The concentration of parliamentary interest on economy led almost every year to changes in the size of the establishment. For some years after 1815 a reduction was necessary. The position in 1819 was regarded as 'normal'. There were 107,000 infantry and cavalry of all ranks, 1,000 engineers, 5,000 artillery-men, including the corps of drivers, and a small wagon train. These numbers were not enough to provide sufficient 'reliefs' for

[1] This experiment was of little value to the commissariat. The men never slept away from their camp: horses and carts were hired by the day, and supplies delivered to the camp by London contractors. Many of the troops in the Crimea had never learned to cook their food in the open air.

foreign stations; the radicals who asked for further reductions were condemning soldiers to death in the tropics. In 1823 three battalions of veterans were formed to deal with trouble in Ireland; a year later more troops were wanted for Ireland, and a strong force was sent to the West Indies owing to the danger of a negro rebellion. In 1825 the first Burmese war meant a reinforcement of 5,000 men for India. Palmerston told the commons that, unless new establishments were created, regiments which had served in India for twenty years, and were under orders for home, would have to remain on foreign service. Palmerston brought some relief from these over-long spells of service in the tropics by instituting reforms on the lines developed more than thirty years later by Cardwell.[1] He found that, when a battalion was sent abroad, only one company was left at home. He increased the number of companies in a battalion from eight to ten, and kept four companies at home stations.

After 1832 commissions of inquiry did something to improve the position of the rank and file. Good-conduct badges, carrying small increases of pay, were instituted, and a proper rotation was arranged for service abroad.[2] Troops in unhealthy stations were given fresh food, and not merely salt beef. Parliament still refused to pay for an establishment large enough to supply enough troops for foreign stations. Macaulay, who introduced the army estimates of 1840, asked for an increase of 10,000 men, and Howick[3] again raised the question of foreign service. In 1841 there were 78 battalions in India and the colonies, 6 battalions on passage, and 19 in the British Isles.[4] Of the latter, 8 had come home within the previous year. Sir Henry Hardinge became secretary at war in September 1841. He carried through a scheme, suggested by Macaulay, for the enlistment of a Royal Canadian Corps and a local corps at St. Helena. He enlarged the West Indian regiment, and cut down the Jamaica garrison

[1] See vol. xiv of this *History*, pp. 8–16, 79.

[2] The soldiers had to pay three shillings for a good-conduct badge or medal. Good-conduct pay earned by private soldiers was withdrawn on their promotion to the rank of sergeant. In 1840 £3,500 was voted to provide schoolmistresses for the children of married soldiers. In 1841 regimental libraries and savings banks were instituted.

[3] Henry George Grey, Viscount Howick, and 3rd Earl Grey (1802–94); educ. privately, and at Trinity College, Cambridge; M.P., 1826; secretary at war, 1835–9; secretary for war and the colonies, 1846–52.

[4] Excluding the household troops.

by two battalions. Henceforward about thirty-one battalions were normally at home. In 1847 a proposal to build up a reserve force by encouraging men to re-enlist after discharge led to a debate on the grievances of the private soldier, but the commons did little more than sanction a slight increase in the military establishment. For the next few years there were slight increases or reductions according to the temper of parliament. Thus, at the outbreak of the Crimean war the total effectives of the British army were about 65,000 at home, 40,000 in the colonies, and 30,000 in India.

The navy suffered almost as much as the army from the economy of parliament and the lack of directing intelligence in the high command. The transition from war to peace in the years following the Napoleonic war was made with a graceless indifference to the welfare of the men who had saved the country from invasion. Between 1813 and 1817 about 120,000 sailors were paid off. Many of them found employment in the mercantile marine or the fishing fleet, but thousands were left to starve. This discharge of men was possible because sailors were under no engagement of continuous service. As a standing force, the British navy consisted of officers and ships. When a ship was put into commission, the captain collected a crew from seamen at the dockyard ports.[1] In times of stress the press-gang was employed, and the numbers of seamen increased by drafting on board convicted smugglers, and even prisoners from towns. As late as 1831 Codrington complained that he had to take a number of men from London jails because the lord mayor wanted to get rid of them from the City. The press-gang was little used after 1815; it was never formally abolished, but 'pressing' was unnecessary owing to the formation of a roll of seamen, and the encouragement of voluntary enlistment by bounties and a higher pension, though a rule of continuous service was not adopted until 1853. Before this time the men were paid off in a lump sum after every commission. A seaman who had served twenty years on different commissions was entitled to a pension; owing to broken service there were few pensioners. In any case serving seamen lost, after a ship was paid off, any higher rating which they might have obtained

[1] Over three-quarters of the British fleet was manned by Englishmen, most of whom came from the south of England.

during a commission. Once at sea, the conditions were harsh, though they were no worse than on most merchant ships. Food and quarters were poor, but the sailors' standard was terribly low.

Officers as well as men suffered from the discharges after the war. The greater part of the fleet was laid up almost for a generation. For twenty years after 1815 there were few changes in type;[1] other Powers also laid up their ships, so there was little risk to be feared. In the year of Navarino only seventeen of the ninety-five capital ships[2] of the British navy were in commission. Although it was necessary to maintain an establishment of officers for employment in war, parliament took little account of the effect of keeping a large number of officers on half-pay.[3] Promotion was given after a certain number of years at sea and, as a senior officer could choose most of his juniors, there was a great deal of jobbery and nepotism. The division between executive officers, who obtained full military commissions, and masters, who were only of warrant rank, was unfair, and made for slackness. The masters were responsible for navigation; the fighting duties of the other officers were of a rudimentary kind in days when gunnery was at close range. The training was haphazard. A small number of boys entered the navy through the Naval College at Portsmouth; others went to sea as volunteers under the control of a ship's captain. After 1836 a system of cadetships was instituted, with instructors on board ship. The navy was a little in advance of the army in opening schools for senior ranks. A gunnery school was started at Portsmouth in 1830, and the Portsmouth College was used after 1836 as a general training school in the higher branches of the profession.

The administrative services of the navy were reformed in

[1] During the first three decades of the nineteenth century English naval architects copied French and American designs. The *Sanspareil*, laid down in 1845, was designed on the lines of a ship of this name taken from the French in 1794, though she was altered before her launch in 1851.

[2] The ships were divided into six 'rates', according to size. The first three rates included all ships of the line-of-battle, i.e. three-deckers and two-deckers. (These ships had five decks and four decks respectively, but their description applies to the decks containing the main armament.) 3,500 full-grown oak trees or 900 acres of forest were used in building a large three-decker. Below these capital ships were frigates—faster and lighter ships—sloops, cutters, and schooners.

[3] In 1841 200 commanders and 1,450 lieutenants had been without promotion for 26 years.

1832 by Sir James Graham,[1] and the admiralty was free from the confusion which cost so many lives in the Crimea, but the habits of routine and the effects of undue economy remained. Owing to the slowness in promotion most of the senior officers were too old for their commands. In 1841 the senior captain was 68; several captains were over 70. Admiral Bowles and Admiral Sir David Milne were 79 when they became port admirals at Portsmouth and Devonport. Two successive admirals at the Nore took up their commands at the age of 74. The control of the service by old men and the low standard of technical education had serious consequences at a time when the introduction of the steamship was changing the conditions of naval warfare. The early steamships were unreliable, uncomfortable, and dirty. Their engines, their coal and water-supply, their large paddle wheels (which were easily put out of action) took up space needed for guns. Sir George Cockburn complained, as first sea lord, that 'since the introduction of steamers he had never seen a clean deck, or a captain, who, when he waited on him, did not look like a sweep'.

Unfortunately the objections of sailors of the old school went beyond dislike of an unpleasing innovation. The senior officers could not adapt themselves to the new conditions of warfare; at first they used steamers as tugs[2] or dispatch-boats, and left the design to the contractors. The contractors handed over an engine-room staff with a new ship; until 1827 steamships did not appear in the Navy List.[3] The screw was regarded at first as unfitted for rough water. In 1845 a screw and a paddle steamer were tied stern to stern, and, after each ship had worked up to full steam, the screw towed the paddle in its wake; henceforward the paddle was abandoned. The victory of iron over wood came later, although there was a shortage of timber in Great Britain and almost a glut of iron. Early tests appeared to show that an iron ship was more vulnerable to shell; the holes could not be stopped, and a single broadside might sink a ship. The composition of the fleet commissioned in the summer of 1853, as a warning to Russia, shows the transition between old and new styles. There were seven screw and three sailing

---

[1] Sir James Robert George Graham, bart. (1792–1861); educ. Westminster and Christ Church, Oxford; M.P., 1818; first lord of the admiralty, 1830–4 and 1852–5; home secretary, 1841–6; offered political offices and the governor-generalship of India by Russell, 1847–8.   [2] As in Turner's picture of the 'Fighting Téméraire'.
[3] A paddle-steamer was built for the navy on the advice of Brunel in 1822.

line-of-battle ships, four screw frigates, four paddle frigates, four screw corvettes and sloops, and one paddle corvette.[1]

A naval expedition to the Baltic formed part of the offensive against Russia in 1854. It accomplished little. The commanding officer, Sir Charles Napier, was too old for his work.[2] The admiralty knew little about the fortifications of the Baltic coast. Most of the ships were too heavy in draught for inshore work in a shallow sea. The fleet had no local pilots, and merely captured merchant ships and blockaded Russian ports; the fortress of Bomarsund in the Åland Islands was taken after 10,000 troops had been brought from France. A second expedition in 1855 bombarded the fortress of Sveaborg, near Helsingfors; the ships could do nothing against the strong walls of Cronstadt.[3] There were minor naval operations off Kamchatka and in the White Sea, but the fighting outside the main theatre of war in the Black Sea made no difference to the final decision.

The first detachments of British troops for the expedition to the Black Sea sailed for Malta in February 1854. Their numbers and the dates of their arrival were announced, without interference from the authorities, in the columns of *The Times*. Lord Raglan[4] was appointed commander-in-chief. Raglan had been on Wellington's staff in the Peninsula, and had lost an arm at Waterloo. He went in 1827 with Wellington to the Horse Guards as military secretary, and stayed there until 1852. When Hardinge succeeded Wellington as commander-in-chief, Raglan became master-general of the ordnance. He was 66 years old in 1854, and had not seen active service for nearly forty

---

[1] In 1853 Queen Victoria watched a sham fight between the ships of the assembled squadron. The whole affair was fought under sail.

[2] Napier's signal to his command on receiving the declaration of war was typical of the old school of admirals. 'Lads, war is declared with a numerous and bold enemy. Should they meet and offer battle, you know how to dispose of them. Should they remain in port, we must try and get at them. Success depends upon the quickness and precision of your firing. Also, lads, sharpen your cutlasses, and the day is your own.'

[3] The admirals decided, for humane reasons, not to attack the city of Helsingfors, although it was strongly fortified. For the Baltic campaigns, see the *Memoirs of Admiral Sir Astley Cooper Key*, ed. Vice-Admiral P. H. Colomb.

[4] Lord Fitzroy James Henry Somerset (1788–1855), 1st Baron Raglan, s. of the 5th duke of Beaufort; educ. Westminster; m. 1814 a niece of Wellington; chargé d'affaires at British embassy in Paris, 1815–18; accompanied Wellington to Verona in 1822, and to St. Petersburg in 1826; M.P., 1818.

years.[1] He was a man of fine presence and conciliatory manner, brave, conscientious, and accurate, but he had little more than average ability. His colleagues at home treated him unfairly and served him badly; if he had not been hampered by the presence of a dying man as commander of the French forces, he might have taken Sebastopol in the first months of the campaign.

Even after Raglan's appointment the cabinet was not clear about the military purpose of the expedition. They wanted the army to keep the Russians out of Constantinople and to drive them from the Principalities. They assumed that a counter-stroke would be necessary, and had some idea of an attack upon Sebastopol. Napoleon III favoured this plan, but the British and French authorities knew little about the strength of Sebastopol, or the number of Russian troops in the Crimea. At the end of May the allied forces arrived at Gallipoli and Scutari; the British troops were without tents. Raglan wanted to move at once to Varna, whence he hoped to deal with the Russians in the Principalities. The commissariat officials doubted whether the troops could be fed at Varna. In June Raglan asked for the organization of a land transport corps, but the war office refused it, and the cabinet did not overrule the decision. Meanwhile Austrian threats forced the Russians to leave the Principalities; they had not taken the fortress of Silistria, and were defeated on the Danube.[2] At the beginning of August they withdrew to the Pruth. Thus the allied armies reached Varna to no purpose. They began to suffer from the malarial conditions of the Bulgarian coast in summer, and from an epidemic of cholera brought in French ships from Marseilles.

The authorities at home now ordered an attack on Sebastopol. Raglan, his chief naval adviser, and at least one of his divisional commanders were not in favour of the plan. They pointed out that little was known about the Russian strength, that the British siege train was incomplete, and the French train had not left Toulon. At home Major-General Shaw-Kennedy, a Peninsular veteran, warned the cabinet that Sebastopol was too strongly fortified to be taken from the sea, and that its capture on the land side would need a large force, which might be

---

[1] In the Crimea Raglan could not rid himself of the habit of describing the enemy as 'the French'.

[2] The defence of Silistria owed much to the work of two British officers, Captain Butler and Lieutenant Nasmyth, who were on their way home from the East. Other British officers directed the offensive against the Russian field army.

attacked by the Russian field armies. The French military staff also objected, but did not venture openly to resist a scheme supported by the emperor. The health of the troops had been so much affected by their stay at Varna, and the transport service was so bad, that an invasion of the Crimea before the autumn appeared impracticable. If the fortress were not taken before the beginning of winter, the armies would be in a dangerous position. There were arguments on the other side. Unless the centre of Russian power in the Black Sea were destroyed, Turkey would not be safe from Russian attack, and the purpose of the war would not have been achieved. Sebastopol was a long way from the military centre of Russia. Many Russian troops marched for three months before reaching the Crimea; it was said that two-thirds of the reinforcements died on their way. The allies had command of the sea, and could land troops at will. The main works of Sebastopol protected only the approaches by sea, and the Russians would have no time to build strong fortifications on the land side. The Crimea was healthier than the Bulgarian coast, and the Allies should be able to transport the armies, take the fortress, and remove the troops before the beginning of winter.

The decision was taken by a weak and divided cabinet, with clamours from the press. *The Times* was particularly vehement,[1] and, as in other details, gave the Russians plenty of warning. Aberdeen, whose conscience was profoundly troubled by the fact of war, made little effort to break through the routine of departmental business, or to assure himself that the ministers concerned with the fighting services were the right men for their posts. He had already given way on critical points to the French. The appointment of St. Arnaud as commander-in-chief of the French forces was a blunder. St. Arnaud owed his rapid promotion to his political support of Napoleon before the *coup d'état*. He was a clever man, but without moral authority, and, apart from his ill health, his temper unfitted him for a high command in the field.

Although an expedition undertaken in this way hardly deserved to prosper, it came near to easy success. The armies began to move from Varna on 24 August. Their movement was

[1] J. T. Delane (1817–79), editor of *The Times*, went to Constantinople in July 1854 to observe the situation at close quarters; he did not go to Varna or to the Crimea.

delayed because the French had not enough steamers to tow their sailing-ships. The French troops were crowded on the ships of war to such an extent that the guns could hardly have been fired if the Russians had attacked the convoy.[1] St. Arnaud suggested that the allies should land on the east coast of the Crimean peninsula, and postpone operations until the following year. Raglan would not accept this indirect method of disobeying instructions. In any case the plan would have allowed the Russians time to prepare for a long siege. Hence the two armies landed in the bay of Eupatoria, to the north of Sebastopol, and on 19 September moved forward over open country broken by small streams. They made no attempt to reconnoitre the ground. Fortunately the Russian commander, Prince Menschikoff, was not an enterprising man. The Russian forces in the peninsula were about 80,000 strong, though 50,000 only belonged to the active regular army. The British force was about 26,000 strong, with 66 guns, the French about 30,000, with 70 guns. There were also some 5,000 Turks.

Menschikoff established himself with 40,000 men and about 100 guns on the rising ground to the south of the river Alma, some fifteen miles from Sebastopol. His army was out of range of the allied ships. The south bank of the Alma consisted of perpendicular cliffs stretching inland for over a mile from the shore, and thence rising less abruptly. Menschikoff did not destroy or block two paths which gave access up the cliffs. He made no defence works, and posted only a few troops at the points where the paths reached the plateau. The allies took advantage of this neglect, but the battle for the heights (20 September) showed the confusion resulting from a divided command. The ground was not properly explored; the French, who were to attack from the side of the coast, were delayed, and left the British force to dislodge the Russian mass. Raglan himself took up a position dangerously in advance of his troops and out of full view of the main battle-field. The heights were gained, and the Russians retreated in disorder. Raglan wanted an immediate advance, but St. Arnaud refused.[2] If the victory

[1] The Russian admiral wanted to attack, but was not allowed to leave Sebastopol harbour. Fourteen French sailing-ships left Varna in advance of the main body and without steam protection. A couple of Russian steam-frigates could have sunk every one of these sailing-ships.

[2] St. Arnaud gave as his reason that the French had left their knapsacks behind them in the valley before marching to the heights.

had been pressed home, the allies might have destroyed the Russian field army, and taken the north side of Sebastopol. Control of the north side of the harbour would have enabled them to destroy the Russian fleet, and to cut off Sebastopol from the north and east of the Crimea. Two days after the battle Raglan again proposed immediate attack, but once more St. Arnaud maintained that the allies had not enough troops to take the Russian works. Sir John Burgoyne, the senior British engineer, also thought an assault too dangerous without a siege-train. The Russians now settled the allies' plans for them by sinking seven ships across the mouth of the harbour. The crews were thus free to help in the defence of the fortress, and, even if the north side of Sebastopol had been taken, the harbour would have been blocked.

The chance of a *coup de main* had been lost. The allies still hoped to take the fortress before the winter, but they could not stay on the north side of the harbour. The landing-beaches and the open roadstead of Eupatoria were too much exposed to form a base for a large army. To the south of the long inlet of Sebastopol—some $3\frac{1}{2}$ miles long and 1,000 yards across—there was a plateau jutting out into the sea, and, on the coast, three small, sheltered bays. If the troops were established on the high ground between the shore and the fortifications, they could be supplied from these bays. The main fortifications, barracks, naval harbour and arsenal, and the city itself were on the south side of the inlet. Therefore the allies took the risk of a flank march, through broken country, from the north to the south side of Sebastopol. Menschikoff was engaged at the same time in getting his army out of the city. His troops crossed Raglan's path, and his rearguard fought a minor action. It was characteristic of the two armies that Raglan should have had no scouts to warn him of Menschikoff's movements, and that Menschikoff took several days to realize what had happened. St. Arnaud was dead before the allies reached the plateau. His successor Canrobert was a pleasant, competent man, popular with his troops and careful of their health and comfort.[1] As a commander he was irresolute, timid, and inactive. Raglan might have dominated Canrobert and obtained a quick decision; but

---

[1] During the winter of 1854–5 Canrobert spent more time than Raglan in the encampments of the soldiers, and showed more inventiveness in mitigating the hardships of his troops.

Raglan himself was not firm enough, and gave way against his own judgement. When the armies had reached the plateau[1] Raglan took a decision which caused immense hardships to the British troops. Two of the three small harbours available as bases were at the west end of the plateau; the third was the inlet of Balaclava, at the south-east corner. Conrobert offered Raglan his choice. On the advice of Admiral Lyons, who looked at the matter from a naval point of view, Raglan chose Bala-clava. Hence he undertook not merely the eastern half of the siege, but the defence of the allied armies against attack from the Russian field army. The harbour was small and the wharves only 75 feet long. One road, unmetalled, climbed the steep hill from the harbour to the plateau. A metalled road[2] from Yalta (some 35 miles distant) to Sebastopol ran parallel with the sea some three miles inland from the harbour. This road reached the plateau about $2\frac{1}{2}$ miles north of the unmetalled track. In the fine autumn weather the position seemed excellent. Raglan did not build metalled roads for the winter or even connect the harbour with the Yalta–Sebastopol road. There was little labour to be obtained, and the troops were preparing for the capture of the fortress.

The Russians were also strengthening their defences. The land between the allied camps and the fortifications of Sebasto-pol was divided by five ravines. On the high ground between these ravines the allies posted guns to silence the Russian batteries

[1] See map. The plateau was 10–11 miles from east to west and 8 miles from north to south at its widest points. In shape it was not unlike the Isle of Wight on a smaller scale. Sebastopol would be, roughly, in the position of Cowes (or slightly nearer to Ryde); the inlet would correspond with the Solent and the inner harbour with the river Medina. The French landing-places would be at Yarmouth and Totland bay. Chersonese, at the extreme west of the plateau, would corre-spond with the Needles. The land border of the plateau would run from the south-west end of the Undercliff near Ventnor to Bembridge; the river Tchernaya, flow-ing into the Sebastopol inlet, would run between Ryde and Bembridge. The British camps were at points on the plateau roughly corresponding with the hinter-land of Sandown and Shanklin. The harbour of Balaclava was on the low ground south-east of the plateau, with isolated hills behind it. The 'crow-fly' distance from the harbour to the plateau was about 3 miles. The distance by road to the summit of the plateau was about 4 miles, though the camps were spread out at some distance from the point where the road touched the plateau, while the trenches, again, were some distance from the camps. These latter facts account for the different estimates, in different authorities, of the distance between Balaclava and the British camps and trenches.

[2] There was a country house and estate of the Woronzoff family at Yalta. The road was generally known as the Woronzoff road.

and open the way for an assault. The bombardment which was to precede this assault was fixed for 17 October. The fleet arranged to engage the coastal works and forts; these forts were three miles from the land front of the allies, and, as the harbour was blocked, the naval bombardment could have no positive effect upon the fortunes of the assault. Unfortunately, after the guns on land had been firing with effect for nearly four hours in the heaviest artillery fire hitherto known in the history of war, the largest French magazine blew up, and disorganized the French plans to such an extent that the assault was postponed. With less excuse, the allied commanders did not keep up their fire during the night; hence the Russians were able to repair the parapets and to bring up new guns from the ships and the arsenal.

The Russians knew that unless they made a great effort to drive off the allies they could not save the fortress. Their best chance of success lay in a surprise attack by the field army. They made two such attacks. The first attack was directed against the British base at Balaclava, where a weak force of 3,000 Turks, 1,000 marines, and the 93rd Highlanders under Sir Colin Campbell[1] defended the harbour. The Russians chose the early morning of 25 October for their move. They took the allies by surprise. Raglan had not kept in touch with the Russian field army; he had news on the previous day of a projected attack, but, as this news had been brought to him more than once, he disregarded it. He had given orders that, in the event of a strong attack in the neighbourhood of Balaclava, two divisions should move down from the plateau. The cavalry division encamped immediately below the heights could be brought quickly into action. The divisional commander, Lord Lucan, was twelve years younger than Raglan; he was a quick, imperious man, unpopular with his troops, and ready to criticize orders from headquarters.[2] Under him, and in command of the light brigade, was his brother-in-law Lord Cardigan.[3] Cardigan was one of the most hated officers in the army. He had

[1] See below, p. 438.
[2] George Charles Bingham, 3rd earl of Lucan (1800–88); educ. Westminster; entered the army, 1816; served on the staff of Prince Woronzoff in the Russo-Turkish war of 1828–9; M.P., 1826.
[3] James Thomas Brudenell, 7th earl of Cardigan (1797–1868); educ. Christ Church, Oxford; M.P., 1818; obtained a commission, 1824; rose, by rapid purchase, to be lieut.-colonel of the 15th Hussars, 1832; prosecuted for fighting a duel, 1841.

quarrelled with Lucan and with the officers of his own regiment, although he was a keen soldier, and spent about a quarter of his income of £40,000 a year on regimental purposes. He was narrow, selfish, and pedantic. In the Crimea he made himself generally disliked, apart from his other unamiable qualities, because he slept on board his yacht in Balaclava harbour instead of sharing the discomforts of the soldiers.[1]

The Russians drove in the Turks from their outlying posts, and the cavalry with the 'thin red line' of the 93rd Highlanders now had the duty of holding up the attack until the infantry came down from the plateau. The cavalry distinguished themselves by two charges unique in British history. The first of these charges, made by the heavy brigade of 900 men under General Scarlett, was uphill against 3,000 Russian horsemen. The second charge was made by the light brigade. As a piece of gallantry it was superb; as a tactical move it was more than absurd, since it was due to a misinterpretation of a badly worded order. The surprise attack had failed to attain its objective, and the Russians appeared to be about to retreat with the English guns which they had captured from the Turks. Raglan ordered Lucan to send his cavalry forward to save these guns. Lucan took the order to mean that he was to attack another section of Russian guns a mile and a quarter distant at the end of a valley.[2] Russian cavalry covered the guns, and other batteries on the sides of the valley protected them. The order was brought to Lucan by Captain Nolan.[3] After the light brigade, at Lucan's orders,

---

[1] For this reason he was on his yacht during the first stages of the battles of Balaclava and Inkerman.

[2] Between the Fedukhine and Causeway Heights. See map 3 at end of volume.

[3] The written order was in these terms: 'Lord Raglan wishes the cavalry to advance rapidly to the front, and try to prevent the enemy carrying away the guns—Troop Horse Artillery may accompany—French cavalry is on your left. Immediate.' But what guns? And what section of the front? It is clear that, if Lucan had interpreted the order in the light of previous orders received, he would have understood that Raglan meant the English guns left unprotected by the Turks. On the other hand, he could not see the guns, whereas he knew of the Russian batteries at the eastern end of the valley, though these guns were also out of sight. Lucan protested to Nolan; Nolan pointed, according to Lucan, to the valley and answered, with some sharpness, 'There, my lord, is your enemy. There are your guns.' Nolan probably did not mean to give an exact direction. He was not pointing to anything which either man could see. He knew the intention of the order, and in any case Lucan may have misinterpreted the sweep of an arm; the angle between the right and wrong direction was hardly more than twenty degrees. The responsibility for the mistake may therefore be divided between (a) Raglan, whose order was not precisely worded—in any case Raglan ought to have waited for th e infantry, and

had begun their charge, Nolan rode across their front pointing
to the English guns; but he was killed before he could make
himself understood.[1] The light brigade, with Cardigan at their
head, thus rode steadily down the valley. They silenced the
guns. Their courage and discipline, and the force of their attack,
so much shook the enemy that, if they had been immediately
supported, they might have driven the whole Russian force into
a disorderly rout. There was no support, and the survivors of
the Light Brigade had to retire along the valley through which
they had come.[2] Their retreat was greatly assisted by the French
chasseurs d'Afrique who drove back the enemy troops and guns
on the northern slopes above the valley. Meanwhile, after too
long delay, the infantry had arrived. The Russians continued
to withdraw. Raglan, still thinking in terms of a prospective
attack upon Sebastopol, did not pursue them, or dislodge them
from the whole of the position which they had taken, although
this position cut the metalled road from Yalta to the plateau.
The British base was secure, but the losses were far greater on
the British side.

The Russians made their second attempt on 5 November.
They left Balaclava alone, and attacked the British lines on the
plateau. On 26 October they had given Raglan warning of
their grand attack by a sally on the east of the British position.
They were driven back, but little was done to improve the
defences in this quarter. The army was busy with the main
siege-works; the French had been more careful in building
works on the edge of the plateau south of the British position,
while the British did not construct anything more than a low

not to have used cavalry alone against a strong force—(b) Lucan, who did not show
common sense, or take care to get precise interpretation of the order given to him
by Nolan; and (c) Nolan, who was sharp to the verge of insubordination, and did
not make sure that Lucan understood Raglan's message.

[1] Cardigan thought that Nolan was guilty of a grave breach of discipline in
taking it upon himself to lead, or encourage, the charge. Cardigan's own conduct
in the charge was entirely to his credit, though he was dazed and bewildered once
the guns had been taken. He rode back without waiting for the troops to re-form.
It is said that he escaped death at the guns because a Russian officer, belonging
to the Radziwill family, recognized him, and promised some Cossacks a reward if
they would take him unhurt.

[2] It is often stated that two-thirds of the brigade were killed or wounded. This
estimate is based upon the number—195—who answered at the first muster after
the charge; but the unwounded men who had lost their horses, and a good many
stragglers, would not have been present at this muster. The actual losses, out of 673
horsemen, were 113 killed and 134 wounded; 475 horses were killed.

stone wall across the main post road leading up from the valley of the Tchernaya. The Russian army, reinforced by a number of battalions from Odessa, was about 120,000 strong, though only 70,000 men could be used for an offensive; the others were needed for the defence of the fortress. The allies had about 65,000 men and 11,000 Turkish auxiliaries;[1] but they had to extend their troops in a semicircle of four miles round the defences of Sebastopol, and to protect their landing-places. Hence the line was weakly held at critical points.

The Russian field army moved to the attack of the British right at dawn under cover of a thick mist; at the same time a strong sortie was made against the British front, and a third force attempted to draw away the allies by a feint to the south of the main attack. The fight has been described as 'a soldiers' battle'. Every battle is a soldiers' battle. Inkerman[2] may have a special claim to the title because there were few large tactical moves; the issue was decided by hand-to-hand fighting of the fiercest kind, and reinforcements were thrown in to hold a line which was continually being broken by the mass of the enemy. In the first part of the battle a British force of 3,600 men, mainly from the 2nd division, held more than 15,000 Russians. Help was long in coming, partly because the British commanders at first refused the offer of French reinforcements, partly because the allies had no proper reserve in a central position. The battle was won by the steadfastness of the British troops,[3] by the superiority of the Minié rifle, with which the greater part of

[1] Under good officers the Turks would have fought well. Raglan had many officers from the Indian army who would have known how to lead Turks, but he would not employ them for the purpose. He did not use the Turks as combatants in the battle of Inkerman; he had already refused Omar Pasha's offer to send him the garrison of Varna.

[2] The name of the battle is taken from the heights on the east side of the Tchernaya. These heights, plainly visible from the British camp, held some old walls and towers known as the ruins of Inkerman. The British troops gave the name Mount Inkerman to the heights on their own plateau between the Tchernaya valley and the first of the ravines leading down to Sebastopol.

[3] General Sir John Lysaght Pennefather (1800-72) was in command of the 2nd division, owing to the illness of Sir G. de Lacy Evans. Pennefather, who had seen active service in India under Sir Charles Napier, never lost his nerve, and insisted on holding the line of his outposts. He rode up and down through the thick of the fight; he was popular with his men, and his 'favourite oaths, roaring cheerily down through the smoke', had an excellent effect. Pennefather knew that small numbers of resolute men, aided by a thick mist, could hold up and even break attacking columns. The moral effect of his refusal to give ground was to make the 'muffin-caps', as the British soldiers called the Russians, believe that the position was held by a force strong enough to resist an outflanking movement.

the British infantry were armed. The Russians lost nearly 12,000 in killed, wounded, and prisoners; the British losses were 2,573, of whom 635 were killed, and the French losses were 143 killed and 786 wounded. No gun, Russian, British, or French, was lost. Ten of the British officers in command of divisions, brigades, battalions, or smaller detachments in the battle were killed or mortally wounded; eleven were wounded, and the other four had their horses shot under them.[1]

The weather had broken since the end of October, but the men still wore the clothes in which they had landed at Varna. Many had lost their knapsacks on disembarkation at Balaclava. Within ten days of the battle of Inkerman a blizzard blew down the tents, destroyed the hospital marquees, and wrecked twenty-one ships off the harbour. One of these ships was laden with warm clothing, another contained ten million rounds of ammunition, and others twenty days' supply of forage. The position was serious because there was no hope of taking the fortress before the spring of 1855. The Russian army, in spite of its losses, was much stronger than the combined force of the allies. Hence the British troops were doomed to spend a winter on open ground. They paid with their lives for the earlier economy of parliament in suppressing the wagon-train and other auxiliary forces, and the refusal of the home authorities to agree to the demand of the supply department for a reserve of forage at Constantinople or to Raglan's proposal for the formation of a land transport corps. The unmetalled clay track to the heights soon became impassable in many places for wagons and carts. There were no skilled road-makers. No one seems to have thought of breaking up a wooden merchant ship, and using her timbers for a 'corduroy' road; the supplies for an army of about 25,000 had to be taken up the steep hill from the narrow harbour. Fuel was short; many of the camp kettles were lost or had become unserviceable, and the supply services at home added to the difficulties by sending out coffee in the form of unroasted green berries.[2] The privations and cold after

---

[1] One battalion of *zouaves* was led into action, according to custom, by a *vivandière* of the regiment, wearing a pretty dress. She was killed almost at once. In the attack of 9 June 1855 the *vivandière* of the Algerian *zouaves* was mounted, and wore a white hat with a feather.

[2] The commissary-general had written as early as Feb. 1854: 'The soldiers will no doubt find some means of overcoming any difficulty that may arise from the want of mills and coffee-roasters.'

the blizzard brought back cholera, dysentery, and malarial fever. During the months of January and February 1855 the number of men in hospital rose almost to 14,000, and, if there had been no reinforcements from home, the British force would soon have ceased to exist. On one day in January the greater part of the British defence and siege-works were manned by 290 men—one-twentieth of the force opposed to them. For a time indeed the reinforcements increased the number of sick. The casualties in the regiments on active service were filled by raw recruits;[1] the authorities at home sent out numbers of boys of sixteen, and even younger, who were unfitted to meet the hardships of winter. There were no ambulances to take men from the camp to the harbour. The hospital ships were ill equipped and over-crowded; nearly one in ten of the sick and wounded died on the sea voyage between the Crimea and Constantinople. The hospitals were insanitary, badly managed, and short of stores. In November 1854 there were no drugs, such as castor oil or opium, for the thousands of cases of bowel complaints. During this month, in one hospital with about 2,000 dysenteric cases, only six shirts were washed. The orderlies were pensioners; many of them were of bad character. In one large hospital more than half of the patients died during the month of February 1855. After this time conditions began rapidly to improve. The French, as their numbers increased, took over some of the works on the British front.[2] A road was built in February from Balaclava to the camp; tram-lines were laid down, and in March a light railway was in operation. The decision to send Miss Florence Nightingale[3] to the hospitals at Scutari was taken at the end of October 1854. Miss Nightingale arrived on the day before the battle of Inkerman. Her position was at first a subordinate one; her thirty nurses, and another forty-six under

[1] Drafting could take place only between battalions of the same regiment. It was thus impossible, in the case of regiments which had already sent their battalions to the field, to fill up gaps by taking seasoned troops from other regiments at home, and using the cadres of these regiments for training recruits.

[2] Raglan thought that the French might have taken over a larger sector. Their numbers increased from 45,000 in Oct. to 65,000 in Dec., and 78,000 in Jan. They did not begin to relieve the British until the third week of January.

[3] Florence Nightingale (1820–1910) began inspecting military hospitals during her first London season. She trained as a nurse at the Kaiserwerth Institute (see below, p. 621) and at the hospital of the sisters of St. Vincent de Paul, Paris. After the Crimean war Miss Nightingale spent her life in the improvement of nursing and hospital conditions, and in public health reform. She was awarded the Order of Merit in 1907.

Miss Stanley, took the places of orderlies, but Miss Nightingale's character, and the support given by the home authorities to her suggestions, soon made her a powerful influence in the management of the hospitals. It is possible to exaggerate her part in the improvement of conditions, but the presence of a number of intelligent and well-trained women of gentle nurture had excellent results upon the details of administration, and an immeasurable effect upon the morale of the sick and wounded men.

On the reassembling of parliament in January 1855, a motion to inquire into the condition of the army and the supply services had the support of a large majority. Aberdeen resigned and Palmerston became prime minister. Palmerston accepted the demand for a commission of inquiry. The commissioners went to the Crimea in March; they gave the highest praise to the fighting troops, and laid responsibility for the breakdown of the supply services primarily upon the cabinet. Their report dealt sternly, and a little harshly, with the shortcomings of the commissary-general and his staff.[1]

Henceforward the worst mistakes were remedied. The main difficulty for the rest of the campaign was not the work of supply but co-operation with the French. The French found reinforcements more easily than Great Britain, in spite of the British efforts to enlist mercenaries from Germany and Switzerland.[2] The laying of a submarine cable from the Crimea to Constantinople[3] in April 1855 made it easier for Napoleon to interfere with his generals; for a time he thought of taking command in person. Canrobert was so much harassed by the emperor's suggestions that he resigned his command in the middle of May. His successor, General Pélissier, was a soldier of greater

[1] The commissary-general defended himself by a counter-statement, in which he maintained that the lack of supplies in the camps was due to the difficulty of transport from Balaclava harbour, owing to lack of forage, and this shortage was the result of the refusal of the treasury to send out the reserve of 2,000 tons for which he had asked. A committee of inquiry appointed in 1856 upheld this statement. Public opinion agreed with *The Times* in regarding the committee as 'whitewashing'. The Naval Brigade, though its camp was farthest from the base, suffered least because the officers had more experience of getting supplies in foreign ports.

[2] Great Britain accepted the Piedmontese offer of a contingent of 15,000 troops largely in order to lessen the disproportion between the size of the French and the other allied contingents. The Piedmontese fought well at Sebastopol.

[3] The land line to Belgrade was extended to Constantinople.

determination;[1] he believed that the capture of Sebastopol was 'difficult, but possible', and wanted to push the attack to a conclusion.

Pélissier supported an expedition to Kertsch (at the mouth of the sea of Azof) which had been postponed by Canrobert. This attempt to cut off the main source of Russian supplies was completely successful. A large number of ships and immense quantities of stores fell into the hands of the allies. Pélissier also agreed with Raglan that an assault should be attempted without delay. On 8 and 9 June the French carried out the first stage of the attack; the main assault was planned for 18 June. Unfortunately Pélissier changed his dispositions on the night of 17 June. He decided to attack at dawn without waiting for a final bombardment. Raglan protested, but, against his better judgement, gave way. The allied troops thus met a heavy fire which might have been silenced; the attack failed, though the Russians lost as severely as the allies. This failure, after the long anxieties of the campaign, was too much for Raglan. He died ten days later. His successor was General Simpson.[2] Simpson had been sent to report on the fitness of Raglan's staff. He was popular, but opinion summed him up as 'a good man, a long-headed Scotchman', hardly good enough for the chief position. After a last attempt on 16 August to use the field army, the Russian commander thought of abandoning Sebastopol; he decided at the end of August to fight to the last. The final bombardment began on 5 September; the allies planned their assault for noon on 8 September; they knew that the Russian reliefs took place at this hour, and that the greater part of the old garrison marched out before their successors came in. Simpson gave the post of honour—the assault on the work known as the Redan—to the second and light divisions. He made this choice because these divisions had been defending the line opposite the Redan for many months; he forgot that, owing to their heavy losses, the regiments had a large number of half-

[1] Changarnier once said of Pélissier: 'If there were an insurrection, I should not hesitate to burn down one of the quarters of Paris. Pélissier would not shrink from burning the whole city.'

[2] Sir James Simpson (1792–1868); fought in the Peninsular war; wounded at Quatre Bras; second in command during the Sind war; described by Napier as 'an officer peculiarly exact in following his instructions'. After the fall of Sebastopol, Pélissier, in his excitement, came to Simpson and kissed him. Simpson's comment was: 'It was a great occasion, and I couldna resist him.'

trained recruits. The Redan was not captured, but the French took the strong Malakoff redoubt which dominated the defence position. The English intended to renew the attack next day; during the night, however, the Russians abandoned their lines, and in the morning their army was on the north side of the harbour. After the capture of Sebastopol an expedition to Kinburn,[1] on the estuaries of the Dnieper and the Bug, destroyed another Russian base, but no further operations of importance were carried out in the Crimea.[2]

While the troops were fighting in the Crimea, attempts were made to end the war by negotiation with Russia. The allies renounced territorial or other gains for themselves. They agreed to remain united in the maintenance of the territorial integrity of the Ottoman Empire and the consolidation of the civil and religious rights of the Christian subjects of this empire. They resolved to find some way of bringing Turkey 'into the general system of the Powers', and invited other Powers to join them in defending the Turks from the menace of Russian imperialism. Austria was as much concerned as Great Britain and France with the defence of Turkey against Russia. The neglect of navigation channels at the mouth of the Danube showed how little Russia cared for Austrian interests. On the other hand, Austria was poor; her internal situation was difficult. The Italians were waiting for their chance to win Lombardy and Venetia. Russian help had enabled the Austrians to suppress the Hungarian rebels in 1849; Russia was the support of monarchical authority in Europe, but, if the Russians were driven to extremes, they might cause trouble in more than one part of the Habsburg monarchy. Owing to their cautious and temporizing policy the Austrians lost the friendship of Russia without getting the support of Great Britain and France; from the Austrian point of view the friendship of France and probably that of England would never have survived the raising of the Italian question. If Austria stayed out of the war, Prussia was unlikely to come into it. Prussia had no direct interest in

[1] This attack was the first naval operation undertaken by ironclads.
[2] The fortress of Kars, in Turkish Armenia, was defended by Turkish troops under the direction of a British commissioner, Colonel Fenwick Williams, R.A. A Russian attack was heavily defeated on 29 Sept. 1855, but the Turks made no attempt to relieve the fortress, although Omar Pasha's army was transferred to Batoum after the fall of Sebastopol. The garrison was starved into surrender on 29 November.

the eastern question, and every motive for keeping on good terms with Russia. Sweden was afraid of Russian imperialism; the fortification of the Åland Islands and the attempts to secure an outlet through the Varanger fiord were a threat to Swedish interests. In November 1855 the Swedes signed a treaty of alliance with Great Britain and France, without definite promise of military aid. The treaty was a warning to Russia, and might have had important results if the war had been prolonged. The alliance of Piedmont meant a great deal to Piedmont, but gave little military assistance to the allies.[1]

The allies were left to fight their own war. In August 1854, with the diplomatic support of Austria (confirmed by treaty in December), they drew up proposals known later as the four Vienna points. These proposals were: (1) The substitution of a European guarantee for a Russian protectorate in the Principalities. (2) The improvement of the navigation channels at the mouth of the Danube. (3) The revision of the Straits Convention of 1841 in the interests of European equilibrium. (4) The abandonment of the claims of Russia to any official protectorate over the Christian subjects of Turkey. A note in the *Moniteur* explained that the third point involved a limitation of Russian naval power in the Black Sea. After the battle of Inkerman the emperor accepted the four points in principle, but refused to limit the size of his Black Sea fleet, or to surrender territory between the Danube and the Pruth. He did not break off negotiations because he was afraid that Austria might join the allies. Nicholas died on 2 March 1855.[2] Opinion in western Europe, and particularly in Great Britain, regarded the war as directed against the policy of the emperor, and hoped for a change under his successor. Alexander II was not strong enough to resist Russian patriotic feeling, and the allies had not won any striking success. Hence, when the Powers met at Vienna to resume discussions, they agreed on the first two points, but negotiations broke down on the question of the Black Sea fleet. Austria proposed, as a compromise, that any increase in the Russian fleet should be balanced by the admission of an equal

[1] In Dec. 1855 the British government introduced a foreign enlistment bill allowing 15,000 foreigners to be enlisted and drilled on British soil. A number of Germans were enlisted in this way.

[2] As Tenniel showed in one of the most famous cartoons in *Punch*, Nicholas was a victim of his own 'General Février'. He went out, with a high temperature, from his palace to a review, and died (18 Feb., o.s.) of the effect.

number of French and British ships into the Black Sea. This plan, which would have led to continual friction, was rejected by Great Britain and France, and the war continued.[1]

The fall of Sebastopol changed the situation. *The Times* described the capture of the place as a 'preliminary operation', but the invasion of Russia from the Crimea was an impossibility. Napoleon had already threatened to take away 100,000 men from the Crimea. He now pointed out that France had on active service nearly four times as many troops as Great Britain. He wanted either to reduce the war to a blockade of Russia, to enlarge it by appeal to national sentiment in Poland, Italy, and Hungary, or to end it by Austrian mediation. Palmerston complained that the Frenchmen in favour of peace were merely a 'cabal of stockjobbing politicians'; but Napoleon knew that a continuation of the war in English interests would endanger his position. Palmerston therefore had to give way. On 16 January 1856, after an ultimatum from Austria, Russia accepted the four points, including the surrender of territory at the mouth of the Danube and the neutralization of the Black Sea.[2] The peace congress opened at Paris on 25 February, and the treaty of Paris was signed on 30 March.[3]

How far did the terms of the treaty of Paris fulfil the purpose for which the Crimean war had been fought? The surrender of southern Bessarabia removed the Russian control of the mouths of the Danube. An international commission was set up to carry out the immediate work of dredging and lighting the channel of the Danube, and a permanent commission, composed of members of the riparian states, received powers to undertake the regulation of tolls and general arrangements for the navigation of the river. The re-enactment of the convention of 1841 affirmed the closing of the Dardanelles in time of peace to foreign ships of war other than light vessels for the service of

---

[1] Russell, who represented Great Britain, and Drouyn de Lhuys, who represented France, agreed to the compromise until they received instructions from home. Drouyn de Lhuys resigned. Russell made a speech in parliament in favour of continuing the war. The Austrian minister disclosed Russell's assent to the compromise, and Russell resigned after notice of a motion of censure. See G. B. Henderson, 'The Eclipse of Lord John Russell', *Cambridge Historical Journal*, Apr. 1935.

[2] i.e. the exclusion of ships of war from the Black Sea.

[3] According to the British representatives, the birth of the Prince Imperial on 16 March diverted Napoleon's interest; but the emperor was already considering a *rapprochement* with Russia, although Great Britain, France, and Austria, in April 1856, pledged themselves to defend the treaty of Paris.

the embassies at Constantinople and the policing of the Danube. The neutralization of the Black Sea rendered 'the maintenance or establishment upon its coast of military-maritime arsenals . . . alike unnecessary and purposeless'. Russian claims to an exclusive protectorate over Turkish subjects or Turkish territory were set aside. Turkey was admitted to 'participate in the public law and system [Concert] of Europe'. Turkish independence was guaranteed by the Powers; the Danubian Principalities were to be given constitutions.[1]

The treaty was not, and could not be, a permanent settlement of the eastern question.[2] Turkey promised to introduce reforms of an enlightened kind; these reforms did not get beyond a high-sounding proclamation. Russia was weakened for the time being, but the Russian government waited for an opportunity to denounce the clause neutralizing the Black Sea. This opportunity came with the Franco-Prussian war. In 1870 Russia announced that she no longer felt bound to respect terms which left her without security on her southern coast even from the attack of a minor Power. Great Britain could do no more than recognize a *fait accompli*, and the only satisfaction which the British government obtained from a conference in London was a declaration that in future no Power should have the right to denounce an international treaty. Within eight years Europe was nearly at war again over Russian pretensions in the Near East.

The lessons of the Crimean war were not fully learned either

---

[1] The treaty laid down that the inhabitants of the Principalities should be consulted about the constitutions, but decided against the union of the two provinces. A plebiscite showed a majority in favour of separation. The French protested that Austrian and Turkish officials in the Principalities had 'managed' the voting. A second vote gave a majority for union. The Powers insisted upon separation, whereupon each Principality chose the same prince. The Powers then accepted the union, and the state of Roumania came into existence, under the nominal suzerainty of the sultan.

[2] The congress of Paris did not confine its business to the Eastern question. Cavour was allowed to make a statement upon the Italian question, and was supported, to the scandal of the Austrian representatives, by Clarendon. Clarendon, on behalf of Great Britain, suggested compulsory mediation before the outbreak of war. The conference passed a general resolution on the subject, but did not carry the matter farther. On the other hand, important decisions were reached on questions of international maritime law: (1) The abolition of privateering was reaffirmed. (2) Neutral flags were held to cover enemy goods other than contraband of war. (3) Neutral goods, except contraband of war, were declared exempt from capture even when carried under an enemy flag. (4) Blockades were declared illegal unless they were effective.

by the British army or by the military Powers of the Continent. The European Powers observed the inefficiency and mismanagement in the early stages of the campaign, and did not notice that, as in previous wars, Great Britain had shown a remarkable power of improvisation. If the war had lasted for another year, Bismark would not have assumed during the Schleswig-Holstein dispute that, from a military point of view, he could ignore British opinion because Great Britain had no *armée de descente*. On the other hand there was no outstanding soldier in England to enforce the reforms which the Crimean war had shown to be necessary. The transfer of the commissariat from the treasury to the war office had been made in December 1854, though the change was not carried out until after the war. In February 1855 the office of secretary at war was merged with the secretaryship of state for war.[1] An army clothing establishment was formed, and colonels no longer made a profit out of the contracts for the uniforms of their men. There were some improvements in the conditions of service during the next decade; the use of Aldershot as a permanent camp improved the health of the troops. Camps were also established at Colchester, Shorncliffe, and the Curragh. Parliament still disliked spending money on the army. The commons voted £7,000 in 1862 for reading-rooms and gymnasia, and £5,000 in 1864 for recreation-rooms, but barracks were still overcrowded, and canteen contractors were allowed to make undue profits. In 1864 it was decided to arm the infantry with a breech-loading rifle; some years earlier musketry schools were opened at Hythe and Fleetwood and a gunnery school was formed at Shoeburyness. A medical school began in 1859 the special study of gunshot wounds and the diseases of armies in the field, and model hospitals were built at Netley and Woolwich; in 1863 the Netley hospital became the army medical school. Miss Nightingale's experience in the Crimea, the reports of the war correspondents, and the institution of the Victoria Cross in 1856—a decoration open to all ranks—did much to raise the standing of the private soldier,[2] but for another generation the country underrated the

[1] The office of secretary at war was not abolished until 1863, but from 1855 the secretary of state for war was commissioned to act also as secretary at war. The change gave the secretary of state for war too many duties, and did not settle his relations with the commander-in-chief.

[2] Apart from the silver Waterloo medal, the first medal conferred upon all ranks was struck after the Afghan war of 1839–42. The issue of this medal caused some

steadiness and devotion of the common man who served in the armed forces on land. The reorganization of the infantry of the line was delayed until the Franco-Prussian war awakened public opinion, and the war office had come under the direction of a man of first-class ability. The system of purchase was modified, though not abolished until 1871. The price of commissions was reduced by a third; purchase was forbidden in regiments taken over by the Crown from the East India Company.[1]

Within three years of the peace of Paris the rapid construction of armoured ships by the French caused a panic in England.[2] The failure of wooden ships before stone fortresses, and the success of the experiments tried at Kinburn with 'floating batteries' of small ironclads, had no immediate result upon English ship-building plans; in 1858, however, the admiralty decided to build an armoured and iron-hulled capital ship. This ship (the *Warrior*) was launched in 1860. A year earlier the French admiralty had changed the design of four large wooden line-of-battle ships in order to give them armoured protection. *La Gloire*, the first of these ships, was launched in November 1859, thirteen months before the launch of the *Warrior*. It was said, with exaggeration, that the new French ships would be able to cover a French invasion. The panic did not last, but armoured ships had now proved their superiority. The naval engagements in the American civil war completed the education of the experts, and, incidentally, brought the term 'ironclad' into common use. There followed a period of some confusion in design. Between 1860 and 1866 the admiralty built large wooden ships protected by iron plates, as well as large ships with iron

discontent among Peninsular war veterans, and a medal for service in the French wars was distributed in 1847 to the navy and army. A copper medal had been issued after the battle of Dunbar.

[1] An incidental reason, or excuse, for the delay in the abolition of purchase was the small size of Sandhurst. Sandhurst was founded for the training of the sons of officers. The cadets were given commissions without purchase. An order that all officers should pass through this establishment was issued in 1861, and cancelled in 1862 because there was not sufficient room for them. The war office refused an offer made by the universities to give candidates a two-year course of training.

[2] At the outbreak of the Franco-Austrian war in 1859, rumours of war between France and Great Britain were so widespread that French shopkeepers at St. Malo sent in their bills to the large English colony in the belief that the English residents would soon be leaving the country. Sidney Herbert drew up a memorandum for the cabinet assuming that war would break out. See also above, pp. 178–9.

hulls.[1] After 1866 no large wooden hull was laid down, but there was considerable difference of opinion over the arrangement of the guns and the disposition of the protective armour. Owing to improvements in the forging of iron, ironclad ships were too heavy to take guns on several decks; consequently the guns were placed along one deck and ships were armed with fewer but larger guns. These changes came with a suddenness comparable with the introduction of the 'all-big-gun' ship about forty years later. The results were similar in one important respect. The *Warrior* could have fought and destroyed every line-of-battle ship built before the Crimean war. The *Bellerophon*, launched in 1865, carried rifled 9-inch guns which threw a shell some four times as heavy as those fired from naval guns five years earlier. The race between ordnance and armour plate had begun. Before the Crimean war, or at all events before 1845, ships laid up for years could be brought out and used in the line of battle. The British lead in capital ships was now much reduced, and greater expenditure was necessary to keep ahead of other Powers. As in the years following the building of the twentieth-century *Dreadnought*, naval estimates went up in an alarming way. The cost of the navy had fallen from £6,547,809 in 1818 to £4,434,783 in 1835. There was a sharp increase between 1835 and 1842, but for the next eleven years the figures were fairly constant. In 1858 they rose almost to £9,000,000, in spite of the heavy expenditure during the Crimean war. In 1861 the estimates were over £12,000,000, and between 1861 and 1869 they remained in the neighbourhood of £10,000,000 or more.[2] This increase resulted partly from the improvements in the conditions of service and the formation of a naval reserve; but the newer type of ship, and the newer type of gun, required more skilled service and a more expensive training. Fortunately for the British tax-payer, the increasing cost of land armaments and the rivalry of France and Germany after 1870 diverted the moneys of the continental Powers from navies to armies. None the less the transition from sail to steam, from wood to iron and shot to shell, from the chequered ships of Nelson's time to the turrets and protective armour of the navy of modern times,

---

[1] Even if the designers had made up their minds at once about the respective merits of wooden and iron hulls, there were not enough yards in the country to build simultaneously more than a few iron-hulled capital ships.

[2] These figures do not include the whole expenditure of the navy. For administrative reasons part of the cost of ordnance was borne on the army vote.

contrasted ominously with the hopes of philosophers and the popular idealism of the Great Exhibition.[1]

[1] Voluntary effort about this time met a long-standing need of the lower deck. In 1852 three officers founded a house at Portsmouth to provide lodging for sailors. Hitherto, men coming ashore with their wages after a ship was paid off (half-yearly payments were not established until 1855) were thrown on the streets and became the prey of thieves, low publicans, and prostitutes. The house at once became a success and was crowded out, although half the men had to sleep on the floors. Within a short time the house was transformed into a club to which the men themselves subscribed.

THE FOREIGN POLICY OF
PALMERSTON, 1856–65

THE years between the Crimean war and the formation of
Palmerston's government in July 1859 were an interlude
in foreign affairs. The main issue during this period was a
war with China. The two Chinese wars fought by Great Britain
in Palmerston's time were due to the irreconcilable differences
of outlook between the societies of East and West. The rulers of
China wished to keep strangers out of the empire and to maintain the classical, 'unprogressive' poise of their state; western
traders, following their acquisitive habits, wanted full admission
to an immensely lucrative trade. Until 1833 this trade was
limited, as far as Great Britain was concerned, to the East India
Company, which brought British goods to India, exchanged
them for silver, and, with the silver, obtained Chinese silks and
tea for the home market. With the abolition of the Company's
monopoly in 1833, friction was likely between the Chinese and
British authorities. The agents of the British Crown could not
be treated like shipping agents or merchant captains; the
emperor of China would not consider any other sovereign as his
equal. There was a further complication. Towards the end of
the eighteenth century the East India Company began to take
part in the opium trade. The Chinese authorities at Pekin had
forbidden this trade. The Company did not wish to disturb its
good relations with the authorities, and obeyed the prohibition.
On the other hand, European trade with China was centred
in Canton, far away from Pekin; the local officials connived at
smuggling, and a large business in smuggled opium was carried
on, mainly in fast-sailing ships called 'lorchas'. When the
representatives of the British Crown appeared in China, the
government was trying to suppress the smuggling of opium.
Thus the efforts of the three British representatives to secure
recognition of their status became confused with the question of
the illicit trade in opium. For some time the British officials

did their best in a tactful way to obtain recognition on terms which should not imply that Great Britain was a tributary power of the Chinese empire. In 1839 the Pekin government sent a high official to put down smuggling. This official asked for the surrender of all British-owned opium in Canton. The opium was given up, but a further quarrel took place over the jurisdiction of Chinese courts in cases involving British subjects. The Chinese attacked a British ship of war, and forbade trade with Great Britain. The British government asked for reparation, and guarantees for the future; they weakened their case by including a demand that compensation should be paid for the opium taken at Canton. The Chinese refused all concessions, and a war followed in which Canton was bombarded. In 1842 the Chinese agreed, in the treaty of Nanking, to open Shanghai, Canton, and three other places as 'treaty ports' for trade under reasonable tariffs, to cede the island of Hong Kong, and to pay outstanding claims of merchants, including the claims for the opium. In the following year the Chinese also allowed privileges of extraterritoriality to British subjects. The concessions made to Great Britain were also granted to other Powers.

This settlement was not likely to last long. Foreign merchants wanted more concessions; the Chinese government (though not the Chinese traders) wanted to cut down the privileges already given. After 1850 the Chinese authorities were in a weak position owing to the outbreak of the fearful civil war known as the Taiping rebellion. In 1856 a French missionary was put to death, after torture, at the order of a Chinese magistrate. The French and British governments agreed upon joint action, but before this action was taken a new and complicated problem arose. In October 1856 the Chinese authorities at Canton boarded the *Arrow*, a lorcha included in the British shipping register because the Chinese owner lived at Hong Kong. The registration of these lorchas was a mistake on the part of the British government; there was no way of controlling small ships in Chinese waters, and lorchas flying the British flag were used for smuggling, for the illicit and cruel trade of transporting coolies to Cuba and the West Indies, and, at times, for piracy. The Chinese boarded the *Arrow* because they claimed that the crew included a notorious pirate; they took twelve of the crew and imprisoned them. The British consul at Canton asked for the return of the men, and also required a written apology for the violation of privileges covered by the British flag. The Chinese authorities, after some delay, sent back the men, but refused to apologize. A British squadron then bombarded the Chinese forts in the Canton river, and the Chinese put a price on the head of every Englishman. Palmerston was accused at home of high-handed action and defeated on a motion in the commons. The attack was not very fair. The technical status of the *Arrow* was a difficult one; the dispute took place thousands of miles away from Palmerston's direct control, and the grievances on each side went far beyond the immediate *casus belli*. Palmerston met the attack in his familiar way. He put the case to the electorate in simple patriotic terms, and, on coming back into office with a majority, sent Lord Elgin to China with a list of demands, including the right to establish a British diplomatic mission in Pekin. France, the United States, and Russia supported these demands, but the French and English were left to use force, the only method of getting any concession from the Chinese. After the capture of the Taku forts at the mouth of the Peiho river (1858), the Chinese allowed everything asked of them. They refused to ratify the agreement. A second expedition reached Pekin, and the Chinese gave way (1860). They opened Tientsin and a number of other ports, accepted foreign diplomatic representatives at Pekin, and agreed to the regulation of the opium trade. As the Chinese authorities could not suppress this trade, the Powers, including the United States, believed, rightly or wrongly, that the best solution was to give it a legitimate status. As a punishment for the murder of about twenty foreigners taken treacherously under a flag of truce, the allies burned down the Summer Palace outside Pekin. Palmerston wrote to Russell his delight that the emperor's palaces had been burned to the ground.[1] A later age, while remembering that no western government could refuse to protect its nationals, may pass a less crude verdict.

Before the end of the Chinese war, serious problems in Europe had diverted public interest from the Far East. The European liberal and nationalist movements of 1848-9 had failed. The Italians did not expel the Austrians from Lombardy and Venetia; except in Piedmont they failed to secure constitutional government, yet the revolutions had not been alto-

[1] W. C. Costin, *Great Britain and China, 1833-60*, p. 337.

gether in vain. Piedmont was now the centre of Italian hopes; her king, Victor Emmanuel, was a man whose public conduct was much better than his private life, and Camillo, Count Cavour, the leading statesman of the country, knew that the Austrians would not be driven out of Italy unless the Italians could get foreign help. He had reason to hope that help might come, at a price, from Napoleon III.

Napoleon's view of the Italian question was a mixture of imaginative insight, calculation, and realism. He believed that the Italian cause was just and that, ultimately, it would succeed. He wanted prestige for himself and his dynasty; he also wanted to break through the treaty settlement of 1815 which had marked the defeat of Napoleon I and deprived France of the Rhine frontier. The rivalry of France and Austria in Italy was centuries older than the second French Empire, and to this rivalry Napoleon III gave a new interpretation. The 'principle of nationality'—a vague conception which had a more sinister meaning when applied to Germany—encouraged the Italian claim to get rid of the Austrians, and might give Napoleon a moral justification for helping in this work; but, on the same principle, Napoleon might claim that the French-speaking province of Savoy and the mixed area of Nice should belong to France. The surrender of Savoy and Nice would be a fair return for French assistance. Moreover, if Napoleon took part in 'freeing' Italy, he could ask for a deciding voice in the political settlement of the country. Thus he might satisfy the French catholics by protecting the Pope against anti-clerical revolutionaries, secure the kingdom of the two Sicilies for the family of Murat, and arrange a marriage between his cousin, Prince Jerome Napoleon, and a daughter of Victor Emmanuel. Napoleon came to an arrangement with Cavour on these terms at Plombières in July 1858. The terms were kept secret, but it was known at once that some agreement had been made. In January 1859 there was a belief in Europe that Napoleon intended to go to war with Austria.

English opinion on the Italian question had long been unfriendly to Austria. Austria was responsible for the harsh methods of repression after the Italian defeats of 1848–9, and, indirectly, for the misgovernment of the Italian states outside Piedmont. Gladstone visited the prisons of Naples in the winter of 1850–1; he agreed with the description of the rule of King

Ferdinand as 'the negation of God erected into a system of government'. Ten years later Palmerston wrote that the temporal power of the papacy seemed to rest on the assumption that 'the Pope would not open the gate of paradise if he had not the power to make some little hell on earth'. Palmerston never concealed his view that the Austrians must leave Italy, and that the Italians were entitled to good government from sovereigns of their own choice. The English middle class was liberal and anti-papal;[1] English commercial interests inclined to a more liberal régime in Italy, in the hope of lower tariffs and increased trade, while long-standing literary connexions gave the Italian movement a wide intellectual public. The Brownings were at the height of their fame; the queen had asked that Robert Browning should dine with the Prince of Wales during the latter's visit to Rome in 1858. The reactionary governments in Italy paid for their banishment of scholars and men of distinction. Mazzini was a friend of the Carlyles; Panizzi, an exile from Modena, became, through the friendship of Brougham, librarian of the British Museum, and was free to carry on a political agitation of a remarkable kind for a public servant. Lacaita, a refugee from Naples, went with Gladstone to the Ionian islands,[2] and was knighted for his services. The Italian nationalists also had friends in the British diplomatic service; Sir James Hudson, minister at Turin, was 'more Italian than the Italians',[3] and ready to disobey his official instructions in the interest of the Italian cause.

The conservatives and the court inclined towards Austria, though Malmesbury warned the Austrian government that public opinion in England would be on the Italian side. Malmesbury himself summed up the matter as one of deliberate aggression on the part of Piedmont; 'that Europe should be deluged with blood for the personal ambition of an Italian attorney and a tambour-major, like Cavour and his master, is intolerable'.[4] Yet the British government could not restrain Louis Napoleon or Austria. Earl Cowley went, in February 1859, on a special mission to Vienna with the suggestion that

[1] Victor Emmanuel, whose private sins made him nervous about his salvation, found to his surprise on a visit to England that he was regarded as a suitable recipient for the gift of a protestant Bible.

[2] See below, p. 304.

[3] Malmesbury, ii. 169.

[4] *The Paris Embassy during the Second Empire from the papers of Earl Cowley*, ed. F. A. Wellesley.

Piedmont should be disarmed under the protection of the great Powers. Austria might well have accepted this solution; it would have left Cavour without excuse that his country was threatened by Austria, and forced him to declare openly that he was fighting for a kingdom of Italy. Austria was indeed beyond help. Russia proposed, and France accepted, the plan of a congress to discuss the Italian question, but Austria made this solution impossible by refusing to allow the admission of Piedmont. Finally, the Austrians put themselves in the wrong by sending an ultimatum to Piedmont asking for disarmament within three days.

The Franco-Austrian war began on 26 April 1859. Napoleon III won victories at Magenta and Solferino, in each case at great cost. He found that Cavour was intriguing to bring about the annexation of the central duchies to Piedmont; that the Lombard peasantry showed little enthusiasm for their Piedmontese liberators. The war was unpopular in France; the Prussians were mobilizing on the Rhine. The French army was suffering from disease, and likely to suffer more heavily during the late summer and autumn in the Italian plains. The emperor was a brave man, but he was alarmed at his own ill health, since he knew the risk to his dynasty if he died while his son was an infant. On 11 July 1859, in spite of his promise to Cavour that he would fight until Italy were free from the Alps to the Adriatic, he met Francis Joseph at Villafranca, and agreed to terms which left Venetia in Austrian hands, gave Lombardy to Piedmont, restored the sovereigns of Modena and Tuscany, and proposed an Italian confederation with the pope as titular head.

In June 1859 Palmerston and Russell came back to office. Their views on the Italian question were close enough for them to work together without friction. They suspected Napoleon III and had no wish to see Austria lose her position as a great Power. They hoped to use English 'moral influence' to bring about a settlement in the Italian interest. Herein they differed from the queen and the prince, who took the side of legitimacy and upheld the rights of a Germanic Power. The disputes between Palmerston and the queen broke out again, and Russell was no longer a buffer between the two contending parties. The queen asked advice outside the cabinet, obtained secret information about cabinet discussions, and used her knowledge to persuade ministers to oppose Palmerston and Russell. The prime minister and the foreign secretary countered the queen's action by taking steps without cabinet sanction; they wrote to her in the grand manner of the whigs. Russell told her in January 1860 that 'according to the doctrines of the revolution of 1688 all power held by sovereigns may be forfeited by misconduct' etc. . . . The queen's answer was sensible. She could not 'make out what the doctrines of the Revolution of 1688 can have to do with this [i.e. a proposal to advise Piedmont as well as Austria and France not to interfere in the status of Central Italy] or how it would necessitate Lord John to abjure them'.[1]

The 'two old boys', in Granville's words, or, as the queen called them, 'those two dreadful old men', had no easy problem. The settlement of Villafranca took them by surprise, but they announced that they would not agree to the restoration of the sovereigns of Modena and Tuscany by foreign arms. Napoleon himself wrecked another attempt at a congress by giving his authority to a pamphlet against the temporal power. The attack had the support of British opinion, but it alienated the French catholics, while the Austrian government refused to come to the congress unless the pamphlet were disavowed. The question of the duchies was settled by plebiscite in favour of union with Piedmont. Up to this point events had favoured Palmerston and Russell. Napoleon was unpopular in Italy because he had not won Venetia for the Italians. If he were not to be equally unpopular in France, he was bound to insist upon the surrender of the territory promised at Plombières. On 1 March 1860 it was announced that the people of Nice and Savoy were to decide by plebiscite whether they would remain with the new kingdom of Italy. The French government made sure that the decision was in favour of joining France, though there is little doubt that, at all events in Savoy, the change was welcomed.

Napoleon had won the 'natural frontier of the Alps'; his next step might be towards the 'natural frontier of the Rhine'. A new phase in the Italian question occupied the attention of Europe. In May 1860 Garibaldi and his thousand volunteers

[1] Q.V.L. 1st ser. iii. 489-90. The constitutional lecture had some effect; the prince wrote, in March 1860, to the prince regent of Prussia: 'As the Italian States have de facto emancipated themselves from their rulers, and these have left the country, we acknowledge a right in the people to determine for themselves their own future destiny.' Martin, v. 49.

landed in Sicily, and overthrew the Bourbon government. Once again Palmerston and Russell were divided between sympathy with the Italians, distrust of Napoleon, and anxiety for the peace of Europe. Opinion in England for the most part supported Garibaldi. Garibaldi was a picturesque figure; every one knew the faults of the Neapolitan Bourbons. Public subscriptions were opened to assist the rebels, and Russell made short work of protests against helping a filibuster: 'We had once a great filibuster who landed in the month of November, 1688.'[1] Napoleon tried to get British co-operation in stopping Garibaldi from crossing to the mainland. It is doubtful whether the British government would have agreed to interfere; but Cavour was afraid of intervention, and, at Hudson's suggestion, asked Lacaita to make a personal appeal to Russell.

Garibaldi was left to cross the straits of Messina. The Neapolitan kingdom collapsed, and, in order to forestall any action against Rome, Cavour sent a Piedmontese force into the papal states. On 15 October 1860 Garibaldi presented the two Sicilies to Victor Emmanuel as constitutional king of Italy; six days later plebiscites in Sicily and Naples accepted the transfer of sovereignty. On 26 October the king and Garibaldi met; there was no longer danger of a republic in south Italy. Any doubts which Russell had felt about the expediency of letting Garibaldi loose on the mainland were now dispelled; the Italian revolution was as successful as the English revolution of 1688. The criterion of success rather than respect for treaty rights was a dangerous one, but for the time Russell made the most of it. He addressed (and published) a despatch to Hudson at Turin on 27 October 1860 in which he argued that a people must be judge in their own affairs; that the misgovernment of the Roman and Neapolitan states was well known; and that the Italians were justified in getting rid of their sovereigns, and in asking for national unity, as the only means of keeping out foreign interference. Then followed the usual reference to William of Orange. The argument, as the Austrian government pointed out, might have been applied to the relations between England and Ireland, but it was clear that England was against intervention, and that Sicily and the south of Italy were among the regions of Europe within the range of British sea-power. Russell wanted to suggest that Rome and Venetia might well

[1] Hansard, 3rd ser. clviii. 1406.

'share in the freedom and good government of the rest of Italy', but the queen wisely pointed out that language of this kind could hardly be used to Austria.[1]

Russell's political philosophy was taken to heart on the east as well as on the west coast of the Adriatic. Since 1815 the Ionian islands had been under British protection. The protectorate was of little value; Malta was of greater strategical importance, and the harbour of Corfu had not been developed. In 1849 the islanders asked for union with Greece. Palmerston refused their demand because he had a low opinion of the ruler of Greece, and of Greek methods of dealing with British grievances. In 1858 Gladstone went as high commissioner to investigate the grievances of the islanders; he did not recommend union with Greece, but the agitation continued, and was supported to some extent in England as a political move by those who disliked the Italian policy of the ministry. The islands were offered to Greece in 1862. A revolution in the kingdom of Greece delayed a settlement; Prince William of Denmark, who became King George I of Greece, accepted the gift.

In the autumn of 1860 English opinion realized that the long dispute between the southern and northern states of America over the question of slavery was reaching a crisis. The election of Lincoln as President in 1860 left no room for doubt; the southern state of South Carolina decided to leave the Union; other states followed the example, and Jefferson Davis was elected president of a new Confederacy. The northern states refused to recognize the right of secession; in April 1861 the war began.

At this time Anglo-American diplomatic relations were quiet. The long disputed question of maritime rights had not been settled; the United States refused to adhere to the declaration of the Congress of Paris in 1856.[2] Two important territorial disputes, however, had been decided between 1840 and 1850 by satisfactory agreements. The first of these disputes concerned the boundary between Canada and the state of Maine. The commissioners appointed under the treaty of Ghent had failed to agree, and the two governments had submitted the dispute to

---

[1] *Q.V.L.* 1st ser. iii. 523. Russell showed his statement to Palmerston; it was not seen by any other member of the cabinet.

[2] See above, p. 291, n. 2.

the arbitration of the king of the Netherlands. The king was invited to determine the true line of demarcation indicated in the treaty of 1783; he suggested a new line which was a compromise between the rival claims, and gave Canada one-third of the area. The American senate believed that the king had acted under British influence; they refused to accept the decision on the ground that an arbitrator asked to decide between two claims had no power to recommend a compromise.[1]

After this refusal Anglo-American relations were further strained by the unwillingness of the United States to recognize a mutual right of search for the detection of slave ships,[2] by local incidents compromising American neutrality in the Canadian rebellion of 1837,[3] and by the large-scale repudiation, on the part of American states as well as private debtors, of loans from Great Britain. Aberdeen, however, and, on the American side, Daniel Webster wanted a settlement of the frontier disputes. Aberdeen sent Alexander Baring, Lord Ashburton, on a special mission to Washington. Ashburton was a partner in the banking house founded by his family; his wife was American. Webster had met him in 1838 while negotiating in London on behalf of United States banking interests. The two men approached the Maine frontier question from a 'business' point of view. The boundary line upon which they agreed was criticized in the house of commons and the American senate, but accepted by both sides.[4] Ashburton and Webster did not go on to settle the Oregon boundary because they realized that a second compromise might have been too much for the public opinion of

[1] President Jackson might have accepted the compromise but the state of Maine objected to it.   [2] See above, p. 241.

[3] See below, p. 380. One troublesome affair arose out of the use of a steamship, the *Caroline*, by American sympathizers to supply a rebel strong point above Niagara Falls. Some Canadian volunteers cut the boat loose to drift over the Falls, and in a scuffle over the affair one American was killed. In 1840 a Canadian named Macleod boasted in New York state that he had killed the American. He was thereupon arrested for murder by the state authorities. The British government claimed that Macleod was acting under orders, and asked for his release. The state of New York, however, insisted on bringing him to trial; the state authorities told the Federal government privately that, notwithstanding his previous bragging, Macleod was known to have a good alibi. The jury accepted the alibi, and Macleod was acquitted.

[4] Each side possessed a map which supported the claim of the other party. In 1933 an eighteenth-century map, discovered in Madrid, with a tracing of the boundary justified the American claim. The treaty (1842) also covered minor rectifications of the boundary between the Lake Huron and the Lake of the Woods and the navigation of certain channels of the St. Lawrence.

their respective countries. The matter could not be postponed much longer; the Oregon territory had ceased to be merely a hunting ground. American immigration into it had increased, and opinion in the United States was hardening against any surrender south of the 49th parallel; the government was interested in possible naval ports on the Pacific coast and an agitation was being carried on especially by the Democrats in the western states in favour of pushing the American frontier up to the line 54·40 agreed earlier as the limit of Russian claims. The United States refused an offer of arbitration—they had more to gain by waiting—but in 1846 President Polk, who was inclined to be violent in public statements and conciliatory in private proposals, persuaded the senate to accept deviations from the 49th parallel which allowed Great Britain to keep Vancouver Island.[1]

Another step towards settling questions likely to cause serious dispute was made in the Clayton–Bulwer treaty (named, as usual, after the principal negotiators) of 1850 which defined the attitude of Great Britain and the United States towards Central America in regard to a possible interoceanic canal. The two Powers agreed to abstain from acquiring dominion or control over any part of Central America or exclusive influence or rights over any interoceanic canal. The interpretation of the treaty caused disputes; the British government maintained that it did not apply to existing British protectorates. One of these was a somewhat loose protectorate exercised over the ominously named Mosquito coast: the British claims to which the Americans objected were abandoned in 1859 under British treaties with Nicaragua and Honduras.

There had been a sharp outburst of feeling in the United States after parliament in December 1854 authorized the formation of a foreign legion in the British army, and agents, with the support of the British minister in Washington and

[1] Even here the lack of accurate maps and descriptions caused trouble. The agreement of 1846 defined the boundary as running midway along the channel separating the mainland from Vancouver Island and thence through the Strait of Juan de Fuca out to sea. There were in fact three channels. In the treaty of Washington (see below, p. 327) the two governments agreed to submit to arbitration the question which channel was meant, but the senate insisted that there should be no 'compromise'; the arbitrator had to choose between the most easterly or the most westerly of the three. The German emperor was asked to arbitrate; he decided in 1872 in favour of the westerly channel which is, in fact, the channel commonly used by shipping from Vancouver to the Strait at the present day.

British consuls, began to enlist American citizens. The British government gave way to American protests, and recruiting was stopped.[1]

Englishmen in 1860 had no two views about slavery; *Uncle Tom's Cabin* had sold more widely in Great Britain than in the United States, though English dislike of American arrogance partly accounted for its popularity. *The Times* had welcomed Lincoln's election, and, if the issue had been merely one of slavery, the sympathies of the English people would have been with the north. Lincoln, however, stated in his inaugural address (4 March 1861) that he would not interfere with the institution of slavery in the southern states. Englishmen began to consider whether, in a war in which both sides had accepted slavery, justice did not lie with those who claimed the right to secede. The news of the northern proclamation of a blockade reached Russell on 2 May; on 13 May a proclamation announced British neutrality, described the confederacy in correct terms[2] as the 'states styling themselves the Confederate States of America', and forbade British subjects to enlist on either side or to equip or deliver commissions to ships of war. The proclamation recognized the southern right of belligerency, without touching upon the right to independence. Russell used firm language in the commons to emphasize British neutrality: 'We have not been involved in any way in that contest by any act or giving any advice in the matter, and, for God's sake, let us, if possible, keep out of it.'[3]

Seward, who was secretary of state in Lincoln's administration, thought that the proclamation was premature;[4] northern opinion in general regarded it as unfriendly to their cause. Meanwhile the southern states wanted to explain their case in

[1] A few years later large numbers of immigrants were enlisted in the United States during the Civil War; there was no actual recruiting in foreign countries, but advertisements in the press encouraged immigrants to go to America and obtain bounties on enlistment.

[2] S. E. Morison (*Oxford History of the United States* (1927), ii. 198 n. 4) considers these terms unusual; but precedents from South American revolutions did not apply, and the British government could not have used any other terms consistent with neutrality.

[3] Hansard, 3rd ser. clxii. 1378–9.

[4] Seward's manner of negotiation had been troublesome before the war. The British minister at Washington wrote privately to Russell about 'the difficulty of keeping Mr. Seward within the bounds of decency even in ordinary social intercourse'. E. D. Adams, *Great Britain and the American Civil War*, i. 129.

London. Russell saw their two representatives unofficially, but would give them no promise. Davis therefore sent to Europe men of greater importance. His choice of James M. Mason and John Slidell was odd; Slidell was a prominent filibuster, and both men were extreme supporters of slavery. The two envoys ran the blockade, and took passages from Havana in the *Trent* (a British ship). They did not conceal their names or their mission. An American warship stopped the *Trent* and took the envoys on board. The American captain had acted without orders; it is said that his own executive officer protested against his action. The news of the capture caused great excitement in America[1] and in England. The Americans felt that they had 'given to Great Britain a dose of her medicine in the previous era'. The governor of Massachusetts congratulated the captain in a public speech; the secretary of the navy spoke of his 'great public service', and congress thanked him for his conduct and asked the president to give him a gold medal.[2] Americans in London wrote home that English feeling was almost out of control. 'The people are frantic with rage, and were the country polled, I fear 999 men out of every thousand would declare for immediate war. Lord Palmerston cannot resist the impulse if he would.'[3] The cabinet decided not to argue the matter, but to ask for the restoration of the prisoners with an apology, and to insist upon an answer within seven days, though the British minister at Washington could lengthen this period by telling Seward of the contents of the dispatch before presenting it to him. The last official act of Prince Albert was a suggestion that the first draft of these instructions should be softened in tone by means of a clause recognizing that the United States had no wish to insult Great Britain. At the same time the government ordered the reinforcement of the garrison of Canada by 14,000–15,000 men. Before the time-limit had expired Seward announced the return of the prisoners. He made no apology, and included in his dispatch a great deal of irrelevant and

---

[1] Adams (i. 206 et seq.) thinks that one reason for the excitement was 'a quite childish fear of the acuteness and abilities of Mason and Slidell'.

[2] The *New York Times* (19 Nov. 1861) was even more enthusiastic about the captain. 'Let the handsome thing be done, consecrate another Fourth of July to him. Load him down with services of plate and swords of the cunningest and costliest art' (Adams, i. 220, n.1).

[3] Adams, i. 217. The British case was unanswerable. The two men were not members of the armed forces; they were civilians travelling on a neutral ship to a neutral port and engaged on a diplomatic mission to a neutral country.

inconsistent argumentation. American opinion had already begun to cool down and in England *The Times* made it plain that Mason and Slidell were 'about the most worthless booty it would be possible to extract from the jaws of the American lion'. These two 'more than any other men' had been responsible for the traditional 'insane prejudice [of Americans] against England'.[1] The envoys found their official reception extremely cold. Russell hoped that Mason 'would find his residence in London agreeable'; he refused to see his credentials.

The slow progress of the war in the summer of 1861 suggested a possibility of English mediation. The cabinet considered the plan, but thought that the time had not yet come for action. At the beginning of the war Palmerston believed that American opinion, jealous of European interference, might regard any offer from Great Britain as 'impertinent'; he thought that 'in the nature of things and in human nature . . . the wiry edge must be taken off this craving appetite for conflict in arms before any real and widespread desire for peace by mutual concession can be looked for'.[2] In October he still held that 'the only thing to do seems to be to lie on our oars and to give no pretext to the Washingtonians to quarrel with us'.[3] A year later Russell inclined to think that mediation was possible. He drew up a memorandum for the cabinet; few members of the government except Gladstone supported him.[4] Thus no official steps were taken, and in March 1863 congress declared that any attempt at mediation would be regarded as an unfriendly act.

A new factor had already been introduced. In September 1862 Lincoln proclaimed that the slaves in the rebellious states would be legally free at the beginning of the year 1863. Only a month before this proclamation Lincoln had declared that his 'paramount object' was 'to save the Union, and not either to save or destroy slavery'. British opinion at first suspected Lincoln of a last gamble,[5] or of using the terrible weapon of a

---

[1] *The Times*, 11 Jan. 1862.

[2] Palmerston to Ellice, 5 May 1861, Ashley, ii. 208–10.   [3] Ibid., pp. 218–19.

[4] Clarendon wrote to Lewis (secretary of state for war) about Russell's plan: 'He [Russell] had thought to make a great deal of his colt by Meddler out of Vanity, and you have shown his backers that the animal was not fit to start. . . . He is therefore taken back to the country, where he must have a deal more training before he can appear in public again.' Maxwell, ii. 266.

[5] *Punch* published a cartoon of Lincoln throwing his 'last card', a black ace, in a game of *rouge-et-noir*. On 21 Oct. 1862 *The Times* denounced the proclamation in strong terms.

slave insurrection. The slaves did not rise, and, on 1 January 1863, Lincoln confirmed his edict of emancipation. This act impressed the English people, though, with the revival of southern success, the break-up of the Union appeared certain, and there was another demand for the recognition of the independence of the south. The British government wisely kept to their neutrality. Henceforward the northern forces moved slowly to victory, and, in the last week of May 1865, the war ended with the surrender of the last Confederate army.

After the *Trent* affair the blockade of the confederate ports had been a source of trouble to the British government. They did not handle the question with much skill. Most of the blockade-runners were English. Russell pointed out that the government had no power to prevent British unarmed ships from trying to reach the southern ports; the owners and captains were acting at their own risk. The foreign enlistment act of 1819 also allowed evasion. The act prohibited the 'building and equipment' of armed ships in British ports for the support of belligerents in a war in which Great Britain was a neutral; there was no rule against the building of ships which might be sailed from British ports and equipped elsewhere unless there was clear evidence that such ships were intended for use as belligerents. English law presumed innocence until guilt had been proved, but in cases of this kind proof might not be available until an offence had been committed at sea.

In October 1861 a representative of the southern states placed contracts on the Mersey for two ships. C. F. Adams, the Northern minister in London, was unable to collect sufficient evidence when he protested to Russell that the ships were intended for the destruction of American commerce. One of the ships sailed from Liverpool as the *Oreto* in March 1862. She ran the blockade, took on arms at Mobile, changed her name to the *Florida*, and did great damage to northern commerce until she was destroyed in the autumn of 1864.[1]

The second vessel, known at first as *No. 290*, was launched in May 1862. The foreign office, on receiving information about the ship from Adams at the end of June, sent the papers to the customs commissioners at Liverpool. The commissioners kept the papers for a week, and then reported that there were no

[1] The *Florida* was arrested at Nassau in the Bahamas, but released by an admiralty court. Sir A. Cockburn afterwards condemned the decision of the court.

grounds for the detention of the ship. On 22 July Adams gave Russell further information. Two days later he followed up his letter with an English legal opinion that the collector of customs ought to detain the ship. The second letter reached the foreign office on 26 July. It was sent, according to custom, to the queen's advocate, who was at this time the senior law officer of the Crown. 26 July was a Saturday. The foreign office did not know that the queen's advocate had suddenly lost his reason. Hence the papers were not dealt with until they reached the attorney-general and solicitor-general (Sir Roundell Palmer and Sir William Atherton) on the evening of 28 July. On this day *No. 290*, afterwards the *Alabama*, left the dock and anchored in the Mersey. Next morning she put out for a trial trip, and did not return; in the afternoon the law officers decided that she ought to be detained. The ship might have been seized before reaching America. Russell wanted to give orders for her detention at any British port, but the cabinet would not agree. Russell afterwards admitted that he ought to have held the ship at Liverpool while he was waiting for the opinion of the law officers; yet when, in November, Adams recited the exploits of the *Alabama*, and announced that he was instructed 'to solicit redress for the national and private injuries already thus sustained, as well as a more effective protection of any repetition of such lawless and injurious proceedings in Her Majesty's ports hereafter', Russell answered that the British government could not accept responsibility. He argued that American precedent justified trafficking in contraband of war; that the government could act only upon evidence, and that they had done their best to detain the ship. In August 1865 Russell again refused to make reparation and compensation, or to refer the question to arbitration.[1]

On the other hand Russell took care to prevent any further offence. He was also afraid that northern privateers might interfere with British commerce, and the shipping interests were equally nervous. The precedent was a dangerous one; the United States might use it in a later war in which Great Britain was engaged, and might fit out privateers on behalf of a belligerent Power. In the spring of 1863 Russell heard that two ships of a peculiar type were under construction at the Laird

---

[1] The *Alabama* was taken in June 1864. For the settlement of the claims by arbitration, see below, p. 327.

yards on the Mersey. These ships, known as the 'Laird rams', were armed with 'piercers' which would be of great danger to wooden ships on blockade duty outside southern harbours. While they were still in course of construction Russell ordered the seizure of another commerce-destroyer, the *Alexandra*; the courts ordered her release, but the case was delayed long enough to prevent the ship from doing any harm. The law officers of the Crown held that the courts would not justify the detention of the rams. None the less the rams were put under supervision early in September, at the moment when the American minister, unknown to Russell, was preparing to announce a severance of diplomatic relations. The British government bought the rams and the crisis passed over.

The English people felt the economic effects of the American civil war more acutely than the conflict over the definition and obligations of neutrality. In 1860 some 530,000 of the working population depended directly, and many others indirectly, upon the cotton industry; about four-fifths of the supplies of raw cotton came from America. The southern states believed at first that their control of cotton would be the dominant factor in the war. Whatever the anti-slavery parties in North America or Great Britain might say, 'in the three million bags of cotton that slave-labour throws upon the world for the poor and naked, we [the south] are doing more to advance civilization . . . than all the canting philanthropists of New England and Old England will do in centuries'.[1] In January 1861 Greville had used much the same language. 'With all our virulent abuse of slavery and slave-owners, and our continual self-laudation on that subject, we are just as anxious for, and as much interested in, the prosperity of the slavery interest in the Southern States as the Carolinian and Georgian planters themselves, and all Lancashire would deplore a successful insurrection of the slaves, if such a thing were possible.'[2] The *Charleston Mercury* of 4 June 1861 announced that 'the cards are in our hands, and we intend to play them out to the bankruptcy of every cotton factory in Great Britain and France, or the acknowledgement of our independence'.[3]

The cards were not in the hands of the south. The cotton-

---

[1] Quoted from *De Bow's Review*, the leading financial journal of the South, in Adams, ii. 3.   [2] Maxwell, ii. 237.

[3] Adams, ii. 5.

factories were in distress; they were not forced into bankruptcy. The American crop of 1860 was the heaviest on record. It was hurried to Europe; most of it arrived before the end of April 1861. Hence there was no shortage of raw cotton at the outbreak of the war. On the other hand in the first quarter of 1861 there was a falling off in demand, and a few mills had already begun to work short-time. No one expected a long war, or a serious shortage of cotton.[1] The price of raw cotton began to rise, and merchants with a large stock in hand made unexpected profits. There was, however, no corresponding increase in the price of the factory products. Foreign purchasers held back in the uncertainty of the market. From the end of 1861 American supplies almost ceased. Whatever the issue of the war the position would not improve quickly. The slave-owners were removing their slaves from the rich lands near the coast; inland fields were being put down to corn, and the cotton in store was deteriorating. There was a boom in shipping, and some industries in the United Kingdom—the mills of Yorkshire and Belfast, and the munition-making firms of the Midlands—sold supplies to blockade-runners, but the cotton industry of Lancashire came nearly to a standstill in 1862. The cotton famine had little effect upon the policy of the government in the question of mediation. The manufacturers at first were anxious to get rid of the stocks on hand. A certain number of them advocated interference when they realized that there would be a shortage of raw material; the more intelligent mill-owners, with the support of other interests, realized that a naval war with the north would only make things worse.

During the winter of 1861–2 there was very great distress in Lancashire and the neighbouring counties. A quarter of a million people were being supported by the rates, and as many others were helped by private charity.[2] Before the end of 1861

---

[1] Palmerston wrote to the president of the board of trade on 7 June 1861 urging an investigation into other sources of supply. 'Has the Board of Trade, or has any other department of the Government any means of procuring or of helping to procure anywhere in the wide world a subsidiary supply of cotton? As to our manufacturers themselves, they will do nothing unless directed and pushed on. They are some of the most helpless and shortsighted of men. They are like the people who held out their dishes and prayed that it might rain plum-puddings.' Ashley, ii. 210–11. The letter shows the empirical attitude of English politicians, and especially of Palmerston, towards the principle of *laisser faire*. The government and the manufacturers did in fact make efforts to get other supplies.

[2] For the organization of relief, see Sir R. A. Arnold, *History of the Cotton Famine*

the boards of guardians in the areas affected received a circular explaining the machinery for the relief of distress. In the summer of 1862 a special commissioner went to Lancashire to inquire into the condition of the workers and the best means of remedy; a bill passed before the end of the session allowed a parish to spread the cost of relief over the other parishes of a union when the expenditure exceeded the amount produced by a 3s. rate. A union could borrow money if the expenditure of all its parishes was above this figure. If the charge reached the sum produced by a 5s. rate, the county could pay the excess. In 1863 these measures were not found sufficient. Public works were begun and a loan of £1,500,000 was promised for the purpose; private subscribers gave nearly £2,000,000. The position improved in the spring of 1863, when new supplies of cotton began to come from Egypt and the East.

At the end of the year 1862 Palmerston and Russell had reason to be satisfied with the results of their foreign policy. They had avoided war with the northern states of America. They had taken an important and satisfactory part in securing Italian independence. They had secured the co-operation of France and Spain (October 1861) in an expedition to Mexico, where the government had broken a promise to use part of the customs revenue for the payment of interest owed to foreign bond-holders, and had taken possession of money collected for those payments in a warehouse sealed by the British consul. Napoleon III had shown signs of ignoring his pledge not to interfere in the internal affairs of the country; but Palmerston did not object to any plans of the French for establishing their influence in Mexico. Napoleon was better occupied in Mexico than in Europe, and, if Mexico became a prosperous monarchy, English interests would not suffer. Palmerston withdrew the British expeditionary force in 1862, and made it clear that he would not prevent Napoleon from setting up the Archduke Maximilian of Austria as emperor of Mexico.

The death of the prince consort on 14 December 1861 affected the conduct of foreign affairs. The prince had never been a

(1864). When a proposal was made in North America to send help to Lancashire, Bright suggested that the North should give something which could be seen, e.g. 50,000 barrels of flour (*Diaries of John Bright*, p. 264, n. 2). Gladstone employed factory workers in making a path in Hawarden Park (Morley, ii. 77, n. 1), and Lord Derby organized relief in Lancashire.

friend of Palmerston, but the prime minister could deal with him more easily than with the queen. Palmerston foresaw one result of the prince's death. He wrote to Russell that the queen's 'determination to conform to what she from time to time may persuade herself would have been at the moment the opinion of the late Prince promises no end of difficulties for those who will have to advise her'.[1] The difficulties were greater because the prince's views on the future of Germany were those which he had learned in his youth from Stockmar. Palmerston himself did not understand the significance of the appointment of Bismarck as minister-president of Prussia in September 1862. Bismarck told Disraeli in 1862 that he wanted to drive Austria out of Germany; Disraeli thought that Bismarck was not talking wildly. Palmerston and Russell belonged to an older genera-tion. They did not know enough about Prussia or Germany to see that, after the disappointments of 1848, the Germans would give up liberalism if they could get unity at this price. Bismarck, in 1862, was forty-seven; his career had not been very remark-able, and his sphere of action as the Prussian representative at the diet of the Germanic confederation and Prussian ambas-sador at St. Petersburg and Paris had been outside the range of English interests. On the other hand Palmerston and Russell ought to have remembered that the effective influence of Great Britain in Europe was limited to regions within reach of British sea-power, and that, without allies, the British army could not fight a great military Power at least during the first stages of a war. From this point of view the affairs of Poland in 1863 should have been a warning.

The Polish rebellion of 1863 was due to Russian misgovern-ment, although its outbreak was largely the work of Poles living in exile. The immediate cause was a measure of conscription introduced into Poland. The British ambassador at St. Peters-burg described the conscription as 'a simple plan, by a clean sweep of the revolutionary youth of Poland, to kidnap the opposition and carry it off to Siberia or the Caucasus'.[2] The Poles began a guerrilla war against the Russians: a war which could only have one ending unless Europe intervened on the Polish side. Public opinion in England, and more strongly in France, supported the Poles. Bismarck, on the other hand,

---

[1] Bell, ii. 298–9.
[2] Ashley, ii. 230.

secured Russian friendship by allowing Russian troops to enter Prussian territory in pursuit of the rebels.

Palmerston had no sympathy with Russia. His letter 'condoling' with the Russian ambassador on the outbreak of the revolt pointed out that the insurrection was a 'just punishment of Heaven for the Russian attempts to stir up similar trouble against the Sultan in the Principalities, Servia, and Bosnia'.[1] On the other hand Palmerston and Russell wanted to avoid war with Russia. They suspected Napoleon's proposals for an Anglo-French protest to Berlin. 'If the Polish revolution goes on, and Prussia is led to take an active part . . . against the Poles, the Emperor of the French is sure, sooner or later . . . to enter the Rhenish provinces as a means of coercing Prussia to be neutral.'[2] For the moment nothing was done. Russell attacked Russian policy in the lords, and, on 2 March 1863, claimed that Great Britain had the right to express an opinion as one of the signatories of the Vienna treaty, which included the settlement of Poland. He suggested to Napoleon III that the chief signatories of the treaty should be invited 'to concur in advising Russia to adhere to its stipulations and to resort to its policy'.

Napoleon thought that Russia would take no notice of the appeal unless the signatories were prepared to support their note by force; he might therefore lose the friendship of Russia and yet do nothing for Poland. Moreover he was not interested in the maintenance of the Vienna settlement. He wrote a personal letter to the Russian emperor. The letter had no effect, and Napoleon then accepted Russell's idea of a joint protest. Austria also joined in the protest. The Russian answer did little more than invite the Powers to repress the international organizations which were responsible for the Polish outbreak. England, Austria, and France made another attempt in June. They suggested concessions and proposed a meeting of the Great Powers to discuss the Polish question. Russia answered by offering to bring the matter before Austria and Prussia; the three Powers which had destroyed Poland were to settle the fate of their victim. Russia knew that Great Britain would not go to war, and the Poles were left to their fate. Napoleon tried once again

---

[1] Ashley, ibid., Palmerston quoted the phrase:
Non lex est justior ulla
Quam necis artifices arte perire sua.

[2] Hansard, 3rd ser. clxix. 564-8.

to secure a congress,[1] but, even if the affairs of Poland could have been dealt with apart from the general situation, it is unlikely that words alone would have kept Russia from her cruel and unwise policy of repression. Russell himself pointed out, after the event, that 'the prospect of a war with Russia for the deliverance of Poland was a very cloudy one. The object to be aimed at must have been, not the fulfilment of the stipulations of the Treaty of Vienna but the establishment of Poland as an independent State.' The basis for the erection of such a state was almost entirely wanting. Neither the Polish aristocracy nor the Polish people were fitted for self-government. Austria would not support the plan. The war, with Prussia as the probable ally of Russia, would have been 'hazardous and expensive beyond calculation'.[2]

The Poles might have had less encouragement to continue a foredoomed revolution if Russell and Palmerston had been more careful to think out their policy, and to recognize at an earlier stage the limits of English power of interference. Unfortunately they made, in a much more complicated issue, the same mistake of using threats which they could not carry out. While the Polish revolution was dragging to its tragic end, the long dispute over the future of the duchies of Schleswig and Holstein revived in an aggravated form. The Schleswig-Holstein question[3] was one of the legacies of the medieval empire. As early as the fifteenth century the two duchies were joined in personal union with the Danish kingdom. The settlement of 1815 confirmed this attachment, and recognized the duchies as independent political bodies under their duke who was also king of Denmark. As duke of Holstein the king of Denmark became a member of the new Germanic Confederation. Holstein and south Schleswig were German-speaking; north Schleswig was mainly Danish. It was inevitable that the growth of nationalism in Europe would affect the attitude of Danes and Germans towards these

[1] See below, p. 321.
[2] Russell, *Speeches and Despatches*, ii. 236. In 1863 Russian naval squadrons (of somewhat antiquated ships) appeared in New York and San Francisco harbours. Their arrival was regarded by northern opinion as a friendly gesture, but was mainly a Russian naval preparation for commerce-raiding in the event of war with Great Britain and France. See T. A. Bailey, *America faces Russia* (1950).
[3] The affair, which included the small duchy of Lauenburg, is also described in contemporary documents as the Danish question, or the question of the Elbe duchies.

lands, and that neither side would be willing either to maintain the *status quo* or to accept any compromise which did not satisfy chauvinist feeling. A further difficulty arose in 1839, when Christian VIII became king of Denmark, and, therefore, duke of Schleswig-Holstein. Christian VIII had one son, who was childless. The rule of succession in the kingdom allowed the crown to pass to a female line. The rule of succession in the duchies recognized only male heirs. If the rule in the duchies were not altered, the personal union between kingdom and duchies would be broken on the death of a king without direct male heirs; the dukedom would revert to a younger branch of the Danish dynasty, the house of Augustenburg. The constitutional and dynastic questions were merged together, because the nationalist party in Denmark, realizing that they could not keep both duchies, decided to allow Holstein to become an independent member of the Germanic Confederation and to incorporate Schleswig in the kingdom of Denmark, while the German nationalists wanted to bring Schleswig into the Germanic Confederation, and Prussia was interested in the port of Kiel.

Christian VIII of Denmark died in January 1848. His son, Frederick VII, tried to satisfy Danes and Germans by dividing the duchies. He incorporated Schleswig with Denmark, and gave Holstein its own institutions, and allowed it to remain within the Germanic Confederation. The solution pleased neither party. Christian, duke of Augustenburg, now came forward as the legitimate heir to the duchies after Frederick VII. In the confused and intermittent war which followed Prussia at first supported and then deserted the German nationalists. Palmerston was asked by the Powers to act as mediator;[1] he and Russell secured an interim settlement between Danes and Germans in 1850, and in 1852 the Great Powers signed a treaty in London assigning (though not guaranteeing) the succession to Denmark and the duchies to Christian of Glücksburg, the nearest heir to Frederick VII in the female line. The king of Denmark agreed not to incorporate the duchies with the kingdom. Augustenburg received back his property, which had been confiscated by the Danes, in return for a promise that he would give up his claims.

---

[1] The position of Denmark at the entrance to the Baltic was a matter of special interest to Great Britain and Russia, though the former no longer depended on naval supplies from Baltic ports.

The agitation went on in spite of this compromise. On 30 March 1863 Frederick VII announced that he intended to separate the financial and military arrangements of Holstein from those of the Danish monarchy; in other words, he proposed to incorporate Schleswig into the kingdom. Austria and Prussia protested. The Diet of the Germanic Confederation asked that Denmark should withdraw this plan. The king refused, and the Confederation ordered military intervention in Holstein.

Russell tried to quiet the Danes and the Germans. He told the Germans that 'the constitution of the whole Danish monarchy could not be subject to the jurisdiction of the German Confederation'. He declared that Great Britain 'could not see with indifference a military occupation of Holstein, which is only to cease upon terms injuriously affecting the constitution of the whole Danish Monarchy'. At the same time he advised the Danes to withdraw from the step taken in March. In November 1863 Frederick VII died, and Christian of Glücksburg succeeded him as Christian IX. Danish opinion forced him to continue the policy of Frederick, and to assent to a new constitution providing for the separation of Holstein and the incorporation of Schleswig.

The affair now became even more confused. Frederick, son of Christian of Augustenburg, came forward, in spite of his father's renunciation, to claim the duchies;[1] liberal opinion throughout Germany supported him. Bismarck viewed this intervention of the German liberals with reserve. His aim was simple, though when he first mentioned it to the king of Prussia the king thought him a little drunk. Bismarck wanted the duchies to become part of the kingdom of Prussia, but the way to this end was not clear. At all events, Bismarck would not support Augustenburg. Austria did not wish to create an awkward precedent in Venetia by recognizing the claims of two provinces to secede from a sovereign whose rights were laid down by treaty. Austria therefore opposed Augustenburg and wanted to keep the question within the terms of the treaty of 1852, and out of the hands of the German liberals, who were ready to fight for Augustenburg.[2] Bismarck was thus able to

[1] Queen Victoria had suggested him as a possible king of Greece, partly on the ground that 'we had been instrumental in depriving him of his just rights to the duchy of Holstein'. Q.V.L. 2nd ser. i. 50. The prince had married a princess of Hohenlohe-Langenberg, the daughter of a half-sister of Queen Victoria.

[2] The Prussian assembly accepted a motion that all German states should

get Austrian support for joint action against the Danes, in opposition to the plans of the liberals.

Palmerston had shown how little he understood the change which was coming over Germany. He described the attempt of the minor German states to decide the sovereignty of the duchies as 'the Duke of Devonshire's servants' hall assuming to decide who shall be the owner of a Derbyshire country gentleman's estate'.[1] He thought Bismarck was 'crazy'[2] and that his policy might lead to French interference and another Jena. He believed that 'all military men who have seen the Prussian army at its annual reviews of late years have unequivocally declared their opinion that the French could walk over it, and get without difficulty to Berlin'.[3] Russell was equally deluded by the views of military men. He thought that the Germans might 'set aside all prudential motives, and give up German unity for ever'.[4] Palmerston had no excuse for his first false step. He was given notice, in July 1863, that the Danish question would be raised in parliament. In March 1863 the prince of Wales had married Princess Alexandra of Denmark, and the Danes hoped that this connexion between the two countries would bring Great Britain to their side. Palmerston therefore had every reason to be careful of his words. He said: 'We are convinced, I am convinced at least, that if any violent attempt were made to overthrow [the rights] and to interfere with [the] independence of Denmark, those who made the attempt would find in the result that it would not be Denmark alone with which they would have to contend.'[5] *The Times*, in September and October, was even more bellicose.[6]

recognize Augustenburg. The motion was proposed by Virchow and Sybel. Virchow was one of the greatest scientists, Sybel one of the greatest historians of the time. Sybel said that 'a victorious war would heal internal dissensions in Germany'. Bismarck was not the only advocate of a policy of blood and iron. The significance of Virchow's motion was noted by Lord Robert Cecil in an article in the *Quarterly Review* (Jan. 1864): 'The great mass of Prussian and Austrian Radicals, with that curious indifference to morality which is characteristic of sentimental politicians, are furiously calling upon their Sovereigns to enter upon the same dishonest course. They do not trouble themselves to argue.'

[1] Bell, ii. 367.
[2] L. D. Steefel, *The Schleswig-Holstein Question*, p. 61, n. 21.
[3] Walpole, ii. 388, n. 1.   [4] Ibid., p. 387.
[5] Hansard, 3rd ser. clxxii. 1252. In a memorandum of 1897 Gladstone wrote that he had not noticed Palmerston's declaration, and that, as far as he remembered, it had attracted little attention at the time, but in Scandinavia the speech was taken, not unreasonably, as a statement of British intentions. Morley, ii. 116.
[6] e.g., 7 and 24 Oct. 1863. *The Times* wrote that it was 'extremely doubtful

If British opinion had been willing to go to war, the co-operation of France was necessary. Palmerston and Russell now lost any chance of this co-operation. In November 1863 Napoleon III suggested a European congress to deal not merely with the Schleswig-Holstein and Polish questions but with the treaties of 1815, which were 'in decay' and yet formed the basis of 'the political edifice of Europe'. The British ministers might have left Russia to refuse Napoleon's plan, but they were afraid that Russia might take the chance of reopening the eastern question. Palmerston thought a French proposal for a general guarantee of the Pope's temporal power was 'probably only one of the traps laid by Napoleon for the silly birds he was trying to lure into his decoy'.[1] Russell hardly ever 'conducted a foreign controversy in which the extreme intelligibility of his words did not leave a sting behind them';[2] he now gave Napoleon a lecture in his most frigid manner. He declared that the main provisions of the Vienna settlement were still in force; he asked whether Napoleon's proposals were to be put into effect by war if there were no general agreement about them. He concluded by saying that 'Her Majesty's Government . . . would feel more apprehension than confidence from the meeting of a congress of sovereigns and ministers without fixed objects, ranging over the map of Europe, and exciting hopes and aspirations which they might find themselves unable either to gratify or to quiet'.

The queen of Holland told Clarendon that Russell's answer was 'deplorable. It is the death blow of an alliance which ought to have dominated the world, managed the affairs of the Continent, and secured us an era of peace.'[3] Even *The Times* thought the dispatch 'unnecessarily explicit'. Bismarck was now secure. Russia was friendly, and Austria on his side; France and England would not act together. In spite of Russell's attempt to gain time for the Danes, Prussia sent them an ultimatum demanding the withdrawal of the new Danish constitution within two days: Austria blindly followed Prussia, and a joint expedition of the two Powers crossed into Schleswig on 1 February

how far our people could be induced to be tranquil spectators of the dismemberment of Denmark', even if the government did not wish to interfere.

[1] Ashley, ii. 244. For once Palmerston and Russell agreed with the queen, who described the suggestion of a congress as 'an impertinence', and hoped that no sovereigns would 'lower themselves by going there'. *Q.V.L.* 2nd ser. i. 114.

[2] W. Bagehot, *Biographical Studies*, 348.   [3] Maxwell, ii. 286.

1864.[1] The Danes were driven back, and, in March, the invading troops had passed through Schleswig into Jutland.

The Danes appealed to Great Britain. Public opinion in England condemned, almost without exception,[2] the action of Prussia and Austria. Palmerston had done much to stir up this opinion, but his own common sense told him that Great Britain could not go to war without allies. Palmerston, and not the peace party in the cabinet, rejected a set of proposals drawn up by Russell for Anglo-French mediation, with a threat that, if Prussia and Austria were unreasonable, Great Britain would send a squadron to Copenhagen, and France 'a strong corps of troops to the frontiers of the Rhine Provinces of Prussia'. Palmerston answered that 'first . . . we could not for many weeks to come send a squadron to the Baltic, and . . . such a step would not have much effect upon the Germans unless it were understood to be a first step towards something more; and I doubt whether the Cabinet or the country are as yet prepared for active interference. The truth is, that to enter into a military conflict with all Germany on continental ground would be a serious undertaking.' Palmerston also thought that France would certainly take Rhenish Prussia, and that 'the conquest of that territory would be an evil for us, and would seriously affect the position of Holland and Belgium'.[3] On this latter point indeed Napoleon III cleverly stated his terms by an indirect method. He refused to join in strong language to the Germanic Powers, 'not being prepared to go to war with them'. French opinion wanted peace, and the emperor was 'determined not to go to war for another reason, viz., that France would look for some compensation on the Rhine, and that would set all Europe against him. The universal belief that he wanted to extend the French frontier in this direction made him doubly

[1] Moltke was second in command of the expedition, but he might have been on the other side. He was born in Mecklenburg, and educated in Holstein and Denmark. He began his career as a page at the Danish court, and then entered the Danish army. He joined the Prussian army in 1822.

[2] The most notable exception was the queen, who fulfilled Palmerston's forecast that her views would be determined by those of her late husband. The queen wrote to the king of the Belgians on 3 Dec. 1863: 'The protocol of 1850 (the basis of the treaty of London) was considered by my Angel as the most flagrant violation of law and justice possible, and I have found all his wise writings on the subject, and have had them recopied.' Q.V.L. 2nd ser. i. 130.

[3] Ashley, ii. 247-8. Palmerston, however, in defiance of the cabinet, warned Austria that Great Britain would sink the Austrian fleet, if it bombarded Copenhagen.

cautious.'[1] It is characteristic of the double dealing of Napoleon that he had already made tentative suggestions to Prussia that France might accept Landau as 'compensation' for allowing the annexation of the duchies by Prussia. A second attempt to sound Napoleon brought a direct answer. If France joined England in a war, 'it would not be the Danish cause which would occupy the attention of the Emperor. The liberation of Venetia would be his first object, something on the Rhine perhaps his second. . . . His Majesty's demands would be very moderate.'[2] Finally the Danes themselves, at a conference of the Powers in London, rejected a compromise put forward by Russell which would have united northern Schleswig with Denmark, and given southern Schleswig and Holstein self-government under the Danish crown. Bismarck's plans could therefore be carried out without risk of interference.

The Danes surrendered on 18 July 1864, and on 1 August the victors took the duchies; a war which began, nominally, to uphold the treaty of London ended with the increase of Prussian territory at the expense of Denmark. It was little consolation to British opinion that the Austrians had also been duped, and now found themselves in possession of Holstein, which they did not want and could not control. The Austrian foreign minister resigned; his place was taken by Mensdorff-Pouilly, an amiable cavalry general who was no match for Bismarck. In 1866 Bismarck was able to carry out the second part of his plan; he expelled Austria from the Germanic Confederation and established a powerful state under Prussian control in North Germany. The inclusion of south Germany, and the creation of a German Empire, could only be a question of time.

Palmerston and Russell were attacked in the press and in parliament. Derby, at the opening of the session of 1864, spoke of the foreign policy of the cabinet as 'a policy of meddle and muddle', and in July a vote of censure was moved in both houses. The government was defeated in the lords, and escaped defeat in the commons by eighteen votes.

The 'two old boys' had not dealt with the Schleswig-Holstein question with any perspicacity, but the temper of the country after the Crimean war was strongly against interference on the

---

[1] Walpole, ii. 390–1.
[2] Ibid. ii. 395.

European mainland. There may have been some truth in a savage criticism passed by Lord Robert Cecil:

Under a more heroic minister, and in a less self-seeking age, it is probable that England would have preferred the risk, whatever its extent, to the infamy of betraying an ally, whom she had enticed into peril. But our Ministry is not heroic; and our generation, though not indifferent to glory, prefers it when it is safe and cheap. A war waged at the other end of the world, which does not send the funds down and only stimulates the iron trade, is not an unacceptable excitement. . . . As long as the public fancied that we could obtain the aid of Russia or France in a Baltic war, the war feeling ran breast high for Denmark; but as soon as the fact dawned on them that some sacrifice might be necessary to save their friends, they contented themselves with what Lord Palmerston euphemistically calls 'honourable sympathies'.[1]

Nevertheless Salisbury and the conservatives were not able to foresee the significance of the policy of Bismarck and the rise of a Prussianized Germany. Palmerston, who fought his first parliamentary election in the year of the battle of Jena, may well be forgiven his blindness to the future when the younger generation understood so little of the change which was coming over Europe.

At the time of Palmerston's death events in Europe had passed beyond the range of interference by Great Britain. The decisions of the next five years belonged to Bismarck and the Prussian army commanders. Russell's cabinet resigned at the time of the outbreak of the Austro-Prussian war. Derby appointed his own son, Stanley, as foreign secretary. Since Clarendon refused to stay in office, Stanley was probably the best man available, but his view of non-intervention went far beyond that of Castlereagh and Canning, and foreign observers began to think that, from a policy of general interference, Great Britain had changed to one of complete indifference to what might happen in Europe. In any case British policy was still determined by fear of France. After the war of 1866 Napoleon's persistent demands for compensation confirmed these fears. In 1867 Napoleon raised the question of Luxemburg. The grand duchy of Luxemburg was of great strategic importance; its inhabitants did not wish to enter the North German Confederation which Bismarck had founded upon the ruins of

[1] *Quarterly Review*, July 1864.

the Confederation of 1815, and it was hard to pretend that the inclusion of the grand duchy in France would be an affront to German national feeling. At the Vienna settlement Prussia was allotted the duty of garrisoning the fortress, but the political sovereignty was never in Prussian hands. In 1839 a part of Luxemburg was given to Belgium; the rest of the country remained under the personal sovereignty of the king of the Netherlands.

If Napoleon III had been allowed to annex Luxemburg, the Franco-Prussian war might have been avoided; but the plan broke down, largely through the influence of Bismarck and the German nationalists. The question was settled at a conference of the Powers held in May 1867 under the presidency of Stanley. The king of the Netherlands kept his rights; the duchy was included in the German Zollverein, or customs union. The Prussian garrison was withdrawn, the fortress dismantled, and the duchy neutralized under the collective guarantee of the Powers. English dislike of interference in continental affairs, and the lessons learned over the Schleswig-Holstein question, may be seen in Stanley's insistence that this guarantee did not require separate action by any one of the guaranteeing Powers if the neutrality of the grand duchy were violated.

The return of the liberals in 1868, with Clarendon as foreign secretary, brought little change in British policy. Clarendon treated the smaller affair of the Belgian railways—a French attempt to obtain control of the lines from Luxemburg to the Dutch frontier—much as Stanley had dealt with the French demand for Luxemburg. He did nothing openly to oppose Napoleon until he was sure of Prussian support. Clarendon died a few weeks before the outbreak of the Franco-Prussian war; Granville took his place, and was completely surprised at the sudden turn of events which ended in war. The foreign office shared this surprise; two hours before hearing of the French protest against the candidature of a Hohenzollern prince for the throne of Spain, the permanent under-secretary told Granville that he had never known 'so great a lull in foreign affairs'.[1]

One positive reason for the reluctance of conservatives and liberals to commit themselves to intervention in European

[1] For the history of British policy during the Franco-Prussian war see vol. xiv of this *History*, pp. 3–8.

affairs at this time was their fear of an American attack on Canada if Great Britain were occupied in a European war. At the end of the Civil War Anglo-American relations were in a dangerous state. The Americans had a large veteran army. They were angered by Russell's refusal to submit the *Alabama* claims to arbitration. They took literally the expressions of view in Great Britain about the inevitability of the separation of Canada from Great Britain.[1] Neither the British nor the United States government indeed wanted war. The British and Canadian authorities had done what they could to put down raids in the confederate interest across the Canadian border into the United States. The American authorities had given no support to Fenian raids into Canada organized on United States territory.

Nevertheless, leading American statesmen were in an annexationist mood. Seward, the secretary of state, in 1867 purchased from Russia the latter's rights over Alaska at a price of 7,200,000 dollars;[2] he annexed the Midway Islands, and would have added the Hawaiian group if Congress had agreed. He aimed at the annexation of Canada, and had the support of a considerable section of American opinion which held the extreme view that the depredations of the commerce-raiders had prolonged the war by two years; that Great Britain could therefore be held liable for the whole cost of the war during those years, and that the account might be liquidated by the cession of Canada and other British possessions in the western hemisphere.

Russell's successors understood more fully the danger to Great Britain if in time of war other countries followed the precedent of the *Alabama*, especially after the house of representatives in 1866 removed from their neutrality law the prohibition against the sale of ships of war to governments at peace with the United States. Stanley was willing to submit to arbitration the question of the damage done by the commerce-

---

[1] See below, p. 384.

[2] In the light of future developments this figure was as derisory as the price paid for the Louisiana purchase. It is of interest that many Russians at this time also took the view that overseas colonial possessions were not worth their cost. Stoeckl, Russian minister in Washington, wrote to Gortchakov in July 1867 (after the Alaska cession): 'L'Angleterre n'a aujourd'hui qu'un seul but, celui de se débarrasser du Canada pour le maintien duquel elle doit faire des sacrifices immenses et des dépenses peu proportionnées aux bénéfices qu'elle retire. . . Si l'Espagne, la France, le Portugal et même l'Angleterre ont dû perdre ou céder leurs colonies sans retirer aucun avantage, pouvions nous espérer d'être plus heureux?' See Hunter Miller, 'Russian Opinion on the Cession of Alaska', *American Historical Review*, xlviii (1943), pp. 521–31.

raiders; he would not accept the American view that the British government had been wrong in recognizing confederate belligerency. Early in 1869 the senate rejected another British proposal for arbitration, and the American demands were stated in their most extreme form. Even so, as in earlier controversies, there were more powerful influences in favour of a compromise. Parliament in August 1870 passed a new foreign enlistment act with more stringent regulations against the building of warships in Great Britain for a belligerent when Great Britain was not at war.[1] Early in 1871 the two governments agreed that a joint commission should meet in Washington to draw up in treaty form a settlement of all questions outstanding between them. The settlement would include the dispute over the channel to the Strait of Juan de Fuca[2] as well as the *Alabama* claims. The commissioners recorded their agreement in the treaty of Washington in May 1871. The treaty contained an expression of regret on the part of the British government for the escape of the *Alabama* and other vessels, and for the depredations which these ships had committed. The way was thus open for arbitration on the claims, but when the tribunal of five jurists began their work, there was another storm because the Americans brought forward the immense 'indirect' claims and the British government, with the support of public opinion, refused to recognize them. The matter was settled by a private agreement between the British and American members of the tribunal to set aside all the 'indirect claims'. This agreement was announced to the tribunal, and accepted by it. The final decision in 1872 awarded the United States fifteen and a half million dollars. British opinion considered this figure outrageously high.[3] The price was well worth while. The treaty of Washington of 1871 has not yet been given its due importance in English history, but Gladstone, if he could have foreseen the future at the beginning of an epoch of German continental hegemony, might well have used Canning's words about calling in a new world to redress the balance of the old.

[1] This act was passed after the outbreak of the Franco-Prussian war but the amendment of the act of 1819 had been under consideration for some time.

[2] See above, p. 306.

[3] It was, in fact, too high; a balance remained over after all the claims had been met. On the other hand the Americans later paid nearly 2,000,000 dollars in claims by British subjects for loss or damage through military operations or the blockade during the Civil War and another 5,500,000 dollars, which American opinion regarded as excessive, for certain fishing concessions.

BOOK III

IRELAND, THE COLONIES, AND INDIA

I

IRELAND

T HE Irish rebellion of 1798 was a sombre background to the act of union of 1800. To the English the outbreak of the rebellion, at a critical time in the war with France, was another of the many instances of Irish treachery; to the Irish, the suppression of the rebels was another example of English ruthlessness. The Irish rebellion was less dangerous to England than the rebellion of La Vendée to the French, and the suppression was less cruel, but the Irish have rarely compared their own treatment with that of other European minorities, and few Englishmen in 1800 asked themselves whether they had any right to expect the loyalty of catholic Ireland. Thus the act of union appeared to one side as a measure of political necessity against rebels, and to the other side a demonstration of force unsupported by right.

The terms of the union were never laid down before the Irish people, and the two houses of the Irish parliament voted their own abolition only after a shameful distribution and acceptance of money and titles. Catholics had some reason for believing that the union would not be altogether to their disadvantage. Although the worst of the penal laws had been repealed, and catholics had the right to vote, if otherwise qualified, they could not sit in parliament, or hold important civil, judicial, or administrative offices under the Crown. The Irish catholics thought that, if they accepted the act of union, the parliament of the United Kingdom would put them on terms of equality with protestants. Pitt wanted catholic emancipation, but the king would not consent to it, and, after Pitt's death, the regent was equally stubborn. There was some excuse, in the tangle of English politics, for the refusal of ministers to fight the Crown on an issue in which popular opinion might well take the protestant view, but the Irish catholics could not accept the subordination of their interests to English party ends. From their standpoint, they had been betrayed.

If the catholics had received emancipation as a gift immediately after the union, and not extorted it almost a generation later, it is doubtful whether Irish opinion would have been conciliated. Irish grievances were not merely religious and political; they were also the result of Irish economic conditions. The source of the trouble was deep-seated, and redress could be found, if at all, only in revolution, and in a revolution affecting property as well as politics and religion. England and Scotland were partly, though not wholly, responsible for the economic distress of Ireland. After the union successive British governments must bear an even greater responsibility for the continuance and aggravation of this distress. British ministers, with the support of parliament and public opinion, would not allow the Irish to carry out their own agrarian revolution, and for too long would not make it for them.

The Irish problem, in simple terms, was the problem of a standard of life. Most people in Ireland lived near the starvation level, and depended for their food upon one staple crop, the potato.[1] The potato crop was precarious; if it failed on a large scale, the greater part of the population would starve. The danger became greater owing to the increase of the population from about six million people in 1815 to eight and a half million thirty years later. There was not a corresponding increase in the amount of land under cultivation, or any improvement in the methods by which this land was cultivated. Owing to the exhaustion of the soil the potatoes became poorer in quality. A parliamentary commission in 1838 pointed out that 'it could scarcely be thought that the customary diet [of the labourers] would admit of any reduction, save in quantity alone, yet it has been reduced as to quality also'.[2]

---

[1] An Irish acre of land (7,840 sq. yards) produced, on an average, enough potatoes (320 bushels) to feed a family of eight for a year. Two acres of land would have been necessary to feed eight people on wheat. About a third of the population lived almost entirely on potatoes, and to an increasing extent on the 'lumper' potato which was first introduced as a cheap food for pigs; others had also a certain amount of milk.   [2] *Irish Railway Commission*, 2nd report, *P.P.* 1838, xxxv. 81.

For the increase of the population beyond the limits of economic safety neither the British government nor the Irish landlords can be held directly responsible. They bear an indirect responsibility, since the penal laws and the selfish attitude of Englishmen towards Irish manufactures caused the migration of a large number of the abler catholics into countries where careers were open to them. The peasants thus lost their natural leaders, and suffered from the degrading conditions in their own country. The mere fact that English and Scottish settlers had introduced a form of land tenure foreign to Irish custom set a barrier between landlord and tenant which was unknown in Great Britain. The priests of the catholic church had an influence which went beyond religion; the parish clergy, owing to the penal laws and the poverty of the church, were closely associated with the peasants, lived in their houses, and belonged to their class.[1] The priests gave to the poor the consolation of the sacraments, and, on the whole, taught them good lessons. On the other hand the particular emphasis of catholic moral teaching, together with the fact that the priests' dues came largely from christenings, marriages, and funerals, did not encourage prudential checks on population. Hence, when there was no check from famine, the population continued to increase. In 1845 there had been no severe famine affecting the whole country for more than three generations.

The Irish labourer lived more by land than by money wages; that is to say, he supplemented his money wage by cultivating a plot of land for which he paid rent in labour. If there had been a scarcity of labourers and an abundance of land, the labourer's position would have been enviable; but there were too many labourers and too little land. Hence the labourer was at a double disadvantage. The owner of land, paid in labour, was sure of his rent; the tenant took the risk of a bad harvest, and in the calculation of his rent his labour was reckoned at the lowest money equivalent. The poorest labourers had neither employment nor resources between June and September, when one year's potato crop was eaten and the next year's crop unharvested; if they could not afford the passage money to England for casual work, they sent their

[1] In 1825 O'Connell warned a parliamentary committee of the danger that the priests 'should be so much under the influence of low people as they necessarily are when all their relatives are in the very lowest stage of society'.

families to beg on the roads.[1] There was little demand for labour in Ireland because small farmers were not much better off than labourers; five-sixths of the population was housed in mud huts or cottages of one single room.

The subletting and subdivision of holdings resulted in a struggle for land 'like the struggle to buy bread in a besieged town, or to buy water in an African caravan'.[2] Until 1829 the landlords added to the confusion by creating small freeholds for political reasons, but this multiplication of inadequate and scattered holdings took place largely outside their control and often without their knowledge. The small tenants held short leases from middlemen, and, if the head rents paid to the landlord were low, the middlemen, who were generally of peasant stock, might be exploiting the rash and urgent demands of the poorer peasants. The high price of Irish corn in the English market during the war period had encouraged corn-growing and subletting at rents which could not be paid after a fall in prices. On the other hand so many intermediaries drew profit from the same piece of land that a reduction of rents was difficult. The position might have been less disastrous, at least for a time, if the land had been fairly treated. There were no proper arrangements for a rotation of crops, for manuring, drainage, or hedging. The soil was used fiercely, and then left to unprofitable fallow. There were few green crops; it was unsafe to grow them since they would be taken by half-starved labourers. Ignorant peasants knew nothing about agricultural improvements; they had no chance of learning habits of thrift since they had nothing to save. The priests were of little help in teaching good farming, and the encouragement given by the Irish agricultural societies had small results; it was useless to offer prizes to farmers who did not know how these prizes could be won.

In any case, the custom of the country worked against improvement and enterprise. Except in Ulster (and to a smaller extent in some of the neighbouring counties), where the tradition of 'tenant right' secured for lessees compensation for improvement or disturbance, the Irish tenant had neither

---

[1] The Devon Commissioners (see below, p. 350) remarked upon the 'patient endurance' with which the Irish poor met 'sufferings greater, we believe, than the people of any other country in Europe have to sustain'. *P.P.* 1845, xix. 12.

[2] Nassau Senior, *Journals, Conversations, and Essays relating to Ireland*, i. 28.

security of tenure nor a right to compensation. If a tenant left his holding at his own or his landlord's wish, the benefit of any improvement went to the landlord. The landlords had some reason on their side. Improving tenants were not common. Improving landlords were also uncommon owing to the habits of subdivision and subletting. If the landlord ignored these habits his tenants might resist him with violence. If he allowed sub-division of small holdings, and if at the same time he were com-pelled to give compensation for any so-called improvement by the tenants, he might find himself liable, at every change of tenant, for hovels and shacks put up against his wish, and against the interest of his property. On the other hand the denial of compensation was an injustice both to the better class of tenant and to the poorer men who had reclaimed pieces of bog or moorland by their own labour. The fact that tenants could be ejected without compensation made it easier for landlords to clear their estates. The improving landlord had every motive for clearances of this kind; there was no other way of consolidating holdings. After 1815 the fall in the price of corn led to the sub-stitution of pasture for tillage; with the use of steamboats the cattle trade with England became more profitable, and, again, favoured pasture. About this time also many thirty-year leases granted to catholics after the relaxation of the penal restrictions in 1778[1] began to expire.

From the tenant's point of view, the landlord's improvements meant ruin. An evicted tenant had neither capital nor alterna-tive employment. He was thrust into the road, and his house pulled down so that he could not come back to it. The Devon commission thought that the 'sweeping charges' of cruelty brought against Irish landlords were exaggerated; but they were stating facts of common knowledge in Ireland when they said that, if evictions were not carried out with care, 'a great extent of misery will often be produced'.[2] Public authority, which might have protected the poor tenant, had encouraged eviction. In 1816 the law allowed distraint of crops and cattle for arrears of rent; a smallholder was thus deprived of his capital, and his eviction was certain. In 1826 an act against unauthorized sub-letting, designed to get rid of the middleman, endangered the security of many poor tenants by annulling illegal arrangements already made. The Irish peasants had one remedy against a

---

[1] See vol. xii of this *History*, p. 389.   [2] *P.P.* 1845, xix. 18–21.

legal system which seemed to be weighted against their interests and to threaten thousands with starvation. They tried to enforce their own code by violence and intimidation. Herein lies the main reason for the lawlessness of a peasantry which, in other respects, was not criminal. The law upheld a land settlement which seemed, from the peasants' point of view, robbery. The law pursued them with ejectment orders; the magistrates were, for the most part, protestant landlords, and the police and military forces acted always on the landlord's side. The peasants reasoned in their own way that, by the combined strength of numbers and of secret organizations, they could enforce a certain wild justice; they answered threats of starvation by threats of murder. To a large extent the plan was effective. A competent observer wrote in 1834:

the peasantry of Ireland do more or less obtain from the Whitefoot associations that essential protection to their existence which the established law of the country refuses to afford. The Whitefoot system is the practical and efficient check upon the ejectment system. It cannot be denied that but for the salutary terror inspired by the Whitefoot the clearance of estates (which in the over-peopled districts of Ireland is considered, justly or not, to be the only mode of improving or even of saving them) would proceed with a rapidity and to an extent that must occasion the most horrible sufferings to hundreds and thousands of the ejected tenantry.[1]

The methods used by the poor in their defence were crude, savage, and horrible; the outrages against man and beast were especially revolting because they were directed more often against the instruments of offence than against the prime offenders. The landlord ultimately responsible for an ejection might be out of reach; his agent might have taken police protection, and the vengeance of the secret societies would fall merely on other peasants. No man's life was safe if he took a holding from which a tenant had been evicted; no witness dared give evidence in an agrarian crime unless he were prepared to leave the country. In any case, terrorism might protect this or that tenant; it was no remedy for the distress of Ireland. There was no attempt at discrimination; evictions of any kind were resisted, even though the landlord might have a good case. The peasants challenged government at its most sensitive point, and

[1] Poulett Scrope, *Letter to Lord Melbourne*, 1834; reprinted and addressed to Sir Robert Peel, 1844, p. 29.

at its first duty, the maintenance of order. They alienated
English opinion; they encouraged landlords to keep away from
their estates, and discouraged improvement. A landlord was
safe only if he allowed subdivision and subletting at will, until
his land was teeming with a population without defence against
the failure of their potato crop. Since improving landlords were
marked out for persecution, there was little incentive to invest
capital in Irish land, and the British public, which was ready
to take absurd risks in South America, left Ireland alone. The
position became worse as time went on. Insurrection acts,
enabling the authorities to proclaim martial law in disturbed
areas, were a regular feature of Irish administration. The
secret societies multiplied—Whitefeet, Blackfeet, Terryalts,
Lady Clares, Molly Maguires, Rockites—until Ribbonism
spread from the north to absorb the lesser organizations into
one body controlled from Liverpool, Manchester, Belfast, or
Glasgow.[1]

The British parliament was bound to pass coercion acts, if it
were not prepared to let Ireland drift into anarchy; but the
agrarian problem could not be solved by coercion. Parliament
took no practical steps to apply positive remedies to the evils
which were the cause of agrarian crime. The position in and
after 1815 was such that no remedy could have been found
except at a cost which British public opinion would have
thought fantastic; there were poor in England as well as in
Ireland, and expenditure which meant little in the later years
of the nineteenth century seemed wild in the generation following the French war. Moreover an attempt to deal with the
problem of the Irish peasantry would have required interference on a large scale with the rights of property. Public opinion
in England would not allow such interference, and enlightened
as well as unenlightened men doubted whether action by the
state, even with good intentions, would not make matters worse.
There was no administrative machinery capable of dealing with
the transfer of half the land of Ireland, and no guarantee that

---

[1] The Ribbon, or Riband, societies began in Ulster among the associations
founded to protect catholics against Orangemen. Ribbonism spread to Sligo about
1820, but still kept its 'religious' character. It became agrarian between 1835 and
1849. Drummond thought that the leaders of the Ribbon societies were 'almost all
publicans . . . of a very low class, and of a very bad character' who returned no
accounts of the moneys paid to them. J. F. M'Lennan, *Memoir of Thomas Drummond*,
pp. 258-64.

the peasantry would change their habits at the dictation of authority.

The immensity of the problem does not excuse the British parliament from failing to attempt any solution. The abolition of slavery was an interference with property, and the British public had been willing to pay £20,000,000 to the slave-owners, but the evils of negro slavery were more easily canvassed in England than the miseries of the Irish peasants. There is no excuse for the general English ignorance of Irish conditions. The legislative union had been forced upon Ireland, and Englishmen could not escape from the responsibility which they had undertaken. Nassau Senior noticed in 1843 that 'the great majority of the members of each House—that is to say, of the two Assemblies which govern Ireland—know less of that country than they know of Belgium or of Switzerland'.[1] Parliament indeed spent many hours each year in discussing Irish affairs, and, between 1810 and 1833, appointed 114 commissions and 60 select committees to investigate matters relating to Ireland.[2] The facts of unrest were known, but this knowledge was at second hand. Few people travelled in Ireland and saw Irish conditions for themselves. The report of the Devon commission in 1845 showed that secondary remedies which left untouched the system of land tenure would neither solve Irish distress nor put an end to agrarian crime. Even this report, and the famine itself, did not bring parliament much nearer to dealing with the prime questions of eviction and compensation.

The reclamation of waste would have lessened the immediate pressure upon land. This reclamation was not economically unsound; a million and a half acres might have been brought into cultivation at a cost of £1 to £10 an acre, and another million and a quarter acres of mountain bog reclaimed for pasture or plantations. Five different committees before the Devon commission suggested this policy. The report of one commission in 1838 stated that 'the policy of rendering such assistance is unquestionable. It is acknowledged to be necessary towards a colony, and must be considered more so in the case of part of the United Kingdom, where neither the land nor the population can continue to be useless without being hurtful at the same time.[3]

---

[1] Nassau Senior, i. 123.
[2] There is a complete list in Hansard, 3rd ser. xxii. 1204–6.
[3] *Railway Commission*, 2nd report, p. 85.

For a generation the government did little. In 1831 a board
of public works was set up, and provision was made for
advancing money to landlords who wished to reclaim land;
the terms were unfavourable, and only two advances were
given in fourteen years for the reclamation of waste. In 1842
an arterial drainage act authorized reclamation on a large
scale, but little work was carried out before the famine. After
the famine loans were offered on better terms, and by this means
some 74,000 acres were drained before 1851.

The attitude of Melbourne's government towards the extension of the English poor law to Ireland shows the refusal to face
the question of state interference. A commission under the
chairmanship of Whately[1] inquired into the condition of the
poorer classes in Ireland. Their reports (1836–7) gave a grim
picture of Irish misery. Outside Dublin there were no arrangements for public relief. The distress was so great and so continuous that, according to the commissioners, an extension of
the workhouse system to Ireland would absorb almost the whole
rental of the country. They limited their proposals for relief
to the sick, the aged, and young children. They looked to other
measures for curing the distress of the able-bodied; their suggestions included the reclamation of land by public authority,
the establishment of model agricultural schools, and the encouragement of emigration. To the British ministers these plans
seemed like asking the state to take over the management of
private property in Ireland. They sent a commissioner of their
own to Ireland, and, on his report, decided to apply the English
system of workhouses. They were right in thinking that there
was no hope of permanent improvement in Ireland unless the
Irish labourer could live by his wages; he could not live by
his wages unless the wasteful arrangement of small holdings
were given up, and the land consolidated, improved, and hus-
banded by substantial persons. The change would cause hardship, and some provision was necessary for those who would
suffer while it was taking place. The poor law was not without
some good effect; otherwise it would not have been a considerable charge upon the landlords who paid the poor rate. It
gave harsh landlords a new excuse for eviction on the ground
that evicted tenants could go to the workhouse, and it did not
succeed in raising the level of a half-starved population.

[1] See below, p. 507.

The failure of parliament to deal with the agrarian problem was more serious, because Ireland as a whole did not share in the immense development of British industry during the nineteenth century. The country had little good coal or other minerals, few skilled labourers, and no capital. The organized resistance to authority which arose out of agrarian conditions spread to the towns; the town labourer was as brutal as the country labourer in his methods, and no less ignorant of the indirect reaction of these methods upon himself. O'Connell told the house of commons in 1838 that during two or three years thirty-seven persons had been blinded with vitriol in the course of trade disputes in Cork, and that similar crimes were common in Dublin.[1] Most of these strikes were a vain effort to retain a standard of living in declining industries; they damaged Irish industries generally, and encouraged the view that Irish workmen, though quick and hardworking outside their own country, were not to be relied upon in Ireland. Irish labour was nominally cheap, but employers found it more expensive than labour in England or Scotland. The Irish poor had not much purchasing power, and Irish manufacturers could not compete even in Ireland with their better-equipped English rivals. There was no steam-engine in a Dublin factory until 1833, in Galway until 1835, twenty-nine years after steam-power had been introduced into Belfast. As late as 1850 there was only 2,646 horse-power of steam at work in Irish textile factories, and about six-sevenths of this power was in the linen factories of the north.

At the time of the union the protective duties of 10 per cent. on manufactured goods imported into Ireland were maintained for another twenty years. In 1820 these duties were renewed until 1825, and their extinction was postponed until 1840. They were withdrawn altogether in 1824; parliament could not resist the pressure of English manufacturers, or understand the difference between Irish and English conditions. In any case the free market for Irish corn in Great Britain weakened the Irish case. It is difficult to say whether this extension of free trade was, on balance, as damaging to Ireland as Irish manufacturers asserted. The decline of the Irish cotton industry did not take place until ten years after the removal of the duties, and was accompanied by an increase in the Ulster linen industry. At all events Irish opinion was justified in holding that after 1824

[1] Hansard, 3rd ser. xl. 1092.

Ireland gained little positive advantage of an economic kind from the union, and even the preference for Irish corn disappeared with the repeal of the corn laws.

The financial arrangements of the union provided that Ireland should pay two-seventeenths of the taxation of the United Kingdom. This figure was contested at the time; neither opponents nor supporters could foresee that the heavy war charges of the years following the union would raise the contribution of two-seventeenths beyond Irish taxable capacity. Ireland, like England, was forced to borrow; the Irish loans came to 51 per cent. of the total sum raised.[1] Between 1801 and 1817 the Irish debt rose from £28,000,000 to £112,000,000, while the British debt increased from £446,000,000 to £737,000,000.[2] The Irish loans were raised mainly in Great Britain; there were no direct taxes in Ireland, and the burden of high taxation fell heavily on the poor. A parliamentary committee in 1815 thought it fair to consolidate the debts and revenues of the two countries, and to equalize the rates of taxation, with exceptions in favour of Ireland. In this way the Irish contribution was halved; Ireland was saved from more loans to meet the annual deficits, but there was no diminution in the Irish taxes. Parliament treated Irish finance with greater consideration than any other Irish problem; little was done to impose increased taxation on the country between 1815 and 1853. On the other hand few of the taxes remitted in Great Britain after 1824 had been levied in Ireland; thus the British tax-payer had relatively greater relief than the Irish tax-payer. In 1820 the taxation of Great Britain was £3. 10s. 3d. per head; in 1850 £2. 7s. 8d. In Ireland the average fell from 14s. 5d. to 13s. 11d.

The peasants took no interest in fiscal questions, except to set up illicit stills while the spirit duty was high; their main grievance, apart from the conditions of land tenure, was the obligation of tithe. Until 1823 Irish tithe was not levied on pasture-land; hence the richer farmers were less affected than the smaller tenants. These sums payable by the humbler peasants were collected by tithe-proctors whose methods were as harsh as those of the middlemen. A better distribution of the burden, and better methods of collection, would not have remedied the main evil; the catholic peasantry, whose church

---

[1] In Great Britain the amount met by loan was 28·4 per cent.
[2] *P.P.* 1893–4, l. 531.

was unendowed, would still have contributed towards the up-keep of a religion known to them as the heresy of their oppres-sors. In any case the Anglican church was too heavily endowed for its needs. In the south and west of Ireland the catholics were in a very large majority, and the concentration of high ecclesiastical offices or rich livings in the hands of a small number of well-born clergymen was even more scandalous in Ireland than in England. The position was so absurd that it found few Irish defenders outside the number of those who lived by its anomalies. Yet it was allowed to remain a major cause of unrest, an insult and an injury to the catholic clergy whose in-fluence was all-powerful with the peasants. The settlement was delayed because English churchmen feared that an attack upon church property in Ireland might be followed by a similar attack in England.

Thus the vicious circle of agrarian unrest, outrage, and co-ercion remained unbroken in Ireland. The greater part of the Irish people were in a constant state of rebellion, open or suppressed, and the Irish administration depended upon the protestant minority. This support had been bought in order to pass the union; it had to be bought again and again in order to maintain an ascendancy without which landlords and pro-testant clergy would have been powerless. Jobbery of a gross kind had always been a feature of government in England, and indeed in every European country. It was being eliminated elsewhere by public opinion. It continued in Ireland because there was no effective public opinion to check it.

There appeared nothing for Irishmen except to wait in the hope that, ultimately, the English people, who were not un-generous and not wholly insensitive to wrong or careless of the freedom of others, should awaken to Irish grievances. As far as agrarian questions were concerned, this awakening was delayed for years; but the political disabilities of the catholic Irish were less difficult to understand, and easier to cure. They could be remedied without interference with private property, and a large and influential section of English opinion, including mem-bers of every administration since the union, wanted to put an end to political disqualifications based on religious intolerance, whether in England or in Ireland. These facts alone might not have been decisive, if there had not arisen in catholic Ireland

a leader[1] who knew how to use the force of numbers in such a
way that he could threaten rebellion without declaring open
war, and unite the majority of Irishmen while keeping their
action, technically at least, within legal bounds. It is one of
the many paradoxes of Daniel O'Connell's career that he was
never a revolutionary. As a schoolboy he had seen the attacks
upon the catholic church by revolutionaries in France. He disapproved of the Irish rebellion of 1798, and, to the last, resisted
the use of armed force against England. On the other hand he
was strongly opposed to the union, though he had no wish for
complete separation from Great Britain. He wanted an Irish
parliament, based upon an electorate in which catholics were
emancipated; he believed that this parliament, together with
the disendowment of the protestant church, would secure for
his country a fair and reasonable government, and break the
power and monopoly of the protestant minority. His interests
were political; he never made agrarian distress a prominent
feature of his agitation. He believed in fixity of tenure, compulsory leases, and a tax on absentee landlords. He was himself
an Irish landlord, kindly and careless, but not 'improving'. He
took Irish habits as he found them, and his own estate of Darrynane was 'a model of everything that ought not to be'.[2]

O'Connell's plan of campaign was simple. The first step
towards repeal must be catholic emancipation. The way to
emancipation, and later to repeal, lay through the pressure of
numbers peacefully organized. O'Connell could keep these
numbers only by means of constant agitation. He soon found
that he could not win the support of the Irish aristocracy,
though he was always ready to accept protestant help. Therefore he turned to the Irish people, and used his splendid powers
of oratory in persuading them that they were strong enough
to free themselves. As the higher legal posts were closed to
catholics, O'Connell earned his large income by pleading in
innumerable small cases which took him all over Ireland, and
gave him practical experience in dealing with the technicalities

[1] Daniel O'Connell (1775–1847), s. of Morgan O'Connell, Cahirciveen, co.
Kerry, and, through his great-grandmother, a descendant of an Elizabethan
settler in Ireland; educ. St. Omer and Douay, 1791–3; entered Lincoln's Inn, 1794;
called to the Irish bar, 1798; married his cousin Mary O'Connell of Tralee, 1802;
inherited the estate of Darrynane from his uncle Maurice O'Connell, 1825, and
the personal property of another uncle, Count Daniel O'Connell, 1833; died at
Genoa, on his way to Rome.

[2] *Sir William Gregory: an Autobiography*, ed. Lady Gregory, p. 73.

of the law. For this work, and still more for the work of agitation, O'Connell relied on his immense physical vigour and
power of concentration. He was a tall man, with fine, blue eyes,
delicate hands, and a strong, musical voice. His faults were
obvious; there was a coarseness as well as a nobility in his face,
in many of his acts, and, above all, in his speeches. He became
over-excited by his own voice and, though he was generally
prudent and ready for compromise, his language often went
beyond the bounds of decent attack. English newspapers and
English politicians attacked him in a similar strain, but his habit
of violent speech was formed before these replies began. On
the other hand he was neither vindictive nor—once away from
politics—intolerant. Furthermore he was not afraid to speak
his mind to his own people. He risked his popularity by attacking agrarian and urban crime, and finally lost it because he
would not allow rebellion. He enjoyed his extraordinary dominion over the Irish people, and it is perhaps his greatest failing
that he never faced the danger that the mass movement which
he had created might not always remain under his control. His
political enemies, in England and later in Ireland, accused him
of making money out of agitation. He was careless about
money, and close enough to his age and the circumstances of
his country to have an easy conscience about finding places for
his relations; but he would have died a much richer man if he
had never touched politics. Before his death a new generation
had grown up in Ireland, and O'Connell shared the fate of reformers who consider their cause more important than their
reputation. O'Connell's best work for Ireland was done before
1830; if his authority declined in his own country after the
failure of his agitation for repeal, and if he was treated with undeserved disdain by younger people who did not know the significance of his work, it is fair to remember that his career had
a European as well as an Irish significance. His methods were
copied by the anti-corn law league in England, and by liberals
in France, Belgium, Poland, and Italy. He represented one
phase, and not the least wise or the least noble phase, in the
nationalist movements of the nineteenth century.

When O'Connell took up the cause of catholic emancipation,
a measure of catholic relief had come near to success. The
chances of success had been destroyed, with O'Connell's approval, to no small extent by the catholics themselves. In 1812

resolutions in favour of considering the catholic claims had passed the commons by a fair majority, and were rejected in the lords by one vote. A new parliament met in 1813; Grattan brought forward a bill of relief. The Speaker proposed that the terms should not include admission to parliament. This limiting resolution was passed, but the majority was only four votes. The decision might have been reversed in another session if the Irish catholics had not refused to allow even an indirect control over the appointment of bishops and the publication of papal rescripts. The refusal was the more serious because the English catholics saw no reason against accepting the principle of 'guarantees', and, for a time, a considerable body of clerical and lay opinion in Ireland had taken the same view. During the absence of the pope at Fontainebleau Cardinal Quarantotti sanctioned acceptance, and the pope himself had been ready to allow the British government to ask for the removal of politically obnoxious candidates from lists submitted to Rome.

Owing to the stiffness of the Irish bishops it was difficult for the English supporters of catholic emancipation to renew their appeal to parliament, but in 1819 Grattan made his last attempt. Although Castlereagh and Canning supported him, he was defeated by two votes. After Grattan's death, William Plunket, member for Dublin University and the son of a Unitarian minister, took up the catholic cause. In 1821 he introduced two bills, including the right of veto in episcopal appointments. The bills passed the commons. The lords threw them out, and the duke of York led the opposition in a speech which, according to Eldon, 'did more to quiet the matter than everything else put together'. For the next three years the usual distress in Ireland was aggravated in many places by famine, and the outbreak of disturbances postponed any chance of getting catholic relief through parliament. O'Connell had already given up hope of carrying emancipation without greater pressure from Ireland. In 1823 he formed the Catholic Association; early in the next year he suggested that the association should appeal to the poorer catholics by asking from them a contribution of a penny a month to provide a fund for the general protection of their interests.[1] Before the end of 1825 the 'catholic

---

[1] The proposal was made at a meeting so small that O'Connell obtained a quorum by bringing in two priests from Maynooth whom he found in a bookshop below the rooms of the association.

rent' was bringing in £1,000 a week, and the association had invested £10,000 in the funds. Moreover, for the first time in Irish history the priests were taking part in politics against the government. The Irish authorities thought the 'catholic rent', and the excitement caused by O'Connell's speeches, a threat to public order; in 1825 they dissolved the Catholic Association, but O'Connell evaded the letter of the law, founded new associations as quickly as they were broken up, and still collected the rent. In the same year emancipation again came before parliament, together with proposals for endowing the catholic clergy and disfranchising the forty-shilling freeholders. The duke of York once more took part in the rejection of the bill, and the protestant party in England raised the 'no popery' cry which for years to come was still to excite the masses. O'Connell thereupon supported a plan which won him his cause within a few years. Hitherto forty-shilling freeholders, in Ireland as in England, had allowed the protestant landowners to control their votes. In the general election of 1826 the catholic party set out to break this custom. They contested the county of Waterford, where the Beresfords considered the seats to be their legal property. The Beresfords lost the election. The plan was tried in county Louth, with a similar result. For the first time in an Irish election intimidation was on the side of the catholics, and fears of hell, or fears of being murdered, were stronger than fears of the landlord.[1]

At a by-election in June 1828, O'Connell had a greater success. Vesey Fitzgerald, a member for Clare, accepted the presidency of the board of trade, and therefore stood for re-election; O'Connell, at first against his own judgement, was persuaded to contest the seat. Fitzgerald was a generous and popular landlord, but the freeholders voted for O'Connell, though, as a catholic, he could not sit in the house. This success put the English government in a difficult position. At the next general election O'Connell would try the same tactics in most Irish county constituencies. Wellington and Peel saw that further resistance would mean civil war in Ireland. Moreover in May 1828, the commons passed by a majority a motion in favour of

---

[1] After the election O'Connell founded the Order of Liberators, largely to protect the freeholders from vindictive action by landlords. The title of 'Liberator' by which O'Connell was generally known (though the peasantry spoke of him more often as 'The Counsellor') was taken from this order. Anyone who had done an act of service to Ireland was entitled to membership.

catholic relief. In view of his previous attitude Peel wanted to resign, but Wellington thought his co-operation essential in dealing with royal and parliamentary resistance. In April 1829 the catholic cause was won; all Irish offices of state, except those of viceroy and chancellor, were opened to catholics.[1] At the same time the forty-shilling freeholders were disfranchised and the qualification for the franchise was fixed at £10 a year. This measure was passed in order to prevent O'Connell from controlling the Irish vote. The Catholic Association was again dissolved, and, in case O'Connell should continue his practice of founding new associations, the lord-lieutenant was given powers to suppress any dangerous society.

O'Connell did not want his movement to end with the grant of civil equality to Irish catholics, but agitation for repeal was more dangerous than agitation for catholic relief. English opinion, divided upon emancipation, would unite in defence of the union. An Irish parliament won by O'Connell would be led by O'Connell, and there was no knowing what he would do with it. In Ireland the more prudent catholic bishops were afraid of supporting repeal. Thus, if O'Connell continued to use violent language, and to organize a mass movement, he might have to choose between a defeat which would be the end of his power and his popularity, or armed rebellion in which he knew that, ultimately, he must be beaten.

This critical decision did not come for fourteen years. It was postponed owing to O'Connell's tactical skill. Until the passing of the reform bill, he kept repeal in the background; after 1832 he was ready to work with the whigs if they would redress Irish grievances. He was bound to raise the tithe question. The priests whose support had been invaluable to him put this question in the foreground; the peasants had never forgotten it, and an act of 1823 which allowed voluntary composition did not remove the religious grievance. In 1832 a tithe act made composition permanent and compulsory, and transferred payment from the tenant to the landlord, or, where the land was sublet, to the last lessor. This measure relieved the poorest

---

[1] Parliament refused to allow O'Connell the benefit of the act of 1829, and thus forced him to stand again for election at Clare. He was re-elected, and this minor piece of spite, for which the extreme protestants in England were responsible, had no political result except to annoy the catholics.

and most numerous class of landholders, reduced the number of tithe-payers by a third or a half, and removed the tithe-proctors. It was opposed in England as an attack upon the church and an interference with property. In Ireland it brought little satisfaction. The Irish peasantry wanted the abolition of tithe, and not merely an improvement in methods of collection; they continued to withhold payment, and to fight the law by means of terrorist societies.

Thus the whigs, in the first reformed parliament, were faced with the old difficulty of maintaining order in Ireland. They tried to find some way of satisfying the Irish without losing their majority in England. Ministers were themselves divided on the two most urgent problems: Should concession follow or precede coercion? To what extent would English opinion allow interference with the property of the Irish church? They decided to introduce, at the same time, an Irish church bill and a coercion bill. They estimated the revenues of the 1,400 Irish benefices serving 850,000 protestants[1] at about £600,000 a year, those of the twenty-two bishoprics at £150,000, and those of the cathedral chapters at £25,000. They proposed to abolish ten sees, to lay a tax of £60,000 a year on bishoprics, chapters, and the richer benefices, and to set up a commission to manage episcopal estates. Any increase in revenues resulting from better administration would be applied to purposes chosen by parliament; the proceeds of the tax would go towards the repair of churches and other expenses hitherto met out of the unpopular church rates. The coercion bill was of the familiar type. It suspended the right of public meeting, partially suspended the habeas corpus act, and applied martial law and a 'curfew order' in disturbed districts.[2] The ministers announced that they would stand or fall by these two measures. The coercion bill satisfied the lords easily, but had a stormy time in the commons; the Irish church bill survived a difficult passage through the commons, and nearly foundered in the lords. The cabinet gave up the proposal to use the increased revenues for purposes not connected with the church, and O'Connell withdrew his approval from the bill.

---

[1] Or, rather, members of the anglican church. There were also 650,000 presbyterians in Ireland, mainly in the north.

[2] Bishop Doyle, one of the most fair-minded catholic prelates, thought that the coercion bill was the alternative to mob rule, and the less obnoxious despotism.

This 'alternation of kicks and kindness' had little effect in pacifying Ireland. In 1833 the arrears of tithe amounted to £1,200,000. Parliament granted an advance of £1,000,000 to the tithe-owners, and took steps to collect the arrears. The cabinet proposed to commute the tithe into a land tax payable to the state at a reduced sum; the plan, described by O'Connell as 'most excellent humbug', had an unexpected result. During the discussion in the commons Russell was afraid that his colleagues might pledge themselves to maintain the revenues of the Irish church. Therefore he stated his own view that parliament might well divert some of these revenues to other purposes.[1] A private member introduced a resolution to this effect. Thus the question at issue was enlarged from the payment of tithes to the partial disendowment of the church. Stanley, Graham, Richmond, and Ripon resigned, and the cabinet could do no more than appoint a commission of inquiry into the position of the Irish church (May 1834).

The troubles of the ministry did not end with these resignations. If the church party thought that Russell had opened the way to the confiscation of church property, O'Connell described the commission as a 'wet blanket'. The coercion act expired at the end of the session. Littleton, the Irish secretary, persuaded O'Connell not to oppose the whig candidate at a by-election at Wexford; he told O'Connell—on the strength of information given him by Althorp and Brougham—that the cabinet would give up the clause in the act allowing the prohibition of public meetings. The cabinet refused to make this concession; O'Connell then published Littleton's offer. Althorp disliked the terms of the coercion act, and resigned from the ministry. Grey refused to continue in office without him, and the whig government thus broke up over differences on the Irish question. Melbourne was in no better position. He introduced a new and milder coercion bill and tried to settle the tithe question, but the house of lords threw out his bill. Peel made another attempt during his short administration. He followed the lines of previous bills in transforming tithe into a rent charge. Once more Russell introduced the wider problem of the revenues of the Irish church, and in the course of the discussions Peel's administration was otherthrown.

O'Connell had taken part in the defeat of Peel; he had

[1] See above, pp. 100–1.

supported an alliance of the different branches of the opposition, known, from its place of arrangement, as the Lichfield House compact.[1] When the whigs came back into office, O'Connell had to settle his tactics. At the time of the coercion bill he had abused the whigs with his usual recklessness. They were 'base, bloody, and brutal'; they had 'brains of lead and hearts of stone and fangs of iron'. O'Connell's language was never a true indication of his policy. He decided to give the whigs a chance. They carried three important measures affecting Ireland, though the terms were not those which O'Connell would have chosen. They introduced the poor law into Ireland, reformed the corporations, and settled the tithe question. On the poor law O'Connell disagreed with the plans of the government and supported, after some hesitation, the views of the Irish poor law commission. The reform of the corporations took five years owing to the opposition of the house of lords. The first proposals, which would have given every existing municipality an elective council, were narrowed down to the more important towns, while the municipal franchise was restricted to householders rated at £10 a year and upwards. The settlement of the tithe question was held up by the refusal of the lords to pass any clause appropriating the revenues of the Irish church to secular purposes, and the refusal of the government to accept any measure which did not allow this appropriation. Finally, in 1838, the government agreed to drop the appropriation clauses. A rent charge, based upon 75 per cent. of the nominal value of the tithe, took the place of the tithe composition. The advances already made to the clergy were left to them as a free gift.

From the Irish point of view the results of co-operation with the whigs were meagre; the English parties spent months and even years in quarrelling over details while they left the most serious problems untouched. O'Connell's exasperation might have shown itself sooner if there had not been an improvement in the administration of Ireland. This improvement was due to the character and abilities of Thomas Drummond, under-secretary from 1835 to 1840. Drummond refused to govern Ireland by exceptional legislation; he repressed Orange as well as Ribbon societies and forbade the packing of juries in the

[1] Lord Lichfield lent his house to the whig leaders for these meetings in February and March 1835.

protestant interest. He reorganized the police, and recruited them freely from the catholic population. He gave catholics their fair share of appointments, and astonished the landlords by reminding them that if they had rights they also had duties.[1] Drummond was largely responsible for the report of the Irish railway commission suggesting state aid in the construction of trunk lines. The plan was not adopted. English opinion applied English conditions to Ireland, and assumed that, if private enterprise could supply capital for railway construction in England, there was no need for state interference in Ireland.[2]

Drummond died of overwork in 1840. At the time of his death it was clear that the Melbourne ministry would not last many months. O'Connell could expect little from Peel and the conservatives. He had never changed his view that repeal must be the aim of the Irish people; on the other hand the Irish themselves showed little enthusiasm for the cause. The number of repealers elected by Irish constituences fell from forty to twelve in the general election of 1841, and the 'tribute' upon which O'Connell depended for his heavy political expenses diminished when there was no longer any widespread agitation. O'Connell was now over sixty-five, and, if he were to succeed in carrying repeal, he could not wait for another whig government. Moreover he knew that the whigs would not support repeal, while he remembered that Wellington and Peel had given way in 1828–9 to the threat of civil war. O'Connell also hoped for presbyterian support, but his close relations with the catholic clergy made this support unlikely. Within two years O'Connell had created a serious problem for the conservative government. In spite of the caution of the moderate bishops, the catholic priests joined the repeal movement. The tribute again reached large figures. O'Connell held monster meetings, and once again excited a whole nation. He took care to avoid incitement to force. His meetings were orderly,[3] but his language was often equivocal, and he certainly intended to use intimidation. The authorities

[1] The earl of Donoughmore, deputy lieutenant of Tipperary, refused to publish the letter containing these words. In 1849 the words were taken as the motto of the first tenant protection society.

[2] The facts were too strong for the British government. Loans were made to the Dublin-Kingstown railway in 1836, and to the Dublin-Drogheda railway in 1842, but at the end of the year 1846 there were only 123 miles of lines open in Ireland.

[3] O'Connell was helped by the temperance movement which, under the leadership of a catholic priest, Father Mathew, swept the country, and, for a time, put an end to drunkenness.

could not ignore these large meetings of disciplined men; they might well ask whether O'Connell could always restrain his followers.

The younger men were affected by influences which never touched O'Connell. They had observed the nationalist movements of the Continent: many of them were excited in a curious way by Carlyle's philosophy of action. They lacked O'Connell's practical experience; they had not seen the terror and the aftermath of rebellion in Ireland. O'Connell thought in terms of Irishmen; the younger men thought in terms of an Irish nation. They borrowed from Mazzini's 'Young Italy' the designation of 'Young Ireland', and brought forward a wide programme of national regeneration, including the revival of the Irish language, for which O'Connell cared nothing. They were more hostile to England, and wanted to be 'free even from the gratitude of the past'. Their speeches were less exuberant, but their attacks had a more lasting effect. The leaders, Thomas Davis, Thomas Francis Meagher, John Martin, Charles Gavan Duffy, Smith O'Brien, John Dillon, Fintan Lalor, and John Mitchel, combined very different talents. Their first journal, the *Nation*, was one of the few Irish papers which printed good poetry.[1] They had few creative ideas of a general kind, and their political philosophy amounted to little more than hatred of England. They showed no power of organization, and within a short time they quarrelled among themselves. Yet, for good or evil, they made it almost impossible for any British government to cure Irish discontent by kindness. In the history of Europe their place is midway between the armed nationalism of the later part of the century and the tolerant liberalism which opposed the European reaction after 1815; in the history of Ireland they bridge the gulf between O'Connell and the Fenians.

The disputes between O'Connell and the 'Young Ireland' party began over the character of the repeal agitation. O'Connell believed that, without going as far as civil war, he could force Peel and his cabinet to give way. Peel took a different view. The majority in favour of maintaining the union was overwhelmingly large, and there was no reason for a strategic

---

[1] Before the appearance of the *Nation* in 1842, the *Dublin University Magazine*, a unionist journal, gave an opening to writers of the Irish literary revival. Moore's *Irish Melodies* had prepared the way for this revival. The *Nation* printed the lines ending 'To do at once what is to do, and trust ourselves alone', from which the Sinn Fein party of later days took its name.

retreat such as Wellington had advised in 1828–9. Peel was not likely to hesitate once his mind was made up. He passed an arms act, drafted troops to Ireland, and made a warning speech that he intended to put down rebellion and would never concede repeal. O'Connell had to choose between insurrection and surrender. In October 1843 he called a mass meeting at Clontarf. The meeting was forbidden, and O'Connell told his followers to obey orders. There was no rioting; but the government had won. O'Connell, in spite of his words, had surrendered. Peel took a second step. O'Connell was arrested and brought to trial on a long count. The jury was packed, and although there were technical faults in the indictment the verdict went in favour of the government. O'Connell's friends persuaded him to appeal against the judgement. His case came before the house of lords; the judges, whose opinion had been asked, upheld by a majority the decision of the Irish court, but the law lords, three of whom were whig and two conservative, voted by three to two in O'Connell's favour.

Although O'Connell came back in triumph to Dublin, his power had gone. He still had the mass of Irish opinion behind him, but he could not repeat his campaign for repeal. A sudden break with his ordinary life of political agitation affected his health, and the quarrels with the 'Young Ireland' party strained his nerves. These younger men disliked O'Connell's mob oratory, his assumption of complete authority, his careless attitude about money;[1] they detested O'Connell's son, who took over the control of the repeal movement while his father was in England. Davis, O'Brien, and Mitchel were protestants, and would not accept O'Connell's views on the ecclesiastical control of education. O'Connell seemed to them to be in danger of betraying the cause of Ireland when he suggested federalism as a possible compromise. Davis's death in 1845 widened the breach. Mitchel was far more violent, and less practical.

On the English side Peel wanted to make concessions. He appointed a strong commission in 1843 under the chairmanship of Lord Devon to study Irish agrarian questions. He told a new viceroy to give as much patronage as possible to catholics. He passed a Charitable Bequests Act to facilitate the endowment of the catholic church. He tried to conciliate the clergy by

[1] O'Connell made himself ridiculous at this time by falling in love with the young daughter of a protestant merchant of Belfast.

an increased grant to Maynooth, and to improve the general level of education by setting up colleges in the north, west, and south of Ireland. These measures raised a storm in England. The objections to the endowment of Maynooth were a little absurd.[1] Parliament had voted a subsidy of £9,000 every year since the union, and the difference between £9,000 and £26,000 could hardly be a matter of principle.[2] The opposition of the catholic bishops to the Irish colleges was scarcely more logical. In 1831 Stanley had set up a board of national education in Dublin for the administration of a grant hitherto given to the protestant Kildare Place Society. The board included catholics as well as protestants, and the schools were open to ministers of either church for religious instruction. The catholics disliked the plan, but it worked fairly well,[3] and gave some kind of primary instruction to one-fourth of the children of Ireland. Catholics could enter Trinity College, though they were in-eligible for scholarships or prizes. Peel hoped to attract the large class which was socially above the level of the primary schools and below the level of Trinity College. He invited catholics to take part in the management of his colleges, and encouraged the establishment of halls of residence and the en-dowment of chairs; but the bishops would not accept 'godless' education, and the language of the church party in England matched the papal rescript describing the colleges as 'dangerous to faith and morals'.

Peel summed his task up as 'the problem of peaceably govern-ing seven millions of people, and maintaining intact the Pro-testant Church Establishment for the religious instruction of and consolation of one million. Great and comprehensive interests, apart from those immediately connected with religion, are involved with the maintenance of that establishment.'[4] He disapproved of governing Ireland 'on the garrison prin-ciple'. It would be unfair to regard his plan of detaching the

[1] Gladstone resigned on the question of the Maynooth grant. He voted for the grant, but thought that the views which he had published in his book on church and state made it impossible for him to continue in office as a supporter of the measure. Gladstone wrote a long letter to Peel explaining his position. Peel sent the letter to Graham with the comment: 'I really have great difficulty sometimes in exactly comprehending what he means.' Parker, op. cit. iii. 164.

[2] A sum of £30,000 was also granted for buildings. It was expected that May-nooth would not be used exclusively for the training of priests.

[3] Irish history was one of the 'controversial' subjects excluded from the schools.

[4] Parker, iii. 114.

prosperous and educated catholics from repeal as an attempt
to isolate the poor. He realized that the peasantry supported
repeal because they hoped that it might bring about some
change in their condition. After the publication of the Devon
report Peel decided to give Irish tenants a legal right to compensation for improvements. His proposals were not very drastic.
They recognized three types of improvement: fencing,[1] draining, and building. They limited the amount of compensation to
£5 an acre. The opposition was so strong that the bill was withdrawn for alteration. Within a short time the Irish famine had
begun.

In the history of Ireland before the nineteenth century famine
had been the grim remedy of over-population. It was said that
300,000 people died during the famine of 1739–40; since that
year there had been no disaster of this magnitude, though
the potato crop had failed in different parts of the country.
The potato disease was known in North America and in Germany. It had broken out in England in 1835 on a scale large
enough to attract the attention of the British Association. It
reappeared in the south of England during the summer of
1845, and spread to Ireland in September. On a rough estimate
4,000,000 people in Ireland and 2,000,000 in Great Britain
lived almost wholly on potatoes. The corn harvest of 1845 was
poor in Great Britain and in neighbouring countries; the supply
from eastern Europe and the Levant could not be increased
sufficiently to meet a sudden demand. The potato crop of 1846
began well, but was blighted over the whole of Ireland at the
end of July.[2] The disease vanished as quickly as it had spread;
the crop of 1847 was good, but the people, weakened by hunger
and distress, could not resist fevers and other epidemics, and
the deaths from disease in the years after the famine outnumbered those of the famine years.

Russell described the disaster as 'a famine of the thirteenth
century acting upon a population of the nineteenth'. The

---

[1] Fencing meant, in Ireland, the removal of the large and wasteful dikes which
separated holdings.

[2] It was estimated that three out of every four acres of potatoes were ruined,
and that one-third of the oats crop was also lost. The value of these crops would
have been about £29,000,000, and the total loss, in terms of money alone, was
about £16,000,000. For the history of the famine see R. Dudley Edwards and T.
Desmond Williams, op. cit.

administrative machinery of the United Kingdom was unfitted
to cope with a catastrophe of this kind. There were British
officials in India who were familiar with famines, but India was
a long way off, and Ireland could not be handed over to a few
civil servants with almost unlimited powers.[1] The temper of the
time was a distrust of interference with the normal course of
trade, and every step taken to relieve Ireland had political or
economic consequences in England which raised serious controversy. The failure of a second year's crop was unexpected; a
new administration came into power during the crisis of the
famine, and the transition added to the difficulties of meeting
an emergency.

The first step taken by Peel lost him the support of the English
agricultural interest. Peel felt that nothing must be allowed to
hinder the import of corn and that the lowering of the corn
duties could not be delayed. He did not prohibit the export of
corn from Ireland. Thus the starving peasants watched the removal of corn to the ports, often under armed guard, for sale
overseas. Even if he had thought the prohibition of export a
wise step, Peel could not have carried it through parliament
owing to the shortage of corn in England. It was the misfortune
of Ireland that the fate of governments was decided at Westminster; with the English poor at their doors, no cabinet could
have survived the inconsistency of lowering the duties on
imported corn and at the same time cutting off one of the
normal sources of supply. Moreover the Irish corn-growers did
not want to lose the British market; Peel and Russell alike held
that the sale of corn would increase the purchasing power of
Ireland, while interference would have paralysed ordinary trading activities and made the situation worse in the long run. Peel's
solution was the import of American maize[2] into Ireland and
the provision of relief works. The maize was retailed at a penny
a pound, and the wages paid on the relief works were intended
to provide destitute labourers with money to buy food.

Peel's measures were successful at least in preventing starvation. Russell was faced almost at once with an even graver situation in which the plan of relief works, supplemented by private

---

[1] Some officials were recalled from the colonies in the latter part of 1846 to
manage the government food depots.

[2] The retailing of maize had some effect in discouraging private trade. The
corn was at first unpopular, and known as 'Peel's brimstone'.

charity on a large scale from England, inevitably broke down. The committees and officials appointed *ad hoc* for the most part did their best; they had to collect information, advance funds, organize work, distribute food, pay labourers, and enforce their plans of relief upon a population distrustful of the government, and unfamiliar with task-work; it is not remarkable that many appointments were unsatisfactory, and that supervision was inadequate, fraud undetected, and needs overlooked. The resident gentry and ratepayers had not the English experience and habits of local self-government; the poorer class had no respect for the law. In many places agrarian outrage continued, and the relieving officers were attacked by labourers who disliked task-work. In order to prevent jobbery, no works could be undertaken to benefit private landowners.[1] Thus a great deal of labour was thrown away on hastily devised schemes of no use to the localities in which they were carried out. Parliament refused to carry into effect a proposal to build railways. The plans could not have been put into operation at once; there was no time for delay, and in any case only one-quarter of the expenditure would have gone to the provision of work for unskilled labourers. The numbers employed on relief works rose from 114,000 in October 1846 to 570,000 in January 1847 and 734,000 in March; at this time, on a moderate estimate, three million persons were being supported from public funds. Abuse of the works was common; the seasonal migration of labourers to England fell to such an extent that there was a shortage of labour in English and Scottish districts where Irishmen normally came for harvesting. In Ireland agricultural work was being neglected. On the other hand road-making was unsuitable for a half-starved population; numbers of men died from exposure and disease, and many others died in remote places out of reach of any relief works.

Russell's government decided at the end of January 1847 to give up the works and to concentrate on providing outdoor relief. They imported large quantities of corn, biscuit, and salt meat for distribution. The new plan could not be put into effect at once, and meanwhile conditions were at their worst. Furthermore, a system of free rations was open to abuse and, if the

---

[1] This rule was relaxed in October 1846, but the terms under which landlords were offered loans for the improvement of their estates were so unsatisfactory that only £180,000 was spent on such work.

country were not to be reduced to pauperism, it was necessary
to prevent fraud. The sale of rations given in relief was checked
by the distribution of cooked food, and, in order to encourage
the resumption of ordinary agricultural work, no relief was
allowed to those who held more than a quarter of an acre.
This restriction was supported in the commons by Irish members, including O'Connell's son, who could not be charged
with lack of feeling towards the Irish poor; but, if it checked the
abuse of relief, it also left thousands of destitute families with a
choice between abandoning their holdings and starvation.[1]

The famine was a turning-point in Irish history. The Irish
now began to leave Ireland for North America in unprecedented
numbers. The emigration figures exceeded 100,000 in 1846, and
were nearly double those of 1844 and more than three times
those of any year before 1842. They rose above 200,000 in 1847,
fell a little in 1848, and remained above 200,000 between 1849
and 1852. At least another million emigrated between 1852 and
1861. Over two-thirds of the emigrants went to the United
States. Some moved westwards into the new lands or as far as
the gold mining areas of California, but most of them worked
as unskilled labourers in the east; they sent home nearly
£2,000,000 in 1850 and 1851 to assist their relations to join them.
At first, with the spread of infection among the passengers, the
conditions on the emigrant ships were scarcely less terrible than
those of the famine; in 1847 about one person in six died on
the voyage.[2] The time and the circumstances of this emigration remained as memories in the minds of those who left their
homes and 'the bones of all the old people' in Ireland; an anti-
English tradition among the Irish outside the United Kingdom
added yet another obstacle to the improvement of Anglo-Irish
relations.

These great evils had an indirect result which might have
turned to the good of Ireland. The question of tenant-right was
still the most serious problem of the country, but a decrease in
the population at least made its solution a little easier. Another

[1] The census commissioners of 1851 estimated the number of deaths in the five
years from 1846 as 'very nearly one million'. The cost of the relief measures, apart
from sums raised by private subscription, was £7,132,268. A little less than half
this sum was a free grant, and the remainder an advance to be repaid within ten
years. A large part of the loan was remitted between 1847 and 1852; in 1853 the
outstanding debt was cancelled in return for the extension of the income tax to
Ireland.   [2] See also below, p. 366, n. 2.

twenty years went by before any large-scale solution was
attempted; during these years the secret societies remained the
peasants' safeguard against eviction, and the savage code of
reprisals was carried out upon offenders against peasant custom.
The British government could not tolerate agrarian crime. The
immediate cause of Peel's fall was a coercion act. Peel asked
for exceptional powers, and Lord Lincoln, the Irish secretary,
also brought forward a bill giving compensation to tenants for
improvements. The fall of Peel's ministry put an end to the
chances of Lincoln's bill. Russell wanted to introduce a measure
on similar lines: he found that he could not avoid asking for
some kind of coercive power, though he was content with less
than Peel had thought necessary. Russell wrote to Lansdowne
in November 1847: 'The war between landlord and tenant has
been carried on for eighty years. It is evident that this relation,
which ought to be one of mutual confidence, is one of mutual
hostility; nor do I see that they can be left to fight out the battle
with any prospect of better result. Murder on one side: ejectment on the other—are as common as ever.'[1] A tenant-right
bill introduced in 1848 was read a second time, and referred to
a committee. That was the end of it. Unfortunately parliament
was more satisfied with another remedy. Before the famine
Irish landlords had mortgaged their property to the extent of
half its gross rental. High rates following the famine, and the
difficulty of getting rent from the tenants during the famine
years, added to their embarrassments. Bankrupt landlords could
neither meet their obligations under the poor law nor improve
their lands. The government decided to disregard vested rights
and to allow the sale of an encumbered estate on the petition of
a landlord or creditor, in the hope that a secure title would
attract English investors with capital for developing the land.
The encumbered estates act came into operation in 1849;
economists, radicals, and many of the best friends of the Irish
tenants welcomed it, but its effect upon the smaller tenants was
unhappy. The chance of buying land cheaply in an over-filled
market did not attract English investors to a country where an
improving landlord might be murdered by his tenants. Between 1849 and 1859 8,952 purchasers bought £23,161,000 of
land; 8,528 of these purchasers were Irish, and the remaining
424 buyers took only £3,000,000 of land. From the tenants'

[1] Walpole, *Life of Lord John Russell*, i. 466–7.

point of view the act brought only an exchange of masters, and the new masters were often harsher in evicting small-holders.

It was unlikely, therefore, that the whigs would be able to govern Ireland without coercion. For a time they had to deal with a threat of political rebellion. The European revolutions of 1848 excited Mitchel and his friends of the 'Young Ireland' party; they were joined by Smith O'Brien, a member of parliament who had given up hope of justice from England. They sent a deputation to ask for help from France; Lamartine, who had talked vaguely about the mission of France to oppressed nations, had no wish to fight England. The ministry thereupon prosecuted O'Brien and his friends. The jury failed to agree, but Mitchel was found guilty under another count, and sentenced to transportation for fourteen years.[1] O'Brien collected a small body of peasants in Tipperary, made a wild attack upon a police force, and was taken prisoner five days later. The other leaders were also captured, and transported with O'Brien to Australia.[2]

Although the Irish had not supported O'Brien's call to armed rebellion, the 'war between landlord and tenant' went on without respite. In the three years 1849–51 36,755 families were evicted.[3] Proposals for extending tenant right and securing compensation for improvement were brought forward again in 1850; the cabinet would not take them up. Russell's attempts to conciliate Irish opinion were genuine enough, but inadequate. Queen Victoria visited Ireland in 1849, and was received with enthusiasm. The visit was followed by a concession which did not touch agrarian grievances. The qualification for the franchise was lowered in the towns to include ratepayers on a £12 valuation, and in the counties to include £5 freeholders. A second measure was dropped owing to its unpopularity in Ireland and England. Russell thought that there was no longer any reason for maintaining an independent administrative government in Ireland. Ireland was, in 1850, about fifteen hours' journey from London; in 1800 this journey had taken sixty hours even with favourable winds. Moreover, the chief secretary had become a more important person in the

[1] Mitchel's *Jail Journal*, the most remarkable example of anti-English literature written by an Irishman in the nineteenth century, is an account of his imprisonment.

[2] Mitchel escaped to the United States in 1853; O'Brien was pardoned in 1854.

[3] The gross total was higher, but about one in every four evicted families was re-admitted. There are no records before 1849; in 1881 an official return (probably incomplete) gave 69,767 evictions (less re-admissions) for the years 1849–80.

administration of Ireland than the lord-lieutenant. Russell proposed to abolish the viceroyalty and to create a fourth secretary of state for Ireland. This plan 'to make Cork like York' was disliked by all parties, and abandoned after a second reading. Irish opinion regarded it as an attempt to destroy the last 'phantom of independence'.

The failure of Russell's cabinet to pass any measure of relief for Irish tenants produced a new agitation. A society, founded to protect the tenants on the estates of the earl of Desart (where protection was badly needed), spread during 1849 and 1850 over the south and west of Ireland and in Ulster, and held a conference in May 1850 to secure united action by north and south. The programme of the movement was the familiar demand for security of tenure and compensation for improvements, together with remission of arrears of rent from the famine period. The catholic priests took a leading part in the agitation, partly because there was at this time a new effort made by the protestant missions in Ireland.[1] Thus, twenty years after catholic emancipation, and twelve years after the settlement of the tithe question, religious and agrarian quarrels were as bitter as ever, and the result of Russell's attempts at conciliation may be seen in the comments of the *Nation* in February 1852, upon the fall of the liberal cabinet. 'The most villainous administration that ever marred Irish affairs is hopelessly foundered. We thank God very heartily for their downfall. Old and bitter enemies fill their places. But if it were Satan himself, instead of Scorpion Stanley, who became Premier of England, the change would be a welcome one to the Irish people.' About fifty members came to the house in 1852 pledged to oppose any government which would not grant tenant-right. The conservatives made some attempt to meet their wishes. Joseph Napier, the Irish attorney-general, introduced bills recognizing the principle of retrospective compensation, and offering loans for improvements. The tenant-right party brought forward a measure of their own which the government refused to accept. Thereupon the fifty Irish members voted

[1] The catholics called the converts 'soupers', on the ground that they were bribed into protestantism. The protestants denied this charge, and accused the catholics of terrorism against converts. The number of converts was greatly exaggerated on the protestant side until the census figures of 1861 showed the facts.

against the conservatives. Their action postponed a settlement for nearly twenty years, and broke up their own organization. The leaders quarrelled among themselves, and, although one catholic archbishop supported them, another archbishop, with the approval of Rome, tried to discountenance secret societies and to keep the priests away from political action.

Once again there was an interlude during which a settlement might have been reached; but the Crimean war and the Indian mutiny occupied English attention. The discussion of Napier's proposals dragged on for two years, and was dropped owing to the opposition of the lords. Year after year agrarian outrages continued; in 1860 Cardwell, as Irish secretary, introduced two bills. The first of them gave to tenants the right to compensation for improvements carried out with the landlord's consent; the second act defined the relation between landlord and tenant as founded upon contract and simplified the assignment of tenancies. The procedure under the first act was so very elaborate that few landlords or tenants made use of it. The second act assumed that landlord and tenant were on equal terms in bargaining about the rent of land, whereas, in fact, the landlord could find tenants far more easily than a dispossessed tenant could find land.

After the collapse of the tenant-right associations, the secret societies continued to stir up resistance. Stephens, the ablest of the younger leaders, had been wounded in the troubles of 1848; he took advantage of the unconditional pardon given by the British government in 1856, came back to Ireland, and began to organize rebellion. The enrolment and drilling of recruits could not be kept secret; the conspiracy was discovered and broken up, but an American society, known as the Fenian brotherhood,[1] was founded in 1858, and spread widely throughout the United States. The Fenians made little headway in Ireland until 1865. In this year the end of the American civil war released from the Federal army a large number of Irish Americans who had no wish to go back to the routine of earning a peaceful living. The success of the Italian nationalists, and the attempt of the Poles to free themselves from Russia, added to the excitement. The Fenians were well supplied with money from America, and Stephens did not conceal his general plan

---

[1] The name was taken from the Fianna, or armed force, which had defended Ireland in legendary times.

for an outbreak which would end in the establishment of an
Irish republic. In these circumstances the British government
could not avoid taking stern measures. The Fenian leaders
were arrested in September 1865. Stephens escaped from prison
with the connivance of a member of the prison staff, but the
other conspirators were sentenced to penal servitude. It was
known that Fenian agents were swearing in recruits, smuggling
arms into Ireland, and trying to win over Irishmen in the
British army. Hence the cabinet decided to suspend the habeas
corpus act in Ireland; the suspension was carried through the
two houses of parliament in a special session on 17 February
1866. Stephens made his way to America, and, from a distance,
announced a general rising before the end of 1866. In May a
band of Fenians attempted a raid across the Canadian border.
Within a few months Stephens had quarrelled with some of his
colleagues. He was deposed from the leadership, and even wilder
men took his place. They tried to raise trouble in England.
A body of men, 1,200 strong, and believed to be Fenians,
assembled at Chester in February 1867; the mayor telegraphed
for help, and a battalion of guards arrived from London during
the night to protect the city and the arms stored in the castle.
There were attacks upon police barracks in Ireland during the
early spring, but the lack of competent leadership, and unusually heavy snowstorms, prevented any concentration or
rising on a large scale. In September two Fenians who had
been arrested at Manchester were rescued from a prison van,
and, in the course of the struggle with the escort, a police officer
was killed.[1] On 13 December another attempt was made to
rescue two Fenian prisoners in Clerkenwell jail. A barrel of
gunpowder was blown up against the outer wall of the prison.
The explosion killed twelve people, and wounded about a
hundred and twenty others.

The Fenian movement ceased to be a danger at the end of
1867. It was clear that the Irish peasantry as a whole had no
wish for a rebellion. Few of the Fenians arrested in Ireland
were holders of land; the bishops had warned the catholic

[1] The rescuers were caught; five of them were condemned to death, in accordance with the legal rule that accomplices in an act resulting in death may be found
guilty of murder. Three of the five were hanged. The sentences caused indignation
in Ireland, and the condemned men were known as 'the Manchester martyrs'.
One of the prisoners, who was reprieved, ended his speech from the dock with
the words 'God save Ireland!' which became in later times a battle-cry of rebellion.

clergy to keep clear of the Brotherhood. Ireland was still un-reconciled to English rule, but the failure of the leaders to obtain anything like the support which O'Connell had secured a generation earlier showed that, perhaps, Ireland was not irre-concilable. The redress of agrarian grievances, and the aboli-tion of the privileges of the Anglican church, might even yet bring about this long-delayed reconciliation. Such was the reasoning which persuaded Gladstone to take up the questions of Irish land tenure and the Irish church.[1] The Fenian move-ment helped to convince him that delay was dangerous. In 1866 and 1867 parliament was occupied with electoral reform; in March 1868 Gladstone declared that the Irish church, as a state church, 'must cease to exist'. He carried a resolution to this effect at the end of April, and, within a week of his success, asked for a bill suspending appointments in the Irish church until parliament had settled the question of disendowment and disestablishment. The bill passed the commons, but was de-feated in the lords.

The new electors who were voting for the first time under the franchise act of 1867 wanted a number of practical reforms which had been delayed during the long old age of Palmerston; they voted on English rather than on Irish questions, but as a class they were not moved by appeals in favour of church estab-lishments or ecclesiastical property.[2] Many of them were non-conformists who supported a measure likely to weaken the anglican church. Disraeli had counted on a revival of anti-papal feeling, but he never understood English dissenters, and his own position was undermined by his failure to persuade his party to agree to concurrent endowment of protestant and catholic clergy in Ireland. Within two months of taking office Gladstone brought forward his bill. He carried it through the commons; the lords were sensible enough to concentrate on securing for the church the largest possible endowment. The moderation and good tactics of the church party had their effect, and the Irish clergy kept between £13,000,000 and £14,000,000 instead of £10,000,000 out of the property of their church. The surplus,

---

[1] For the evolution of Gladstone's views on Ireland see above, p. 189.

[2] A large meeting of protest against Irish disestablishment was held in St. James's Hall. The conservative organizer thought the meeting a success. Shaftes-bury wrote that 'it was one mass of clergy with a sprinkling of peers. . . . The time is gone by when the country could be be-bishoped and be-duked on public matters.' Buckle, v. 26.

after the failure of an attempt to obtain concurrent endowment, was divided between various public purposes.[1]

The settlement of the church question left Gladstone free to turn to Irish land-tenure. The two parties agreed that something must be done to improve the position of the tenants, but there were differences of opinion, cutting across party lines, about the remedy. There was also the long-standing ignorance of Irish conditions. Gladstone gave three months in 1869 to a study of the intricacies of land-tenure; Disraeli wrote in 1870 that he could get no help and no information from his party about the question.[2] The history of the land bill was remarkable; only eleven members, including several Irishmen who thought the bill did not go far enough in the tenants' interest, voted against the second reading, and the conservatives limited their criticism to points of detail. The house of lords did not divide upon the second reading, and the act passed with less opposition than any measure of its kind since the union.

This agreement was obtained because Gladstone did not wish to interfere with the rights of property, but merely to protect tenants from unfair treatment. He allowed loans of public money to tenants for the purchase of their holdings, although he did not expect much use to be made of this provision. The bill limited the landlord's powers of arbitrary eviction, and enforced compensation; it recognized the custom of tenant-right in Ulster, and similar usages which had been growing up elsewhere. Over the greater part of Ireland, where the tenant was unprotected, a 'scale of damages' was established for eviction. The scale varied according to the size of the holding; no payment for disturbance was made in cases of eviction due to a failure to pay rent, but all tenants, including those turned out for non-payment of rent, received compensation for improvements.[3]

The Irish land act of 1870 was not a success, though it did much to save tenants from the worst kind of eviction. It was not wholly fair in its working. Unscrupulous landlords could evade

[1] Between 1871 and 1882 £1,000,000 was given to Irish intermediate education, £1,300,000 to a pension fund for national school teachers, £1,271,500 to distress works, £950,000 to cover payments under the arrears of rent act (1882), £250,000 to sea-fisheries. The Maynooth grant and the *regium donum* paid to the presbyterian church were discontinued, in return for compensation.

[2] Buckle, v. 118. A series of articles in *The Times* during 1870 did much to instruct English opinion.

[3] The right to compensation was retrospective, in view of the fact that its recognition had been so long delayed.

its provisions by raising rents and thereby forcing their tenants into arrears which they could not pay. Good landlords found that if they improved land at their own expense, and let it at a higher rent, they might be charged compensation at an unfair rate.[1] Moreover, the smaller the holding the higher the rate of compensation; thus a measure intended to protect the small tenant gave the landlord a new interest in getting rid of him. The tenants themselves wanted fixity of tenure and fair rents; Gladstone's bill did not satisfy either of these demands. Once again an English parliament, with the best intentions, had refused to look at the holding of land from an Irish point of view, or to recognize that Irish tenants thought of themselves as part-owners of the land on which they worked. During the long agricultural depression after 1875 many Irish tenants were unable to pay rents which were not too high in 1870. The act provided no means of adjusting rents, and therefore did not touch the difficulty which came with a general fall in agricultural prices.

Thus in 1870, after the passing of two measures which Grattan, O'Connell, and many of the leaders of 'Young Ireland' would have thought an astonishing surrender by Great Britain, the problem of reconciling Ireland to the union was still unsolved. It is possible to think that, even if the land act had given the Irish peasant the security which he believed to be his right, agrarian reforms alone would not have reconciled Irish opinion to union with Great Britain. Ever since 1800 the leaders of Ireland had asked not merely for redress of grievances but for repeal of the union. If, at times, they had been willing to accept half-measures, these compromises were not lasting, and the younger generation always rejected them. The bitterness of the leaders of the Irish people had increased with the years. O'Connell was more violent than Grattan, 'Young Ireland' more violent than O'Connell. The Fenians introduced a new element into Irish agitation: the hatred of England felt by the emigrants from Ireland. Disraeli once said of the Irish that, 'if they led that kind of life which would invite the introduction of capital into the country, . . . instead of those feelings which they acquire

---

[1] i.e. if a landlord reclaimed 100 acres of bog land worth, before reclamation, 6d. an acre, he might charge a rent of £1 an acre. If he divided the land into 10 holdings, each of 10 acres, he would be liable to a charge of £700 for disturbing his ten tenants; but the compensation would be based upon a rent which included interest upon the capital expended in reclamation.

by brooding over the history of their country, a great part of which is merely traditionary, you would find men acquiring fortunes and arriving at conclusions . . . entirely different from those which they now offer'.[1] The Irish in the United States and in the British Dominions acquired fortunes; they still 'brooded over the history of their country'.

The years 1869 and 1870, when Gladstone was passing his Irish church and Irish land bills, brought an increase of agrarian crime, and the liberal government was compelled to introduce a peace preservation act. In the autumn of 1870 a body known as the 'Home Government Association of Ireland' was founded in Dublin. It included catholics and protestants, liberals and conservatives. The aim of the association was the establishment of an Irish parliament. Four years later, nearly sixty home rulers were returned to the house of commons. A new phase in Anglo-Irish history had begun.

[1] Buckle, v. 91–92.

II

THE COLONIES

THE hundred years which began with the treaty of Utrecht and ended with the settlement at Vienna decided the political sovereignty of a large part of the temperate zones of the world. The significance of these decisions was not understood in 1815. After the Napoleonic war Great Britain did not give back the Cape of Good Hope, Mauritius, Demerara and Essequibo (in Guiana), Trinidad, St. Lucia, or Tobago. She kept these places, as she kept Heligoland, Malta, and the Ionian islands, mainly for strategic reasons, but British opinion was less concerned with the future of the British Empire than with the future of the American colonies of Spain. The revolt of these colonies, following the successful revolt of the British colonies in North America, confirmed the view that colonies ripened to independence as soon as they grew wealthy and developed interests of their own. The remaining British colonies, however, were not rich enough to think of independence even if they had wanted it. From the point of view of the mother country territorial sovereignty over these vast and distant spaces was a privilege for which the taxpayer was heavily charged at a time when the British exchequer had to meet interest on war debts and the transition from war to peace. Thus the colonies seemed merely a burden. This attitude lasted for half a century and indeed reached its climax after 1850. There was a logical connexion between free trade, which abrogated colonial preference in the home market, the repeal of the navigation laws which had restricted colonial trade in the interests of British shipping, the grant of responsible government and the withdrawal of British garrisons. The new industrial economy in its earlier stages discounted the value of an empire acquired to serve an outworn mercantilist system. Free traders had no use for colonies, and for a long time the colonial market was small and unimportant. The West Indian possessions depended upon slavery; Englishmen had come to regard slave labour as immoral and a disgrace to their name. South Africa was a military and trading outpost, a naval station, and a port of call.

Australia was a penal settlement, largely unexplored. Canada was of greater economic importance, though its advantages were reckoned in terms, not of wheat, but of lumber, furs, and fish.

The colonists were out of mind as well as out of sight. The West Indian planters alone were fashionable. French settlers in Canada, Dutch farmers at the Cape had no English connexions. New South Wales had associations with convicts. The English, Scottish, and Irish settlers in Upper Canada were mainly poor folk, belonging to the voiceless majority of the people of the British Isles.[1] The harsh Canadian winter took a heavier toll of these settlers than Turkish misrule took of Greek peasants, but it was easier to interest the English upper class in the freedom of Greece than in the fate of their fellow countrymen in Ontario. Although there was public indignation about the horrors of slave-ships, the mortality among emigrants during a transatlantic crossing passed too long unnoticed.[2] There was little imaginative response to the hardships endured by men and women in Canada. Byron and Shelley never concerned themselves with the practical development of liberty among English-speaking people overseas; Chateaubriand was the only European writer of genius who had set foot in Canada before 1800. There is but one mention of the colonies in the poems of Wordsworth.[3]

Colonial patronage, the most important element in colonial administration, was largely used to find places for the trouble-

---

[1] Wakefield wrote in 1849 that 'the whole emigration to Upper Canada and New Zealand furnishes no instance of the ultimate settlement of a gentleman's family with satisfaction to themselves and their friends at home' (quoted in *Cambridge History of the British Empire*, ii. 451).

[2] The larger number of emigrants crossing the Atlantic were Irish who, even more than the English or Scottish emigrants, were at the mercy of unscrupulous agents. Supervision of emigration from the chief British and Irish ports was suggested in 1831 by the British consul in New York, and by a philanthropist named R. Edwards. A small corps of emigration officers was established in 1833. In spite of many obstacles a good deal of progress of an *ad hoc* kind was made in inspecting ships and supervising the general conditions of passage. An agent-general for emigration was appointed in 1837, and an act of 1842 did much to assist the work of supervision. The immense increase in the number of emigrants during and after the Irish famine put too great a strain on this machinery, and was followed by other acts of parliament imposing more stringent regulations. The development of steamships led to an improvement in conditions, and after 1855 the traffic was easier to control owing to a sharp fall in the number of emigrants. See O. MacDonagh, 'Emigration and the State, 1833–55', *Trans. R. Hist. S.* 5th ser. v (1955), pp. 133–59.

[3] *The Excursion*, Bk. ix, 363–82.

some members of the families of the governing class in Great Britain. Colonial problems as such provided little intellectual interest. The whigs considered these problems in general terms, and mainly from the standpoint of political liberty. Russell had sat in parliament for more than a quarter of a century before he became colonial secretary, but, after taking this office, he could write naïvely: 'I soon became interested in colonial affairs.'[1] Peel did not mention the colonies in the Tamworth manifesto; Palmerston did not much concern himself with them; Disraeli found Canada a diplomatic embarrassment. From 1801 to 1854 the secretary of state for war also had control of the colonies. Lord Bathurst held the office from 1812 until 1827; his successors were either well-intentioned nonentities or men of first-class ability who might expect early promotion to higher places. The third Earl Grey was the first of this line of secretaries who combined a knowledge of his subject with a recognized authority in the cabinet.[2] The rapid succession of ministers, and the moderate abilities of the more obscure holders of the office, gave much power to the small permanent staff who managed the business of the department. Sir James Stephen[3] was for many years the real director of colonial policy—the 'Mr. Mother-Country' ridiculed by Charles Buller. Stephen had never seen any of the colonies. He gave to their service the best years of his life although his high abilities were, perhaps, as much suited to scholarship as to administration. Yet he always looked upon the empire as a liability, a trust which could not be given up, but which brought little or no advantage to the trustee. He thought that in time Canada and Australia would break away from the mother country; like most of his contemporaries, he hoped that the severance of legal ties would be gradual and friendly. He wrote in 1849 that 'it remains for

[1] Walpole, *Life of Lord John Russell*, i. 339.

[2] Huskisson may also be reckoned an exception, but he held the office only from Sept. 1827 until May 1828.

[3] Sir James Stephen (1789–1859), s. of a master in chancery; b. London; educated privately, and Trinity College, Cambridge; counsel to the colonial department, and in private practice, 1813–25; permanent counsel to the colonial office and board of trade, 1825–34; assistant under-secretary for the colonies, 1834–6; under-secretary, 1836–47; regius professor of modern history at Cambridge, 1849–59; professor at the East India College, Haileybury, 1855–7. The Stephen family enjoyed a good deal of colonial patronage. A brother of Sir J. Stephen became in turn solicitor-general, judge of the court of requests, and a judge of the supreme court of New South Wales. Three other members of the family, and a relation, Mr. Forbes, held good posts in New South Wales.

the Canadians to cut the last cable which anchors them to us. But it is for them, not for us, to take that step and assume the consequent responsibility. . . . The same process is in progress in the Australian colonies.'[1] As for the smaller colonies—including South Africa and, apparently, New Zealand—these 'detached islands with heterogeneous populations' were 'wretched burdens which in an evil hour we assumed and have no right to lay down again'. Stephen's successors held similar views. Herman Merivale[2] and Frederic Rogers[3] believed that sooner or later the colonies would ask for national independence. The general pessimism about the political future of the colonies, and the relative indifference of parliament and public opinion to colonial questions, threw into stronger relief the enthusiasm of a small group of radicals. The philosophy and practical aims of Jeremy Bentham might not appear to give much encouragement to any school of empire. Bentham agreed with Adam Smith that colonies were economically useless. He addressed a pamphlet to the Convention in Paris in 1793 entitled *Emancipate Your Colonies*; but he made the important reservation that colonies might serve as an outlet for a surplus population. James Mill fastened upon this aspect of the colonial problem in his article on 'Colony' in the *Encyclopaedia Britannica* (8th edition). Molesworth, Gibbon Wakefield, Durham, Charles Buller, and other radicals of remarkable ability supported the view. For different reasons these men failed to reach or to keep high office in English politics,[4] but in spite of their waywardness and, at times, their lack of scruple in the choice of means they brought about a great change in colonial policy. They wanted to direct and control emigration, and to mitigate its hardships. Their belief in self-government on democratic principles led them to oppose the bureaucratic methods of the colonial office, and the misuse of colonial patronage; they believed also that the good

[1] K. N. Bell and W. P. Morrell, *Select Documents on British Colonial Policy, 1830–60*, p. xxiv.

[2] Herman Merivale (1806–74), on his father's side probably of Huguenot descent, and, on his mother's side, a grandson of a German merchant settled in Exeter; b. Dawlish; educated Harrow, and Oriel and Trinity Colleges, Oxford; fellow of Balliol College; professor of political economy at Oxford, 1837–42; assistant under-secretary for the colonies, 1847; permanent under-secretary, 1848–59; under-secretary for India, 1859–74.

[3] Frederic Rogers (1811–89), 1st Baron Blachford; b. London; educated Eton, and Oriel College, Oxford; fellow of Oriel, and a friend of Newman; a member of the staff of *The Times*, 1841–4; under-secretary for the colonies, 1860–71.

[4] See above, pp. 95–96.

sense and British sympathies of the colonists would keep the new territories bound to the home country. The catchwords of 'systematic colonization' and 'representative government' for the colonies offered a robust and positive programme. This programme was opposed for different reasons. Tories of the older school inclined to think of the colonists as dangerous republicans. Many economists doubted whether emigration was the best method of dealing with unemployment. Emigration was expensive, and the money might be spent to greater advantage in improving conditions at home. Moreover the men likely to make their way in the colonies were those whom Great Britain did not want to lose, while their places would be filled at home by immigrants from Ireland. From a different point of view the missionary societies distrusted 'systematic colonization'. Many supporters of missionary work were ill-informed sentimentalists who condemned planters and colonists abroad, while caring little about social evils at home. The missionaries were often narrow-minded; their teaching did not always improve or enlighten savage minds. Some of them were not always free from love of the power or even of the goods of this world. On the whole, however, the 'saints' of the Clapham sect, and the men and women whom they and other protestant denominations sent into the mission field, justified their faith. The missionaries upheld standards of behaviour too rare among early traders; they were concerned with the well-being of the natives, and in many cases protected them from exploitation. Their letters and reports had an effect upon English opinion at home, and did much to relieve the inevitable confusion and tragedy accompanying the intercourse between backward races and an acquisitive western society. The missionary societies had access to the colonial office. Sir James Stephen was a member of the committee of the Church Missionary Society, and the fact that a man in his position could feel 'thankful for the many opportunities' offered to him of 'mitigating the cruel wrongs inflicted' by his countrymen 'on so great a portion of the human race' may be set against the extravagances and exaggerations of Exeter Hall.[1]

For two decades after Waterloo this mitigation of wrong meant to most Englishmen the abolition of slavery and the

[1] A hall in London where evangelical societies held their meetings.

improvement in the condition of the West Indian negroes. The prohibition of the slave-trade (1807) to British subjects and ships flying the British flag was the first stage in a long and difficult task. It was necessary to persuade other nations to follow the example of Great Britain, and, ultimately, to change the economy of the West Indies. In 1814 the restored Bourbon government in France promised that French subjects should be forbidden to engage in the slave-trade after 1819. Napoleon attempted to conciliate British opinion during the Hundred Days by abolishing the trade throughout the French dominions. In 1815 Portugal agreed to abolition after a period of years— finally extended to 1830—and received £300,000 in compensation from British taxpayers. Spain forbade the trade after 1820, in return for £400,000. These payments and promises did not stop the traffic. Slaves were smuggled across the Atlantic; the business became more horrible because the risks were greater, and the traders crammed more negroes into their ships. Great Britain was the only country which made a serious effort to track down and seize slave ships. There was a large import of slaves into Brazil and Cuba. Most of the Cuban trade was in American hands; the United States not only did little to stop it, but continued until the Civil War to raise difficulties with Great Britain about the mutual right of search of suspected vessels flying the American flag.[1] Moreover, although the treatment of the slaves in the West Indies had improved, there were still many cases of cruelty; British opinion tended to judge the planters by these bad examples. Thus the abolitionists in Great Britain became convinced that they must work for the ending of slavery as they had worked for the ending of the slave-trade.[2] In 1820 the colonial office took the first step by forbidding slavery in the new South African settlement of Albany. In 1821 Wilberforce, who was now sixty-two, obtained the help of Thomas Fowell Buxton.[3] Wilberforce wrote a pamphlet in

---

[1] See also pp. 240–1. The fearful havoc caused by the slave trade from East Africa to Arab countries was little known to Englishmen before Livingstone (see below, p. 553) published the accounts of his journeys of 1852–6 and 1858–64. As early as 1822, however, the British government had obtained the consent of the sultan of Zanzibar to a restriction of the trade, and to the operation of a British naval squadron for the interception of slave ships. After Livingstone's revelations, further efforts were made to stop the trade. The Zanzibar slave-market—the principal depot—was closed down with the sultan's agreement in 1873.

[2] Wilberforce always had this end in view.

[3] Sir Thomas Fowell Buxton, bt. (1786–1845); b. Essex: educ. Trinity College,

favour of abolition, and in 1823 Buxton asked the house of commons to abolish slavery in British possessions by allowing freedom to all children born of slaves. Slave-owners would receive compensation for the loss of their property. Canning agreed that, ultimately, the slaves ought to be freed; he thought that freedom should be given by stages if it were not to ruin planters and negroes, and that the first stage should be an improvement in the treatment of slaves.

This policy of 'melioration' was begun by recommending the West Indian colonies to abolish the flogging of women and the use of the lash in field work. The planters, whose interests were strongly represented in the unreformed parliament, protested against this interference. They believed that the emancipation of their slaves would mean a shortage of labour, and much higher costs of production. They had increased their output of sugar during the Napoleonic war, and the fall in prices after 1815 was already a serious problem. They were afraid that the talk of emancipation in Great Britain would excite the negroes and cause a slave rising. An insurrection took place in Demerara, where the negroes thought that the governor and planters were keeping from them news of their liberation. The planters over-reached themselves. They suppressed the Demerara outbreak with great harshness, and wrongly accused English missionaries of inciting the slaves to rebellion. In 1824 Canning laid before parliament a draft order in council for the amelioration of the 35,000 slaves in the crown colonies of Trinidad, St. Lucia, and Demerara. Canning hoped that the other colonies would extend the order to the 650,000 slaves under their rule. The planters did little to carry out the wishes of the home government. They were warned in 1828 that an improvement in their slave laws was a 'matter of necessary policy'. They did nothing. Three years later Sir James Stephen answered the argument that the slave-owners were the best judges of the expediency of the legislation proposed to them.

It is one of the inveterate illusions under which the resident West India Body labour, to suppose this proximity of observation an infallible and necessary guide to sound conclusions. . . . They have not watched the progress of public opinion throughout the civilized world and are unconscious of the rapid progress of that day in which

Dublin; brewer; married, 1807, a sister of Mrs. Fry; M.P., 1818; wrote and spoke in favour of reform of prisons and the criminal law.

it will be impossible to sustain Slavery in the British Dominions. . . .
Their lives are passed in a contracted circle amidst petty feuds and
pecuniary embarrassments. There is no civilized Society on earth
so entirely destitute of learned leisure, of literary and scientific inter-
course and even of liberal recreations.[1]

In the latter part of 1832 Howick, as under-secretary for the
colonies, proposed immediate emancipation, together with a
land tax which would safeguard the planters by compelling
the freed negroes to work. The West Indian interest, as usual,
objected to the plan and the cabinet postponed action. Buxton
raised the matter in parliament, and Stanley, who became
colonial secretary in 1833, carried through a different scheme
of emancipation. All slaves were to receive their freedom within
twelve months; slaves employed in agricultural work would be
apprenticed to their former masters until 1840, domestic or
non-predial slaves until 1838. The planters were allowed
£15,000,000 in compensation. During the debate the sum was
raised to £20,000,000 by the efforts of the planters' friends,[2]
while the friends of the negroes persuaded the house to make
the payment a free gift and not a loan to be repaid by the freed
slaves.

For a time apprenticeship worked fairly well. It broke down
for several reasons. The abolitionists in England wanted complete and immediate emancipation, and used cases of cruelty
to discredit the system. The bad treatment of negroes in the
prisons of Jamaica had nothing to do with apprenticeship, but
British opinion assumed that free negroes would be in a better
position to resist abuses. In any case the planters themselves
found the system unworkable when their mechanics were counted
as 'non-predial' slaves whose term of apprenticeship came to
an end in 1838. The colonial legislatures abolished apprenticeship in July 1838. The results of complete freedom differed
according to the conditions of the colonies. Antigua had accepted emancipation without apprenticeship because there was
little risk of a labour shortage. The slaves were in a better
condition than in other islands, and unlikely to find free land
on which they could live without working in the plantations.
In most islands there was a scarcity of labourers, and a decline

[1] Bell and Morrell, op. cit., p. 373.
[2] The government estimated the compensation payments at about £37. 10s. a
slave; the average selling price of a slave was £38. Hansard, 3rd ser. xx. 134-5.

in production. The British government expected the decline to be lasting, but made no objection to plans for encouraging labourers to come into the islands.[1] The real solution lay in improved methods of cultivation, and in the education of the negroes.

A solution of this kind would take time, and required a change of mind and habit among the planters. Meanwhile the decline in the production of sugar had led to a rise in prices in the British market, where the planters were protected by very high duties on foreign sugar. For some years after the war the average consumption of sugar in Great Britain was about 20 lb. per head;[2] the demand rose and fell with the fluctuations in price, and was likely to increase if the price fell considerably; in 1829 Huskisson estimated that two-thirds of the people of England drank their coffee unsweetened. In 1840 the price of sugar in Great Britain was $7\frac{1}{2}d$. per lb., while foreign artisans could buy better sugar at $4\frac{1}{2}d$. per lb. With the consumption of sugar at a figure above 240,000 tons, the planters were getting a large subsidy. In 1846 the whigs decided to lower the duties on foreign sugar annually until in 1851 foreign and colonial sugar would be admitted on equal terms. There had been little profit in the colonial trade since 1838, and the planters had a reasonable case in asking for the postponement of a measure which would ruin many of their number. The date of equalization was changed from 1851 to 1854. This delay gave time for adjustments of wages to meet the new situation. The adjustments were desirable on general grounds; the negroes were becoming demoralized by the high wages which could be paid only in a protected market. The development of crops other than sugar, the use of machinery, and the provision of coolie labour slowly eased the situation. The days of large fortunes were gone; there were many hard cases and heavy losses, but henceforward the position was not altogether hopeless.

Although the difficult transition to a new economy in the West Indies did not raise any serious constitutional problems,

[1] At first the immigration of Indian hill coolies was thought undesirable. The coolies might become slaves under other names, and the regulation of their long sea voyage would be difficult; after experiments had been tried in Mauritius (resulting in the indianization of the island), the planters were allowed to recruit labour from India.

[2] The average annual consumption at the present day is about 100 lb. per head.

the assembly of Jamaica provided in 1838–9 the rare example of a legislative body refusing to perform its functions. The members were exasperated by the insistence of the home government upon prison reform[1] and hoped by this new form of protest to assert their right to manage their own affairs. The whigs could not allow such an act of defiance, and proposed to suspend the Jamaican constitution. The tories, who were not as a rule the champions of democracy, resisted the proposal although they had agreed to measures of a drastic kind in Lower Canada. The government resigned on the question; on their return to office they introduced a second Jamaica bill, giving the legislature two months' grace to consider the position. The legislature resumed public business, and for the next twenty-five years Jamaican affairs were not a major issue in British politics. They became important, suddenly, in 1865, owing to a negro rising in the island. The rising was a small affair, limited to one area, and the grievances of the negroes were economic, not political; they asked for the abolition of rent on their lands. The governor, E. J. Eyre, who was known in Australia as a protector of the aborigines, proclaimed martial law; he put down the trouble quickly, but allowed far too severe measures of repression. No one in England could estimate the seriousness of the danger which Eyre had to meet, but the matter caused a great stir.[2] J. S. Mill called Eyre a tyrant; Carlyle thought him almost a hero. The lasting effect of the crisis was the abolition of representative government in Jamaica. The planters made little protest because they did not wish either to take the blame for the unpopular measures of the executive or to share their responsibilities by giving votes to the negroes.

Four years later the white population of British Honduras asked, mainly on financial grounds, for the abolition of their representative assembly; in 1876 similar petitions came from St. Vincent, Grenada, and Tobago. Thus, at the time when the larger colonies were developing an independent political life, the colonies in the tropics were coming more directly under the control of the home authority. An increase of control had already taken place in the settlements on the West African coast. Until 1821 the trading stations at the mouth of the

---

[1] The legal arguments of the planters were far better than their moral case.

[2] At the time of the Jamaica rising public opinion was already indignant at the treatment of natives in New Zealand which led to the Maori war. See below, p. 395.

Gambia river, at Sierra Leone, and on the Gold Coast were in the hands of the Africa Company. The company was wound up in 1821, and there seemed no reason for maintaining these small and unhealthy outposts.[1] On the other hand they were bases for use against the slave-trade, and the missionary societies protested against the removal of British protection. The Gold Coast settlements were entrusted in 1828 to a committee of London merchants, but, owing to reports that an illicit trade in stores was being carried on with foreign slave-traders, the imperial government resumed direct control in 1843. Seven years later the Danes sold their stations on the Gold Coast to Great Britain, and in 1871 the Dutch followed their example. In 1861 a settlement was established at Lagos in order to cut off the slave-traders. In this way Great Britain became the dominant Power on the west coast of Africa; here, as elsewhere, expansion was due more to circumstance than to imperial design. As late as 1865 a select committee of the commons recommended withdrawal from all the western African settlements, with the possible exception of Sierra Leone. Four years later Clarendon wrote, in a private letter: 'There is no care in this country for our African possessions. I believe that an announcement of intention to get rid of them would be popular.'[2] The economic importance of the hinterland of tropical Africa was as yet unrealized, and, apart from the journeys of Livingstone and others, three—Niger, Nile, and Zambesi—of the great river basins were hardly known, and the fourth—the vast Congo basin—was altogether unexplored.

In the larger as in the smaller colonies the political life of the settlers was determined narrowly and obviously by the needs of existence; there were few refinements of art or temperament, and little superstructure of principle. The size of the colonies was an all-important consideration. Canadian roads were so bad and distances so great that it was almost impossible to collect a representative body of men except in the season when

---

[1] In 1824 a small British force was overwhelmed and massacred by an army of 10,000 from the neighbouring Ashanti kingdom. The Ashanti warriors had bought munitions from the Danish and Dutch trading posts. The Ashanti were heavily defeated in 1826. They did not succeed in invading British territory again until 1863. The British government would not allow a punitive expedition to go into Ashanti territory and destroy their military power.

[2] Quoted in *Camb. Hist. of B.E.* iii. 35.

the representatives were busiest at their farm work. The standard of education was low, but the colonists knew from sharp and direct experience their elementary wants. The question of the clergy reserves of land in Canada was not discussed, as Gladstone or Newman might have discussed it, from the point of view of the relation between church and state. To the Canadian farmers these blocks of waste forest land allocated to the anglican church hampered the work of clearing, and isolated one settlement from another. Sheep-farmers in Australia did not concern themselves with the neat economic balance of Wakefield's 'systematic colonization';[1] they knew that complete and clear-cut allocation of lands within a restricted area did not suit sheep-farming in Australia. Thus political issues were not stated in philosophical terms; they were practical matters concerning land, and labour on the land. English traditions affected colonial politics; these traditions could be summed up in the view that British citizens were always free to manage their local affairs. The demand for self-government—the term 'responsible government' meant control of local affairs by local men—did not imply a wish for separation. Separation was never a real question in the first half of the nineteenth century. French Canadians, descendants of United Empire Loyalists, and British immigrants were not likely to want the union of Canada with the United States; in any case this union would not necessarily bring local self-government. Great Britain alone could supply capital and labour for the development of Australia. In South Africa the Dutch went out into new country beyond the limits of British territory, but the Great Trek did not take the Boer farmers away from the shadow of the British Crown, and if the colonists who remained directly under British jurisdiction had been left to provide for their own defence, the trekkers could not have survived.

The colonies were therefore asking for something like municipal independence. The colonial office did not object to this demand, or wish to dominate local affairs; the colonists were content to leave the conduct of foreign affairs to the British government. The difficulty lay in the fact that the colonies were not municipalities, and therefore 'self-government' was not like the local management of the business of a large city. The issue was fought on the question of the control of revenues,

[1] See below, p. 387.

the classical disputing-ground for British subjects at variance with sovereign authority. The imperial government claimed for the executive an independent revenue, drawn mainly from Crown lands; otherwise the colonies would be, not self-governing municipalities, but separate states. The imperial government also claimed the right to supervise the distribution of land in the interests of immigrants from Great Britain; these unoccupied spaces were not the private appanages of first-comers on colonial soil, but the patrimony of the English people.

On the other hand, from the colonial point of view, the demand for local self-government could not be satisfied as long as the executive officials disposed of an independent revenue which freed them from local control. The colonists, therefore, wanted to control the whole of the revenue, and to be sure that the governor and his officials would take the advice of men who knew local opinion. Hence the demand for local self-government led to the demand for 'responsible government' in the sense known to English-speaking people; an executive responsible to an elected assembly, and an elected assembly with financial control. This demand took a slightly different shape in different colonies. It was put more clearly in Upper Canada than elsewhere, but the main issue was the same in Lower Canada and in Australia. Ultimately, there could be only one answer to this demand. Sooner or later, directly or indirectly, by open grant or by implication, the imperial government would give the full ministerial responsibility and popular control for which the colonists asked. Englishmen after 1832 were unlikely to deal with Englishmen in any other way.

The concessions were first made to Canada. The settled, or partially settled, areas of British North America consisted in 1815 of three areas: Upper and Lower Canada, and the Maritime Provinces. There were vast tracts of land west of these areas, but the fertile plains beyond the forests were too far from the coast to attract settlers before the development of railways. An attempt at settlement in the Red River district in 1812–15 ruined the promoters and did little more than open up an important strategic and trading centre; in 1871 there were only 241 people in Winnipeg. The small outposts on the Pacific coast were interested mainly in trade with China; the rivalry of the Hudson Bay and the North-West Companies, until their amalgamation in 1821, and the activities of the fur traders in the

North, belong more to tales of adventure than to political history. Access to Upper Canada was difficult and expensive before the development of steamship services on the St. Lawrence and the opening of canals which avoided the rapids. Hence the Maritime Provinces took most of the immigrants from the United Kingdom before 1820. The greater part of these immigrants came from Scotland and Ireland, where conditions favoured emigration, and the timber ships offered passengers low rates for the westward voyage.[1] The Maritime Provinces were more interested in lumber and fishing than in farming;[2] shipping and shipbuilding were corollaries of the timber business, while there was a profitable trade with the West Indies. As late as 1852 Nova Scotia had nearly a third as much tonnage on the sea as France, though the coming of the iron ship had a serious effect upon the economy of the Maritime Provinces, and the rapid growth of Upper Canada after 1820 brought a relative decline in the importance of the seaboard area. In 1820 the two provinces of Nova Scotia and New Brunswick had as many people as Upper Canada; in 1850 Upper Canada was twice as populous.

The conflict between the local and imperial governments took place in Upper and Lower Canada. The existence of a large French population in Lower Canada made this conflict peculiarly difficult. The French settlements in Lower Canada were spread along the St. Lawrence; the banks of the river formed 'one continuous white-cottaged street'. Ten miles away the land was still uncleared. The French settlers lived in intellectual isolation. There was no emigration from France. The catholic church held absolute dominion in matters of conscience, and the anti-clericalism of the French Revolution had broken the last connexion with French life. Differences of language, custom, and religion kept the French population apart from the English settlers. The French farmers were almost self-sufficing. The church did not encourage commercial enterprise; the timber trade was capitalized, with its headquarters in London and Glasgow. A small and not well-educated class of lawyers dominated political life. These men might have been a very

---

[1] Fares from Ireland were even cheaper than from Scotland because the lower range of timber duties in Ireland encouraged ships to discharge their cargoes at Irish ports.

[2] Conditions in the lumber trade were very severe; it was said that few lumbermen lived much beyond the age of forty.

strong force if their leaders had not attacked the privileges and position of the church, and therefore set the clergy on the side of authority. In any case a slow-moving, placid body of farmers, long accustomed to control and organization from above, would not have troubled the colonial office if they had not been brought into contact and opposition with restless, energetic neighbours in Upper Canada.

The growth of Upper Canada dated from the arrival of the United Empire Loyalists.[1] Some ten thousand of the immigrants made their homes in Ontario, where the soil gave a good return after the woods had been cleared. The work of clearing broke the spirit and exhausted the small capital of many of these settlers; here, as elsewhere, the rewards were taken too often by those who came after the first laborious attack upon the trees. After much land had been cleared, difficulties of communication made life hard and dreary, especially for women accustomed to the conditions of Great Britain. The position improved with the increase in population, but the environment was such that only the vigorous and alert could survive. These tough individualists would not sit quietly under grievances for which they saw an obvious cure. The constitutional act of 1791 had separated Upper and Lower Canada as the simplest method of avoiding racial friction.[2] The form of government provided under the act was aristocratic in intention. This government was representative, not merely by custom, but also because the Loyalists in Upper Canada were familiar with representative assemblies and would never have tolerated any other régime. On the other hand the assemblies had little or no control of policy. British opinion in 1791 thought that the democratic character of the American colonies had been one of the chief reasons for their revolt. The Canadian colonies were provided with nominated legislative and executive councils—corresponding, in some measure, to the British upper house—as well as assemblies, while the executive authority rested finally with the governor.

The grievances of the French colonists could be reduced to fear of encroachment by their British neighbours; French nationalism, which had long been dormant, developed, on lines familiar to European observers of the last hundred years, as a protest against alien absorption. The British colonists complained that

---

[1] See vol. xii of this *History*, p. 254.　　　　　[2] See ibid., p. 302.

they were not given a fair share of the customs duties on goods passing through the French province on the way to Upper Canada. They objected still more strongly to the clergy reserves, and to the concentration of political power in the hands of a small number of families who formed an oligarchy round the governor. In 1831 the imperial governmert made concessions on the revenue question; the colonists in Upper Canada were not satisfied with half-measures, while nothing could be done to remove the fundamental grievances of the French. The assembly of Lower Canada was almost wholly French, the legislative council mainly British. In 1834 there was a complete breach between these two bodies. A commission of inquiry sent out from England could find no remedy except in the withdrawal of the concessions made in 1831. This was too much for the whigs, but they proposed to allow the governor of Lower Canada to spend money, if necessary, without the consent of the assembly. In other words, representative government would be suspended if the representatives did not provide for the needs of the executive. In Upper Canada the tactlessness of Sir Francis Bond Head, who was lieutenant-governor from 1836 to 1838, aggravated the situation. In 1837 there were disturbances in each province. These disturbances, led by W. L. Mackenzie, a political journalist, in Upper Canada and by Louis Papineau, a French Canadian, in the province of Quebec, were easily put down; but the British government took them as a serious warning. The decision to send Lord Durham to report on the situation had lasting effects, though it cannot be regarded as a deliberate act of statesmanship. Melbourne was not interested in the colonies; Glenelg, the colonial secretary, was soon to be driven from office because his colleagues did not feel able to defend him. Durham was chosen partly to satisfy the radicals, partly because Melbourne did not mind sending a possible rival out of England on a task which was unlikely to add to his reputation. Melbourne wrote to Durham: 'The final separation of these colonies might not be of material detriment', but it would be 'a serious blow to the honour of Great Britain' and a blow 'certainly fatal to the character and existence of the ministry under which it took place'.

Durham reached Canada in May 1838 and sailed for England in November of the same year. One of his first acts was his political ruin. He had to settle the fate of a number of prisoners

implicated in the troubles of 1837. His instructions did not
allow him to give these men a free pardon. No jury would
convict them, and the time for a court martial had passed.
Durham banished some of the ringleaders who had already
left the country, and sent eight of the prisoners to Bermuda.
He had gone beyond his powers, since he had no authority in
Bermuda. He was attacked with great unfairness in the imperial
parliament; Melbourne took no steps to defend him, and allowed him to resign his commission. On his return he wrote the
report which made his name famous. To some extent the report
has been overpraised. Durham was confused over the issue, and
did not foresee the consequences of his wider suggestions. He
proposed the union of Upper and Lower Canada in order that
the French might be outnumbered in one large province; the
plan had been suggested to the cabinet in 1821. He advised
forbearance in the use of imperial authority. Canning had
already laid down that the power of the imperial parliament
should not be used 'upon trifling occasions, or in case of petty
refractoriness and temporary misconduct'. The colonial office
also held this theory, although its action sometimes belied it.
Yet, if Durham was not altogether an innovator, his common
sense and democratic convictions, strengthened in colonial
affairs by the arguments of his friend Charles Buller, showed
him that nothing less than responsible government would satisfy
the colonists. He accepted this plain fact without drawing pessimistic conclusions about separation. A sentence in his report
summed up his views. The governor must look for 'no support
from home in any contest with the legislature except on points
involving strictly Imperial interests'. Imperial interests included
the disposition of land as well as matters of foreign and commercial policy, but the implication was clear. The executive
officials in Canada must be responsible to the representatives
of the Canadian people.

The whigs acted upon the less liberal suggestion in Durham's
report and united the provinces of Upper and Lower Canada
in 1840. The grant of responsible government was not long
delayed. Russell, who became colonial secretary in 1839, saw
the difficulty which Durham had put aside too easily. The
question of responsibility could not be divided neatly between
domestic and imperial affairs; these affairs did not fall neatly
into two compartments. Russell laid down that the principal

offices in Canada should not be held merely at the pleasure of the Crown but that office-holders should retire when retirement was expedient for reasons of public policy. These officials, including members of the council, were to be treated as members of an administration responsive, if not responsible, to popular control. Lord Sydenham,[1] the first governor-general under the new regime, was the first of a new type of colonial governor. Hitherto, mainly for economy, soldiers trained in the rigid and unimaginative school of Wellington had been sent to deal with equally rigid and unimaginative colonial politicians. Sydenham, with his experience of British politics, tried to carry through his policy by persuasion. His successors were less happy, and at the end of 1846 the position was as dangerous as in the period before the Durham report. The repeal of the corn laws affected Canadian interests, since Canada suddenly lost the advantages of low duties on colonial wheat which had diverted American wheat to Canadian mills, and favoured the St. Lawrence route to Europe. At this critical moment Lord Elgin was appointed governor-general. Elgin was a Scotsman, a liberal, and the son-in-law of Durham; Grey, at the colonial office, supported him in a policy of wise conciliation. In 1847 the conservative party in the Canadian administration lost a general election. Elgin accepted ministers from the liberal party on condition that they did not hinder measures necessary for maintaining the imperial connexion or commit him to anything which would prevent future co-operation with an administration of a different character. Henceforward responsible government was recognized in Canada. It is characteristic of English political practice that this immense change rested upon convention and not upon statute law. The Canadian ministers soon used their powers to bring forward a bill compensating those who had suffered from unnecessary, unjust, or wanton damage in Lower Canada during the troubles of 1837. The bill was denounced in Canada and Great Britain as rewarding treason, but Elgin did not oppose it, and Russell and Grey refused to discuss it on its merits in the imperial parliament. They asked for, and received, a majority on the larger question of responsible government.

[1] Charles Edward Poulett Thomson, 1st Baron Sydenham (1799–1841); s. of a merchant; b. Wimbledon; educ. privately; worked in a branch of his father's firm at St. Petersburg, 1815–17 and 1821–3; M.P., 1826; vice-president of the board of trade, 1830–4, president,1834, and 1835–9; killed in a riding accident.

The federation of the different provinces was now only a matter of time. The motives on the Canadian side were partly economic; the desire for greater commercial bargaining-power in dealing with other countries, and, in particular, with the United States; the demands for an inter-colonial railway, and the removal of internal tariffs. On the political side the continued friction between Upper and Lower Canada led the English in the two provinces to hope that federation might solve the problem of finding a stable government. The American civil war raised the question of Canadian defence and put an end to the small but vociferous agitation in favour of annexation by the United States. The civil war made it clear that the American constitution was not ideal. Moreover, since the grant of responsible government, the Canadian provinces had settled two questions which might have led to difficulties with Great Britain. In 1853 the imperial parliament handed over the clergy reserves to the Canadians; six years later the Canadians showed that they would not accept the principle of free trade adopted by the mother country. The first Canadian tariff on British goods met with a strong protest from the manufacturers of Sheffield; the duke of Newcastle as colonial secretary merely lectured the colonists on the merits of free trade, but the Canadians claimed, a little sharply, the right 'to adjust the taxation of the people in the way they deem best, even if it should unfortunately happen to meet the disapproval of the Imperial Ministry'.[1]

The British North America act of 1867,[2] which provided for the federation of Canada, made little difference to the relations with Great Britain. The imperial government still controlled foreign relations, though the colonists had already asked permission to send unofficial agents to Washington to discuss the terms of a commercial treaty with the United States, and in 1865 the foreign office agreed that Canadian representatives should confer with British ministers in foreign countries on

---

[1] Bell and Morrell, p. 369. The tariff was, nominally, for revenue purposes.

[2] The act included the provinces of Ontario, Quebec, New Brunswick, and Nova Scotia. Rupert's Land and the North-Western Territory were added in 1869–70; British Columbia joined in 1871 with the promise of a transcontinental railway. Prince Edward Island joined in 1873. Newfoundland remained outside the union. The federation was called a Dominion. A section of Canadian opinion wanted the title 'Kingdom of Canada', but the term was refused owing to a fear that the use of the word 'Kingdom' might be offensive to the United States. There was no suggestion that the word implied separation.

questions of trade agreements. The leading supporters of federation in Canada complained that the duke of Buckingham, as colonial secretary, and the imperial parliament failed to realize the importance of the British North America act. The measure was passed as though it were 'a private bill uniting two or three English parishes . . .'. From the British point of view the act, which was mainly the work of the Canadians, was regarded as another step towards friendly separation; little enthusiasm could be felt either for the road or for the end of the journey. In 1870 Granville and Kimberley—who succeeded him at the Colonial Office—made public statements repudiating any desire to further the dismemberment of the Empire; the fact that each thought it necessary to make these statements was indirect evidence of the view generally attributed to liberals at this time.[1]

At the beginning of the nineteenth century Canada at least had its modern name, though this name belonged in law only to two provinces. The name 'Australia' was not suggested until 1814; it was used officially three years later, but the term was not fixed for many years.[2] Gladstone never took to it readily, and if Bentham's plan of a settlement had been carried out, South Australia might today be called Felicitania. Before 1813 only the coastal fringe of the country had been explored; the Blue Mountains were an uncrossed barrier. Settlements were made outside New South Wales in order to forestall the French at a time when Napoleon was showing an interest in the *terra australis*. These settlements were given up after 1812, and British authority was not claimed over the whole continent until 1829, when the French once again showed signs of establishing a colony. New South Wales was founded as a penal establishment in 1788, and Van Dieman's Land (later Tasmania)[3] settled in

[1] One important step which gave an appearance of leaving the colonies, and particularly Canada, to look after themselves was the withdrawal of the larger part of the British defence forces. This withdrawal had been recommended by a select committee and approved by parliament in 1862, on the ground that 'colonies exercising the right of self-government ought to undertake the main responsibility for their own order and security. . . and assist in their own external defence'. The recall of the troops was begun under Derby's administration, and continued by Gladstone as part of Cardwell's army reforms. See also below, p. 401.

[2] The article on Australia in the ninth edition (1875) of the *Encyclopaedia Britannica* begins with the words: 'Australia, or New Holland.'

[3] Tasman, who discovered the island in 1642, named it after his patron, Van Diemen, governor of the Dutch East Indies. The change of name took place in 1853.

1804 by a few soldiers, convicts, and six free men. The population of New South Wales in 1820 was about 24,000; the convicts had given the country a bad reputation; a colony in which there were more than twice as many men as women could hardly avoid grave social evils. New South Wales had little to offer free settlers; development in the years after 1815 was slow, and was due more to sheep than to men. The first sale of Australian wool in Great Britain took place in 1817; five years later this wool was judged to be as good as the best wool from Saxony. The Australian export, which equalled the export from Spain to Great Britain in 1834, was only two-thirds of the German export in 1840. Ten years later it was four and a half times greater; while the mining of gold in 1851 brought a new and disturbing source of wealth. In 1860 the population of New South Wales was 350,000, and of Victoria 538,000. Tasmania had been declared a separate colony in 1825, Western Australia in 1829, South Australia in 1836, New Zealand in 1840, Victoria in 1850. The first railway was opened in New South Wales in 1850; the first Australian university was founded at Sydney between 1849 and 1852.

A rapid awakening of political self-consciousness accompanied this growth in wealth and numbers, but the earliest demands made to the home government had little to do with constitutional theory. These demands arose out of the distinction between officials and the most important free settlers and, on the other side, free settlers of a humbler sort, freed convicts and their descendants. The names of the political groups—'parties' would be too definite a term—show the line of division: 'exclusives' were ranged against 'emancipists'. The emancipists asked in 1819 not for 'responsible government' but for changes in judicial arrangements affecting the status of ex-convicts; the act of 1823 establishing a nominated council for New South Wales was entitled, significantly, the New South Wales judicature act. The colonies could not develop as free settlements while they remained dumping-places for criminals. Public opinion at home was uneasy about transportation.[1] Many of the convicts were criminal types; the majority were poor creatures who had fallen through weakness or ill luck in the harsh conditions of urban life, and in many cases their sentences were unnecessarily severe. Humanitarian reformers at home, led by Archbishop Whately,

[1] See below, p. 471.

pointed out that the voyage was sentence of death to large numbers, and that the system under which prisoners were collected and transported led to general demoralization, while the conditions of convict life in Australia offered no terror to the clever criminal and little chance of reform for the dull or the weak. A committee of the house of commons in 1832 attempted to improve the system while keeping the punishment of transportation. A second committee, appointed five years later, recommended its abolition. Molesworth, as chairman of this committee, wanted to free the new settlement of South Australia from the competition of cheap convict labour in New South Wales; in any case the evidence against transportation was very strong.

Although the recommendations of the committee of 1837 were not fully carried out, no convicts were sent to New South Wales after 1840, and the plan of assigning convict labourers to employers was abolished. The home government could not easily discover a substitute for transportation. Imprisonment in Great Britain was expensive; discharged prisoners found it difficult to get work, while the number of prisoners serving long sentences had increased with the abolition of capital punishment for minor crimes. For a time the stream of convicts was diverted to Tasmania; sixteen thousand were sent to the island in four years. Conditions in Tasmania became even worse than they had been in New South Wales, while the state of Norfolk Island, where the worst cases were drafted, was horrible beyond description. In 1846 Gladstone, as colonial secretary, suspended transportation to Tasmania for two years; Grey in 1848 proposed only to send out convicts who had passed through Pentonville or other new reformatory prisons in Great Britain; these men would go with tickets of leave either to Tasmania or to such colonies as were willing to receive them. This plan also broke down. Tasmania did not want criminals at any stage of their sentences; public feeling in Melbourne and Sydney was strongly against receiving ticket-of-leave men, although employers up country would have taken convict labourers at a cheap price. An attempt to land convicts at the Cape was met with such indignation that the governor sent the ship on to Tasmania. After the discovery of gold in Australia it was essential to avoid flooding the country with convicts; by 1855 transportation in any form had been abolished in the eastern colonies and

Tasmania. The system lingered on for another thirteen years in Western Australia.

There is a certain irony in the fact that the first discovery of gold in Australia was made by a convict who was whipped on the supposition that he must have stolen some gold, melted it down, and pretended to have found it. Later discoveries by a Pole and a clergyman were accepted as genuine, but kept secret owing to the danger of exciting the convict population.[1] The colonial office was afraid that a rise in prices and the diversion of labour would have a bad effect upon the wool trade. The discoveries could not be concealed for ever. Other people found gold in 1851 in Victoria and in New South Wales. The news caused a rush to the gold-producing areas. At the beginning of 1852 there were only two policemen left in Melbourne; the rest had gone to look for gold. Wages and prices rose at once, and there was wild speculation in real property. The number of emigrants to Victoria increased sevenfold in a year, and the population of Australia nearly trebled between 1850 and 1860. The wool-growers ultimately gained from the increase in population and local purchasing-power. The demand for meat increased the value of sheep and brought a new market for cattle. Roads were built to carry traffic to the mining areas; larger ships were necessary to deal with the increase in imports, and the shipowners were anxious to get return cargoes. There was also a rise in the world price of wool.

Meanwhile the political demands of the Australian colonists grew with the passing of time. During the third decade of the nineteenth century the main problems were the disposal of land and the attraction of free settlers. For some years the theories of the English radicals, and particularly of Gibbon Wakefield, affected the policy of the home government. Wakefield justified 'systematic colonization' on economic grounds. He suggested that the failure of many colonial ventures was due to the shortage of labour resulting from cheapness of land. If land were sold at a fair price, settlers without capital would have to work for some time as labourers before they could buy farms of their own. If the sales were confined to suitable areas, the settlements would not be too scattered. The proceeds of the sales of land could be used to assist emigration.

[1] The governor of New South Wales is reported to have told the clergyman: 'Put it away, Mr. Clarke, or we shall all have our throats cut.'

Wakefield's idea was not entirely new, but it had not been applied on a large scale or supported with much ingenuity. The plan attracted Howick, who applied it to the land of New South Wales.[1] This application took no account of the needs of sheep-farmers under Australian conditions. In spite of official regulation, it was impossible to prevent 'squatters'[2] from occupying land outside, or even inside, the settled areas. Most of the early squatters were ex-convicts; after the development of the wool trade men of substance and good family began sheep-farming on a large scale. As late as 1835 the colonial office refused to recognize the squatters, although the governor of New South Wales pointed out that '100,000 soldiers scattered throughout the bush' could not drive back the sheep. In 1836 the legislative council of New South Wales gave the squatters a legal position on payment of an annual licence fee of £10, irrespective of the size of their holdings. They were without security of tenure, and the colonial office still compared the squatters' occupation with the act of a Berkshire farmer attempting to feed his oxen on the queen's demesne at Richmond or Hampton Court. A settlement reached in 1846 continued the yearly leases in districts near towns; elsewhere the sheep-farmers had longer leases, with the right to purchase their runs.

The increase in the number of settlers and the abolition of transportation led to demands for self-government as such, and not merely as an incidental accompaniment of local control of land questions. The example of Canada affected Australian opinion: many of the immigrants after 1840 were chartists, who brought with them a feeling of resentment against authority. The New South Wales act of 1842 provided for the election of two-thirds of the legislative council; but this concession did not satisfy the colonists. Five years later Grey sent to New South Wales a plan for modifying the constitutions of all the Australian colonies. He added, in 1848, that he had no wish to impose

[1] Wakefield wanted to found a new colony as a private venture in South Australia where his plans could be given full trial. The colony was authorized in 1834 and established two years later. It was not a success, though later settlers reaped the benefit of the pioneer work. Wakefield's main contribution to the development of the colonies was not his land theory, but his view that, under proper control, Australia could take an almost unlimited number of suitable settlers.

[2] The term 'squatter' was taken from the United States, where it had a different meaning, and referred to men who had taken small strips of land between legally occupied farms. In New South Wales, where, on a rough estimate, three acres were needed for a sheep, a 'squatter's' sheep-run might cover thousands of acres.

upon the colonists 'a form of government not in their judgment suited to their wants', and explained that the legislative councils would have power to make changes for themselves, on condition that any such changes were accepted by the Imperial government. The Australian colonies government act of 1850 gave the colonists very wide powers of choice. Grey even suggested a general assembly for the whole of Australia. There was some support for this plan in the colonies, but the population was too small, the distances too great, and common interests too few; the federation of Australia did not take place for another fifty years. Meanwhile, new constitutions were worked out in detail by the colonists and accepted in 1855, with slight modifications, by the imperial government. The transition to 'responsible government' was comparatively smooth, and the new system produced few conflicts with the mother country; the main difficulty lay not in relations with Great Britain but in the absence of broad principles dividing colonial parties and in the instability of administrations. Between 1856 and 1900 the average life of a ministry in an Australian colony was eighteen months, and a great deal of the work of government passed from the hands of transient ministers to the permanent civil service.

The history of New Zealand illustrates most of the colonial problems of the first half of the nineteenth century: the reluctance of the imperial parliament to extend its obligations and annex new territory; the changes in the situation brought about by the action of foreign states and by the restless, individual enterprise of British citizens; the antagonism between missionaries and settlers; the protection of native rights; discussions over self-government, and, finally, the burden of native wars caused largely by the mistakes and greed of the colonists.

Although missionaries had established relations with the Maoris of New Zealand in 1814, the first scheme of colonization was suggested by a Belgian, Baron de Thierry, who had served in the British army. The colonial office pointed out, in 1823, that New Zealand was not a British possession; Thierry then applied to the king of the United Netherlands and to Charles X of France. Meanwhile trading-posts set up by adventurers had led to trouble with the natives and protests from the missionaries.[1]

---

[1] One of the most profitable forms of trade was the purchase of preserved Maori heads for sale at a high price to curio-hunters in Australia and Europe.

The importation of firearms and spirits disorganized native life far away from the trading-posts. The British government still refused to annex the country, though the Revolution of 1830 appears to have cut short a French plan of sending catholic missionaries as the precursors of annexation. In 1836 Gibbon Wakefield mentioned New Zealand when he was giving evidence before a parliamentary committee on the methods of disposing of colonial lands. He pointed out the evils which were following the arrival of landsharks, escaped convicts, and other bad types; he added that 'we are, I think, going to colonize New Zealand, though we be doing so in a most slovenly and disgraceful manner'. The banker Francis Baring, and others interested in Wakefield's evidence, agreed to support a plan of 'systematic colonization'. They founded a New Zealand association, but Stephen thought their projects would involve the British government in the conquest of the country and lead to the extermination of the natives. Although the missionaries in New Zealand had come to the conclusion that British intervention was necessary, the Church Missionary Society at home was in favour of allowing time for the organization of a Christian native government. The report of a parliamentary committee on the treatment of aborigines in British settlements[1] strengthened feeling against the association.

The committee reported that the misery inflicted upon the natives was comparable with the ancient evils of slavery and the slave trade. This new evil had grown up without even the colour of sanction from the legislature. 'We have not even the poor excuse that it contributes to any interest of the state.' The oppression of aborigines was 'morally indefensible', and a shameful misuse of the many advantages bestowed 'by Providence upon the British empire . . . for some higher purpose than commercial prosperity and military renown'. This maltreatment was 'in point of economy, of security, of commerce, of reputation . . . a short-sighted and disastrous policy'. It was due to ignorance, lack of system, and 'the difficulty which distance interposes in checking the cupidity and punishing the crimes of that adventurous class of Europeans who lead

---

[1] *P.P.* 1837, vii. 75–76. This report is the most remarkable expression of liberal opinion on the treatment of aborigines put forward by any parliamentary inquiry during the nineteenth century. Extracts from the report are printed in Bell and Morrell, pp. 545–52.

the way in penetrating the territory of uncivilized man'. The committee considered Wakefield's scheme for the colonization of New Zealand, and suggested delay until a proper policy had been devised. The reports from New Zealand convinced Glenelg at the end of 1837 that the establishment of a settled form of government was necessary in the interest of the natives. 'The only question is between a colonization, desultory, without law, and fatal to the natives, and a colonization organized and salutary.' Glenelg was ready to recognize the New Zealand association if it were transformed into a chartered company, with the right of the Crown to exclude undesirable persons from membership of the governing body and the staff.

The association appealed to parliament. Molesworth attacked Glenelg's administration of the colonial office, and blamed him for not taking steps to put down scandals in New Zealand. No one outside his own department defended Glenelg, but the association found little support, and its promoters had to accept Glenelg's conditions. In August 1838 a private joint-stock company was formed for the colonization of New Zealand. Normanby, who succeeded Glenelg in February 1839, refused to recognize the company. Wakefield and his friends took matters in their own hands, and sent a ship to New Zealand. Meanwhile the discussions in parliament and the formation of the company revived French schemes of colonization. French traders suffered from the anarchy in trading-stations. In 1836 Gregory XVI appointed a bishop of New Zealand; French newspapers had begun to talk of obtaining for France at least a share in the country. The British government, therefore, ordered Captain Hobson, the senior naval officer in Australian waters, to treat with the Maoris for the cession of sovereignty. His instructions are a curious example of the way in which an unwilling government was constrained by facts.

The Ministers of the Crown have deferred to the advice of the Committee appointed . . . to inquire into the state of the Aborigines . . . in the vicinity of our colonial settlements; and have concurred with that Committee in thinking that the increase in national wealth and power, promised by the acquisition of New Zealand, would be a most inadequate compensation for the injury which must be inflicted upon this kingdom itself, by embarking on a measure essentially unjust, and but too certainly fraught with calamity to a numerous and inoffensive people, whose title to the soil and to the sovereignty of New Zealand is indisputable and has been solemnly recognized by the British Government. We retain these opinions in unimpaired force, and though circumstances entirely beyond our control have at length compelled us to alter our course, I do not scruple to avow that we depart from it with extreme reluctance.[1]

These instructions, published, without authorization, in the *Globe* newspaper, excited opinion in France. The French government arranged with a French company to convey settlers to New Zealand, and to provide them with supplies for seventeen months.[2] In return for this help, the company would give to the government one-fifth of any lands which it might acquire. The French expedition did not leave Rochefort until March 1840; it arrived to find New Zealand under British sovereignty.

On 6 February 1840 Hobson made a treaty with the native chiefs. This treaty of Waitangi became a subject of dispute and criticism, but without it the British company would have been unable to secure a settlement. From the Maori point of view the treaty was the best bargain made by any native race. The Maori chiefs ceded their sovereign rights, and obtained a guarantee of their lands, with a right of pre-emption for the British Crown if any land should be sold. Hobson proclaimed British sovereignty before all the chiefs had signed the treaty because he wanted to forestall action by the company's settlers. The company now tried to attract German settlers, and even proposed to sell the Chatham Islands to a German colonization company and to establish a separate German colony in New Zealand. The first years of colonization were difficult and unsatisfactory. The colony was poor. There was confusion over grants and purchases of land. The 'adventurous class of Europeans' caused trouble with the Maoris, since colonists and natives misunderstood the conditions of sale and ownership of land. A colonist might think that he was buying land outright; the native seller would assume that he was disposing only of right of occupancy, or that he was admitting a white man merely to the privileges enjoyed by a tribe over land. In June 1843 one of the many disputes led to fighting, in which the Maoris defeated the settlers and killed a number of prisoners. The home government refused to send a punitive expedition

---

[1] *P.P.* 1840, xxxiii. Correspondence relative to New Zealand, p. 37.
[2] The Maoris called the French 'the tribe of Marian', after a French captain taken by them in 1772.

because the settlers were in the wrong. The Maoris took this refusal as a sign of weakness, and in 1845 began a rebellion in the North Island. The trouble was suppressed and a free pardon was granted to the rebels.

Thus the company was soon in conflict with the colonial office. Many of its landowners were absentees; the attitude of some of its high officials towards the natives may be seen in a letter of January 1843 from the governor of the company to the colonial office. 'We have always had very serious doubts whether the Treaty of Waitangi, made with naked savages by a consul invested with no plenipotentiary powers, without ratification by the Crown, could be treated by lawyers as any thing but a praiseworthy device for amusing and pacifying savages for the moment.'[1] Stanley, as colonial secretary, sent the reply which the letter deserved, but the company, as usual, appealed to parliament. A parliamentary committee reported in 1844 that the company had acted improperly in sending out colonists in defiance of the Crown; on the other hand the Treaty of Waitangi did not imply a recognition of the right of the natives to all 'wild land' in New Zealand. Stanley disputed the view that 'the uncivilized inhabitants of any country have but a qualified dominion over it', and, in spite of another appeal from Wakefield and Buller, upheld the treaty. Finally, in 1850, the company unwillingly surrendered its charter in return for a money compensation. The end of this experiment coincided with another of Wakefield's schemes: the establishment of a colony in collaboration with the missionary societies. This plan had already been tried on a small scale by an arrangement between the company and the Free Church of Scotland. Wakefield formed a Canterbury association, with the two archbishops and seven bishops among its members. The settlers were carefully chosen, and a new Canterbury was founded in New Zealand in 1848.

After formal annexation in 1840 New Zealand received the institutions of a Crown colony. The seat of government was fixed, not very wisely, at Auckland; owing to the distances between the capital and the outlying settlements the colonists wanted local and municipal independence. Hence the constitution proposed for New Zealand in 1846 was of a federal type. There were two provinces; each province had its own executive government, and a legislature of two houses. Delegations

[1] *P.P.* 1844, xiii. (Committee on New Zealand, appendix, p. 30.)

from the provincial legislatures formed a general assembly of two houses for the discussion of common affairs. The creation of six different assemblies, as well as municipal councils, in a thinly populated country, was more an act of faith in the future than a solution of present difficulties. Moreover, the constitution gave the Europeans too great powers over the natives; it limited the franchise to those who could write and read English, and set aside certain areas as native reserves, but left the natives elsewhere under European control. Sir George Grey,[1] as governor of New Zealand, thought that this control would lead to injustice, and that the natives would not submit to it. A new act in 1852 created six provinces, each with an elected provincial council and an elected superintendent. The general assembly of the country consisted of the governor, a nominated legislative council, and an elected house of representatives. Four years later full ministerial responsibility was conceded on the request of the colonists, and without any objection from the colonial office.

Thus New Zealand passed quickly through the stages of colonial evolution to which British opinion was now resigned. In one respect alone the colonists had not fulfilled the expectations of pessimists. They had not asked the imperial government to fight any large native war. They soon made this demand. Between 1847 and 1860 the European population of New Zealand doubled; at the end of the year 1859 the Maoris had sold to white settlers 32 million acres in the South Island, and nearly seven million acres in the North Island. The chiefs were becoming anxious about the effects of this transfer of land. The natives employed on public works learned the use of European tools and implements; others obtained money from trade and from the sale of land. These new habits undermined the authority of the chiefs and did not always lead to the improvement of the tribesmen. Moreover the Maoris disliked the attitude taken by Europeans towards them; their opinion of the morals of white men was not high, and they could see that, if they allowed events to take their course, there would be a general disintegration of Maori custom before European individualism.

[1] Sir George Grey (1812–98), s. of an officer who was mortally wounded at Badajoz eight days before his son's birth; b. Lisbon; served with 83rd foot, 1829–39; explored N.W. Australia, 1837; governor of South Australia, 1841–5, New Zealand, 1845–53 and 1861–8, Cape Colony, 1854–9; worked in England in favour of state-aided emigration, 1868–70; returned to New Zealand, 1871; prime minister of New Zealand, 1877–9; returned to England, 1894.

Hence the more active natives began a movement in 1854 for the union of all the tribes under a paramount chief or king. They wanted to put an end to tribal feuds, to limit the sales of land, and to regulate the traffic in liquor and arms. The government did not treat the movement with tact or goodwill. The assembly brought forward a measure to recognize private ownership of native land, and thereby to destroy the tribal rights guaranteed under the treaty of Waitangi. War broke out in 1860 over a disputed title to land in which the governor and his ministers were in the wrong. The Maoris acted with great restraint, and prominent church leaders like Selwyn,[1] who knew the wishes of the natives, protested against the governor's policy.

The military operations were not creditable to the Europeans. The Maoris were good fighters, and skilled in choosing and fortifying positions. The regular troops who took part in the fighting thought better of their enemy than of the settlers. The main fighting was over at the end of 1864, but the war was prolonged until 1869 owing to the vindictive policy of land-confiscation carried out by the New Zealand government. The New Zealand ministers at first proposed to take eight million acres. Great Britain was bearing the greater part of the cost of the war, and the governor put pressure on the colonial authorities to reduce their demands. They insisted on taking nearly three million acres. The Maoris were confirmed in their view that land-grabbing was the real motive of the war, and submitted only when they could fight no longer. For some years they remained sullen and despondent. Fortunately there was a change for the better in the policy of the colonists after the early fears and resentment of the war period had passed. In 1862 a native land act forbade transfers of land until ownership had been proved; a native land court was set up in 1865. Two years later the Maoris were given direct representation in the house of representatives, and in 1872 two Maori chiefs were nominated as members of the upper house. Sir Donald Maclean, the minister of native affairs between 1869 and 1876, did much to conciliate native opinion, and from 1871 the native population ceased to decline.[2]

[1] George Augustus Selwyn (1809–78), s. of a legal author; b. Hampstead; educ. Eton, and St. John's College, Cambridge; first bp. of New Zealand, 1841; learned Maori on his voyage out to New Zealand; organized New Zealand church; bishop of Lichfield, 1868–78. Selwyn College, Cambridge, was founded to commemorate his work.   [2] Intertribal war, aggravated by the introduction of firearms, and

After the Napoleonic war Great Britain held Cape Colony as a port of call and a strategic place which she could not allow to fall into French hands. There was no idea of making a large colony, and for many years the increase of white population came mainly from within the settlement.[1] The colony was based upon slave labour. This fact led, in South Africa as elsewhere, to the view that most types of manual labour were unsuitable for white men. In 1820 the British government voted £50,000 to assist in sending out to the Cape emigrants of some means who would increase the English element in the colony and form a barrier against the Kaffirs on the eastern border. The first settlers did not prosper. Few of them knew anything about farming. They were not given large enough holdings of land; they soon began to complain that they were not allowed to keep predial slaves. Many drifted to the towns, but those who could survive the first difficult years ultimately prospered. The experiment was not repeated, and for the next quarter of a century the authorities at the Cape had not to meet the grievances of dissatisfied and ruined emigrants. There was little agitation for constitutional change, and the imperial government was unlikely to create a new legislative body in a slave-holding colony at a time when these legislatures were giving trouble elsewhere. In 1833 Sir Benjamin D'Urban[2] was sent to the Cape as governor to introduce a modified constitution which made no provision for popular election. D'Urban's main business was with administrative problems: financial economy, emancipation of the slaves, compensation of slave-owners, and the settlement of frontier problems. Economy was easy, if distasteful. The Imperial parliament had already fixed the amount to be paid to slave-owners.

The problem of the frontier meant, in practical terms, the relation between the settlers and the native tribes. British opinion did not understand the significance of the native question in

epidemics of measles and influenza had caused heavy mortality between 1820 and 1840, but in 1858 the native population was over 56,000; in 1871 it was only 37,502. After an increase to 45,400 in 1874, the figures remained about this level for thirty years, when a further increase took place.

[1] As late as 1841, 23,950 emigrants sailed from the United Kingdom for Canada, 14,552 for Australia and New Zealand, and only 130 for the Cape.

[2] Sir Benjamin d'Urban (1777–1849), s. of an army officer; joined 2nd dragoons, 1793; served in the Netherlands and West Indies, 1794–7; and in the Peninsula, 1808–14; governor of Antigua, 1820, Demerara, 1824, British Guiana, 1831, Cape Colony, 1833–7; commander-in-chief in Canada, 1847–9.

South Africa. The warlike tribes to the north and east of the border of Cape Colony were unlike the helpless negroes of the West Indies. Few of these tribes had any more right of long-standing occupation than the Dutch or British settlers. Between 1817 and 1828 Chaka, king of the Zulus, had devastated large areas of South Africa; tribal life was broken, and the country between Natal, Nyasaland, and the Kalahari desert was in chaos and disorder. This pressure of armies and their victims affected the Kaffir tribes on the uncertain borders of the British colony. D'Urban was ordered to make friendly alliances with the Kaffirs. He decided, after a Kaffir attack in 1834, that he could not protect the farmers on the frontier without annexing the territory between the rivers Keiskamma and Kei. At first he wanted to drive out the tribes; he decided against this plan, in the hope that British rule would civilize the Kaffirs. The colonial office refused to accept the annexation. Glenelg thought that the encroachments and violence of the settlers had goaded the Kaffirs into attack. The extension of the frontier would add to the difficulties of defence, and bring the colony into contact with new enemies. There would be no end to this extension: 'we should be engaged in a series of contests desolating to Africa and ruinous to ourselves'. The colonial office suggested a new series of treaties, and recommended the greatest care to avoid in Africa the evils which had followed elsewhere from the inter-course between civilized and savage peoples.

It was impossible to avoid the misfortunes introduced by this contact. The 'adventurous class of Europeans' could not be brought to order on a wild, remote, and sparsely populated frontier; the Kaffirs could not be restrained from acts of reprisal or provocation. Farmers living in isolation, and afraid of raiding bands, were impatient of the enlightened humanitarianism of officials in London; missionaries anxious to protect native rights at times exaggerated their case, and included all settlers in the same condemnation. The policy recommended to D'Urban might be just and reasonable. It was unlikely to satisfy the colonists. The Dutch settlers already had grievances against the imperial government. They thought that the missionaries were encourag-ing natives to withdraw their labour. They objected to the emancipation of slaves, more for general social reasons than for any economic distress caused to themselves; the protesting Dutch farmers did not own many slaves. These farmers were migratory by habit and economic necessity, since by migration alone could they escape from disaster in times of drought. They wanted more land for their cattle, and knew of vast areas of fertile land beyond the frontier; they were used to relying upon themselves for defence against native raids, and there would be little change of condition in this respect if they went out beyond the frontiers of the colony.

The reversal of D'Urban's project of annexation was the final incentive to the 'great trek'. Between 1835 and 1837 some 5,000 men, women, and children—followed in the next few years by many others—crossed the Orange river, and set up their homes in new country. The history of every frontier advance had been a trek of ox-wagons; this movement differed from earlier advances in that the farmers decided to set up a state of their own. They declared in a manifesto of February 1837: 'We quit this colony under the full assurance that the English Government has nothing more to require of us, and will allow us to govern ourselves without its interference in future.' The colonial office thought badly of the migration. Glenelg wrote to Sir George Napier, who had succeeded D'Urban in 1837, that

the motives of this emigration are sufficiently obvious . . . they are the same motives as [*sic*] have, in all ages, compelled the strong to encroach on the weak, and the powerful and unprincipled to wrest by force or fraud, from the comparatively feeble or defenceless, wealth or property or dominion. . . . Opportunities of uncontrolled self-indulgence and freedom from the restraints of law and settled society, are, it would appear, in all countries, irresistible temptations to the inhabitants of the borderland of civilization.

Glenelg could not agree that the settlers had ceased to be British subjects; they had only removed themselves 'beyond the reach of Her Majesty's protection, by measures which Her Majesty altogether discountenances and condemns'.[1]

Within a few years the trekkers raised a difficult question. The greater number, after fighting with the Zulus, went to Natal. The British government had already refused to annex Natal, though a small number of traders were settled there. The establishment of an independent Boer republic in Natal was another matter. In 1843, after a good deal of hesitation, Natal was proclaimed a British colony, and the Dutch retired.

[1] Bell and Morrell, pp. 488–9.

The restoration of order attracted large numbers of natives, many of them refugees whose tribal organization had disappeared. On the advice of local opinion, the government decided in 1849 to create 'locations', or special areas of settlement for these natives. The decision was taken during Grey's period of office at the colonial office. Grey disliked any plan of segregation; he was afraid that 'if the policy of isolating the natives should be adopted, it would too probably end, sooner or later, in their expulsion or extermination when the European inhabitants should increase in numbers so as to require additional space. No Government would be strong enough to save them from this fate.'[1] He agreed that, for some time, separation might be necessary; but he looked forward to the absorption of the natives in a colonial economy which would meet the needs of the two races.

In any case another Kaffir war interrupted the plan. The treaty system failed to work on the eastern frontier. Cattle-raiding, accompanied at times by murder, was as bad as ever. The border farmers wanted a return to D'Urban's plan of annexation, but the colonial office pointed out that this plan would mean a war fought by British troops and paid for by British taxpayers. English opinion was becoming restive at the expense of these wars, and thought that the colonists ought to provide and pay for their own defence. Stephen put the case in language which showed that the official view in London was not unreasonable.

I am quite aware that [the] grievances [of the settlers] have a very different aspect to the sufferers and to observers at many thousand miles' distance and I can well understand that the insecurity of a man's cattle is a sore annoyance. But that it should be a cause of War or of Military inroads is not equally clear: If men will settle in the neighbourhood of marauding Tribes they cannot, I think, claim of their Government that at the National expense they should be rescued from the natural penalty of that improvidence any more than the vine dressers and farmers at the foot of Vesuvius can expect indemnity against the effects of an eruption.[2]

Grey was no less opposed than Glenelg a decade earlier to any increase in British territory in South Africa; he thought that the only way of civilizing the border tribes was by an intermediate stage between annexation and *laisser faire*. The

[1] Ibid., p. 519. [2] Ibid., p. 501.

chiefs might be compelled to accept British protection, and to recognize the authority of a British official—a commandant of Kaffraria—but farmers should not be allowed to settle in their country. On the other hand Sir Harry Smith,[1] as governor of the Cape, believed that direct annexation was the remedy. Grey's change of view is another example of the constraint of facts upon a government anxious to protect natives and unwilling to add to its colonial territories. In November 1846 Grey supported his compromise with the old argument that acquisitions of African land would be 'not merely worthless, but pernicious—the source not of increased strength but of weakness—enlarging the range of our responsibilities, while yielding no additional resources for properly sustaining them'. Nineteen months later Grey wrote: 'I certainly should have preferred that the British territory in South Africa should have been contracted instead of being enlarged, but I am inclined to believe that practically its enlargement was inevitable.'[2] Once again, therefore, British territory was extended to the Kei. Elsewhere Grey also accepted a forward policy. Sir Harry Smith annexed the country between the Orange and the Vaal rivers. Most of the Dutch settlers were ready to accept this solution as the only way of escape from the anarchy beyond the old frontier, while the colonial office thought that there was no other method of protecting the natives.

Neither annexation turned out well. Trouble with the Kaffirs broke out again in 1850, and the assumption of British sovereignty did not put an end to the confusion in the Orange River Territory. *The Times* protested against the cost of Kaffir wars which brought profit to Cape Colony at the expense of the British taxpayer: 'It is generally believed that a large portion of the two millions paid for the last Caffre war found its way into the pockets of jobbers and that the colony could well afford a similar evil if sure of a similar indemnification. . . . We cannot afford to encourage this extravagant taste.'[3]

[1] Sir Harry George Wakelyn Smith, bt. (1787–1860); s. of a surgeon; joined 95th foot, 1808; fought in S. America, the Peninsula, United States, and at Waterloo; sent to Cape Colony, 1828; took part in Kaffir war, 1834–5, and rode 700 miles over rough country in 6 days; adjutant-general of the queen's troops in India, 1840; fought in war against Gwalior; won battle of Aliwal, where he led the final charge; a divisional commander in the battle of Sobraon; governor of the Cape, 1847–52; commanded northern military district of England, 1854–9.

[2] Bell and Morrell, pp. 502 and 510.

[3] *The Times*, 7 Mar. 1851; Bell and Morrell, pp. 519–21.

The failure of Smith's optimistic plans and the growing indignation in Great Britain led Grey to limit British responsibility. The Sand River Convention of January 1852 recognized the Boers beyond the Vaal as possessing a full right 'to manage their own affairs and to govern themselves', on condition that they did not allow slavery within their territory. Two years later the Bloemfontein Convention handed over the government of the country between the Orange river and the Vaal 'to the representatives delegated by the inhabitants to receive it', and freed these inhabitants from their allegiance to the British Crown. The annexation of Kaffir territory could not be undone, but Grey warned the colonists that they must learn to live on better terms with the natives. He repeated language which had been used for many years past.

While it is due to those persons and their descendants who were induced with the direct sanction of Parliament to leave this country for the purpose of settling in the Eastern division of the Colony, that they should not be abandoned without aid. . . in a position of so much danger, their right to look for the support of the mother country is by no means without its limits. . . . Beyond the very limited extent of territory required for the security of the Cape of Good Hope as a naval station, the British Crown and nation have no interest whatever in maintaining any territorial dominion in Southern Africa.[1]

Throughout this troubled period the grant of representative institutions to Cape Colony was settled without much difficulty. The principle had already been conceded elsewhere; the details mattered little. In 1849 the imperial government decided to give a bicameral legislature to the colony. The grant was made in 1853. Natal was separated from the Cape Colony in 1856, and allowed a partially elected assembly. The grant of responsible government was not a particularly pleasant gift to Cape Colony, because the colonists found that responsibility implied duties as well as privileges. They were told that they must pay for the troops employed for their protection. They objected to this payment, and maintained that the troops were necessary owing to the mistaken policy of an executive over which they had no control. They had thus to choose between taking on the burdens attached to responsible government and leaving power in the hands of the governor and his officials. The officials themselves did not approve of giving full responsibility to a colony

[1] Bell and Morrell, p. 529.

in which there was a large majority of natives, while the white population was not homogeneous, and was scattered over areas so far apart that the eastern settlers could not afford to spend long periods of time in Capetown. The final decision was taken in 1872, in spite of resistance from the eastern districts. The history of the next fifty years shows how little any of those concerned with the politics of South Africa were able to foresee the future; but this future belonged to a different and a new age. Already, before 1870, the discoveries of diamonds and gold were foreshadowing this new age,[1] in which there was a change of opinion about the British Empire, and a period of conscious imperialism succeeded a period of resigned acceptance of dissolution. In any case the transition to a new age was less abrupt than is sometimes thought. Among the governing class in Great Britain before 1870 'separatism was only an opinion, not a policy,' and as an opinion it was based to a considerable extent on the belief that the colonists themselves would insist on full independence. There was, however, little or no demand of this kind from the colonial side. It is commonly argued that the reason for the change in British opinion was a matter of 'big business' interests. There were, obviously, such interests, but it should not be forgotten that the change of opinion coincided with the enlargement of the franchise in Great Britain. The relations and friends of the British emigrants to the colonies, and the emigrants themselves, already looked on the 'empire' not as a political or military embarrassment, but as a 'Greater Britain'[2] beyond the seas.

[1] The discovery of diamonds in Griqualand after 1865 resulted in the reluctant annexation of the area by the British government, partly to suppress the anarchy of the early mining settlements and partly to prevent an extension westwards of the slave-hunting areas under the control of the two Dutch republics. The rich Witwatersrand goldfield was not discovered until 1886.

[2] Sir Charles Dilke's book with this title was published in 1868.

III

INDIA

IN the year 1813, a quarter of a century after the opening of his trial, Warren Hastings appeared before the house of commons in committee to give evidence in the matter of the renewal of the East India Company's charter. As he left the house the members rose to their feet and stood bareheaded. This gesture was not merely an act of reparation; it was a sign that English opinion was beginning to take a pride in the work done by the subjects of the Crown and servants of the Company in India. In 1786 the lands under the control of the Company were Bengal, Bihar, Chittagong, and Benares in the valley of the Ganges, the Circars north of the Coromandel coast, Madras and a small area in the hinterland of the Carnatic, the town of Bombay and the adjacent island of Salsette. In 1813, when Lord Moira[1] became governor-general, the Ganges valley (excluding territory left to the nawab of Oudh) from Rohilkhand and the upper waters of the Jumna to the sea, the west coast from Goa to Travancore, and the whole of the east coast were British possessions. The greater part of Oudh, Travancore, Mysore, where the raja had lost a great deal of his territory, and the large kingdom of Hyderabad were under the protection of the Company. Ranjit Singh in the Punjab, the most powerful prince of the north-west, was a faithful if somewhat overwhelming ally. The power of the Mahrattas was broken; the French danger had vanished. The Company might well give orders that no more annexations were to be made.

It was unlikely that the existing limits would be kept. The frontiers of British territory were politically ragged and strategically unsound. For more than seven hundred miles along the valley of the Ganges the frontier was open on the north to hill tribes who would recognize defeat only on an overwhelming scale. The watershed dividing the river systems of the Ganges from those of the Indus was less than a thousand feet high; there was no physical obstacle in the way of extending the

[1] Created marquis of Hastings, 1817. For his early career see vol. xii of this *History*.

hinterland of British power on the west coast until it reached the valley of the Ganges. The interests of commerce and of peace made this extension desirable. The amirs of Sind, who controlled the lower waters of the Indus, misgoverned their subjects and took toll of traffic on the river. Mahratta chiefs in the country north-east of Bombay tolerated and even supported the robber bands, known as Pindaris, who plundered Central India every year. Moreover Indian society was, politically, in a state of decomposition. The Indian states bordering the areas of British rule went the way of all eastern despotisms based on conquest without administrative organization. Few treaties lasted the lifetime of the prince who signed them; fewer still outlived the anarchy and disputed successions which followed the death of a conquering raja. No treaties could be made with robber bands.

If agreement on a stable frontier were difficult, conquest was easy, and might be justified because it brought law and order. Cornwallis once wrote that 'a brigade of our sepoys would easily make anybody Emperor of Hindostan'. Since Cornwallis's time the military strength and prestige of the army had increased. The British troops were better; the possibility of a coalition of Indian enemies was more remote, and after 1812 there was no danger that this coalition would be supported by a European power. The chief difficulty about a policy of conquest was the cost of operations and the upkeep of a large army. Here again it might be held that, in the long run, an increase in the extent of territory under British control would mean a saving of money. Sir Charles Metcalfe,[1] one of the great administrators of the early nineteenth century, wrote that if the lands already acquired could not provide an efficient army 'we must look to an increase of territory by conquest over our enemies in the interior of India. There is no doubt that opportunities will arise for effecting such conquests, for with the utmost moderation and justice upon our part, misunderstandings and wars in the

[1] Charles Theophilus Metcalfe (1785–1846), bt., 1st Baron Metcalfe; s. of a major in the Bengal army, who became a director of the E.I.C.; educ. Eton; appointed to a Bengal writership, 1801; sent on a special mission to Lahore, and negotiated treaty with Ranjit Singh, 1809; resident at Delhi, 1811, and Hyderabad, 1820; member of the supreme council, 1827; provisional governor-general of India, Mar. 1835 to Mar. 1836; retired from the service of the Company owing to differences of opinion over the removal of restrictions on the liberty of the press in India, 1838; governor of Jamaica, 1839–42; governor-general of Canada, 1843–5; resigned owing to ill health.

course of time will be occasionally unavoidable.' The aim of British policy should be 'to apply the net revenues of conquered countries to the maintenance of additional force, and the acquisition of additional force to the achievement of new conquests, on just occasions—thus growing in size and increasing in strength as we proceed, until we can with safety determine to confine ourselves within fixed limits, and abjure all further conquests'.[1]

British India was already large enough to make the Company's rule anomalous, and its trading monopoly absurd. On the renewal of the charter in 1813 the Company kept its political and administrative functions because parliament was afraid of the powerful instrument which the control of Indian patronage would put in the hands of the government at home. The India act of 1784[2] had given the direction of policy to six commissioners for the affairs of India, known as the board of control; the president of this board soon overshadowed his fellow commissioners; after 1812 he was always a member of the cabinet. The orders of the board were transmitted to India by a secret committee of three directors of the Company. The 'proprietors', or shareholders, could not annul or even suspend any resolution of the directors which had the approval of the board. Executive authority in India was vested in a governor-general and a council of three members. Thus the Company remained a body which 'maintained armies and retailed tea'; on the other hand, the fact that, at least in name, it carried out the work of government led to the restriction, and finally, in 1833, to the abolition of its trading activities. The search for markets during the Napoleonic wars had strengthened the demand that trade with India should be free to all Englishmen. In 1813 the directors agreed to give licences to traders who sailed ships of not less than 350 tons—a fair tonnage for this trade. The Company retained for itself a monopoly of the China trade, and of the export trade with the mainland of Europe. Ten years later trade with India in all commodities except tea was freed from restriction, but the China monopoly was maintained.

The India act of 1833 ordered the Company 'with all convenient speed [to] close their commercial business, and make

---

[1] Quoted in E. Thompson and G. T. Garratt, *The Rise and Fulfilment of British Rule in India*, pp. 266–7.
[2] See vol. xii of this *History*, pp. 274–5.

sale of all their merchandise, stores and effects, at home and abroad, distinguished in their account books as commercial assets'. As compensation the proprietors received an annuity of £630,000 charged on the territorial revenues of India. The bargain was not a bad one, since the average annual profits of the Company's trade had declined by a half in fifteen years. Even before 1815 the character of Indian trade was changing. The export of cotton to Great Britain began, on a small scale, with the exclusion of the American supply in 1812–14. On the other hand manufacturers in Great Britain undersold imported cotton piece-goods from India, and found a market for British cotton goods in the East. The adoption of blue uniforms in the navy encouraged the development of indigo-planting in India. Indian jute had already been tried, in 1795, as a substitute for hemp, and the invention of new processes in 1833 gave a sudden impetus to the trade. A greater demand was created twenty years later, when the Crimean war cut off Russian supplies of hemp and flax. Few Europeans took advantage of the opening of Indian trade between 1813 and 1833. There were in 1828 only 2,016 Europeans in India unconnected with the service of the Crown or the Company; but the majority of these were traders, and the exploration of new lines of business was better left in their hands. Between 1834 and 1856 the export trade of India increased by 188 per cent., from £7,990,000 to £23,000,000. and the import trade increased by 227 per cent., from £4,260,000 to £13,400,000.[1]

This economic transformation was the background to the extension of territory and improvement of administration under successive governors-general between 1815 and 1857. The Company's servants showed in peace and war the characteristics of their country and their time. Their sense of responsibility for the welfare of India increased as more of the country came under British control. Sir Thomas Munro, who governed Madras between 1820 and 1827, wrote that

we should look upon India, not as a temporary possession, but as one which is to be maintained permanently, until the natives shall in some future age have abandoned most of their superstitions and prejudices, and become sufficiently enlightened, to frame a regular government for themselves, and to conduct and preserve it.

[1] These facts were stated in a memorandum drawn up by J. S. Mill, addressed by the Company to parliament in 1858.

Whenever such a time shall arrive, it will probably be best for both countries that the British control should be withdrawn.[1]

Munro did not attempt to consider how long this process of enlightenment would take, since he was arguing against those who believed any such improvement impossible. His arguments were those of liberal and radical reformers at home; he pointed out that the change for which he hoped in India 'was at one time in Britain itself at least as hopeless as it is here'. In India, as elsewhere, reformers looked to education as the means of fitting a people for self-government. Mountstuart Elphinstone,[2] governor of Bombay from 1819 to 1824, drew up a minute on the need for an educational system in India.

It is now well understood that in all countries the happiness of the poor depends in a great measure on their education. It is by means of it alone that they can acquire those habits of prudence and self-respect from which all other good qualities spring. . . . If there be a wish to contribute to the abolition of the horrors of self-immolation, and of infanticide, and ultimately to the destruction of superstition in India, it is scarcely necessary now to prove that the only means of success lie in the diffusion of knowledge.[3]

Elphinstone was a fine scholar, but the knowledge which he wanted to spread in India was that of western Europe, and, although there might be differences of opinion about the extent to which Indians should be encouraged to study their own classics, the weight of opinion inclined to Macaulay's cocksure judgement that 'a single shelf of a good European library was worth the whole native literature of India and Arabia'.[4] There was, indeed, little modern vernacular literature, and not much prose literature of any kind. On this 'westernizing' view, which was shared by progressive Indians, higher education must be given in a European language; obviously the English

[1] Quoted, from a minute by Sir Thomas Munro in 1824, in Ramsay Muir, *The Making of British India, 1756–1858*, pp. 284–5.

[2] Mountstuart Elphinstone (1779–1859), s. of 11th Baron Elphinstone; b. Dunbartonshire; educ. Edinburgh high school, and privately; went to India, 1796; attached to Wellesley's staff, and fought at Assaye and Argaum; resident at Nagpur, 1804; ambassador to Afghanistan, 1808; resident at Poona, 1810–19; governor of Bombay, 1819–27; declined governor-generalship of India and a special mission to Canada; wrote a *History of India*. Elphinstone was almost alone among the great Indian civil servants and soldiers of his time in having no strong religious views. He was much influenced by Bentham, and designed a *Panopticon* suitable for Indian conditions. [3] Ramsay Muir, p. 297. [4] Ibid., p. 299.

language had the strongest claim. The subjects of literary study would be the classics of western liberalism, the books which had trained Englishmen, and, doubtless, would train Indians, in the art of self-government.[1] Elphinstone assumed that, as a result of education, Indians would want self-government. He argued plainly and honestly that the only other policy was one of 'depressing the natives', and that, ultimately, it would be better 'for our honour and interest, as well as for the welfare of mankind, that we should resign our power into the hands of the people for whose benefit it is entrusted'.

Education would be useless without an improvement of material conditions. Here again the English rulers of India were true to the practical, positive spirit of their age. The improvement of conditions was carried out under great difficulties, and required persistence of will and constructive ability of the highest order. The value of this work to India cannot be over-rated; the strong hand of English administration kept most of India clear of the financial speculators, of every European nation, who would otherwise have fastened upon Indian potentates as they exploited the resources of other oriental states. This service, considered merely in terms of money, was an immense gain to the Indian taxpayers.

Dalhousie's report on his governor-generalship in 1856 ended with a statement that henceforward every lieutenant-governor, and the chief officer of every province, would be required to make an annual report upon the progress made during the year in the principal departments of the civil and military administration. It was assumed that this progress would be unbroken, and that the Indian population welcomed the improvements which western science and western enterprise were bringing to India. Yet there is one significant fact. Dalhousie's account was written in the year before the outbreak of the mutiny. He was careful to say that war or rebellion might break out in India

[1] Although official encouragement was given primarily to the diffusion of western knowledge, the presence of Englishmen in India had many indirect effects upon the development of a purely Indian culture. The Company's college of Fort William at Calcutta (opened in 1801) did much to interest civil servants in Indian languages, history, and customs, and gave Bengali a recognized standing. The missionaries introduced printing in the vernacular; William Carey (1761–1834), Baptist missionary, scholar, and professor at Fort William, composed dictionaries of Bengali and other languages, and wrote five Indian grammars. Elphinstone (who described the education of Indians as 'our highroad back to Europe') defended the maintenance of a chair of Sanskrit at the Company's college at Poona.

at any time 'in quarters where they were the least to be expected. . . . No man, therefore, can ever prudently hold forth assurance of continued peace in India.'[1] He did not ask whether British rule in India was attractive as well as successful and advantageous. The question would not have been entirely fair. Indian civilization was at a low ebb before the English conquests, and government was little more than military authority, competent or incompetent, according to the temperament and capacity of the ruler and his agents. The habit of passive acquiescence could not be changed in a generation. British methods and western technique were bound to make some inroads into this age-long acceptance of arbitrary power. An attitude of mind in the governing class entirely strange to Indian ways and expectations would not be understood at once. The results of the age of reform in Europe did not correspond with the hopes of reformers. In India the reformers were less optimistic, and already some of the clearest minds had realized that the peace and justice of British rule were not bringing content. Thirty years before the mutiny Sir John Malcolm wrote that 'our administration, though just, is cold and rigid. If it creates no alarm, it inspires little, if any, emulation. The people are protected, but not animated or attached. It is rare that any native of India living under it can suffer injury or wrong; but still more rare that he can be encouraged or elevated by favour or distinction.' Hastings, as governor-general, believed that British officials were 'too dry with the natives, who give us high credit for justice, but I fear they regard us in general as very repulsive'.[2]

Reforms of a material kind did little to bridge 'the immeasurable distance between us and the natives'. In many respects this distance widened after 1815. The parliamentary committee which reported upon the renewal of the charter in 1833 advocated greater employment of Indians in the administration. The charter act contained a clause that 'no native of India, nor any natural-born subject of His Majesty, . . . shall be disabled from holding any place, office, or employment, by reason only of his religion, place of birth, descent or colour', but little was done to give positive effect to this recommendation in any of

[1] Ramsay Muir, p. 355.
[2] Malcolm, *Memoir of Central India*, ii. 264, and Hastings, *Private Journal*, i. 338, quoted in Thompson and Garratt, p. 281.

the higher posts. The reformers wanted energetic officials, and suspected that Indians would be half-hearted in putting down barbarous and cruel customs. Moreover, the new type of Englishman in India was more withdrawn and aloof than the English of the eighteenth century. Elphinstone wrote to Malcolm in 1819: 'The fault of our younger politicians—who have never seen the Indian States in the days of their power—is a contempt for the natives, and an inclination to carry everything with a high hand.'[1] Elphinstone regarded Malcolm as the last of the older type: 'the later statesmen are more imperious and harsher in their notions, and reckon more on force . . . and less on affection'.[2] There were other and better reasons for the change. The new generation was less complacent over the corruption of Hinduism and the cruelties which it allowed. British officers and administrators of India, affected by the revival of religion and the greater strictness of moral tone in English society, refused to live the semi-Indianized lives of their predecessors, while the Indian Christian communities, limited mainly to the south, had no effect in bridging the gulf between a western and an eastern culture. The increase in the number of Englishwomen in the country made social relations less easy and more self-conscious. The voyage to India took less time in steamships than in sailing-vessels; hence fewer Englishmen spent very long periods in India without intervals of leave.[3] There was less inclination to regard India as a home. The increasing lack of interest in Indian architecture and craftsmanship was partly due to this change in attitude. The bungalows of the British garrison and officials were not built as permanent homes. The events of the mutiny added terribly to this estrangement between rulers and ruled, but the antagonism had been latent throughout the first half of the nineteenth century, in spite of the unselfish devotion to Indian interests of men like Metcalfe, Elphinstone, Bentinck, Dalhousie, Outram, the two Lawrences, and a host of unnamed soldiers and servants of the Company.

For some years after the arrival of Hastings as governor-general the consolidation of British power involved serious war.

[1] Quoted in Thompson and Garratt, p. 306.
[2] J. S. Cotton, *Elphinstone*, p. 128.
[3] From 1840 the Peninsular and Oriental Steamship Company ran regular services on either side of the Isthmus of Suez.

The first of these wars settled the northern frontier of Bengal, and put an end to the plundering raids of the Gurkhas of Nepal. Attempts had been made to stop the raids by an exchange of lands. The Gurkhas would not give up their claims to country under British control, and Hastings decided to deal with them once and for all. The campaign began in November 1814. It was not glorious. The Gurkhas were only some 12,000 strong; but they were brave soldiers, fighting in territory well suited to their raiding tactics. The older British commanders were used to war in the plains, where the enemy ran away from a resolute attack.[1] In the mountains of Nepal it was not easy even to find the enemy. The troops and transport animals suffered from the extremes of heat and cold, and the officers learned caution only after sharp reverses. Major-General Sir D. Ochterlony was the one commander to escape these minor defeats; it was due mainly to his patience that the war ended in March 1816. The Gurkhas gave up most of their claims to the lowlands, and surrendered the provinces of Kumaon and Garhwal in western Nepal. The treaty left the site of Simla in British possession, and the experience of the war showed the advantage of bringing troops to the hills in the Indian summer.

During the Gurkha war Hastings was anxious about the safety of central India. The Calcutta government had one battalion of Indian infantry to guard the frontier line from Bundelkhand to Cuttack, and robber bands of Pindaris had appeared in force in the autumn of 1814. In 1815 a large party passed from end to end of the Nizam's dominions, and was kept out of British territory only by the unusually high waters of the river Kistna. Another party early in 1816 crossed the river and for twelve days plundered land in British possession. In 1817 Hastings decided to attack the raiders in the country from which they came and to destroy their organization. This plan meant operations on a large scale. Hesitation or defeat would bring the Mahratta chiefs against the British forces. One section of the

---

[1] Elphinstone's account of the beginning of the battle of Assaye—one of Wellesley's hardest-won victories—may be taken as typical of many battles fought in the plains. 'Somebody said, "Sir! that is the enemy's line." The General said, "Is it? Ha, damme, so it is." ' Elphinstone's description of the battle of Argaum—two months after Assaye—shows how lightly he could take a lesser engagement against Indian cavalry. 'All the time I was at pains to see how the people looked, and every gentleman seemed at ease as much as if he were riding a-hunting.' Sir T. E. Colebrooke, *Life of Elphinstone*, i. 89.

army was directed to cut off and encircle the robbers, while another section prevented the Mahratta princes from breaking into central India to help the Pindaris. Hastings thought that the enemy, with full Mahratta support, might bring 130,000 horse and 87,000 foot into the field. His own armies included about 10,000 Europeans, 70,000 Indian regular troops, 34,000 irregulars, and 303 guns.

The British forces were none too many. The enveloping movement was begun in the summer of 1817, but floods in the Deccan delayed the concentration of the southern army, and the northern army suffered from cholera. Three of the Mahratta princes, Holkar of Indore, Appa Sahib Bhonsle, regent of Nagpur, and the peshwa of Poona, turned against the British but were defeated before the end of 1817. Appa Sahib of Nagpur was taken as a hostage. Sindhia of Gwalior showed signs of attempting to join the rebels, but was compelled to sign a treaty promising to intervene on the British side. The fifth Mahratta chief, the gaikwar of Baroda, dared not move. The peshwa held out until the summer of 1818, and the last native stronghold, Asirgarh, fell in April 1819. The settlement after the war brought the boundary of British influence to the Sutlej, and left the amirs of Sind and the Sikh Ranjit Singh in the Punjab the only independent princes in India. The Pindaris disappeared for ever. Holkar lost half his territory. The raja of Nagpur also lost territory, and became a British vassal. Nineteen small Rajput states came under British protection. The peshwa of Poona was deposed, and retired to live near Cawnpore. The British commander promised him a pension of £80,000 a year; Hastings thought the sum much too large, but the promise was kept. The raja of Satara, whose effective powers the peshwas of Poona had long usurped, was re-established in a small principality.

Two other annexations, outside India, took place while Hastings was governor-general. Between 1803 and 1814 the British had occupied the coast-line of Ceylon, and left the interior of the island to the king of Kandy. Towards the end of the year 1814 a revolution broke out against the cruelties of the king. The king's forces attacked rebels who escaped into British territory. Sir John Brownrigg, as governor, had already protested against the mutilation of native traders from the British area; early in 1815 he decided to attack Kandy. The king's own subjects handed him over within a month to the British forces, and his territory was annexed.

In 1819 Sir Stamford Raffles[1] persuaded Hastings to recommend to the East India Company the purchase of the island of Singapore from the Sultan of Johore. Raffles had found that the Dutch had overlooked this small and almost uninhabited island in their attempts to secure all the important positions in the Malay archipelago.[2] He realized the strategic and commercial possibilities of the place, and directed its early development with such zeal and competence that within four years a bare swamp had become a settlement with an annual trade of £2,500,000.

Hastings settled the north-west frontier of India for twenty years. His successor, Lord Amherst, had to deal with the ill-defined eastern boundary of the province of Bengal. To the north of Chittagong lay the kingdom of Assam; to the east and south the military principality of the kings of Ava in Burma. The kings of Ava had begun their conquests as minor chieftains in the middle of the eighteenth century. By 1793 they had taken upper and lower Burma, and were near to Chittagong. Their rule was very cruel, and numbers of Burmese took refuge in British territory. The counter-raids organized by these refugees sometimes gave the king of Ava a pretext for invading British territory. In 1816–17 the king began to threaten Assam; in the following year he claimed Chittagong and other border towns. Hastings wisely treated his letter as a forgery and took no notice of the claim. The Burmese were now defeated by a Siamese army, and for the next four years did not trouble the

---

[1] Sir Thomas Stamford Raffles (1781–1826), s. of a sea-captain, and born at sea off Jamaica; appointed to a clerkship at East India House at the age of fourteen; sent to Penang, 1805, where his skill in languages and administrative ability soon brought him promotion; took part in the reduction of Java, 1811; lieutenant-governor of Java, 1811–15, and resident at Bencoolen, Sumatra; explored Sumatra, and given charge of British interests east of the straits of Malacca; advised the purchase of Singapore, 1819, and organized its administration, 1822–3; sailed for England, 1824, on a ship which caught fire (Raffles lost all his notes and memoranda and collections worth £20,000–£30,000); assisted in the foundation of the Zoological Society, of which he was the first president. In spite of his weak constitution, and the time which he gave to administrative work, Raffles was an oriental scholar, botanist, and anthropologist of high reputation, while his work in freeing slaves, including those belonging to the Company, and in supporting Christian missions and native education was of great social importance.

[2] Java was given back to the Dutch in the treaty settlement after the Napoleonic war. They obtained Bencoolen in exchange for Malacca in 1824.

Indian government. In 1822 they annexed Assam; less than twelve months later they landed soldiers on the island of Shahpuri, near Chittagong, and drove out a small British guard. Amherst only remonstrated with them, and thereby made them more insolent. They came back to Shahpuri early in 1824, and invaded British territory on the mainland. Amherst was now forced to declare war.

War in Burma was a difficult undertaking. The country was little explored and extremely unhealthy. It was almost impossible to lead a large force through the mountainous and tangled country east of Chittagong, and the military authorities decided to attack by water.[1] The principal cities of the kingdom were on the banks of the Irrawaddy, and a fleet of boats could be brought some four or five hundred miles up stream. Unfortunately the high command in India assumed that the native population, out of hatred for their governors, would take the British side, and supply the expedition with boats and provisions. No other arrangements were made for a force of eleven thousand officers and men. This force occupied Rangoon without much resistance in May 1824. The troops arrived just before the rains. As the Irrawaddy was impassable for nearly six months, the expedition was held up at Rangoon with no land transport and no supplies except salt pork, rice, and biscuit, most of which went bad in the hot climate; five months passed before the Indian command sent transport animals and proper food. Meanwhile the troops were too weak to resist disease. The five British regiments which landed at Rangoon in May numbered about 3,500 rank and file. More than 3,100 were dead before the end of the campaign, and nineteen out of twenty deaths were due to disease. Little was done even on the military side. Sir Archibald Campbell, the British commander-in-chief, was not ready to move up stream until February 1825. The Burmese were very skilful in building stockades and earthworks, but in April their ablest leader, Bandula, was killed and the expedition reached Prome, the chief city of Lower Burma. It was impossible to cover the remaining two hundred miles to Ava before the breaking of the monsoon. Fighting began again in November after the rains. The Burmese were heavily

[1] Among the naval commanders in the expedition was Captain Marryat (see below, p. 554) and among the ships the first steamboat used by Great Britain in war.

defeated in December, but would not accept the British terms until the troops were within forty-five miles of Ava. If the enemy had left Ava as they left Rangoon, they would have put the British expedition in an awkward position, but the king's hold on his subjects was not strong enough to allow further resistance. The king agreed to cede Arakan and Tenasserim, to renounce all right of interference in Assam, Cachar, and Jaintia, and to pay an indemnity of a million pounds. The delta of the Irrawaddy remained in Burmese hands, but British territory now extended along the sea coast from the Irrawaddy northwards without a break to Chittagong.[1]

For the next ten years there were no military operations on a large scale in India. These years of peace were a gain to the finances of the country. The Burmese war had cost over £13,000,000, and the first business of the governor-general was to put an end to a long series of financial deficits. Lord William Bentinck,[2] who succeeded Amherst in 1828, was a whig of the old school, a cold, unsympathetic man, distrusting those who worked with him, and disliked in spite of his courage and public spirit. Bentinck's economies were not likely to make him popular.[3] He reduced the charges of the civil and military services, and recovered part of the land revenues alienated by fraud. He simplified the judicial system, increased the number and the salaries of native judges, and substituted vernacular languages for Persian in the law courts. He began the ten years' work of settling the taxation of the north-west provinces, a vast affair affecting an area inhabited by 23,000,000 people. On his own responsibility he abolished *suti*, the burning of widows, a practice based upon a doubtful interpretation of Hindu sacred texts, and maintained largely owing to the financial interest of heirs

---

[1] The Burmese war had repercussions in India. There were signs of unrest in the Mahratta country, and a usurper at Bharatpur turned out the sovereign recognized by the Company. The capture of Bharatpur, the strongest fortress in India, by Lord Combermere in January 1826 had a sobering effect upon the rest of the country.

[2] William Cavendish-Bentinck (1774–1839), 2nd s. of the 3rd duke of Portland; entered the army, 1791; attached to Suvorov's headquarters, 1799; governor of Madras, 1803–7; recalled because the directors thought him partly responsible for the mistakes leading to the mutiny at Vellore (see below, p. 430); served in the Peninsular war, 1808–10; envoy at the court of Ferdinand of the Two Sicilies, and commander-in-chief of the British forces in Sicily, 1811–14.

[3] There appears to be no reliable evidence for the story that Bentinck wanted to pull down the Taj Mahal, in order to sell the marbles, and that the building was saved because the auction of material from the palace at Agra proved unsatisfactory.

to property. He supported Sleeman[1] in the suppression of the *thugs* (i.e. 'cheats'), a fraternity of professional assassins who sheltered themselves under vows to the goddess Kali. Bentinck did not want to interfere with the native princes of India, but he deposed the raja of Coorg for cruelty, annexed Cachar, at the request of the inhabitants, and assumed the entire government of Mysore owing to the maladministration of the raja. He renewed the long-standing alliance with Ranjit Singh, and, just before leaving India, obtained a treaty with the amirs of Sind opening the Indus to merchants and traders. He took these last measures partly because he was afraid of Russian aggression. Fear of Russia led his successor, Lord Auckland,[2] into the most disastrous policy undertaken by any governor-general.

Auckland's appointment was a result of the change of government in England. Peel had chosen Lord Heytesbury;[3] Melbourne returned to office before the nomination was confirmed, and gave the post to a whig politician.[4] Auckland agreed with Palmerston's anti-Russian policy; unfortunately the state of affairs within and without the frontiers of British India allowed him every chance of reckless action. Bentinck had already noticed evidence of Russian designs. Persia had fallen under Russian influence since the Russo-Persian war of 1826–8, and was being encouraged to look in Afghanistan for compensation for territory lost to Russia. Afghanistan had been unusually disturbed for a quarter of a century; Shah Suja, who had been expelled from the kingship in 1809, was supported by the British in honourable exile at Ludhiana. Dost Mahomed, the chief of

[1] Sir William Henry Sleeman (1788–1856), of yeoman family; b. Stratton, Cornwall; obtained a cadetship in the Bengal army in 1809; served in the Nepal war, and thenceforward employed in political work; suppressed *thugs* and *dacoits*, 1839–41; political resident in Gwalior, 1843–9; resident at Lucknow, 1848–54, when he opposed Dalhousie's annexation of Oudh.

[2] George Eden, 2nd baron and 1st earl of Auckland (1784–1849); a supporter of the whigs in the house of lords; president of the board of trade and master of the mint, 1830; first lord of the admiralty, 1834 and 1835; governor-general of India, 1835–41; first lord of the admiralty, 1846–8.

[3] William A'Court, Baron Heytesbury (1779–1860); secretary of legation at Naples, 1801; envoy extraordinary at Naples, 1814, and Madrid, 1822; ambassador at Lisbon, 1824–8, and St. Petersburg, 1828–32, where he formed a high opinion of Nicholas I; lord-lieutenant of Ireland, 1844–6.

[4] Auckland was the first governor-general to be appointed with the title of 'governor-general of India'. Hitherto the title had been 'governor-general of the presidency of Fort William in Bengal'. Until 1854 the governor-general continued to administer Bengal (see also below, p. 429).

the Barakzai clan, was amir at Kabul, but his authority was hardly recognized by his brothers at Kandahar, and not recognized at all by a prince of Shah Suja's allegiance at Herat. Ranjit Singh had seized Peshawar in 1834, and in 1837 the Persians began the siege of Herat. This important strategical post might become the gateway for a Russian approach to India, although there was, in fact, no likelihood of a Russian invasion. Auckland was therefore ready to listen to advisers in India who suggested a great strategical combination to secure the north-west frontier. This advice came from men who had been seconded for political service mainly owing to their linguistic ability. Sir William Hay Macnaghten,[1] one of the ablest of the political officers, persuaded Auckland that if Afghanistan were left to its fate Russia and Persia would threaten the Indian frontier. If the British authorities supported Dost Mahomed they would have trouble with Ranjit Singh over Peshawar. On the other hand, if they could persuade Ranjit Singh to restore Shah Suja in Afghanistan, they would be free from any Russian danger. They could obtain Ranjit Singh's help by a promise of British co-operation and a guarantee of the territory which he had taken from Dost Mahomed.

This scheme had obvious faults. Shah Suja was incapable and unpopular. A prince restored by Sikh and British arms would not win the loyalty of the Afghan chiefs. Ranjit Singh's terms were high; during the negotiations he forced the Indian government to promise to take the leading part in restoring Shah Suja. Dost Mahomed himself wanted to keep on good terms with the British authorities, and turned to Russia only when he found that he could not get British help. Auckland was a conscientious mediocrity, without experience of war or of Indian affairs. The commander-in-chief in India disapproved of the plan. Wellington, who knew India, thought that it would mean a 'perennial march into Afghanistan'. On the other hand the cabinet encouraged the scheme, though with some misgiving.

[1] Sir William Hay Macnaghten (1793–1841), s. of an Indian judge; b. Bushmills, co. Antrim; educ. Charterhouse; went to India as a cadet in the E.I.C. in 1809; appointed to the Bengal civil service, 1814; distinguished himself for his knowledge of Indian languages and customs; published works on Moslem and Hindu law, 1825–9; accompanied Bentinck on a tour of the upper and western provinces, 1830–3; in charge of the secret and political departments of the government secretariat, 1833–7; went with Auckland on a tour of the north-west provinces, 1837; sent on a special mission to Ranjit Singh, 1838, and negotiated the treaty between the governor-general, Ranjit Singh, and Shah Suja.

Hobhouse, the president of the board of control, approved of it before he heard that Auckland had decided to carry it out, and Palmerston wrote to Melbourne that Great Britain would regain her lost ascendancy in Persia, and thereby add to the security of the sultan and 'place the Dardanelles more securely out of the grasp of Russia'.[1] Meanwhile all pretext for the undertaking had gone. The Persians gave up the siege of Herat; the Russian envoy to Dost Mahomed was disavowed by his government.

Auckland's plan of campaign was bad. Since Ranjit Singh refused to allow British troops to march across his country, Auckland agreed that the Sikhs should use the Khyber pass, while the main British army went through Sind to the Bolan pass. The passage through Sind was a violation of the treaty of 1832 opening the Indus to trade on condition that no munitions of war were carried on the river. Auckland made the mistake of putting Shah Suja's own forces under the command of Macnaghten, and omitting to define Macnaghten's relations with the commander-in-chief. The plan involved collaboration between the Bengal and Bombay armies in very difficult country. The authorities in India did not arrange for enough transport. The political officers attached to the expedition suggested military operations without sufficient knowledge of the force, above all of the transport and supplies, necessary to carry them out. The senior military officers were men of little capacity, who repeated the errors of the Nepal and central Indian campaigns; they also quarrelled with Macnaghten and the political staff.

Kandahar was occupied in April 1839 and Ghazni taken by storm in July. Dost Mahomed left Kabul, and Shah Suja was installed in August. Shah Suja now held the three most important strategical points of the country. No military movements on a large scale were possible in winter, and the shah had time to win over the most powerful Afghan chiefs to his side. The Indian government could not keep a large force in Afghanistan, and if Shah Suja were unable to maintain his position with his own troops, trained by British officers, Auckland should have withdrawn the expedition and restored Dost Mahomed. It was soon clear that the shah depended upon the British force, but Macnaghten refused to face the situation. Meanwhile Ranjit Singh died, and there was a risk that the

[1] W. M. Torrens, *Life of Melbourne*, ii. 274.

Sikhs might endanger communications between British India and Afghanistan.

Matters remained in this unsatisfactory state throughout the summer of 1840. In November Dost Mahomed surrendered, and the Indian government failed to use the last chance of withdrawal without too great loss of prestige. Auckland and Macnaghten (whom Wellington described as 'the gentleman employed to command the army') believed that they could take their time about withdrawal. Auckland wanted to cut down the expense of the expedition, and refused to allow proper fortifications to be built for the garrison of Kabul, where Shah Suja had taken the citadel for his seraglio. Auckland also reduced the large subsidies paid to the chiefs to keep open the passes, and the chiefs began to break their agreements. In April 1841, against the wishes of his own commander-in-chief in India, Auckland appointed Major-General Elphinstone[1] to command the forces in Afghanistan. Elphinstone had been a good soldier; but he had no experience of eastern wars, and was a very sick man. He protested against his appointment, and took the command only out of a sense of duty. He was unable to deal with the evils of divided control at Kabul, and merely watched the inevitable beginnings of rebellion.

The end came suddenly. In November 1841 Macnaghten was just about to leave Kabul to take up the governorship of Bombay when his successor, Sir Alexander Burnes, was murdered by a mob. No attempt was made to punish or even to disperse the rebels. No transport or supplies were collected. The British force at Kandahar could not march through the snow to Kabul; a force at Gandamak fell back, through lack of transport, to Jallalabad, in order to keep open the way to India. At the beginning of December, when the garrison was almost starving, Elphinstone and Macnaghten agreed with the rebel chiefs to leave Afghanistan and to release Dost Mahomed. Before the retreat Macnaghten suspected the good faith of the chiefs with whom he had signed a treaty; he opened negotiations with a rival Afghan faction. He was betrayed to Akbar Khan, Dost Mahomed's son, and assassinated. In spite of this murder, Elphinstone went on with the negotiations. He refused to take

[1] William George Keith Elphinstone (1782–1842); s. of a director of the E.I.C. and cousin of Mountstuart Elphinstone; entered the army, 1804; decorated for his conduct at Waterloo; saw no active or regimental service, 1825–39; appointed to the command of the Benares division of the Bengal army, 1839.

the advice of some of his officers that he should seize the citadel, and hold out until relief came in the spring. He would not let the garrison fight their way to Jallalabad. On 6 January 1842 he began a disorderly and dangerous retreat without the greater part of his stores and guns. The army, hampered by a mass of Afghan camp-followers, had to protect the British women and children of the garrison. Akbar Khan could not or would not help them against the tribesmen who attacked at every point. At last the women and children and some of the officers, including Elphinstone himself, were given up as hostages, but the attacks continued. The troops made their last stand in the pass of Jagdallak. One survivor, Dr. Brydon, reached Jallalabad.

As soon as Auckland heard of this disaster he wanted to withdraw from Afghanistan. A force which marched into Kabul and out again would do nothing to restore British prestige, and there was no chance of holding the country. In any case the defeat of British arms would have a serious effect in India, and it might be impossible to spare a large force for an Afghan war. Some steps had to be taken, however, to rescue the prisoners in the hands of Akbar Khan, and the garrisons at Jallalabad and Kandahar.

Auckland's time of office was now over. His successor, Lord Ellenborough,[1] arrived in India at the end of February 1842. Ellenborough first decided upon an expedition on a large scale, to be followed by withdrawal to the east bank of the Indus. Meanwhile the military position improved. India was quiet, and in the north-west a relieving force under General Pollock marched through the Khyber pass to find that the garrison of Jallalabad had defeated its besiegers. Nott was holding out at Kandahar, and there was no reason for an immediate retreat. Ellenborough did not realize the full extent of the recovery, and suddenly ordered the retreat of the armies without even rescuing the prisoners. Nott and Pollock made the excuse that they had not enough transport to move back to India; Ellenborough repeated his instructions for withdrawal, but left it to the

[1] Edward Law, 2nd baron and 1st earl of Ellenborough (1790–1871); educ. Eton and St. John's College, Cambridge; M.P., 1813; lord privy seal in the Wellington administration of 1828; president of the board of control, 1828–30, 1834–5, and 1841; governor-general of India, 1842–4: first lord of the admiralty, 1846, but resigned with Peel; president of the board of control, 1858. Ellenborough held, during his father's lifetime and until his own death, a sinecure office in the court of queen's bench said to have been worth £7,000 a year.

discretion of Nott to retire directly, or through Ghazni, Kabul, and the Khyber. Nott took advantage of this permission; he recaptured and destroyed the fortress of Ghazni, entered Kabul, and joined forces with Pollock. The prisoners were released and the two armies returned to India. Ellenborough published a bombastic proclamation, and ordered the troops to bring back from Ghazni the gates taken from the temple of Somnath in Gujrat in A.D. 1024.[1] The campaign of 1842 had done much to recover lost prestige, but the fact remained that Shah Suja had been assassinated, and that Dost Mahomed had been allowed to return to Kabul.

The conquest of Sind was an indirect result of the Afghan war. Auckland had broken the treaty with the amirs of Sind, and had also insisted on collecting from them tribute formerly paid to Shah Suja. This tribute had been in abeyance for thirty years, and the amirs produced documents sealed by Shah Suja releasing them from payment; Auckland forced upon them a new treaty in 1839 obliging them to pay three lacs of rupees a year for the upkeep of a subsidiary force in their country, and warned them that 'neither the ready power to crush and annihilate them nor the will to call it into action were wanting, if it appeared requisite however remotely for the safety and integrity of the Anglo-Indian Empire or frontier'. After the disaster in Afghanistan the amirs had every temptation to break this treaty. It is possible that they had taken steps to do so, but the Indian government had no proof of the fact. James Outram,[2] one of the bravest and most sympathetic British soldiers who ever served in India, had been political agent in Sind since 1839. The amirs liked him, and might have come to terms with him, but Sir Charles Napier[3] was given charge of the negotiations.

[1] The gates were not, as Ellenborough believed, original, but late copies of those removed from Gujrat.

[2] Sir James Outram, bt. (1803-63); s. of a civil engineer; b. Butterley, Derbyshire; educ. Aberdeen; went to India as a cadet, 1819; served in infantry, 1819-25, and on special work, 1825-38; took part in first Afghan war; agent in Sind, 1839-42; took part in Sind campaign; Resident at Satara, 1845, and Baroda, 1847-51; withdrawn owing to disputes with the Bombay government over methods of suppressing corruption; reinstated in 1854 but soon afterwards appointed governor of Aden; returned to India owing to ill health and appointed Resident of Oudh; recommended the annexation of Oudh; given command of military forces in Persian expedition, 1856-7; took part in relief of Cawnpore and siege of Lucknow; military member of the governor-general's council, 1858-60.

[3] Sir Charles James Napier (1782-1853); s. of an army officer; b. London;

This fierce and indomitable man, a strange figure on his campaigns with his dark spectacles, great aquiline nose, and a beard reaching almost to his waist, made up his mind that the charges against the amirs were well founded. Napier believed, rightly, that the British occupation of Sind would benefit the inhabitants, and that sooner or later there would be trouble with the amirs if they were left alone. He noted in his diary that 'we have no right to seize Sind, but we shall do so, and a very advantageous, useful, humane piece of rascality it will be'. Outram, on the other hand, thought that the treatment of the amirs was 'most tyrannical'. Napier insisted upon the surrender of territory, including Karachi, in return for a release from the tribute. Outram was given the difficult work of persuading the amirs to accept these terms. They agreed to them in February 1843, but could not keep their troops from attacking the residency at Hyderabad. Napier had already destroyed the fortress of Imam Garh—without even declaring war. He wanted to deal with the amirs before the heat of summer, and used the attack on the residency as a pretext for a direct advance. He marched at once with 3,000 men against 20,000 of the enemy, whom he fought at Miani. The battle was typical of English fighting on the plains of India. Napier misjudged the enemy's position, and was saved from disaster by his bravery and determination, and, curiously enough, by the refusal of the sepoys to obey the first orders given to them. The victory settled the fate of Sind. Six of the amirs were captured; others, including the amir of Hyderabad, submitted when Napier told them that the only terms he would offer were 'life and nothing else'. Sher Mahomed, one of the amirs of Morpur, a chief known as 'the Lion',

entered the army, 1794, but went back to school in Ireland; took part in resisting the Irish rebellion of 1798; served in the Peninsula, and was five times wounded at Corunna; had two horses killed under him in 1810, and three months later was again badly wounded; took part in the war of 1812 against the United States; fought as a volunteer against the French in 1815; Resident at Cephalonia, 1822–30, and twice offered commands in the Greek army; declined the governorship of South Australia in 1836; commanded the northern district during the chartist troubles, 1839; accepted an Indian command, 1841; appointed to Sind in 1842, and severely hurt by a rocket soon after landing; fought in the first Sikh war; appointed to succeed Sir Hugh Gough in the second Sikh war; quarrelled with Dalhousie, 1850. His many published works include a number of military pamphlets, a *Dialogue on the Poor Laws*, a treatise on *Colonization, with Some Remarks on Small Farms and Overpopulation*, an historical romance on William the Conqueror, translations from the French, an edition of his wife's book, *The Nursery Governess*, and an unfinished treatise entitled *Defects, Civil and Military, of the Indian Government*.

held out; he was defeated in March, in another of Napier's blind and furious battles. Sind was annexed, though the cabinet disapproved of Ellenborough's policy, and agreed to the annexation only because it had already taken place. The directors, with the approval of Ripon, president of the board of control, censured the governor-general, but left him time for another piece of aggression before recalling him to England.

Ellenborough's attack on Gwalior was more justifiable than the expedition to Sind. The maharaja of Gwalior died without direct heir at the beginning of 1843; his widow, a child of twelve, adopted a boy of eight as an heir. Ellenborough approved of the appointment of a regent. Within a few months the regent was dismissed, and power fell into the hands of the army. The Sikh army had also assumed power in the Punjab. There was a danger that the two armies might unite. Ellenborough therefore revived the treaty of 1804 which entitled the Indian government to keep a subsidiary force in Gwalior. The army of the country was defeated in two battles, and a new treaty transformed Gwalior into a protected state. This step was too much for the cabinet, the directors, and public opinion. Ellenborough was recalled. His own exaggerated language made it difficult to put a moderate interpretation upon his acts, but he found the Indian army depressed by defeat and left it with a new reputation for invincibility. His open preference for soldiers made him many enemies in the civilian administration; after the Afghan expedition, a governor-general might well think it desirable to cut down the power of the political advisers. The annexation of Sind had been an act of doubtful morality, yet Napier was right in describing it as a humane measure from the point of view of the inhabitants. Napier himself set up a model administration in the country, and began a tradition which was imitated with lasting success in the Punjab. Although Ellenborough had little time to carry out any civil reforms, he showed a certain insight in writing to Queen Victoria in 1843 that the position and prestige of the native princes would be better if they were 'the feudatories of an Empress'. His administration was free from any kind of nepotism, and there was a sincerity about his hopes for the 'future prosperity of India if it be governed with due respect for the feelings and even the prejudices, and with a careful regard for the interests, of the people with the resolution to make their well-being the chief object of the Government, and not the pecuniary advantage of the nation of strangers to whom Providence has committed the rule of this distant Empire'.[1]

Ellenborough's fears that the Sikh army would cause trouble were soon justified. His brother-in-law, Sir Henry Hardinge,[2] who succeeded him as governor-general, began to strengthen the garrisons in the north-west. The Sikhs had been in a state of anarchy since the death of Ranjit Singh in 1839. In 1843 Maharaja Sher Singh was murdered. Sher Singh had been friendly to the Indian government, but the Sikh military leaders who now controlled the Punjab were less willing to watch the British annexation of small neighbouring territories. In December 1845 the Sikhs crossed the Sutlej, and met the British and Indian troops at Mudki. The Sikhs were afraid of their own daring; the sepoys were no less frightened of the Sikhs, but, as usual, the direct methods of the British commander, Sir Hugh Gough, defeated the enemy. Gough fought a second action at Firozshah a few days later. If he had been allowed to continue his frontal attacks, he would have won a decisive victory; but Hardinge, as a soldier, insisted on serving under Gough, and, at the same time, as governor-general, ordered that the army should wait for reinforcements. The battle therefore did not begin until late in the afternoon, and, after a night of confusion, ended in an attack at dawn upon the Sikh entrenchments. The Sikhs then went back over the Sutlej into their own country, only to cross the river again when they found that they were not pursued. Sir Harry Smith[3] cut off and defeated one force at Aliwal in January 1846. In February the British won a complete victory at Sobraon. The Sikh army agreed to give up their claims to land on the left bank of the Sutlej, and the Jalandhar Doab between the Sutlej and the Bias. They promised to pay an indemnity of £500,000, and to surrender Kashmir instead of a further payment of £1,000,000. The Indian government

---

[1] *The Indian Administration of Lord Ellenborough*, ed. by Lord Colchester, pp. 64–65, quoted in Thompson and Garratt, pp. 363–4.

[2] Sir Henry Hardinge, 1st Viscount Hardinge of Lahore (1785–1856); s. of a clergyman; fought in the Peninsular war; attached to Blücher's headquarters in 1815, and lost his left hand at Quatre Bras; M.P., 1820; secretary at war, 1828–30; Irish secretary, 1830 and 1834–5; secretary at war, 1841–4; governor-general of India, 1844; retired at his own request, 1848; master-general of the ordnance, 1852, and, after the death of the duke of Wellington, general commanding in chief the forces, 1852–6; field-marshal, 1855.

[3] See above, p. 400.

had neither men nor money to hold Kashmir in sufficient force, and gave the country to the raja of Jammu for a million pounds.

These terms were not likely to be lasting. A British agent and garrison remained at Lahore to maintain the interests of the young Maharaja Duleep Singh. If the troops had been withdrawn, the Punjab would have collapsed again into anarchy. The agent, Henry Lawrence,[1] knew, as few men, how to win the support of high-spirited Indians; the Sikh chiefs themselves soon asked that the garrison should stay. In December 1846 a new treaty continued the British garrison for eight years. Lawrence now became Resident, with a council of regency under his direction. He went home on leave in January 1848, and the Sikh army took their last chance of rebellion.

The rebels had to deal with a new governor-general. The earl of Dalhousie,[2] who landed in India at the beginning of 1848, was not yet thirty-six years old. Wellington and Peel had noticed his ability, and made him vice-president of the board of trade in 1843. In 1845 he succeeded Gladstone as president. His work, largely concerned with the new railways, taught him much that was of service to India, but he knew nothing of Indian conditions or of war. Within three months of his arrival at Calcutta, two British officers were murdered at Multan, apparently with the connivance of the governor of the province. The governor, Mulraj, then proclaimed a holy war, and called upon all Sikhs to join him. A force hastily collected by one of Lawrence's officers defeated Mulraj, but the rebellion extended throughout the Punjab and a large force sent from Lahore to help in the siege of Multan went over to the enemy. Dalhousie had been trying to save money, and there were not enough supplies for a strong expedition to start before November 1848. Gough, who was in command, fought his battles in

[1] Sir Henry Montgomery Lawrence (1806-57); 4th s. of Lieut.-Col. Alexander Lawrence; b. Ceylon; educ. Londonderry grammar school and at Bristol; 2nd lieut. Bengal artillery, 1822; fought in 1st Burmese war, and invalided home, 1826; returned to India, 1829; worked on revenue survey of north-west provinces, 1833-8; took part in Afghan expedition, 1842; Resident at Nepal, 1843-5; took part in Sikh wars; agent for the Punjab, 1846, Resident, 1847; agent in Rajputana, 1853; chief commissioner in Oudh, 1857.

[2] James Andrew Broun Ramsay, 10th earl and 1st marquis of Dalhousie (1812-60); b. Dalhousie; educ. Harrow, and Christ Church, Oxford; Dalhousie's term of office was extended for three years at the request of the directors, although his health was suffering very badly from h⸱⸱ stay in India.

the familiar way. The Sikhs were magnificent soldiers; at Chilianwala their resistance was so stubborn that Dalhousie and the British government decided to supersede Gough and appoint Napier in his place. Before Napier's arrival Gough won a battle at Gujrat; for once he was persuaded to reconnoitre the enemy position and to use his artillery before sending infantry against entrenchments. Multan had already fallen and Mulraj was a prisoner. In March 1849 the rest of the defeated Sikh army gave up the war. The Punjab was now in British hands, but the British authorities did not know what to do with it. Dalhousie thought that if the Sikhs remained independent they would believe that the English were afraid of them. The support of a titular maharaja would mean responsibility without control. Annexation was the only other course, and although the cabinet, the directors, and Sir Henry Lawrence disagreed with this policy, Dalhousie acted on his own judgement, and thus extended the frontiers of British India to the border of Afghanistan. Henry and John[1] Lawrence organized the province. Their work was well done, though they disagreed on the treatment of the chiefs to such an extent that in 1853 Dalhousie had to give Henry another post and leave John in sole command. The measure of their success can be seen in their roads and canals, the reduction of the land tax, the organization of a system of justice, the disappearance of slavery, *thuggee*, and other forms of crime, and, above all, in the remarkable loyalty of the Sikhs during the Mutiny.

Within three years of the second Sikh war Dalhousie had to meet troubles in Burma. A new generation was growing up in the Burmese kingdom; and the experience of the first war with the British was forgotten. The complaints of British merchants became so very serious that in 1851 Dalhousie asked for the removal of the governor of Rangoon and the payment of an indemnity to merchants who had suffered from Burmese extortion. The new governor was worse than his predecessor, and

---

[1] John Laird Mair Lawrence, 1st Baron Lawrence (1811–79); 6th s. of Lieut.-Col. Alexander Lawrence; b. Richmond (Yorks.); educ. at private schools at Bristol and Bath, and at Londonderry grammar school; entered Haileybury, 1827, and Fort William College, Calcutta, 1830; held appointments in city and district of Delhi, until 1840; invalided home, 1840–3, and advised not to go back to India; brought to the notice of Hardinge, 1845; administrator of the Jalandhar territory, 1846–9; member of the board of administration of the Punjab, 1849–52; chief commissioner for the Punjab, 1853–9, when his health broke down through overwork; viceroy of India, 1863–9.

in January 1852 the commodore of the British squadron on the Irrawaddy brought all British residents at Rangoon to his flag-ship, took a Burmese warship as a hostage, and declared a blockade of the river. The Burmese attacked him. He sank one of their war vessels and bombarded their stockades. After this attack the British could not draw back, and the king of Ava still refused to pay any compensation. Dalhousie decided to send a strong expedition to the country. The lessons of the first Burmese war were not altogether neglected. The troops were better fed, and were trained in stockade fighting. The period before the breaking of the monsoon was chosen for the attack, and a fleet of steamers went with the expedition. The Burmese did not make a very serious defence. Rangoon fell in April, Bassein in May 1852. After the capture of Pegu Dalhousie annexed the whole province. The Burmese did not formally acknowledge the surrender, but made no effort to continue the war. The king of Ava was now shut off from the sea, and the new territory put in order without any opposition from the inhabitants.

The annexation of the Punjab and of the province of Pegu was criticized a little unfairly in England. Dalhousie's peaceful absorption of native states within the borders of British India was more open to question. He thought that the relationship between the British authorities and the rulers of 'protected states' too often compelled the governor-general either to tolerate misrule or to break an agreement with an incompetent prince in the interests of his subjects. He found a precedent for lessening the number of native princes in the doctrine of 'lapse'. According to this principle, invented by Dalhousie's predecessors, the sovereignty of a native state 'lapsed' to the paramount power in default of natural heirs in a ruling family. The working of the principle was difficult because Hindu custom encouraged childless rulers to adopt sons. Dalhousie claimed that in such cases sovereignty could not pass to an adopted son without the consent of the governor-general. He distinguished between states which had been independent before the British régime and those set up by the British themselves or, again, states which were subject to princes conquered by British arms. He settled the financial differences between the British government and the nizam of Hyderabad on terms which strengthened the nizam's position. He declared in this settlement that the nizam had been a faithful ally for over fifty years, and that the British government would do nothing to impair his independence; but it was not always easy to make distinctions of this kind, and, in any case, native opinion did not understand them. No native ruler thought himself secure, and Dalhousie's methods seemed to be part of a plan for the gradual extinction of dependent states.[1]

It happened that there were an unusual number of deaths of rulers without direct heirs during Dalhousie's governorship. He was able to take, among other states, Satara in 1848, Sambalpur in 1849, Nagpur in 1853, Jhansi in 1854. The state of Satara had been created by the British government in 1818. Jhansi was a tributary state of Bundelkhand which had passed into British hands with the other dominions of the peshwa of Poona. Nagpur, the most important of these principalities, contained 80,000 square miles of territory, including good cotton-growing land, and a population of 4,000,000. Its annexation secured greater control of the road from Bombay to Calcutta. The annexation of Oudh was a more important matter. Here there was no question of 'lapse', though the king of Oudh provided Dalhousie with a strong argument against the maintenance of dependent princes. The king misruled his subjects, but was loyal in his relations with the Company. Furthermore one of Auckland's many mistakes had given the king a grievance. In 1837 Auckland had signed a treaty binding the king of Oudh either to improve his government or to hand over the administration of the country to British officials. The directors refused to recognize this treaty. Auckland did not inform the king of this fact, and Hardinge accepted the treaty as valid in his correspondence with the king. The misgovernment of Oudh in Dalhousie's time was beyond hope of improvement; the king could not control his own agents. The condition of the peasantry justified interference, yet if the king refused to abdicate the British government had no legal right to depose him. Dalhousie suggested that the king should retain his rank and titles but give up the control of his administration. The board of control would not accept this compromise, and ordered Dalhousie to take over the kingdom. The king would not abdicate; Dalhousie proclaimed his deposition in February 1856, and annexed his kingdom. Dalhousie claimed that the internal

[1] The doctrine of 'lapse' was officially withdrawn in 1859–60.

reforms which he was introducing into the whole of India were a benefit to the states which he annexed. He had nothing of Napier's vivid imagination. Napier might write:

> Would I were king of India! I would make Moscowa and Pekin shake. . . . Were I king of England I would, from the palace of Delhi, thrust forth a clenched fist in the teeth of Russia and France. England's fleet should be all in all in the west, and the Indian army all in all in the east . . . India . . . should suck English manufactures up her great rivers, and pour down those rivers her own varied products.

Dalhousie thought in more commonplace terms of railways, canals, and telegraph poles. He began the Grand Trunk Road and finished the Ganges Canal, which was longer 'than all the irrigation lines of Lombardy and Egypt together'. He reformed the prison administration, looked after the forests, opened a college of engineering, and established village schools. He set up a central legislative council, and freed the governor-general from special duties of local administration by creating a lieutenant-governorship of Bengal. Hardinge had already considered a plan for an Indian railway system, though many engineers thought that the lack of skilled labour, and the difficulties of the Indian climate, would make it impossible to build and maintain railways in India except at ruinous cost. Dalhousie projected lines from the port of each presidency into the interior of the country, with connexions to the neighbouring presidency. Private companies would build the railways, and receive a government guarantee of five per cent.; the government had the right of buying the companies after twenty-five or thirty years.[1] Dalhousie came back to England in 1856, and was voted a pension of £5,000 a year by the Company. Within a year his administration was held responsible for a revolt which seemed to threaten the position of Great Britain in India.

The potential danger to British power, the suddenness of the outbreak, and the ferocity of the fighting gave to the Indian

---

[1] Dalhousie's plan was adopted in 1859, when the construction of 5,000 miles of railways was sanctioned. Indians invested heavily in Indian government loans, most of which paid 3½ per cent. The railway loans paid 5 per cent. and offered the same security, but attracted curiously little Indian capital. Out of nearly 50,000 holders of the railway loans in 1868 only 397 were Indians. See *Camb. Hist of B.E.*, ii. 790.

Mutiny an importance which it did not altogether deserve. From a military point of view it was an affair on a small scale. It might have been suppressed at once if the senior officers in the Indian army had been abler men. It was never a war of independence; it scarcely affected more than a third of the area of British India, though the rest of the country looked on passively, uncertain whether, after all, the hundredth anniversary of the battle of Plassey would not see the end of British rule. No foreign Power attempted to interfere. The frontiers were not disturbed; there was no trouble in Afghanistan. The Sikhs were quiet. Gurkhas were recruited in Nepal, and fought with Campbell at Lucknow. Sindhia's loyalty in Gwalior was of untold value. Only one of the three Presidency armies mutinied, and hardly more than a quarter of the sepoys of the army of Bengal took part in the fighting. There was no organized leadership of the Mutiny. Even at Delhi there were two rival commanders. Few Moslems and few peasants joined the rebels. Most of the population in the disturbed areas was unarmed, and only wanted peace. The rebellion was broken within five months, and during these months the civil administration was undisturbed south of the Narbada. Mutinies of native troops were not new in India. There was a serious outbreak at Vellore in 1806, caused by changes in the regulations which appeared to be an attack upon caste and religion. Another outbreak took place at Barrackpore in 1824 because the sepoys feared that they would lose caste if they were taken oversea to Burma. Two regiments mutinied on the Sikh frontier in 1844. In 1809 the European troops nearly broke into rebellion. Discipline in the army had declined during the two decades before 1850. The best officers of the army were often taken away for political work, and the increasing centralization of authority lessened the power and influence of the regimental officers. In the Madras army little attention was paid to caste, but in Bengal the habit of enlisting men of high caste was bad for discipline. A Brahmin recruit thought himself superior to a non-Brahmin captain, and the captain took the same view. The sepoys were irritated by the minor economies of the Indian government. In 1849 Napier checked a mutiny over the question of allowances to native troops by disbanding a native regiment; after showing that he was not afraid of them he gave the sepoys what they wanted. Dalhousie censured Napier for making concessions, and Napier's resignation in 1850 increased the native soldiers' distrust of authority.

Thus there were grounds for thinking that the native troops might cause trouble. Dalhousie warned the home government that there were not enough British soldiers in India. At the outbreak of the Mutiny there were less than 40,000 European troops in the combatant services, while the native army was some 230,000 strong. Three infantry battalions of European troops were away on an expedition in Persia. The expedition was justified, since the Persians had occupied Herat in violation of their treaty with Great Britain. The British forces took Bushire, defeated the Persians, and expelled them from Herat. This campaign weakened the forces in India at a critical time, though it had a valuable result in confirming the neutrality of Dost Mahomed in Afghanistan. Three more battalions of European troops were in Burma, twelve were stationed in the Punjab; a detachment was at Aden. There remained less than eleven full battalions of infantry for the rest of India south and east of the Sutlej. Hence the lines of communication were dangerously unguarded. On the road between Calcutta and Peshawar there were no British troops at Benares, Mirzapur, or Allahabad, though Allahabad, at the meeting-place of the Jumna and the Ganges, was the key point on the way to the north-west, and contained a large arsenal. At Cawnpore there was only an infantry depot, with a weak reserve company of artillery; at Agra a battalion of infantry not at full strength. Delhi was another important strategical point between mountains and desert; it contained a great magazine guarded entirely by native troops. Lucknow, in Oudh and on the line from Allahabad, was held by a weak infantry battalion, Meerut by a cavalry regiment, an infantry battalion, two troops of horse artillery, and a field battery. The only railway in operation ran for a short distance from Calcutta. Owing to Dalhousie's economies in the transport service, it was almost impossible to move troops without collecting tents and baggage. There was a shortage of medical stores and ammunition, and the army had little mobile siege-artillery.

The native troops could judge for themselves the weakness of the British position. The withdrawal of troops for service in the Crimea seemed to show that there was a limit to the numbers of Englishmen; many credulous natives thought that the whole population of England had settled in India. The state of affairs was thus dangerous even before several new and serious grievances disturbed the troops. In 1856 the government decided to alter the conditions of service in the Bengal army. Six only of the Bengal regiments were liable for service outside India. Three of these regiments were in Burma, and two of them were due for relief. The other three could not be spared from their stations. The land route to Burma was closed, and reinforcements would have to be taken by sea. The troops would thus lose caste. The question of caste in the Bengal army wanted careful handling, but the governor-general settled the matter at a stroke by ordering that recruits in the Bengal army should be liable for service anywhere. Henceforward no high-caste Indians enlisted, and the sepoys already serving began to suspect an attack on their caste. They also thought that the government was trying to build up a new force of Sikhs, Punjabi Moslems, and Gurkhas, in order to deprive the sepoys of their privileged position. A second reform, also reasonable in itself, caused discontent. Privates of the Bengal army, if certified unfit through illness, were allowed to take their discharge, after fifteen years' service, with a small pension. This regulation was much abused; men would starve themselves for months in order to qualify for the pension. A new rule in 1856 exempted invalids from active service, but kept them on the strength of their regiments for camp duties. Finally, in January 1857, a rumour spread that the grease used for the cartridges of the new Enfield rifle was made of the fat of cows and swine. Every cartridge had to be bitten before insertion into the rifle; therefore every Hindu or Moslem using the new rifle would be polluted. There was some truth in the story. Beef-fat had been used in the factory at Woolwich, though not at the Dum-Dum factory in India, and, after the complaints began, no cartridge greased with beef-fat or lard was issued to any sepoy regiment.[1] The British regimental officers did not know the facts; their denials were taken as deliberate lies.

The troubles of the soldiers might have been settled if there had been no civilian discontent. Dalhousie had given a number of powerful personages grievances against the government. The dispossessed rani of Jhansi was a most determined enemy

[1] One Gurkha regiment, at the request of the men, was given cartridges greased with such fat. *Cambridge History of India*, vi. 174.

during the Mutiny. Dhandu Pant, generally known as the Nana Sahib, the adopted son of the deposed peshwa of Poona, had lost the large pension allowed to the peshwa at the time of his deposition. The landowners of Oudh, the home of 40,000 sepoys in British service, thought themselves harshly treated after the annexation. The Brahmin priests disliked attacks on religious practices, such as the abolition of *suti*, or the act of 1850 which protected the civil rights of converts from Hinduism and the act of 1856 which removed legal difficulties in the way of the re-marriage of widows. They were scarcely less afraid of the indirect attacks on Hindu custom. They feared the spread of education, particularly the education of women. They distrusted the introduction of railways in which people of different castes travelled together. Rumours even spread that the government was planning the forcible conversion of India to Christianity. Finally, British rule in India had destroyed the rich careers for adventurers, at the expense of the peasantry, which existed before the nineteenth century. If a chance offered the old opportunities of plunder, numbers of men would be ready to take it.

The disturbances began at Barrackpore, near Calcutta, in January 1857. Four regiments showed signs of open mutiny. As soon as they were reassured about the cartridges, they began to suspect the glaze on the cartridge-paper. In February the troops at Berhampore would not touch the cartridges. In March further trouble occurred at Barrackpore. A native regiment was disbanded; no other steps were taken because there were no European troops available. In April some troopers of a cavalry regiment at Meerut who refused to use the cartridges were tried by court martial, sentenced to imprisonment, and, on 9 May, publicly stripped of their uniforms. A native officer warned Lieutenant Hugh Gough that the sepoys intended to break open the prison and rescue the troopers. Gough's senior officers refused to believe the story. Next day an attempt was made to cut off the British garrison while the troops were in the garrison church. The attempt failed because the time of service had been changed, but in the evening three regiments mutinied and killed their British officers. They broke open the prison, and marched on Delhi. If they had been followed and captured, further outbreaks might have been stopped; but the commander of the garrison, General Hewitt, who had seen fifty years of service, was too old to deal with an emergency. In any case, his small force of cavalry consisted mainly of recruits with unbroken horses. The mutineers reached Delhi. They were admitted by treachery into the citadel, and murdered all the British men and women whom they could find. Other mutineers attacked the European quarter of the city. The native regiments joined the mutineers, and killed those European officers who were unable to escape from the lines. Lieutenant Willoughby and eight men in charge of the magazine, with great courage, fought to the last and then blew up the building. The rebels now proclaimed the old king of Delhi, Bahadur Shah, as Moghul emperor of India.[1] For the next three weeks nothing happened, and, in spite of British blunders, the rebels missed their chances of success.

Lord Canning[2] had been in India since February 1856. The news of the capture of Delhi reached him on 14 May 1857. He ordered the troops returning from Persia to sail to Calcutta, and intercepted other troops on their way to China. He sent a steamer to bring back the regiments in Burma, but refused to send another fast steamer with the news to England. He made little use of the troops at his hand and refused the offer of volunteers at Calcutta. The commander-in-chief, General George Anson, was at Simla; he could not order an immediate advance on Delhi because he had not enough transport or supplies. Meanwhile the mutiny began to spread. The commanders at the different stations were blindly confident in the loyalty of their native regiments, and in most cases refused to disarm them. Early in June Rohilkhand was lost. The two sepoy regiments at Jhansi, with the connivance of the rani, murdered the European men, women, and children in the place, and the British hold on the north-west provinces was limited to Agra.

The stations of Cawnpore and Allahabad maintained communications between Lucknow, Agra, and Calcutta. In the first week of June the garrison of Allahabad could not leave the fort. At Cawnpore Sir Hugh Wheeler expected attack at any moment, though he trusted the loyalty of the Nana Sahib. He decided that it was his duty to keep open the road to Allahabad; he therefore left his protected position, and began to fortify two

[1] The king lived in his ancestral palace as a pensioner of the company.

[2] Charles John, Earl Canning (1812–62); 3rd s. of George Canning; educ. Eton and Christ Church, Oxford; under-secretary for foreign affairs, 1841–6; chief commissioner for woods and forests, 1846; declined the foreign secretaryship, 1852; postmaster-general, 1853; governor-general of India, 1855; viceroy, 1858–62.

barracks on the edge of the cantonments near to the road.[1]
Henry Lawrence at Lucknow also prepared the residency for
a siege, and collected a large store of provisions. Troops began
to move slowly from Calcutta, but Canning did not disarm the
native regiments below Benares until the middle of June. He
told Anson to march directly on Delhi, instead of using a longer
route which would have allowed him to take up the siege-train
at Agra. Anson died of cholera on 27 May before he was half-
way to Delhi. His successor, Sir Henry Barnard, after troops
from Meerut had joined him, disposed of three and a half
British battalions, one and a half regiments of British cavalry,
one field and three horse batteries, a hundred and fifty gunners
with the siege-train, and one weak Gurkha battalion. With this
force of 3,500 men he defeated 30,000 rebels, and took the long
ridge—some fifty to sixty feet above the plain—which commanded the line of communication from Delhi to the Punjab.
This ridge was the best point from which to attack the city; but
Barnard's force was too small to attempt the assault. Canning
had expected him to take Delhi; actually he was holding, at the
height of an Indian summer, a position none too strong in itself,
against an enemy ten or even twenty times as numerous as his
own force.

Meanwhile the Nana Sahib had shown his treachery, and
Cawnpore was surrounded by mutineers. Three hundred
British officers and men and about a hundred loyal native
officers, a hundred European civilians, and four hundred
women and children were crowded in the fortified camp. The
garrison was attacked by 3,000 sepoys, trained by British officers, and now under the leadership of the Nana Sahib and his
lieutenant, Tantia Topi. The rebels had seized the heavy guns
and ammunition left in the magazine. The camp was ill provided with water, and ill protected from the sun. From 6 June
to 26 June the garrison held out against continuous bombardment. Their food-supplies were running short, and there seemed
no chance that reinforcements would arrive before they were

---

[1] Rice-Holmes thinks that Wheeler did not attempt to occupy the magazine,
a strong building to the north-west of the city protected on one side by the Ganges,
because he was afraid that, if he withdrew the sepoy guard from the magazine
buildings, he might precipitate a rising (*Camb. Hist. of India*, vi. 183). Fortescue's
view is that Wheeler considered it safer to establish himself on the road to Allahabad
(whence he might expect relief) south-east of the city (J. Fortescue, *History of the
British Army*, xiii. 261).

starved out. The women and children could not die fighting, and Wheeler accepted the Nana's offer of a safe-conduct to Allahabad for the garrison and civilians. On 27 June the Europeans and native officers set out in the boats provided to take them down-stream. As soon as they cast off, they were fired on by the Nana's troops. The men were killed, and the women and children who survived the sabres of the mutineers were imprisoned. The advance guard of a relieving force under Sir Henry Havelock[1] left Allahabad on 30 June. The force was a mixed body only 2,000 strong, including a number of civilian volunteers. They had not enough transport animals, and could not move quickly, though at every point they defeated the rebels. On 15 July they were within twenty-two miles of Cawnpore. The Nana on this night ordered his troops to kill all the women and children in his prison. The sepoys refused. The Nana then found five villains who hacked the prisoners to death with knives and threw the bodies into a well.

The massacres at Delhi and elsewhere had already excited the British troops to savage reprisals against the enemy. Havelock's troops entered Cawnpore on 17 July. Few British soldiers have seen a sight more horrible than the place of massacre. Wolseley, who was serving as a young officer with the force, wrote nearly half a century later: 'Had any Christian bishop visited that scene of butchery when I saw it, I verily believe that he would have buckled on his sword.' It would be difficult to find troops who, after an event of this kind, would show mercy or even discrimination to their opponents. The English forces had dealt out grim punishment to rebels on their way to Cawnpore: officers and men now went to terrible lengths in their revenge, and on each side, British and Indian, the memory of the atrocities and the reprisals has been one of the most sinister results of the Mutiny.

[1] Sir Henry Havelock (1795–1857); s. of a shipbuilder; b. Bishop-Wearmouth; educ. Charterhouse; entered at the Middle Temple, 1813, but gave up the bar after a quarrel with his father, and obtained a commission in the army, 1815; went to India, 1823; took part in 1st Burmese war; A.D.C. to Sir Willoughby Cotton in 1st Afghan war, wrote an account of the campaign in 1839, and returned to Afghanistan, 1840; took part in Gwalior campaign, and 1st Sikh war; on furlough—after 26 years' continuous service in India—1849–51; q.m.g. of the Queen's troops in India, 1854; held a command in the Persian expedition, 1856–7; returned to India just before the Mutiny. Havelock was a very religious man, of somewhat narrow views, stern in character and conduct; he did not obtain a command equal to his abilities until the Mutiny, when he suddenly became famous. Before his death was known he was created a baronet and awarded a pension of £1,000 a year.

For the time, in July 1857, Havelock's position in Cawnpore was as unsafe as the position of the force outside Delhi. He could not advance to Lucknow until he was reinforced. The mutineers, after their success at Cawnpore, had attacked Lucknow. The garrison went out to meet them, but, owing to the carelessness of Henry Lawrence and his officers, had to retreat with a loss of three guns. Lawrence was mortally wounded on 2 July and died two days later. His successor, General Inglis,[1] miscalculated the amount of stores at his disposal and added to the trouble of the garrison by cutting down their rations. The fighting men and the women and children, closely besieged in a comparatively small enclosure, suffered from disease, but 60,000 rebels—including 10,000 trained soldiers—failed to take the residency from the garrison of less than a thousand English troops, 150 civilians, and 700 loyal sepoys. Outram[2] joined Havelock on 15 September, and ten days later the troops fought their way into Lucknow. In their haste to save the residency they had left the greater part of their transport behind them. Thus the relieving force had not raised the siege of Lucknow, but only reinforced the garrison. On the other hand the general situation had improved with the capture of Delhi. This feat was largely due to the arrival of troops from the Punjab. John Lawrence and his officers had been in a difficult position. They wanted to send a force to Delhi, but could not feel sure of the loyalty either of the Sikhs or of the Afghans across the frontier. For a time Lawrence thought of giving up Peshawar to Dost Mahomed, and retiring across the Indus. His own staff, as well as the governor-general, opposed this plan. At the end of July Lawrence allowed Nicholson[3] to lead a column from Lahore to Delhi. He reached the place early in August after marching twenty-seven miles a day for three weeks. He found that Barnard was dead. John Nicholson, tall, iron-willed, and as quick as he was brave, soon became the dominant figure at Delhi, although he was not in command. A force attacking the British

[1] Inglis had a Canadian mother and an American grandmother.

[2] Outram had orders to take command, but he would not deprive Havelock of the honour of relieving Lucknow, and continued to serve under him until the force reached the residency.

[3] John Nicholson (1821–57); s. of a physician; b. Dublin; educ. Dungannon College; obtained a commission in the Bengal Infantry, 1839; served in Afghanistan, and captured at Ghazni; took part in Sikh wars and in the administration of the Punjab; engaged in frontier administration, 1852–7, where he impressed the natives to such an extent that a sect was formed to worship him.

rear was driven back; the heavy artillery was brought up, and on 14 September the assault began. Nicholson forced his way into the city, but was mortally wounded while encouraging his men. After six days' fighting the small British force captured the palace and drove the rebels away in disorder.

A month before the fall of Delhi Sir Colin Campbell[1] arrived in India to take command of the British armies. He had come by the overland route in advance of the reinforcements from England; the only new troops at his immediate disposal were a well-organized naval brigade, with eight heavy guns, and three companies of infantry who had been wrecked on their way to China. The collection of transport and supplies took a long time, and Campbell did not leave Calcutta until 27 October. He then moved to Cawnpore, and took up a detachment of troops from Delhi. He found that a body of mutineers, mainly from Gwalior, under Tantia Topi was concentrating at Kalpi for an attack upon Cawnpore. He decided to march at once to Lucknow, although he heard from Outram that the garrison could hold out until the end of November. He brought his men into Lucknow between 14 and 17 November, and raised the siege. Havelock died of exhaustion a few days later, but Outram was left in the strongly fortified Alam Bagh, a large walled garden outside the city. Campbell went back to deal with Tantia Topi. He found that the rebels had reoccupied Cawnpore and plundered the British baggage and stores. He attacked at once, scattered the rebels, but was unable to take Tantia himself.

Thus at the beginning of 1858, seven months after the outbreak at Meerut, British authority was restored. The British troops easily defeated the enemy in the field, whenever they met them, in spite of the sepoys' superiority in numbers, and a handful of British soldiers could keep a large army at bay for many weeks, while an army of mutineers, in an immensely strong position, could not resist a British assault. This superiority

---

[1] Sir Colin Campbell, Baron Clyde (1792–1863); s. of John Macliver, a Glasgow carpenter, and of Alice Campbell, of the Campbells of Islay; educ. by his uncle, Colonel John Campbell; given the name of Campbell owing to a mistake of the duke of York; fought in the Peninsular war and took part in the Walcheren expedition; led a forlorn hope at San Sebastian in 1813; served in the China war, 1842; and in the second Sikh war; held commands in the Crimean war; offered the command-in-chief in India by Palmerston on 11 July 1857, and sailed next day for India; left India in 1860; field-marshal, 1862.

increased as the months passed. In February 1858 Outram held
the Alam Bagh with less than 4,000 British and about 1,000
Indian troops against 120,000 rebels, 20,000 of whom were
trained sepoys; yet the enemy did not dare to make a serious
assault. Lucknow was finally captured in March 1858. Of
the rebel leaders the Nana Sahib was in hiding. Tantia Topi
had escaped, but could not hope to do more than worry his
enemies. The rani of Jhansi was alive, and fought like a man,
but she was merely a fierce barbarian leader. The king of Delhi
was a prisoner. The mutineers were becoming little more than
bands of brigands out for plunder.

At this point a policy of conciliation might have done much
to restore order. Against the advice of Outram and John Lawrence, Canning proclaimed that, as a punishment for their aid
to the rebels, the landowners of Oudh, with certain exceptions,
would forfeit their lands.[1] Surrender on these terms was unlikely, and fighting of a desultory kind continued in Oudh until
the end of the year 1858. Elsewhere Sir Hugh Rose,[2] the ablest
soldier to hold a command in the Mutiny, carried out a brilliant
campaign in the disaffected area of central India. Rose had
never fought in India, but he had learned soldiering under
Prussian officers, and his methods were different from the un-
military slowness of Indian officers of the old school. He dressed
his men in khaki, and took with him a sufficient baggage-train.
He reached Jhansi on 21 March. The city was enclosed by a
high wall, four and a half miles round. The garrison was about
12,000 strong. Rose had less than half this number of men,
and under 3,000 British troops. While he was investing the
fortress he detached 1,900 men from his main body, and defeated Tantia Topi, who suddenly appeared with 22,000 men
and 28 guns. Rose would have taken the whole force if he could
have spared men to follow them. Two days later he began the
assault on Jhansi. After four days' fighting he took the city and
the fort. His own losses were 343; the enemy lost between 3,000

---

[1] Canning thought this punishment a light one for rebels who might have been
sentenced to death.

[2] Sir Hugh Henry Rose, Baron Strathnairn and Jhansi (1801–85); son of a
diplomat; b. and educ. Berlin; served in Ireland, 1820–33; chosen for special duty
in Syria 1840–8; secretary of embassy at Constantinople, 1851, and for a time
chargé d'affaires; liaison officer between the French and British staffs in the
Crimean war, where he distinguished himself for exceptional bravery; commander-
in-chief in India, 1860–5, and in Ireland, 1865–70; field-marshal, 1877.

and 5,000 men. As soon as he had collected supplies, Rose set out for Kalpi. The march was a wonderful feat of endurance over a dusty and waterless country in hot weather. A rebel army near Kalpi was defeated with about twenty times the loss which it inflicted on the British force. Rose took Kalpi at the end of May, after he had suffered no less than five attacks of sunstroke. He now heard of a new danger. Tantia Topi and the rani of Jhansi had made a dash for Gwalior in the hope that the maharaja's army would join them. The plan succeeded, though the maharaja himself escaped with his bodyguard to Agra. The treasury and fortress of Gwalior were now in rebel hands. Tantia Topi and the rani might try to cut the road between Bombay and the north-west, or they might cross into Mahratta territory with the Nana Sahib. Rose marched at once on Gwalior, defeated the rebels in a battle in which the rani was killed, and took the fortress. Tantia escaped again, and carried on a guerrilla war as an independent bandit. He moved from place to place over an area of central India as large as England, and across country filled with jungle and tropical forest. The population was, on the whole, friendly to him; even if they wished him elsewhere they could not resist him, because he was entirely ruthless. He could always take horses, and as his object was not to defeat the British but to escape from them he was hunted down only with great difficulty. In April 1859 he was betrayed. The British authorities tried him by court martial and hanged him for high treason. With his death there remained the final subjugation of Oudh, and the difficult work of pacification. The Nana Sahib was chased into the jungle of southern Nepal and vanished for ever.

The Mutiny had a deep and lasting effect upon British India. The efforts of 'Clemency' Canning to stop indiscriminate revenge were of great value, but they did not prevent outbursts of racial hatred in Great Britain and in India. The vindictive punishments against which Canning protested were unnecessary even from a military point of view. It was clear to the Indians that the English were too strong to be driven out of India, and that, if they were just in times of peace, they could be terrible in war. For psychological reasons which it is not difficult to understand, Indian opinion turned back to religious obscurantism. In the generation before the Mutiny Indian reformers had founded the Brahmo Samaj, a society which had in view the reform and purification of Hinduism and the acceptance of western culture. After the Mutiny, a new generation associated this movement with the domination of Great Britain and the disintegration of Indian ideas. The leaders of the Brahmo Samaj lost influence, and a school of thinkers who could not hope to turn the British out of India went back to orthodox Hinduism as a shield against absorption by their conquerors. On the English side the Mutiny left feelings of distrust, contempt for the Brahmins who had rebelled in spite of their privileges, and for the whole body of Indians, who had failed, in spite of overwhelming numbers, to continue their attack for more than a few months. Henceforward there was little of the optimism of the liberal reformers of the earlier years of the century. The British officials no longer held the view that by slow infiltration of western culture the Indian peoples would give up their superstitions and prejudices. For this reason the government was more cautious about introducing reforms. There was a greater care for efficiency, but a deeper gulf between rulers and ruled.

After the Mutiny the Company's rule disappeared, and the Crown took over the full control of the government of India. To some extent the change was formal, since executive power had long been in the hands of the president of the board of control, and the opening of the Indian civil service to public competition in 1853[1] had taken from the Company the patronage left in their hands in 1813. The act of 1858 transferred the territories and properties of the Company to the Crown, and set up a principal secretary of state and a council of fifteen members for the government of India. The governor-general was given the title of viceroy, and the European troops of the Company were transferred to the Crown. The proportion of Europeans in the army was increased: there were 65,000 in 1863, and the artillery was kept in British hands. A penal code, based upon Macaulay's draft of 1837, was introduced in 1860. The material progress of the country became even more rapid, at least as far as public works and trade were concerned. The Crown officials encouraged settlers and planters: they were

---

[1] The service was thus opened to Indians, but only rich men could send their sons to England, and orthodox Hindus would not cross the sea. One Indian candidate entered the service in 1864; there were no others until 1871.

anxious to show that they could outdo the Company's servants in suggesting reforms, and it was easier for the Imperial government to obtain loans for large capital undertakings. On the other hand, English opinion lost interest in Indian affairs within a few years after the transfer, and Indian debates in parliament were rarely followed by a large house.

In India the political and constitutional changes were not very noticeable. Canning remained in his post until 1862. His successor, Lord Elgin, died after little more than twelve months in India. Elgin was succeeded by John Lawrence, who held office until 1869.[1] Lawrence created the Indian forests department, reorganized the native judicial system, and extended the railways; after the severe famine of 1866, when relief was badly mismanaged in Orissa, he spent large sums on irrigation canals. His economies at Government House were unpopular, but, as earlier in the Punjab, he was concerned mainly to protect the poorer cultivators, whose interests he upheld in a settlement between landlords and peasantry in Oudh. Lawrence's knowledge of India was of particular importance in his treatment of Afghanistan. Dost Mahomed died in 1863. He left sixteen sons; twelve of them began to fight over his inheritance. Civil war lasted until 1869, when Sher Ali, Dost Mahomed's favourite son, established himself on the throne. Lawrence refused to take any part in this war, and rejected proposals to annex the wild territory, inhabited by tribes under nominal Afghan suzerainty, between Afghanistan and the Punjab. This policy of non-interference had one important result. The expansion of Russia in central Asia was bringing her armies within reach of the northern frontiers of Afghanistan. The absorption of the three khanates of Khokand, Khiva, and Bokhara was only a matter of time. Tashkend fell into Russian hands in 1865, Samarkand in 1868. Although this advance was looked upon with suspicion in Great Britain and in India, Lawrence saw that the best policy for Great Britain lay in recognizing Russian influence between the Caspian sea and the western frontier of China. The wisest officials in India hoped that the Russians would civilize one of the most barbarous regions of the world, and believed that an attempt either to partition Afghanistan or to make a close

---

[1] In 1868 an expedition to Abyssinia, led by Sir Robert Napier (Lord Napier of Magdala), for the release of British and other European prisoners, consisted largely of Indian troops. The force captured and destroyed the fortress of Magdala.

alliance with Sher Ali would be a mistake. Lawrence and his supporters wanted to leave Russia undisturbed north of an agreed frontier and to oppose any further advance beyond this frontier, Lawrence's successors, Lord Mayo and Lord North-brook, continued this policy. The change under Lord Lytton to a 'forward' policy, bringing Afghanistan under direct British influence, was a mistake which led to another Afghan war.

BOOK IV

THE AGE OF REFORM

I

THE ORGANIZATION OF A CIVILIZED SOCIAL LIFE

THE development of an honest, competent, and properly supervised system of local government stands out as one of the most original features of the nineteenth century. This development may be described as the organization of a civilized social life; it produced far-reaching and profound results, the measure of which can be understood only by comparison with the conditions and standards of earlier generations. Improvements in the management of their common affairs made life easier, safer, healthier, and more kindly for citizens of every class, and the change from a haphazard to a scientific administration in town and country was as essential to the mechanism of a complicated industrial society as the provision of new methods of transport.

This administrative superstructure of the nineteenth century was built on a very ancient foundation; in spite of its novelty, it kept a good many features of the old-style ground-plan. At the same time it is not surprising that there should have been hesitation, confusion, and the widest differences of opinion about the additions required by the age, and that these cross-currents of opinion did not follow party lines. The administrative changes were indeed discussed and sanctioned in parliament, hastened or delayed by the ideas and prejudices of the political parties, but the attitude of these parties towards problems which they had not foreseen and did not fully understand was more often a matter of accident than of principle. Thus tory and conservative justices of the peace accepted the introduction of Benthamite principles into the new poor law. They did not approve of Bentham; they were not supporting any general plan of administrative reform. They believed that the new poor law was necessary; they did not want the unpopularity of carrying out its drastic proposals. On the whole tories and conservatives laid the greatest stress upon property and the claims of vested interests. Whigs and liberals were less afraid of popular control and more hopeful of its results; radicals were more nervous about increasing the powers of the state because, reasoning from past history, they were afraid that such powers would be used in the interest of aristocratic privilege and patronage. In 1821 Sydney Smith, who was in this respect more of a radical than a whig, objected to the appointment of inspectors of prisons 'for reasons so obvious that it is hardly necessary to enumerate them. The prison inspector would have a good salary; that, in England, is never omitted. It is equally a matter of course that he would be taken from among Treasury retainers, and that he would never look at a prison.'[1] On the other hand, the radicals also wanted efficient public services; thus they were led by the logic of facts, and often against their will, to accept the interference of the state. The principle of buying in the cheapest market did not mean buying at the cheapest price, especially in the matter of local government.

This uncertainty about the proper sphere of state action gave particular weight to the views of political economists. The economists disliked committing themselves to opinions on the subject, and disclaimed the authority thrust upon them by the public, but they were interested in the application of their views, and their theoretical analysis touched practical life at every point. Although the older generation of economists and writers on public matters, James Mill, Ricardo, and Malthus, were suspicious of state interference, they recognized the limits of private action, and the need for equality of opportunity, if competition were to be fair between individuals. Ricardo concerned himself mainly with questions of banking and finance; James Mill took an active part in educational and other movements. Malthus believed that the state could support emigration, prevent the exploitation of the labour of children, assist in education, and even help families with more than six children. McCulloch included housing and health regulations, factory laws, the building of canals and railways, and some recognition

[1] Quoted in S. and B. Webb, *English Prisons under Local Government*, p. 75.

of employers' liability among the permissible activities of the state. J. S. Mill and Nassau Senior went farther, though they also shared the belief that the state never did things well. Senior's justification of building regulations shows this tentative and inconsistent attitude of mind. 'No one denies the right of the State to interfere to prevent a man from injuring others. It exercises this right when it forbids him to build a row of un-drained cottages. But the right of the State to interfere to prevent a man from injuring himself supposes that the legislator knows better how to manage the affairs of an individual than the man himself does.'[1] Therefore Senior was doubtful about factory legislation applicable to grown-up men and women. He thought that the state might provide parks, open spaces, museums, picture galleries; yet his final view was that 'it is as difficult to elevate the poor as it is easy to depress the rich. In human affairs . . . it is much easier to do harm than good.'[2]

If the political economists could not give more than vague and often inconsistent guidance, it is not surprising that men engaged in the day-to-day business of government should have hesitated before problems which were too new to fit into existing political categories. It is plain enough, now, that these ad-ministrative experiments were far more important than most of the personal rivalries and party alinements of the day. To those who lived in the first half of the nineteenth century, and parti-cularly to those who were accustomed to consider themselves, and to be considered by others, as the governing class, such experiments were hardly more than incidental to the grand work of government, that is to say, the enforcement of law, public order, and justice, the control of public money, the supervision of the executive power, the decisions of war and peace. The prestige of long tradition belonged to the high offices of state concerned with the major exercise of sovereignty. Thus ad-ministrative offices of great social importance were merely stepping-stones in a political career; their sphere of action did not often include matters of first-rate parliamentary importance until Disraeli and Joseph Chamberlain made public health a national question of the highest rank.[3] The amount of adminis-trative reform obtained in any department depended upon the

[1] M. Bowley, *Nassau Senior*, p. 266.   [2] Ibid., p. 272.
[3] The Young England party had this intention though they could not carry it into effect. See above, p. 114.

capacities of the holder of a particular office, or the influence of an outstanding member of the department concerned. A minister of the Crown might be associated for years with departmental work and spend his active life in parliament without understanding the change in the character and emphasis of public business. Russell remarked in 1840 that when he first entered parliament (in 1813) 'it was not usual for governments to undertake generally all subjects of legislation. Since the Reform Bill, it has been thought convenient that the Government should propose changes in the laws.' Russell never thought out for himself the reasons for this new procedure.

From another point of view these administrative changes may be studied without much reference to politics. They came through political channels; they were due, not to the inventiveness of politicians, but to the advance of knowledge and to improvements in productive technique. The first public health acts were measures of precaution against the spread of Asiatic cholera. There was a rough understanding of the connexion between dirt and disease, or at all events, an empirical correlation of stench and the spread of infection, but until the work of Lister and Pasteur had revealed a new world of living organisms, the direct and immediate danger of filth was not known; an operating-theatre was as unclean as a slaughter-house. Moreover a science of bacteriology was impossible before the improvement of microscopes, and the invention of technical devices which allowed the study and isolation of germ-cultures. The interaction of improvements in technique and improvements in administrative organization can be seen equally well in the development of new means of transport. The old road system of the country broke down because people made more things than they could move by the old methods and heavier things than the roads could bear. The experts who worked out better methods of road-construction wanted facilities which could not be provided under the traditional system of unpaid local supervision and maintenance, or even by the new turnpike trusts.

The rise of the expert had other effects upon the development of a new type of administration. Jobbery, ignorance, and neglect had been the great faults of the old haphazard ways of local government. The expert, by definition, knew what could be done, and what he had to do. He expected to be paid for his work, and, in return, maintained a relatively high standard of personal and professional conduct. Moreover the increase in the size and efficiency of commercial undertakings led to the discovery of methods of preventing jobbery; the administrative expert came into existence, with his improved systems of audit and accounting, and the control of expenditure. Manufacturers, professional men, and merchants, conscious of their own importance, familiar with large-scale undertakings and with precise and accurate management, had standards in which there was no place for bumbledom.[1] This demand for a more rational administration of the common affairs of society came mainly from one class, but it affected the well-being of other classes.

There is another point of view. The 'business man' wanted a business-like direction of his local affairs. He disliked 'nuisances': he believed in 'progress', and measured it by standards of external efficiency. At the same time these new men, serious-minded in their conduct of affairs, were not without a sense of duty and obligation. The business man's sense of duty lacked magnificence and imagination; it was in many respects stupidly insensitive. Earlier aristocratic régimes had not been less insensitive, and were often, especially in their decline, more frivolous and irresponsible. It is not possible to separate this growing sense of justice and obligation from a consciousness of self-interest, and a separation of this kind is necessary only on a pessimistic view of human society and human affairs. The reform of the poor law, for example, was due partly to the desire of landowners to escape the ruinous charges on their property. It was due also to a belief that the old poor law was demoralizing those who received relief and unfair to other labourers who did not receive it. The expenditure of public and private money on the education of the poor shows something more than a fear of illiterate and uncivilized mobs. The reform of penal legislation and of the prison system was undertaken to protect society from the multiplication of criminals and the spread of disease from the common jails. It was also the result of an increasing dislike of the infliction of pain, a better conception of justice, and a consciousness that punishment should not be merely retributive or deterrent.

The reform of the poor law shows nearly all the features common to the treatment of administrative problems in the

[1] For the rise of the professional class see above, pp. 17–19 and below, pp. 618–23.

early nineteenth century: fear of state action; respect for the
new science of political economy; hesitation before the size of
the problem and the strength of vested interests; lack of clear-
ness in defining the aim of reform, and timidity in execution;
and, at the same time, a willingness to try a new plan, without
fully understanding what it meant.

The working of the Elizabethan poor law, with its accretions
of over two centuries, might well cause disquiet in the years after
1815.[1] The cost of poor-law administration had risen from
£619,000 in 1750 almost to £8,000,000 in 1818, or 13s. 3d. per
head of the population of England and Wales. These charges
fell only on real property or tithes; they were distributed un-
equally over this limited field of wealth, since assessment to the
poor rate was strictly parochial. The law of settlement, which
had been grafted into the Elizabethan system towards the end
of the seventeenth century, enabled manufacturers in towns
to escape the burden of maintaining unemployed workmen in
times of depression; they could take men from their villages
in good times, and send them back again when there was no
work for them. The administration of the law was expensive
owing to the jobbery and corruption of the minor persons
employed. The 'general mixed workhouse', in spite of legislation of 1782 permitting better arrangements, still housed the old
and the sick, the disabled and unemployed, young children,
ne'er-do-wells, and mad people. Life within its walls, for most
of the young or old, could be described as a kind of mental
breaking on the wheel. Furthermore the subvention of the
wages of able-bodied paupers by grants from the poor-rate had
become a grave, though different kind of evil. To contemporaries
this subsidy of wages was even more serious owing to the acceptance of Malthus's view that population tended to increase
beyond the means of subsistence. Hence allowances in aid of
wages, received as a matter of course by labourers and based
upon the size of their families, would lead to an increase in
numbers until every one was poor. This view was reinforced by
the economic theory of the 'wages fund', which assumed that at
any given time there was a definite and fixed amount of capital
available for the payment of rates, taxes, and wages; the greater
the amount paid in rates, the less the sum available for wages.
Malthus admitted that his view of life had a 'melancholy hue'.

[1] For the early history of the poor law see vols. viii–xii of this *History*.

It happened to be a wrong view. The 'wages fund' theory was also wrong; but there was no doubt that the allowance system weakened the independence and self-respect of the labourers, and prevented any rise in agricultural wages. The competition of subsidized labour lowered the rate of wages in areas where the subsidy was not paid, and was therefore unjust to good employers and unsubsidized labourers.

If the allowance system were to be abolished, and the administration of the poor law freed from corruption and abuse, the work could be done only by a central authority with power to enforce its regulations. There was no other way of securing uniformity among the 15,000 different parishes and townships each of which was responsible for the treatment of the poor in its own area. Furthermore, there would be strong local resistance to the curtailing or abandonment of the allowances in aid of wages. These subsidies were general in the home counties, East Anglia, southern England as far west as Wiltshire, and as far north as the north riding of Yorkshire; they were not unknown elsewhere.

The enforcement of reform was delayed because the central authorities were afraid of the temper of the people. A committee appointed in 1817 to consider the question of poor-law reform made no positive recommendations. There was much discussion, but no attempt to deal with the problem. The agrarian disturbances of 1830 brought matters to a head. These disturbances were most severe in the areas where allowances were paid; the labourers were now claiming the allowances as of right. The whigs were bolder than the tories in facing the problem. They believed that the allowance system ought to be abolished. They appointed a commission early in 1832 to study the question, and took care that membership, and, therefore, responsibility for unpopular proposals, should not be confined to their own party. The chairman, Dr. Blomfield,[1] bishop of London, and the two senior members were tories; the remaining six were whigs. The younger members were Benthamite in sympathy. The assistant-commissioners appointed to collect information were determined to show that the existing system was entirely bad; their reports were summarized and published in order to influence public opinion before the recommendations of the commission were announced in March 1834.

[1] See below, p. 508.

The commissioners gave few carefully prepared statistics, and exaggerated the number of able-bodied labourers in receipt of outdoor relief. They did not inquire into the cause of destitution or unemployment in towns. They recommended that outdoor relief should no longer be provided for the able-bodied; relief would be given in 'well-regulated' workhouses, but, if the labouring poor were to regain habits of self-respect, the workhouses must be as unattractive as possible. In the commissioners' words, the situation of the pauper 'must cease to be really or apparently so eligible as the situation of the independent labourers of the lowest class'. At the same time the commissioners were neither inhumane nor unenlightened in their recommendations. They proposed to continue outdoor relief for those who were unable to work owing to old age or sickness. For the old and the sick who could not be relieved at home, and for orphan children, they recommended treatment in workhouses, but they suggested a rigid classification: able-bodied men, able-bodied women, old people and children, each in a separate workhouse. The old were to 'enjoy their indulgences', and the children were to be educated by qualified schoolmasters. The work done by the able-bodied was not to be 'repellent'.

This policy required a new type of administrative organization. Here the commissioners borrowed from Bentham. They recommended the creation of a central authority consisting of three commissioners, a grouping of parishes into unions,[1] and the election of local boards of guardians to supervise paid officials in carrying out the policy dictated by the central commissioners.[2] They did not propose a national system of relief, which would have avoided inequalities of rates in different districts and disposed of the troublesome law of settlement. They modified the settlement law, but they held that a national system would break down. 'Vigilance and economy, unstimulated by any private interest ... would be relaxed ... candidates for political power would bid for popularity, by promising to be good to the poor.'[3] On the other hand the poor-law commissioners were to be given full powers; parliament could not discuss every detail and every experiment in poor-law administration.

---

[1] Few parishes had made use of the act of 1782 allowing the formation of unions.

[2] The electoral franchise for the boards of guardians included all ratepayers, and did not exclude women.

[3] Report of poor law commissioners, 1834 (reissued, 1905 [Cd. 2728], 179–80).

The report was accepted by men as different in their opinions as the duke of Wellington, Brougham, the two Mills, and Grote. Most of the proposals passed into law in the poor-law amendment act of 1834, and members of parliament were glad to be rid of a difficult problem. Public opinion outside the house was less sure that the act was a good one. Nearly every important newspaper was against it, and the fact that the report had exaggerated the number of labourers who would lose their wage-subsidy led to an overestimate of the strength of popular resistance. The whigs therefore took care that one at least of the new commissioners under the act was a tory.

The poor-law commissioners appointed Edwin Chadwick[1] as their secretary. Chadwick was tactless, impetuous, and cock-sure. He worked against his own commissioners when he disagreed with them, and, after endless quarrels, left the service of the poor law for the board of health in 1848. He made himself and the board so very unpopular that in 1854 a general outcry led to its abolition and his own retirement. Yet, if the road behind Chadwick was strewn with his enemies, it was strewn also with his ideas. His harsh, domineering mind was lit up by a passion for administrative efficiency and the reform of public health. He was endlessly inventive; he worked at high pressure, and had a sharp and unerring power of finding his way through masses of figures and details. It has been well said that Chadwick represented the 'official mind' in its most ruthless and impersonal form; his very faults supplied a driving power of the greatest value in carrying through measures which were new, unpopular, and full of unexpected complications and difficulties.

With Chadwick as guide and gadfly, the commissioners of 1834 began to unite parishes and to build workhouses. They started in the south, where the evils of the allowance system were greatest. Two good harvests, bringing cheap bread, and new openings for employment in railway building worked in their favour; but they soon found that they could not get

[1] Edwin Chadwick (1800–90); b. Longsight, near Manchester; entered an attorney's office, after a very slight education; took to journalism while reading for the bar; called to the bar, 1830, but never practised; brought to the notice of Bentham by his articles on social questions; lived in Bentham's house, and received a legacy from him; appointed (through the influence of his friend Nassau Senior) to the poor-law commission; served on a number of commissions dealing with social and administrative questions, 1834–47; contested London University, 1867; knighted, 1889.

uniformity, even in the treatment of the able-bodied. In the manufacturing districts of the north and indeed in all large cities, including London, the prohibition of outdoor relief to the able-bodied was impracticable; large numbers of able-bodied men suddenly lost their employment in bad times, and there were not enough workhouses to hold them. Even in agricultural districts the commissioners were compelled to tolerate outdoor relief in cases of sudden necessity. They tried to make the status of able-bodied pauper less desirable than the position of the worst-paid labourer, and, if they did not always succeed, the reason lay more in the grim condition of the worst-paid labourers than in the compassion of the central or local authorities. In 1850 the central authority refused to sanction a dietary proposed by the Bradfield board of guardians, on the ground that it was 'decidedly less nutritious than those of other unions'. The Bradfield guardians answered that their scale gave the paupers more to eat than independent labourers of the district could buy for themselves and their families out of their wages.

The commissioners were attacked throughout the country, and, when bad times came, the revolt against the poor law, the new 'Bastilles', and the 'three bashaws' at Somerset House was among the causes of chartism.[1] None the less, before 1840, in spite of the resistance of the north, six-sevenths of the population of England and Wales lived in areas covered by the unions. In one matter of great and ominous significance for the most helpless people in England the commissioners did not carry out the recommendations of the report of 1834. They did not insist upon the provision of different workhouses for different classes of the indigent poor. There were practical reasons for this change of policy, or, rather, neglect of duty. Separate houses meant division of families, greater expense, difficulties of supervision. Many unions were too small to provide enough paupers for each class of workhouse. In any case the commissioners thought that they could prevent the abuses of the old 'mixed workhouse' by separating different types of pauper in different parts of the same house.

It would have been well if commissioners and guardians had remembered Cobbett's large-hearted question and answer: 'What is a pauper? Only a very poor man.' This simple fact was too often forgotten, and a régime intended to deter the

[1] See above, pp. 134-5.

able-bodied was too often applied to the sick, to old people, and to children. The commissioners were afraid of demoralizing the labouring classes if the workhouses were too comfortable a refuge for the old. They criticized in 1840 'a strong disposition on the part of a portion of the public so to modify the arrangements [of the workhouses] as to place them on the footing of almshouses'.[1] If the workhouses were too inviting, even for the aged and the infirm, labourers would lose any encouragement to save, and children would make no efforts to keep their parents in their declining years. The risks were not great; few workhouses were too comfortable. The commissioners, after giving up the idea of separate establishments, did little more than publish a few plans to enlighten guardians about the size or arrangement of a good general workhouse. An outbreak of sickness at Sevenoaks in 1842 due to overcrowding led to the issue of some elementary rules on the question of numbers; the system of classification, based merely on age and sex, took no account of sickness, infection, or mental infirmity. Some of these omissions were remedied in the course of time. Guardians were warned that they must take care about infectious diseases, that dangerous lunatics must be sent to asylums, and vagrants housed in separate wards. Married women of good character were to be put with the aged, though nothing was said about unmarried women or young girls. In 1842 the commissioners explained that loose women ought to be kept away from women and girls of good character, but until 1847 there was no rule on the subject. Before 1842 married couples, whatever their age, were not allowed to live together.

The conditions of life in a workhouse depended very much upon the temperament and methods of the master or matron; but these officers had little freedom. They were bound to insist upon the same hours, the same meals, and the same work for all inmates except children under seven and the aged and infirm. There were no rules about exercise. No pauper was allowed outside the workhouse except for urgent and special reasons,[2] though the rule was relaxed to permit attendance at church, and, after 1842, children could be sent out to school.

[1] Report of 1840, quoted in S. and B. Webb, ii. 158.
[2] No one could be detained in a workhouse against his or her will. Able-bodied persons, including loose women, could therefore evade this rule by leaving the workhouse, and coming back when they needed support. The rule therefore weighed most harshly upon children and old people.

Until 1842 all paupers, even children, took their meals in silence. There were no books, not even bibles, and the education upon which the report of 1834 had laid stress was of a perfunctory kind. Smoking was forbidden inside the house, and might be forbidden in the yards. Visitors were allowed only at the discretion, and in the presence, of the master or matron. Until 1842 parents had no right to see their own children in the same workhouse even once a day. The attempt to find work which was not 'repellent' proved too difficult, and the able-bodied were taught the merits of self-help by means of stone-breaking, hand-grinding of corn, and oakum-picking. Bone-grinding was given up after it had caused a bad outbreak of disease.

The act of 1834 was a five years' experiment. Public feeling disliked the rigour and bureaucratic methods of the commissioners to such an extent that in 1839 and 1840 the whigs merely renewed the measure for another year. In 1841 Russell brought forward a proposal to continue the act until 1851. Peel persuaded him to limit the extension to five years, and in this form the conservatives passed the proposal in 1842.

After the transfer of the powers of the commissioners in 1847 to a poor-law board,[1] under the control of a minister, there was a gradual improvement in conditions, especially in the treatment of children and sick and old people. The change was due to the rising standards of the age, and the increasing sensitiveness of public opinion; the authorities themselves led the way in reform. The 'allowance system' had disappeared, and there was less reason to fear the effects of outdoor relief to the able-bodied. The problem of the workhouse child was taken seriously, though it was not approached with much imagination. The board advised that the children—there were between 40,000 and 50,000 of them in 1848—should be sent to special poor-law schools. Within the next twenty years most pauper children between the ages of five and fourteen were brought up in these large, barrack-like places. There was a reversion, about the years 1866-9, to the boarding-out system, though under proper safeguards.

The board took longer to improve the treatment of the sick. Between 1863 and 1865 outbreaks of dangerous diseases in poor-law infirmaries led to parliamentary debates on the question.

[1] In 1871 the local government board took over the work of the poor-law board.

In 1865 guardians were told to supply 'expensive' medicines, such as quinine and cod-liver oil, to the sick poor. In 1867 poor-law dispensaries were started in London on a system which had already worked well in Ireland. The sick, excluding those disabled by age, formed about 13 per cent. of the recipients of outdoor relief, while there were 50,000–60,000 cases under treatment in poor-law infirmaries. There had been even less advance in the methods of dealing with mental defectives who were not dangerous enough to be sent to asylums. The lunacy commissioners had no need to fear that good treatment would demoralize their patients, but such a view seemed extravagant to boards of guardians who had learned a different tradition. Hence, for reasons of economy, the guardians left too many cases in workhouses, to the discomfort of the wretched defectives and their sane companions. On the other hand there was a general improvement in the standard of workhouse comfort. The cost of maintaining paupers (apart from buildings and salaries) rose by 10 per cent. between 1863 and 1870. The evils of the mixed workhouse, the 'common Malebolge', had aroused educated opinion. The poor-law board took greater care to secure proper separation, though before 1860 they did not order that new workhouses should have quarters to suit the different categories of inmate. Another eight years went by before they laid down detailed regulations about air-space and lighting.[1]

The poor-law amendment act of 1834 established a new form of authority to deal with a particular problem. This special treatment was possible because the relief of the poor could be kept apart from the more general matters of local government. Other spheres of local government needed reform, but the methods applied could not be the same. No one, outside a small group of Benthamite enthusiasts, wanted to sweep away the traditional institutions of local government. The justices of the peace in the counties, the municipal corporations in the

[1] Two small facts are enough to illustrate the long story of unnecessary hardship imposed upon old people and young children who had the misfortune to be maintained out of the rates. In the year 1868 the guardians of the poor were told that the benches for the old and infirm 'should have backs, and be of sufficient width for reasonable comfort', and that little armchairs and rocking chairs should be provided for the children's sick wards. About the same time children were given milk, instead of tea or coffee, at breakfast and supper.

chartered boroughs, had long been the authorities through which Englishmen regulated their common affairs. The boroughs were enclaves of independence within the counties; the parish was subordinate in civil affairs to the justices. The justices were appointed by the Crown, on the advice of the lord lieutenant of the county; they maintained the authority of the Crown, ensured the execution of the laws, and punished offenders. Their executive work had given to their more formal and larger meetings in quarter sessions something of the character of a legislative body. They had a wide discretion; they developed policies of their own in administrative questions without always realizing the importance of their action. A few Berkshire justices, not even in quarter sessions and without consultation with any higher authority, had systematized the plan of subsidizing wages out of the poor-rates.

There was little objection to the rule of the justices in country districts. The country gentlemen who gave their time to the work were, on the whole, tolerant and careful; the clerical justices were generally the most educated men in their parishes. These squires and parsons were tory in sympathy, and often heavy-handed in punishing offences against the laws which restricted the killing of game to owners of freehold estates worth at least £100 a year, but they did something towards the repression of public abuses, drunkenness, and brutal sports. They were not unenlightened in their attitude towards public works, and a good deal of the radical opposition to them was based either upon political differences or upon dislike of interference with popular liberty even when this liberty was being misused.[1] The county magistrates were, however, unfit to deal with administrative problems of great complexity. The growth of new towns outside the old municipal boundaries added to the difficulties. There were not enough gentlemen to be found in the mining and manufacturing areas, and the unwillingness to appoint newly enriched manufacturers to the bench was not due to social exclusiveness alone. After 1815 a great deal of the justices' work passed out of their hands, or came more directly under the supervision of the central government. The new poor-law

[1] The removal of some of the powers of the justices was not always a social advantage; thus the freedom allowed to any ratepayer, after 1830, to open a beerhouse, on payment of two guineas, led to a great increase in the number of small and undesirable public houses.

authorities took away from the justices their most important
financial business. The factory act of 1833 set up independent
inspectors of cotton-factories and the prisons act of 1835 inspectors of prisons; the act of 1835 also put prison administration directly under the home secretary. The justices lost their
highway duties in 1835; their control of licensing regulations
and of the police was gradually weakened. For some time their
judicial powers remained untouched. No one wanted elected
judges; whigs and radicals, in their dislike of bureaucracy and
suspicion of the executive power, were long opposed to the
employment of stipendiary magistrates, outside the metropolitan area.[1]

The administrative work of the justices in crowded districts
was more troublesome because the old system of parish meetings had also broken down under a strain for which it was not
fitted. Parish government had been government by consent.
There was no uniformity about parish meetings or vestries. In
most cases a small group of important ratepayers met on Easter
Monday or Easter Tuesday to discuss the business, and allot
the parish offices, for the year. This rough and ready method
often developed into a 'select', or close, vestry in which a small
and self-constituted oligarchy filled vacancies by co-option.
Elsewhere open meetings were held, and the business was discussed by the parish as a whole. In the new urban centres these
open meetings meant a democracy of the worst kind; here and
there a local 'boss' maintained a rule of organized corruption.
Bethnal Green was an instance of this kind; the domination of
the 'boss' lasted for fifty years, and survived his imprisonment
in 1818 for misappropriation of funds. A few towns produced
order out of this confusion, and, without legal authority, obtained the consent of their parish meetings to the appointment
of an executive committee and a salaried staff. Liverpool was
the most remarkable instance of enlightened self-help under the
direction of a small number of prominent citizens; but these
extra-legal committees were at the mercy of self-interested demagogues who might use the weight of numbers at the open parish
meeting. Parishes varied so much in size, wealth, character,

---

[1] Sydney Smith described the justices of the peace as 'a bulwark of some value
against the supreme power of the State'. S. and B. Webb, *English Local Government,
The Parish and the County*, p. 606. Stipendiary magistrates had been appointed in
the metropolitan area in 1792.

and needs that any attempt between 1815 and 1832 to apply the Liverpool system generally would have failed; the tory ministers were not likely to make this attempt. There was, however, a double movement towards closing the open vestries and opening the close vestries. The reform of the open vestries was an indirect result of the increasing anxiety of landowners about the cost of poor-relief; the reform of the close vestries was due largely to the outcry against the corruption of several of the London metropolitan bodies, and to the protests of middle-class ratepayers and radicals like Francis Place. A parliamentary committee appointed in 1829 reported in favour of elected vestries; in the autumn of 1831 Hobhouse introduced a measure which passed without much criticism. This act applied to vestries where two-thirds of the ratepayers were in favour of adopting it. It established vestries to be elected by all ratepayers, men or women, voting by ballot. As one third of the vestry retired every year, the act required annual elections. Hobhouse's bill thus carried into law features of the radical programme which were resisted for many years when it was proposed to apply them to parliamentary elections. The facilities under the act were little used outside the metropolitan area, owing to the decline in the importance of the vestry after the poor law amendment act of 1834. The parish thereby lost its most important administrative function. There remained the expenditure and collection of church rates, and with their abolition in 1868[1] the parish as a unit of government fell into decay.[2]

The municipal corporations of England and Wales, nearly 250 in number, varied in size and in constitution; some had remained open democracies, others had developed, like the select vestries, into close oligarchies. The standard of honesty and efficiency in the administration of corporate property did not depend upon the degree of democratic control. On the whole the close corporations were less irresponsible than the open boroughs. The practice of using corporation funds for bribery at parliamentary elections worked more in the tory interest because the borough oligarchy was generally tory in sympathy, but the tories themselves were becoming alarmed at the failure of the borough magistrates to keep order: the

---

[1] See below, p. 511.
[2] For the parish councils established under the local government act of 1894 see vol. xiv of this *History*, pp. 213–14 and 295–6.

nonconformists were jealous of the anglican control of the boroughs through the 'shabby, mongrel aristocracy', and the radicals disliked close corporations on principle. The reform of parliament left these municipal corporations without means of defence. Their title to their property was legal, but they could not expect much tenderness from a whig ministry which had refused to recognize a title to property in 'pocket' boroughs and parliamentary seats; the first stage in reform had already come with the repeal of the test and corporation acts.[1] In 1833 the whigs set up a commission to inquire into the state of the municipalities in England and Wales. The commission appointed a number of young barristers to investigate the facts. These assistant commissioners were whigs, with Joseph Parkes a radical, as their secretary. One of them wrote to Francis Place: 'We shall do our duty . . . our chief is an excellent Radical, Ballot, etc., and the majority of our men are Balloteers.'[2] The report of the commission was rhetorical and unfair. It attributed to all boroughs the gross corruption of a few, and assumed that popular control was a guarantee of administrative purity and competence, though the neglect of the London docks by a democratic corporation was in striking contrast with the efficient and oligarchic management of Liverpool. On the other hand the main case was unanswerable. Peel did not try to answer it or to oppose the dissolution of the old corporations, and the transfer of their property, debts, and powers to municipal councils elected by ratepaying householders of three years' standing. The municipal corporations act of 1835 affected 178 boroughs, with a population of 2,000,000.[3] Political wirepullers considered it a great blow to toryism; Creevey thought that it would mean government by dissenters. It was not without some results upon the borough representation, and, as there were few administrative issues in the new corporations, elections were fought on traditional party lines. The administrative significance of the change was hardly realized because the old corporations had done little to provide public services.

The improvement commissioners, who came into existence during the century before the municipal reform act, were the

---

[1] See above, p. 76.
[2] S. and B. Webb, *The Manor and the Borough*, ii. 715–16 n.
[3] The unchartered municipalities could avail themselves of the act only after a complicated procedure.

pioneers of modern municipal work; in 1835 there were about two hundred of them in the provinces, and another hundred in the metropolitan parishes. They were fairly uniform in type, and represented the first attempts to deal with the nuisances abounding in towns without building regulations, public paving, street cleaning and lighting, without drains or sewers in the modern sense of the term, and with few means of keeping public order or protecting property. The commissioners generally included the senior officers of the municipality, a few justices, and the most public-spirited inhabitants of the town. In most cases the members were elected, or co-opted for life; sometimes the commission included all householders of a certain standing. They obtained their powers by private act of parliament; their efficiency depended upon local feeling and ability. They were least competent in the metropolitan areas, possibly because in these areas there was not much local patriotism or continuity of occupation. In many places they were the most important feature of the government of the town. The police commissioners of Manchester were independent of the vestry, and carried out scavenging and paving as well as police work. They numbered houses, and tried to get powers to widen streets and to control the water-supply. In 1817 they built a gas-works and prevented a private company from laying down another set of mains.

The commissioners did work of an experimental kind, limited in character by the rudimentary state of sanitary knowledge and mechanical invention, and the extent of public demand. They were often hampered by the ignorance and prejudice of their fellow townsmen; the poorer ratepayers objected to any charge for services such as paving or cleaning. There was some point to their objections because the areas paved and cleaned were generally the most important streets, and little was done in side-streets or courtyards; in any case the commissioners were not concerned with positive amenities, such as open spaces, libraries, or education. The radicals disliked the undemocratic constitution of many commissions, and considered that their powers were incompatible with the principle of free competition. The Manchester gas-works, for example, were described as 'a false step in political economy. We have converted the Commissioners of Police into dealers and chapmen, and have secured to them the exclusive sale of their wares at such price as they shall deem reasonable.'[1] Some critics thought that this price was fixed at a high figure in order to give a profit which could be spent on town improvements. Others complained that the commissioners provided fire-engines for the town. 'If the town would keep none, the fire-offices would keep engines for themselves, and such would be the competition that the town would be better served, and at no expense.'[2] The opposition in Manchester took advantage of the constitution of the improvement commission under which any one assessed at £30 rental could attend the commissioners' meetings. When the conduct of business became impossible owing to organized obstruction, the leading citizens appealed to parliament for a change in the constitution. The new constitution, which limited the commission to 240 elected members, came into force in 1828; it gave the town a progressive and business-like government. The commissioners circulated agenda before meetings, and agreed to the auditing of accounts by professional accountants and the assessment of valuations by professional valuers. They increased the police of the town, built a town hall, and sent out deputations to observe experiments tried elsewhere. The radicals still distrusted any extension of corporate activities; in 1834 they wanted to sell the gas-works to a private firm. They opposed the compulsory purchase of houses for street widening, and objected to the cost of these 'cursed improvements'. Few towns were as enlightened as Manchester, and yet the condition of the poor in the slums, and the general sanitary defects of the city, were serious enough. Elsewhere the defects were greater, and there were less strenuous efforts to remedy them. The residents in Parliament street, at the very doors of the house of commons, complained in April 1799 that their street had not been cleaned since the previous November. There was some improvement in London towards the end of the eighteenth century when the value of manure was realized; the discovery that ashes, cinders, and dust mixed well with clay for brick-making caused a boom in refuse.[3]

The act of 1835 allowed the new municipal corporations to take over the duties of the improvement commissions, but there

---

[1] S. and B. Webb, *English Local Government, Statutory Authorities*, p. 265.

[2] Ibid., p. 267, n. 1.

[3] Large quantities were shipped from London after 1812 for rebuilding Moscow. The boom did not last long, because the sweepings of macadamized roads contained too many granite chippings.

was no pressure upon the councils to make use of their optional powers, and up to 1848 only twenty-nine boroughs had taken advantage of them. On the other hand the central government had already begun to consider the question of public health. The first measures were temporary precautions taken during the cholera outbreak of 1831–3. This epidemic spread westwards from Russia. Before it reached England two doctors were sent to St. Petersburg to report upon preventive and quarantine measures, and a central board of health established to advise about precautions. The disease appeared at Sunderland in the autumn of 1831, and spread rapidly over the country. Local boards of health were created, and, as some places objected to paying for them, an act of parliament made payment obligatory. After the epidemic was over, the boards were allowed to lapse. Their revival was due to Chadwick and the poor-law commissioners. The commissioners employed a number of doctors to inquire into the causes of destitution and death in London. The conditions described by these doctors in a report of 1838 were such that one cabinet minister, Lord Normanby, refused to believe them. At the request of Blomfield, Russell in 1839 asked for a further report from the poor-law commissioners to include all England and Wales. This report of 1842 on 'the Sanitary Condition of the Labouring Classes' narrowly avoided being shelved owing to personal disputes between Chadwick and his political and administrative 'superiors'; it was, however, an immense propagandist success, and, incidentally, redounded all the more to Chadwick's credit because the commissioners would allow its publication only under Chadwick's name. The report showed a situation of grave danger to the whole community; the remedies proposed were stated not in terms of medicine but of sanitary engineering. This latter fact came out even more clearly in the next stage when in 1843 Peel's government appointed a royal commission on 'the state of Large Towns and Populous Districts'. The commission, which reported in 1844 and 1845, inquired into the water-supply of fifty large towns; in six cases the supply was good, in thirteen cases indifferent, and in thirty-one cases insufficient or impure. In Birmingham four houses out of five, in Newcastle eleven houses out of twelve, were without water. There were two water companies in Liverpool, paying high dividends, but the city had no public fountains or pumps, no standpipes for street-cleaning, few cattle troughs, and not enough water to put out fires.[1] A bill introduced in 1845 to deal with these general evils was withdrawn for further discussion. Then came the crisis over the corn laws. Russell's government in 1847 brought forward another bill which also was withdrawn for alteration, and brought back again in 1848. Meanwhile the cholera reappeared, and public opinion became interested in the questions of health and sanitation. The act of 1848 set up a central board of health on the lines of the poor-law board, with Chadwick as one of its three members. The central board had powers to create local boards on the petition of 10 per cent. of the inhabitants of a district and to enforce boards in places where the death-rate was above 23 per 1,000. The central authority had little powers of coercion once a local board was established, and, after five years of strenuous persuasion, there were local boards covering only two millions of the population and hardly touching the rural areas. Chadwick, with his incessant attacks upon the vested interests in the way of sanitary reform, made himself and the board as unpopular as the poor-law commissioners. In 1854 parliament altered the character of the central board, and in 1858 distributed its duties among other departments of state. For some years after 1854 no important legislation was passed,[2] but the return of cholera in 1865-6 once again stirred opinion. An act of 1866 (planned before the cholera outbreak) compelled local authorities to provide sanitary inspectors, and allowed the central

[1] Chadwick drew attention to the 'atmospheric impurities' which were the cause of disease, and suggested better drainage, the removal of refuse, purer water-supplies, and more air and space in housing. He pointed out that deaths from diseases due to dirt and bad ventilation were greater annually than the losses from death or wounds in any British war of modern times. He recommended the appointment of medical officers of health, and the promotion of cleanliness as 'necessary to the improvement of the moral condition of the population'. Liverpool appointed a medical officer of health in 1847; Manchester did not follow this example until 1868. To the end of his life, in spite of the work of Pasteur and Lister, Chadwick believed in the 'atmospheric' theory of epidemics.

[2] There was one important exception, affecting London. In 1855 a metropolitan board of works was set up to bring order into the chaos of administrative authorities in the metropolitan area. Before this time there was no definition of the area of London (outside the ancient boundaries of the City). The area chosen for the board of works was based on the thirty-six registration districts used for the census of 1851 (see also below, p. 600). 'London as a governmental unit began as a statistical area.' G. Gibbon and R. W. Bell, *History of the L.C.C.*, 1939, pp. 22-23. The acceptance of the plans of the board for a general sewage system for London was assured in the hot summer of 1858 when the stench of the Thames was intolerable in the houses of parliament.

government to insist upon the removal of nuisances, the provision of sewers, and a good water-supply. In 1871 a more comprehensive attempt was made to deal with the problem of educating public opinion and providing better administrative machinery. A strong royal commission, appointed in 1868, laid down a number of requirements 'necessary for civilized social life'. These requirements included a good water-supply, a proper drainage system, the prevention and removal of nuisances (for the first time, pollution of the air by smoke was defined as a nuisance), healthy houses in healthy streets, the inspection of food, proper provision for burial, and the suppression of the causes of disease. On the administrative side, the commissioners recommended the creation of a new department responsible for the services connected with public health. The local government board was established in 1871 to undertake this work.

The requirements of modern social life include an efficient police force. No such force existed in 1815. 'Thief-taking' was a local business, dependent on the activities of the high constable of the county, and the parish constables appointed by the justices of the peace. The office of constable was unpaid; every citizen was liable to serve, but, as substitutes could be provided, the service was generally undertaken by a few men who were paid for their work. In country districts, before the age of rapid transport and a mobile population, bad characters were soon known, and, in a rough and ready way, the system worked. In towns the burgesses hired watchmen, and in rural areas a few public-spirited property-owners sometimes paid special thief-takers. London, the centre of the government and wealth of the country, had a more elaborate system of watch and ward, but there was no organization covering the whole area; the West Indian merchants, for example, began the policing of the river to stop the pilfering of cargoes. Public opinion was suspicious about putting a new instrument into the hands of the executive, and afraid that a strong police force might be used to subvert liberty. A parliamentary committee of 1816–18 thought that 'the police of a free country was to be found in rational and humane laws, in an effective and enlightened magistracy . . . above all in the moral habits and opinions of the people.'[1] Three years after the committee's report the behaviour

[1] *P.P.* 1818, viii. 3rd report of committee on the police of the metropolis.

of the London mob at Queen Caroline's funeral showed that the habits of the people needed some stronger external check, while a second committee, appointed in 1822, with Peel as chairman, pointed out the comparative immunity enjoyed by thieves under a system which left the thief-takers weaker and less well organized than the criminals. The committee suggested a police office, under the control of the home office, to deal with London and the suburbs. In 1829 Peel was responsible for the metropolitan police act, setting up a commissioner and assistant-commissioner of police, with headquarters at Scotland Yard.[1]

The municipal corporations act required borough councils to appoint watch committees who in turn were to set up adequate police forces. These instructions were not everywhere obeyed with promptness.[2] There was little central control over the local committees; their authority ended with the borough boundaries, and the criminals were free to take up their quarters in the suburban slums, but the improvement in the boroughs if slow, was continuous. The country districts were the last to be adequately policed. The justices of the peace could not cope with the problems of a larger population and the demands for higher standards of security within their areas of jurisdiction. They had not enough constables; they had no arrangements for pursuing criminals from district to district, and in many cases they had no 'lock-ups'. A royal commission of 1839 (including, as usual, Chadwick) recommended wider police areas which would allow exchange of information, the transfer of constables to troubled districts, and better facilities of training. The commissioners did not propose a national system, because this plan would have offended local feeling. The government therefore introduced an act permitting the justices to appoint chief constables for the direction of the police in their areas. In many districts the justices did not take advantage of the act, and the ratepayers disliked the cost of a police force. Hence the criminals moved from the policed into the unpoliced counties. An inquiry

---

[1] Peel was afraid that the police force might offer yet another opportunity for jobbery for the upper class. He wrote to Wellington in Nov. 1829, in reply to the latter's congratulation on the new force, 'The chief danger of the failure of the new system will be, if it is made a job, if gentlemen's servants and so forth are placed in the higher offices. I must frame regulations to guard against this as effectually as I can.' Quoted in A. Aspinall and E. A. Smith, op. cit., p. 376.

[2] See J. Hart, *E.H.R.* lxx. 411–27.

in 1853 showed that twenty-two counties has set up a constabulary, while seven counties had adopted the act for particular areas. There was no co-ordination between the different areas. In 1856 parliament insisted upon this co-ordination and gave the home office power to inspect the police system of counties and boroughs. This act was opposed on the old ground that it interfered with public liberty; that the inspectors would be spies; that a system of inspection would destroy initiative and local responsibility and reduce England to the level of the continental 'police-states'. However, these risks to liberty were accepted when the home office offered an increased grant to local bodies for an efficient police force.[1]

The improvement in public order and the diminution of crimes against life and property were not due merely to better methods of detection. The English prisons in the eighteenth century were centres of demoralization, disease, and the spread of criminal practices. John Howard[2] had brought the state of the prisons to public notice, but, here as elsewhere, the long period of war interrupted reform. About 1810 there was a revival of public interest in the question; in 1814 the grand jury of Middlesex presented Newgate prison as a public nuisance, and a parliamentary committee was set up to investigate the condition of the prisons in the city of London. A group of members of parliament, including Romilly and Burdett, with the support of Lord Holland, led an agitation for reform, and the work begun by John Howard was taken up by Elizabeth Fry, a quaker woman of great strength of mind and character.[3]

[1] There were no municipal services for the prevention of fire in 1815. The insurance companies encouraged the provision of fire-engines and an act of 1833 allowed parishes to provide engines and pipes at the ratepayers' charge, but these precautions were useless without a good water-supply. In 1862 the metropolitan board of works took over the private fire-engines and staff in London, and established the metropolitan fire brigade. As late as 1867 a parliamentary committee which collected information from 86 towns of over 20,000 inhabitants found that only 78 of these towns had fire brigades and 51 had regulations about fire-escapes in buildings; there were no building regulations designed to prevent outbreaks of fire. A committee of 1842 on building regulations had pointed out the danger of back-to-back houses, and recommended the enforcement of rules about flues and the isolation of workshops using combustible materials.

[2] See vol. xii of this *History*, pp. 38-39.

[3] Elizabeth Gurney (1780–1845); d. of John Gurney, banker; b. Earlham, Norfolk; married Joseph Fry, 1800; took part in the quaker ministry; formed an association for the improvement of female prisoners in Newgate, 1817; persuaded the government to improve the conditions of transportation and the settlement of prisoners in New South Wales; instituted an order of 'nursing sisters'.

Mrs. Fry began to visit Newgate prison in 1812, in order to reform the prisoners by means of personal instruction in the Christian religion. Others followed her example and prison committees were started in many towns. The emotional methods of approach used by pious visitors were not always wise, though in many cases they provided the psychological liberation which the prisoners needed to get away from their own past. This evangelical interest was, however, of great importance in giving publicity to the scandals shut away behind prison walls. Peel, with his usual administrative efficiency, carried through the first stage in prison reform. He compelled justices to organize their prisons on a prescribed plan, to inspect them regularly, and to send quarterly reports on their condition to the home secretary. Jailers were to be paid, and not to live by fees; women warders were to be given charge of women prisoners, and the prison chaplain and surgeon were required to visit every prisoner in the cells. Prisoners were to be graded for work, to receive religious instruction, and to be taught to read and write.

Peel's measure applied only to the prisons of the county justices and those of London, Westminster, and seventeen provincial towns. The debtors' prisons in London and the prisons of the smaller municipalities and franchises were left untouched. The worst evils of the larger prisons were remedied, but Peel's successors at the home office did not follow up the first measures of reform. There was little understanding of the complexity of the problem. It was obvious that prisons ought not to be centres of disease; that the prisoners should not live under conditions harsher than those required by the law; that young offenders should not be contaminated by contact with hardened criminals. Yet there was not even a clear idea about the purpose of imprisonment; most people failed to distinguish between retributory, deterrent, or reformatory punishment. James Mill did much to introduce clear thinking on these large questions by his article on prisons in the *Encyclopaedia Britannica* of 1823; he suggested that the purpose of imprisonment should be 'reform by industry'; but it was difficult to find profitable work which could be done under prison conditions. In any case, how were the profits to be shared? If the tasks chosen required collaboration among the workers, there was a danger that the hardened criminals would corrupt those with whom they worked.

The whigs appointed a committee in 1835, and accepted its recommendations. The committee explained the need for uniformity of treatment throughout the country, and concluded that this uniformity was possible only under a system of state inspection and the enforcement of regulations by a central authority. The treadmill was introduced as a substitute for productive labour, but its effects could hardly be called reformatory, and, in the hands of careless or callous officials, it became an instrument of torture. Enough was known, from American experiments, about the fearful results of complete solitary confinement to prevent the application of this method of avoiding the contamination of prisoners. As a compromise, prisoners were kept in separate cells, but employed as far as possible on productive work, allowed to read books, and, when at work or exercise, to talk to their neighbours. Here, almost for a generation, the reforms came to a standstill.[1] The abolition of transportation created a new problem for prison authorities in the treatment of men serving long sentences. The judges who passed these sentences often knew little or nothing about the conditions to which they were assigning condemned criminals. The study of mental pathology was in its earliest stages, and, in any case, did not form part of the training of those charged with the administration of law. Criminals who had served their sentences did not feel inclined to advertise their status by agitating against the prison regime, and the public would not have put much trust in their evidence. Prison management did not often attract imaginative or sensitive men, and the sum of human pain inflicted unintentionally, and as a result of invincible ignorance, by the prison system in the nineteenth century is likely to astonish posterity far more than it worried contemporaries.

The reform of the criminal law was an easier matter than the reform of prisons, though the demand for a less barbarous penal code came mainly from outside the professional body of lawyers. The attitude of parliament was not particularly enlightened. In 1808 Romilly persuaded the commons to accept transportation

[1] Prison diet, for example, remained entirely unsuitable for men and women living in enclosed conditions. The prisons act of 1865 secured greater uniformity in administration, but in other respects did nothing to improve the treatment of criminals. One measure—the youthful offenders act of 1854—was socially important in sending young people to special establishments where they had at least the chance of reform.

for life, instead of hanging, as a punishment for picking pockets. Two years later he brought forward a bill repealing an old statute which made the theft of five shillings from a shop a capital offence. The commons passed the bill and the lords threw it out; the archbishop of Canterbury, the bishop of London, and five other bishops voted against it. In 1813 Romilly again introduced his bill, and again the lords rejected it; two royal princes, an Irish archbishop, and four bishops supported the majority. In 1816 the lords destroyed the bill without even dividing on it. In 1818 Romilly pointed out that the law might well be repealed because it was not carried out, but the peers still refused to accept a formal repeal. Romilly died in 1818. Mackintosh took up his proposals for reform of the criminal law, and carried a proposal for a special committee to report on capital offences in the penal code. The committee recommended the repeal of a large number of obsolete statutes enjoining capital punishment for offences such as injuring Westminster Bridge or impersonating out-pensioners of Chelsea Hospital. The opposition of the house of lords blocked still wider reforms until in 1823 Peel took up the question. Canning's toryism did not include the belief that harsh and obsolete laws had a token value, and Peel was able to carry five statutes exempting about a hundred felonies from the death penalty. Opinion was changing quickly,[1] and in 1832 housebreaking, horse-stealing, sheep-stealing, and the coining of false money ceased to be capital offences. The house of commons would have included all cases of forgery, but the lords thought it necessary to keep the death penalty for criminals who forged wills, powers of attorney, or transfers of stock. In 1837, and again in 1841, more statutes were repealed. A proposal that the death sentence should be inflicted only for murder was lost merely by one vote. After 1838, and for the rest of the century, no person

[1] From a different angle, legislation forbidding cruelty to animals is another sign of this change of view. The first bill to prevent ill treatment of horses and cattle was passed in 1823, largely through the efforts of Richard Martin, a Galway land-owner and a friend of George IV, who gave him the name of 'Humanity Martin', Martin tried again and again to persuade parliament to forbid cruel sports like bull-baiting and dog-fighting. Although the Royal Society for the Prevention of Cruelty to Animals was formed in 1824, Martin was attacked in the press and ridiculed in the commons. In 1833 bull-baiting and similar cruelties were forbidden within five miles of Temple Bar, and in 1835 the prohibition was extended to the whole country. There were cases in which soldiers were used to enforce the law against the 'sport' of ox-driving.

was hanged except for murder or (up to 1861) attempted murder.

In 1841 transportation, as an alternative to capital punishment, was near to its end. Colonial opinion was becoming restive about it, and the English supporters of 'systematic colonization' did not want the colonial lands filled by convicts.[1] The system was expensive; an estimate of 1837–8 put the cost at about £500,000 a year. It was not deterrent, and not often reformatory. It gave a few men the chance of starting a new life in Australia; as a rule, it made bad men worse, and weak men into hardened criminals. As a punishment for women it was nearly always degrading. For a short time a modified system was tried. Convicts served for a time on public works; they passed to private service, and were then released with a conditional pardon. This 'ticket-of-leave' plan broke down because most of the colonists objected to it; there were also great practical difficulties in the way of securing adequate supervision and the selection of men of good behaviour. The substitution of penal servitude in England for transportation abroad was the last stage in the reform of the criminal code, and if there had been a more humane and intelligent attitude towards prison life, the diminution in crime which followed the removal of the most savage punishments of the law might have been even more remarkable.

The reform of the common-law courts and of the court of chancery was in many respects more difficult than the civilizing of the criminal code. The delays, obscurity, and expense of legal processes affected larger and more influential classes of the population, but the opposition of vested interests and the timid conservatism of the lawyers were more serious because the technical side of reform required professional knowledge and goodwill. The court of chancery was supposed to correct the rigidity of the common law, and to provide remedies where the common law did not apply; but the 'equity' of the court had almost disappeared under a mass of cumbersome rules and practices. The common-law courts were hardly less of an obstacle to cheap and speedy justice,[2] and the lower courts which existed for the recovery of small debts had only limited areas of

---

[1] See above, pp. 385–7.

[2] For the reform of the common-law courts (1873) see vol. xiv of this *History*, pp. 16–19.

jurisdiction. Eldon opposed as long as possible all changes in an antiquated system which caused loss and misery to thousands of suitors;[1] he gave way in 1812 before the pressure of public opinion, and agreed to allow an additional judge to clear off some of the arrears of his own court; twenty years was not an unusual length for a chancery case. The procedure of the court remained unchanged until in 1828 Brougham raised the whole question of legal reform. Peel began, in his cautious way, by substituting payment by salary for payment by fees in the courts for the recovery of small debts. He thus bought off the opposition of a number of minor legal officials. Within a short time Brougham himself became chancellor; he simplified the procedure of the high courts, laid down new rules for the court of chancery, abolished many sinecure posts, and, in spite of the opposition of chancery lawyers, set up a new court to deal with bankruptcy cases. Hitherto only traders could declare themselves bankrupt, and imprisonment for debt remained an absurd and cruel anomaly until an act of 1844 did away with this penalty in cases of debts under £20, and allowed private debtors to go into bankruptcy. Seventeen years later all persons imprisoned for debt were classed as insolvent, and the debtors' prisons were thus emptied, although imprisonment for debt, as distinct from a refusal to carry out the order of a court, was not abolished until 1869. Meanwhile the establishment of county courts[2] in 1846 was an immense advantage to creditors who could recover small debts without great cost and inconvenience.

The law of real property remained a lumber-room of pedantry and a rich source of income for lawyers; the establishment of a registry of titles in 1862 had little effect, partly because solicitors did not encourage their clients to use it. On the other hand the criminal code was consolidated in 1860, and, in 1863, after the preparation of an index to the statutes, parliament began the repeal of a large number of obsolete or unnecessary laws. No attempt was made to simplify the language of the laws, or to compile a civil code, and the English legal system in 1870,

---

[1] It is an interesting comment upon the state of equity jurisdiction that when a prizefighter put his opponent at his mercy he was said to hold him 'in chancery'.

[2] The name is misleading; every poor-law union had a county court, and neighbouring courts were grouped into circuits under the jurisdiction of a single judge. Bentham had suggested courts of this kind. The facilities for recovering debts led to an increase in small credits, and hence to the imprisonment of more small debtors.

though far less of an anomaly and a hindrance to a reasonable social order than it had been in 1815, was still very far from an ideal code in which rights and remedies were clearly stated, and processes like the buying and selling of land could be carried out easily and cheaply.[1]

[1] For the reform of legal education see below, pp. 618–19. Two other legal reforms deserve special mention.

1. An act of 1833, due to Brougham's efforts, transferred the judicial work of the privy council to a judicial committee of the council consisting of the lord chancellor, two privy councillors, and certain high judicial officers, with the addition, in ecclesiastical cases, of prelates who were members of the council.

2. After the failure of previous attempts, including his own and those of Peel, Russell carried in 1836 a measure allowing civil marriage and dispensing non-conformists from the publication of banns in churches. Russell's act is of interest for the general administrative history of the period, since it made use of the new machinery provided by the poor law, and appointed registrars of births, marriages, and deaths in every poor-law union. The act required a medical certificate of the cause of death, and was of great social value in preventing and detecting crime.

Reform of divorce procedure was the logical consequence of the introduction of civil marriage, but until 1857 divorce required a special act of parliament. An act of 1857, in spite of strong opposition from the clergy (and from Gladstone, who is said to have spoken a hundred times in the debates), created a special court for the hearing of divorce petitions, put divorce on the same footing as other civil actions, and allowed the remarriage of divorced persons.

II

EDUCATION, 1815–70

THE changes in the character, scope, and extension of schools and universities throughout the United Kingdom between 1815 and 1870 might well be taken as the central feature of the age of reform. These changes, which affected the manners, outlook, and capacity of every class in society, were part of the general movement towards a higher standard of life. Furthermore, while the political and administrative measures of the time were directed towards a better arrangement of things, the educational reformers aimed at the improvement of people, though by increasing the supply of persons qualified to serve the administrative and technical needs of an industrial society they were solving a problem as practical as the problems solved by the engineers. The new schools were as necessary as the new machine tools and the new railways.

There were deep-seated prejudices against educational reform, and an indifference which was almost more troublesome than prejudice. The engineers and inventors also had to deal with opposition of this kind; but their discoveries and processes offered immediate results, and appealed to motives of personal gain. Educational reform was expensive; it brought no immediate results, and was concerned, in the hands of its best advocates, with values which could not be measured in commercial language. Self-made and successful men, quick to see the possibilities of a new machine or the importance of a good water-supply for their towns, did not show the same alertness of mind in considering the economic advantages of an educated working class. From their point of view an educated working class meant an increase in labour troubles. They were less likely to agree with Carlyle's view: 'Who would suppose that Education were a thing which had to be advocated on the ground of local expediency, or indeed on any ground? As if it stood not on the basis of everlasting duty, as a prime necessity of man.'[1]

The prejudices against book-learning were not altogether unfounded. 'Education' as a subject was not properly studied;

[1] T. Carlyle, *Chartism*, p. 98 (1842 ed.).

existing schools and universities were not producing very striking results. They did little to improve the standard of technical efficiency. Artisans, engineers, and inventors learned their trade as apprentices, or as 'hands' in workshops; for many years the backwardness of English technical instruction was due to the number and efficiency of the workshops and factories where a man was taught his business in a practical way. Technical education in Germany advanced more rapidly because Germans had fewer workshops in which to learn. If higher education, such as it was, appeared to be merely a form of vocational training for clergymen, lawyers, and doctors, and an ornament of a harmless kind for those who wanted to be 'gentlemen', elementary education was equally unsatisfactory. In 1815 the most common method of education in Great Britain, and in many other European countries, was a plan described by Joseph Lancaster,[1] one of its chief advocates, as 'a new mechanical system for the use of schools'. This plan was simple: the elder children in a school taught the younger children. Andrew Bell,[2] another pioneer of the movement, summed up the method: 'Give me twenty-four pupils to-day, and I will give you twenty-four teachers to-morrow.' Lancaster and Bell were not men of any depth of character; each claimed priority as the inventor of the 'monitorial' system, though it had been discussed in France long before it became popular in England. The plan had certain advantages. It was cheap; it reduced the cost of educating a child to seven shillings a year, and, as little money was spent on teaching the poor, there was something to be said for spreading the rudiments of knowledge by the least expensive method. In any case there was a shortage of teachers, and until 1846 little was done to meet this shortage by training people for the work.

[1] Joseph Lancaster (1778–1838); s. of a soldier; b. Southwark; served for a short time as a naval volunteer; joined the Society of Friends; opened a school in Southwark, 1801, and tried the monitorial system because he could not afford to pay assistants; published an account of his school, 1803; went to America, 1818, where he lived for the rest of his life. Lancaster, though vain and unbalanced, was less mechanical than Bell in his methods; he did not want to associate them with denominational teaching.

[2] Andrew Bell (1753–1832); s. of a barber; b. St. Andrews; educ. St. Andrews University, 1769; ordained in church of England; sailed for India, 1787; superintendent of the Madras Male Orphan Asylum, 1789, where he began the plan of using the elder children to teach the juniors; published an account of his system, 1797; rector of Swanage, 1801; spent most of his time in spreading his methods of teaching; superintended the work of the National Society. Bell was a domineering and conceited man, with a great love of money.

The monitorial system had merits of its own. It introduced discipline, responsibility, mutual aid, and corporate life into the schools of the poor; it bridged the gulf between teachers and taught which was one of the greatest obstacles to reform in the public schools of the professional and upper classes. The faults of the system were obvious; it would have broken down at once if education had been regarded as more than a mechanical process of instilling a number of facts into the minds of children. It lasted for a generation largely because the supporters of popular education had nothing better to suggest. The utilitarians believed in knowledge, but they never understood small boys. James Mill's treatment of his own son is an example of over-intellectualism, while Bentham's *Chrestomathia*, with its 'new system of instruction . . . for the use of the middling and higher ranks of life', is a curious mixture of absurdity and good sense. Bentham thought that his Panopticon[1] was equally suited for a prison or a school. He based discipline on 'the Universal Delation principle, or Non-connivance-tolerating principle'; in other words, sneaking.

There were wiser and better views of educational method. The education of children in their own homes was influenced indirectly by Rousseau, and directly by the work of R. L. Edgeworth and his daughter.[2] Their book, *Practical Education*, first published in 1798 and reissued as late as 1822, taught the importance of play and of handwork in the training of children's minds, and began the great change in the relations between parents and their children which developed slowly throughout the nineteenth century. The civilizing of children before they went to school was one of the great aids to the civilizing of the public schools. The Edgeworths' book affected mainly the upper and upper middle classes; Robert Owen's introduction of infant schools in connexion with his factories touched a wider class. Here, as in other spheres, Owen's influence might have been greater if he had taken more care to respect popular prejudice. Owen found himself in trouble with the fellow directors of his business (three of these directors were quakers) because he included music, dancing, and preparation for military drill in his schools. Above all, his opposition to religion put him out of

---

[1] The Panopticon was a building with a number of rooms or cells radiating from a central observation-point, so that an observer at this point could supervise the circle of which he was the centre.   [2] Maria Edgeworth, the novelist.

court with the only bodies who were carrying out educational work on a large scale.

No political party in Great Britain accepted the well-known phrase, adopted by the French jacobins, that education should be 'universal, compulsory, gratuitous, and secular'. Gratuitous education was impossible without state control, and this control was suspect in a country where the establishment of religious freedom was a recent memory, and every form of governmental interference was open to doubt. Compulsory education appeared to be an attack upon the liberty of the individual. Few people in England, fewer in Scotland, and practically no one in Ireland or Wales wanted secular schools. The force of vested interests was as powerful as the force of habit. Elementary education in England was in the hands of religious societies. The first stage had been the Sunday schools in which children were taught to read the bible. The next development was an extension of the Sunday school: an attempt to spread education of a religious type among the children of the poor. The motives of those who supported this attempt were a mixture of pure charity, a desire to relieve misery and ignorance, and a fear of the possible dangers of an increasingly large and illiterate urban population. There was also a rivalry between the established church and the nonconformists; neither party could leave the other in possession of the field. In 1815 the two most important religious societies were the 'National Society for promoting the education of the poor in the principles of the established church' (founded in 1811) and the 'British and Foreign School Society' (founded in 1814); the former society taught the liturgy and catechism of the church of England, the latter enforced bible-reading, but excluded denominational teaching.

It would be unfair to criticize too harshly the work of these societies. They were doing something which no one else was attempting; they gave the rudiments of education to thousands of children who would otherwise have remained illiterate. They did not create the denominational rivalry which, for years to come, stood in the way of a plan of national education. Yet they could not cover the whole of the country; there were limits to the means and the generosity of their subscribers. They were more interested in religious instruction than in general education, narrowly jealous of their religious principles, and ready to oppose grants by the state which might be of greater advantage to their denominational rivals than to themselves. State aid had been suggested before the foundation of these two societies. In 1807 Whitbread introduced a bill allowing the establishment of rate-aided schools, under the supervision of the clergy, in every parish. There had been a school in every parish in Scotland since the seventeenth century, but in Scotland the religious difficulty did not exist because most people, until the disruption of 1843,[1] supported the established presbyterian church. The commons accepted Whitbread's plan; the lords rejected it because they thought that it did not safeguard the interests of religion, or, rather, of the established church. Nine years later Brougham moved for a parliamentary committee to inquire into 'the education of the Lower Orders in London'. After the presentation of the report he asked for a royal commission to consider the position of educational charities in England and Wales. In 1820 he introduced an education bill which required that all teachers should be members of the church of England; that the clergy should control the plan of teaching in the schools, and that religious teaching should be limited to the bible, without the use of any denominational catechism. Neither churchmen nor nonconformists would accept a compromise of this kind; the bill was dropped, and the rivalry of the denominational societies blocked the way until 1833. In this year a sum of £20,000 was voted 'for the purposes of education'; the National and the British and Foreign Societies shared the grant and used it for the building of schools. Preference was given to schools in large towns, and the grant was available only in cases where voluntary contributions met half of the cost of a new school. Parliament continued the grant after 1833, and also voted £10,000 for school-building in Scotland.

The number of children at school doubled between 1820 and 1834, but more buildings and more teachers were needed;[2] a committee of the commons reported in 1838 that an increase in the grants to the societies was the only practicable way of attaining

---

[1] See below, pp. 526-8.

[2] Estimates of school attendance vary considerably. One estimate in 1833 suggested that about a third of the children of the working classes in England had no schooling. Inquiries by the Manchester Statistical Society showed that one-third of the children in Manchester and one-half of the children in Liverpool did not attend any school. These figures included a large Irish population, and were not typical of Lancashire, where about 60 per cent. of the children went to some kind of school. On the other hand only 10 per cent. were at schools of reasonable educational standard.

this end. The cabinet was less satisfied with the voluntary system, and decided that the question wanted more careful study. They did not ask parliament to set up a board of education; the lords would certainly have opposed the plan. On Russell's initiative a special committee of the privy council, with the lord president as chairman, was appointed to administer the grant made by the house of commons.[1] The committee proposed to establish a training college and to adopt the principle that general religious teaching would be given in schools under state authority, and denominational teaching by ministers. The plan broke down because the church asked for complete control, and the nonconformists thought that any kind of state management was contrary to the principle of religious liberty. The storm was so great that the committee nearly foundered in it; an increase in the parliamentary grant was carried only by two votes, and the lords, led by the archbishop of Canterbury, protested to the queen against the establishment of the committee.

The secretary of the committee, Dr. Kay (later Sir James Kay-Shuttleworth), told Russell that he was working for 'the claims of the civil power to control the education of the country'. He knew a good deal about the condition of England and the new problems of administration, since he had served as a poor-law commissioner and also practised as a doctor in the poorer parts of Manchester. He gave way before the opposition of the religious denominations to a single training college. On the other hand he sent inspectors to schools receiving state help; he gave grants only to schools where voluntary contributions were provided, and tried to obtain clauses in the trust deeds of schools guaranteeing the liberty of parents in matters of doctrinal instruction, particularly in single-school areas. There was little demand for secular schools. The political parties were alarmed at the irreligion and 'pernicious opinions' of the masses, and felt that 'all instruction should be hallowed by the influence of religion'.

The inspectors reported depressing facts about the working of the monitorial system and the inefficiency of the schools. In 1846 the committee proposed a new system of training which

---

[1] Russell, in his best high whig manner, wanted the committee 'to afford gratuities to deserving schoolmasters; there is no class of men whose rewards are so disproportionate to their usefulness to the community'.

would get rid of the monitors. They apprenticed 'pupil teachers' for five years to schools recommended by their inspectors; these pupil teachers were eligible for grants to a training college, and teachers with a training college certificate received an annual government grant in addition to their ordinary salaries. The parliamentary grant was now raised to £100,000; public opinion began to accept the fact of state aid and supervision on an increasingly large scale, but was still opposed to the idea of a state educational service. On the other hand, although the religious societies protested that state control meant stagnation and that religion was not a 'subject' which could be separated from secular instruction, the problem of finding enough money by voluntary subscription was becoming insoluble. There was an alternative; the local rates might be used to supplement parliamentary grants and private subscription, but the religious question was once more an obstacle. Many ratepayers objected to paying for schools of religious denominations other than their own. In 1853 Russell introduced a bill giving towns of more than 5,000 inhabitants power to levy an education rate. The bill was not accepted. This failure did not prevent the privy council committee from giving capitation grants to schools in rural areas on condition that a certain sum was raised locally. Three years later the grants were extended to the towns. These measures brought further increases in the parliamentary grant. The sum was raised, in 1857, to £541,233, and the cost of administration was now greater than the whole educational charge in 1843. A department of education was set up in 1856; this measure was little more than a minor administrative reform bringing under one authority the work done by the committee and the business of the department of science and art established in 1853 under the board of trade.[1] On the other hand the part played by the state in education was at last important enough to justify direct representation in parliament. For this purpose a new office was created under the Crown; the holder of the office had the title of vice-president of the committee of the privy council for education, but he was, in practice, minister of education.

A further step of great importance was taken in 1858. The rising cost of education, and increasing uneasiness at the growth of bureaucratic control, led to a demand for a parliamentary commission of inquiry. This commission was appointed, with

---

[1] See below, p. 500.

the duke of Newcastle as chairman, to inquire 'into the present state of popular education in England, and to consider and report what measures, if any, are required for the extension of sound and cheap elementary instruction to all classes of the people'.[1] The commissioners estimated that only 4·5 per cent. of the children of school age were not attending school. This estimate was too low, but the report was not optimistic about the amount or value of the education given in the schools. Most children left school at the age of eleven; among the poorer classes only one child in twenty received any sort of education after the age of thirteen. The commissioners had no means of judging the efficiency of private schools; they believed that in most case these schools were less efficient than the state-aided schools visited by government inspectors. The cost of education in inspected schools was 28s. to 30s. a year for every child. The training of teachers and the administrative expenses of the state added another 4s. 6d. Of this sum the parents paid less than a third, and the state contributed more than one half; the remainder came from endowments or subscriptions.

The report did not recommend compulsory education; the commissioners were not agreed in principle on the question, and in any case public opinion was not ready to compel parents to send their children to school or to accept the view that 'the state' has an obligation to educate its citizens. For similar reasons, the commissioners did not think it practicable to suggest raising the school-leaving age. They proposed the establishment of boards of education in counties and in boroughs of more than 40,000 inhabitants. These boards would have power to levy rates, to examine children in reading, writing, and arithmetic, and to pay grants on the results of these tests; they would not appoint teachers, or interfere with the management of schools. In this way the commissioners hoped to avoid the religious difficulty.

The government was unwilling to risk another storm of denominational jealousy over local rates. They did not set up the local boards, but Robert Lowe,[2] as head of the education

---

[1] The commissioners took account of systems in other countries; Matthew Arnold was sent to report on the French, Dutch, and Swiss methods.

[2] Robert Lowe, 1st Viscount Sherbrooke (1811–92); s. of a clergyman; b. Bingham, Notts.; educ. Winchester and University College, Oxford; fellow of Magdalen College, 1835–6; called to the bar, and went to Australia, 1842; member of the New South Wales legislative council, 1843–50; M.P., 1852; joint secretary of

department, welcomed the principle of payment by results, and applied it in a narrow, inflexible way. There was at the time a good deal to be said for this principle. The commissioners believed that many children leaving school at the age of eleven were badly taught because the teachers neglected the 'drill of the three R.s' for work more interesting to themselves. Payment by results would put an end to this neglect; the only way to test results was by examination. The system raised the standards of the worst schools, and gave mediocre teachers and school managing committees an incentive to greater efficiency. Since the majority of schools and teachers were inefficient this way of raising the general level was not entirely against the interests of the children. On the other hand the system was drearily mechanical; it forced the pace for the dull children, led to the neglect of those who could be trusted to pass the examinations, and concentrated too much attention upon elementary work. Unfortunately Lowe accepted payment by results as an end in itself, and for two decades or longer, after his years of office, the central authority enforced this deadening system.[1]

During the next ten years the demand for a national system of education increased in force. English education was known to be backward in comparison with that of many continental countries, and the wars of the period 1860-70 seemed to show that an educated nation could provide better soldiers than a less educated rival. The north beat the south in the United States; Prussia defeated Austria in Europe. The reform bill of 1867 made the education of the masses an urgent problem. Thus in 1868 the liberal government, with W. E. Forster[2] in charge of the education department, was in a strong position for carrying a far-reaching measure. The supporters of 'unsectarian' education tried to force the government to give up the denominational

the board of control, 1852-5; vice-president of the board of trade, 1855-8; vice-president of the committee of the privy council on education, 1859-64; chancellor of the exchequer, 1868-73; home secretary, 1873-4.

[1] Men who were more liberal-minded than Lowe did not object to examinations. Mill, in his inaugural address as rector of St. Andrews in 1867, approved of the compulsory examination of children every year until they reached a minimum standard. The examinations begun by the College of Preceptors in 1853, and the Oxford and Cambridge local examinations, first held in 1858, were of great use in widening the field of studies and raising the standard of secondary education.

[2] William Edward Forster (1818-86); b. Bradpole, Dorset; educ. Tottenham quaker school; entered woollen business, 1836; M.P., 1861; under-secretary for the colonies, 1865-6; vice-president of the committee of the privy council for education, 1868-74; chief secretary for Ireland, 1880-2.

principle. The centre of this radical agitation was the National Education League, founded at Birmingham in 1869 by Joseph Chamberlain, R. W. Dale (a well-known congregational minister), and others. The supporters of the religious principle formed a National Education Union. The government, not unreasonably, chose a compromise, and aimed at a sufficient number of schools, open to state inspection, and allowing complete religious liberty. The denominational schools were left untouched in areas where they were working well, and met the local needs. Elsewhere locally elected school boards were given powers to levy rates, build schools, provide teachers, and, if they thought fit, insist upon the attendance of all children who were not being educated in any other way. A clause suggested by W. Cowper-Temple laid down that religious instruction in the 'board schools' should exclude any 'catechism or religious formulary distinctive of any particular denomination'. On the other hand the grants to denominational schools were increased, though no rate aid was allowed to them.

The bill passed its final reading on 9 August 1870. It was limited to children under thirteen. It did not provide free education, because only those parents who could not afford payment were excused fees. The exclusion of denominational teaching was hardly logical; it kept ministers of religion out of the state schools, and established, in Disraeli's words, 'a new sacerdotal class' of schoolmasters with the duty of interpreting the bible in any way they pleased, as long as their interpretation was not that of any existing church formulary. Yet the bill was a great step forward. For the first time it secured local expenditure on education. The 'board schools' had more resources than the voluntary schools; the first step towards compulsion had been taken, and, although religious differences were still an obstacle to the smooth working of a national system of education, henceforward there were no areas in England without schools, and no children grew up without elementary education merely because their parents were poor.

For many years the problems of elementary education were the building of schools, the training of teachers, and, above all, the development of a public opinion which would look beyond the rivalry of the denominations. The obstacles in the way of the reform and extension of secondary education were different in kind. There could be no question during these years of secondary education for the poor; the demand could not be effective until elementary schools were established throughout the country. Secondary education in England and Wales was therefore limited to the middle and upper classes. In Scotland a superstructure had already been built on the foundation of the parish schools, and, in the towns, the burgh schools and academics. These schools were perhaps too much interested in preparing children for a successful career; the first headmaster of Loretto[1] encouraged games as a corrective to the concentration of many of his fellow countrymen upon getting on in the world.

With all its faults, the Scottish system was better than the unreformed system of secondary education in England. There were three types of English secondary school: grammar schools, private schools, and public schools. The distinction between public schools and grammar schools had grown up during the eighteenth century; the former were merely those grammar schools which had escaped the general decadence of educational foundations, increased their staff, and taken boarders. The boarders solved the financial problem; the salaries of the grammar schools were fixed by their statutes, and in many cases the schools had decayed owing to the decline in the purchasing-power of these fixed stipends. The old statutes were a hindrance in other respects; they laid down a curriculum which took no account of subjects developed since the sixteenth or seventeenth centuries. In 1805 a judgement of Lord Eldon declared that this limitation of subjects was binding, and, until an act of 1840 gave the courts power to change the statutes of a school, a grammar school founded in the reign of Elizabeth to teach Latin and Greek could teach only Latin and Greek in the nineteenth century.

The decline in the grammar schools was also the result of a change in social habit. During the eighteenth century many tradesmen's sons went to Eton and Winchester; the next hundred years brought a stricter segregation of classes. The change

[1] H. H. Almond, headmaster of Loretto, 1862-1903. Almond also began the change from stuffiness to fresh air. He started in 1862 with rules enforcing open windows, tweed knickers, and open flannel shirts; in 1864 he added compulsory cold baths; in 1866 no coats; in 1867 no waistcoats, and runs in wet weather; in 1869 no food between meals; in 1870 no hats; and in 1874 the regular use of flannels for games.

was due not merely to social exclusiveness but also to a greater care about the environment in which children were brought up. The private schools came into existence for the same reasons. Many of them were founded, like King's College and University College schools, by reformers dissatisfied with public and grammar schools. Middle-class parents tended to choose these private schools; farmers and shopkeepers with ambitions for their children would certainly choose them. They gave more supervision than other types of school; they were readier to take up modern subjects. Private-school masters often led the way in reform; Rowland Hill and his family introduced into their school at Birmingham separate form-rooms, instead of the large class-rooms customary elsewhere, and tried experiments in self-government. On the whole the private schools inclined towards mechanical methods of teaching, and wearisome cramming out of little handbooks.

The public schools were, in 1815, the survivors in a struggle for existence, but they would not have outlasted the age of reform if they had not been remodelled under the direction of a few remarkable men. Their curriculum was narrowly classical and linguistic; their methods of teaching put too great a burden on memory, and their textbooks were out of date and unimaginative, though in these respects other schools were not in a better position. The discipline of the classics (or, in the less complimentary words of Sydney Smith, 'the safe and elegant imbecility of classical learning') was not without value, and, if boys were compelled to learn most of their work by heart, they were as well employed in learning Greek and Latin authors as in any other form of memorizing. The boarding arrangements at the public schools were not as bad as might have been expected.[1] The maintenance of order was the great difficulty. The schools were understaffed, and order was kept by terror. Relations between masters and boys were nearly always unfriendly; organized games were slowly taking shape, though their educational value was entirely neglected. When the duke of Wellington talked about the playing-fields of Eton he had in mind not games but fighting. As late as 1818 two companies of

---

[1] In 1838 Hawtrey, a reforming headmaster of Eton, answered a deputation asking for water to be laid on in college: 'You will be wanting gas and turkey carpets next', but the answer would not have seemed unreasonable to Hawtrey's contemporaries.

soldiers with fixed bayonets were brought into the buildings at Winchester to put an end to a school 'rebellion'. Traditions of this kind could be broken down only by men of strong character, who knew how to gain the respect as well as the fear of boys; for this reason the reform of the public schools, with its immense effect upon the habits of mind of the governing class, was the work of a few men. Thomas Arnold[1] is the best known of the first generation of reforming headmasters. He was one of the products of the reform movement in the universities. He went up to a working college, and won an Oriel fellowship at a time when Oriel was almost alone in setting the highest intellectual standard. At Oxford Arnold learned that the study of the classics could be used as an introduction to the study of living problems. Arnold was a liberal by temperament, and his methods of teaching were intended to stimulate interest and free inquiry; he asked questions about the subject-matter as well as the syntax of the books read by his boys. He included French and mathematics as regular subjects at Rugby; hitherto they had been 'extras'. His main work was the civilizing of school life. He did not invent many of the methods which he used. Samuel Butler, headmaster of Shrewsbury from 1798 to 1836, had introduced modern subjects, and tried to make his senior boys govern the school in a responsible way. A housemaster from Eton, who was Arnold's predecessor at Rugby, had already increased the prestige of the school and nearly quintupled its numbers. Arnold deserves his reputation because his personality impressed boys and masters. Others had found the prefectorial system a nuisance; the prefects were the ringleaders of disturbance. Arnold won their confidence, and used them to raise the discipline and moral tone of the school. School chapels had been part of the dry routine of education. Arnold was the first headmaster to make the chapel a centre of school life. Many of his assistant masters spread his methods elsewhere; Cotton, for example, introduced Arnold's ideas at Marlborough, and encouraged rugby football to keep his boys from poaching and other mischief.[2]

Edward Thring, headmaster of Uppingham from 1853 to

---

[1] Thomas Arnold (1795-1842); s. of a collector of customs; b. East Cowes; educ. Winchester and Corpus Christi College, Oxford; settled at Laleham, where he took pupils, 1819; headmaster of Rugby, 1828-42; published *Principles of Church Reform*, 1833; regius professor of modern history at Oxford, 1841.

[2] See below, pp. 627-8, for the development of football and other games.

1887, introduced another type of reform. Thring came from Eton and King's, and knew the best and worst features of the old system. As a young clergyman in Gloucester he was interested in elementary education. A breakdown in health made him give up parish work for private coaching. In 1853 he was offered the headmastership of Uppingham, a small grammar school with 2 masters and 25 boys. He raised the numbers to 30 masters and 320 boys, and refused to go beyond this figure. Thring was not less of an autocrat than Arnold, but he had not to fight a bad tradition, and could give more time to educational experiments. He thought that a school should aim at educating every boy, and not merely the clever boys; for this reason he would not allow large forms. He carried Arnold's work of civilizing schoolboys one stage farther by improving the appearance of class-rooms, hanging pictures on the walls, and providing good desks on which boys were not allowed to carve their names. He limited to the mornings the ordinary subjects of school work—classics, mathematics, English composition, scripture, history, and geography—and gave the afternoons to optional subjects, including drawing, carpentry, and turning. It is characteristic of Thring and of the public-school masters of his time that he distrusted the training of secondary-school teachers. He thought that this training was too mechanical, and wanted his masters to work out their methods for themselves.

The Newcastle Commission on elementary education was followed within a few years by two other inquiries covering the field of secondary education. The first of the commissions was appointed in 1861, with Lord Clarendon as chairman, to report on the great public schools; the second commission, appointed in 1864 and presided over by Lord Taunton, dealt with schools not included in the other two inquiries. The Clarendon commissioners were mainly concerned with the administrative side of the schools, though they reported, in a guarded way, a general impression of idleness. They believed in a classical education, but thought that the methods of teaching Latin and Greek were old-fashioned. They did not suggest very sweeping changes. The Taunton commissioners had a much wider subject of inquiry. Their report showed the great need of secondary schools. A hundred towns of 5,000 or more inhabitants had no endowed grammar schools, and, in spite of the opportunities given in 1840 to endowed schools to change their statutes, few of them

made provision for education in non-classical subjects. There had
been an increase in the number of public schools: Cheltenham
was founded in 1841, Marlborough in 1843, Rossall in 1844,
Wellington in 1856, Clifton in 1862, Malvern in 1865, Radley
in 1847, Haileybury (formerly a training college of the East
India Company) in 1862. Some of these schools took day boys,
but their pupils were drawn from a social class above the level
of the grammar schools. A few proprietary schools were started
in county towns, and Nathaniel Woodard (1811-91), an anglican
clergyman, began an ambitious plan for the higher education of
the middle classes. He proposed to divide the country into five
areas and to found three schools in each area; the schools would
be graded according to their fees and the type of education
provided. Woodard's first school was at Lancing; two other
schools, Hurstpierpoint and Ardingly, soon followed, but the
scheme never had enough financial support. In any case
Woodard's aims were strictly anglican; he wanted to reconcile
the middle classes to the church and to defeat the radicalism
of his time; a plan of this kind needed a religious order of
trained teachers. The Woodard schools merely touched the
fringe of a problem which, as the Taunton commissioners
realized, could be solved only with the assistance of the state.
The commissioners believed that most middle-class parents
desired a religious education for their children, though they did
not trouble themselves about denominational differences. The
report suggested the establishment of rate-aided secondary
schools, controlled partly by local boards of education, but this
recommendation was not put into effect. The endowed schools
act of 1869 did little more than appoint three commissioners to
revise the statutes of the grammar schools.

Neither the Clarendon nor the Taunton commissioners recommended any change in the 'class' basis of English secondary
education. Even if they had disapproved of separating children
according to the social status of their parents, it is improbable
that they could have altered a system which had established
itself in English life. Class distinctions existed outside the schools;
the schools did nothing to mitigate them, and, in the course of
time, a great deal to intensify them. From one point of view it
may be said that the public schools performed a certain service
in mixing the old aristocracy with the new professional middle
class; on the other hand they separated both these classes from

the poor. Thus, before the reform of the grammar schools, and long before the resources of the state were used to provide a good secondary education for the children of the poor, the richer classes of the country had become attached to certain schools, familiar with the segregation of their own class in these schools, and accustomed to a particular code of habits, manners, and social behaviour which, for better or worse, the children of the poor had no opportunity to learn.

The religious question was no obstacle in the way of the reform of secondary education. The reforming headmasters gave to their schools the type of religious teaching which most middle and upper class Englishmen wanted; those who disliked it were not asked to pay for it, or to assist in enforcing it upon others. On the other hand the reform of the universities was never free from religious and political controversy. The condition of Oxford and Cambridge invited criticism. Oxford was governed by Laudian, Cambridge by Elizabethan statutes. Internal reform was not easy. The colleges were independent societies jealous of outside interference; the governing body in each university was composed mainly of heads of houses, elderly and safe men who did not wish for change, and the clerical vote was almost always in a majority in the general assemblies of masters of arts. The college tutors had little part in the direction of university affairs, and, although many of them were able men, they were burdened with large classes of an elementary kind. There was no inducement for them to stay in the university, since they could not hold their fellowships after marriage. The relation between the colleges and the university was unsatisfactory. The universities were poor; many of the colleges were rich, and made little contribution to higher studies. The restriction of many fellowships and scholarships to founder's kin or to persons born in particular localities or educated at particular schools led to abuse, and filled the colleges with idle and useless members.

In spite of these shortcomings reform of studies had begun. Jackson, as dean of Christ Church from 1783 to 1809, did much to encourage work. Oriel since 1795 elected fellows by examination from outside its own body. Balliol in 1828 elected most of its scholars by open examination. Cambridge was in many ways in advance of Oxford; college examinations were held in St. John's as early as 1772. Written examinations, and a real viva voce examination instead of the formal disputation, were established for the degree of B.A. at Oxford in 1800, and an honours list was added to the ordinary pass school. Mathematics and physics became a separate school in 1807, and in 1830 different subjects of examination were prescribed for pass and honours candidates. The Cambridge mathematical tripos had a high reputation long before 1815; a separate classical tripos was instituted in 1824, though, until 1850, it was open only to honours graduates in mathematics.

The critics of the universities were concerned as much with their religious exclusiveness as with their educational shortcomings. At Oxford no one could matriculate without subscribing to the thirty-nine articles; at Cambridge nonconformists might become members of the university, but they had not access to scholarships, fellowships, or university degrees. The universities were the training-places of the anglican clergy; each college had its chapel, at which attendance was compulsory, and the endowments of religion could not easily be separated from those of learning. The movement outside the universities in favour of university reform was part of a larger attack upon the anglican church; it was supported not only by the enemies of the establishment but also by the enemies of religion. If churchmen believed that they were defending the connexion of religion with the state, many of their opponents held similar views about the nature of their attack. The tractarians were driven to the defence of vested interests, of which in other respects they disapproved, because they feared that the secularization of the universities was one stage in the movement towards the secularization of national life.[1] On the other hand a number of members of each university, including Thirlwall, later bishop of St. David's, Turton, later bishop of Ely, and Musgrave, later archbishop of York, supported the removal of religious tests. The question was raised in parliament, and a bill, discussed with much heat, passed the commons in 1834, only to be thrown out by the upper house.

Sixteen years later, when churchmen were less panic-stricken about the threat to religion, two commissions were appointed to report on the state of Oxford and Cambridge. They were not well received. The two vice-chancellors refused to give information; the dean of Christ Church would not even answer letters from the commissioners, and the bishop of Exeter, as visitor

[1] See below, p. 515.

of Exeter College, compared their work with the attempts of James II to subject the university to his 'unhallowed control'. The two members for Oxford University, Gladstone and Sir Robert Inglis, joined in the protests; Gladstone said that there was not 'the shadow or the pretext of a case for inquiry'. The report on Oxford was more severe than that on Cambridge. It was not altogether fair. Scottish critics did not understand the tutorial system or the reasons why professors were less important in the English universities than in Scotland, but there was more reason in the view that Oxford paid too little attention to the advancement of knowledge, and that too large a place was given to classics. Neither commission dealt directly with the admission of nonconformists; the Oxford report disapproved of the rule requiring subscription to the thirty-nine articles, and the Cambridge report suggested that the university ought to 'throw open the advantages of its system of education . . . as widely as the State has thrown open the avenues to civil rights and honours'. Although the church interest was strong enough to keep nonconformists out of fellowships and university or college offices,[1] the acts of 1854 and 1856 which embodied the main proposals of the commissioners freed from religious tests matriculation at Oxford and admission to degrees at either university (except in the faculty of theology). Bills were introduced annually from 1863 for the abolition of the remaining tests; in 1871 'the citadel was taken'.

Meanwhile the universities had been enlarging their field of studies. In 1851 Cambridge had begun triposes in the natural and moral sciences; a year earlier Oxford founded honour schools of natural science, and law and history. Oxford built laboratories between 1855 and 1860; the Cambridge buildings were a little later, but with the gift of the Cavendish laboratory by the duke of Devonshire in 1871, during his chancellorship, Cambridge had a better centre of research than the smaller and earlier laboratories of Oxford. As early as 1825 there was a movement in favour of a non-sectarian university in London. Brougham, Russell, and the poet Thomas Campbell[2] decided to form a public utility company on Benthamite lines, and, with

---

[1] In 1860 and 1861 the senior wranglers at Cambridge were debarred from fellowships owing to the religious tests.

[2] Thomas Campbell (1777–1844); b. and educ. Glasgow; wrote *The Pleasures of Hope, Ye Mariners of England,* and published *Specimens of the English Poets* (7 vols.).

money raised in this way, to build a college. Macaulay, Grote, James Mill, and other liberals and radicals supported them, and in 1828 a college was opened under the ambitious name of the 'University of London'. Religious opposition, and the jealousy of Oxford, Cambridge, and the medical associations, delayed the grant of power to give degrees. Churchmen, and a good many nonconformists, feared that the university might develop on secular lines; for this reason King's College[1] was founded as a rival institution on anglican principles. In 1836 the two colleges were incorporated as the university of London, and the secular foundation took the name of University College. The university received power to confer degrees, to examine students, and (in 1850) to include in its membership other institutions of higher education. The arrangement was not a very good one. The university had 'no concrete existence between the recurring throes of examination'; and the affiliated colleges and institutions had no common life. In 1858 the examinations of the university were thrown open to all men who applied to sit for them. The gulf between teaching or research departments and the examining or administrative work of the university increased, and for many years the university of London did not take the prominent place in the national life which its position and resources would otherwise have allowed.

Elsewhere the development of university institutions was slow. The establishment of the university of Durham gave effect to a plan favoured by Cromwell during the Commonwealth. In 1832 the dean and chapter of the cathedral granted a sum of £3,000 a year from their large revenues towards the maintenance of a university predominantly theological in its studies.[2] The grant was increased in 1841, and in 1852 the College of

[1] The foundation of King's College provoked the last duel fought by an English prime minister. Lord Winchilsea, who was a strong opponent of catholic relief, accused the duke of Wellington of using the plan as a cloak 'for his insidious designs for the infringement of our liberties and the introduction of popery into every department of state'. Wellington challenged Winchilsea, and the two peers met in Battersea Fields on 21 March 1829.

[2] The motives behind this grant were not entirely disinterested. One of the members of the chapter wrote in Aug. 1831: 'It appears to be morally certain that, as soon as the Reform Bill is disposed of, an attack will be made on Dean and Chapters, and as certain that Durham will be the first object. It has occurred to us that it will be prudent, if possible, to ward off the blow ... by annexing an establishment of enlarged education to our college [i.e. to the dean and chapter]. No doubt sacrifices would be required of us. We regard them as a premium to be paid to insure the remainder.' Quoted in 'The Bishops and Reform', *E.H.R.* lvi (1941), p. 461.

Medicine at Newcastle was connected with the university. The number of students was never large, and fell after 1860 with the development of technical education in the great towns of the north. An undenominational college was founded at Manchester in 1851, with a benefaction left by John Owens;[1] there were colleges of medicine at Leeds (1831), Birmingham (1828), Sheffield (1828), and a college at Lampeter (1822), intended mainly for the education of the Welsh clergy. Throughout this period the four universities of Scotland[2] were untroubled by the religious difficulties and accumulation of vested interests which harassed reformers at Oxford and Cambridge. The Scottish universities were cheap; fees were low, and lodging far less expensive than in the colleges and university towns of the south. Hence the Scottish students were drawn from a wider field, and included many more boys of poorer families. The age of matriculation was lower than at Oxford and Cambridge, and the standard of examination tests not very high. More than a third of the students were under seventeen, and more than half under eighteen.[3] The classes were often too large, owing to the number of students; on the other hand, the reputation of the Scottish professoriate and, particularly, of the Edinburgh medical school was deservedly high. Moreover, the greater diffusion of university education had one important result of a general kind. More secondary-school teachers were graduates in Scotland than in England.

In 1815 working men had few chances of adult education. Long hours of labour, bad housing, low wages, and the meagreness of elementary schooling might well have limited the numbers of those wanting to learn; the striking fact is, however, the persistence of the demand. Brougham was among the few public men who gave a great deal of time and energy to meeting this demand. He founded, and took part in managing, the

[1] Owens was a radical nonconformist who wanted to leave his money to his friend George Faulkner, an anglican tory. Faulkner suggested that he should found a college, and the legacy of £97,000 was used for this purpose. In 1868 both Disraeli and Gladstone refused state aid for the enlargement of the college.

[2] St. Andrews, Glasgow, Aberdeen, and Edinburgh. There was a plan in 1830 to use a bequest at Dumfries for the foundation of a new university, but the money appears to have gone to a lunatic asylum.

[3] The junior Greek classes at the universities often began with the Greek alphabet.

Society for the Diffusion of Useful Knowledge (1827),[1] which published informative literature at a cheap price. A good many critics complained that the 'information' was superficial and disconnected; the same criticism might have been applied to most of the textbooks in use at schools, and to the classical learning accepted as culture at the universities. The *Penny Encyclopaedia* was in advance of anything of its kind, and a movement which aimed at giving to working men a general idea of the principles underlying the tools and machinery in common use may well be considered the first stage in modern technical education. Within a few years other and better works, such as Cassell's[2] *Popular Educator*, were published to meet the new demand. The effect of these cheap books was greater because the working class had no access to libraries. The first public libraries act was not passed until 1850,[3] and the only serious non-theological literature which had a circulation comparable with these informative booklets was revolutionary and anti-clerical in character.

Brougham's plans included the provision of mechanics' institutes where small libraries could be collected, and working men meet for lectures and discussions. These institutes arose out of the foundation of Anderson's Institution in Glasgow; John Anderson, a professor at Glasgow University, started evening classes in 1760, and, at his death, left property for the foundation of a college in which his work might be continued. George Birkbeck, the first professor of natural philosophy at the institution, was

[1] From 1831 to 1835 the society published, quarterly, a journal of education which summarized information about educational experiments in other countries, notably Switzerland.

[2] John Cassell (1817–65); s. of an innkeeper; apprenticed to a joiner; became a lecturer in the temperance movement, and, in order to spread the movement in a practical way, set up as a tea and coffee merchant in London. His interest in social improvement led him to turn author and publisher. He founded in 1850 the *Working Man's Friend and Popular Instructor*, in 1852 the *Popular Educator*, and in 1861 the *Quiver*. It is interesting to compare Cassell's well-known advertisement 'The child: what will he become?' with Hogarth's series 'The two apprentices'.

[3] The promoters of the movement for public libraries were William Ewart, a Liverpool merchant, educated, like Gladstone, at Eton and Christ Church, and Edward Edwards, first librarian of the Manchester public library. The act of 1850 applied only to boroughs with more than 10,000 inhabitants, and required the consent of two-thirds of the ratepayers, at a special meeting called for the purpose. The library rate was limited to ½d., and could not be used to buy books. Between 1850 and 1860 twenty-five towns took advantage of the act. The provisions were extended to Scotland and Ireland in 1854, the population clause repealed in 1866, and the permissible rate raised to 1d. in 1855.

impressed by the intelligence of the mechanics whom he employed to make his apparatus, and invited them to his lectures. In 1804 Birkbeck left Glasgow for London, to take up
practice as a doctor. The classes were held by his successor,
but in 1823, after a dispute with the governors of Anderson's
Institution, the working men set up an institute of their own.
Birkbeck, Brougham, and Francis Place suggested a similar
mechanics' institute in London. The London Institute was
opened in 1824, and in 1860 there were 610 institutes, with
102,050 members.[1] Unfortunately the working-class element in
the institutes soon declined, though a new start was made in a
few places like the People's College at Sheffield. The methods
of teaching were not always good; the average lecturer did not
know how to explain his subject to an untrained student, and
the lectures were not attractive to mechanics or factory hands
tired after a long day's work. The institutes became centres of
recreation for clerks, mechanics, and shopkeepers, and their
educational side was limited to a few popular lectures.[2]

There were other attempts to meet the working-class demand.
The failure of the chartists and the breach between the popular
movements and the established church had impressed a small
group of men, of whom Charles Kingsley,[3] Thomas Hughes,[4]
and F. D. Maurice[5] were the leading figures. These men thought
that the chartist programme was not unreasonable. They set

[1] The Prologue to Tennyson's *The Princess* has a good account of an 'outing'
of a mechanics' institute from a neighbouring town to a country gentleman's
park.

[2] To a certain extent the Young Men's Christian Association fulfilled the same
purpose—the organization of leisure with indirect educational results. The Association, founded by George Williams in 1844, began with a few young men, mainly
drapers' assistants. It developed a good deal between 1855 and 1864; its objects
were mainly religious, but it also provided reading-rooms and libraries.

[3] Charles Kingsley (1819–75); s. of a clergyman; b. Holne, Dartmoor; educ.
Helston grammar school, King's College, London, and Magdalene College, Cambridge; curate of Eversley, Hants, 1842, rector, 1844–60; regius professor of
modern history at Cambridge, 1860–9; canon of Chester and Westminster.

[4] Thomas Hughes (1822–96); s. of a clergyman; b. Uffington; ed. Rugby and
Oriel College; M.P., 1865; Q.C., 1869; principal of the Working Men's College,
1872–83; chairman of the first co-operative congress, 1869; county court judge,
1882; wrote *Tom Brown's Schooldays* and *Tom Brown at Oxford*.

[5] John Frederick Denison Maurice (1805–72); s. of a unitarian minister; educ.
Cambridge; editor of the *Athenaeum*; largely through the influence of Coleridge, left
unitarianism for the church of England; professor of history and literature at
King's College, London, 1840; professor of divinity, 1846; deprived of these chairs
for unorthodox views, but held the chaplaincy of Lincoln's Inn; vicar of St. Peter's,
Vere St., 1860–9; professor of moral philosophy at Cambridge, 1866.

about making chartists into Christians and Christians into social
reformers. Their political work was of indirect importance in
awakening opinion among their own class, though the small-
scale economie experiments of the 'Christian socialists' came to
little more than a few co-operative workshops which did not
pay their way. The series of pamphlets, *Politics for the People*, to
which Kingsley contributed as 'Parson Lot', were soon forgotten.
On the other hand Maurice and Hughes began a new experiment by opening an adult school in a rough slum district in
London; in 1854 Maurice and his friends established the Working Men's College. They avoided the mistakes of the mechanics'
institutes, and tried to educate as well as inform their students.
The outbreaks of cholera turned the attention of the Christian
socialists to the teaching of elementary hygiene and physiology.
Here again their influence went beyond their immediate field
of work, though it was probably greater in promoting the development of games in the public schools than in bringing
the principles of public health to the notice of the children of
the poor.

The Taunton commission had reported severely upon the
endowed schools for girls, and suggested that girls should be
given a larger share in the endowments of secondary education.
Women's education, where it existed, tended to be superficial
and dreary. Classics and mathematics were generally excluded,
and, as there was no other subject with an educational tradition
of any value, the standard of teaching was not high. Girls played
no games, and took little exercise other than an hour's walking
in a 'crocodile'. The cheaper girls' schools were poor imitations
of the expensive and fashionable schools, and the 'governess' in
well-to-do homes was too often the average product of a girls'
school. Fortunately for the education of women, the movement
for reform came under the direction of Kingsley and Maurice,
who were good judges of character, and cared as much for
physical as for mental training. Maurice's sister was a governess,
and interested her brother in the training of women teachers.
In 1847 the Governesses' Benevolent Association tried to start a
scheme of training, and about the same time Miss Murray, one
of Queen Victoria's maids of honour, collected funds for a
women's college. The two plans were combined in the foundation of Queen's College, London. Maurice became the first

Principal, and Miss Beale[1] and Miss Buss[2] were among the first students. Miss Buss, while at Queen's College, continued to teach at her own private school in North London; in 1850 she changed the name of the school to the North London Collegiate School for Ladies.[3] Miss Beale became Principal of Cheltenham Ladies' College in 1858. These two women, with patience, good humour, and much worldly wisdom, overcame a great deal of prejudice and ridicule. The evangelical governors of Cheltenham Ladies' College nearly rejected Miss Beale because they suspected her theological views; Miss Buss had to be careful not to overstep the lines of social distinction adopted by the parents of her pupils; she could take the children of tradesmen as her pupils, if their fathers did not live over their shops.

The improvement of girls' schools brought a demand for the admission of women to university examinations. These examinations would test the standard reached by the schools, and, if girls could pass the same examinations as their brothers, they might well ask for university education on equal terms. In 1856 a woman was refused admission to the examination for the London medical diploma, and in 1862 another woman was not allowed to sit for the London matriculation. Lord Granville, as chancellor of the university, gave his casting vote against a proposal to admit women to this examination; the defeat led to a movement in favour of throwing open the examinations. In 1868 Cambridge university accepted girls as candidates for the local examinations. Many girls who left school too early to sit for these examinations had leisure to continue their reading. For this reason Miss Clough, sister of Arthur Hugh Clough, suggested to the Taunton commission that courses of lectures, open to women, should be organized in large towns. This was the beginning of the university extension movement. The plan was a great success; it brought a demand for an examination of a standard higher than the ordinary locals. The establishment of the Cambridge higher local examinations led in turn to the

[1] Dorothea Beale (1831–1906); d. of a surgeon; b. London; educ. partly at home and partly at a school in Essex; mathematical tutor at Queen's College, 1849; head teacher of the Clergy Daughters' School, Casterton, 1857.

[2] Frances Mary Buss (1827–94); d. of a painter-etcher; b. and educ. London; assisted her mother in keeping a school at Kentish Town, which was moved to Camden street in 1850.

[3] The term 'ladies' was dropped for 'girls' in 1871, when Miss Buss handed over the school to a trust. Cheltenham Ladies' College still keeps its original name.

provision of more advanced teaching. Twenty years earlier, at the time of the foundation of Queen's College, Mrs. E. J. Reid had opened her house in Bedford Square for lectures to women; the house became a centre of higher education, and took the name of Bedford College for Women. The college was incorporated in 1869, and moved in 1874 from Bedford Square to Baker Street. Meanwhile the supporters of the extension lectures in Cambridge thought that time might be saved if women came to hear lectures in Cambridge. Henry Sidgwick therefore asked Miss Clough to become principal of a small hall of residence, established in 1876, which was called Newnham Hall (later Newnham College). Miss Emily Davies started another hall at Hitchin, and transferred it in 1873 to Cambridge, where it continued as Girton College.[1]

The Taunton and Clarendon commissioners felt a little uneasy about the neglect of science in education. This neglect was not due merely to the dead hand of tradition or the pressure of vested interests in other subjects, though the conservatism of the older universities, from which most public-school masters were drawn, had a good deal to do with the maintenance of the classical routine. Furthermore, after the publication of the *Origin of Species* (1859), science, in the eyes of clerical headmasters, became tainted with irreligion. On the other hand, the classics, taught on the lines suggested by Thomas Arnold, were a good instrument of education and mental training, and the scientific critics of this literary discipline were not always free from professional jealousy and obscurity of thought. The introduction of science as an important subject in schools was not easy. The experts disagreed about the branches of science to be taught and the best way of teaching them; the sciences were in rapid process of change, and their tentative conclusions were not well adapted for training the minds of boys. There were few textbooks; practical work in laboratories was expensive and brought new problems of discipline. Between 1854 and 1859 Herbert Spencer[2] published four articles on the value of scientific education; these articles, reissued in 1861 as a book on *Education, Intellectual, Moral, and Physical,* were translated into thirteen

---

[1] The name was taken from the village of Girton on the outskirts of Cambridge.
[2] Herbert Spencer (1820-1903); s. of a schoolmaster; b. Derby; worked for some years as a civil engineer; sub-editor of the *Economist,* 1848-53; henceforward his life was spent in writing. See also below, p. 548.

languages (including Arabic and Mohawk), and had a great influence on public opinion. Spencer was not clear in explaining what he wanted. He believed that a knowledge of science would be of value at every stage of life for every one, but he did not work out a curriculum suitable in turn for elementary schools, secondary schools, and universities, or meet the old difficulty that knowledge which is practically useful in later life may not be of much use in the education of children.

A stronger, and in many ways a less muddled, support of science came from John Ruskin.[1] Ruskin pointed out that English education set much store by training the mind, and yet gave little attention to the subjects upon which the trained mind could direct its powers. Ruskin was more concerned with nature study than with science, and his aim was moral rather than intellectual. He attributed 'the vices of the upper classes' chiefly to the 'single fact that they had been taught the study of words and not the study of things'. Thomas Henry Huxley, though less original in his views, had more influence than any other educational reformer upon the development of science as a branch of school education. Huxley assumed that a liberal education was an end in itself. He put aside arguments in favour of education brought forward by politicians who wanted an educated electorate, manufacturers who wanted more educated workmen, and clergymen who wanted to reconcile people to religion. He followed Ruskin in attacking the older educational subjects on the ground that they did not do what they claimed to do and that they gave too much importance to a knowledge of literary forms. Huxley overrated the educational value of elementary science, and failed to understand that the ordinary child would take science, like any other subject, on authority, and would not necessarily learn from it any wide or general rules of life and conduct. From this point of view Matthew Arnold[2] gave an effective answer when he pointed out that there could be no substitute for the 'moralizing' effect of letters, poetry, and religion. Arnold had more practical experience of education than Spencer or Huxley. Like Ruskin, he was not afraid of state action. He wanted more and better schools,

[1] See especially *The Stones of Venice*, iii, Appendix vii.

[2] Matthew Arnold (1822–88); b. Laleham, Middlesex; s. of Thomas Arnold (see p. 486); educ. Winchester, Rugby, and Balliol College, Oxford; fellow of Oriel College, 1845; private secretary to Lord Lansdowne, 1847; inspector of schools, 1851; professor of poetry at Oxford, 1857; published his first volume of verse in 1849.

especially secondary schools; his arguments might have carried greater weight if he had been less priggish in his manner of stating them, and less ready to assume that foreign models were always better than anything in England.

If the movement in favour of widening the curriculum of secondary education suffered to some extent from the exaggerations and vagueness of its supporters, there was considerable demand for a good system of technical training. This demand was not met in any enlightened way, and here, rather than in the secondary schools, the domination of the classics was directly harmful. The control of education was in the hands of men who knew little science, and the 'practical' business man and manufacturer found that a literary training was not of much use in commerce. In 1837 the board of trade established a school of design, but little interest was taken in providing theoretical instruction in subjects connected with industry and manufactures. The Royal Society of Arts, under the influence of the prince consort, was more active than any government department. The society took part in planning the exhibition of 1851; the profits of the exhibition—£186,000—were spent on buying land in South Kensington. The prince wanted to build a large institution for the 'dissemination of a knowledge of science and art among all classes'; there was a good deal of opposition, and the site was used only for a museum and headquarters of the newly formed science and art department of the board of trade.[1] The Royal Schools of Mines and of Science as applied to the Arts were also founded in 1851. In 1853 Professor Lyon Playfair[2] published a pamphlet, *Industrial Education on the Continent*, in which he pointed out the superiority of technical instruction in Germany. No official action was taken, though for a time Playfair became secretary of the science and art department. Meanwhile, after a discussion with representatives of the mechanics' institutes and other bodies interested in technical education, the Royal Society began to hold examinations. The Royal

[1] See above, p. 480.

[2] Lyon Playfair, 1st Baron Playfair (1818-98), son of a medical officer of the E.I.C.; b. Bengal, educ. St. Andrews, Glasgow, and Giessen; professor of chemistry at the Royal Institution, Manchester, 1842; chemist to the Geological Survey, 1845, and professor at the School of Mines; professor of chemistry at Edinburgh, 1858; M.P., 1868. Playfair's work as a chemist was done mainly before 1860; he carried out investigations into nitro-prussides, coals for steam navigation, and gases of the blast furnace. He took part in a number of royal commissions of a scientific kind.

Institution of Great Britain, founded in 1799 to promote a better unstanding of the application of science to the common purposes of life, had been providing lectures of a popular kind. The institution appointed Humphry Davy and after him Michael Faraday[1] as professors, but their lectures, though well attended, reached only a small number of the public.

The department of science and art gave grants and bounties to teachers; its work was on a small scale, and did not meet the demand in the country for well-taught and intelligent teachers. Playfair brought the question before the Taunton commission, and the commissioners reported in favour of an inquiry. A detailed questionnaire was sent to the educational authorities of these European countries which had a good system of technical education, and in 1868 the results of this inquiry were published in a volume of 500 pages. Meanwhile the education department asked the chambers of commerce in Great Britain for information about the needs of technical instruction, and the effect upon British trade of the competition of countries where this instruction was already given. The Nottingham manufacturers pointed out that their great rival in the hosiery trade was Chemnitz, where excellent technical instruction was available at low fees. Nottingham had only a school of art, where the fees excluded the poorer classes. The manufacturers of Leeds had already been disturbed by the evidence at the Paris Exhibition of 1867 that their continental competitors produced work far in advance of English goods. Leeds had a population of 250,000; most of its industries depended upon applied science. The only technical instruction given in the city was in a cellar where one teacher, who received an annual grant of £11, held a class in chemistry. These facts were enough to produce in 1872 a royal commission of inquiry into the teaching of science. The results of this inquiry fall within the last three decades of the nineteenth century, but the neglect of the training of teachers in earlier years meant long delay before technical education could be at all widespread, and, owing to this delay, British industry lost much ground in relation to Germany between 1870 and 1900.

[1] See below, pp. 565–6.

III

RELIGION AND THE CHURCHES

THE established church of England, richly endowed and privileged, had in 1815 at least the external support of almost the whole of the upper class, and, in most country districts, of the greater part of the population. There was a small Roman catholic minority, denied full civil rights, but living quietly and without political importance. Irish immigration increased the number of Roman catholics, but most of these immigrants were very poor people whose troubles were economic rather than political. There was a much larger minority of protestant dissenters,[1] also without full civil rights, though less hampered in practice by disabilities than the Roman catholics. In Wales, and in some parts of England, there were more dissenters than churchmen; in Scotland presbyterianism was far stronger than any other denomination. Except in the west of England and parts of East Anglia and the north, the nonconformists belonged mainly to the shopkeeping and lower middle class of the towns. The poor, at least in the great towns, were largely pagan, with a veneer of religious observance and much hidden superstition. The effect of religious belief upon conduct was most marked in the middle class. It is impossible to reduce the significance of personal religion to averages; religious indifference is not a mean between atheism and faith, but personal religion would seem to have been widespread, though it was far less orthodox than the official custodians of doctrine in church or chapel were inclined to believe.

It has been said that the consolation of belief and the emotional character of protestant dissent in England saved the country from political revolution and that the atheism of

---

[1] The term 'nonconformist', though of venerable use in England, was less commonly employed than 'dissenter' in the early years of the nineteenth century; the words 'dissent' and 'dissenter' were less frequently used during the latter years of the century because they were associated too closely with the dislike of strict anglicans for the nonconforming denominations. The terms were rarely given their strict legal meaning, and, in common speech, a dissenter was always a nonconformist, and vice versa.

English jacobins lost them much support.[1] There is some truth in these views, but the association of jacobinism with foreigners, the belief that England was already the most free country in Europe, the interest of all classes in sport—the rough sport of the eighteenth century—and the common sense of the English magistrates were factors of equal importance in keeping the peace. The danger-centres of revolution were in the great towns, and among a population least affected by religious sanctions, or diverted from immediate grievances by hope of redress in another world. There was a large circulation of atheistical and anti-clerical literature among politically-minded working men, but Wellington's judgement that the people of England were 'very quiet' may explain the character of English religion; to some extent, the English were religious because they were quiet, and not quiet because they were religious. On the other hand the democratic character of the nonconformist denominations had an important political effect in training their members in administration, self-government, and public speaking. Radicalism, trade-unionism, and, to a lesser extent, the chartist movement owe much to this training; it is unsafe to regard it as diverting into religious channels an enthusiasm which might otherwise have turned to revolutionary politics. Chapel stewards and local preachers tended to be cautious-minded men, of good standing in their own circles, and not the type of which revolutionaries are made.

The church of England contained members of very different theological opinions. The anglican settlement was, in intention, a compromise; it accepted authority, and tolerated considerable liberty of judgement. It required conformity, and left some doubt about the doctrines to which the faithful conformed. It maintained a hierarchy which was never a priestly caste, and never jealous of the interference of laymen in religious matters outside the restricted field of ecclesiastical duty. The division of the church into parties was no sign of weakness; the strength of Anglicanism lay in the fact that these parties remained within the same communion. The extrusion of the methodists[2] —a mistake for which the church paid heavily—was not due

---

[1] 'It was God's mercy to our age that our Jacobins were infidels, and a scandal to sober Christians. Had they been like the old Puritans, they would have trodden Church and King to dust, at least for a time.' S. T. Coleridge, *Table Talk*, ii. 68.

[2] See N. Sykes, *Church and State in England in the Eighteenth Century* (1934).

to differences of opinion on matters of doctrine; the seceders did not carry with them all those who shared their views, and the evangelical movement within the church reached its full development after the secession had taken place.

Although this movement had passed its climax in 1815, it still represented the most active section of the church. The leaders set a pattern of strict and pious life in an age of low moral standards. They maintained a serious and unselfish attitude towards public affairs. They used their wealth conscientiously, and, on the whole, to good and noble purpose. They cared nothing for popularity; their doctrines taught them at all times to save souls, and they preached by example as much as by exhortation. Their weakness was on the intellectual side. They neglected theology and history; they held narrowly to a literal interpretation of the received text of the bible, and too much of their zeal came from a belief in the eternal punishment of unconverted sinners. They took for granted the framework and organization of the church, but their idea of a church was an aggregate of individuals, each concerned with his own salvation. Owing to their failure to understand the social significance of the church as an institution the evangelicals did not give enough thought to the responsibility of Christians for the economic and social system from which clergy and laity drew their incomes. The evangelicals had one thing to impress upon the world of their time; a renewal of personal religion. Without this revival of personal religion the Oxford movement could not have taken place; Newman grew up as an evangelical, and in many respects his early training was the only barrier which kept him from complete scepticism. Similarly, in the course of time, the evangelical insistence upon personal holiness transformed the old low church party, which represented in religion the most arid type of whiggery, into the low churchmen of the middle years of the century; no church could have survived the shocks of these middle years if it had consisted of men with the religious views of Palmerston or Russell.

The evangelicals had no serious rivals for nearly twenty years after 1815, but the two centres of the party, Clapham and Cambridge, had begun to lose their importance. Henry Thornton, the leading member of the 'holy village' of Clapham, died in 1815, Granville Sharp in 1813; John Venn's many years' tenure of Clapham rectory ended in 1813. The survivors did not live through the most controversial years of the Oxford movement. Wilberforce and Hannah More died in 1833, Zachary Macaulay in 1838, Charles Simeon in 1836. These leaders had no successors of their own calibre or influence, and the younger generation drifted away from a society which had always been afraid of ideas and tended to see in Bentham, Paine, Shelley, and Byron only different examples of the revolt against orthodoxy. Shaftesbury alone continued the tradition of public and political activity; his evangelicalism heightened his own sense of duty, but added to his isolation from the class which he did so much to help, and kept him a lonely and unhappy man.

Although the evangelicals lost in permanent influence owing to their failure to understand the place of the church in the world, they did a great deal to found institutions within the church itself, and their societies revived the activity of older associations. Here again most of their work was done before 1815. The Religious Tract Society was founded in 1799, and the Church Missionary Society in the same year.[1] The British and Foreign Bible Society came into existence to provide bibles in Welsh. The founders resolved at their first meeting (1804) to promote 'the most extensive circulation of the Holy Scriptures both at home and abroad'. These societies had episcopal sanction, though the Bible Society included dissenters among its members, and rigid churchmen were afraid that the circulation of the bible without the prayer book would encourage the growth of dissent. The Church Missionary Society accepted the liturgy and maintained the episcopal system, but its leaders encouraged collaboration with other denominations. They used methods of propaganda which were disliked owing to their novelty; no other society sent deputations from parish to parish to preach about its work. The question of Christian missions in India was also controversial. Wilberforce thought that the attitude of Christian opinion towards missionary work in India was 'by far the greatest of our national sins', while the Vellore mutiny of 1806,[2] due partly to a belief that the English intended to suppress native religious observances, frightened the East India Company. The quiet persistence of the evangelicals turned opinion to their side, and in 1813 Wilberforce and his

[1] It did not take its present title, 'The Church Missionary Society for Africa and the East', until 1812.   [2] See above, p. 430.

friends persuaded parliament to agree to the appointment of a bishop and three archdeacons for India.

The high church party differed little from the evangelicals in matters of ritual and ceremonies or in distrust of Roman catholicism. The high churchmen were orthodox followers of the anglican divines, disliking the 'enthusiasm' common to the evangelicals and the dissenters. A few high churchmen raised those problems which were later to trouble Newman; on the whole they did not criticize the reformation settlement or inquire into the relations between the anglican communion and the older churches of Christendom. The high churchmen had centres in Clapton and Hackney which were the counterpart of the Clapham sect. They too supported foreign missions,[1] and published their own journals and reviews. Their strength lay rather in their hold of doctrine than in their philanthropic activity. In politics they were inclined to extreme conservatism, and there was little reason for them to make a stir, since the tory government suited their views. They took considerable part in the foundation of the National Society, though their interest in education was not free from a fear that if churchmen did not exert themselves dissenters would take their place. They also wanted to build new churches in populous districts; here they had the support of the government, of the universities, and of high personages in the state. In 1818, the year of the foundation of the Church Building Society, parliament voted £1,000,000, and in 1824 another £500,000, for church-building; before 1833 about £6,000,000 had been raised from all sources. Bishop Blomfield warned the subscribers that the support of church-building was a matter of political prudence as well as of charity. Few churchmen suggested that a better distribution of ecclesiastical property would have gone far to meet the need.

Between the high churchmen and the evangelicals there was a smaller group of latitudinarians[2], for the most part scholars, whose influence was greater outside than inside the church. They never formed a school, and their ideas ranged from the romantic and philosophical views of Coleridge to the practical-minded and business-like tolerance of Blomfield. They were more prominent after 1830 because they took the liberal side in the agitation for administrative reform in the church, while

---

[1] The Universities' Mission to Central Africa was founded, under high church influence, in 1858–9.   [2] Known from about 1850 as 'broad churchmen'.

their opinions on doctrinal questions were welcomed by laymen who distrusted the Oxford movement. At Oxford they were known as the Noetics, or intellectuals; two of their three ablest members, Whately and Arnold, were fellows of Oriel College, and Milman a fellow of Brasenose. If Milman[1] is the only dean of St. Paul's whose work has been produced on the London stage, Whately[2] remains the only professor of political economy who has been promoted to an archbishopric. Whately was a liberal in politics and religion; his mind was hard, logical, unimaginative, and to some extent intolerant. He refused to allow Pusey to preach in his archdiocese, or to receive Newman in Dublin. He was a strong supporter of education and of the reform of the penal system: his writings did much to create a public opinion in favour of abolishing transportation. Arnold also left Oxford, after three years' residence at Oriel, and developed his views in a different environment. These views offended low church and high church. It was said of Arnold that 'he woke up every morning with the conviction that everything was an open question'. He wanted the national church to include all sects except Roman catholics, quakers, and unitarians; he proposed that all ministers of the church should receive episcopal ordination, and that non-liturgical services should be held in parish churches. He cared so little for ecclesiastical dogma that he described the doctrine of apostolical succession as 'a profane heraldic theory'. Milman was hardly less disliked by the high church party owing to his liberal views and the realistic treatment of Old Testament figures in his *History of the Jews.*

[1] Henry Hart Milman (1791–1868), 3rd s. of Sir F. Milman, bt., physician to George III; b. London; educ. Eton and Brasenose College, Oxford; professor of poetry at Oxford, 1821–31; vicar of St. Mary's, Reading, 1818; canon of Westminster and rector of St. Margaret's, 1835; dean of St. Paul's, 1849. Milman published a drama called *Fazio*, which was acted, at first without his knowledge, at the Surrey Theatre, under the title of *The Italian Wife*, and subsequently played by Charles and Fanny Kemble in England and America, and also translated into Italian. Milman turned from poetry and play-writing to history after 1826; and wrote, successively, a *History of the Jews* (1830), a *History of Christianity under the Empire* (1840), and a *History of Latin Christianity down to the death of Pope Nicholas V* (1855). As dean of St. Paul's Milman in 1858 introduced evening services under the dome.

[2] Richard Whately (1787–1863), s. of a clergyman; b. London; educ. Bristol and Oriel College, Oxford; vicar of Halesworth, Suffolk, 1822; principal of St. Alban Hall, Oxford, 1825; succeeded Nassau Senior as professor of political economy, 1829; archbishop of Dublin, 1831; chairman of the Irish poor-law commission, 1833–6.

The liberal churchmen were more concerned than high or low church clergy with the reform of the administration and finances of the church, because they were more in touch with lay opinion. To the ordinary layman, and particularly to the increasing number of those wanting a thorough overhaul of every institution in the country, the church was as full of abuses as the unreformed parliament. The highest authorities accepted pluralism and non-residence; even those who saw the need of change set a bad example. Blomfield was wise enough, after his promotion to the see of London in 1828, to realize that unless the church submitted to reform there might be a general confiscation of ecclesiastical property; yet from 1810 to 1828 he held more than one benefice. During part of this time he was also making a good income from private pupils; from 1820 to 1828 one of his benefices was the living of Bishopsgate, with an income of £2,100 a year, and between 1824 and 1828 he was bishop of Chester.[1] If a reforming bishop could accumulate money and preferment in this way, the average prelate or well-born incumbent might well go farther. Bishop Sparke of Ely, his son, and his son-in-law enjoyed more than £30,000 a year of church endowments. Archbishop Manners-Sutton (1755–1828), an active high churchman, presented seven of his relations to sixteen benefices; his predecessor in the see of Canterbury, who is said to have left a million pounds, provided his elder son with £12,000 a year and his younger son with £3,000 a year from benefices and other well-paid offices. The *Extraordinary Black Book* of 1831,[2] which gave an account of the misappropriation of funds in the interest of the upper class, was directed as much against the abuse of church preferment as against the scandal of pensions and secular places. The compilers of the book maintained that the ecclesiastical revenues of the whole of Europe were less than those of England; that

[1] Towards the end of his life, and after he had taken part in the suppression of pluralism, Blomfield wrote to Palmerston that he would like to resign the see of London, if he could receive an annuity of £6,000. This sum, in his son's words, was 'rather less than one-third of the income which he was then enjoying'; Blomfield asked for it 'in order to enable him to continue the life-insurances which constituted almost the sole provision that he had made for his family'. A. Blomfield, *A Memoir of Bishop Blomfield*, p. 386. Blomfield had eleven children. The annuity required a special act of parliament. The act was passed, after some opposition, and Blomfield was also given the use of the Fulham estate for his lifetime.

[2] See above, p. 28.

bishops and clergy generally voted against reforms, and that, even when they showed some interest in measures of public importance, such as education, their purpose was more to weaken nonconformity than to strengthen religion.

Practical men in the church wished to remedy a state of things which they could not defend and the public would no longer tolerate. At the same time a number of churchmen who disliked the liberalism of their time began to ask whether the attack upon the church was due to a cause deeper than irritation over the misapplication of endowments; the church had lost the support of a nation which was at least nominally Christian because clergy and laity had forgotten the meaning of institutional religion. Thus two movements, one for administrative reform, the other for a revival of the conception of the church as a divinely appointed society, worked simultaneously to change the outward form and internal character of the church of England. These movements were interdependent. The administrative reforms enforced a more careful performance of spiritual duties, the revival of a belief in the sacred mission of their office made the clergy more anxious to observe outward forms, to avoid scandal, to attend to the upkeep and repair of their churches, and to look upon the church as something more than a department of state.

The first surrender of privileges came before administrative reform. This surrender was begun before 1832; it was not made willingly or with much grace. The repeal of the test and corporation acts in 1828 merely removed a formal grievance; annual acts of indemnity had long safeguarded dissenters from penalties for breach of the law. On the other hand only ten bishops voted for, and nineteen voted against, catholic emancipation.[1] After the passing of the reform bill, the whigs turned to the question of church property. They prepared a draft scheme for the appointment of a body of commissioners to manage episcopal and cathedral endowments. They proposed to forbid non-residence, to create new sees, and to cut down the incomes of the richest bishoprics in order to apply the surplus revenues to poor parishes. They could not put their scheme into effect before they went out of office in 1834, but Peel did not intend to fight public opinion on behalf of clerical abuses. He accepted the principles of the whig plan, and

[1] On the second reading of the bill.

appointed a commission to inquire into the state of the church in England and Wales. The first report of the commission, issued in 1835, recommended the creation of new sees at Ripon and Manchester and the rearrangement of other dioceses, including the enormous diocese of Lincoln. The commissioners suggested large reductions in the incomes of the richer sees. Durham, which had a revenue of £17,000–£20,000, was cut down to £7,000, and Canterbury reduced from about £18,000 to £15,000. A second report, published in 1836, advised the limitation of cathedral chapters to a dean and four residentiary canons, and the use of the revenues of stalls and offices beyond this number for the augmentation of poor livings.

The whigs were back in office before the publication of the second report. They accepted most of the recommendations, and set up a permanent board of ecclesiastical commissioners to administer the property taken for new uses. They also passed a church pluralities act forbidding a clergyman to hold more than two livings; they allowed the subdivision of parishes, and settled at least for the time the troublesome question of tithes in England and Wales.[1] This question did not affect the church alone; a great deal of tithe was in lay hands, and few people objected to tithe-payment as such. On the other hand the incidence of tithe was capricious and the mode of collection and assessment bad; commutation of tithes hitherto paid in kind had taken place in about 2,000 parishes, but in most places the annual amount was fixed by bargaining between incumbents and farmers. The whigs proposed in 1833 and 1834 that tithe should be commuted for a rent-charge based upon a septennial valuation made by special commissioners. The house of lords would not accept the details of the whig bill; Peel was not in office long enough to settle the matter, and in 1836 Russell introduced a bill based to a large extent on the earlier proposals. Henceforward all tithes were paid in money; the basis of valuation was the average market price of wheat, barley, and oats over a seven-year period, and a board of tithe commissioners settled disputed assessments. Finally, the abolition of the old court of delegates[2] and the substitution of the judicial committee of the privy council as the final court of appeal in matters of church discipline and clerical

---

[1] For the Irish tithes see above, pp. 344–7.
[2] For this court see vol. vii, p. 434 of this *History*.

misdemeanour removed some of the anomalies of the ecclesiastical courts.[1]

The whigs also tried to settle the problem of church rates levied for the repair of the fabric of parish churches. As late as 1811 there was little opposition to these rates, but the dissenters, especially in the towns, began to refuse to pay for the upkeep of churches which they did not attend. The legal position was curious. If the churchwardens and a vestry meeting levied a rate, payment could be enforced. If the parish meeting refused to levy a rate, the only sanctions which could be applied were ecclesiastical, but it was hardly possible to use the ancient instruments of interdict and excommunication, and in any case the punishment would have fallen not upon the dissenters but upon the churchmen. In 1834 the whigs proposed to abolish church rates in return for a charge of £250,000 on the land tax. The churchmen thought the sum too small and the dissenters thought it too large. Three years later Spring Rice, chancellor of the exchequer, suggested that, if the property of the bishops were handed over to the management of commissioners, there would be a saving of about £250,000. The bishops refused to become 'annuitants of the government', and denied the right of parliament to make good from their estates the loss of other revenues to which the church was legally entitled. The matter was left unsettled, and remained as a source of local disputes and bitterness until Gladstone in 1868 abolished compulsory church rates.

To the average Englishman, and certainly to the average middle-class voter, the legislation of the years 1836–40 set the church in sufficiently good order; there were further anomalies to be removed, but, for the time, nothing to cause a scandal. The dissenters would not allow any encroachment of church influence, particularly in the sphere of education; they were not inclined to begin an attack upon the establishment as such, and an attack of this kind would have had little political support. Nevertheless it was not clear to churchmen that the reform of ecclesiastical finance would satisfy their enemies. In any case there were men who had already seen that the liberal

---

[1] At this time churchmen made no objection to a measure establishing the judicial committee of the privy council as the final legal authority in ecclesiastical causes, although these causes might involve the definition of doctrine.

opposition went beyond an assault on the outworks of anglicanism. The liberal critics might be discreet, and even respectful;
they might fear the social consequences of any sudden dissolution of belief. Sooner or later, after due preparation, they would
attack the citadel and centre of Christian doctrine. Therefore
it was not enough to make the church respectable, or to limit
the incomes of bishops and improve the position of the lower
clergy. The intellectual content of liberalism was more dangerous than the pages of the *Extraordinary Black Book*. The liberal
thesis, which would substitute a vague theism, or even agnosticism, for dogmatic belief, could be met only by a direct negative.
The church must assert her position as a divine society, proclaim her infallible authority, and revive the traditions of a
time when this authority was unquestioned. The universities
were the obvious centres of a movement reasserting the super-
natural claims of the church to obedience. The colleges of
Oxford and Cambridge were places of leisured discussion and
easy friendship; the visible signs of economic change had not
touched them. Their members lived in a kingdom of their own,
where they were strong enough to maintain their privileges and
to resist invaders who refused at least nominal allegiance to the
established church. They belonged to the secure and well-
provided classes of society; their most ascetic practices were
carried out against a background of comfort. They had no
anxieties about their own livelihood, and their subjects of study
increased their isolation from the most urgent social problems
of the age.

The Oxford movement appears out of scale with the early
railway age because it was the product of a university which
was itself a curious anomaly. It was scarcely possible for
sensitive and clever men like Keble, Pusey, Newman, or
Hurrell Froude to understand the world of George Stephenson
or Feargus O'Connor or Edwin Chadwick. The fascination of
Oxford was too much for them. There was interest enough in
her ancient intellectual discipline; her internal disputes had
the vividness of the politics of a city state. The domination of
ecclesiastical subjects and religious beliefs was a real domination; everything else was seen at second hand. There was something feverish, a touch of absurdity, about the language of these
Oxford attacks upon the religious indifference of the time. The
occasion of Keble's sermon on 'National Apostasy' in 1833 was

the proposal to secularize a portion of the revenues of the Irish bishoprics.[1] The appropriation clause was withdrawn, and the government merely followed Tudor or Stuart or even medieval precedents in uniting a number of sees; yet Newman described the situation as 'critical', while Keble accused parliament of a 'direct disavowal of the sovereignty of God', and denounced the country, in its support of parliament, as guilty of apostasy.

It is doubtful whether these extravagant warnings and fears expressed by a country clergyman with Oxford connexions and a reputation for quiet, well-phrased verse would have led to an important movement in the church if Newman had not given Keble[2] his support. Four friends of Keble met at a Suffolk rectory in July, but could not agree upon a course of action. Newman[3] was of a different type. He wrote to Pusey, six months before leaving the church of England, that 'general scepticism' was something which 'might easily come' on him; his enemies have described him as 'essentially sceptical and sophistical', and on this line of interpretation his conversion to Roman catholicism has been called 'an act of pure self-will. He bowed to an image which he had first himself set up.'[4] Acton described Newman as 'the manipulator and not the servant of truth'.[5] It is difficult to read Newman's *Essay on the Development of Christian Doctrine* (1845) without noticing that his tests of truth rested upon nothing more than the power of a theory, dogma, or belief to survive. Newman, at all events in later life, was aware that this interpretation might be put upon his views. He wrote of his friend Lord Blachford: 'My surmise is that he thinks me a profoundly sceptical thinker, who,

[1] See above, p. 346.

[2] John Keble (1792–1866), s. of a clergyman, b. Fairford, Glos.; educ. privately, and at Corpus Christi College, Oxford; fellow of Oriel; vicar of Hursley, 1836–66; professor of poetry at Oxford, 1831–41; published *The Christian Year*, 1827.

[3] John Henry Newman (1801–90), b. London, s. of John Newman, a banker, possibly of Dutch origin, and of Jemima Fourdrinier, of Huguenot descent; educ. Ealing and Trinity College, Oxford; fellow of Oriel College, 1822; curate of St. Clement's church, Oxford, 1824; vicar of St. Mary's, 1828; travelled in Italy and the Mediterranean, 1832–3; began the *Tracts for the Times*, 1833; withdrew from Oxford to Littlemore, 1842; joined the Roman catholic church, 1845; re-ordained priest at Rome, 1846; commissioned by Pius IX to introduce into England the institute of the Oratory of St. Philip Neri, 1847; rector of the newly founded catholic university of Dublin, 1854–5; published an *Apologia pro Vita Sua* in answer to attacks by Kingsley, 1864–5; created a cardinal, 1879.

[4] O. Elton (quoting Thirlwall), *A Survey of English Literature, 1830–80*, ii. 147.

[5] *Letters of Lord Acton to Mary Gladstone*, ed. W. H. Paul, p. lx.

determined on not building on an abyss, has by mere strength
of will, bridged it over, . . . but that my bridge, like Mahomet's
coffin, is self-suspended, by the action of the will.'[1] Newman's
habit of reasoning to the limit of any set of words or ideas does
not represent the whole man. There was another side to his
character, a depth of religious conviction which was nearer to
mysticism than to logic. He was not capable of the magnificent
surrender of the saints of the church; he was too much self-
centred, and too much interested in the attitude of other people
towards himself. Isaac Williams, one of the quieter but not the
least brilliant of the tractarians, distrusted Newman's 'habit
of looking for effect'.[2] On the other hand his distinction of
mind was beyond question. He might be over-subtle, but he
was never cheap. His English style was, in its own sphere, un-
equalled by any other writer of his time; his books are not less
readable because their long passages of argument and controversy are rarely without a touch of irony and even of un-
christian spite. No other member of the tractarian party
approached Newman in genius. It is difficult to find in Hurrell
Froude[3] any of the charm which impressed his contemporaries.
Froude's irresponsibility, incessant paradoxes, and petty dislikes represent the worst products of a literary university, while
the pathological elements in his character are more obvious
today than they could have been a hundred years ago. Pusey[4]
joined the movement at the end of 1833. His accession was of
great importance. He was already one of the most remarkable
scholars of his age; unlike the other leaders of the Oxford movement he had studied abroad, and his appointment to the chair
of Hebrew in 1828 had given him a leading position in the
university. He came of better family than most of his Oriel
colleagues, and hitherto his political views had been of a liberal
kind, though the success of the whigs in 1832 had alarmed him.
Pusey fell too easily under the influence of Newman, whose
judgement was less sound and less charitable than his own;
Newman in turn was influenced by Pusey's learning.

[1] W. Ward, *Life of Newman*, ii. 90.   [2] I. Williams, *Autobiography*, p. 54.
[3] Richard Hurrell Froude (1803–36), s. of a clergyman, b. Dartington; educ.
Eton and Oriel College, Oxford; fellow of Oriel; died of tuberculosis.
[4] Edward Bouverie Pusey (1800–82), s. of a Berkshire landowner; educ. Eton and
Christ Church, fellow of Oriel, studied in Germany, 1825–7. In his youth Pusey
was a good horseman and a good shot. His wife's early death (1839) was a loss
which affected his whole way of life.

Newman, Keble, and Froude formed an 'Association of Friends of the Church' in the autumn of 1833, and decided to publish a number of *Tracts for the Times*. They believed that a revival of the doctrine of apostolical succession would reawaken the clergy to the significance of their church, and they realized that this doctrine was the logical foundation of ecclesiastical authority. The *Tracts* were addressed mainly to the clergy; Newman's sermons in the university church expounded the same theses in less technical language. The leaders of this movement for the restoration of authority were comparatively young men; in 1833 Newman was thirty-two, Froude thirty, Pusey thirty-three, and Keble forty-one. They knew little of the world to which their teaching was addressed, and there was an air of unreality about their hints at martyrdom while they were defending privilege, and about the 'emergency' which they alone had discovered. To the ordinary man, whatever his party, there was no emergency. The church was not in danger; there were no martyrs, unless this name could be applied to the non-resident clergy, the pluralists, and highly paid bishops and canons whose emoluments were threatened. Thus the teaching of the tracts appeared to be an unnecessary assertion of clerical authority, set out in words which offended most sections of church opinion; the insistence upon doctrines which the reformers had condemned, and Englishmen in general, rightly or wrongly, had long regarded as Roman errors, seemed unnecessary and to a large extent dishonest. Whately even suspected that the tractarians were secret infidels.

The agitation in 1834 for the removal of university tests also put the tractarians in an unfortunate position. They too wanted to reform Oxford, but they intended the university to be the centre of a revival of the church, and the admission of nonconformists would cut at the root of their plans. On the other hand Oxford was a national university, and in limiting its endowments to members of the church of England the tractarians were again defending privilege and aligning themselves with vested interests which on other grounds they wished to remove. Their position was even more difficult when in 1836 Melbourne appointed Dr. Hampden to the regius chair of divinity. Hampden was neither an original thinker nor a great scholar; the tractarians thought his views on the authority of the creeds unorthodox. Yet Bishop Copleston had suggested

Hampden's name to the prime minister, and the archbishop of Canterbury had not objected to his appointment. Thus, if they opposed Hampden, the tractarians were opposing ecclesiastical authority in the interest of an authoritarian view of the church. They could not prevent the appointment, and they made the mistake of taking the lead in a movement to exclude Hampden from a vote in the nomination of select preachers to the university. From this time their attack on liberalism and their attempts to revive a more spiritual conception of the church were never free from the narrow associations of university politics.

The need of caution was greater because the movement was becoming known outside Oxford, and indeed outside England.[1] Moreover the leaders were facing, inevitably, a more serious question than anything raised by the appointment of Hampden. They were putting forward high claims for the authority of the anglican church, and giving to every formula and ceremony of the church a meaning which they considered implicit and most of their critics thought sophistical. They believed that they could answer their critics by an appeal to history. Yet the Roman catholic church held that anglican orders were invalid, and that anglican clergymen could not appeal to the catholic doctrine of apostolic succession. The evangelical party, most broad churchmen, and the greater number of the laity accepted the Roman logic, and pointed out that, if the tractarians followed their views to a conclusion, they ought to join the Roman church. Over this problem the Oxford movement was wrecked.

Newman came to the conclusion that the faults of the Roman church were not more serious than the defects which he and his friends were trying to cure in the church of England. He found that he could not fairly use the arguments of his favourite anglican divines against the Roman church, and that every claim brought forward for the church of England applied even more strongly to the church of Rome. For a time a pragmatic type of reasoning satisfied him. The church of England was in possession; it could assert its apostolical character. This line of thought did not answer the Roman claim based upon St.

---

[1] The terms 'Newmanism' and 'Puseyism' were used as early as 1838 to denote the movement. 'Puseyism' was adopted by French, German, and Italian writers, and appears even in modern Greek as πουζεισμός. The Puseyites were not known commonly as tractarians before 1840.

Augustine's phrase: *securus iudicat orbis terrarum*. Other members of the party shared the difficulties which oppressed Newman; they also wanted to show the critics who were accusing them of dishonesty that anglican teaching was not incompatible with catholic doctrine. Newman himself made an effort of this kind, in one of the *Tracts for the Times* (No. XC), which ultimately turned the scale for him against the church of England. He tried to prove by a logical interpretation of words that in the thirty-nine articles, to which every anglican clergyman was bound to subscribe, there was nothing contrary to traditional catholic belief. Thus, if Article XXII condemned 'the Romish doctrine' of purgatory, it did not condemn all doctrines of purgatory, but merely a perverted and exaggerated view of the true doctrine. The attacks on this tract were not altogether fair to Newman. He was not always right in his historical interpretation of the articles, or of the intentions of those who drew them up; his method of analysis was curt, uncompromising, and often opposed to common sense. He did not try to gain the sympathy of his opponents. At the same time the protestant view of the thirty-nine articles was also unhistorical. These articles did not state a creed; they defined an intellectual position. They were drawn up not to exclude but to bring in as many different views as possible.

The authorities of the university treated Newman as Newman himself had treated Hampden. Tract XC appeared in February 1841. In March the heads of colleges accused Newman of breaking the statutes of the university by 'reconciling subscription [to the articles] with the adoption of errors which they were designed to counteract'. The opinion of the heads of Oxford colleges was not the voice of the church; the bishops disapproved of Newman's interpretation, but passed no collective censure. For some time longer Newman stayed in the anglican church. He was shocked by measures such as the establishment of a bishopric in Jerusalem to which Great Britain and Prussia agreed to nominate candidates in turn, but Oxford questions still had the greatest effect upon him. In 1843 Pusey was delated for heresy, and forbidden to preach within the university for two years. The final blow came, in a curious way, from Newman's own side. W. G. Ward, a young fellow of Balliol, had been attracted by Newman's preaching and had joined his party. Ward was an eccentric man, not learned outside the field of pure mathematics, full of prejudices, and a master of formal dialectic. After Froude's death in 1836 Ward became the *enfant terrible* of the tractarian movement. It is a sign of the academic and unpractical side of this movement that the leaders allowed Ward, with his schoolboy love of shocking his opponents, to take over the editorship of the *British Critic*, the organ of the party. Ward encouraged Newman to publish Tract XC; in the discussions which followed the publication he went beyond Newman's extreme position. He maintained that the articles were protestant in intention and tendency, but that it was possible to give them a catholic interpretation. This thesis destroyed the reasoning upon which Newman had distinguished between the abuses which the articles condemned and the doctrines which they took for granted. Ward went out of his way to wreck the party by announcing in 1844 that in subscribing to the articles he had renounced no Roman doctrine, and that although he did not hide his opinions he had not been censured by ecclesiastical authority or asked to give up his fellowship. The most tolerant authorities could not have avoided a challenge of this kind. The authorities of the university were not tolerant, and ten years of goading from clever and sophistical young men had exasperated them. In February 1845 they deprived Ward of his degree. Ward left Oxford, married, and joined the Roman church. The convocation which condemned Ward also passed a vote of censure on Tract XC.[1] Oxford was the centre of theological and historical study in the church. If the university rejected, year after year, catholic doctrines, and if the bishops differed from the university merely in the method of condemnation, there could be no place for the tractarians in the anglican church.

Newman was received into the Roman church in October 1845. Many of his supporters followed him. A second secession in 1851, which included Manning, a friend of Gladstone and a future cardinal, was due to an abstruse doctrinal question. The bishop of Exeter had refused to institute the Rev. G. C. Gorham to a living in his diocese because he objected to Gorham's views on the precise effect of baptism upon the spiritual state of the baptized person. Gorham appealed against the bishop's decision, and the judicial committee of the privy council

[1] The vote was carried in the house, but the two proctors used their traditional right of veto.

declared, in March 1850, that Gorham's views, which were opposed by the high church party, were not contrary to the doctrines of the church of England as legally enjoined upon the clergy. Pusey, Keble, and their friends protested that the church could not accept the decision of a lay court on matters of doctrine. They tried to obtain the recognition of the upper house of convocation as a special court of appeal in purely doctrinal cases, but the house of lords would not agree to a measure likely to strengthen the romanizing party in the church.

In spite of the secessions to Roman catholicism the Oxford movement continued to be the most important factor in the internal history of the anglican church. Pusey and Keble remained faithful to the earlier view of the tractarians that the church of England was an integral part of the catholic church, and this view satisfied most high churchmen. Moreover, the tracts published during the first ten years of the movement and the sermons preached by the leaders had an influence which Newman's changes of opinion could not destroy. The Oxford movement, like the whig legislation against which the tractarians protested, had encouraged a greater care for external order and ceremonial, a deeper conception of the clerical office. The change of attitude was not entirely due to the tractarians; it did not bring unmixed benefits to the church. The general improvement of professional and administrative standards would have affected the clergy even if there had never been an Oxford movement. The revival of interest in church architecture and ritual was part of a broader revival of historical studies; the Oxford reformers owed a good deal to the new interest in the middle ages.

On the other hand the uncompromising ecclesiasticism of the tractarians broke the unity of the church; the clergy were more divided in opinion in 1870 than in 1815. This division showed itself in the character of their services. Questions of ritual had played a small part in the first campaigns of the tractarians; they were of great importance after 1850, and many clergymen came near to asserting a right of private judgement in defiance of their bishops and in opposition to the wishes of the laity. The prayer book rubrics defining vestments and ceremonial were not very clear; a ritual commission, appointed in 1867, published inconclusive reports, to which the innovating party gave little attention. This insistence upon externals did much to alienate public opinion, which was uninterested or stubbornly conservative in matters of ritual. It also gave the impression that the new high church party, unlike the old evangelical and high church parties, took no account of laymen. The revival of convocation in 1852, after the Gorham case, seemed an attempt to increase the authority of the clergy at the expense of the laity. The revival was otherwise of little importance, since convocation had no legislative power, and, in view of the general fear of the romanizing party, parliament was unwilling either to give it such power or even to alter its ancient composition.

Finally, the relative success of the Oxford movement did not make it easier for the church to meet the disruptive attacks of nineteenth-century thought. The leaders of the Oxford movement had concentrated attention upon historic doctrines largely forgotten or even rejected by protestant churchmen: they never met the liberals on their own ground. For all their intellectual ability, the Oxford reformers knew little or nothing of the physical and biological sciences. Analogies between Newman's theory of the development of doctrine and the theory of the evolution of species by natural selection are far-fetched, and, in any case, these analogies emphasize the pragmatic character of Newman's arguments, and destroy rather than confirm his main assumptions. In many respects the tractarians were as rigorously literal as the evangelicals in their interpretation of the bible; they were more rigorous in their attitude towards church doctrine. Their formula *securus iudicat orbis terrarum* might be a justification of ancient catholic beliefs; it was worthless as an argument against a theory of human development which ran counter to the literal acceptance of these ancient beliefs, since, in its century-old view of a special creation of man, the judgement of the world and of the catholic church had been demonstrably wrong.

After the first storms caused by the Oxford reformers had passed, there was an attempt at a liberal movement within the church. This new movement had no leader of the genius of Newman, no clear intellectual programme, no centre from which to direct its action. The interests of the small group headed by Maurice and Charles Kingsley were social rather than intellectual. Maurice was as brilliant as he was sincere, but he was too restless, and spread his work over too many subjects. Kingsley was never a learned theologian, and the

series of *Tracts for Priests and People* which the two friends began
to publish in 1854 were concerned mainly with current social
questions.[1] The Christian socialists showed churchmen that
Christianity was a way of life and not merely a series of intellectual propositions. This revival of a sense of corporate
responsibility for the well-being of their fellow countrymen
counterbalanced the over-emphasis on doctrinal and ceremonial
questions resulting from the Oxford movement.[2] Kingsley's
novels reached a public untouched or repelled by the high
anglicanism of Oxford, while Maurice, though he wrote nothing
of original value, did a great deal to prepare lay opinion for a
revision of doctrine in a liberal direction, and to encourage the
work of scholars like Westcott and Hort, but the protests over
the publication of *Essays and Reviews* in 1860[3] showed that
liberalism, at all events in matters of theological opinion, did
not have a wide following among the clergy.

The secession of a considerable number of anglican clergymen had an effect upon the progress of Roman catholicism
in England, though the fact of catholic emancipation was of
greater importance. To some extent the anglican converts
were not easily assimilated; they tended to adopt ultramontane
views, while the English catholics held to an older tradition.
The Oxford movement brought a new interest in the catholic
church, and at the same time a revival of historic distrust and
prejudice. This ancient distrust caused a sudden outburst of
popular feeling about the time of the Gorham judgement.
Public interest in ecclesiastical affairs was unusually strong, and
the storm raised by the tractarians had not died down. Englishmen sympathized with the liberals in Italy, and considered that
Pius IX was partly responsible for the liberal defeat. In 1850
the pope decided to abolish the long-standing régime of apostolic
vicariates in England and to establish a regular diocesan hierarchy. Rumours of this plan had reached England a few years
earlier, and it is possible that Pius IX thought that the British
government would make no objection. The whigs had reopened

---

[1] For the educational work of Maurice, Kingsley, and other liberal churchmen
see above, pp. 495–6.
[2] Acland's report on the cholera outbreak at Oxford (1856) gives a grim picture
of the sanitary conditions in the poorer parts of the city. A good deal of the slum
property stood on land belonging to colleges of which some of the leading tractarians were members.   [3] See below, pp. 575–6.

diplomatic relations with Rome in 1847, and Lord Minto, on his mission to Italy,[1] appears to have been told of the diocesan plan. It was not unreasonable that catholic bishops appointed to administer dioceses in different parts of England should take territorial titles denoting these dioceses. On the other hand the announcement of the change was made in terms which implied the return of Englishmen to the catholic church. Cardinal Wiseman, who became archbishop of Westminster, was well known in England; his sympathies were entirely English, though he had been born in Spain and had lived for many years in Rome. No one familiar with Wiseman's flowery and pompous style of writing would have paid much attention to sentences proclaiming the restoration of England 'to its orbit in the ecclesiastical firmament', but English protestants gave them a sinister and aggressive meaning.

There was a general outcry, in which most of the anglican bishops took part. Wiseman's statement that 'we shall continue to administer with ordinary jurisdiction the counties of Middlesex, Hertford, &c.', appeared to ignore the authority of the Crown, and the catholic press in England and abroad pointed out that the pope had taken no notice of the anglican episcopate. Russell might have tried to explain the facts. He chose a path which a true whig usually disliked; he followed the prejudices of the crowd, and wrote an open letter to the bishop of Durham in which he complained of papal aggression, and put the blame largely upon the 'Puseyites'. In 1851 Russell brought forward a bill prohibiting the assumption of ecclesiastical titles already taken by clergy of the church of England. Although the bill was opposed by Gladstone and the Peelites, it passed both houses by a large majority. It was not even suited for its purpose, since the catholics named their sees from places not taken to designate anglican bishops. In any case no prosecution was ever started under the terms of the act; there was general agreement when Gladstone repealed it in 1871.

The internal history of the English nonconformist bodies in the period between 1815 and 1870 was for the most part quiet and uneventful. The nonconformists gained from every successful attack upon anglican privilege, and, on the whole, their attitude towards the church was unfriendly and often bitter.

[1] See above, p. 245.

The Wesleyans were nearer, by tradition and belief, to the evangelical party in the anglican church. The organization of the main nonconformist bodies was not uniform; here again the principle of authority was strongest among the Wesleyans. The nonconformists, like the evangelicals, were less attentive than high churchmen to doctrinal questions, but they held definite views which were not by any means liberal in the intellectual sense of the term. They accepted a literal interpretation of the bible; the baptists were as rigorous as the tractarians in their attitude towards their particular doctrines. At the same time there was less cohesion in the nonconformist denominations; they represented an individualist tradition and an emphasis upon the right of private judgement. They had little sense of the corporate existence or catholicity of the Christian church; they suffered from schism and division on points of minor importance. On the other hand, the fact that they did not give prominence to statements of doctrinal belief, and that they were not bound to fixed liturgical services, made it possible for them to adapt themselves easily to changes of opinion, and to escape from the burden of tradition which made adaptation of this kind more difficult for the established church.

Of the 'three denominations' of the eighteenth century, presbyterians, independents, and baptists, the presbyterians alone had changed their theological position; they had adopted Socinian views, and chosen to call themselves 'unitarians'.[1] They had thus separated themselves from the presbyterianism of Scotland and northern Ireland, and a new presbyterian organization, on orthodox lines, was begun in England, first as a branch of the Scottish church, and, after 1836, as an independent body. The unitarians were strongest in London and in the older manufacturing and mercantile towns; most of their members came from the middle class, and their intellectual influence was out of proportion to their small numbers. The independents had maintained their theological views but changed their name and organization. They recognized the weakness of a system of entirely autonomous churches, and decided to form a closer association while maintaining as far as possible their local traditions of self-government. They showed the change by the revival of the term 'congregational', which had been used in the sixteenth century, and by the establishment of a

[1] See vol. xi of this *History*.

congregational union of England and Wales (1832). In 1833 the union published a declaration of faith and order, not as 'a standard to which assent should be required', but as a statement of the principles accepted by its members. The baptists, who differed from the independents solely on the mode and application of baptism, had never been united among themselves about this abstruse theological question; it remained as a symbol of differentiation in the nineteenth century, although the doctrinal implications tended to recede into the background, and the different sections of baptists were hardly to be distinguished from the congregationalists. A baptist union was formed in 1813, and the baptists, who had been active in missionary work since the foundation of their missionary society in 1792, collaborated for this purpose and for the education of their clergy, but the union safeguarded the right of every congregation to choose its own minister and to arrange its own affairs.

The constitution of the main body of methodists was more unitary than that of the older denominations;[1] the problems of administration were therefore more complicated, and the difficulty of finding agreed solutions more serious. There were indeed four schisms of importance between 1797 and 1850. The first seceders disliked the hierarchical form of government given to the society by John Wesley; another secession about 1810 produced the sect of primitive methodists, who worked among the very poor and tolerated extreme 'revivalist' services which other methodists thought unseemly. The trouble between 1828 and 1850–2 was due to another democratic movement against the dominant position of the ministers. The growth of radicalism and chartism, the excitement over the European revolutions of 1830 and 1848 affected many of the laity, though the methodists were not inclined to violent political action, and were generally on the side of authority. The establishment of a theological college for the training of ministers, the adoption of the practice of laying on of hands in ordination, and even the official use of the term 'reverend' offended the more democratic element. In 1849–50 a large group of malcontents joined the seceders of earlier years, and formed a society of 'Methodist Free Churches'. For a time there was a fall in the numbers of the main body; the losses between 1850 and 1855 amounted, in

---

[1] For the rise and constitution of methodism see vols. xi and xii of this *History*.

Great Britain and Ireland, to 100,000, but after 1855 the older society regained much ground.[1]

Two new sects of some importance came into existence between 1820 and 1830. Edward Irving, a friend of Carlyle and until 1833 a Scottish presbyterian minister, founded the catholic apostolic church; the Plymouth brethren formed a loose but at the same time an exclusive organization under the direction of Henry Groves and the Rev. J. N. Darby. These two bodies were at first sight entirely apart in ideas and in practice. The Irvingites adopted an elaborate ritual and a curious apocalyptic terminology; the Plymouth brethren had no priesthood, published no creed, and accepted no ecclesiastical order. On the other hand, each of the two sects represented a certain wild literalism in the interpretation of the bible, based its principles upon the nearness of the Last Judgement, and made an extremely narrow estimate of the number of the elect. It is probable that, although neither of these bodies was large, they were typical in many respects of a much greater number of earnest and religious-minded men and women belonging to the anglican and nonconformist churches, and that, among the uninstructed majority of Englishmen, many thousands grew up in this atmosphere of literal and somewhat bleak piety.

The history of the church of Scotland during the years after 1815 is an interesting example of the attempt of a large section of a religious society to free itself from state control. This attempt was in some ways more logical than the Oxford movement, or, at all events, more uncompromising as far as concerned the majority of its supporters. The Scottish movement did not become involved in the defence of privileges which bore little relation of fact to the conception of a Divine society on earth; it had far more support among the laity than was given to the tractarians. It demanded a financial sacrifice which few of the tractarians had to meet, and it put more clearly one of the most difficult problems of modern society; the delimitation between the spheres of authority of church and state. Finally, it was nearer in its main ideas to the general tendencies of nineteenth-century thought, as expressed in the idea of 'a free church in a free state'.

[1] Wesleyan methodism owed much to the wise guidance of the Rev. Jabez Bunting (1779–1858).

The reformation in Scotland had been made by the people against the Crown. Hence the organization of the church took the democratic form of a claim for self-government. During the religious struggles of the sixteenth and seventeenth centuries the two main questions at issue had been the restoration of episcopacy and the right of patronage. On the first question the Crown was beaten. The question of patronage was affected by the decline of militant presbyterianism in the eighteenth century. The patrons, in this age of 'indifference', regained most of the rights they had lost. The revival of organized religion, and the necessity for strong action if the church were to survive, led to the reopening of the question after 1830.

The revival of presbyterianism was due largely to the work and character of Thomas Chalmers,[1] but his efforts would have had less result if there had not been a general movement to raise the religious standards of the presbyterian ministry. The obvious way to secure the appointment of suitable candidates and the exclusion of unsuitable men was to make the 'call' to a parish something more than a formal invitation by the faithful to a candidate already chosen by the patron. Petitions to this effect were presented to the general assembly of the church of Scotland in 1832. The assembly refused to take action because they did not wish to raise the whole question of the relations between church and state. The petitions were renewed in 1833. In 1834 the reformers won their case; they secured the right of a congregation to exclude by a majority vote a candidate who was thought unsuitable. It was doubtful whether the assembly was within its legal rights in agreeing to a veto of this kind. Almost at once the matter was put to the test. In August 1834 Lord Kinnoul nominated one Robert Young to the living of Auchterarder in Perthshire. The congregation of the parish would not accept him; the presbytery[2] upheld their objection. Young brought his case before the court of session. Eight out of thirteen judges held that the rejection was illegal. The

---

[1] Thomas Chalmers (1780–1847), s. of a merchant, b. Anstruther, educ. St. Andrews; minister at Kilmeny, Fife, 1803–15, and lecturer in chemistry at St. Andrews; minister at Glasgow, 1815–23; professor of moral philosophy at St. Andrews, 1823–8; professor of divinity at Edinburgh university, 1828–43; principal and professor of divinity at the Free Church college, Edinburgh, 1843–7. Chalmers was a strong supporter of foreign missions and of evangelical work among the 'home-heathen' in the cities of Great Britain.

[2] i.e. a local court or council of ministers and chief elders of churches.

president of the court used remarkable language. He said: 'That our Saviour is the head of the Kirk of Scotland, in any temporal, or legislative, or judicial sense, is a position which I can dignify by no other name than absurdity. The Parliament is the temporal head of the Church . . . from whose acts alone it exists as the national Church, and derives all its powers. . . .'

In 1838 the general assembly passed a resolution pledging itself to defend the jurisdiction of the church courts in all matters touching church doctrine, government, and discipline. It appealed to the house of lords, but the lords decided that the presbytery in Scotland could reject a patron's nominee only on grounds of heresy, ignorance, or immorality. On Chalmers's advice the assembly decided to accept the decision as far as concerned the temporalities of a benefice, but to insist upon the right of a congregation to keep out a minister whom they did not want. They appealed both to the government of the day and to the opposition. The whig government was nearing its end. Aberdeen, on the conservative side, was prepared to introduce a bill giving the presbytery a right to decide upon objections made to a nominee, if these objections were formulated in specific terms; a general objection would be invalid.

The assembly would not accept this compromise. Meanwhile another test case occurred. Lord Fife's trustees, as patrons of the living of Marnoch, in the presbytery of Strathbogie, appointed a minister named Edwards to the living. The congregation would not give him a 'call'. He appealed to the court of session; the court ordered the presbytery to take Edwards on trial, and the presbytery obeyed. The standing committee of the assembly thereupon suspended those presbyters who had voted in favour of accepting the decision of the court. The majority of the presbytery then appealed to the court against the minority, and won their case. Finally the presbytery was ordered to receive Edwards. The church was forced open, and Edwards was installed. The assembly formally expelled the ministers. The duke of Argyll tried to settle the question by getting parliamentary sanction for the veto, but the house of lords refused to support his bill.

The change of government brought no advantage to the assembly. Peel's views were opposed to the political liberalism of most of the dissentient Scottish presbyterians, and the conservative party was unlikely to sympathize with resistance to law. The new cabinet suggested a compromise whereby the patron kept his right of presentation, the church its right of objection, and the church courts the duty of deciding upon the validity of the complaints. The assembly refused this compromise, made a violent declaration against the court of session, and asserted that 'all acts of the parliament of Great Britain passed without the consent of the church and nation, in alteration of, or derogatory to the government, discipline, rights, and privileges of the church . . . and also all sentences of courts in contravention of the same government, discipline, rights, and privileges, are and shall be null and void'. This document was sent to the queen. No cabinet could accept a defiance of this kind, and no agreement between the parties was now possible, though one more effort at settlement was made within the church. At a meeting of the Scottish convocation in November 1842, two sets of resolutions were drawn up expounding grievances and suggesting remedies under threat of secession. In the view of the government there could be only one answer. The protesting party were told in January 1843 that their demands were unreasonable and that the cabinet would not recommend the queen to accept them. The result was a schism in the church. On 24 May 1843, 474 ministers left the established church of Scotland and formed the Free Church of Scotland. Within four years of the disruption, the seceders had raised £1,254,000, and built 654 churches. No other religious body within the dominions of the Crown showed such energy and self-sacrifice during the Victorian age.

IV

ENGLISH LITERATURE AND THE
DEVELOPMENT OF IDEAS

ALTHOUGH it is dangerous to set precise limits of time to movements in literature or to attempt too close a correlation between the literature and art and the political or economic structure of an age, an historian of the nineteenth century can hardly avoid taking the reform bill as the beginning of a new artistic epoch. During the first three decades of the century the best work in English literature was in poetry; between 1832 and 1870 the best work was in prose. There was indeed nothing in the conditions of English life after the reform bill particularly unfavourable to the writing of great poetry; Tennyson and Browning came very near to imaginative genius of the highest order, and the work of other men was of good quality and remarkable for variety as well as for technical skill. On the other hand the continual inventiveness of the time, the incessant search after improvement, and the criticism of existing institutions and social habits encouraged and even required the development of a new type of literature in prose. There was an increase in the range of subjects and, for that matter, in the number of words in current use.[1] It has been said that for every new word or term invented by Bentham there were at least a score in the next generation. There were more readers, more writers, and more books. Here again it is unsafe to put too much emphasis on any one year as a dividing line. The popularity of the literary and political reviews before 1832 already showed a wide extension in the subjects of literary and public discussion and in the number of writers who could expect to sell their books; the increase in the national income, which allowed more people to give their time to writing and provided more readers with leisure to exercise their curiosity, had begun before the third decade of the century.

The years before and after 1832, however, make a dividing

[1] e.g. altruism, scientist, sanitation, mobilize, mauve, estate agent, and the whole terminology of the physical and biological sciences. Other words, such as handbook, subjective and objective, were reintroduced into the language or given new meanings.

line, if only because many of the imaginative writers of the earlier period of the century died about this time. Blake died in 1827, Hazlitt in 1830, Scott and Crabbe in 1832, Coleridge and Lamb in 1834. Wordsworth, who lived until 1850, and Southey, who lived until 1843, had done their best work many years earlier.[1] De Quincey's attempt to revive the sonorous language of the seventeenth century was made in *The Confessions of an Opium Eater* (1821) and other essays written about the same time; although his own disordered and drug-haunted life did not end until 1859 his articles and papers written after 1830 were not of much importance. Landor[2] was also an isolated figure, an aristocrat with revolutionary sympathies of a classical republican type. He survived his contemporaries, but he owed little to them as an artist, and had little influence upon any of the younger generation of writers except Swinburne, though his poetical prose tended, like the writings of Lamb, De Quincey, and the novelists, to widen the range of English style. Tennyson published his first volume of verse in 1830, and Browning in 1833. The originality of their work was recognized at once, though not always with favour. Coleridge thought that Tennyson 'did not very well know what metre is' and that his verses hardly scanned. Carlyle's *Sartor Resartus* appeared in serial form in 1833–4. Macaulay's essay on Chatham, one of the most brilliant of his *Edinburgh Review* articles, was published in 1834. Newman's most remarkable series of prose writings began about 1833; Dickens began to write the papers collected in *Sketches by Boz* in 1834–5, and *The Posthumous Papers of the Pickwick Club* appeared in 1836–7.

The new prose literature, written for a wider public than the governing class of the eighteenth century, was connected with politics in the larger sense but far less concerned with politicians; the writers were less in contact with the narrow world

---

[1] Thomas Moore (1779–1852) had also written his best poetry before 1823.

[2] Walter Savage Landor (1775–1864), s. of W. Landor, a Staffordshire landowner, who, through his second wife, Elizabeth Savage, inherited estates in Warwickshire; educ. Rugby and Trinity College, Oxford; a jacobin in youth; went to Spain to take part in the rebellion against the French, 1808; a great deal of his life was spent in violent quarrels and in disputes or financial difficulties caused by his temper and unbusinesslike habits; Coleridge admired his work in 1798, and Swinburne went to Florence to see him in 1864. Landor's aristocratic republicanism was based on his admiration for Milton. He disliked both Pope and Wordsworth, and his style is nearer to the architecture of the classical revival than to the work of any of his literary contemporaries.

of upper-class society and more interested in movements than in parties. Disraeli and Trollope were the only writers of good novels about contemporary politicians; Peacock's[1] novels, though they touched politics, were concerned mainly with social and literary satire. For the first time a revolutionary movement in English politics produced no literature of importance. The poetry of chartism is bad, and the prose is inferior to the writings of Cobbett. Carlyle's *Chartism* and Kingsley's novels were the work of men outside the movement, and if philosophic radicalism inspired the political writings of Mill, there was no one in the nineteenth century to compare either with Burke or with Tom Paine. There was indeed little dissatisfaction with the forms of government; most writers accepted the institutions of the country, though they might support or distrust this or that reform. It is more remarkable that there should have been little good prose and practically no verse about machinery, and that an achievement such as railway building should have had so small an influence upon imaginative literature. The character of English education was responsible for a good deal of the open or indirect hostility to mechanical invention. Most poets and prose-writers of the age, if they were not gentlemen by birth, at least accepted the tradition which put a low and almost a servile value upon technical skill and merely functional achievement.[2] If there are exceptions, they represent the moods rather than the permanent outlook of writers or artists. Ruskin was entirely sincere when he thought that a railway line spoiled a landscape, and yet described a ship of the line in 1856 as 'the most honourable thing that man, as a gregarious animal, has ever produced'. Matthew Arnold is a better example of a blind devotion to literary form which came near to giving an aesthetic value to the old Greek view that manual skill and mechanical invention were the marks of an unfree mind. From a sociological point of view it is an interesting paradox that the *bourgeois* writers of the age of high capitalism should have been almost unanimous in failing to discover beauty in the technique upon which middle-class life and the capitalist system were based.[3]

[1] Thomas Love Peacock (1785–1866), b. Weymouth, s. of a London glass-merchant; clerk in the E.I.C., 1825–56; a friend of Shelley, 1812–18.

[2] Turner used a railway train in one and steam-boats in two of his best pictures, but the modern inventions were a foil to the central theme.

[3] As an inspector of schools Matthew Arnold owed a great deal of his leisure and comfort to rapid travel, and yet he merely sneers at railways.

The conditions of the time explain two other features of this prose literature. The moral ideas of western Europe, and, in particular, the current moral judgements of public opinion, rested upon a Christian foundatioñ, and upon standards of sexual behaviour sharply different from those of the ancient pagan world. The structure of an orderly society, the safeguards of family life and honour, depended upon the observance of these Christian standards; they were in danger of collapse during the last years of the eighteenth century and the licence of the regency. Hence the reaction after 1832.[1] This need of order and deliberate restraint was not felt in England alone, and it would be unwise to infer from the 'gentility' and even from the prudishness of the period, or from the avoidance of direct reference in literature to the physical phenomena of sex, that the writers of the age were either hypocritical or squeamish. Every age has its conventions about words; the eighteenth century was in many respects more sentimental in its treatment of the relationships of men and women, and even more conventional in its treatment of the characters of women. The conventions of the mid-nineteenth century affected certain fields of literature, particularly novels and light comedy. The habit of reading aloud, more widespread a century ago than it is now in an age of smaller and better-lit rooms, meant, as a rule, the reading of stories, and therefore a demand for stories suitable for a family circle. Thackeray, with his imaginative insight into the 'underworld' of London and Paris, was certainly hampered by the fashion of the time. It is doubtful whether any other writer of high talent was much troubled. Browning, for example, never hesitated in his choice of subject;[2] Tennyson's best work was unaffected by the belief that it was the duty

[1] It is necessary to add that in many respects the reaction was slow. Prostitution was one of the gross evils of London and other great cities. The evil was aggravated by the fact that employment open to women was for the most part drab, ill-paid, and often 'sweated'. On the other hand the difference between the Victorian age and the eighteenth and earlier centuries is that social evil of this kind was at last recognized as a scandal, and not merely condoned or exploited. The harshness of the respectable to the non-respectable was neither new nor, again, a specially English phenomenon, and must be linked, however incongruously, with the general desire to raise standards. Victorian writers at least did not wallow in the mud of their social disorders.

[2] For example, 'Porphyria's Lover'. It is possible that a good deal of the Victorian 'nonsense' verse is a psychological substitute for the bawdy of earlier periods. Browning's love of the grotesque may have a similar origin.

of poets to safeguard and improve household morality. Dickens represented more liberation than repression of emotion, and the reaction against the mid-Victorian conventions did not come from the most vigorous and inquiring poets or prose-writers. Swinburne's literary paganism was little more than the manipulation of words.

A second, though less universal, feature of the age was a search after a substitute for doctrinal religion. In this respect there is a curious contrast with the period of Shelley and Byron. Shelley's 'atheism' was a figure of speech, a form of attack upon the abuses and vested interests of church establishments. The scepticism of the eighteenth century was mainly the worldly indifference of frivolous-minded people. The irreligion of the nineteenth century was deeper; Mill, Arnold, and George Eliot were not 'pleasure-lovers'. There was a good deal of selfishness and cant, but few grave abuses remained for attack in the church of England after 1850. The scientific thought of the age was not concerned with the scandals of church organization; it was undermining the very foundations of belief. No one could foretell what would happen to society after these disintegrating theories had passed into general circulation and affected the masses. The French Revolution was a lesson in the behaviour of men who had lost the restraining influence of religion; atheism and revolutionary politics seemed to flourish together. For this reason there was an anxious sense of mission and, at the same time, of foreboding among writers who felt that they ought to provide some guidance for the common man, and yet doubted the social effectiveness of their own trust in 'the larger hope' or in the providence of 'some Power, not our-selves, which makes for righteousness'.

Finally, it should be remembered that, even in an age of rapid change and active intellectual curiosity, few people read new books, and most people who read new books read bad books. Among the old books widely read, the bible still held the first place. It was read uncritically, and with a literalism which was often harmful to unbalanced or untrained minds, but its imaginative power, consolation, and magnificence were within reach of the humble. The language of the authorized version was independent of literary fashion; the psalms indeed were the only poems, and the gospels the only biographies known in common to Englishmen and women of all classes.

After the bible *Robinson Crusoe* and *The Pilgrim's Progress*[1] were among the most widely read classics of the middle years of the nineteenth century. On the other hand there was a very large sale for sentimental and religious novels of a worthless kind.[2] The Rev. L. Richmond's *The Dairyman's Daughter*[3] had a sale of two million copies. Mrs. Bennett's *Vicissitudes Abroad, or the Ghost of My Father*, in six volumes (1806) sold 2,000 copies on the day of publication. Tracts had an even larger sale. *The Sinner's Friend* was translated into thirty languages.[4] Martin Tupper's *Proverbial Philosophy, a Book of Thoughts and Arguments, Originally Treated*, appeared in instalments over a period of nearly thirty years from 1838, and had an enormous sale; a million copies were sold in the United States before 1881. Even among readers of 'literature', second-rate and noisy poems such as *Festus* (1839) by Philip James Bailey (1816–1902), or the jejune historical tableaux of Sir H. Taylor's[5] *Philip van Artevelde*, were given high praise in their time, while writers like Francis Smedley, the author of *Frank Fairleigh* (1850), or sporting novelists like G. J. Whyte-Melville, sold large quantities of third- and fourth-rate novels. Children's books were largely the result of the changed attitude towards education and a realization of the importance of play. It was fortunate that both *Robinson Crusoe* and *The Pilgrim's Progress* were books which few children disliked. Most Victorian books written for children (even Mrs. Ewing's (1841–85), and Kingsley's *The Water-Babies*) were choked with moral and religious lessons, but the simplicity of many of the writers, with a natural gift for story-telling, made the books less unsatisfactory than their intention, and the readers were acute enough to choose their own pages and chapters. In

---

[1] Francis Place read *The Pilgrim's Progress*, though, with his cocksure lack of imagination, he classed it with 'other equally absurd books'.

[2] For the best-sellers see A. Cruse, *The Englishman and his Books in the Early Nineteenth Century*, 1930, and M. Dalziel, *Popular Fiction a Hundred Years Ago*, 1957.

[3] The book is a lugubrious account of a girl who, after her own religious conversion, also converted her sister, mother, and father. The two sisters died, and, before her death, one of them wrote to her parish clergyman a series of letters about her religious life.

[4] The number of copies printed is not necessarily an indication of the numbers read, since tracts were given away to doubtful recipients more freely than other works.

[5] Sir H. Taylor (1800–86) disapproved of the romantic writers of his youth because they had no subject-matter. Byron's *Don Juan*, for example, gave 'only such light observations upon life and manners as any acute man of the world might collect upon his travels'.

spite of the large sale of bad new books, the remarkable feature of the age was the popularity of 'good literature'. The writers of the time wrote for the public, and not for one another; poetry was less esoteric, and prose less technical, than in the next two generations. The intellectual movements within the arts were intelligible to the general reader because they were connected with the main currents of thought in other fields. The sciences were less professionalized; Lyell's *Principles of Geology*, Mill's *Political Economy*, Darwin's *Origin of Species*, and Maine's *Ancient Law* could be read by laymen. History was more of an art than a science, and historians were less afraid of picturesque generalization and more occupied with presenting the broad outline of events. The number of readers and writers, though large, was still not too large for high ability to pass unobserved, while the development of organized publicity had not thrown popular standards of judgement into confusion. On the whole, the critics in every field were fairly sure in their estimates, and the judgement of posterity is nearer to that of contemporaries than is often the case in periods of rapid change.

Among the poets Tennyson,[1] after 1850, had the greatest reputation. No other English poet has been made a peer on the strength of his poetry. Tennyson was an ideal candidate for this honour. His poetry was on the side of authority; his political opinions were those of an intelligent country gentleman and his moral standards beyond reproach. In religion he was, ultimately, on the side of the church, and in economics on the side of the middle class. Tennyson's work was neither disturbing nor calming, except in those passages where he used, sharply and often with splendid dramatic effect, his power of observing natural things. Yet, although there is little profound emotion in his poetry,[2] few English poets have been

---

[1] Alfred Tennyson, 1st Baron Tennyson (1809–92), b. Somersby, Lincs., s. of a clergyman; educ. Louth grammar school and Trinity College, Cambridge. Tennyson's family was sufficiently well off to make it unnecessary for him to earn his living, though, after the greater part of the family capital was lost through bad investment, Tennyson accepted a civil list pension of £200 from Peel. He published only two poems between 1833 and 1842, partly owing to reviewers' attacks on his first volume of poems, partly owing to the death of his close friend Arthur Hallam. His great popular reputation began with the appearance of *In Memoriam* during the year (1850) in which Tennyson succeeded Wordsworth as poet laureate. Tennyson was offered a baronetcy by Gladstone in 1873 and Disraeli in 1874; he accepted a peerage in 1884.

[2] Verlaine once told W. B. Yeats that he had tried to translate *In Memoriam*,

more skilled in the use of words, in the attainment of simplicity, and in the poetic harmonizing of experience which is neither unbearably tragic nor entirely commonplace. This poetry belongs, like Constable's paintings, to the long hours of an English summer; it is content with the visible world, and content, ultimately, to leave unanswered questions to which there is no easy answer. For this reason there was little development in Tennyson's mind, and it is difficult to find any development in his poetry other than a greater control over his material. For this reason also, because his genius was sensitive to things rather than to people and to harmony rather than to conflict, there was hardly any decline in his power of writing. He published *Mariana in the Moated Grange* in 1830; *Tiresias* was written over half a century later. Tennyson went on revising his earlier poems, and repeated certain themes after many years. He worked on his longest poem, *In Memoriam*, for seventeen years before he published it. He took his position very seriously after his appointment to the laureateship, and to some extent spoiled his work by his belief that, as Virgil celebrated the triumphs of Augustus, an English poet laureate was committed by his office to a moralizing panegyric upon English life and the excellence of the English system of government. The heroic directness of *The Lady of Shalott* and the *Morte d'Arthur* gave way to the symbolism of the *Idylls of the King*; there is a note in Tennyson's handwriting: 'King Arthur ... Religious faith ... The Round Table ... Liberal Institutions.'

A great deal of Tennyson's work may be described as the poetry of escape;[1] it would be difficult to apply this term to the poems of Robert Browning. Browning, like Tennyson, was concerned with problems of conduct and with the reaffirmation of belief, but he was not satisfied merely to state the case in exquisite language, and to hope for the best in spite of the evidence. He wrestled with his problems, enjoyed their subtlety, and found their solution in the concept of freedom. It is typical of the two men that Tennyson delayed his marriage for more than ten years owing to want of money—though he could well

but had failed to do so because Tennyson was 'too noble, too *anglais*, and, when he should have been broken-hearted, had many reminiscences'. Yeats, *Discoveries*, p. 12, quoted in Elton, i. 344.

[1] The hero in *Maud* (Tennyson thought *Maud* his best poem) is shocked by the cruelty of nature, and yet, a few stanzas afterwards, decides to go for consolation to 'the quiet woodland ways'.

have supported himself by writing—while Browning[1] eloped with Elizabeth Barrett.[2] Browning's vitality was his artistic undoing; he allowed himself too many tricks of language, and his refusal to keep ordinary rules obscured his meaning even from contemporaries, and has made a great deal of his work unintelligible to later generations; yet even in his longer poems, and in spite of the tortured lines or the suppression of articles, relative pronouns, and auxiliary verbs, there is again and again a rare lyrical beauty. His plays were meant more for reading than for acting. They are often more like novels than plays, but the men and women in them are real; they are not embodiments of the cardinal virtues, the deadly sins, or the British constitution. Browning's vigour saved him from the bathos of Tennyson at his worst, and, if Tennyson represented, in poetry, the settled life of his age, the leisured culture of the *rentier*, the softening of manners, and the increasing uncertainty about the ultimate destiny of man, Browning's 'impassioned curiosity' is more typical of the individual energy and force of the period of high capitalism. Shelley and Byron went to Italy to escape from England. Browning exploited Italian richness and colour as whole-heartedly as a Victorian entrepreneur seized upon a new machine or attacked some newly revealed source of mineral wealth.[3] In each case there is the same naïve and magnificent vulgarity, the same astonishing result.

No other Victorian poet approached Tennyson in the handling of words or Browning in creative energy. Swinburne[4]

[1] Robert Browning (1812–89), b. Camberwell, s. of a clerk in the bank of England, and great-grandson of a Hamburg merchant named Wiedemann; educ. at home, though in 1829–30 he attended Greek classes in London university; decided at that time to give his life to writing poetry; met Miss Barrett in 1845, and eloped with her in 1846. Browning's reputation was high among the literary public after the appearance of *Paracelsus* in 1835, but until he published *The Ring and the Book* in 1868–9 his poems were less well known among the general public than those of Mrs. Browning. Browning spent a great deal of his time abroad, before and after his marriage, and gave some of his best poems an Italian setting which did not originally belong to them (e.g. 'Pippa passes' was suggested by the sight of a girl in a wood near Dulwich).

[2] Elizabeth Barrett Browning (1806–61), b. nr. Durham, d. of Edward Moulton, who took the name of Barrett on succeeding to some property; injured her spine as a young girl, and remained an invalid for many years; published several volumes of poems and wrote literary articles before meeting Browning, though her best work was done in his company.

[3] 'Italy is stuff for the use of the North, and no more.' *Letters of R. and E. B. Browning, 1845–6*, i. 53.

[4] Algernon Charles Swinburne (1837–1909), s. of an admiral, b. London; educ. Eton and Balliol College, Oxford; went down without taking a degree. After 1862

continued the romantic tradition in his passion for a political liberty which was neither more nor less than aristocratic individualism, but, except when he is writing of the sea or the landscapes of southern England and the border country, his work is too literary. He was too good a classical scholar to be a modern poet; he could repeat the whole of the *Oresteia*, and his Latin and Greek verses are better than those of any professional scholar of his time. His imitativeness comes out in a curious way in *Atalanta in Calydon*. The play is written on a classical theme and follows a Greek arrangement, but its construction is lyrical rather than dramatic; the characters are pre-Raphaelite, and the diction owes more to the bible than to antique models. Moreover, in spite of his attempt to break away from the didactic morality of his time, Swinburne was as much of a moralist and even a preacher as his contemporaries. He was born a quarter of a century later than Tennyson and Browning, and the disintegration of accepted standards had gone farther. Tennyson wrote of the insufficiency of the creeds; Swinburne denounced Jehovah with a certain boyish enthusiasm; yet the pantheism of *Hertha* and the chorus in *Atalanta* castigating the high gods are not far removed in thought from *In Memoriam*. Matthew Arnold, fourth in succession of greatness as a poet, and midway in time between Tennyson and Swinburne, also wanted to persuade people that in poetry alone could they find liberation from the doubt and falseness of the age. Arnold was more free, in his poetry, to develop his imaginative powers without hampering them with moral teaching, because he had another sphere of practical activity as a prose-writer. His best poetry was written before 1867, and his best prose in the last twenty years of his life. Arnold's poetry is grave and measured, more classical in form than Swinburne's work, less bold in metrical experiment. To a certain extent his verse lacks vitality. Arnold was in fact as little of a rebel as Tennyson or Swinburne; his attacks on the middle class were made from a middle-class point of view. *Fin de siècle* was mainly a middle-class disease in the later years of the century, and Arnold was among the early sufferers, as Rossetti, in his carefully phrased verse, was among the earliest of the conscious aesthetes.

Swinburne suffered from a form of epilepsy; he spent the last thirty years of his life almost in seclusion at T. Watts-Dunton's house at Putney.

These four poets were above their contemporaries in the quality and quantity of their work. There were others who produced remarkable poetry on a smaller scale, and reflected, in their differences of manner and outlook, the variety and individualism of the age. Edward Fitzgerald (1809–83) and Coventry Patmore (1823–96), John Keble and Arthur Hugh Clough, Christina Rossetti and William Johnson Cory (1823–92), Ferguson's *Lays of the Western Gael* and Macaulay's *Lays of Ancient Rome* could have belonged only to an age of comparative freedom for individual development, and an age in which no received standards and rules had final authority. Keble was the most conventional, and, in his time, the most popular, of the lesser poets, and *The Christian Year* has the characteristics of minor poetry. It is more about the liturgy than about religion; it is derivative in style—a critic described it as 'Wordsworth for women'—and often jejune in expression; at the same time it is a quiet and accurate reflection of anglicanism in the nineteenth century. Christina Rossetti's[1] religious poetry is deeper and more passionate; her range of subjects was greater, and there is no shrinking from emotion. It is curious that the religious revival of the century brought little good poetry; Newman's verse was inferior to his prose.[2] Reginald Heber (1783–1826) was a common-sense regency figure, hard-working and heavy-handed. Patmore's *Angel in the House*—a final version of three separate poems published in 1854, 1856, and 1860—was immensely popular. Patmore was, officially, on the side of the conventions. He was a religious man, and wrote about legally married lovers; it is possible that he was largely misunderstood, and that his philosophy was much nearer than that of any other of his contemporaries except Browning to an understanding of the significance of sexual passion.

Clough[3] was a typical 'intellectual' of the middle years of the century. After a brilliant career at Rugby he joined, and

---

[1] Christina Georgina Rossetti (1830–94), b. London; sister of D. G. Rossetti; contributed to *The Germ* (see p. 591); gave most of her time to religious work and devotion; her health broke down after an illness in 1871. Christina Rossetti's 'In the Round Tower at Jhansi' is one of the few good poems about the Indian Mutiny.

[2] Richard Chenevix Trench (1807–86), archbishop of Dublin, wrote sonnets which give him a high place among the minor poets.

[3] Arthur Hugh Clough (1819–61), s. of a Welsh landowner; educ. Rugby and Balliol College, Oxford; fellow of Oriel; resigned his fellowship, 1848; head of University Hall, London, 1849; examiner in the education office, 1853.

left, the tractarians, and spent the rest of his life in a restless agnosticism. Fitzgerald was a man of means, with many literary friends, who persuaded himself that he liked 'rough sailors and fishermen' better than 'lettered society'; in other words he was a sophisticated dilettante who gave up any attempt to deal with the age. He translated Calderon in 1853, and printed the first edition of the *Rubaiyat of Omar Khayyam* in 1859. Although the work was little noticed, except by the pre-Raphaelites, it sold steadily; Fitzgerald issued revised editions in 1868 and 1872.[1]

The pre-Raphaelite movement belonged more to painting than to poetry, though its canons of painting were affected by literary themes, and its poetry was much like decorative art. Rossetti's[2] poetry was violently attacked in 1871 as 'the fleshly school of poetry'. The attack mattered little, since Rossetti's influence had already encouraged a poet of greater ability whose work had nothing of the finickiness and eroticism of his master. William Morris[3] suffered from entirely different defects. He wrote too easily, especially in later life; he 'composed' poetry to fill pages for his printing-press, and once put together seven hundred lines in an afternoon. On the other hand *The Defence of Guenevere* (1858), *The Life and Death of Jason* (1867), and even the over-long *Earthly Paradise* (1868–70) have a vigour and sensitiveness which bring them near to great poetry.[4]

[1] Fitzgerald's version is more than a translation. The Persian originals were separate units not set out in any sequence of thought, and written in two manuscripts. Fitzgerald rearranged, paraphrased, and combined these units, and added to them at least two pieces from other Persian poets.

[2] Dante Gabriel Rossetti (1828–82), s. of a refugee from Naples who became professor of Italian at King's College, London, b. London; studied drawing under Cotman, and later, after he had written some of his best poems, under Ford Madox Brown. For some time after 1852 Rossetti had an arrangement with Ruskin whereby Ruskin agreed to buy all those of Rossetti's pictures which pleased him. Ruskin also paid for the publication of Rossetti's translations from the Italian poets. Rossetti's poems had a curious history. Most of them were written between 1847 and 1853; a number appeared in *The Germ* and others in the equally short-lived *Oxford and Cambridge Magazine*. In 1862 Rossetti buried his manuscripts in his wife's coffin, only to exhume them in 1869. The first edition in book form was published in 1870. Rossetti continued to revise his work—there are four different versions of *The Blessed Damozel*—and reissued a collected edition in 1881.

[3] William Morris (1834–96), s. of a bill-broker, b. Walthamstow; educ. Marlborough and Exeter College, Oxford, where he met Burne-Jones; pupil of G. E. Street (see p. 584); went into business in order to reinstate decoration as one of the fine arts. See also vol. xiv of this *History*.

[4] A list of the minor poets would be incomplete without the writers of light verse. Edward Lear's *Book of Nonsense* (1846) popularized the 'limerick'; the

The prose-writers of the middle years of the century fall into three classes. Some wrote to inform, others to exhort or to criticize, and others, again, merely to entertain. The division is not clear-cut. Entertainment was not the sole purpose of novelists like Dickens or Disraeli, and still less of the Brontës; Carlyle, Ruskin, and J. S. Mill combined information with advice. Macaulay's history was, from one point of view, a political pamphlet. It is equally impossible to assign distinctive styles to each of these categories of writers. The influence of oratory upon prose style lessened; the prose of the middle years of the century becomes less violent and more rapid, less pungent, more business-like, and freer in its choice of words and sentences; but it is not safe to make any generalization covering the art of Newman and Carlyle, Ruskin and Macaulay, Dickens and J. S. Mill. Here again the age is one of individualism; originality or wide variations from the normal type did not offend the public taste.

Macaulay[1] was the first though not the oldest in years of this group of writers to gain a great reputation. He was never a graceful speaker, yet his speeches in the commons were heard with more attention than those of any of his contemporaries. His official work in India settled the penal code and determined the character of Indian education for nearly a century. His

Rev. Richard Harris Barham's *Ingoldsby Legends* (1837–47) introduced comedy into the tales of horror popular in the early years of the century. Charles Stuart Calverley (1831–84), a fine classical scholar, produced a number of excellent parodies of contemporary poets. The Rev. C. L. Dodgson (Lewis Carroll), in *Alice's Adventures in Wonderland* (1865), carried on Lear's tradition in a mixture of prose and verse. Sir W. S. Gilbert's work belongs mainly to the period after 1870; his *Bab Ballads* were published in 1869.

[1] Thomas Babington Macaulay (1800–59), Baron Macaulay, s. of Zachary Macaulay, b. Rothley Temple, Leicestershire; began to write a summary of world history at the age of seven, educ. at private schools and Trinity College, Cambridge; fellow of Trinity, 1824; called to the bar, 1826, but had already begun to write for the *Edinburgh* and other reviews; appointed by Lyndhurst to a commissionership in bankruptcy, in spite of his whig views, 1828; M.P. 1830; commissioner of, and, later, secretary to the board of control, 1832; went to India as member of the gov.-gen.'s council, 1834–8; secretary at war, 1839–41; wrote essay on Warren Hastings, 1841; published *Lays of Ancient Rome*, 1842, and his collected essays, 1843; paymaster-general, 1846–7; published the first two volumes of his *History of England*, 1848, and sold 13,000 copies in four months; on the publication of the third and fourth volumes in 1855, 26,500 copies were sold in ten weeks. Macaulay was a short, stout, plain-looking man, of great physical powers of work until the breakdown of his health in 1852. He was apt to monopolize the conversation at a party. Sydney Smith once said to him towards the end of a dinner, 'Macaulay, when I'm dead, you'll be sorry you never heard me talk.'

History of England became a classic on the day of the publication of the first volume. There is a swing about his verse which lifts it above commonplace rhyming; it is characteristic of the man that he should have written only one love-poem. Macaulay accepted his age, admired its care for liberty, order, and improvement, assumed that the future as well as the past belonged to the whigs. His unusual memory, strong pictorial imagination, and quick mind fitted him for the writing of history. Even his faults turned to his advantage. He was not troubled by subtleties of thought, or disturbed by the heroic and the mystical. He never doubted the justice and truth of his own standards of criticism. He was interested in detail but not in *minutiae*, and content to widen rather than to deepen human knowledge. Such a man was ideally fitted for the prosperous middle-class public of his time. Sensitive or rebellious minds, more subtle or more profound thinkers, found him intolerable. Carlyle spoke of his 'essentially irremediable, commonplace nature'. John Mitchel, sentenced to transportation for high treason against an authority which he refused to acknowledge,[1] described Macaulay's religion as 'a tone of polite, though distant recognition of Almighty God, as one of the Great Powers. . . . British civilization gives Him assurances of friendly relations.'[2] Few writers have had so great a fame and yet left so small a mark upon the development of English thought or upon the work of their intellectual equals.

The place of Thomas Carlyle[3] in English letters is curiously different from that of Macaulay. Macaulay overrated the importance of material progress; Carlyle distrusted material progress. Macaulay took for granted the rightness of the scheme of

---

[1] See above, p. 357.　　　　　　　[2] Mitchel, *Jail Journal*, p. 22.

[3] Thomas Carlyle (1795–1881), s. of a mason; b. Ecclefechan, Dumfriesshire; went to Edinburgh university to study for the ministry, 1809; schoolmaster, 1814–18; took pupils, 1818–22, and began translations from German; married Jane Baillie Welsh (b. 1801), 1826; settled in London, 1834, after a period in Scotland, and little success in literature, and wrote *The French Revolution*; part of the MS. was accidentally destroyed in Mill's house, but Carlyle rewrote the book, and from 1837 began to earn a satisfactory income as a literary figure of established reputation; he published *Chartism* in 1839, *Heroes, Hero-Worship and the Heroic in History*, 1841, *Past and Present*, 1843, *Life and Letters of Cromwell*, 1845; henceforward *The Life of Sterling* (1851) and *The History of Friedrich II* (1858–65) were his only long works. Carlyle's life and work were much affected by the severe dyspepsia from which he suffered after 1819. Froude's *Life of Carlyle* is a full and in many ways an unfair account of Carlyle's life, and of the stormy but deeply affectionate relations between Carlyle and his wife.

things because the whigs had won their cause. Carlyle was for ever struggling with the problem of triumphant evil. His roughness of manner came partly from ill health but mainly from extreme sensitiveness and, in Harriet Martineau's words, 'an intolerable sympathy with suffering'. This sensitiveness affected his political and historical judgement. In his search for the expression of Divine justice in history he made Frederick the Great into a good man, and assumed that the fury and confusion of the French Revolution were an equitable retribution for the sins of the French monarchy and aristocracy. His sense of personal responsibility and duty blinded him to the importance of institutions and impersonal forces in history. Carlyle's contempt for government by discussion and for liberals who believed in the voting-power of the people led him, as an old man, into impracticable dreams about the merits of a landed aristocracy, in other words, of the class which he had once thought largely responsible for the French Revolution, while no man given to praising action above speech has ever expressed his choice in a wilder torrent of sentences. His English style had many of the faults which he attributed to parliaments. It was verbose, egoistical, noisy, full of repetition and overstatement.

Nevertheless Carlyle's writings affected a whole generation, including men as different as J. S. Mill and the enthusiasts of the 'Young England' and 'Young Ireland' groups. His inconsistencies mattered little because he was in any case more critical than constructive. He attacked the principle of *laisser faire* and refused to be impressed by the progress of material invention because he realized intensely the 'condition of England'. If he ignored the importance of statistics or the hard and directly relevant work done by parliamentary inquiry, he was right in thinking that politicians often used soft words to disguise injustice and indifference. Carlyle's standards were deeper than those of the Manchester school; he 'stirred the mass of readers rather by antagonism than sympathy', but, in spite of his harshness, he was the chosen author of the young and the generous. Even his way of writing did much to break up the heavy, conventional prose of the professional historians of his time. He introduced a wider and less stilted vocabulary; his powers of description were often superb and his insight into human character and motives far above those of other English historians. In an age which trusted overmuch to machinery, and believed that the self-interest of the majority worked automatically towards the general good, it was no bad thing that one man should insist that the progress of the world has depended, ultimately, upon the energy and heroism of individuals unwilling to leave things to chance or to the action of their neighbours.

J. S. Mill,[1] like Carlyle, was a reformer, but a reformer of a different type, basing his arguments upon positive and exact knowledge and a carefully elaborated philosophical and economic theory. Carlyle decided early in life that he would have 'nothing more to do with metaphysics', and by metaphysics he meant any systematic study of philosophy. Mill's life was spent in trying to discover a scientific basis for a theory of society, though he too gave little attention to metaphysics, and occupied himself too long in explaining away the superficial ethical system of Bentham. Mill had little help from his British contemporaries; he complained in 1835 that

England once stood at the head of European philosophy. Where stands she now? . . . Out of the narrow bounds of mathematical and physical science, not a vestige of a reading and thinking public engaged . . . in the prosecution of thought for the sake of thought. Among few except sectarian religionists—and what they are we all know—is there any interest in the great problems of man's nature and life; among still fewer is there any curiosity respecting the nature and principles of human society, the history or the philosophy of civilization; nor any belief that, from such inquiries, a single important practical consequence can follow.

There is a certain petulance in this outburst. Bentham and the utilitarians, and on the other side Burke, were to some extent responsible for the neglect of philosophy, while from the 'narrow bounds of mathematical and physical science' there were soon to develop discoveries of immense social importance, such as those of Pasteur and Lister, and a new foundation for the theory of society which Mill wanted to build up. Thirty years

[1] John Stuart Mill (1806–73), s. of James Mill, b. Pentonville, London; educ. by his father on a severe system which included elementary Greek at the age of three, and a complete course of political economy at the age of eleven; travelled and worked in France, 1820–1; junior clerk at the East India House, 1823; head of his department, 1856, retired 1858; married, in 1851, Mrs. Taylor, whom he had known for twenty-one years; after her death in 1858 Mill lived for half the year at Avignon; M.P., 1865–8.

later Mill himself wrote a study of the work of Sir William Hamilton.[1] In the main, however, Mill was right. Hamilton was almost alone as a teacher,[2] and the philosophical schools of Oxford and Cambridge were almost entirely unoriginal. Little attention was paid to German philosophy; there was no translation of Kant's *Kritik* until 1841.[3]

Mill himself was more of a reformer than a philosopher; he wrote the *System of Logic* (1843) and the *Principles of Political Economy* (1848) for practical ends, and the influence of the Saint-Simonians and Comte upon his thought was strong because he believed that they were working out a way of life. Mill was one of the earliest scientific humanists of the modern age. The changes in the different editions of the *Political Economy* show his concern with welfare and his desire to use economic doctrine as a guide to legislation and policy. The essay *On Liberty* (1859) was as much an address to the age as Carlyle's *Past and Present* or his *Shooting Niagara, and After*. Mill agreed with Tocqueville and with most liberal thinkers of his time in distrusting the tyranny of the commonplace majority. Macaulay criticized the essay *On Liberty* as a defence of eccentricity, but Mill was defending qualities which Macaulay did not understand, and a European culture beyond the limits of Macaulay's knowledge of fact. It is characteristic of Mill that he should have been one of the few Englishmen of his time who were closely in touch with French thought; and that while Macaulay believed that poetry was declining[4] Mill was among

[1] Sir William Hamilton (1788–1856), b. Glasgow, s. of a merchant; educ. Glasgow, Edinburgh, and Balliol College, Oxford; practised as a lawyer; professor of civil history at Edinburgh, 1821; professor of logic and metaphysics, 1836; his lectures were not published until 1858–60, but he wrote philosophical articles for the *Edinburgh Review* as early as 1829.

[2] Alexander Bain (1819–1903), professor at Aberdeen after 1860, was also of importance in the development of the study of mental processes and their physical background; his two books, *The Senses and the Intellect* (1855) and *The Emotions and the Will* (1859) belong to a later period than the time about which Mill was writing.

[3] J. H. Stirling wrote on Hegel's philosophy in 1865, and W. Wallace, later professor of moral philosophy at Oxford, translated Hegel's *Logic* in 1874. H. Sidgwick (1838–1900) and T. H. Green (1836–82) did not publish books until after 1870.

[4] 'We think that as civilization advances poetry almost necessarily declines. . . . In an enlightened age there will be much intelligence, much science, much philosophy, abundance of just classification and subtle analysis, abundance of wit and eloquence, abundance of verses, and even of good ones; but little poetry. Men will judge and compare, but they will not create.' It is interesting to set this forecast against the views of Wordsworth at the beginning of the nineteenth century:

the first to recognize the greatness of Tennyson. Mill's prose style, exact, sober, and finely modelled, was well fitted to introduce into the English language the new technical terms of the social and economic sciences. Mill did this work without jargon or pedantry, and if the general effect of his careful exposition is a little colourless and monotonous, it reflects the persistent melancholy and pessimism of his own mind.

The style, subject-matter, and purpose of Ruskin's works appear at first sight to be very different from anything written by Mill, yet there are parallels in the history of the two men. Ruskin,[1] like Mill, was affected throughout his life by the type of home education which shelters a boy too much from experience. Ruskin again, like Mill, was influenced by Carlyle.[2] In Ruskin's case this influence extended to his style, though the diction and rhythm of the bible were more important in determining his semi-poetical mode of writing. Ruskin, like Mill, wrote to convince and not merely to expound. He was less content to leave the statement of truth to produce its own effect; he preached too much, and was too ready to think that abundance of goodwill made up for deficiencies of knowledge, and that he could neglect the more arid types of statistical information. Ruskin approached the 'condition of England question' from the point of view of art. His earliest work was on geology and architecture; his first important book, the first volume of *Modern Painters* (1843), was an interpretation of Turner, who was already admired but, according to Ruskin, admired in the wrong way. The second volume of *Modern Painters* (1846) took

'If the labours of the men of science should ever create any material revolution, direct or indirect, in our condition, and in the impressions which we habitually receive, the Poet. . . will be ready to follow the steps of the man of science, not only in those general and indirect effects, but he will be at his side, carrying sensation into the midst of the objects of the science itself. . . . The remotest discoveries of the chemist, the botanist, or mineralogist, will be as proper objects of the poet's art as any upon which it can be employed' (quoted in W. J. Courthope, *The Liberal Movement in English Literature*, p. 24).

[1] John Ruskin (1819–1900), s. of a wine merchant; b. London; travelled as a child with his parents over most of England and Wales, and the lowlands of Scotland, and, after 1833, many European countries; matriculated at Christ Church, Oxford, 1836; married in 1848; his marriage was annulled in 1855, and his wife afterwards married Millais; Slade professor of fine art at Oxford, 1870–84; Ruskin inherited a fortune from his father and made large sums from his books; he gave away most of his capital and a great deal of his income, though much oi it was wasted on social experiments which came to nothing.

[2] Carlyle himself described Ruskin rather unkindly in 1852 as 'a bottle of beautiful soda-water. . . very pleasant company now and then'.

him into a wider field, and included a theory of beauty. The last volume of *Modern Painters* did not appear until 1860; meanwhile Ruskin had written other books suggested by his study of painting. He defended pre-Raphaelitism (1851) as he had defended Turner, and made an analytical study of architecture, especially the architecture of Venice. This study, which resulted in *The Seven Lamps of Architecture* (1849) and *The Stones of Venice* (1851–3), brought him to the connexion between art and social life. He laid too much stress upon moral aspects and overlooked the importance of material and economic facts and forces in determining the character of the buildings and pictures of an age; yet it must be remembered that the historians whom he studied had scarcely begun to investigate these impersonal factors, while the moral decline of the Italian city states was written large in every work. Ruskin applied to the conditions of the nineteenth century his view that good art cannot be produced by bad men or in a corrupt epoch, and explained why the art of his own time was inferior to the art of the middle ages. There was some truth in the view that gothic art was good art because it did not sacrifice the craftsman to a system of mass production, but further study might have shown Ruskin that medieval conditions were not what he thought them to have been, while, from the point of view of the well-being of the workman, modern conditions offered ways of improvement unknown to the gothic ages. On his own presuppositions, and with his strong ethical ideas, Ruskin was almost bound to make a direct attack upon the social and economic structure of modern life. He developed this attack in some lectures on *The Political Economy of Art*, delivered in 1857, and republished nearly a quarter of a century later as *A Joy for Ever*. In 1860 Ruskin turned to the economists. He wrote the four essays printed in *Unto this Last* for the *Cornhill Magazine*, but Thackeray, as editor, stopped their publication after the fourth number owing to the outcry against them. In 1862–3 *Fraser's Magazine* accepted other essays which appeared in 1872 under the title *Munera Pulveris*; no publisher would take any more of these strange outbursts against authority. Although Ruskin did not know enough about the economics which he was attacking, nearly all his first principles would be accepted today; his insistence upon the welfare of the community as something more important than the profit-seeking of individuals had a good effect upon a generation fatigued by the incessant thunderclaps of Carlyle. Ruskin's preoccupation with the conduct of men in society took him a long way from his starting-point in the study of art, but this confusion of art with ethics had one important consequence. Ruskin did a great deal to change the attitude of the English middle classes towards the fine arts. Here his work, in spite of his prejudices and his puritanical judgement, was one of liberation. He freed Englishmen from the delusion that art was 'immoral' and associated with an 'immoral' aristocracy. He showed them that artists and their patrons were not the enemies of religion or of good behaviour; that art was based on a deep observation and study of nature; that the good taste of which the upper class tended to claim a monopoly was to a large extent bad taste, and that the English people had a long tradition, not entirely lost, of sound and noble craftsmanship and enjoyment.

Ruskin's generosity of mind was also a prophylactic against the influence of Herbert Spencer. Herbert Spencer carried to an extreme the mid-nineteenth-century sense of mission and belief in material progress. He was trained as an engineer, and his idea of the world was one of convenient gadgets subject to continuous improvement; yet, with all his superficiality, there is in his work a sense of the vastness and even of the mystery of created life. He began to write about the concept of evolution before the publication of the *Origin of Species*, and although his first works were a defence of individualism—*The Proper Sphere of Government* (1843), and *Social Statics* (1850)—he turned to science and philosophy, and spent nearly forty years in working out a complete system of the universe, applicable to every detail of thought, conduct, and social life. This synthesis had little influence upon first-class minds, but it was one of the major intellectual forces affecting public opinion in the third generation of the century.[1]

The popularity of works dealing at second hand with scientific theory was a result of the conflict between the hypotheses of the scientists and the traditional views taught by the clergy. This conflict of opinion had at first a certain unreality about it. The retailers of science were far more cocksure than the majority of those scientists who were producing work of original

[1] Spencer's influence was even greater outside Europe. His works had a very large sale in America, Russia, India, and Japan.

quality, while popular theology rested too much upon a literal and unhistorical interpretation of the bible. Darwin, for example, took no part in the controversies over the social or theological implications of his theory, and the deepest religious thinkers were unperturbed by the discovery that Lyell's[1] *Principles of Geology* (1830–3) and *The Antiquity of Man* (1863) seemed to contradict the narrative of the creation in the first chapter of Genesis. On the other hand, the attack upon dogmatic religion was many-sided, and there was scope for fluent and superficial writers to construct rival syntheses of the universe. Most of these works—Huxley's, for example—belong to the period after 1870, but Spencer was not alone in providing a complete and water-tight system of thought. Harriet Martineau's[2] summarized translation of Comte's *Positive Philosophy* had a great vogue on its appearance in 1853, and influenced George Eliot. Similar attempts were made to free history from the theological presuppositions of Christian writers. These attempts also suffered from the over-confidence of their authors in using data insufficient to bear their generalizations. H. T. Buckle's[3] *History of Civilization in England* (1857–61) (though the author never properly reached English history) was the best known of these explanations of history in terms of climate, food, and soil.

W. E. H. Lecky[4] had a more profound, though not less sceptical, mind than Buckle; his best work in English and Irish history belongs to the last quarter of the century, but he made his name by two general works; the *History of the Rise and Influence of the Spirit of Rationalism in Europe* (1865) and a *History of European Morals from Augustus to Charlemagne* (1869). Lecky explained these books as 'an attempt to examine the merits of certain theological opinions according to the historical method. They belong to a very small school of historical writings which began with Vico, was continued by Condorcet, Herder, Hegel, Comte,

---

[1] For Sir C. Lyell see below, p. 572.

[2] Harriet Martineau (1802–76), b. Norwich, d. of a manufacturer, of Huguenot descent; began to publish stories as 'Illustrations of Political Economy' in 1832; recovered from a serious illness after treatment by mesmerism, 1844; wrote *A History of England during the Thirty Years Peace*, 1848–9.

[3] Henry Thomas Buckle (1821–62), s. of a London shipowner, educ. privately; travelled on the continent 1840–3, and subsequently settled in London; died at Damascus on an eastern tour.

[4] William Edward Hartpole Lecky (1838–1903); b. co. Dublin, s. of an Irish landowner; educ. Cheltenham and Trinity College, Dublin; thought of taking Orders after leaving the university; M.P. 1895; spent his life in historical study and writing.

and found its last great representative in Buckle.' The list of names is imposing, but much of the work of this school of philosophical historians was premature because their speculations were not based upon critical study of the subject-matter of history.

The critical methods of modern historical scholarship date mainly from the latter years of the eighteenth and the early years of the nineteenth centuries. They were directed at first to a reinterpretation of ancient history; the use of archaeological and philological evidence, and the historical treatment of law brought the most remarkable results. The 'new learning' was applied more easily to the history of Greece and Rome, because the material was readily available; for a long time scholars had been providing editions of texts and maintaining high standards of research. There was much less work of this kind to help the students of medieval or modern times. Public and private archives were not open to investigation; their contents were unclassified and unarranged. The Benedictine order in France, a succession of great antiquarians in England, and a few scholars like Muratori in Italy collected material of the highest value, but their interpretation of this material was less sound. The romantic revival, especially in Germany, and the desire to use the history of the past as an instrument of patriotic education led to a new interest in the middle ages. This interest spread to later periods of history, and the methods of the classical scholars were extended to other fields. The work was slow and difficult. It required patient application and a good deal of financial help if the new material were to be published. In England this financial help was not easily obtained. The universities were not much interested in literary subjects outside the range of theology, classics, and philosophy. The Society of Antiquaries, founded in 1751, was of little help in historical work. A record commission was set up in 1800 to supervise the preservation and arrangement of the national archives; the commissioners were men of affairs who were not much interested in documents, and until Sir Harris Nicolas (1799–1848) published a series of attacks upon the Society of Antiquaries, the record commission, and the British Museum library, little was done for the assistance of scholars. In 1836 Nicolas, who had begun his career as a naval officer and turned to antiquarian research almost by accident, secured the appointment of a parliamentary committee of inquiry into the state of the public records. As a result, the public record office was established in 1838 but another twenty years passed before the publication of an authoritative series of editions of the sources of English history. In 1857 Lord Romilly, as master of the rolls, persuaded the treasury to pay for a work of this kind. Sir Thomas Duffus Hardy (1804–78), who was largely responsible for the appointment of an historical manuscripts commission in 1869, was at first in charge of the *Rolls Series*; Stubbs became editor in 1863. Hardy made a number of valuable contributions to the study of British archives, but his work was overshadowed by the immense range and learning of Stubbs.[1]

The development of the scientific side of historical study led to a partial separation between history and literature. This separation was never complete. Stubbs had imagination as well as learning, and Maitland was to show that abstruse legal points could be set out in fine English prose. Yet the scholars most fitted by temper of mind for the difficult and original work of editing chronicles or arranging documents were not necessarily good writers. The study of Anglo-Saxon history, begun by Sharon Turner's *History of England from the Earliest Period to the Norman Conquest* (1799–1805), was continued by Sir Francis Palgrave (1788–1861) and J. M. Kemble (1807–57). Palgrave was, and is, almost unreadable; Kemble was mainly a collector and editor of documents; J. Lingard (1771–1851), who complained that 'the philosophy of history' often appeared to him 'the philosophy of romance', was a better writer than Palgrave; he had not Macaulay's vigour and strength, but it is easy to see that Macaulay was a protestant, while few readers of Lingard's *History of England* would guess, at least from the earlier volumes, that the author was a catholic priest. Henry Hallam (1777–1859) was as superior to Lingard in constructive power as Lingard was superior to Palgrave, but Hallam's *Constitutional History from the Accession of Henry VII to the Death of George II* was more of a political manifesto, a learned and magnificent exposition of whig principles. J. A. Froude (1818–94), whose English prose is in many respects better than the prose of Macaulay, was

[1] William Stubbs (1825–1901), s. of a solicitor, b. Knaresborough; servitor at Christ Church, Oxford; fellow of Trinity College, Oxford; regius professor of modern history at Oxford; bishop of Chester, 1884, Oxford, 1888.

able to make use of the critical work of his predecessors. A great deal of his work was entirely new; he went to manuscript sources, though he could be careless in using them. At the same time he had more of an artist's passion than a scholar's detachment: his own intellectual changes affected his judgements upon the characters and events of the English reformation. He began as a tractarian and a disciple of Newman; he became an agnostic and a disciple of Carlyle, and based his interpretation of the character of Henry VIII not merely upon the evidence of historical documents but on opinions which Carlyle had reached without examining this evidence. S. R. Gardiner's work on the Stuarts began to appear while Froude was still writing on the Tudors. The contrast between these two men is again the contrast between the artist and the student. Gardiner (1829–1902) made a more careful use of his material; his mind was humbler and more evenly balanced, and his estimates of men and institutions less affected by his emotions.

The increasing specialization of history destroyed the unity of the subject, but historians had a very great effect upon the general outlook of the age. Law and economics might claim a place in history once monopolized by the actions of the great; lawyers and economists could not ignore the historical method. Sir Henry Maine's *Ancient Law* (1861) applied this method to the study of primitive law and custom. Walter Bagehot,[1] as an economist and essayist, was deeply influenced in his thought by the new attitude towards law and history as well as by the application of the principle of natural selection to the rise and fall of political societies. Bagehot's writings, especially his *English Constitution*, which attacked the old theory of 'checks and balances', reached a very wide public; his *Physics and Politics* was 'an attempt to apply the principles of natural selection and inheritance to political society', and to show the importance of common habits and modes of thought as steadying and unifying influences in national life.[2]

---

[1] Walter Bagehot (1826–77), s. of a banker; educ. Bristol and University College, London; called to the bar, 1852, but went into his father's business; began to write for reviews, 1852; editor of *The Economist*, 1860–77.

[2] British interests in the East, as well as the comparatively unworked field of study in Arabia and Turkey in Asia, led to a number of remarkable and original works of travel. Sir Richard Burton's *Pilgrimage to El-Medinah and Mecca* (1856), W. G. Palgrave's *Narrative of a Year's Journey through Central and Eastern Arabia* (1865), Sir A. H. Layard's archaeological accounts of Nineveh and Babylon, R. Curzon's

The most popular form of English prose in the middle years of the century was the prose of the novel. The successors and later contemporaries of Scott continued the tradition that a novel was written primarily to entertain, though entertainment included satire and political conversation, and might include attacks upon social abuses. The conventions of the drama still affected the form of the novel. A novel must tell a story, generally with a happy marriage as the ending; there must be a hero, a heroine, and a villain. There was little attempt at subtlety either in character-drawing or in language; for this reason the earlier Victorian novelists had a wider range than their successors. They described any one who might come into the story, and used their observation and imagination in a business-like way, with the knowledge that the plot would carry them along, and bring characters and readers alike to the end of the diversion. The social conditions of the time increased the attraction of the novel. The theatre suffered from every obstacle; there was no playwright of any importance

Visits to Monasteries in the Levant (1849), and, above all, Kinglake's* _Eothen_ (1844) were the best written of these books. Burton also travelled widely in Africa, but the most remarkable series of African journeys were those of David Livingstone (1813–73). Livingstone had educated himself while working in a cotton factory. He joined the London Missionary Society in 1838, and from 1841 travelled in the interior of Africa.

The most original English books of travel were those of George Borrow.† Borrow's travels did not take him outside Europe, and his most interesting explorations were in England and Wales. From 1835 to 1840 he was an agent of the British and Foreign Bible Society in Spain. His account of these years, in _The Bible in Spain_ (1842), was one of the oddest expressions of protestant orthodoxy and anti-papal feeling. Borrow liked 'low company' and good fights; he had a very remarkable power of learning languages, and these different qualities led him, while in Spain, into the company of Spanish gipsies. When he came back to England he went on with his gipsy studies. _Lavengro: The Scholar, The Gypsy, The Priest_ (1851) and _The Romany Rye_ (1857) introduced, without self-consciousness, a new type of book and a new field of study. Borrow's last book of travel, an account of _Wild Wales, Its Peoples, Languages, and Customs_, surveyed mainly those subjects which ordinary 'intellectuals' allowed to pass unnoticed. It is a curious fact, reflecting upon the character of British rule in India, that there are no mid-nineteenth-century books on Indian life and customs at all comparable with the travel books about the Near and Middle East. Travel in the Ottoman Empire was more of an adventure, and the traveller was not embarrassed by the presence of British officials.

* Alexander William Kinglake (1809–91), s. of a banker, b. Taunton; educ. Eton and Trinity College, Cambridge; called to the bar, but did not practise a great deal; M.P. 1857; went to the Crimea, and wrote a _History of the Invasion of the Crimea_ in eight volumes (1863–87).

† George Borrow (1803–81), b. East Dereham, s. of a recruiting officer, educ. Edinburgh.

before T. W. Robertson,[1] while the development of cheap magazines encouraged the writing of stories which could be printed in instalments. Most of the novels of the age are too long because they appeared chapter by chapter in magazines before they were published as books. The novel, as a literary form, was new enough to attract original minds, and already well enough developed to allow great diversity of method and interest; *Jane Eyre, Tancred, Vanity Fair, Wuthering Heights,* and *Dombey and Son* appeared in the same twelvemonth (1847). There was plenty of elbow-room for these novelists of different temperament and method. They wrote for the great public, and the great public bought their books. Their mutual relations, as authors, had little of the jealousy of literary coteries working in a restricted field.

Dickens and Thackeray, Trollope, Charlotte and Emily Brontë, and George Eliot far excelled their contemporaries, but there were other writers whose work was not without value. Samuel Warren (1807–77), the author of *Passages from the Diary of a Late Physician* and *Ten Thousand a Year,* had some influence upon Dickens. Robert Surtees's *Jorrocks' Jaunts and Jollities* (1831–4) has remained a classic of a sort. Captain Frederick Marryat (1792–1848) had a good deal of the eighteenth-century tradition in his stories of the sea. There was a school of Irish novelists, of whom Charles Lever (1806–72) was the most popular, and the historical novels of Lytton-Bulwer had a certain vitality, though little else except words and false pathos.

Dickens and Thackeray were outstanding both in popularity and in power. Dickens[2] was largely self-taught, and most of the books from which he learned anything were stories: *Don Quixote, Gil Blas, Tom Jones, The Arabian Nights,* and *The Vicar of Wakefield.* He knew no foreign language, classical or modern. He ventured to write a history of England for children, but it is not a credit to his historical knowledge. He was not a profound

---

[1] See below, p. 625.

[2] Charles Dickens (1812–70), b. Portsea, s. of a clerk in the navy pay office, and of the daughter of Charles Barrow, a lieutenant in the navy; Dickens's father settled in Camden Town in 1822–3, and was imprisoned for debt; his son found work at a blacking warehouse near Hungerford Steps. His family had a legacy in 1824 and Dickens went to school until, in 1827, he was articled to a solicitor; he learned shorthand, became a reporter, and began to write articles for magazines; the *Pickwick Papers* established his reputation.

thinker; Acton once said that Dickens knew nothing of sin when it was not crime. Carlyle wrote that Dickens's theory of life was 'entirely wrong. He thought men ought to be buttered up, and the world made soft and accommodating for them, and all sorts of fellows have turkey for their Christmas dinner.' For the characters whom Dickens described, and whose needs he understood, this solution of the problem of existence was not a bad one. It was not Dickens's only solution. His sense of justice was always leading him to attack abuses, particularly abuses in law and administration, and he certainly believed that humbug, cruelty, spiritual pride, and hardness of heart were sins. He was one of the few great writers of the nineteenth century who saw the world from the point of view of the urban poor, and did not merely sympathize a little remotely with their sufferings. It was for this reason that he put a comfortable dinner high in the scale of values; that his work is full of melodrama, wildly inaccurate and exaggerated in the description of gentlefolk, over-sentimental about women, and yet exact to the smallest detail in the talk of the common people. Dickens, like all great novelists and playwrights, had a magnificent power of words, so immense a power that the Victorian conventions never stood in his way. His novels are all 'family books', and yet they are full of coarse-minded and hardened criminals, men and women, whose foulness is conveyed, and often over-heightened, without blenching or burking, in language which never shocked his readers. To a certain extent Dickens's sense of the grotesque enabled him to keep his middle-class public in spite of his assumption that all dissenters were canting, and 'to break every Victorian convention while observing the whole code to the last letter'. The fundamental cause lies in Dickens's almost incredible optimism and belief in human nature. The wickedness and humbug of his bad characters are cloaks which they might, and often do, cast away suddenly. Dickens was 'more afraid of institutions than of men', because it was easier to change the habits of a man than to reform an institution. This belief in the spontaneous goodness of human beings, and a corresponding distrust of institutions, brought Dickens into the political currents of his age. He talked the language of radicalism without knowing it, just as he tried to bring about a number of practical reforms without ever basing them on an intellectual system.

Most of Dickens's characters belonged to the lower social world of London—the men and women who provided the amenities of the well-to-do. Thackeray[1] was also a townsman, but he concerned himself more with 'society', or with the adventurers who preyed upon the vices of the upper class. He knew little about the common people, other than those who lived as servants in the houses of the rich. He did not take much interest in moral or political reform; he accepted the conventional religious standards of the fashionable world. His critical and detached attitude expressed itself rather in satire upon the pharisaism of the social system. *The Book of Snobs* is more than a satire on snobbery; it is an attack upon the false pride of caste of the respectable and governing classes. *Vanity Fair* is a similar attack, made with greater subtlety and artistic power. Thackeray was less unequal than Dickens; his characters are more consistent, and if they are less heroic they are much less exaggerated for dramatic effect. Thackeray's creative vitality showed itself more in extension than in depth. His novels record family history, and take an immense number of characters in their stride; the plots are loosely drawn and vague, but never mechanical. Charlotte Brontë, whose intense imagination made up for her lack of experience, admired Thackeray's books, as Thackeray in turn recognized her genius.

The measure of the greatness of Dickens and Thackeray may be seen by comparing their novels with those of Trollope.[2] Trollope had talent, power of observation, and a capacity for making up characters on very little direct knowledge. His 'Barsetshire' novels about the anglican society of a cathedral city are exact to the letter, though he never lived in this society. Yet his novels, like the furniture of his age, lack fineness and distinction. He was too modest about his own skill; his reputation

[1] William Makepeace Thackeray (1811–63), b. Calcutta, s. of an Indian civil servant, educ. Charterhouse and Trinity College, Cambridge; inherited a fair income from his father, but soon lost the greater part of it; went to Paris to study art, 1834, but took up journalism; in 1836 he asked Dickens to employ him for the illustrations in the *Pickwick Papers*; an early contributor to *Punch*, in which he published *The Book of Snobs*; *Vanity Fair* (1847) first established his position as a novelist, though *The Luck of Barry Lyndon* had appeared in 1844.

[2] Anthony Trollope (1815–82), s. of a barrister who lost his money in speculation and died in 1835, leaving his wife to maintain her children by novel-writing; Trollope obtained a clerkship in the post office in 1834, and retired from the civil service in 1866; he published his first novel in 1847, but had little success until the appearance of *The Warden* (1855) and *Barchester Towers* (1857). Trollope claimed to be the inventor of the pillar-box.

suffered, absurdly enough, from his explanation that he went ahead with the business of writing so many words an hour. No one could write sentences, at Trollope's pace, for years on end, without treating words in a casual and slip-shod way, but Trollope had a good deal of Dickens's enjoyment and gusto, and something of Thackeray's irony. He took the world as he found it; the unhappiness of his childhood and the snobbery with which he was treated at two public schools saved him in later life from unction about success. He knew that a description of life must be a criticism of life, and that, in his own words, 'the novelist must teach, whether he wishes to teach or no'.

George Eliot[1] was less cautious in her view of the duties of a novelist. It is hardly true to say that in her books, for the first time, the English novel ceased to be merely an 'entertainment' and became 'a medium for the discussion of the serious problems and preoccupations of mature life'. This view has the support of Acton, who thought George Eliot 'the most illustrious figure that had arisen in literature since Goethe', and of Herbert Spencer, who believed that no other novelist deserved a place on the shelves of the London Library; but it has been answered by W. E. Henley's summary of George Eliot as 'the apotheosis of pupil-teachery'. George Eliot was not the first English novelist to be concerned primarily with the meaning of life. The Brontës,[2] and especially Emily Brontë in *Wuthering Heights*, had less learning but far more imagination of

---

[1] Mary Ann Evans (1819–80) ('George Eliot'), b. Chilvers Coton, Warwickshire, d. of Robert Evans, a builder and estate agent; learned Latin, Greek, Italian, and German from teachers in Coventry; took part in editing the *Westminster Review*, 1851, and, through Herbert Spencer's friendship, met George Henry Lewes, with whom she lived from 1854 to his death in 1878; began to write novels, 1856; published *Scenes from Clerical Life*, 1858, and *Adam Bede* in 1859; married J. W. Cross, a New York banker, 1880.

[2] Charlotte Brontë (1816–55) and her sisters Emily Jane (1818–48) and Anne (1820–49) were d. of the Rev. Patrick Brontë (who changed his name from Brunty before leaving Ireland in 1802), vicar of Haworth, near Keighley. Charlotte and Emily Brontë and their two elder sisters went to a school for clergymen's daughters in 1824; the two elder children died within a year, and Charlotte and Emily were kept at home until 1831. After a short time at a school near Leeds Charlotte became a governess in 1839; in 1842 she went with Emily to Brussels in order to learn French and thus improve her chance of success as owner of a school; in 1846 Charlotte, Emily, and Anne published a volume of poems under the names of Currer, Ellis, and Acton Bell; Emily's *Wuthering Heights* and Charlotte's *Jane Eyre* appeared in 1847; Charlotte published *Shirley* (1849) and *Vilette* (1853). In 1854 she married her father's former curate, the Rev. A. B. Nicholls.

a mystical kind, and the background of their novels is a wild and lyrical questioning of existence. Charlotte and Emily Brontë were never afraid of passion; their direct and violent emotions carried them through faults which would have ruined ordinary writers; faults of construction, improbabilities of fact, and a lack of humour. It has been well said that Charlotte Brontë was 'about as well equipped to be a satirist as she was to be a ballet-dancer'. George Eliot was equally unsuited for distinction in either of these spheres, but her work had a touch of priggishness which separated her as much from Charlotte and Emily Brontë as from Shelley or Byron. George Eliot's extraordinary reputation as a profound thinker was due to the fact that her philosophy was of a very ordinary kind, and that she was troubled precisely with those doubts and problems which belonged to her own age. Her novels were written between 1856 and 1876. During these years the early creative exuberance of the industrial age had passed out of the times. The improvement of material conditions had left thoughtful people more free to consider problems of conduct and belief which went beyond the organization of social life or an attack on vast and obvious abuses. At the same time the development of biblical criticism, and of materialist thought represented by Spencer and Buckle, had begun seriously to shake the middle class. George Eliot herself translated Strauss's *Leben Jesu* in 1846 and Feuerbach's *Wesen des Christenthums* in 1854. Her readers were ready to accept her presentation of the moral law as a substitute for religion because they were looking for a substitute of this kind. Within her own limits, George Eliot had a sharp and clear mind. She knew the middle and lower class of the English midlands, and, if there was a certain heaviness in her treatment of character, English provincial life had little grace or nonchalance about it. Here again George Eliot was not original. Mrs. Gaskell was the first novelist to describe the manufacturing towns of Lancashire from the point of view of a resident; Charlotte Yonge and Mrs. Oliphant were equally quick observers of middle-class and professional society, though they contented themselves with quiet and amusing description, and, except for death-bed scenes, left high tragedy alone.

There was no sudden change in the novel after 1870. The influence of readers from a lower social class, and, above all, the steady pressure of the woman reader upon the type of novel

produced, were not felt for another decade. The curious interlude of high imperialism, bringing an immense sale for novels
of action, from those of Rider Haggard to those of Kipling,
belongs almost entirely to the period after 1870 and has a
different political and economic background.[1] Kingsley was
unaffected by the imperialist current; *Westward Ho!* is a glori-
fication not of the British Empire but of protestantism, robust-
ness, and personal energy.

Of the three greatest novelists of the last quarter of the nineteenth century—Henry James, Meredith, and Hardy—Meredith alone had begun to write before 1870.[2] Meredith's work
shows once more the danger of overlooking the great diversity
of Victorian talent, and of submerging poets and prose-writers
too closely in their age. The first version of *Love in the Valley*
was published in 1851, while Macaulay was writing his
History, six years before the appearance of *Tom Brown's Schooldays*, and two years before the appearance of *Villette*. *The
Shaving of Shagpat*, like all humorous books, is more of a period
piece, but *The Ordeal of Richard Feverel*, one of the most lyrical
of Victorian novels, was contemporary with *The Virginians*.
Meredith's Italian novels belong to the years just before and
after his experience as a war correspondent in the war of 1866;
they represent a liberalism which was already a losing cause
in Europe. Their political side is unimportant; it is more interesting to notice that Meredith, like his contemporaries, was
a moralist, and that, like George Eliot, he used the novel as
a means of enlightening his readers, though he was subtler
in his drawing of character. Finally, it might be said that
Meredith's work shows sign of the 'fatigue of artistic perception'
which marks the end of an epoch. The decades of simple,
straightforward English prose were over, and a long period of
sophisticated and self-conscious writing had begun.

It is possible that, with different limiting conditions, the
theatre might have had a greater effect upon English literature
and English political life, and that the light social comedy of
the eighteenth century might have developed into a wider
school of criticism of contemporary conditions. The evangelical

[1] See vol. xiv of this *History*, pp. 331–3.
[2] Hardy's first novel, *The Poor Man and the Lady*, written in 1868, was never published.

revival was unfriendly to the theatre, but the main reason for the low standard of plays was the régime under which the theatre was allowed to exist. There were great critics and great actors; the critics tended to neglect the plays and to criticize the acting, while the plays were poor because the English licensing regulations confined the serious theatre to three licensed houses in London—Covent Garden, Drury Lane, and the Haymarket—and the theatres of Bath, Bristol, and Liverpool. Occasional licences were given elsewhere and other theatres existed, but only for the production of opera and musical entertainments, or melodrama, in the proper sense of the term. The licensed theatres in London were so large that their proprietors were compelled to produce plays with large and sensational effects; the comedy of manners, with its subtle plots and quiet acting, became impossible. Meanwhile the unlicensed houses kept playwrights to turn out anything which came to hand; the educated public left the theatre to the shopkeepers, and went only to hear opera or to see well-known actors and actresses in familiar plays. A committee of the house of commons in 1832 recommended the abolition of the monopoly of the licensed houses; henceforward the law was not strictly observed, though 'free trade' in the 'legitimate drama' was not formally permitted until 1843. The improved status and conditions of the theatre did not attract writers of outstanding ability to the stage before 1870.[1]

Music in England was dominated by the prestige of foreign composers, and, apart from the deference paid to continental musicians of high reputation, the status of performers in England was low. If musicians were asked to entertain the guests at a reception in a great house, a silken cord divided them from the rest of the company. The earl of Westmorland (1784–1859), a soldier and diplomat by profession, was one of the very few violinists and composers of high social standing. He founded the Royal Academy of Music in 1823 in order to improve the position and training of English musicians, but the effect of an institution of this kind could be felt only after a period of years, and it is not surprising that between 1815 and 1870 there were only two English professional musicians of very considerable reputation: J. Field (1782–1837), who lived mainly out of

[1] See also below, pp. 625–6.

England, and Sir William Sterndale Bennett (1816–75), who
spent most of his time in teaching music for a living. The
English composers of the sixteenth and seventeenth centuries
were forgotten. Tom Moore saved many Irish melodies from
oblivion, but he took no interest in the surviving English songs.
The cathedrals were not yet centres of English church music,
and their choir schools did not train boys in musical knowledge
or appreciation. There was no musical education in public or
grammar schools. In these circumstances the wonder is that
there were so many societies up and down the country giving
performances and practising as best they could. These societies
kept alive an interest in music; they touched only a fringe of
the public, and the influence of music was not at all comparable with that of poetry or even of painting in the culture
of the nation.[1]

[1] For the attempts to develop a more popular interest in music see below, p. 624.
The London Philharmonic Society (1813) and the Antient Concerts (1776–1848)
maintained a high standard in London. The Antient Concerts were limited to
music at least twenty years old; the Philharmonic Society often invited distinguished
continental composers to write music for its concerts; Beethoven's Ninth Symphony
was one of these commissioned works. Handel's *Messiah* was one of the few great
works of music familiar to a very large public.

V

MOVEMENTS IN THE SCIENCES AND ARTS

AT every point in a survey of English life in the nineteenth
century it is possible to see the increasing importance of
the progress made in the physical and biological sciences.
Imaginative work in literature has an absolute value; Shelley's
poem on 'The Cloud', as a work of art, remains unaffected by
developments in the science of meteorology, and Wordsworth's
poem on the daffodils has nothing to do with a botanical survey
of the lake district. Yet it is not unfair to describe the nineteenth
century as the first age in which the accumulation of scientific
knowledge was more important than law, religion, art, and
letters in determining the direction of ideas and the attitude
of the public at large towards accepted values. It is certainly
true that the influence of science upon literature was far greater
than the influence of literature upon science. At the same time
this view needs qualification. The development of experimental
science in the nineteenth century was a chapter in a long story,
and the result of an intellectual preparation, covering several
hundred years, in which the contribution of 'pure' as well as
'applied' literature was of great significance. The social conditions under which intellectual work was carried out were also
directly relevant to the character and direction of this work.
Scientific investigation could hardly have advanced so quickly,
and might never have advanced at all, if society had not valued
freedom of thought; freedom of thought is, in the long run,
impossible without political liberty, and political liberty must
be embodied in law and institutions. Writers of imagination
and scholars in the humane studies thus took an important part
in providing these essential conditions of scientific work. Furthermore, the methods of the sciences applied also to other fields of
investigation, though in the 'humane' studies it was more difficult to formulate general laws because the isolation of the
subject-matter was less easy. An historian might well claim that
the greater part of many branches of science is 'natural history',

and that their discipline is the historical method. From another point of view, it may be said that the scientists were using in the investigation of nature methods similar to those which manufacturers and business men were applying to industry and commerce; that is to say, methods of rational calculation and measurement, without reference to the authority, habits, or traditions of the past. The differences between astrology and astronomy, alchemy and inorganic chemistry, are not unlike the differences between the presuppositions of economic life in the middle ages and the assumptions of high capitalism in the nineteenth century.

Thus the science of a hundred years ago is not altogether as original as it appears; it belongs to the general intellectual phenomena of the age, and owes a great deal to its social, economic, and political setting. On the other hand, scientific discovery, like movements in art and letters, did not merely reflect in a passive way other features of the time. Science had a life of its own, and made an active contribution, in return for freedom to carry out investigations without fear of authority and under conditions which allowed and encouraged individual effort. It would scarcely be possible to exaggerate this contribution. The economic progress of the country was increasingly dependent upon applied science; a deeper and more extensive knowledge of the laws governing the world of life and matter affected most problems of government and administration. These effects were constructive not merely in matters such as the improvement of public health or the cheapening of comforts and amenities, but also in the sense that they seemed to establish upon a firm basis the idea of progress which, in the eighteenth century, was more or less an act of faith in the reasoning powers of man. They were destructive because they provided data which conflicted with received ideas of conduct and belief. To a large extent the constructive effects came first, and, as far as the sciences were concerned, set the tone and determined the attitude of investigators. The general conclusions applicable to other spheres of thought were not drawn by the scientists themselves; the most original and powerful minds engaged in scientific work were content to take this work as an end in itself. Davy, Faraday,[1] and Thomson were men of simple religious belief,

[1] The elders of Faraday's sect suspended his membership because he missed a Sunday service in order to obey the queen's command to dine at Windsor.

who directed their creative energy to the solution of specific problems within their own subjects. Darwin was equally outside the conflict of opinion aroused by the bearing of his theories upon religious or political questions.

Davy's *Discourse Introductory to a Course of Lectures on Chemistry* at the Royal Institution in 1802 is one of the earliest and most remarkable examples of the constructive belief in progress. It is an important statement because it shows that the belief in progress was not a vulgar deduction from the increasing comfort of life, but an intellectual conclusion based upon positive knowledge. In this respect it followed the line of thought already begun in the seventeenth century, and was untouched by the shock of the French Revolution, which overthrew the literary and political optimism of many writers of the old régime. Davy contrasted human beings 'in what is called a state of nature . . . unable to discover causes, and quietly and passively submissive to the mercy of nature and the elements' with the position of civilized man, 'informed by science and the arts, and in control of powers which may be almost called creative; which have enabled him to modify and change the beings surrounding him, and by his experiments to interrogate nature with power, not simply as a scholar, passive and seeking only to understand her operations, but rather as a master, active with his own instruments'.[1] There were in these early days almost no limits to the optimism of physicists and chemists. They were amazed and excited by their own discoveries, and the indifference of the educated public often led them to think in exaggerated terms. Most scientists during the first half of the nineteenth century believed that the main lines of knowledge had been laid down and that the classical Newtonian scheme of physics was adequate to describe all phenomena.

The method of progress in these various fields of investigation was by hypothesis, verification, and the formulation of laws based upon recorded experience. To a large extent the method might be described as 'the application of the experimental and mathematical methods of dynamics to the other subjects of physics, and, as far as applicable, to chemistry and biology

---

[1] *Collected Works of Humphry Davy* (1839), ii. 311–26. Davy also thought that 'the student of natural philosophy, perceiving in all the phenomena of the universe the designs of perfect intelligence [would] be averse to the turbulence and passion of hasty innovations, and [would] uniformly appear as the friend of tranquillity and order'.

also'. The technical details of this work do not fall within the scope of political history. To a large extent the development of the sciences was international; the names Volta, Faraday, Oersted, Ampère, and Ohm represent five different nationalities; an account of the study of electricity would be incomplete if it did not include every one of these five men, and of others whose nationality is hardly relevant to a general estimate of their work. On the other hand the political historian must be interested in the conditions under which the scientists of any one country studied particular problems, the reasons why these problems were attacked and solved in a certain order, and the effects of scientific discovery upon the general state of opinion.

There were in 1815 few facilities in Great Britain for the investigation of the subjects grouped loosely under the heading of natural philosophy. The association of physical and chemical research with philosophy showed that the importance of experimental work was hardly understood. The foundation in London of the Royal Institution in 1799[1] was an example of individualist and almost haphazard methods of providing for research. The Institution was established by private subscription 'for diffusing the knowledge and facilitating the general and speedy introduction of new and useful mechanical inventions and improvements, and also for teaching, by regular courses of philosophical lectures and experiments, the application of these discoveries in science to the improvement of arts and manufactures, and in facilitating the means of procuring the comforts and conveniences of life'. This foundation, designed more for the diffusion and application of knowledge than for original investigation, had the good fortune to appoint to its staff two men of genius, Davy[2] and Faraday.[3] It became in

[1] See above, p. 501. The American Philosophical Society, founded at Philadelphia in 1743 'for the promotion of useful knowledge', is an earlier example.

[2] Sir Humphry Davy, bt. (1778–1829), b. Penzance, educ. Penzance grammar school and Truro; apprenticed to a surgeon; superintendent of the Pneumatic Institute at Clifton, 1798; studied the effects of inhaling various gases, and discovered that nitrous oxide, or laughing-gas was respirable; director of the chemical laboratory of the Royal Institution, 1801; professor of chemistry at the institution, 1802–12; lectured on agricultural chemistry and electricity; invented the miner's safety lamp, demonstrated the elementary nature of chlorine, and prepared metallic sodium and potassium by electricity; president of the Royal Society, 1820.

[3] Michael Faraday (1791–1867), s. of a blacksmith, b. Newington Butts, London; apprenticed to a bookbinder; assistant to Davy at the Royal Institution; travelled with Davy, 1813–15; director of the chemical laboratory of the institution, 1825; professor of chemistry, 1833–67; Faraday's earliest work was in collaboration with

their hands something far more than a technical institute or a centre of popular instruction, though its lectures were well attended and even fashionable. A similar foundation was set up by subscription in Manchester; there were other institutions on a smaller scale. Unless a student of chemistry or physics happened to possess independent means he depended upon these private societies for any chance of experimental work. John Dalton (1766–1844) maintained himself by giving lessons in mathematics at half a crown an hour and by elementary analytical work long after he had won a European reputation for his isolation of the rules of combination of the elements and his determination of atomic weights.[1] In London, University and King's Colleges opened laboratories for general instruction, but there was no state institution for scientific research or teaching until the foundation of the Royal School of Mines in 1851. The application of chemistry to agriculture was a matter of interest to landowners, and a parliament of landowners which gave up the corn laws with reluctance might have been expected to ask for state aid in investigating means to increase production; belief in private enterprise and the distrust of state interference were so strong that the Royal College of Chemistry and the experimental station at Rothamsted were founded without assistance from public funds. The Rothamsted station, which began a systematic programme of agricultural research in 1843, was maintained by Sir John Lawes; the College of Chemistry was the result of a subscription among landowners impressed with Liebig's work of 1840 on *Chemistry in its Application to Agriculture and Physiology*. This book was itself the work of private initiative. The British Association for the Advancement of Science, founded in 1831 as a meeting-ground for members of different scientific societies, invited Liebig to draw up a report on the position of organic chemistry. Liebig did not write the report, but published a book in which he showed the close relation between the growth of plants and the chemical qualities

Davy on the properties of chlorine. He liquefied a number of gases and conducted experiments in the production of optical glass. In 1831 he began to examine the phenomena of magneto-electricity, and henceforward made a number of discoveries of far-reaching importance. Faraday belonged throughout his life to a peculiar religious sect, known as the Sandemanians, named after one of its founders in the eighteenth century.

[1] In 1818 Dalton was offered, and refused a house, a laboratory, and an income of £400 a year. He was given a civil list pension in 1833.

of the soil. The College of Chemistry lasted only a few years as a private institution. It was unable to fulfil undertakings to provide analyses of soil or to meet other demands made by subscribers; its funds therefore fell away, and it was absorbed after 1853 in the Royal College of Mines.

The delay in giving state assistance to chemistry was curious because the state had long recognized the practical importance of astronomy. The growth of British possessions and trade interests in southern seas had led to the foundation of observatories outside Great Britain. The East India Company maintained stations at Bombay, Calcutta, and Madras; in 1829 a Royal Observatory was opened at the Cape of Good Hope. Astronomical studies were important not merely for navigation but for the rapidly developing work of cartography and land surveying. Geology also had a direct practical importance for the mapmaker and for mining prospectors; in 1832 a geological survey was undertaken at state expense. The royal navy and the merchant service required good charts[1] and a better general knowledge of tropical waters; there were already precedents in the voyages of Cook and others for the expeditions after 1815 beginning with the five years' tropical survey made by the *Beagle*, on which Darwin sailed as botanist, and followed by the exploration of the Antarctic by the *Erebus* and the *Terror* between 1839 and 1843, and the voyage of the *Rattlesnake* between 1846 and 1850.

At least until 1850 the 'accumulated experience of craftsmen',[2] the skill of individual designers, and methods of trial and error had done more for the development of industry in

[1] The hydrographic department of the admiralty made their charts available to the merchant navy and the public after 1822. It is an interesting sign of the activities of the British navy in the general protection of trade that, apart from the coasts of the United States and of France and the French Empire, these charts in the nineteenth century covered practically all the seas of the world. In 1855 a special committee of ship-owners and scientists was set up at Liverpool to investigate the magnetic conditions and compass errors of merchant ships. This committee sent three reports to the board of trade during the next seven years and recommended that all navigators of merchant ships should have a general knowledge of magnetism and compass-correction. Between 1800 and 1850 the use of chronometers became almost universal on well-equipped British ships.

[2] *A History of Technology*, ed. C. Singer and others, vol. v, Preface, p. vi. Adam Smith, while recognizing the importance of applied science, did not put it in the highest place. 'Some [improvement] came to be by the ingenuity of those men of speculation, whose trade is not to do anything, but to observe everything; and who, upon that account, are often capable of combining together the powers of the most distant and dissimilar objects' (see ibid., iv. 150).

Great Britain than any planned collaboration with scientists. In any case the public indifference to scientific research which did not promise an immediate practical return cannot fairly be taken as a sign of vulgarity or indifference to knowledge. Laboratory research, even in chemistry and physics, was relatively new; its potentialities were unrealized, while in mechanical engineering the early practical applications of science were disliked, and accepted only because it was impossible to reject them. Steam power and machinery seemed to create at least as many social and economic problems as they solved. Scientifically minded men might find in these new sources of power and control over nature almost limitless chances of betterment; the mass of opinion still regarded laboratory research as a private hobby, with results of occasional, and at times disputable, value. Hofmann, a pupil of Liebig who came to England to direct the work of the College of Chemistry, had to apologize for investigating the properties of aniline since his researches seemed to be merely academic. Moreover, if Davy was a popular and well-known social figure, ready to call attention to the intellectual and cultural meaning of his work, other masters, like Faraday, lived almost in seclusion, and were content to make their discoveries without telling every one of their value, originality, and practical importance. Even Davy addressed an audience which did not know how to draw the most obvious consequences from facts brought to their notice. Davy's safety lamp for coal-mines might have been a lesson in the significance of experimental research; yet medical opinion, though interested in his work, did not infer more than superficial conclusions from Davy's studies in the effects of inhaling gases. Faraday's work on electrolysis and electromagnetic induction formed the basis of the modern investigation and utilization of electricity. Faraday was given a pension in 1838 and a house in Hampton Court twenty years later; but the inventions of George Stephenson and other engineers seemed more dramatic and more important for everyday life. The generation of electric charges and currents might be a curious study, but to the practical man Joule[1] said the last word when he demonstrated in 1841 that the efficiency of the most perfect electromagnetic motor hitherto

---

[1] James Prescott Joule (1818–89), b. Salford, Lancs., s. of a brewer; educ. privately; studied under Dalton for a time, but was mainly self-taught, and worked in his private laboratory.

made was, for every pound of zinc used in the battery, about one-fifth of the efficiency of one pound of coal used to drive a good Cornish pumping-engine. Joule himself thought this comparison so unfavourable that he almost despaired of 'the success of electromagnetic attractions as a means of power'.[1] For a time even the military possibilities of scientific discovery were ignored. The electric telegraph had been foreshadowed by many scientists before Wheatstone and Cooke in 1837 devised instruments which put telegraphy on a paying commercial basis; in 1844 the first telegraph line in England ran between Paddington and Slough. Electric lighting by means of the carbon arc as well as by incandescence was already known, but hardly beyond the experimental stage. Parliament and the civil and military authorities did little more than gape at these inventions until they were in common use.

The public might well have underrated the utilitarian side of chemistry and physics; it is more remarkable that the philosophical and aesthetic aspects of these new and startling investigations made little general appeal. The English educational system was almost wholly literary. Neither Oxford nor Cambridge gave an honorary degree to Davy. Dr. Butler of Shrewsbury, who was an active educational reformer, disapproved of Charles Darwin and his brother spending time in an amateur chemical laboratory when they might have been reading the classics. To minds unfamiliar with scientific method the aesthetic side of science was hidden by the technicalities in which it was expressed. Even scholars trained in mathematical precision and method ignored the importance of experimental work. Brougham, whose restless mind and universal knowledge gave him an unusual interest in scientific discovery, thought that Thomas Young's application of the principle of interference to light (1817) contained 'nothing which deserves the name either of experiment or discovery', because it appeared to offer mathematical difficulties. In 1843 Joule announced his discovery of the primary facts of the conservation of energy, that is to say, of the first law of thermodynamics. He made his statement at a meeting of the British Association in a paper 'on the calorific effects of magneto-electricity and on the mechanical value of heat'. Joule added in a postscript his conviction that 'the grand

---

[1] Faraday, however, showed how to turn the energy liberated by burning coal into electric energy capable of easy distribution.

agents of nature are by the Creator's fiat indestructible, and that wherever mechanical force is expended an exact equivalent of heat is always obtained'. The technical expression of his views had little attraction for the layman: 'The quantity of heat capable of increasing the temperature of a pound of water by one degree of Fahrenheit's scale is equal to . . . a mechanical force capable of raising 838 pounds to a perpendicular height of one foot.' It is significant that the *Annual Register* for 1843 does not mention even the meeting of the British Association.

This public indifference must not be exaggerated. The intellectual significance and practical corollaries of the new discoveries were gradually understood. The ever-increasing number of learned societies[1] in every branch of science, the development of popular lectures, and the cumulative results of research changed public opinion. The annual meetings of the British Association, held in different towns of the United Kingdom, did much to interest laymen, and even the social side of these gatherings gave an impression of the increasing importance of scientific workers. Railways made people more familiar with applied science. The Great Exhibition of 1851 had a similar effect. Henceforward the facilities for scientific work were greatly extended. William Thomson,[2] afterwards Lord Kelvin, went to Paris in 1845 because he could get better laboratory experience in France than in Great Britain; James Clerk-Maxwell (1831-79), a few years later, found at Aberdeen and Cambridge the resources which he needed. Maxwell was a man of means; he retired from professorial work in 1865, after holding chairs at Aberdeen and London, but in 1871 he accepted the chair of experimental physics at Cambridge and supervised the construction of the Cavendish laboratory presented to the university by the duke of Devonshire. The laboratories at Oxford, built largely through the influence of Acland and Ruskin, were opened in 1861, and Lyon Playfair's work on behalf of technical education was already influencing public opinion. Thomson's incessant inventiveness brought him a large private fortune without diverting him from studies proper to his genius; he also demonstrated, year after year, the connexion

---

[1] Many of the societies of today which combine scientific work with a large popular membership were founded between 1820 and 1850.

[2] In 1851 Thomson (immediately following Clausius) enunciated the second law of thermodynamics which is the basis of a great part of modern physical chemistry and engineering.

between theoretical and applied science, the quickening rate of discovery, and the contributions made by different branches of science to the solution of a complicated problem. The establishment of telegraphic communication between England and America is a good example of the convergence of different lines of investigation upon a single problem. The first cable had been laid, successfully, in 1858, but Thomson's instructions were not obeyed, and the employment of high potential currents ruined the insulation. A new cable was laid in 1865-6 by the *Great Eastern*, the largest ship afloat. The insulation of the copper core was the result of a long series of experiments by Thomas Hancock (1786-1865) in 'vulcanizing' india-rubber; gutta-percha had already been tried in 1848 in a cable across the Hudson. The use of an efficient wire rope was due to the experiments of Robert Newall, who also invented special machinery for cable-laying, while Thomson devised a special instrument for recording the currents at the end of a long cable.

The indifference of the educated public retarded the development of chemistry and physics in the first half of the nineteenth century; there was, however, no obvious conflict of ideas between the leaders of discovery in these subjects and the leaders of received opinions in the church. On the other hand the conclusions reached in other branches of scientific study were less easy to harmonize with the accepted interpretation of religion. If the two great religious parties in England, the high church and the evangelicals, with the protestant nonconformists, had been less rigid in their outlook, this conflict of opinion need not have been so strong. The overthrow of the Ptolemaic theory of the universe had involved a greater adjustment of orthodox opinion than anything suggested in the nineteenth century, and, in the course of time, liberal Christianity found nothing in the Darwinian hypothesis incompatible with a belief in Divine purpose. The immediate shock was bound to be severe. The first attack came from the geologists. The progress of geology was similar to that of other sciences. The work was done outside the older educational endowments, and, for many years, with little help from the state.[1] J. Hutton's *Theory of the Earth* (1785) was the result of observations made by a landowner and student of agriculture. William Smith, whose *Map*

[1] In 1813 a readership in geology was founded at Oxford and maintained out of public funds.

of the Strata of England and Wales (1815) was the first example of accurate geological cartography, worked as a land surveyor and gave scientific currency to many local terms, such as 'lias' or 'clunch', in use among his own workmen; the Geological Society, founded in 1807 and incorporated in 1825, owed its development mainly to men of private fortune who could afford the travel necessary for geological study. The received views of the geological history of the world fitted into the biblical story of the creation and the flood. It was assumed that periods of calm had followed periods of great disturbance, and that the creation of men and other living things had taken place during the latest period of calm. It was also assumed that there was evidence of a vast deluge. The study of fossils, of the stratification of rocks, and of the remains left by primitive man upset these views; the new hypotheses could not be brought into agreement with the literal interpretation of the Old Testament, still less with the chronology established by Archbishop Ussher and accepted by uneducated opinion almost as part of the inspired text of the Bible. The transitional state of the subject may be seen in W. Buckland's *Reliquiae Diluvianae* (1823), in which the remains of animals found in caves are taken as evidence of the character of living creatures in the world before the flood. Buckland, who became dean of Westminster in 1845, wrote in 1836 a summary of geological knowledge as a proof of 'the power, wisdom, and goodness of God as manifested in the Creation'. At this same time Charles Lyell[1] was bringing forward convincing proof against any sudden creation, and demonstrating that the older catastrophic views were wrong, and that the facts of the earth's surface could be explained only by the action of slow upheavals followed by denudation. Lyell himself did not assume any conflict between science and religion, though he refused to be bound by a literal reading of Mosaic texts. The change of view in geology naturally had a great effect upon the study of the antiquity of man; towards 1860 there was evidence enough to show that men had lived in Great Britain at periods when animals extinct for many thousands of years had flourished in the country.

[1] Sir Charles Lyell, bt., (1797–1875), s. of Charles Lyell, botanist and Dante scholar, b. Kinnordy, Forfarshire, educ. Exeter College, Oxford; entered Lincoln's Inn, but was prevented by weakness of the eyes from continuing professional work; joined the Geological Society in 1819, secretary in 1823, and five times president; first published *The Principles of Geology* in 1830–3.

Other work of a specialist kind which was also accessible to the ordinary reader contradicted received opinions about the place of man in the scale of life. The general idea of the development of higher from lower forms of life was not new in 1860. Robert Chambers's *Vestiges of Creation* (1844) and, ten years later, Herbert Spencer's work accepted this hypothesis; Lyell used the term 'evolution' in a sense not very different from the meaning given to it in Darwin's[1] book *The Origin of Species by Natural Selection*. Darwin himself noted that at the time he was writing 'almost all naturalists admitted "evolution" under some form'. The importance of Darwin's work lay in the accumulation of a large mass of evidence, collected from every region and examined with the insight of genius. Darwin combined in an interesting way a number of different lines of research. He began the study of botany and geology on the advice of the scientists whom he knew at Cambridge, and found that in each subject notions about the nature and history of species were imperfect. He was influenced by books of travel, notably those of Humboldt; his five years' voyage with the *Beagle* gave him an opportunity of studying tropical regions and carrying out original research in the new science of oceanography. Already in 1837 Darwin had begun to consider the 'laws of change' affecting species. At this point another science came to his help. In 1838 he read Malthus's *Essay on Population*; the book provided an answer to the central problem of his work. Selection was the keystone of man's success in raising domestic animals and plants; yet it was difficult to understand 'how selection could be applied to organisms living in a state of nature'. Malthus's argument suggested to Darwin that, in the struggle for existence, 'favourable circumstances would tend to be preserved, and unfavourable ones to be destroyed'. The result would be the formation of new species. Darwin worked for twenty years upon this hypothesis that certain qualities had 'survival-value' and that these qualities spread owing to the elimination of those organisms which did not possess them. In

---

[1] Charles Robert Darwin (1809–82), grandson of Erasmus Darwin(1731–1802) and of Josiah Wedgwood, b. Shrewsbury, s. of R. W. Darwin; educ. Shrewsbury, Edinburgh, and Christ's College, Cambridge; studied medicine, and thought of taking Orders; sailed as naturalist on the *Beagle*, 1831–6; married his cousin Emma Wedgwood, 1839; settled at Down, Kent, 1842, where he worked for the last forty years of his life. Owing to ill health Darwin rarely attended scientific meetings, and knew only a few of the scientific scholars of his age.

1844 he felt sure that he could disprove the old doctrine of the immutability of species, but he continued to read, to collect evidence, and to make experiments by crossing pigeons. In June 1858 he received an essay in manuscript from A. R. Wallace,[1] a naturalist working in the Malay peninsula. Wallace had also read Malthus, and had come to the conclusion towards which Darwin was working. Wallace's essay was a brilliant piece of reasoning, planned in two hours, and written in the course of three evenings' work. Darwin, after much pressure from Lyell, had already begun to expound his theory in a book. Lyell and Hooker, one of the greatest botanists of the time, now advised him to send Wallace's essay, with an abstract of his own work, to the Linnean society. The two essays were published in a joint communication to the society on 1 July 1858. In November 1859 Darwin published the *Origin of Species*. The first edition of 1,250 copies sold out on the day of publication. Many scientists accepted Darwin's views at once; others, including Virchow in Prussia, were unconvinced at first, but within five years opinion had come round. T. H. Huxley, already known for his original work in morphology and the study of marine organisms, was among the earliest supporters, while Herbert Spencer's phrase 'the survival of the fittest', though open to philosophical question, summed up the Darwinian theory for the public. Darwin followed up his book by three other studies: *The Variation of Animals and Plants under Domestication* (1868), *The Descent of Man* (1871), and *The Expression of the Emotions in Man and the Animals* (1872).

Darwin's magnificent work was not free from a certain confusion. He failed to distinguish between the hypothesis of an evolutionary origin of living forms and the hypothesis of natural selection as giving the mechanism of this evolution. He also assumed the inheritance of variations possessing 'survival-value'. He was too cautious to try to answer the deepest problem—

---

[1] Alfred Russell Wallace (1823–1913), b. Usk, Monmouthshire, educ. Hertford; English master at Leicester collegiate school; went with H. W. Bates on a voyage to the Amazon, 1848; explored the Malay peninsula between 1854 and 1862; in his later years Wallace wrote in favour of spiritualism, and also published books supporting land nationalization and attacking vaccination as useless and dangerous. Wallace and Darwin remained close friends after the publication of their joint paper: it is typical of the difference in character between the two men that, while Darwin rarely left Down after 1842, Wallace, after his final return from the East in 1871, lived in seven different houses during a period of less than twenty years, and made long tours in Europe, the United States, and Canada.

the relation between selection and purpose. He was concerned, not with the origin of life, but with the development of living organisms. Later study has settled some of the technical difficulties in his theory; others remain unsolved. In either case the problems were outside the range of laymen, and their solution required the patience and scientific discipline which Darwin imposed upon himself. On the other hand the general implications of the idea of evolution, supported by natural selection, could not fail to startle the public. The gulf between the Darwinian view of the development of created life and the view implicit in Christian doctrine seemed far greater than in the new theories introduced by the geologists. The geologists merely demonstrated that the Mosaic cosmogony could not be taken as a literal statement of fact; the Darwinian theory abolished the dividing line between men and animals, denied any sudden creation of man, and therefore any literal interpretation of the fall of man, with its theological consequences. Theologians might have reconsidered the fundamental significance of Christian doctrine, and distinguished between essential and accidental elements in their beliefs. The older views were embodied in the formulae and practical teaching of the church, and associated, in the minds of Christians, with their deepest hopes and experience. It was therefore not surprising that the first attitude of the leaders of the church was entirely hostile. Samuel Wilberforce, bishop of Oxford, rashly attacked the *Origin of Species* in the *Quarterly Review*, and, still more rashly, at a meeting of the British Association, although he had no technical knowledge to set against the long years of work which supported Darwin's conclusions. The result was merely to make matters worse from the point of view of the church. Wilberforce might call the Darwinian hypothesis atheistical and unsound in philosophy and logic; he could not disprove this hypothesis by argument.

The shock to orthodox interpretations of Christian belief was greater because the publication of the *Origin of Species* nearly coincided with another attack upon received opinion starting from a different angle, and based upon different types of evidence. The seven writers, including Temple, Jowett, Mark Pattison, Baden-Powell, and C. W. Goodwin, who contributed to *Essays and Reviews*, reached their conclusions before the appearance of Darwin's work, though their book was not published until the spring of 1860. They argued in favour of a less rigid interpretation of the bible, and a revision of the historical doctrines based upon the literal meaning of biblical and patristic texts. The Christian church was not bound to the opinions of Bishop Wilberforce; a generation later scholars and theologians accepted most of the arguments put forward in *Essays and Reviews*. In 1860 most of these arguments were new; they were stated by men of academic temperament in language which, in some cases, seemed designed to shock the reader. Anti-Christian writers, such as the positivist Frederic Harrison, seized upon the most liberal and 'advanced' expressions of opinion as evidence that the essayists denied every important doctrine of their faith. It was difficult for the official leaders of the church to avoid giving an opinion. Wilberforce once again supported conservatism, and defended the Mosaic view of the creation. The bishops could hardly refuse to give the book some kind of condemnation. They condemned its general teaching in a pastoral letter; their own clergy compelled them to be more explicit. One of the essayists was a beneficed clergyman in the diocese of Salisbury; the bishop of Salisbury took proceedings against him. In 1862 the case, and an action against another of the essayists, came before the court of arches. The judgement was against the defendants, but the judicial committee of the privy council reversed the decision on appeal. A number of clergymen organized a protest on behalf of orthodoxy. The protest was likely to widen the gap between the reflections and doubts of thinking men and the doctrines of the church; it took the form of a declaration, drawn up at Oxford and signed by 11,000 of the clergy, recording a belief 'without reservation or qualification' in the inspiration and divine authority of the Scriptures, and in everlasting punishment. About the same time Keble published a 'litany of our Lord's warnings' and preached a sermon on 'the spirit of God's most holy fear'. The controversy over *Essays and Reviews* ended, as far as direct ecclesiastical action was concerned, in a condemnation of the book in convocation, though this measure had no legal effect. The refusal of the majority of the clergy to reconsider the statement of Christian doctrine was echoed and discussed in the press and the reviews. The matter was outside the work of Darwin, but the intolerance and obscurantism of a large section of religious opinion was in open contrast with the exact methods of scientific investigation, and the attitude of the church towards biblical criticism seemed to shut out any hope of reconciling science and religion. The imaginative literature of the time is full of this conflict; on the whole the scientific view had the stronger support and, in Spencer and Huxley, combative, if superficial, defenders who knew how to explain technical questions in popular language. Moreover the general acceptance of the Darwinian hypothesis led to the extension of the principle of evolution to other spheres, and not least to the study of the early stages of religion. Tylor's *Primitive Culture*, published in 1871, applied Darwin's method to the science of anthropology, and was the precursor of a new school of thought which educated men could not ignore and appeals to traditional authority could not suppress.

Ruskin's correlation of the state of the arts with the general condition of social life applies with particular force to architecture. It is possible to avoid reading poetry or looking at pictures; every one has to use and pass judgement on buildings, even if this judgement is made only from the standpoint of convenience. An architect works, as it were, in public; his importance depends more closely upon the immediate verdict of public opinion than the work of poets or painters. In any case the capital, labour, and materials necessary for carrying his ideas into effect are limiting factors directly related to the social conditions of his time. An architect of genius can impress his individuality within these limiting conditions. There was no architect of genius in England between 1815 and 1870, and the architecture of the period therefore tended to be a pedestrian record and reflection of social and economic conditions, undisturbed by creative imagination of the highest kind.

Thus the buildings of the first half of the nineteenth century reflect the rapid changes in habit, mental outlook, social organization, and technical equipment during this age. Political conquest, foreign influences, a sudden increase of wealth, or a greater knowledge of ancient models had brought rapid transitions in architectural style at earlier epochs in English history. The rate of change was quicker after the eighteenth century partly because the long domination of the Palladian style, which required exact plans and measurements, had led to the rise of the professional architect. There was, however, little organized instruction, and, as few public buildings in the eighteenth century offered work on a large scale, an architect depended for success upon private patronage. This patronage was, on the whole, well bestowed. The conventions of the age and the habit of the grand tour taught the upper class certain standards of taste and judgement in buildings as in pictures. The foundation of the Royal Academy in 1768 gave an independent standing to architecture, and the Academy school was the first stage in the development of professional training. In 1791 the architects of London formed a dining club which became the Royal Institute of British Architects (incorporated in 1837). The multiplication of drawings and books of models allowed greater variety in the choice of style, although it put too much emphasis upon authority and upon 'academic' canons of building.

In the early nineteenth century there was a sudden increase in the number and type of new buildings. The planning of great houses ceased to be the main source of an architect's income; patronage disappeared, at least in its cruder forms, and young architects had a more systematic apprenticeship in the offices of leading practitioners. The growth of the cities brought a revival of church building on a scale unknown since the time of Wren, and, with the rising standards of comfort, there was a demand for larger and better houses of moderate size, and for the planning of residential areas, at least in the richer quarters of towns. 'Pleasure towns', of which Bath is the best example, had been growing up before 1815 at inland spas and sheltered coastal watering-places. Cheltenham remains to this day a remarkable instance of a small market town enlarged on a plan to attract wealthy residents and visitors.[1] Brighton was a neat, new-built town as early as 1788.[2] Tenby and Buxton, Leamington

---

[1] The centre of the town, already built over, and including the most valuable sites, was left out of the scheme. Apart from Regent Street (see vol. xii of this *History*, pp. 546-7), and the terraces adjoining Regent's Park, two main pieces of large-scale planning were carried out in London between 1815 and 1870. One was Belgravia (named after a Grosvenor property in Leicestershire), built by Thomas Cubitt after 1825 in an area much of which was waterlogged. Cubitt took off the clay top-soil for brick-making, and then covered the gravel subsoil with earth from the excavations of St. Katherine Docks. The other was a slum clearance in Westminster to allow, between 1845 and 1851, the construction of Victoria street—in its early days one of the sights of London. Another bad slum area, Agar's Town (known as 'Ague Town') was cleared in the late 1860's for St. Pancras terminus and goods yards.

[2] In 1815 the name 'Brighton' was already in common use, though it was still regarded by many as a vulgar abbreviation of Brighthelmstone.

and St. Leonards are also good examples of this planning, but nearly every important town had a small suburb, a few streets or a terrace, neatly laid out. Improvements in inland transport gave more chances of bridge-building, though the civil engineers took a good deal of such work out of the hands of the architects.[1] Telford's suspension bridge carrying the Holyhead road over the Menai Straits, Brunel's suspension bridge at Clifton, and many of his viaducts and bridges on the Great Western railway survive as outstandingly successful works of this 'imaginative engineering'. The railways and the new factories required buildings of a type hitherto unknown. The modern conception of 'functional' architecture was hardly understood, or, at all events, not applied to these new buildings, and the idea of dignity remained distinct from suitability to purpose. A railway station was 'dignified' only if it possessed some of the attributes of display usually associated with buildings of a formal kind. It would have been useless to suggest that a railway station should 'look like a railway station', because no one knew what a railway station ought to 'look like'.[2] The one purely functional building of any size in the Victorian age was the hall of the Great Exhibition; this building was removed to Sydenham Hill, where, as the Crystal Palace, it became the butt of architectural critics for two generations. It was designed to serve a temporary purpose by a landscape gardener who had built large glass-roofed conservatories for rich patrons; its height was determined by the needs of the exhibition, and the accident that the site included some elm-trees which the promoters did not want to cut down. The building did not suit the conditions of the English climate, and could not be kept clean. It is not surprising that this example of 'functional design' was not followed elsewhere.

The commercial needs of the age were unlikely to encourage

[1] There is a story, not fully authenticated, that Rennie obtained the designs for Waterloo bridge from a broken-down architect in prison. See Sir R. Blomfield, *The Touchstone of Architecture*, p. 109. It is a curious instance of the combination of empiricism with exact scientific observation that the effect of wind on bridges was little studied before the collapse of the Tay bridge in 1879. Until this time most engineers were content with the observations made by Smeaton in the middle of the eighteenth century.

[2] The earliest termini 'looked like', and indeed were sheds, since they were used for goods traffic and as carriage depots as well as for passengers. Paddington station (departure side) in London is one of the few remaining examples of an early terminus in which functional design and decoration fit harmoniously.

the development of a new architectural style. Few good architects were asked to design factories; few people of taste could find any pleasure in these centres of smoke and noise. The change in style was therefore the result, not of an adaptation of architecture to new purposes, but of the inevitable 'fatigue of the eye' which brings about changes in fashion for which there is otherwise no particular reason or justification. In earlier ages, when builders who knew only the work done in their immediate neighbourhood handed down a traditional style from generation to generation, this 'fatigue of the eye' and desire for new patterns brought small modifications, until, in the course of time, a new style appeared. In the nineteenth century the accumulation of exact knowledge of different styles, the versatility and professional training of the architects, and the demands of the public introduced new factors. The mixture of Greek and Pompeian styles used by the brothers Adam went out of fashion after 1815, but two other revivals took place almost simultaneously. Two churches were completed in St. Pancras parish, London, between 1822 and 1827; one was an amalgam of four Greek buildings. The other had a west front based on that of York Minster.

From an academic point of view the classical revival was more logical. It did not involve a sudden break with existing canons, and it was based upon a good understanding of ancient models. On the other hand the gothic revival had more historic justification. The traditions of gothic architecture, especially in the perpendicular style, had survived in cottages and houses throughout many parts of the country; this style suited English materials and weather conditions; it was the style most fitted in northern Europe for churches, which were still the largest public buildings. Gothic buildings were cheaper and more adaptable to modern needs; therefore, for technical reasons alone, the gothic was likely to outlast the classical revival. There were other reasons for the return of gothic styles. The romantic movement in literature and the development of historical studies brought a new interest in medieval art, and the ecclesiasticism of the tractarians introduced a serious element which distinguished nineteenth-century gothic from the playful and dilettante garden-pieces of the eighteenth century. Ruskin upheld the gothic style on moral grounds; he made the common mistake of limiting sincerity to one mode of expression, but here, as in other branches of art, there was much to be said for freeing architecture from its associations with the 'display' expenditure of the rich, or the caprices of patrons, and connecting it once more with ordinary life and with the work of simple craftsmen. In any case, the classical revival was over long before 1870 and the architects of the regency period were in disfavour. A leading critic wrote in 1862 of Nash and his contemporaries: 'With the aid of a few columns stuck here and there, or rich window dressings and rustications in another place, and aided by the fatal facility of stucco, they managed to get over an immense amount of space with a very slight expenditure of thought.'[1]

These architects of the early nineteenth century who 'put an end to the dreadful monotony . . . of plain brick walls with oblong holes cut in them' had none of Ruskin's moral scruples about style. They were ready to build in classical or oriental or gothic styles according to the demand. Nash[2] is remembered for his use of 'the fatal facility of stucco'; he also restored the west front and chapter-house of St. David's cathedral in the gothic style, and encouraged the elder Pugin, one of his own draughts-men, to produce a book of practical designs of gothic character. Wilkins[3] thought himself equally competent to construct classi-cal or gothic buildings, and has left Downing College in the Greek style and gothic work in King's and other Cambridge colleges. James Wyatt[4] and his nephew Sir Jeffry Wyatville[5] were equally sure of their talents; they did great harm to West-minster Abbey and to Salisbury cathedral by their unscholarly attempts at restoration, though Wyatville's rebuilding of Wind-sor, on the lines of a residential castle of the later middle ages, was much more successful, and, in many respects, nearer to the traditions of Strawberry Hill.

[1] J. Fergusson, *History of Architecture*, vol. iii, p. 302.

[2] For John Nash see vol. xii of this *History*, pp. 546–7. Nash made great use of cast iron (often painted to look like stone) in his buildings. Cast iron was commonly employed during the first half of the nineteenth century—wrought iron came in later—for buildings, such as mills, where there was danger of fire.

[3] William Wilkins (1778–1839), s. of an architect, b. Norwich; educ. Norwich grammar school and Caius College, Cambridge. Wilkins even made a plan for gothicizing Gibbs's classical building at King's College, Cambridge.

[4] James Wyatt (1746–1813), s. of a farmer and timber-merchant, b. Burton Con-stable, Staffs.; attracted the notice of Lord Bagot, who took him to Rome; surveyor of Westminster Abbey, 1776; designed Fonthill Abbey; see vol. xii of this *History*.

[5] Sir Jeffry Wyatville (1766–1840); studied in his uncle's office: the addition to his name is said to have been sanctioned by George IV after the restoration of Windsor castle.

The work of the classical revival was based to some extent on a series of drawings beginning with Dawkins and Woods's *Illustrations of Palmyra and Baalbec* (1750), Adam's *Spalatro* (1760), Stuart and Revett's *Antiquities of Athens* (1762), and the publications of the Society of Dilettanti.[1] During the years when the French wars interrupted continental travel[2] English students were able to study the buildings of the classical revival in France through drawings, notably those collected by the banker Hope, a connoisseur of art, who came to London in 1796 after the French occupation of Holland. The Elgin marbles, brought to England between 1806 and 1812, were even more important in their effect upon taste and design than the Portland vase acquired nearly fifty years earlier.

Nash's work had a certain monotony, but he was not often content with scholarly imitations of Graeco-Roman work like the Marble Arch (originally designed to stand in front of Buckingham Palace); his younger contemporaries kept more exactly to ancient models. St. George's Hall, Liverpool (designed in 1839), is the largest and best of these pieces of erudition, where the character and, as far as possible, the site of a building followed classical precedents. The gateway of Euston station,[3] copied from a Greek temple at Agrigentum, and the colonnade and gateways at Hyde Park Corner were successful because they offered no structural difficulties; the façade of Apsley House and the superimposed imitations in St. Pancras' church were unsuitable for their purpose, and the attempts to make English country houses look like Greek temples were absurd. Wilkins was unfortunate in his two largest London buildings, University College and the National Gallery. The college had a very poor site, and Wilkins had to set back the wings of the National Gallery in order to avoid interference with the view of St. Martin's church; the treasury compelled him to use columns taken from Carlton House, and to cut down by half the sum originally allowed for the building. Two other architects, Sir John Soane (1753–1837) and Sir Robert Smirke (1781–1867), designed buildings of importance in London; Soane's Bank of

---

[1] See vol. xii of this *History*.

[2] The character of the classical revival was affected by the fact that it was easier during the Napoleonic period for Englishmen to travel in Greece than in Italy.

[3] There is a less-known triumphal arch at the Holyhead terminus of the former L.N.W. railway, set up earlier to commemorate the landing of George IV on his return from Ireland in 1821.

England has gained from recent alterations, but his picture-gallery at Dulwich (1802) was a better piece of work. Smirke's façade at the Custom House and the embankment front of Somerset House have the advantage of a river aspect; the British Museum is less suited to the site,[1] and is little more than an academic exercise on a large scale.

A certain purity of style saved most of these cold imitations of antique work from complete nullity, but even the severity was lost when Cockerell[2] introduced more decorative and Palladian features into his buildings at Oxford, Cambridge, and London. Meanwhile the gothic revival had made considerable progress. In 1805 John Britton began to publish a series of drawings of *The Architectural Antiquities of Great Britain and Ireland*. Between 1814 and 1835 he produced another series, *The Cathedral Antiquities of England*, for which the elder Pugin took measurements. Thomas Rickman's *Attempt to Discriminate the Styles of Architecture in England from the Conquest to the Reformation* (1817) was the first work of accurate scholarship dealing with gothic, while the younger Pugin's[3] many publications on gothic design gave the movement an abundance of examples and ideas. Pugin was not primarily an architect. His earliest work was the reform of scenery for the stage and the designing of gothic furniture; he even made designs for the confectionery on the royal table at Windsor. In spite of his enthusiasm for medieval styles and his contribution to the exact study of medieval architecture, there was always something theatrical about his buildings; the detail might be right, but the plan was often wrong. Barry[4] took Pugin as his assistant for the decorative work and detailed drawings of the new houses of parliament.

[1] Smirke's original plan, which included a large square approached diagonally by a wide street, would have set off his building to greater advantage.

[2] Charles Robert Cockerell (1788–1863), s. of an architect; educ. Westminster; travelled in Greece, Asia Minor, and Sicily, 1810–17; surveyor of St. Paul's cathedral, 1819, where he renewed the ball and cross, 1821; professor of architecture at the Royal Academy, 1840–57; Cockerell's work includes gothic buildings.

[3] Augustus Welby Northmore Pugin (1812–52), s. of Augustus Pugin, a Frenchman who settled in England in 1798, b. London, educ. Christ's Hospital. Pugin, whose main interest apart from his work was in sailing, was shipwrecked in 1830; lost his reason in 1851 owing to pressure of work.

[4] Sir Charles Barry (1795–1860), s. of a well-to-do stationer, b. London, articled as a surveyor, 1810–16; travelled abroad, 1817–20, and, like Cockerell, was well known for his drawings before he practised as an architect. Barry had built in the Italian renaissance style (Reform Club, Pall Mall) and in English perpendicular (King Edward VI school, Birmingham) before he designed the houses of parliament. He was also a good landscape-gardener.

The neighbourhood of Westminster Abbey and St. Stephen's Hall partly determined the choice of gothic for the site. In any case the classical revival had already spent its force; public opinion hesitated between the perpendicular and Elizabethan or Jacobean styles. Barry would have chosen as his model Inigo Jones's river façade for Whitehall palace; he built a gothic exterior on a classical plan, with too many towers of different heights and sizes. He also missed the chance of bringing the river front of his building to the water's edge. On the other hand he showed that gothic styles could be adapted to very large modern buildings, and his careful study of the internal decoration of the various rooms and chambers had an important effect upon the development of craftsmanship.

In the middle years of the century the influence of Ruskin, and the desire for change, led to the substitution of thirteenth- and fourteenth-century models for the perpendicular style of the early gothic revival. The change was unfortunate, particularly for domestic buildings, where large window-space was necessary. Gilbert Scott[1] and George Street[2] designed a number of churches and other buildings in these middle years on strictly gothic lines. Scott, however, did not limit himself to early gothic. In 1834, as a young architect needing money, he realized that the poor law amendment act would create a demand for workhouses. Modern rules of professional etiquette were not yet in force: Scott went from union to union on horseback offering his services, and, with the collaboration of W. B. Moffat, a builder's son, put up about fifty workhouses, many of them in the Elizabethan style. Scott's St. Pancras station was a copy of Flemish gothic, and Street's royal courts of justice were based on French models. The different stages in the Gothic revival may be seen in Scott's Martyrs' Memorial (1840) at Oxford and his Albert Memorial in London (1864); the design of the

[1] Sir George Gilbert Scott (1811–78), s. of a clergyman, b. Gawcott, Bucks.; articled to an architect; won open competition for the church of St. Nicholas, Hamburg, 1844. It is characteristic of the time that the *Ecclesiologist* attacked Scott for building a Lutheran church, and that Scott himself believed that gothic architecture began in Germany, though he later changed his view. The drastic methods of restoration used by Scott and his school led to the formation of the Society for the Preservation of Ancient Buildings.

[2] George Edmund Street (1824–81), s. of a solicitor; b. Woodford, Essex; articled to an architect at Winchester, and worked as assistant to Scott. Street was a learned architect whose best work was done in parish churches, though he restored a number of cathedrals. Street's design for the law courts was hampered by the fussiness and parsimony of the first commissioner of works.

latter—'a kind of *ciborium* to protect the statue of the prince'—
was much bolder and finer, though it was spoiled by poor
colouring and bad sculpture.

The Gothic revival was never without rivals, even in official
buildings; it was associated, in the course of time, with conservatism and 'Puseyism'. A conservative government chose a
gothic style for new offices in Whitehall in 1858; Palmerston
and the whigs refused to accept the plans, and ordered in their
place a Palladian building which they regarded as less traditional—so quickly had fashion changed. There was no attempt
to develop a style less fettered by imitation of the past. The
functions and character of industrial society were well established and better known than they had been in the first years
of the century, but the visible expression of the activities of
modern Englishmen in factories, warehouses, shops, and railway stations fell increasingly into the hands of men who were
content with cheapness, or whose ideas of beauty were limited to
a gothic façade, a few battlements, or a cluster of pillars badly
carved. If people of traditional taste and manners were no
longer in control of the designs of public or private buildings,
the fault lay in the shortcomings of English education. The distinction between a gentleman and the 'cads of counting-houses'
is written large in the architecture of Victorian England; the
gentlemen took for granted the baseness of the counting-houses,
and made not the least attempt to educate the common people
in matters of artistic appreciation. There was indeed little grace
in the houses of the middle class and the poor. The opportunity
of money-making was too much for the speculative builders;
the town-planning and even the trimness of the earlier decades
disappeared, and, in their place, the suburbs of the new towns
contained mean imitations of rich men's houses, or street after
street of clumsy boxes far worse than 'the plain brick walls with
oblong holes cut in them'.

On the other hand there was some attempt at least to lay
down and enforce building regulations in cities. Here the problem was difficult almost beyond solution, among other reasons
because it was not a new problem. The nineteenth century did
not create the slum; the novelty of the age was rather that it
recognized a slum as such. Through long acceptance of misery
the inhabitants of slums took them for granted; the Irish immigrants herded in the worst tenements of Liverpool, Manchester,

or Glasgow had not known better conditions in their own country. There was another complication. It was hard enough to secure a reasonable standard of new building; although there were many new Victorian slums, the gravest scandals were in old buildings. A policy of large-scale demolition, paid for by the ratepayers, was beyond the dreams of the average municipal officer or ratepayer of the early nineteenth century. The efforts to improve the housing of the poor belong more to the history of public health than to the history of architecture, and the small number of enthusiasts who worked for these improvements had little time or money to spare for architectural niceties. They were fighting to keep people alive, and this fight demanded a concentration of energy. It is also fair to remember that if the Victorian reformers were content with houses and streets which were an offence to the eye, their work had an aesthetic as well as a sanitary value in getting rid of the stench and dirt accepted as inevitable by earlier generations.[1]

The social and economic changes of the age affected sculpture and painting as well as architecture. Since the renaissance sculpture had been an academic art in England, dependent upon cultured patrons and foreign examples. The English climate was not thought suited to the display of statues out of doors. There was little room in English streets for decorative or even for portrait sculpture, and, apart from the formal ornamentation of Palladian buildings, the use of statuary was limited to funeral monuments inside churches, many of which were badly lighted, and to the galleries of great mansions. In this narrow field of demand English sculptors had to compete with foreigners with greater prestige and more opportunities of practice. Roubiliac in the eighteenth century, Dalou after 1871, had the most important influence upon the development of sculpture in England; both these men were refugees.[2] The English upper class, whose classical education gave them a taste in sculpture, were too often content with the purchase of antiques or reproductions of ancient works. The middle class did not understand sculpture; neither the unreformed nor the reformed municipalities were likely to spend money in the patronage of

[1] See above, pp. 461–3.
[2] For Roubiliac (or, more correctly, Roubillac) see vol. xi of this *History*. Dalou came to England after the fall of the Paris commune.

the arts. The strict tenets of the Wesleyan and evangelical movements affected the art schools; no unmarried student at the Royal Academy was allowed to draw or model from the nude.[1] The Gothic revival was of little use to sculptors; the art schools did not teach the technique of gothic sculpture, and the perpendicular style of the first period of the revival was not suited to architectural statues. Unfortunately, at the time when two great English sculptors, Nollekens and Flaxman, might have founded a distinctive school, the influence of the Elgin marbles and the European reputation of Canova and Thorwaldsen prevented any break-away from the tradition of imitating classical models. Portrait sculpture also became formalized and pompous, and even the standard of technical efficiency declined. Thomas Woolner,[2] a member of the pre-Raphaelite brotherhood, did good work, but the choice of artists for the monuments of the rich or the great was generally in the hands of committees, who took care to appoint 'safe' men such as Chantrey[3] and Westmacott;[4] Matthew Wyatt's[5] George III and Chantrey's George IV were among the very few good statues put up in London. The position hardly changed for a generation.[6] There was a bold attempt to revive outdoor sculpture in the decoration of the Albert Memorial, but the feeble workmanship and commonplace grouping of the figures show the low state of carving in England. The great reputation of Alfred Stevens (1818–75) was due to the lack of rivals; Stevens was hardly more than a deliberate copyist of Michelangelo.

[1] This rule encouraged early and improvident marriages among art students.

[2] Thomas Woolner (1825–92), s. of a civil servant, b. Hadleigh; went to Australia to look for gold, 1852–4.

[3] Sir Francis Legatt Chantrey (1781–1841), s. of a carpenter and small farmer, b. Norton, Derbyshire; apprenticed to a Sheffield carver and dealer in prints and models; a portrait-painter and wood-carver in Sheffield and London before he turned to sculpture in 1804; married a rich wife in 1807, and began to obtain important commissions for portrait busts. Chantrey left the reversionary interest of his property—about £150,000—to the Royal Academy, in order to make some financial provision for the president and to provide a fund for the purchase of works of art carried out in Great Britain by artists of any nationality.

[4] Sir Richard Westmacott (1775–1856), s. of a sculptor, b. London; studied in Rome under Canova; exhibited regularly at the academy, where he succeeded Flaxman as professor of sculpture in 1827; his practice was almost as important as Chantrey's. His work included a large number of statues in Westminster abbey and St. Paul's cathedral, and the statue of the duke of York on a column in Waterloo Place. His son Richard Westmacott (1799–1872) was also a sculptor, and succeeded his father as professor at the academy.   [5] Son of James Wyatt.

[6] The Crimean war memorial in Waterloo Place is a fine exception.

If there was little good sculpture in the country partly because there was nowhere to put it, the amount of wall space for pictures largely increased. The houses of the upper middle class had not the long 'display' galleries of great mansions, but there were dining and drawing rooms where paintings could be hung. The owners of these new houses, and the shipping or cotton magnates and manufacturers who built on a scale not far short of the mansions of the eighteenth century, did not inherit family portraits or collections of pictures. The puritanism which associated sculpture with classical paganism or aristocratic immorality found no fault with portraits and landscape or *genre* paintings, though the artist had to avoid the naturalism of the Dutch school and the savagery of Hogarth. Wilkie's[1] village scenes are taken from Dutch models; they are of great social value as portraits of village life, but there are no drunkards or loose women or indecorous gestures at his village feasts. Etty's nudes were regarded as improper.[2] On the other hand the tyranny of the classics affected painting almost as much as sculpture, and the picture-dealers, who had extended their business from the sale of prints, began to exploit the demand. A very large number of pictures were imported annually from the continent, and aristocratic patrons continued the tradition of buying old masters, though on a smaller scale than in the eighteenth century; the galleries of great houses were full, and few of their owners cared to sell or exchange their inheritance for modern works. The newer purchasers, who did not know what they were buying, followed the fashion, and the rise in the value of the works of established painters, living or dead, convinced shrewd but inexperienced buyers that the dealers could supply them with safe investments, if they kept within the beaten track. Thus royal academicians could be sure of a sale for their works, and these favoured few were unwilling to encourage originality or new methods which might displace their own paintings. Constable made his reputation, after he had been painting for years, by an exhibition of his work in France. For a long time he sold little in England, and, as late as

[1] Sir David Wilkie (1785–1841), s. of a Scottish minister, b. Cults, Fife; studied design at Edinburgh; came to London, 1805. Wilkie's last two paintings were portraits of the sultan Abdul Mejid and of Mehemet Ali.

[2] Not by Queen Victoria, who showed interest in them when the curator of an exhibition had been uncertain whether he ought not to hide them from the queen's view.

1826, advertised his pictures at so much a square foot.[1] At the same time discontented artists exaggerated the tyranny of the academicians. The academy, under royal patronage, gave to artists a standing which had more than a social and economic value. Most good painters were elected to its membership, and the academy exhibitions took too many rather than too few pictures. The academy schools provided almost the only means of training for poor students; few painters took pupils, and in these few cases the charges were high. Moreover the alternative to a self-governing academy was state control. Public opinion would not accept this control, and the artists did not want it. Here, as in other spheres, it was felt that state management would lead to jobbery. The patronage of the Crown was of more value; though, in the prince consort's time, this patronage did more to encourage the decorative and applied arts than to develop painting. The prince was an early collector of 'primitives'; his taste in pictures was neither puritanical nor jejune, but it was not very good.

There were two painters of genius in the first half of the nineteenth century whose work stood out from the conventional habit, European as well as English, of filling large canvases with historical or literary pictures of an obvious kind.[2] Constable[3] was never very popular mainly because his landscapes were different from the brown trees and drab-coloured scenes of his contemporaries. He painted English landscapes as he saw them; he complained that the 'great vice' of his age was '*bravura*, an attempt to do something beyond the truth'. Constable was not unaffected by the example of earlier masters, but in the main he was content with work of an entirely unacademic and unimitative kind. He was equally content with the landscapes of his own country, without lakes, castles, mountains, ruins, or any of the romantic trappings of ordinary landscape painters. He never went to Italy even when he could afford to travel

---

[1] He charged a fairly high price per square foot.

[2] Benjamin Haydon (1786–1846) has left in his *Autobiography* a good, though wild and erratic, account of this type of work, of which his own huge paintings were extravagant examples.

[3] John Constable (1776–1837), s. of a prosperous corn-miller, b. East Bergholt, Suffolk; encouraged by Sir George Beaumont (painter and friend of Reynolds) to study art; from 1803 he realized his own talents as a landscape-painter, and went his way without thought of fame or recognition. He described his own quiet methods: 'I imagine myself to be driving a nail. I have driven it some way, and by persevering I may drive it home; by quitting it to attack others, though I may amuse myself . . . the particular nail stands still.'

abroad. He wanted nothing more than the morning or high afternoon of the English spring or summer. He did not often paint in winter, and there is sunlight in nearly all his work. Turner[1] was a more splendid painter of sunlight; in many ways indeed he was the greatest artist of his age in Europe, great enough to borrow freely from earlier masters, and even to imitate them directly. He left instructions in his will that his 'Building of Carthage' and 'The sun rising through mist' should be hung next to the Bouillon Claudes in the National Gallery. Turner was fortunate in that he came of extremely vigorous peasant stock and that his family received a small legacy which enabled him to study. He made a reputation in early life; he was free to travel, and never embarrassed by money troubles. He was too robust and individual to be spoiled by success, though he was sensitive to criticism, especially in his later years when some of his artistic extravagances laid him open to ridicule. On the other hand his carelessness about materials has done his work irretrievable harm. Fortunately he left an immense number of paintings; he painted quickly and worked hard. His technique in water-colours was even greater than in oils, and few artists in modern times have equalled his power of colour or his bold imagination.

In 1845 English art was in a low period. Turner had done his work. Constable was dead. Etty's health had failed.[2] Raeburn (1756–1823) and Lawrence (1769–1830) had left no successors approaching their own talent. John Cotman, one of the best English landscape-painters in water-colours, died in 1842, and, even before his death, the school of Norwich painters begun by John Crome (1768–1821) had broken up. Bonington's[3] early

[1] Joseph Mallord William Turner (1775–1851), s. of a barber, b. London; sold drawings before he was ten; exhibited at the R.A., 1790; became a 'romantic' landscape-painter after a tour in the north in 1797, and began to paint studies of light in 1807. Ruskin pointed out that Turner's work falls into three periods: 1800–20, when he imitated various old masters; 1820–35, when he attempted ideal compositions; and 1835–45, when his work began to take a wilder form, though during this period he painted some of his most famous pictures, including 'The Fighting Téméraire' and 'Rain, Steam, and Speed'.

[2] William Etty (1787–1849), s. of a baker, b. York; apprenticed as a printer; given money to study painting, 1805; R.A., 1828.

[3] Richard Parkes Bonington (1801–28), s. of a prison governor who lost his post and settled in France, b. Arnold, nr. Nottingham; studied at Calais and Paris; exhibited in London after he had already made a reputation in France, but was so little known in England that the *Literary Gazette* denied his existence and attributed his work to another artist.

death in 1828, in his twenty-eighth year, brought to an end the career of a painter of greater promise than any of his contemporaries. David Cox (1783–1859) continued to paint in a quiet way the landscapes of north Wales which brought him all the fame he ever desired, but Cox was never fashionable.[1] Landseer's[2] animals, Leslie's[3] humorous paintings, and Maclise's[4] *genre* pictures contented the public; their conventional methods did not satisfy younger artists, eager to break away from styles which had lost artistic interest.

The leaders of the movement of revolt were Rossetti, Holman Hunt,[5] and Millais. Rossetti was neither the best painter nor the clearest thinker of the pre-Raphaelite brotherhood (or clique, as the members first named their group), but he provided the movement with a name, a doctrine, and a journal (*The Germ*) which lasted long enough for the public to learn the aims of the new school. Other groups of artists had worked together and followed a particular school or method of painting. The pre-Raphaelites were more consciously influenced by intellectual considerations taken from other fields, even if they were not original in their ideas or accurate in their scholarship. Rossetti and his friends did not depend for a living entirely upon the sale of their pictures, though their sales were by no means inconsiderable. Holman Hunt was for some time in money difficulties, and thought of giving up painting for farming. After 1851 he was in no trouble; he received 400 guineas in 1854 for 'The Light of the World' and much higher prices for his later works. Millais's 'The Carpenter's Shop' sold for £150 in 1850, when

[1] Samuel Palmer (1805–81), one of the artists personally influenced by Blake, also painted good landscapes.

[2] Sir Edwin Landseer (1802–73) was the favourite painter of the court as well as of the public.

[3] Charles Robert Leslie (1794–1859), of American parentage, b. London; apprenticed to a bookseller in Philadelphia; the head of his firm and other leading merchants of the city sent him to study in Europe, where he began by aiming at 'high art', but soon turned to light humour; professor of painting at the Royal Academy, 1848; published a *Handbook for Young Painters*, 1852.

[4] Daniel Maclise (1806–70), s. of a Scottish highlander who had settled in Cork; made a sketch of Sir Walter Scott, 1825; opened a studio, and after painting portraits at Cork for two years came to London and studied at the Royal Academy; published a series of portraits in *Fraser's Magazine*, 1831–8, including most of the literary figures of his time; a friend of Dickens; decorated the royal gallery in the house of lords with historical frescoes.

[5] William Holman Hunt (1827–1910), s. of a London warehouseman; went to the Near East in 1854 for three years to study the surroundings of the life of Christ; awarded the Order of Merit in his last years.

the artist was a young man of twenty. In any case the pre-Raphaelites did not have to wait long for success. Ruskin's support was of great value to them, and, even without Ruskin's help, their purpose was simple enough for public opinion to understand and accept it. Rossetti's 'Childhood of the Virgin' (1849) and 'Ecce Ancilla Domini' (1850) caused some scandal and more surprise, but as early as 1857 pre-Raphaelitism was taken for granted. Lesser men had begun to copy its methods, and the doctrines of the group tended to disappear as each of the leaders went his own successful way.

The pre-Raphaelites claimed, simply, to paint nature as they saw it. Their test of truth was accuracy in detail. Their drawing was more careful, honest, and accurate than most of the academic work of the time, but other artists had painted things as they saw them and produced results no less honest and far less mannered than the 'Childhood of the Virgin'. David Cox summed up the whole matter in 1853 in his reply to critics of the roughness of his drawings: 'They forget that they are the work of the mind, which I consider very far before portraits of places.' The pre-Raphaelites, like all artists, painted things seen in and through a particular mode of the imagination; their realist presentation of detail was too often an exotic romanticism tinged with religious emotion. They tried to bring back the sense of awe and reverence which, according to their theories, had been lost to art since the development of academic painting. It is easy to find in the pre-Raphaelites many of the faults which they condemned in others, and to think of them as the artistic counterpart of the 'Young England' movement in politics. A deliberate imitation of fifteenth-century workmanship was itself a form of academic painting. It was not necessarily insincere; it was bound to lack originality and intellectual liveliness, and the emphasis upon awe and reverence could easily go too far. The pre-Raphaelites attacked Frith's 'Derby Day', not because it was a bad painting—it is a good painting—but because it had a vulgar subject. Reproductions of the paintings in the Campo Santo at Pisa had a great influence upon the work of the pre-Raphaelites; a closer study of fourteenth- and fifteenth-century art and a better knowledge of history might have shown Rossetti (who never went to Italy, in spite of his exploitation of Italian subjects) that this early period was hardly less sophisticated than the age of Raphael. Constable and Turner had proved in a

masterful way that concentration upon detail was not essential
to 'honesty of purpose', and the German school of Nazarenes
had already practised the religious attitude towards painting.
Furthermore, the pre-Raphaelites were not the only people
interested in early Flemish or Italian art. A room was set aside
for works of these schools in the National Gallery in the very
year of the foundation of the brotherhood. Thomas Stothard[1]
had already chosen medieval literary subjects for his pictures
and illustrations; his son Charles Stothard knew more than
Rossetti ever knew about medieval art, while Ford Madox
Brown[2] had begun to paint in the pre-Raphaelite manner some
years before the appearance of *The Germ*.

In spite of faults of theory and execution, the pre-Raphaelites
had a lasting and, on the whole, a sound effect upon English
painting. At least they worked with some idea in view, and
were ready to make experiments. Holman Hunt, the least gifted
of the group, was the only member who kept faithfully to the
principles throughout his long life. Millais was the first to leave
the brotherhood, but his early experience set a mark upon all
his work. G. F. Watts followed Rossetti only in the use of
symbolism, and here Blake was a sounder and healthier master.
On the other hand Watts's peculiar methods of flattery in his
portraits show the effect of the pre-Raphaelite sense of mission
and responsibility. Lawrence had pleased an earlier generation
by making his high-born and distinguished sitters more handsome than they really were. Watts transformed Victorian politicians into philosopher-kings, publicists into sages, and poets
into bards. Moreover, through Burne-Jones and his friend
William Morris, the influence of pre-Raphaelitism reached the

---

[1] Thomas Stothard (1755–1834), s. of a publican, b. London; apprenticed to
a designer of patterns for flowered silks; most of his best work was in book-illustra-
tion, but he did a good deal of decorative work in houses, and painted a number
of pictures in oils, of which the best known is 'The Canterbury Pilgrims setting
forth from the Tabard Inn'. Charles Stothard (1786–1821) published a series of
Monumental Effigies of Great Britain to show the changes in English medieval costume,
and made a close study of the Bayeux tapestry.

[2] Ford Madox Brown (1821–93), s. of a retired commissary in the navy, b. Calais,
studied in Belgium and later in Italy; declined to join the pre-Raphaelites owing
to their exaggerated realism, though he was on friendly terms with them and contributed to *The Germ*, and was influenced by their work as they were influenced by
his paintings. Brown was one of the earliest artists to take part in teaching working
men. He became a regular teacher at the Working Men's College (see p. 496) and
his 'Work', which included portraits of Carlyle and F. D. Maurice, is a good example
of the ideas of the social reformers.

decorative arts, where an attack upon commercialism was even more necessary than in painting. Burne-Jones soon produced better work than his master Rossetti; his collaboration with Morris was important in the revival of good stained glass.

The popularity of the pre-Raphaelites, once their methods had become familiar, was due partly to the growing interest in art among the middle class. Ruskin was largely responsible for this change, but with the opening of public galleries in many cities there were more pictures to be seen, and with the gradual increase in the leisure and culture of the professional class there were more people to see them. Improvements in engraving and printing, and the removal of the excise duty on glass in 1845, brought a large demand for reproductions of pictures of every kind, from the prints of the Arundel Society (founded in 1849) to the cheap patriotic or religious or sporting scenes which decorated cottage walls. From the point of view of the trained artist and connoisseur much of this popular appreciation was misplaced; for the social historian the very existence of these cheap reproductions is significant. They were an improvement, not merely upon the bare walls of a poor man's room, but upon the few crude and ill-printed patches of colour within reach of humble purses in the eighteenth century. Middle-class houses rarely had good prints before 1840. The development of photography was equally important.[1] Photographs even in their early days were better than bad portraits, and could be bought by people who could not afford pictures. They had an educational value in giving the ordinary man a clearer and better idea of people and places outside his own knowledge; they provided, for the first time in history, an accurate visual record of events. A few faint-hearted people feared that they might be the death of painting, or at all events of portrait-painting. Artists themselves had sharply to remember that their own work had always been something more than the representation of objects.[2]

[1] The development of photography was the result of parallel investigations in Great Britain and France. In Great Britain W. H. Fox-Talbot (1801–77) and J. B. Reade (1801–70) secured pictures on sensitized paper about 1839. Talbot gave his name to the 'talbotype', or 'calotype'—words, now forgotten, describing early photographs. Photography advanced rapidly after the introduction of the collodion process by F. S. Archer (1813–57). A civil list pension was given to Archer's children, on the ground that their father had gained nothing from discoveries which had brought wealth to others.

[2] An exhibition of Japanese art in London in 1862 had an important influence on this 're-thinking'.

VI

THE CONDITION OF THE PEOPLE
1850–70

ASSUME that an American, who had known England at the death of Sir Robert Peel (1850), came back again in 1870 or 1871; what changes would he notice in the structure of English society, and in the political, social, and economic life of the people?[1] He might perhaps observe from his ship that there were lighthouses on the Bishop and the Wolf Rocks.[2] He would certainly notice that there were more steamships and that most of the new ships were of iron; in 1865 the steam tonnage added to Lloyd's register for the first time exceeded that of sailing ships.[3] The adaptation of the compound engine to marine use in 1854 and the increase in boiler-pressure had saved fuel and water and added to the speed and cargo-room of steamships. A traveller would find that railways had become part of the landscape, and that at least on the main lines the cuttings and embankments were no longer bare. The mileage of lines had more than doubled, and in 1868, after the completion of the Midland line from Bedford to St. Pancras, there was only one long section of main line—Settle to Carlisle —to be built until the Great Central came to London in the twentieth century. The pirate age of railway speculation ceased

---

[1] Henry James's *The Middle Years* may be taken as a good example of the impressions of an American who came to England in 1868.

[2] There was a lighthouse—completed in 1848—on the Bishop Rocks at the beginning of 1850, but it was destroyed by a storm in February of that year.

[3] On the other hand, in this year steam tonnage was only 15 per cent. of the total, and sail tonnage had actually reached its maximum. Steam had ousted sail for passenger and mail traffic, but sail could compete successfully in the carriage of bulky commodities (including coal for steamships) over long distances. The design of sailing ships was greatly improved in the early middle years of the century, and the development of oceanographical studies after 1850 (see above, p. 567) had provided ampler and more reliable information about winds, currents, &c. See G. S. Graham, 'The Ascendancy of the Sailing Ship, 1850–1885', in *Econ. Hist. Rev.* 2nd ser. ix (1956), pp. 74–88. Although there were as yet no steam trawlers, fresh sea fish were in 1850 no longer a luxury for the inland population. The change was made possible by railways, and was due also to better methods of fishing and the use of ice for chilling.

with the fall of George Hudson, the 'railway king', in 1849, and in England the period of great amalgamations ended with the formation of the North Eastern in 1854 and the Great Eastern in 1862. More ambitious plans, including a scheme for the union of the London and North Western, Great Western, and London and South Western lines, had broken down, though the railways were forming agreements among themselves to avoid undue competition. An agreement affecting the traffic to Scotland was made as early as 1851. The state had taken little part in directing railway policy, and had confined itself to matters affecting the safety of travel. Even here the government inspectors had no compulsory powers of obtaining information until 1871. The block system of signalling was in force only on one-fifth of the lines of the country. In technical matters, indeed, the railways had more opportunities than the state for trying experiments. Parliament might have dealt more narrowly with railway rates, but the subject was extremely complicated, and the railways were not making large profits. On the whole people were satisfied with them. The 'express' trains did not go much faster than in 1850, but rolling stock was more comfortable than in the days when a 'parliamentary carriage' was described (1849) as 'very like a rabbit-hutch', though the status of the third-class passenger did not improve to any great extent until, in 1872, the Midland company put third-class carriages on all their trains in order to attract traffic from other lines.

The canals never recovered from the first heavy blows of rail competition.[1] The larger companies paid their way, but many of the smaller canals could have survived only by subsidy, and there were no strategical or industrial reasons why a subsidy should have been given. In many cases the railways bought out canals, or secured control of a majority of shares in them. Fear of the abuse of monopoly caused parliament to pass an act in 1845 'to obtain greater competition for the public advantage' by enabling canal companies to make arrangements among themselves about tolls. The act gave to railways which already controlled canals the chance of extending this control elsewhere, and, to the dismay of the promoters of the act of 1845, an increasing number of amalgamations took place between

[1] The value of the £100 shares in the Grand Junction company which at one time had reached £330 fell to £155 in 1846 and to £60–£70 in 1853.

railway and canal companies. In 1865 the railways owned about one-third of the canals of the country.

The roads had been improved to take the increase in transport to and from the railways. This improvement was slow because the administrative machinery was inadequate. The turnpike trusts were never very popular or efficient, and a generation which had learned the possibilities of railway speed and through travel was not likely to endure toll-gates. Moreover, within ten years of the building of railways nearly every turnpike trust was bankrupt, and the work of keeping the roads in repair had fallen on the ratepayers who also paid the tolls. Riots in Wales[1] in 1842–3 led to the establishment of road boards which took control of the management of the trusts, lowered the tolls, and removed a number of gates. The system might have been extended to England if the governments of the day had been willing to face the problem of dealing with the debts of eleven hundred trusts, the vested interests of their employees, and the opposition of the county justices to any extension of central control. Opinion became restive at the wasteful and inefficient way of keeping up the roads; in 1864 a parliamentary committee reported in favour of handing over the trusts to a public authority. Henceforward the trusts began rapidly to disappear; there were 854 of them in 1871 and only two in 1890. There was similar slowness in improving the administration of the ordinary roads not controlled by trusts. The general highway act of 1835 set up ratepayers' meetings in each parish as the governing authority with power to levy rates and appoint a surveyor; the larger parishes elected boards of management, but the unit of administration was too small. An act of 1862 allowed the justices in quarter sessions to combine parishes into districts, but the home office took little interest in the practical working of the act, and the district areas varied in size and efficiency. No further step was taken until after 1870. Three years earlier the first bicycles had appeared on the roads; henceforward the road-constructors had to meet new problems. The telegraph[2] pole was becoming a common

---

[1] These disturbances were known as the Rebecca riots, because the gangs of men who pulled down toll-houses justified themselves by the prophecy (Gen. xxiv. 60) that Rebecca's seed should possess 'the gate of those which hate them'. Resentment against the new poor law was a contributing cause of the riots.

[2] Purists objected to the introduction of the word 'telegram' instead of 'telegraphic dispatch' or 'telegrapheme'. Messrs. Longmans promised to introduce the

feature of the roads. Between 1850 and 1860 a number of private companies had opened telegraph lines; parliament authorized the Post Office in 1868 to take over the private companies, and to establish, as in the case of inland letters, a uniform charge irrespective of distance. Meanwhile, in 1866 the *Great Eastern* had completed the laying of the Atlantic cable, and in 1870 telegraph lines were open to India.[1]

The omnibus was twenty years old in 1850; a French company had established a dominating position in London in 1855 and transformed itself three years later into an English concern, with Chadwick as one of the directors. Horse-drawn tramways, almost forgotten after the introduction of the locomotive, had reappeared on the streets, but there were not many of them.

The face of the countryside changed little between 1850 and 1870. The period of inclosures was over, except in Wales and the hills of the north-west, and in the neighbourhood of cities the tide had turned in the other direction. Common land was now beginning to have a value as open space. Little had been done to replace the lost English forests: with the disappearance of the oak fighting ship the admiralty had no interest in afforestation. On the other hand foreign conifers had become respectable; Meredith, for example, writes of them in language which would have been a scandal to Cobbett. Wire fences were an unpleasing innovation, kept down largely through the influence of hunting men. Owing to improvement in land drainage, especially on heavy soils, a traveller in winter would notice fewer bogged fields. Threshing machines had become common earlier in the century; at harvest time there were many more reaping and mowing machines, and, at other seasons, mechanical drills had come into use, but the configuration of the country was not favourable to steam ploughing. The mechanization of agriculture indeed had begun in the eighteenth century; the process did not gain momentum until after 1850. Small farmers were slow to change their methods; they had little knowledge or capital, and left 'improvement' to the gentry who were better able to risk losses. There had been little change, since the years following the French wars, in the distribution of

word into a new dictionary in 1858, but as late as 1873 one authority described the word as 'lawless'. The earliest 'private company lines' were laid along the railways.

[1] See above, pp. 569 and 571. A cable between Dover and Calais was laid in 1851. Reuters News Service was founded in this year.

land between tillage and pasture, though the railways had been of immense value to the dairy-farming areas of the south and middle west. The soil itself was given more varied treatment owing to the development of manufactured fertilizers; Peruvian guano had been imported in large quantities since the 1820's, and, a little later, Chilean nitrates were also common.

Few mansions on the eighteenth-century scale were built after 1850, but there was a steady increase in the number of houses of large or moderate size in the home counties, or, in the midlands and north, within reach of the great towns. A returning traveller would have been impressed by the multitude of new small houses, particularly in the suburban districts of London and the manufacturing towns. The figures show that the increase in the number of houses was proportionally greater than the increase in the population.[1]

| Year | Houses | | | Population |
	Inhabited	Uninhabited	Building	
1821	2,088,156	69,707	19,274	12,000,236
1831	2,481,544	119,915	24,759	13,896,797
1841	2,943,965	173,247	27,444	15,914,148
1851	3,278,039	153,490	26,571	17,927,609
1861	3,739,505	184,694	27,305	20,066,224
1871	4,259,117	261,345	37,803	22,712,266

These figures do not give a complete picture of the change, since they take no account of houses pulled down and replaced, or of houses enlarged or put into better repair. At every census since 1801 one house in five contained two families, and the average number of persons in a family had not fallen by more than 0·40 since 1801. The average number of persons to an inhabited house in 1871 was 5·4 in England, 4·9 in Wales, 8·2 in Scotland, and 5·6 in Ireland. The improvements, however, applied mainly to the towns; agricultural housing was little changed, and, by the rising urban standards, was coming to be regarded as disgracefully backward.

[1] Census report, 1871, vol. iv, Appendix A, Tables 1 and 9. The figures refer only to England and Wales, and in the census returns of 1871 'flats' are put into inverted commas, and are counted as separate houses. A certain number of 'model blocks' of flats had been built, mainly by philanthropic effort, in the congested districts of central London, but they were not very popular, and formed only a very small proportion of the new buildings. Flats for middle and upper class householders were still a curiosity, though bachelor chambers had been familiar for many years. Nearly one-half of the houses in England and Wales were assessed at a rental below £10.

The people of England formed nearly 21,500,000, and of Wales 1,217,000, of the 31,845,379 inhabitants of the United Kingdom. 3,360,000 lived in Scotland; an increase of nearly 475,000 since 1851. 5,412,265 lived in Ireland; a decrease of 1,160,000 since 1851.[1] The mean age of the population of England and Wales had been constant at 26·4 since 1851. The distribution of age showed that there were living in 1871 nearly 125,000 men and women born before the French revolution. Nearly seven million people were between 20 and 40; 10·4 million were 20 or under 20 years of age. The increase of population in Great Britain since 1831 had been greater than the total figures (8,892,536) for England and Wales in the census of 1801. The birth-rate in England and Wales rose from 33·9 per 1,000 in the period 1851–5 to 35·3 in the period 1866–70; during these same periods the death-rate fell from 22·7 to 22·4 per 1,000. The average annual natural increase of the population therefore was about 1·24 per cent., and the birth-rate figures showed that, on an average, every married woman between the ages of 20 and 40 bore a child every three years. The death-rate in England and Wales during the period between 1850 and 1870 was slightly lower than the rate in France and Belgium, and considerably lower than the rate in Prussia. The tables of mortality show that most English towns were less unhealthy than in the earlier years of the century; London and Liverpool were healthier cities than Berlin. Although most of the population lived in urban areas, the average length of life had risen slightly. The population of London and of 102 other towns of more than 20,000 inhabitants was 3,480,593 in 1821, 6,753,734 in 1851, and 9,543,968 in 1871. London[2] alone contained in 1871 nearly as many people as the whole urban areas of England and Wales in 1821. On the other hand the percentage increase in rural areas and in towns containing less than 20,000 inhabitants was about a third of the urban rate of increase. Moreover, a greater number of townsmen were born

---

[1] The remaining 350,000 came from the Isle of Man or the Channel Islands, or were in the army, navy, and merchant service abroad on the date of the census.

[2] London included, for census purposes, the area bounded on the north-east by the Lea and the Thames, in the south-east by the parishes of Plumstead and Eltham, on the south by Sydenham, Lower Norwood, Streatham, Tooting, and Putney Heath, on the west by Chiswick Eyot and Wormwood Scrubbs, thence, roughly, east to the Edgware Road, and thence north via Hampstead, Kentish Town, Highbury, and Clapton to the Lea.

in towns: 2,055,576 of the 3,254,260 Londoners of 1871 were born in London, while another 436,000 London-born people were living in other parts of England and Wales. Scottish-born people in England and Wales had increased from 103,768 in 1841 to 213,254 in 1871; one-half of these immigrants were in the northern or north-western counties, and one-fifth in London. The Irish-born population in England and Wales had increased from 290,891 in 1841 to 566,540—a number equal to more than a tenth of the population of Ireland—in 1871. The Irish-born population in Scotland was 207,770 in 1871. It was estimated that almost one-eighth of the Scottish population was of Irish stock. These figures alarmed the Scottish census commissioners to such an extent that they used language which brought a protest from the Irish commissioners. They noted that the Irish immigrants 'undoubtedly produced very deleterious results, lowered greatly the moral tone of the lower classes, and greatly increased the necessity for the enforcement of sanitary and police precautions where they have settled in large numbers. . . . It is painful to contemplate what may be the ultimate effects of this Irish immigration on the morals and habits of the people, and on the future prospects of the country.' The number of people born in foreign parts (including the children of British parents) rose from 39,446 in 1841 to 139,445 in 1871.

The population of the United Kingdom would have been even larger if there had not been a continuous stream of emigration, mainly towards the American continent.[1] American statistics show that the number of people born in the United Kingdom and resident in the United States was 1,364,986 in 1850, 2,224,743 in 1860, and 2,626,241 in 1870. In 1850 nearly a million, and in 1870 over 1,800,000, of these immigrants were Irish-born. It is also clear from a comparison between British and American figures that about half a million English-born immigrants to the United States came back to England or settled elsewhere between 1850 and 1870.

The occupations of the people of the United Kingdom show

[1] The figures for decennial periods (excluding foreigners) were as follows:

Census Years	Number of Emigrants in the intervals	Census Years	Number of Emigrants in the intervals
1821–31	225,878	1851–61	2,054,578
1831–41	655,747	1861–71	1,674,594
1841–51	1,545,543		

a considerable change between 1850 and 1870. Agriculture
still employed more men and women than any other industry.
The numbers had fallen slightly over twenty years, but it is
probable that there were in 1851 more workers than the land
could properly support. The decrease in Scotland was very
much greater; it reached the high figure of 38 per cent. between
1861 and 1871, though the population of the Scottish islands
was in 1850 dangerously high in relation to means of livelihood.
The textile industries were far ahead of any other urban occupa-
tional groups in the United Kingdom. They employed about
1,100,000 workers in 1851. The number had not changed very
much in 1871, though there were more factory workers. The
metal, engineering, and shipbuilding industries, as might be
expected, showed a large expansion. Iron-workers in Great
Britain had increased from under 80,000 in 1851 to a figure
not much below 200,000 in 1871. Owing to the greater volume
and complexity of business the number of commercial clerks
more than doubled, while the rising standards of living and
increase in the numbers of the middle class resulted in the
employment of some 200,000 more men and women as domestic
servants in England and Wales. The rise in the number of
machine-makers in Great Britain was even more striking; the
figures had increased from 61,000 to 106,000 during the years
1861-71.

The change in the distribution and daily work of the people
of Great Britain can be studied from another angle. One might
take new industries, such as rubber, iron ship-building, or jute
manufacture, or the heavy chemical industry; one might consider the consequences of particular inventions or discoveries.
The Bessemer steel-making process,[1] patented in 1856 and
developed commercially during the next few years, began the
transformation of an age of iron into an age of steel, though,
as late as 1860, no one anticipated this change. Whitworth's
standardization of screws and screw-threads, measuring-
machines and gauges, had been highly commended at the Great
Exhibition. Whitworth went on improving his inventions, and

---

[1] The essential feature of this process was the use of a powerful blast to burn
out the carbon and silicon from pig-iron in the molten state. The iron produced in
this way could be turned easily into steel by the addition of manganese to return
the necessary amount of carbon. This process required ores free from phosphorus.
Hence the large imports of Spanish iron-ore. Siemens devised another process of
steel-making in 1866.

in 1870 most engineers had recognized the immense economies of time and labour which could be gained by the adoption of standard types. In the textile industries the wool-combing machinery invented by Donisthorpe and Lister was in use after 1851. After the terrible years of decline before 1850 the number of hand-loom workers in the cotton industry had fallen to a few thousands; the decline in the woollen industry was slower and less disastrous for the workers. The mechanization of the hosiery trade was postponed even longer; the American sewing-machine began to affect the tailoring and bootmaking trades after 1856, but for the next fifteen years the machines were worked by hand or foot. In 1871 there were only 65 h.p. of steam in the 58 tailoring and clothing factories and about 400 h.p. in the 145 boot and shoe factories of Great Britain. The increasing demand for coal in the heavier and mechanized industries and on the railways and ships of the high seas had extended coal-mining to lower levels. At first there were many serious explosions in these lower depths; hence the development of ventilating machinery, and, for economy as well as for safety, stronger and more powerful winding-machines.

These changes in production brought larger factories and workshops.[1] Water-power had almost gone out of use; in 1870 electrical power was undeveloped, while the horse-power of steam reached nearly a million. The textile factories had already reached a considerable size in the first year of the Victorian period. The average number of persons employed in a single cotton-mill was 137 in 1838 and 177 in 1870–1. Ship-building had long been organized in works employing many hands, and as the ships grew larger so too did the ship-building yards. The greatest of the Thames yards employed 700 men in 1825; a northern yard in 1870 might employ about 800 men. Twenty-six of the chief iron-works of South Wales employed an average of 650 men in 1870–1, but the number of small units in the Sheffield, Birmingham, and Black Country area brought down the average throughout the metal manufactures to 34·5.[2] The general background of industry was thus still one of small firms. The census of 1851 for England and Wales was the first in which

---

[1] The changes must not be exaggerated. In 1875 the total amount of fixed capital in the manufacturing industries was less than that in the railways. The capital investment in the cotton industry in 1875 was about £100,000,000.

[2] The figure is probably too high because numbers of small workshops are likely to have been overlooked in the count.

masters were asked to state the number of their operatives. Some
130,000 replied to the question. A third of them had no hired
workers (or returned none). Of the remaining two-thirds, about
76,000 had under 10 hired workers, 9,000 had between 10 and
49, 1,000 between 50 and 99.

The late application of the principle of limited liability had
some effect upon industrial organization, though the conditions
of earlier industrial enterprise did not require much more than
a family firm, or a firm of partners. Most businesses were
founded from private savings and financed out of earnings.
In any case a manufacturer could generally obtain credit from a
bank for a scheme with reasonable prospects. It was partly for
this reason that the legal changes which permitted limited
liability companies were not introduced at an earlier date.
Until the year 1825 the promotion of companies of any kind
was difficult. The South Sea Bubble had given the joint-stock
principle a bad name, and an act of 1720 forbade the formation
of any company except by royal charter. A charter was expensive,
and grants were not readily made. In spite of the difficulties
there were in 1820–5 a large number of unincorporated companies, representing about £160,000,000 of capital. The legal
position of these partnerships was doubtful. They could not
sue or be sued except in the names of every shareholder; the
principle of unlimited liability worked harshly in cases where it
was applied to the whole property of a man who had only a
small interest in the profits of a large concern. The act of 1720
was repealed in 1825; between 1825 and 1844 steps were taken
to allow suing-rights and some degree of limited liability to unincorporated companies. There was no difficulty about granting
incorporation to railway and other companies, where no single
group of partners could be expected to provide the required
capital; most business men and economists hesitated to recommend any large extension of limited liability to ordinary commercial undertakings. In 1844, after a parliamentary inquiry
into the abuses of company-promoting, an act was passed to
allow the registration of companies with an official registrar;
companies thus registered were given the privileges and status
of incorporation, though the liability of their shareholders was
unlimited unless they obtained a charter or an act of parliament. Mere registration did not remove the possibility of fraud,

and the leading business men and bankers of the country were still nervous about removing the last check upon speculation. On the other hand small investors were increasing in number with the rising wealth of the country, and the example of the railway companies stimulated the demand for investments in which the holder did not risk the whole of his resources. Hence in 1855-6 legislation was introduced to allow limited liability. The first results were not encouraging. Thirty-six per cent. of the companies formed between 1856 and 1865 ceased to exist within five years; 54 per cent. did not survive ten years. For a long time the larger part of joint stock capital was in railway shares and banks; few non-speculative issues were open to 'outsiders'.

The growth of speculation was indeed largely responsible for the serious commercial crisis of 1866. Commercial crises had occurred in 1825, 1836-9, 1847, and 1857.[1] The intervals between these crises appeared so regular that there was a good deal of rather vague conjecture about their causes. The memory of speculators was short; a few years after one collapse the lessons were forgotten and rash-minded men began once again to act rashly, but there were also special reasons for each crisis. In each case the nature of the speculation was different, and the 'boom' was brought to a close by different external causes.

The crisis of 1857 happened after a good harvest which brought down the price of wheat and affected the American market and many English houses with commitments in this market; the suspension of the bank charter act limited the failures to a few large banks and bill-broking houses. In 1866 the trouble was due largely to the development of finance companies. These companies, formed to subscribe and acquire stock in financial enterprises, had their origin in France during the early days of the Second Empire.[2] The extension of the principle of limited liability gave them an opening in England,

[1] For a short account and a bibliography of the commercial crises of the period see W. O. Henderson, 'Trade Cycles in the Nineteenth Century', *History*, July 1933.

[2] The Crédit Mobilier was the most important of these companies. It was founded under official patronage (the French government wanted to be independent of the Rothschilds) mainly by a group of Portuguese Jews at Bordeaux, who were themselves influenced by Saint-Simonian theories and wanted to 'socialize the Rothschild business' by mobilizing the capital of small investors. At certain periods one-third of the shares of the Crédit Mobilier were in English hands. In 1864 English investors held two-fifths of the shares of the Great Russian railway, which was controlled by the Crédit Mobilier.

and a number of hopeful enterprises with high-sounding names —'The International Financial Company', 'The Imperial Mercantile Credit Company'—attracted investors. The tendency was dangerous, since, apart from the chances of fraud, the companies were selling shares in large concerns which had not yet come into existence. One of the most important finance companies was the firm of Overend and Gurney. This firm was of long standing and high reputation as a discounting and bill-broking house. After the death of the two senior partners in 1856 and 1857, Overend and Gurney began to undertake business of a risky character, and soon over-reached themselves. They wanted more capital and decided in 1865 to make use of the goodwill of their business and to transform themselves into a limited company. The public did not know the real position of the house, and eagerly took up the shares. In May 1866 the company failed to meet its liabilities; its fall brought a run on the banks and the collapse of many of the speculative ventures which had offered themselves since 1856. The directors of the Bank of England asked for the suspension of the act of 1844. The government agreed that suspension was necessary, but required that the rate of discount should be raised to 10 per cent.; it remained at this figure for three months. The crisis alarmed foreign opinion to such an extent that the foreign secretary sent a circular to the British embassies and legations in Europe explaining the reason for the panic.

The improvement in banking facilities, the greater stability of banks since the legislation of 1844, and the amalgamation of the smaller houses acted as a safeguard against financial collapse; at the same time these improved conditions concealed the first symptoms of distress, and therefore made matters worse when a crisis could no longer be staved off. For the same reasons recovery was a more difficult process; after 1870 long periods of depression took the place of these sudden and sharp set-backs to speculation. During the twenty years after 1850 there were only two years, 1858 and 1861, in which there was anything more than a slight fall in the amount of exports from the United Kingdom. The fall in 1858 left the total higher than in 1856, and the fall in 1861 was due to the effect of the American civil war upon the cotton industry. There was a further fall in 1862, but the figure for 1863 was higher than in any previous year. The total in 1855 was under £100,000,000 and in 1870 nearly

£200,000,000. During the same period imports (including re-exports) rose from about £150,000,000 to about £300,000,000. The excess of 'visible' imports over 'visible' exports continued to be paid for in services—shipping, banking, insurance, and by the interest on British capital invested abroad. This investment was taking place, especially after 1850, at an increasing rate. It is hardly possible to give an accurate estimate, but, all in all, the total seems to have been more than £800,000,000 in 1870; over half of this sum was in European and United States government bonds, and much of the remainder in railways. Without such an outflow of capital there would have been less employment for British and Irish emigrants in the colonies and the United States, and the introduction into India of western techniques and modes of communication would have lagged as much as in China or the Ottoman Empire. On the other hand one may ask whether the working class would have gained if less money had been invested abroad and more spent on social betterment at home. The question is an academic one, since opinion in Great Britain did not consider the alternatives of foreign or domestic investment from the point of view of welfare. The state did not 'take sides' in this matter. It maintained, with general approval, a rigid economy in its own expenditure. Throughout the period of expansion between 1850 and 1870 the revenues employed to meet the cost of government, justice, and defence, and the service of the debt, rose only from about £57,500,000 to about £75,000,000. The cost in money of the Crimean war was slightly less than the revenue of 1856. In times of economic depression, governments tried to spend less. A few erratic thinkers who stumbled on different views had little influence or, like Attwood, misinterpreted their own discoveries.

It is again not easy to allocate the increasing national income between different classes. The amount of wages divided into the number of wage-earners shows a rise of about 50 per cent. in money wages between 1850 and 1870. Trades which were badly paid in 1850 gained more than trades in which the rate of wages already allowed a fair standard of living. If these occupations underpaid in 1850 were excluded, the rise for the average working man would probably have been about 30 per cent. On the other hand the cost of living also rose, and until 1865 the rise in prices was a little greater than the rise in wages.

After 1865 wages increased at a higher rate than prices, and in
1870 most working-class families were absolutely as well as
relatively better off by about 10 per cent. than in 1850.[1] The
agricultural labourers had a slightly smaller increase in wages,
but their cost of living probably increased less than that of the
urban workers. If the improvements in the amenities of towns,
in conditions of public health, and in hours of labour are taken
into account, the common people of Great Britain were certainly in a happier position. The risks of unemployment had
changed little, but the numbers displaced by new machinery
and new processes had diminished, and, in any case, the working
class was better equipped to meet changes in technique. There
were fewer illiterates, and a smaller proportion of people in
receipt of poor-relief.[2] The deposits in the savings banks of the
country rose from under £30,000,000 in 1850 to £53,000,000 in
1870. These deposits represented the savings of the middle as
well as the working classes, but they were spread over a very
wide area. The post office savings bank, established in 1861,[3]
dealt at the end of 1862 with 180,000 accounts representing
nearly £1,750,000. In the years 1869–74 there was an average of
1,373,000 depositors, with accounts amounting to £18,000,000.

The improvements in conditions of labour between 1850 and
1870 were beyond question. Most branches of the textile trades
had obtained a working day of ten and a half hours and a working week of sixty hours, with a Saturday afternoon holiday; the
worst scandals of children's and women's labour in coal-mines
had been remedied, but in the year of the Great Exhibition
there were no legal restrictions upon the hours of employment
of adult men, and no legislation affecting the hours of any
workers outside the textile and coal-mining industries. For the
next twenty years parliament was unwilling to lay down any
limits to the working hours of men, though it was realized that
in many industries the protection of women and children also

---

[1] There was an improvement of about 60–70 per cent. between 1870 and 1914,
excluding free social services.

[2] Between 1850 and 1859 the number of paupers was 48 per 1,000 in England
and Wales. There was an increase during and after the bad years of the cotton
famine, but the figure fell in the period 1870–9 to 34 per 1,000.

[3] Gladstone fixed the rate of interest on deposit accounts at $2\frac{1}{2}$ per cent. because
consols, which were below par in 1861, brought a return of 3 per cent. The depositors' money could thus be re-invested, and the difference in the rates of interest
paid for the cost of management. These savings came mainly from the working and
lower middle classes, and from the children of all classes.

brought shorter hours for all workers. Even in the case of women and children public opinion was curiously slow in asking for information, and assumed that the worst evils of the industrial system occurred in mines and factories. Only a minority of the men, women, and children in industrial employment worked in coal-mines and mills or in establishments known to the law as factories. There was no reason to suppose that conditions were better outside these new establishments. On the other hand the fatalism of earlier years had disappeared; factory acts had not ruined the cotton industry, and after 1850 manufacturers were inclined to reverse Nassau Senior's argument that the profits of a manufacturing business were made in the last hour of the day's work. It appeared more probable that, if the minds and bodies of the workpeople were overtaxed, the amount of spoiled and defective work done in the last hour brought not profit but loss. This view could be pushed a stage farther. If children were stunted and broken in the first years of a premature working life, if men and women were overtired day in day out, what would happen to the labouring classes of Great Britain? How could the country compete with foreign rivals if the quality and skill of English labour deteriorated? There was also no doubt about the effectiveness of legislative interference. Unscrupulous employers might add five minutes here or there to the day's work in a mill, but gross evasions of the law were detected. It was no less clear that a well-drafted law, devised after expert inquiry and carried into effect by official inspectors, was the only effective means of securing reform and of protecting the good employer and his workpeople against abuse.[1]

The first industries to be dealt with were those allied to the textile group, or near to them in locality. The workers in these allied trades, or in areas where the experience of the cotton mills was well known, wanted to share the benefits of regulation, and the textile manufacturers were not unwilling that other industries should be treated to a dose of inspection and control. About 1853 the operatives in the bleaching and dyeing industries agitated for a sixty-hour week. The employers pointed out that they were in a different position from the cotton-manufacturers, who bought their own raw material and determined their own rate of production. The bleachers and dyers worked for cloth-merchants who were themselves bound under con-

[1] For earlier factory legislation, see above pp. 12–13 and 148–55.

tract; the dispatch of orders was seasonal, and the bleaching and dyeing trade suffered from an alternation of heavy and slack times which made regulation difficult. There was an answer to this argument. If the merchants knew that their orders could not be carried out unless they gave longer notice, they would adjust their contracts accordingly. Most employers recognized the force of this answer, and were ready to accept a regulation of hours. Hence there was little opposition in 1860 to the inclusion of women and children employed in these trades under the protection of the factory acts. During the parliamentary debates on the subject Graham, Roebuck, and Brougham admitted that they had changed their opinions. The change of opinion was shown in ways characteristic of the men. Graham said plainly that he had been wrong in thinking that the factory acts would have a bad effect upon trade, and that he wanted to make amends for his earlier votes. Roebuck turned round to attack the employers whom he had defended. Brougham did not acknowledge that he had made a wrong forecast, but told the house of lords that he 'had been unable to dismiss from his mind the evidence brought forward by the committees of inquiry'. Four years later Gladstone, who had never gone the whole distance with Ashley, announced his conversion to protective legislation in one of his embossed sentences: 'It is an interference, as to which it may be said that the Legislature is now almost unanimous with respect to the necessity which existed for undertaking it, and with respect to the beneficial effect it has produced both in mitigating human suffering, and in attaching important classes of the community to Parliament and the Government.'[1]

In 1861 the debate on the inclusion of lace-factories in the protected industries showed this change in opinion even more clearly. The bill laid before the house allowed work on Saturdays until 4.30 p.m. and fixed at eleven the age-limit for part-time workers. The commons raised the age-limit to thirteen and decided that the half-holiday should begin at 2.30 p.m. In 1861 Shaftesbury obtained a general commission of inquiry into the employment of children in trades and manufactures. This commission sat for five years, and investigated a large number of trades. It would be difficult to exaggerate the burden of human suffering which it brought to light. The first report,

[1] Quoted in J. L. and B. Hammond, *Lord Shaftesbury*, p. 151.

published in 1863, dealt with the work of children in the potteries. There was the familiar story of the employment of little boys and girls of six, seven, or eight in unhealthy conditions for very long hours. The grim evidence of doctors may be summed up in the words that 'each successive generation of potters becomes more dwarfed and less robust than the preceding one'. Even before the publication of the report the masters themselves asked for legislation. Conditions were worse in the lucifer-match industry, since the workers tended to develop 'phossy jaw' (necrosis of the jawbone). These and other trades were dealt with in an act of 1864. This act extended the definition of a factory to 'any place in which persons work for hire' in the trades concerned. The definition was widened in 1867 to cover small workshops, foundries, glass factories, and blast furnaces. The experience of the earlier acts and the volume of information collected by the commission of inquiry and the factory inspectors showed the need for greater flexibility and comprehension in factory legislation. Parliament was learning to make special rules for 'dangerous trades', and to require something more than a limitation of hours. Another act of 1867 went a stage farther in regulating the conditions of industries not carried on in factories by defining a workshop as 'any room or place whatever, whether in the open air or under cover, in which any handicraft is carried on by any child, young person, or woman, and to which and over which the person by whom such child, young person, or woman is employed has the right of access or control'. The term 'employed' meant 'occupied in any handicraft, whether for wages or not, under a master or under a parent', and therefore included home industry.

These laws were not accepted, like the act of 1844, as a leap in the dark, but as a matter of decency and common sense. *The Times* noted in March 1867 that 'to employ women and children unduly is simply to run into debt with Nature', and that 'the old system of unrestricted freedom' merely 'tempted men to indulge in alternate fits of idleness and excessive labour. They would be drunk for two days at the beginning of the week and would then endeavour to recover their lost wages, not only by overworking themselves during the remainder of the week, but by compelling their wives and children to work unreasonable hours'.[1] Drunkenness as a habit, on working-class wages in

[1] *The Times*, 4 Mar. 1867. Quoted in Hutchins and Harrison, p. 167.

the early years of the nineteenth century, was less universal than the readers of *The Times* in 1867 might believe; the important point was that, at last, public opinion was becoming less frightened of interfering directly with the 'liberty' of the adult workman. There was ample room for improvement in hours and conditions of work and in the wages even of the best-paid workers. The large class of 'general labourers' was still unorganized and unprotected; lowest of all, numbers of 'sweated workers', hardly known to the 'decent poor', lived in permanent misery. Their turn was not to come for a good many years; it was nearer, not merely in time but in the intentions of the public, than it had been in 1815 or in 1850.

The development of trade-union action between 1860 and 1870 also shows the results of a generation of reform. The older men alone could realize the improvement in wages and conditions of work since the hard days of chartism. There were still deep-seated grievances. The unions were still looked upon as dangerous combinations led by agitators and as a standing threat to public order and liberty. There was a good deal of jealousy between overlapping or competing trades, and, in their efforts to maintain standards continually threatened by technical change, economic depression, and the shift of demand, the unions were on guard against interlopers of their own class as well as against the tricks of capitalists. On the other hand the general softening of manners due to improved conditions of life and the spread of education had affected the ideas of working men. They took more care to keep the strike as a weapon in reserve, and to investigate alleged grievances before asking for redress. The failure of chartism had not turned English working men towards a more consistent and more developed theory of class antagonism and revolutionary thought. The writings of European revolutionaries, though composed to a great extent in London, had little influence upon the leaders of trade-unionism. The International Association of Working Men, which alarmed the governments of Europe in 1870, was founded in London in 1864;[1] most of the leading figures of the association were foreign exiles who had settled in London. Officials of the English

---

[1] The foundation of the First International was due more to political than to economic reasons. The association arose out of a visit of two French delegates to London in 1863 to arrange joint action by working men of different countries on behalf of the Polish rebels.

unions took part in the meetings and discussions; they knew little of continental conditions, and their collaboration did not go much beyond general sympathy. The London trades council refused even to use the association as an agency of communication with trade societies in other countries. A few of the smaller unions maintained a local terrorism, but the repudiation of violent and criminal methods by the larger associations had a greater effect upon public opinion. The unions were supported by men outside the working class. Although Frederic Harrison, Thomas Hughes, and A. J. Mundella had less imaginative insight and originality than Robert Owen, they understood more clearly the immediate issues upon which working men could enforce their claims. In 1869 Thomas Brassey, the son of the great railway builder, defended trade unions in the commons on the ground that they had lowered the cost of labour because they had improved the character of the labourer.

The increase in the size and resources of the unions had its effect upon the leaders. The amalgamated society of engineers was an insurance society on a large scale; Robert Applegarth,[1] secretary of the amalgamated society of carpenters and joiners from 1862 to 1871, wanted to give the trade unions a recognized and respectable place in national life. The secretaries of the large societies, with headquarters in London, worked together, and learned a good deal from the radicals of a different social class. In some respects they learned too much; the submerged elements in the working class might have gained more if the trade-union movement had been more revolutionary and less content with radical individualism. On the other hand a more pugnacious movement would have had less public support and probably fewer lasting gains. In the end the worst-paid trades did not lose by the cautious policy of the large and better-organized societies. The negotiation of agreements with

[1] Robert Applegarth (1834–1925), b. Hull, s. of a quartermaster in the navy; worked as an errand boy at the age of eleven, learned cabinet-making without regular apprenticeship; settled in Sheffield, 1852; emigrated to the U.S.A., 1855, but came back in 1856 owing to his wife's health; joined the Sheffield carpenters' union, and became the prime mover in the formation of the A.S.C.J.; stood for the London school board, and for parliament at Maidstone, 1870, but retired in favour of Sir J. Lubbock; member of the royal commission on the contagious diseases act, 1871; war correspondent for an American newspaper during part of the Franco-Prussian war; foreman, and ultimately owner, of a firm manufacturing engineering and diving apparatus.

employers for regulating wages gave the trade-union leaders considerable practical experience, and brought to the front men of administrative ability who were not merely nimble-witted platform orators; piece-work rates in the cotton industry, for example, were most complicated, and their settlement needed some knowledge of mathematics as well as of the technical questions of a highly specialized trade. The revival and extension of the miners' national association between 1858 and 1863, largely owing to the skill and work of Alexander Macdonald,[1] brought about the appointment of checkweighers to secure an independent control of the weight of coal hewn by each miner; for some time the mine-owners did their best to hinder the work of the checkweighers, but this fact made it necessary to appoint men who were reliable, acute, and of some education. These men soon became the leaders of unionism in every mining area.

The unions were also learning to break down the sectional and inter-trade suspicions which hampered their development. Between 1857 and 1867 trades councils were set up in large towns. The franchise act of 1867 gave votes to a large number of town artisans; the question of direct parliamentary action by trade-unionist members was now much less remote. In the same year the amendment of the law of master and servant brought a parliamentary success in a field curiously neglected at the time of the repeal of the combination laws. Hitherto breach of contract had been punishable with a fine in the case of employers, and imprisonment up to three months in the case of workmen. A justice of the peace could try these cases in his own house, and from his decision there was no appeal. In 1863 the Glasgow trades council invited other councils to work for a change in the law. It was pointed out that 10,339 cases came before the justices in a single year. In 1864 a conference of all trades was held in London to discuss the matter; two years later a parliamentary committee inquired into the law, and an act was passed in 1867 to enforce the hearing of cases in open court,

---

[1] Alexander Macdonald (1821–81), b. Airdrie, s. of a sailor who became a miner; went into the mines at the age of eight; saved money to go to Glasgow university, 1846, and continued to work as a miner in the long vacation; mine manager, 1850; opened a school at Airdrie, 1851–5; gave his whole time to the formation of the national union of miners, 1855–63; secretary of the union, 1863–81; obtained financial independence by good investments; M.P., 1874; served on the commission on the labour laws, and presented a minority report.

and before more than one justice. Henceforward fines or damages generally took the place of imprisonment.

On the other hand a number of outrages at Sheffield, for which some small local craft unions were held responsible, brought about a royal commission of inquiry which put all unions into a difficult position. Before this inquiry opened the magistrates at Bradford, supported on appeal by the judges of the high court, decided that the boilermakers' society could not proceed against a defaulting official because trade unions did not come within the scope of the friendly societies act of 1855 enabling registered associations to settle disputes in this way. If this decision remained valid, a union had no protection for its accumulated funds. Furthermore the ruling implied that trade-unionism was against public policy, since one of the reasons given by the court of queen's bench was that the boilermakers' union, though not a criminal association, was an association 'in restraint of trade'. The leaders of the large unions at once held a conference in London which continued more or less in permanent session. The most important innovation, however, at this time, was a proposal by the Manchester and Salford Trades Council for an annual trades congress. The first of such congresses met at Manchester in June 1868. The idea of the promoters was that the congress should be not so much an instrument for economic bargaining as a meeting, on the lines of the British Association and the Social Science Association, where trade unionists could discuss their affairs and interests. The facts of the situation, and the wishes of most trade unionists were to lead to developments far beyond this original conception. A second congress was held in Birmingham in 1869, and a third in London in 1871. At this London meeting the congress took the decisive step of appointing a parliamentary committee.[1]

---

[1] The London Trades Council was formed in 1860 after a builders' lock-out in 1859 when other unions had come to the financial help of the building workers. Until 1871 there was intermittent friction between the London Council and the northern and midland associations largely owing to the distrust felt by the leaders of the older and established unions for one George Potter. Potter (1832–93), a carpenter by trade, had become prominent during the building dispute. In 1861 he founded a paper, *The Beehive*, which for a short time had a considerable influence on working-class opinion. Potter was an aggressive, flamboyant orator, exhibitionist by temperament and opportunist in opinion. He headed a deputation of working men in 1864 to welcome Garibaldi on the latter's visit to London, and rode on horseback at the side of Garibaldi's carriage. He made his peace with the London leaders—more or less on terms of surrender—in 1871.

Meanwhile the commission of inquiry widened its scope to include a general examination of unionist activities, and handed over the Sheffield cases to a special committee of investigation. In spite of the change of public opinion towards trade unions, there was likely to be a temporary but sharp reaction against them. The change in the status of unions had come about in the lifetime of many employers who tended to judge them by their past history. To the smaller masters unable to meet demands for higher wages the constant pressure of the unions was often irritating and at times threatening. It was therefore to be expected that every employer who disliked and feared the power of organized labour would try to persuade the commission that the unions were illiberal, exclusive, and tyrannical. The larger societies had no difficulty in showing that they had nothing to do with outrages, that they did as much to discourage strikes as to organize them, and that, in their insurance and benefit arrangements, they were providing services of value to the community. The majority of the commission recognized these facts, and suggested that henceforward no combination should be prosecuted for 'restraint of trade' unless its action involved breach of contract or refusal to work with any particular person. On the other hand they proposed to allow the privilege of registration as a friendly society only to associations which did not attempt restrictive measures such as limiting the number of apprentices or the use of machinery in the trades with which they were concerned. A minority report, signed by Frederic Harrison, Thomas Hughes, and Lord Lichfield, was more favourable to the unions, and put forward as a guiding principle that no act by a combination of men should be regarded as criminal if it could be done legally by one man. Harrison drafted a bill which allowed trade unions to be registered as friendly societies, and at the same time retained for the unions the exceptional legal position which prevented them from being sued in their corporate capacity. Without the former privilege, the funds of the unions were insecure; without the latter, they were liable to attack by any one who thought himself wrongfully excluded from membership.

The liberal government accepted Harrison's proposals, after a good deal of hesitation; they added a clause providing for the severe punishment of persons using violent threats of molestation against employers or workmen. The interpretation given to 'molestation' by the courts might include ordinary picketing, and from 1871 to 1875 the unions agitated against this clause in the law. They were not in an easy position, because they were not and could not be logical in their demands. They were asking, ostensibly, that every workman should be free to bargain for the sale of his labour as he thought fit, and according to his interest; but his interest lay, according to the unions, in giving up his separate power and accepting the principle of collective negotiation and agreement. If collective bargaining were to be an effective weapon, it must be accepted as such by a majority of the workmen in any trade. Thus the unions really wanted to compel all workmen to accept the principle of collective bargaining, and to coerce a minority who might refuse. Coercion might not imply physical violence; it was none the less a denial of free choice. Fortunately the practical solution of this problem was not alarming to a people accustomed to the principle of majority rule, and, in 1875, a conservative government accepted the facts, recognized peaceful picketing as legal, and safeguarded the essential features of collective bargaining while leaving the ordinary criminal law to deal with acts of violence or physical intimidation.

After the failure of the co-operative movement as a means of transforming the economic structure of society, the supporters of co-operation as a principle limited themselves to doing what they could within the existing framework of capitalist production and exchange. The society founded in Lancashire in 1844 and known as the 'Rochdale Pioneers' was a transitional stage in this development. The promoters did not give up hope of realizing Owen's ideas; at the same time they were practical enough to invent the system of returning profits to members of their society according to the amounts of purchases made. This new movement appealed to large numbers of working-class families; wages were beginning to rise above a bare subsistence-level, and with an increase in prosperity working men had every inducement to save, including the threat of unemployment and the workhouse. The co-operative profit-sharing societies provided a convenient means of making small savings; their difficulties came when they began to attempt production as well as distribution. After a good many failures, the Rochdale system was applied to a wholesale co-operative producing society of which the retailing associations were members, and from which they received dividends in proportion to their purchases. Meanwhile, in addition to the benefits conferred by trade unions as friendly societies, there was a great extension of benefit organizations of a non-political character. The Oddfellows' society was reorganized in 1833, the Foresters in 1834. Better management and a clearer understanding of the actuarial side of their business gave these societies a stability which earlier organizations had lacked. The establishment of a registrar of friendly societies[1] in 1846 was also a protection against fraud and mismanagement.

Working men formed associations to defend and raise the standard of life of their members. Associations of professional men had a similar aim, and a similar result in increasing the part and influence of organized and representative bodies in the national life. The professional organizations developed a greater sense of responsibility than the trade unions towards the 'consumer'. Their members received higher pay than working men, and had less cause to be discontented with the existing regime of society. They were not resisting employers whose interests appeared to be in direct economic conflict with their own. The older professions inherited a form of organization which was not based primarily upon profit-seeking. Their technique was generally of a highly specialized kind, and required a longer course of training than apprenticeship to a trade. Even in cases where the technique was not always particularly advanced, the professional man held a position of trust and was anxious to safeguard the public as well as his colleagues against dishonest and untrained interlopers.

Each of the three professions already organized in 1815 had taken care to introduce reforms. The clergy were forbidden pluralism and non-residence; patronage was bestowed with a stronger sense of responsibility, and the standard of clerical duty had been raised. The legal profession had rid itself of a great deal of formalism and pedantry. The procedure of the courts had been simplified,[2] and, with the establishment of the Council of Legal Education[3] in 1852 by the four inns of court, the lawyers

---

[1] J. Tidd Pratt, who held the office until 1870, was an extremely wise counsellor to the societies.   [2] See above, pp. 469-73, for the reform of the civil and criminal law.

[3] The council, which was partly the result of an inquiry ordered in 1846 by the house of commons into the question of legal education, provided lectures and held examinations, though the latter were not compulsory before 1872. Suggestions were made for the foundation of a legal university in London.

had at last taken in hand the reform of legal education. The solicitors[1] had already begun to improve the education of members of their profession. The Law Society, incorporated in 1831, made provision for lectures in 1833; three years later the judges of the common-law courts agreed to require all candidates for admission as attorneys to pass a written examination in common law. In 1837 a similar rule was applied to solicitors at the court of chancery. In 1843 the Law Society was authorized to keep a register of solicitors.

In the medical profession the rise of the general practitioner and the development of advanced studies by a few outstanding physicians and surgeons had raised the standards of knowledge and training. Sir Henry Acland, for example, remodelled the Oxford medical course in order to give students general instruction in science before they began practical work in hospitals. The British Medical Association was founded in 1854; a few years later, as the result of parliamentary inquiry, the medical act of 1858 created a general council of medical education and registration for the United Kingdom. This council was a new type of organization entrusted with the performance of important social functions under the supervision of the state. The council had powers to keep a register of qualified practitioners, to approve the bodies giving these qualifications, and to bring before the privy council cases in which the licensing bodies were not insisting upon a proper examination or previous course of study.[2]

Meanwhile certain branches of medicine and surgery had become specialized. Ophthalmology was a distinct field of inquiry as early as 1804; the invention of the ophthalmoscope, the use of type for testing the sight and of astigmatic lenses for correcting defects of vision gave the subject a new importance after 1850. Orthopaedic and aural surgery were treated as special branches of investigation about 1830, laryngology about 1860. The stethoscope, invented about 1819, came into general use for auscultation a few years later, and, together with percussion,

[1] The old distinction between 'attorneys' practising in the common law courts and 'solicitors' practising in the court of chancery was losing its meaning; in the nineteenth century attorneys were generally admitted also as solicitors. After 1873 the term 'solicitor' was used to cover both branches of the profession.

[2] In 1860 an adulteration of food and drink act provided for the first time in the nineteenth century some protection against a serious danger to health. The campaign for legal measures against the evils of adulteration was greatly assisted by the publicity given to the facts in the medical journal *The Lancet*.

led to improved methods of diagnosis. The clinical thermo-
meter had been invented in 1797, but few doctors had taken
advantage of it. It was reintroduced in 1844, but again was not
in common use until more than twenty years later. An Edinburgh doctor, Alexander Wood, invented the hypodermic
syringe in 1855.

The greatest advance was made in surgery. In 1844 W. T. G.
Morton, an American dentist, showed the value of ether as an
anaesthetic; a year later James Simpson tried it in obstetrical
operations at Edinburgh. Within a few months after these
experiments Simpson adopted chloroform, which Liebig had
discovered in 1832. Chloroform brought an entirely new sur-
gical technique. Speed became of less importance; the shock to
the patient was less severe, and surgeons and patients alike were
willing to try more intricate and drastic operations. In spite of
the immense improvement resulting from the use of anaesthetics,
the mortality of patients continued to be high owing to the
inflammation and morbid affections of wounds. Joseph Lister
(1827–1912), working on the results obtained by Pasteur, came to
the conclusion that the cause of the trouble lay in germs carried
in unfiltered air on the operators' hands. Lister became professor
of surgery at Glasgow in 1861; within the next two decades he
had made antiseptic treatment an essential feature of surgery.

Dentistry, as distinct from mere tooth-drawing, developed as
a branch of scientific surgery in the latter years of the eighteenth
century; the duchess of York had a surgeon dentist in 1808, but
even in 1838 it was possible to remark that dentistry 'was growing into a profession'. The dentists were trying to raise the
status of their work, and to protect the public from quackery.
For a long time they had to fight the conservatism of the surgeons; they found an able leader in Sir John Tomes (1815–95),
who was apprenticed to an apothecary at Evesham in 1831 and
specialized in dentistry. In 1858 Tomes persuaded the College
of Surgeons to grant special licences in dentistry; in the same
year he was one of the founders of the Dental Hospital.

The use of anaesthetics and the rise of antiseptic surgery, and
the realization that cleanliness was essential to health, made it
necessary to train nurses and to secure women with high professional standards; public opinion was no longer willing to tolerate
the employment of characters like Dickens's Mrs. Gamp. At the
same time the revival of sisterhoods devoted to medical and

social work—one of the results of the Oxford movement—gave a new position to nursing. In 1840 Mrs. Elizabeth Fry[1] took part in founding an institute of nursing in connexion with Guy's hospital; the institute was modelled on the Prussian establishment at Kaiserswerth, which was itself the result of an impression made by Mrs. Fry's work upon a German pastor. The horrors of the Crimean war hospitals and the work of Miss Nightingale brought the question of nursing before public opinion. Miss Nightingale was trained at Kaiserswerth; after the Crimean war she was able to found a home and school for nurses at St. Thomas's hospital.

Parliament used the associations of professional men as an indirect method of raising and controlling the standards of work done by them for the community. It was also necessary to raise the standard of efficiency in the departments of state, and to make sure that the taxpayer obtained as good a return for public expenditure on administration as individuals obtained from fees paid to professional men. In 1853 a strong commission, including Sir Stafford Northcote and Sir Charles Trevelyan, reported in favour of choosing civil servants in the higher grades by examination.[2] The commission suggested that this examination should be of a literary kind, and on subjects studied at the universities. They also recommended that greater care should be taken in the government departments to distinguish between work of a routine character and work which required high intellectual attainments. The report met with the usual type of objection. It was said that clever men were not necessarily trustworthy; that an examination was not a good test of 'character'; that candidates of ability would not care to sit for an examination. On other grounds it was still doubted whether a cabinet could keep the allegiance of a party without the use of patronage. Public opinion, however, supported the report and three civil service commissioners were appointed in 1855 to conduct examinations. The heads of departments were not bound to fill vacancies with candidates who had passed the examination, but no civil servant appointed after 1859 could

---

[1] See above, p. 467.

[2] The report noted (with some exaggeration) that 'those whose abilities do not warrant an expectation that they will succeed in the open professions . . . and those whom indolence of temperament or physical infirmities unfit for active exertions, are placed in the Civil Service, where they may obtain an honourable livelihood with little labour, and with no risk.'

qualify for a pension unless he had a certificate from the civil service commissioners. The examination was of a qualifying kind until 1860; in this year real though limited competition was allowed, and after 1870 the examination was open to all candidates who applied to sit for it.[1]

The increase in the number and variety of professions changed the character of middle-class life, and did more than any other feature of the time to bring about a change in the position of the landed aristocracy. The landed class maintained its old social prestige. County society was still closed to most professional men, though it was more easily accessible to rich industrialists who bought land. These *nouveaux riches* might be the butt of their contemporaries; their children were soon absorbed into the upper class. There was no great increase in the peerage. In 1870, excluding the bishops and the representative peers, some 470 names were on the roll of the house of lords. Most of the new peers were whigs or liberals. Grey made forty-three peers, Melbourne fifty-two, Peel only five between 1841 and 1846.[2] As the majority of them were among the purchasers of estates the upper house remained predominantly a house of hereditary landlords, renewed by the addition of men eminent in politics, law, diplomacy, and the fighting services. Until Gladstone's cabinet of 1886 no administration contained less than seven peers or sons of peers, but the decline of direct and indirect aristocratic influence was already seen in local government. The old ruling class was being edged out in the country, and, except for occasional honours, had no place in the great towns. On the other hand the gibe that government by the middle class meant government by small shopkeepers had already lost its force. The essential fact lay in the control of technical knowledge by the professional members of the middle class; there was no longer any need of aristocratic direction, and, unless they joined the professional classes, the upper class had little or nothing to contribute to the management of the common affairs of a highly organized society. It is also important to notice that

[1] The control of departmental expenditure became stricter about this time. The report of a select committee on public moneys in 1857 was followed in 1861 by the establishment of the committee on public accounts for the purpose of reviewing expenditures; the exchequer and audit act of 1866 set up a general supervision of all spending of public money.

[2] These figures include legal appointments and grants of higher rank in the peerage.

in this age of capitalism an increasing amount of the administrative and regulating work of society was being done by methods not strictly or entirely capitalistic. The professional organizations allowed competition and high differential profits; but competition was limited, and in many cases charges were regulated and a standard of service and code of behaviour laid down and enforced.

The growth of professional technique lessened the distinction between the middle and upper classes from the point of view of general culture. A greater cultural and aesthetic value was put upon technical knowledge as such; a higher degree of education was necessary for acquiring the new technical qualifications, and the exercise of these qualifications had a broadening effect. The problems of society, reflected as always in literary and artistic movements, were problems more familiar to the professional than to the upper class. Clubs and dining societies were founded in most of the large provincial towns for the discussion of political, literary, and social questions; as early as 1850 Leeds had a club of this kind for women, though they met, not for dinner, but for tea.[1] The rise in the circulation and fall in the price of newspapers had a similar effect upon the formation of public opinion.[2] The habits of professional work also brought a much greater equality of manners. Newman's description of a gentleman and Matthew Arnold's attacks upon *bourgeois* philistinism were more widely read among the middle than among the upper classes. Moreover the daily life of the middle classes and, to some extent, of the poor was less harassed by minor discomforts and inelegances than a century earlier. It

---

[1] In spite of Cobbett's view of tea-drinking as a 'destroyer of health...a debaucher of youth, and a maker of misery for old age', the consumption of tea per head increased steadily after about 1842. The average for the years 1858–62 was double that of the years 1838–42. About the middle of the century Indian tea began to take the lead over China tea in British taste.

[2] The circulation of *The Times* was 6,000–7,000 in 1817, 10,000 in 1834, 18,500 in 1840, 40,000 in 1851, and 70,000 in 1861. The price fell from 7*d.* in 1815 to 5*d.* in 1836, 4*d.* in 1855, and 3*d.* in 1861. In 1861 the *Morning Advertiser* had a circulation of about 5,000, the *Daily News* 6,000, the *Standard* (morning and evening) 130,000, the *Telegraph* (evening) 150,000. *Reynolds's Weekly* sold 350,000 copies, many in the manufacturing districts, and the *Morning Post* 4,500. The *Illustrated London News* first appeared in 1842, though few of its illustrations were taken from life. Other papers, e.g. the *Observer*, had occasional illustrations, mainly of royal functions. The *Sunday Times* published a picture of the house of commons after the fire of 1834. *Punch or the London Charivari* appeared in 1840 on the lines of the French satirical paper, *Charivari*, and owed its success to two cartoonists of great talent, John Leech (1817–64) and Richard Doyle (1824–83).

is scarcely possible to exaggerate the social effect of the many inventions which made life less troublesome for persons of moderate means; inventions and discoveries such as sulphur and phosphorus matches,[1] paraffin oil,[2] cheap soap, sewing-machines, macintoshes. The middle classes could afford sea-side holidays; trips by train or boat to Gravesend or Margate were within the purse of so many Londoners that already there was a distinction between the more and the less crowded watering places. The railways opened up cheap continental travel. After the opening of the Mont Cenis tunnel (1871) Turin was only 33 hours' journey from London. Already in 1836 Murray began to publish his series of guide books to foreign countries. Thomas Cook, who had organized cheap excursions for the Midland railway in 1845 and sold hotel coupons in 1846, arranged a special trip from Leicester to Paris in 1855. The Great Exhibition 1851 and the Paris Exhibition of 1861 encouraged the habit of excursions, and before 1870 Cook's Swiss and Italian excursions, 'including a good deal of the Cockney element', were a feature of the summer.[3]

Music and the theatre attracted larger audiences in London and in the provinces. The Monday popular concerts in St. James's Hall were started in 1859; cheap editions of musical scores were common after 1844, and about ten years later the invention of valves for brass instruments encouraged the formation of brass bands which did much for musical education. Attempts were made in many places to provide cheap concerts for the working class. Unfortunately these concerts, like the mechanics' institutes of a generation earlier, did not attract the people for whom they were intended. A few gentlemen of Leeds formed a 'Rational Recreation Society' in 1853 to provide concerts on Saturday evenings. The prices charged ranged from 3d. to 1s. a seat, but the cheapest seats did not have the

[1] In 1827 a druggist of Stockton invented a sulphur match which he named a 'congreve', after Sir William Congreve, the inventor of a rocket. A few years later 'promethcans' and 'lucifers' took their place, and in 1833 phosphorus matches were imported from Germany. Browning's mention of matches in 1845 is one of the early examples of the introduction of a recent and humble scientific invention into poetry. ('The quick, sharp scratch | and blue spurt of a lighted match', *Meeting at Night*.)

[2] Petroleum was used for lighting about 1847, and imports from the United States became of importance soon after 1860.

[3] A report on the effect of Cook's tours was made, at Dickens's suggestion, for *All the Year Round*. See *Early Victorian England*, ed. G. M. Young, ii. 311-12.

largest sale, and a writer on the education of the working classes in Leeds[1] admitted in 1860 that 'the taste for good and refined music . . . has not yet reached the operative classes to any considerable extent, and it may be doubted whether the attendance at the lowest places of entertainment has been appreciably diminished. When there is a circus, however, or any popular spectacular entertainment, the beerhouse keepers are loud in their complaints of the serious diminution in their receipts.'[2]

The theatre in London had gained from the repeal of the restrictive licensing regulations, but there were still many difficulties in the way of producing good plays which would fill a house. The prejudices against the type of 'spectacular entertainments' were not altogether ill founded. On the other hand for nearly twenty years after 1844 Samuel Phelps and Mrs. Warner maintained a high standard of production, plays, and acting at Sadler's Wells theatre, and between 1850 and 1857 Charles Kean and his wife played Shakespeare and attempted to introduce exact scholarship in scenery and costume at the Princess's Theatre in Oxford Street. The queen's patronage of the theatre had a great effect upon changing the attitude of public opinion towards the stage. In 1848 professional actors and actresses appeared for the first time in the royal theatricals at Windsor castle during the Christmas festival. The queen and the royal family went to plays in London, and not merely to the opera; the upper and middle classes followed their example. One important result was an improvement in the comfort of theatres; the rowdier spectators went away to the music-halls and less reputable entertainments, while the theatres began to increase the number of seats of fair price for the well-to-do middle classes. The new type of theatre-goer wanted a quieter type of acting and greater realism. Ellen Terry made her first appearance on the stage as a child in 1856, and in the next decade Robertson's[3] plays set a new standard of theatrical

---

[1] J. Hole, 'Light, More Light.' On the present state of education amongst the working classes of Leeds, and how it can be improved. 1860.

[2] The beerhouse keepers still did far too large a trade, but drunkenness was much less common among all classes than in 1815 and drunken behaviour less easily condoned.

[3] T. W. Robertson (1829–71), s. of an actor, b. Newark; first appeared on the stage in 1834; produced his first play 1851; David Garrick (1864), Society (1865), and Caste (1867) were his most popular works.

interpretation, though they were somewhat derided at first as the 'teacup and saucer school'.

The change in the character of outdoor sports shows the softening of manners which had taken place since 1815; it is also an interesting example of the indirect effect of administrative improvement and organization. Sports were less haphazard partly because people became accustomed to higher standards of organization in their work, and therefore applied these standards to their recreation. The cruel and demoralizing entertainments of the eighteenth century were disappearing. Cock-fighting had ceased to be a gentleman's amusement even before the first reform bill; in 1870 it was generally discredited among decent people, though it still survived in low company of every class. Bear-baiting and bull-baiting were forbidden by law in 1833 and 1835.[1] The old prize ring went out with, or soon after, the Regency, though an occasional fight still stirred public curiosity. Boxing-gloves, or muffles, were already in use at the beginning of the nineteenth century.

Hunting had become more elaborate, and therefore more expensive, in the early years of the century; its traditions were stereotyped, and there was already a good deal of conscious snobbery about them. Shooting had changed more rapidly with the improvement in guns, though, at all events for partridge-shooting, conditions were less easy because the stubble was shorter. Grouse-driving began about 1840. Horse-racing, which had declined during the French wars, had a great revival after 1815. The classic races—the St. Leger, Derby, and Oaks —were established before this time, and annual meetings were held at Goodwood. The Ascot meeting was a familiar event before the end of the eighteenth century; the race for the gold cup[2] was first held in 1807. Steeplechasing on regular courses was also popular, though the Grand National at Aintree was not run before 1839. There was less organized betting off the course, and far less reporting of race-meetings, than in the later years of the nineteenth century, but the lack of proper control and supervision allowed a great deal more fraud. Lord George Bentinck did much to clear away the worst abuses, and public opinion

[1] See above, p. 470.
[2] Between 1845 and 1853 the cup was presented by the emperor of Russia, and known as the emperor's cup. In the first year of the Crimean war the cup took its modern name.

supported his work. The development of handicap races added much to the interest of racing.[1]

The change in manners was hardly less important in cricket, already in 1815 a national game. Cricket in the first half of the century was a rough and often violent game, played on grounds which made the long-stop the most important man in the field. Popular matches were associated with betting and rough crowds. The M.C.C. established themselves as the leading club early in the nineteenth century; Lord's ground occupied its present site in 1827, but the rules of the game were still uncertain. Bats had a sweeping curve at their base in 1815, and did not take their present shape until some ten years later. Round-arm, or over-hand, bowling began about 1830; for the next forty years old-fashioned cricketers regarded it with suspicion. The development of the game owed a great deal to two teams which toured the country: the amateur club of I Zingari, founded in 1845, and an All-England team, mainly professional, which began to play exhibition matches in 1846. The rise of the first-class amateur was the most novel feature of cricket. The family of which W. G. Grace was the best-known member is an example of the spread of games to the middle classes. This development was the result of the growing importance of organized games at the old and new public schools. The larger schools began to hire professional cricket coaches; the increase in the number of reasonably good amateur players led to the formation of many clubs, which continued, and extended, the seriousness and even moral fervour about games which boys were beginning to acquire at school.[2]

Football had never been a game regularly and formally organized except in a few schools, where the rules were a matter of local tradition. Throughout the country there were local games played on Shrove Tuesday, often in the streets of towns —a custom which lingered on into the twentieth century.[3] The game spread in the schools, and as more boys left school with a common set of rules, football clubs became possible. The

[1] The Cesarewitch and Cambridgeshire races at Newmarket were begun in 1839, the City and Suburban in 1851, and the Lincoln in 1853. The Thousand and Two Thousand Guineas at Newmarket date from 1809.

[2] The first recorded use of the phrase 'it isn't cricket', with a moral connotation, occurs in 1900 (*O.E.D.*).

[3] In the writer's own childhood, a game of this kind was played in the high street of Dorking, only twenty-four miles from London.

volunteer movement, which brought numbers of young men together, had the incidental result of encouraging matches; in 1863 the Football Association was founded as a regulating body. 'Association' football was played by most of the members, but the Rugby game, introduced by schoolmasters to other schools, kept its popularity among public schoolboys, and in 1871 a separate Rugby Union was formed. Neither game was professionalized in 1870, but, after the establishment of the competition for the English cup in 1871, first-class 'association' football began to attract large 'gates' and the leading clubs found it worth while to employ full-time players; though, for every important professional club, there were scores of small amateur clubs, and an even larger number of games played on pieces of waste or common land, while the attendances at the association games showed that the English working class had at last found a cheap and amusing way of spending Saturday afternoons. 'Athleticism' was a new word in 1870, but athletic sports, in their modern sense, had been revived before this time.[1]

The railways and improved roads had made possible these meetings in every sport, and were to allow an indefinite extension of inter-county or other competitions. It is also significant that an ancient sport was revived and a new game became fashionable in the twenty years after 1850, and that in each case women could take an equal part with men. Archery indeed had never died out as a sport, and the romantic movement had much to do with its revival. A great meeting at York in 1844 was the first of similar annual competitions in important centres. Croquet became popular since it was suited to the gardens of the more substantial middle-class householders. The game reached England about 1852 from the north of Ireland, where it seems to have been played in a French convent. It spread rapidly from the great country houses, and readers of *Alice in Wonderland* will remember that in 1865 every middle-class child might be expected to know the rules. Tennis, as a game played on lawns, was patented in 1874. Scotsmen in London had long played golf on Blackheath, but there were only two golf clubs south of the border, Hoylake and Westward Ho!; neither club

[1] The first Oxford and Cambridge sports meeting took place in 1864 and the A.A.A. was founded in 1866; athletic meetings were held at the Royal Military College, Sandhurst, in 1812, and at Woolwich and a few public schools in 1840.

was ten years old in 1870. Polo, a sport of the rich, was not introduced into England until 1869, though it was played a few years earlier by Englishmen in Calcutta and in the Punjab.

For leisure or work, for getting or spending, England was a better country in 1870 than in 1815. The scales were less weighted against the weak, against women and children, and against the poor. There was greater movement, and less of the fatalism of an earlier age. The public conscience was more instructed, and the content of liberty was being widened to include something more than freedom from political constraint. Taken in the large, the age from 1815 (and in some respects the age before 1815) was a period of reform, and justified a robust belief in progress. Yet England in 1871 was by no means an earthly paradise. The housing and conditions of life of the working class in town and country were still a disgrace to an age of plenty. The great productive powers discovered and set into operation during the course of a century were too often running to waste through lack of good planning and bold common sense. There was a certain levelling up of classes in the sense that the standards of all save the very poor had risen. The gulf between rich and poor was in some respects hardly as wide as in 1815; there was less fear on the one side, less violence on the other, but the fundamental distinction between the owners of property and the common man remained the great unsolved problem. Although the dividing line between capital and labour was not easy to draw, a far greater number of Englishmen than in 1815 belonged by occupation and surroundings to an industrial proletariat. In these circumstances it would be idle to talk of fraternity; Englishmen of different classes were unable to sit at the same table without a sense either of patronage or awkwardness. A few people believed that social justice could be secured only through revolution. An historian may perhaps find greater significance in the fact that political power was passing to a larger electorate, though little attempt had been made to fit the new electors for their responsibilities, and the people as a whole scarcely knew what they wanted.

If society in England had grave defects, they were equally serious dangers in the international situation. The political consequences of the industrialization of western and parts of central and northern Europe had been considered in too hopeful a light. It was supposed that an increase in wealth would mean an increase of goodwill, and that the exploitation of the markets of the world would bring an interlocking and interdependence of interests necessarily peaceful in kind. When there was so much more to divide, there would be fewer quarrels about the division. These high hopes were disappointed. The transition from the rationalization of the acts and aims of individuals to the harmonizing of these countless separate purposes was far more difficult than the work of liberating private enterprise from traditional control. The transition in the international sphere was even more complicated; the obstacle of national sovereignty blocked the way, and, in the course of the nineteenth century, nationalism increased in force and in unreason.

In the international sphere the extension of markets did not mean an improvement in the relations between states; an increase in the value of the prizes to be won brought greater covetousness and more intense competition. Moreover it was possible to use the new productive resources, and every new instrument and invention, to resist the social and political changes which, logically, they implied. The failure of political liberalism in central Europe left the way open for the unification of Germany in the interest of the class least affected in its habits of thought and scale of values by the 'age of reform' and, ultimately, put the control of the surplus wealth created by the labours of a great nation into the hands of a backward, feudal, land-owning, and military caste which never understood the 'living logic' of industrialism and refused to accept the adjustments of traditional values required of it. Such a 'return of the past' was a European calamity on a scale so vast that its meaning could not be realized at the time, and Englishmen went about their affairs without comprehending more than the most obvious, and often the least significant, political effects of the rise of Bismarck, Prussia, and Germany. In any case the future of Great Britain lay in the hands of the children to whom, at last some measure of training was being given on a generous scale. If these children listened to the stories of their fathers and grandfathers, they heard of an England upon which they were not likely to look back with regret; few people born in 1850 would have chosen, even upon a slight knowledge of the facts, to have been born half a century earlier. Few people growing up to manhood in 1870 could feel altogether in despair of their country. Census commissioners are not given to fine writing; the writers of the census report in 1871, surveying the increasing numbers, increasing well-being, and far-reaching achievements of the people of England, felt justified in quoting the words of Milton: 'Lords and Commons of England, consider what nation it is whereof ye are and whereof ye are the governors; a nation not slow and dull, but of a quick, ingenious, and piercing spirit; acute to invent, subtile and sinewy to discourse, not beneath the reach of any point the highest that human capacity can soar to.'

This proud saying has been a challenge to successive generations of Englishmen; it may well be taken as a general verdict upon the age of reform.

BIBLIOGRAPHY

IN the following list of authorities no title is given in more than
one place, so that each section is to be supplemented from
the others related to it. The books referred to above in footnotes or in the text are not all mentioned here, and critical
observations already made in the volume are not here repeated.
Only one edition of each book is mentioned. In a few cases a
reason is given for the choice, but in others it is sometimes the
best, often, where later editions are not materially better, the
first, and in a few instances the only edition available in any of
the chief English libraries.

GENERAL

(*a*) PARLIAMENTARY DEBATES AND PAPERS. The most important sources of English political history during the age of
reform are the debates in parliament and the sessional papers
presented to the house of lords or the house of commons. The
debates covered every field of activity (including, for example,
the fine arts) and reflected, directly or indirectly, almost every
shade of opinion in matters of policy. The parliamentary papers,
available after 1836 for purchase by the public, have an equally
wide range. They provide material on the subjects about which
the houses of parliament asked for information; governments
dependent for tenure of power upon the free consent of the
governed also supplied a great deal of information on their own
initiative. During the period 1815–70 presentation to parliament was the normal, and indeed almost the only, means of
publishing this information. Thus the number and importance
of parliamentary papers increased rapidly; these papers include
the reports of royal commissions and parliamentary committees
of inquiry, diplomatic correspondence with foreign Powers,
matters affecting internal or foreign trade, census returns and
other statistical abstracts, annual reports of government departments, and statements of revenue and expenditure.

In 1813 the publication of the parliamentary debates was
taken over entirely from Cobbett[1] by the printer T. C. Hansard,
who gave his name to the work. For the years 1815–70 *Hansard's
Parliamentary Debates* fall into three series: (i) vols. xxix (Nov.

[1] For Cobbett's parliamentary reports see vol. xii of this *History*.

1814) to xli (Feb. 1820); (ii) new series, vols. i (Apr. 1820) to xxv (July 1830); (iii) third series, vols. i (Oct. 1830) to cciii (Aug. 1870).

There are two classes of sessional papers: (*a*) papers presented at the request of either house, or in accordance with the requirements of an act of parliament; these papers include the reports of select committees; (*b*) papers presented by command of the sovereign, that is to say, at the discretion of the executive; these papers include reports of royal commissions. The best guide to the arrangement of these papers (with a description of official indexes, &c.) is P. and G. Ford, *A Guide to Parliamentary Papers* (1955). A reprint in facsimile by P. and G. Ford (1953) of *Hansard's Catalogue and Breviate of Parliamentary Papers, 1696–1834* (1834), and a *Select List of British Parliamentary Papers, 1833–1899* (1953), by the same scholars, are indispensable. An unofficial index of 8,500 papers, with short descriptive summaries of the most important papers, published in 1901 by H. Vernon Jones (*Catalogue of Parliamentary Papers, 1801–1900*), is also useful. There is a *Guide to the Principal Parliamentary Papers Relating to the Dominions* compiled by M. I. Adam, J. Ewing, J. Munro, 1913, and a chronological index of papers relating to India (*Annual Lists and General Index of Parliamentary Papers Relating to the East Indies, 1801–1907*, H. of C. 1909 (89), lxiv. 757). H. W. V. Temperley and L. M. Penson, *A Century of Diplomatic Blue Books, 1814–1914* (1938), is most valuable for papers on foreign policy.

Sir Lewis Hertslet, librarian and keeper of the papers of the foreign office, edited a series of *British and Foreign State Papers* 'to comprise the Principal Documents which have been made public, relating to the Political and Commercial Affairs of Nations, and to their Relations with each other' from 1814. The series has been continued as an official publication; each volume normally covers one year.

A valuable summary of the parliamentary debates on economic questions, and of the most important statistical information contained in parliamentary papers, was published in 1919 in *Commerce and Industry*: vol. i, *A Historical Review of the Economic Conditions of the British Empire from the Peace of Paris in 1815 to the Declaration of War in 1914*; vol. ii, *Tables of Statistics of the British Empire from 1815* (ed. W. Page). Another important summary, mainly for the period after 1850, is in *Statistical*

Memoranda and Charts prepared in the Local Government Board relating to Public Health and Social Conditions (1909 [Cd. 4671], ciii. 669). Lists of the royal commissions and parliamentary committees of inquiry since 1815 have been published from time to time as parliamentary papers. H. M. Clokie and J. W. Robinson, *Royal Commissions of Inquiry* (1937), may also be consulted.

(*b*) WORKS OF REFERENCE. The *Annual Register* gives a convenient summary of the parliamentary history and main events of the year. The *Register* improved in style, methods of selection, and objectiveness during the latter part of the period. For the early years, and particularly for the reign of William IV, the political history is described with a considerable tory bias.

The *Dictionary of National Biography* (founded in 1882 and reprinted, with some corrections, in 1908–9 in 22 vols.) is generally reliable, though the quality of the work varies, and the longest articles, or those dealing with the most important figures, are not always the best. Supplementary volumes covering the lives of people who died during the years 1901–11 and 1912–21 were published in 1912 and 1927: vol. i of the 1908–9 edition and the supplementary volume of 1927 contain accounts of the method of composition of the *Dictionary*. From time to time corrections of fact appear in the *Bulletin* of the Institute of Historical Research. Each article in the *Dictionary* has a short bibliography.

The *Encyclopaedia Britannica* also contains an immense mass of reference material dealing with every aspect of the period. Articles in early editions are often important as evidence of contemporary opinion or the state of knowledge at the time they were written. Editions of the *Encyclopaedia* were published in 1815–17 (5th), 1823–4 (6th), 1830–42 (7th), 1853–60 (8th), 1875–89 (9th); the most useful editions for the student are the 10th (1902–3), which was a reprint of the 9th edition, together with eleven supplementary volumes, and the 11th (1910–12). Files of newspapers, especially of *The Times*, are of obvious value, and have obvious limitations; Palmer's *Index to The Times* began publication only in 1866.

Historical Portraits, 1700–1850, pt. ii, *1800–50* (ed. C. R. L. Fletcher and Emery Walker, 1919), give the best general collection of reproductions of portraits of the period, with short historical notes.

(*c*) GENERAL HISTORIES OF THE PERIOD. Sir Spencer Walpole's

History of England from the Conclusion of the Great War in 1815 (6 vols., rev. ed. 1890) is the earliest, and remains the best, general survey of the political history of the period from 1815 to 1856; the first two volumes of Walpole's *History of Twenty-five Years* (1904) continue the political history to 1870. Herbert Paul's *History of Modern England* (1904–5) deals in vols. 1–3 with the years 1846–70; his work is on a smaller scale than that of Walpole, and is far less balanced in judgement. E. Halévy's *Histoire du peuple anglais au dix-neuvième siècle* (vol. i, 3rd ed. 1923, vols. ii and iii, 1923; Eng. tr., 3 vols., rev. ed. 1949–50) was left unfinished at the author's death; the third volume reached the year 1841. A part of the fourth volume (left incomplete) was published in 1946 (in French) and in 1948 in English, as *The Age of Peel and Cobden*, under the editorship of P. Vaucher. This work was reprinted in 1951 as the fourth volume of the English translation of the history with a supplementary essay by R. B. McCallum linking it with the two concluding volumes covering the period 1895–1915. Halévy described himself as a 'philosophical historian'; his history begins with an introductory survey which has already established itself as a classic, and the whole work ranks with books like Tocqueville's *La Democratie en Amérique* as a brilliant interpretation of the life of an English-speaking people. Of the older histories, W. J. Cory, *A Guide to Modern English History, 1815–35* (1880–2), and H. Martineau, *History of England during the Thirty Years Peace* (1849), are of interest more for the opinions of the writers than for their value as historical works.

G. M. Trevelyan, *British History in the Nineteenth Century and After* (new ed. 1937), and A. Briggs, *The Age of Improvement, 1784–1874* (1959), are the best short general histories covering the period. The last two volumes in the series *English Historical Documents*, ed. D. C. Douglas, vol. xi, 1783–1832, A. Aspinall and E. Anthony Smith (1959), and vol. xii (1), 1833–71, G. M. Young and W. D. Hancock (1956), contain short introductory notes for each subject treated, and excellent bibliographies. Vol. x of the *New Cambridge Modern History* covering the period 1830–70 was published in 1960 and vol. ix (from 1793) is in course of preparation.

The *British Museum Catalogue of Printed Books*, of which a new edition has been in preparation since 1931, is essential for checking titles of books. Supplementary volumes in the form of

a *Subject Index* record from time to time accessions since 1880.
R. A. Peddie, *Subject Index of Books* (*in the B.M.*) *published before
1880* (4 series, 1933–48), is of great use.

Important articles dealing with the history of the period, and
often including documentary material not otherwise printed,
appear in the leading historical reviews, of which the most
important are the *English Historical Review*, *History*, *American
Historical Review*, *Economic History Review*, *Economic History* (a
supplement to the *Economic Journal*), *Economica*, *Journal of
Economic History*, and the *Journal of Modern History* (the two
latter published in the United States). *Victorian Studies*, a review
published at Indiana University, covers all aspects of the
period. The *Transactions of the Royal Historical Society* and the
Journal of the Royal Statistical Society should also be consulted.

POLITICAL AND CONSTITUTIONAL HISTORY

The classification of printed sources for the history of parties
and politics during the period 1815–70 is difficult because there
is no clear line of demarcation between primary and secondary
authorities. *Queen Victoria's Letters* contain material of a documentary kind of importance for understanding the development
of the constitution; so too do the volumes of Morley's *Life of
Gladstone*. Most of the memoirs and lives of nineteenth-century
public men were written at the request of friends or relations
who wished the subject of a work to appear in a favourable
light, and most of the writers, even if they were not directly in
contact with affairs, shared the parliamentary tradition of the
Victorian age that the political institutions of the country required a certain forbearance and a sense of limits in controversy. Hence, unlike the writings of earlier periods, there is a
great deal of personal reticence, too much *couleur de rose*, and not
a little make-believe about the biographies of the nineteenth
century. On the other hand no period has produced political
memoirs in such abundance; the habit of letter-writing was not
yet affected by modern inventions such as the telephone. Thus
members of the same cabinet exchanged letters or short notes
far more often than in modern times because it was quicker to
write a note than to arrange a conversation or even to drive
from one London house to another. In the earlier part of the
period the *tempo* of business was much slower, and ministers had

more time for writing. No modern prime minister is ever likely to write as many letters in his own hand as Peel or Gladstone or Salisbury.

The relation between ministers and the Crown is illustrated in the *Letters of King George IV, 1812–30* (3 vols., ed. A. Aspinall, 1938), and the *Correspondence of William IV and Earl Grey from November 1830 to June 1832* (ed. Henry, Earl Grey, 2 vols., 1867), but the most important material is to be found in the *Letters of Queen Victoria*. For the period 1837–78 these letters have been published in two series: the first series (published in 1907), consisting of three volumes and covering the years 1837–61, was edited by A. C. Benson and the first Lord Esher. The second series, in two volumes (issued in 1926), was edited by G. E. Buckle. The editing and selection of the second series are better than in the first series. The letters chosen for publication represent a small amount of the queen's correspondence, which filled 500–600 bound volumes for the years 1837–61. The editors had less freedom than the writers of biographies of the queen's subjects. A selection, on a larger scale, of the queen's correspondence with Gladstone has been edited by P. Guedalla in *The Queen and Mr. Gladstone* (2 vols.: vol. i, *1845–79*, 1933). *The Life of the Prince Consort*, by Sir Theodore Martin (5 vols., 1876–80), is written almost entirely as a panegyric, and contains little material of first-class importance. The *Memoirs of Baron Stockmar* (ed. E. von Stockmar; Eng. trans., ed. Max Müller, 2 vols., 1872–3) are hardly less discreet, though they contain interesting chapters. R. Fulford, *The Prince Consort* (1949), and F. Eyck, *The Prince Consort* (1959), are more critical studies.

The biographical material for the lives of the prime ministers varies in quality and quantity. C. D. Yonge's *Life and Administration of Robert Banks Jenkinson, 2nd Earl of Liverpool* (3 vols., 1868) is jejune: A. G. Stapleton's *Political Life of George Canning, 1822–7* (3 vols., 2nd ed. 1831), is more valuable for foreign than for domestic affairs, and contains few documents, but Stapleton, as Canning's secretary, wrote from first-hand knowledge. The third series[1] of Wellington's papers, *Despatches, Correspondence, and Memoranda of the Duke of Wellington* (ed. by his son, 8 vols., 1867–80), includes the years 1819–32. *The Correspondence of Princess Lieven and Earl Grey* (ed. G. Le Strange,

[1] For the first and second series see vol. xii of this *History*.

3 vols., 1890) is important for party history as well as for foreign policy. *The Memoirs of Sir Robert Peel* (ed. Earl Stanhope and E. Cardwell, 2 vols., 1857) were prepared by Peel himself; they deal mainly with catholic emancipation, Peel's first administration, and the repeal of the corn laws. C. S. Parker's *Sir Robert Peel from his Private Papers* (3 vols., 1891–9) is on a larger scale than the *Memoirs*. N. Gash, *Mr. Secretary Peel* (1961), is the first volume of an authoritative biography of Peel. *The Melbourne Papers* (ed. L. C. Sanders, 1889) are less full than those of Peel. No comprehensive study has been made of Lord Derby, though there is a short essay on him by G. Saintsbury, *The Earl of Derby* (1892), and a longer work by W. D. Jones, *Lord Derby and Victorian Conservatism* (1956). Neither of the two biographies of Aberdeen (*The Earl of Aberdeen*, by Sir A. Gordon (Lord Stanmore), 1893, and *The Life of George, 4th Earl of Aberdeen*, by Lady Frances Balfour, 2 vols., 1923) is adequate, though each contains correspondence otherwise unpublished. P. Guedalla, *Palmerston* (1926), has a very full bibliography. Sir S. Walpole's *Life of Lord John Russell* (2 vols., 1889) contains a great deal of correspondence; Russell's own *Recollections and Suggestions, 1813–73* (1875), are of interest, though they make only a small contribution to the history of politics. *The Early Correspondence of Lord John Russell* (ed. R. Russell, 2 vols., 1913) covers the years 1805–40; the *Later Correspondence* (ed. G. P. Gooch, 2 vols., 1930) deals mainly, though not entirely, with foreign affairs. Morley's *Life of Gladstone* (3 vols., 1903) is a model of its kind, though it assumes too easily that liberalism was the righteous cause. P. Guedalla, *Gladstone and Palmerston* (1928), contains the correspondence between the two men from 1851 to 1865. The *Life of Disraeli* published between 1910 and 1920 (vols. i and ii, W. F. Monypenny (to 1846); vol. iii (to 1855), W. F. Monypenny and G. E. Buckle; vols. iv–vi (1855–81), G. E. Buckle), is on a larger scale, and, though less a work of art than Morley's biography, has more information about the history of parties.

Other memoirs or biographies written by contemporaries or by authors with personal knowledge of ministers or prominent leaders of the parliamentary opposition include G. Pellew, *Life and Correspondence of Henry Addington, Lord Sidmouth* (3 vols., 1847), Lord Holland, *Further Memoirs of the Whig Party, 1807–21* (ed. Lord Stavordale (afterwards earl of Ilchester), 1905), H. Twiss,

Life of Lord Eldon (3 vols., 1844), Sir D. Le Marchant, *Memoir of Lord Althorp* (1876), Disraeli, *Life of Lord George Bentinck* (1852: later ed. 1874), John Morley, *Life of Cobden* (1881: rev. ed. 1903), the earl of Malmesbury, *Memoirs of an ex-Minister* (2 vols., 1884), Sir G. O. Trevelyan, *Life and Letters of Lord Macaulay* (2 vols., 1876), the (8th) duke of Argyll, *Autobiography and Correspondence* (ed. Ina, duchess of Argyll, 2 vols., 1896), A. P. Martin, *Life and Letters of Robert Lowe, Viscount Sherbrooke* (2 vols., 1893), Lady Gwendolen Cecil, *Life of Robert, Marquis of Salisbury* (vols. i and ii, 1921), E. Hodder, *Life and Work of Lord Shaftesbury* (3 vols., 1886), Lord E. Fitzmaurice, *Life of Earl Granville* (2 vols., 1905), the (first) earl of Selborne, *Personal and Political Memoirs* (pt. 2, vol. i, 1898), Sir Wemyss Reid, *Life of W. E. Forster* (2 vols., 1888). Lord Campbell's *Lives of the Chancellors* (vols. vi–viii, 1848–69) contains valuable information, though the standard of accuracy is not uniform. J. B. Atlay, *The Victorian Chancellors* (2 vols., 1906–8), is worth consulting.

J. K. Laughton's *Memoirs of the Life and Correspondence of Henry Reeve* (2 vols., 1898) contain a great deal of political information. Lord Brougham's *Life and Times of Henry, Lord Brougham* (3 vols., 1871), includes a number of letters written to the author, but is otherwise of little value. The memoirs of J. C. Hobhouse (Lord Broughton), *Recollections of a Long Life* (ed. Lady Dorchester (6 vols., 1909–11)), are more interesting for Hobhouse's connexion with Byron than for his political career. W. Bagehot's *Biographical Studies* (ed. R. H. Hutton, 1881) are short but brilliant sketches based on personal knowledge or reliable information.

Of the letters and diaries of the period published as such, and not used as material for memoirs and biographies, Charles Greville's diary is far the most important: *The Greville Memoirs*: (i) *A Journal of the Reigns of King George IV and King William IV* (3 vols., 1874: new ed. 1888), (ii) *A Journal of the Reign of Queen Victoria (to 1860)* (5 vols., 1880). Greville was clerk to the privy council from 1821 to 1859, and therefore in a position to know a great deal about the details of party politics and the methods of business and personal qualities of the leading men of the country. He was not a strong party man, and, owing to his genial character, social habits, and assured position, he knew also all the social gossip of his time. Henry Reeve, the first editor of the diaries, omitted a certain number of personal references. The most recent edition is *The Greville Memoirs*, ed. L. Strachey and R. Fulford (8 vols., 1938).

Mrs. Arbuthnot's *Journal, 1820–1832*, ed. F. Bamford and the duke of Wellington (2 vols., 1950), and Charles Arbuthnot's *Correspondence*, ed. A. Aspinall (Camden Society, 3rd ser., vol. lxv, 1941), are of special interest owing to the friendship of the Arbuthnots with the first duke of Wellington. The *Letters of Dorothea, Princess Lieven, during her Residence in London, 1812–34* (ed. L. G. Robinson, 1902) and the *Political Diary of Lord Ellenborough, 1828–30* (ed. Lord Colchester, 2 vols. 1881) are of considerable importance for the personal side of party politics. *The Croker Papers* (ed. L. J. Jennings, 3 vols., 1884) are of more value. Croker was secretary of the admiralty from 1809 to 1830, and in the confidence of the leaders of the tory party. *The Creevey Papers* (ed. Sir H. Maxwell, 2 vols., 1903), though of lighter weight, are important. Creevey was a whig member of parliament and treasurer of the ordnance from 1832 to 1834; his correspondence contains a great deal of amusing gossip, but is of more value on the social side than for the history of politics. Another selection, mainly illustrating the social history of the time, has been made from Creevey's manuscripts by J. Gore (*Creevey's Life and Times*, 1934). John Bright's *Diaries* (ed. P. Bright, 1930) are of importance for the history of middle-class radicalism in the early and middle Victorian age.

The *Memoirs of the Court of England during the Regency* (2 vols., 1856), *Memoirs of the Court of George IV* (2 vols., 1859), and *Memoirs of the Courts and Cabinets of William IV and Victoria* (to 1840) (2 vols., 1861), edited by the duke of Buckingham, include the correspondence of the Grenville family, but otherwise make little contribution to history. The third volume of the *Diary and Correspondence of Lord Colchester* (ed. by his son, 3 vols., 1861) is of some political interest.

There are few contemporary works of value dealing with the leaders of the popular and extreme democratic movements. *The Life and Struggles of William Lovett* (written by himself, 1876) is of pathetic interest, but its historical importance lies mainly in showing the lack of any defined class philosophy among the leaders of working-class movements.

Recent historical biographies and studies are based upon the material already described, and upon research into private archives and into correspondence and papers in the British

Museum library and elsewhere. The most important political works of a biographical kind are A. Brady, *William Huskisson and Liberal Reform* (1928), W. R. Brock, *Lord Liverpool and Liberal Toryism, 1820–7* (1941), Graham Wallas, *Life of Francis Place* (1898), G. M. Trevelyan, *Lord Grey of the Reform Bill* (1920), A. Aspinall, *Lord Brougham and the Whig Party* (1927), J. R. M. Butler, *The Passing of the Great Reform Bill* (1914), G. S. R. Kitson Clark, *Peel and the Conservative Party* (1929), A. A. W. Ramsay, *Sir Robert Peel* (1928), C. S. Parker, *Life and Letters of Sir J. Graham* (2 vols., 1907), C. Whibley, *Life of Lord John Manners and his Friends* (2 vols., 1925), R. Coupland, *Wilberforce* (1923), C. W. New, *Life of Lord Durham* (1929), G. D. H. Cole, *Life of William Cobbett* (1924), F. Podmore, *Life of Robert Owen* (1906), R. E. Leader, *Life and Letters of J. A. Roebuck* (1897), G. M. Trevelyan, *Life of John Bright* (1913), C. Driver, *Tory Radical; the Life of Richard Oastler* (1946), Lord David Cecil, *Lord M.* [Melbourne] (1954), Sir P. Magnus, *Gladstone* (1954), and A. Briggs, *Victorian People* (1954).

Other studies dealing with movements or particular aspects of politics are F. O. Darvall, *Popular Disturbances and Public Order in Regency England* (1934), H. W. C. Davis, *The Age of Grey and Peel* (1929), R. L. Hill, *Toryism and the People, 1832–46* (1929), K. G. Feiling, *The Second Tory Party, 1714–1832* (1938), F. E. Gillespie, *Labor and Politics in England, 1850–67* (1927), and N. McCord, *The Anti-Corn Law League* (1958). S. Maccoby, *History of English Radicalism* (3 vols.), *1786–1832* (1955), *1832–52* (1935), *1853–1886* (1938), includes excellent bibliographies. G. D. H. Cole, *A Short History of the British Working Class Movement, 1789–1947* (rev. ed. 1948), is a convenient, though not unbiased summary. Two older books, S. Buxton, *Finance and Politics, an Historical Study, 1783–1885* (2 vols., 1888), and H. Jephson, *The Platform: its Rise and Progress* (1892), are of value. R. G. Gammage, *History of the Chartist Movement* (1st ed. 1854, rev. ed. 1894), was written by a former chartist, but E. Dolléans, *Le Chartisme* (2 vols., 1912–13), and M. Hovell, *The Chartist Movement* (1918), give a better account of the movement; Hovell's book has a good bibliography. *Chartist Studies*, ed. A. Briggs (1959), is a good regional survey. E. Dolléans, *Histoire du mouvement ouvrier* (vol. i, *1830–71*, 1936), and M. Beer, *History of Socialism in England* (2 vols., Eng. trans. 1919–20), deal more directly with the development of anti-capitalist thought; S. and B. Webb (Lord and Lady Passfield), *History of Trade Unionism* (1894; rev. ed. 1920), is a standard work.

The contemporary view of the British constitution is given at length in Sir T. Erskine May (Lord Farnborough), *The Constitutional History of England since the Accession of George III, 1760–1860* (2 vols., 1861–3: new ed., edited and continued in a third vol. to 1911, F. Holland, 1912), and, more shortly but with greater insight, in W. Bagehot, *The English Constitution* (1867; rev. ed. 1872). Sir W. Anson, *Law and Custom of the Constitution* (vol. i, *Parliament*, ed. Sir M. Gwyer, 1922; vol. ii, *The Crown*, ed. A. B. Keith, 1935), A. V. Dicey, *Introduction to the Study of the Law of the Constitution* (8th ed. 1915), and J. Redlich, *The Procedure of the House of Commons* (3 vols., 1908), are standard authorities. Sir D. L. Keir, *Constitutional History of Modern Britain, 1485–1937* (6th ed. 1959), and A. B. Keith, *The Constitution of England from Queen Victoria to George VI* (2 vols., 1940), are the most recent works. W. I. Jennings, *Cabinet Government* (3rd ed. 1959), is mainly concerned with modern practice, but has good historical sections. E. and A. Porritt, *The Unreformed House of Commons* (2 vols., 1903), and C. Seymour, *Electoral Reform in England and Wales* (1915), are standard works on parliamentary history. N. Gash, *Politics in the Age of Peel* (1953), is a most important study of the electors and the electoral system. H. J. Hanham, *Elections and Party Management; Politics in the time of Disraeli and Gladstone* (1959), is of value for the period following the reform act of 1867. C. S. Emden, *The People and the Constitution* (1933) and K. B. Smellie, *A Hundred Years of English Government* (1937), are suggestive and informative works in short compass. J. A. Thomas, *The House of Commons, 1832–1901* (1947), is another interesting study. A. S. Turberville, *The House of Lords in the Age of Reform, 1784–1837* (1958), is important for the first part of the period. H. D. Traill, *Central Government* (1881 ed.), is a good description of the administrative work of the departments of state at the end of the period, and the *Whitehall* series (1925–35) of monographs on the government departments contain historical chapters. E. W. Cohen, *The Growth of the British Civil Service, 1780–1939* (1941), is also of value. Sir W. S. Holdsworth, *History of English Law*, vol. xiii (ed. A. L. Goodhart and H. G. Hanbury, 1952), is a standard work, though its political and constitutional references are not always up to the high level of its legal conclusions.

FOREIGN POLICY

The authorities for the foreign policy of Great Britain are less accessible in print than those dealing with domestic policy. Parliamentary debates give a fairly accurate statement of the policy which a government thinks it possible to carry out, and a summary of negotiations connected with the execution of such a policy; diplomatic correspondence is often printed at length in parliamentary papers. Material of this kind is especially rich for the period of Palmerston's tenure of the foreign secretary-ship, and for the administrations in which he was prime minister. On the other hand there are obvious reasons why a government cannot publish in detail negotiations undertaken with foreign Powers, or explain fully in parliament its own plans, still less its own failures. Furthermore, the foreign policy of one country cannot be understood without reference to the policies of other Powers, including Powers which are not bound to give an account of their acts to parliamentary assemblies. The historian of foreign policy is therefore more dependent than an historian of domestic policy upon unprinted archival material and private correspondence; this material was not, as a rule, available during the period 1815–70; while few writers of political biographies knew enough about foreign affairs to make the best selection from among the papers open to them. Thus recent investigations have brought a greater revision of opinion in this field than in other branches of political history.

The *Cambridge History of British Foreign Policy* (vols. ii and iii, 1923) contains chapters of unequal merit; in some cases later works by contributors to the *History* have made their chapters out of date. The bibliographies are of permanent value. H. W. V. Temperley and L. M. Penson, *Foundations of British Foreign Policy from Pitt (1792) to Salisbury (1902)* (1938), is a well-chosen selection of documents. The best short survey of the results of modern investigation is R. W. Seton-Watson, *Britain in Europe, 1789–1914: a Survey of Foreign Policy* (1937); this book contains an excellent bibliography. A. Cecil, *British Foreign Secretaries, 1807–1916* (1927), gives a short biographical account of the ministers in charge of foreign affairs, and a study of their policies. A. J. P. Taylor, *The Struggle for Mastery in Europe, 1848–1918* (1954), is a general history of European diplomacy. Foreign policy between 1815 and 1841 has been described at length, in its international setting, by Sir C. K. Webster, *The Foreign Policy of Castlereagh, 1815–22* (2nd ed. 1934), H. W. V. Temperley, *The Foreign Policy of Canning, 1822–7* (1925), and Sir C. K. Webster, *The Foreign Policy of Palmerston, 1830–41* (2 vols., 1951). Each of these books contains references to earlier works or printed collections of material such as the *Memoirs and Correspondence of Viscount Castlereagh* (ed. 3rd marquis of Londonderry, 12 vols., 1848–53). Dr. Temperley's book has a full bibliography. H. C. F. Bell, *Life of Palmerston* (2 vols., 1936), is the best account hitherto written of Palmerston's foreign policy as a whole, but the scale is too small, and the archival material has not been fully examined. J. Hall, *England and the Orleans Monarchy* (1912), R. Guyot, *La Première Entente cordiale* (1926), and E. Jones-Parry, *The Spanish Marriages, 1841–6* (1936), are important for the history of Anglo-French relations. A good deal of excellent work has been done on British policy in the Near East. C. W. Crawley, *Greek Independence, 1821–33* (1930), is very good within a limited field; W. M. Miller, *The Ottoman Empire and its Successors, 1801–1921* (rev. ed. 1927), and H. Dodwell, *The Founder of Modern Egypt: a Study of Muhammad Ali* (1936), are not concerned primarily with British policy, though they give a clear and reliable account of this policy in their respective fields of study. H. W. V. Temperley, *England and the Near East*, vol. i, *The Crimea* (1936), is an authoritative history of British policy in relation to Turkey, with an exhaustive bibliography. S. Lane-Poole, *Life of Stratford Canning, Lord Stratford de Redcliffe* (2 vols., 1888), is the best of the biographies of ambassadors. F. A. Simpson, *Louis Napoleon and the Recovery of France* (1923), throws much light on British policy before and during the Crimean war, though the book has been corrected in some important respects by Dr. Temperley's work. H. L. Hoskins, *British Routes to India* (1928), a study by an American scholar, is of value for the Near and Middle East. V. J. Puryear, *England, Russia, and the Straits Question, 1844–56* (1931), and *International Economics and Diplomacy in the Near East, 1834–53* (1935), contain interesting material, though the conclusions drawn are often controversial. G. B. Henderson, *Crimean War Diplomacy and other Historical Essays* (ed. W. O. Henderson, 1947), is especially interesting for the diplomacy of Lord John Russell. Mrs. R. Wemyss, *Memoirs and Letters of Sir Robert Morier from 1826 to 1876* (1911), is particularly good for German affairs. Sir H. Maxwell, *Life of the Fourth Earl of Clarendon* (2 vols., 1913), and Lord Newton, *Life of Lord Lyons* (2 vols., 1913), contain important material. Other works of importance on different questions are C. Sproxton, *Palmerston and the Hungarian Revolution* (1919), L. Steefel, *The Schleswig-Holstein Question* (1932), P. Knaplund, *The Foreign Policy of Mr. Gladstone* (1935), A. A. W. Ramsay, *Idealism and Foreign Policy* (1925), A. J. P. Taylor, *The Italian Problem in European Diplomacy, 1847–9* (1934), and W. C. Costin, *Great Britain and China, 1833–60* (1937). Sir J. W. Headlam-Morley's *Studies in Diplomacy* (ed. A. Headlam-Morley, 1930) include valuable material for the period 1815–70, particularly in relation to the Near East. Among the best works on Anglo-American relations are S. F. Bemis, *A Diplomatic History of the United States* (4th ed. 1955), J. F. Rippy, *The Rivalry of the United States and Great Britain for Latin America, 1808–30* (1929), M. W. Williams, *Anglo-American Isthmian Diplomacy, 1815–1915* (1916). E. D. Adams, *Great Britain and the American Civil War* (2 vols., 1925), is the best work on the subject. Sir C. K. Webster, *Select Documents on Britain and the Independence of Latin America 1812–30* (2 vols., 1938), is useful.

Of the older biographies or general works, Sir H. Bulwer (Lord Dalling), *Life of Viscount Palmerston (to 1846)* (3 vols., 1870–6), and E. Ashley, *Life of Viscount Palmerston* (2 vols., 1879), are inadequate as biographies and as studies of British policy, but they include a great deal of Palmerston's correspondence; neither book is altogether reliable. Sir H. Rawlinson, *England and Russia in the East* (1875), is a polemical work, but interesting as the statement of a point of view by an expert. Sir E. Hertslet's *Map of Europe by Treaty* (4 vols., 1875–91) is a useful book of reference for material otherwise contained in the *British and Foreign State Papers*. Hertslet's *Recollections of the Old Foreign Office* (1901) is unique of its kind.

Students of foreign policy will also find it useful to consult Sir E. Satow, *A Guide to Diplomatic Practice* (3rd ed. revised by H. Ritcher, 1932), and Sir G. Butler and S. Maccoby, *The Development of International Law* (1928).

NAVAL AND MILITARY AFFAIRS

There is no adequate history of the army or navy during the period between 1815 and 1870. Sir W. L. Clowes (and others),

History of the British Navy, vol. vii (1897–1913), is hardly more than a bare outline, with few references to authorities, and superficial in its treatment of administrative questions or the development of naval construction. The best account of the transition from sail to steam is in an American work, J. P. Baxter, 3rd, *The Introduction of the Ironclad Warship* (1933). A few memoirs, of little value, describe the life of a naval officer: *The Memoirs of Admiral Sir Astley Cooper Key* (ed. Vice-Admiral P. H. Colomb, 1898) are the best of their kind. There is no comprehensive history of the British mercantile marine.

The history of the army has received more attention, partly because there was more active service on land than at sea, and military affairs, especially in connexion with India, took a more prominent place in public attention and in parliamentary discussions than the navy. The Hon. (Sir) J. W. Fortescue's *History of the British Army* deals with the nineteenth century (to 1870) in vols. xi (1923), xii (1927), and xiii (1930). This work, though well written and sympathetic, is not altogether satisfactory; the campaigns are dealt with at length, but the administrative history of the army is summarized only in a superficial way, and the author's political bias distorts his judgement on many questions of policy, though his description of the conditions of life of the rank and file is a useful corrective to the neglect of the subject in most general histories of the period. A. W. Kinglake, *The Invasion of the Crimea: its Origin, and an Account of its Progress down to the death of Lord Raglan* (8 vols., 1863–87), is a full and dramatic account, based upon personal knowledge and upon a minute scrutiny of the evidence. The military side of the work is better than the narrative of diplomatic negotiations. Kinglake was unfair to Lord Stratford, and had a personal as well as a political bias against Napoleon III; in matters affecting Anglo-French co-operation, and the part taken by French commanders in the war, it is necessary to consult P. de la Gorce, *Histoire du second Empire*, vol. i (6th ed. 1902). W. H. Russell, *The British Expedition to the Crimea* (rev. ed. 1876), is an account written by *The Times* correspondent at the war. General Sir E. Hamley, *The War in the Crimea* (1891), is a short but good summary of the military operations. Lord Stanmore, *Sidney Herbert: a Memoir* (2 vols., 1906), and C. Woodham Smith, *Florence Nightingale* (1950), are important for the administrative history of the war. Joan Wake, *The Brudenells of*

Deene (2nd ed. 1954), adds details regarding Lord Cardigan from unpublished manuscripts.

IRELAND

There is a very large and scattered literature dealing with the history of Ireland and of Anglo-Irish relations; this literature includes a number of short and good objective studies, but the greater part of it is of a controversial kind. The Irish point of view is generally stated more explicitly in contemporary polemical works than the English standpoint, though the assumptions of English nationalism are not less strong.

The best textbooks of Irish history are E. Curtis, *History of Ireland* (6th ed. 1950), and S. Gwynn, *History of Ireland* (1925). *Daniel O'Connell*, by D. Gwynn (1930), is also good. W. E. H. Lecky's *Leaders of Public Opinion in Ireland* (2 vols., 1861; rev. 1871; vol. ii deals with O'Connell) is less impartial than might appear from the author's restrained style. *Two Centuries of Irish History (1691–1870)*, ed. J. (afterwards Lord) Bryce (1888), is a composite work, containing a good deal of useful material but polemical in character. A. E. F. Murray, *A History of the Commercial and Financial Relations between England and Ireland from the period of the Restoration* (1903), and G. O'Brien, *The Economic History of Ireland from the Union to the Famine* (1921), also include valuable information and statistical material, but leave much to be desired from an historical point of view. R. B. McDowell, *Public Opinion and Government Policy in Ireland, 1801–46* (1952), T. W. Freeman, *Pre-Famine Ireland* (1957), and K. H. Connell, *The Population of Ireland, 1750–1845* (1950), are good studies; *The Great Famine, Studies in Irish History, 1845–52*, ed. R. Dudley Edwards and T. Desmond Williams (1956), is an excellent collection of essays also covering more ground than the title suggests, and including a useful select bibliography. Sir Charles Trevelyan, *The Irish Crisis* (1848, later ed. 1880), gives an account of the famine and of the relief measures of which he was in charge. Nassau Senior, *Journals, Conversations, and Essays relating to Ireland* (2 vols., 1868), is a fair-minded approach to Irish economic questions. Sir William Gregory's *Autobiography* is one of the few books of its kind written by an Anglo-Irish landlord. J. F. M'Lennan, *Memoir of Thomas Drummond* (1867), describes the best type of English government in Ireland. W. R. Trench, *Realities of Irish Life* (1869), throws some light on

Ribbonism; Sir C. Gavan Duffy's *Young Ireland* (2 vols., 1880; rev. ed. 1896) and *The League of North and South* (1886) are important histories of the Irish nationalist movement which developed in opposition to O'Connell, though they are written with a strong bias. J. O'Leary, *Recollections of Fenians and Fenianism* (2 vols., 1896), is even more partisan; the most striking expression of hatred of England is in John Mitchel's *Jail Journal* (1868). J. L. Hammond, *Gladstone and the Irish Nation* (1938), J. A. Reynolds, *The Catholic Emancipation Crisis in Ireland, 1823–9* (1954), and J. H. Whyte, *The Independent Irish Party, 1850–9* (1958) are good recent studies.

THE COLONIES

The amount of material dealing with colonial development, though far smaller than the material for the period after 1870, is very large: full and classified bibliographies, together with a compressed but accurate narrative, may be found in the *Cambridge History of the British Empire* (vol. vi, *Canada and Newfoundland*, 1930; vol. vii, pt. i, *Australia*, pt. ii, *New Zealand*, 1933; vol. viii, *South Africa*, 1936; vol. ii, *The Growth of the New Empire*, 1940). E. A. Walker, *History of South Africa* (2nd ed. 1935) and *The Great Trek* (1934), are of interest. J. A. Williamson, *A Short History of British Expansion*, vol. ii (4th ed. 1953), is a good summary. The first volume of L. C. A. Knowles, *Economic Development of the Overseas Empire, 1763–1914* (1924), is an excellent general economic survey; the second and third volumes, containing special studies of Canada (1930) and South Africa (1936), were completed for publication by C. M. Knowles after Mrs. Knowles's death. C. A. Bodelsen, *Studies in Mid-Victorian Imperialism* (new ed. 1960), is of interest. Sir Charles Lucas (and others), *Historical Geography of the British Colonies* (6 vols., 1888–1911), is particularly useful for the smaller tropical colonies. V. T. Harlow and F. Madden, *British Colonial Developments, 1774–1834: Select Documents* (1953), and K. N. Bell and W. P. Morrell, *Select Documents on British Colonial Policy, 1830–60* (1928), are the best collections of original material. Lord Durham's *Report on the Affairs of British North America* has been published in separate form, with an introduction, by Sir Charles Lucas (3 vols., 1912); Charles Buller's *Responsible Government for the Dominions* (1841) has been reprinted in E. M. Wrong, *Charles Buller and Responsible Government* (1926). Sir Charles Lucas also reprinted (1891) Sir G. Cornewall Lewis's *An Essay on the Government of Dependencies* (1841). J. L. Morison, *British Supremacy and Canadian Self-Government* (1919), is a good study. R. L. Schuyler, *The Fall of the Old Colonial System: a Study in British Free Trade, 1770–1870* (1945), and J. B. Brebner, *North Atlantic Triangle* (1945), are important.

INDIA

The *Cambridge History of the British Empire* deals with British India in vols. iv and v (1929 and 1932). These volumes, which also form part of the *Cambridge History of India*, contain an excellent bibliography of primary and secondary sources; the text is often less satisfactory. E. Thompson and G. T. Garratt, *The Rise and Fulfilment of British Rule in India* (1934), is written with sympathy for the modern movements in India; Sir E. Blunt, *The I.C.S.* (1937), is a useful survey, with a short but good bibliography. E. Thompson, *The Life of Charles, Lord Metcalfe* (1937), is the best of recent biographies of Indian administrators. Sir P. J. Griffiths, *The British Impact on India* (1952), is a good study of British rule in retrospect. Among books published before the Cambridge *History* Ramsay Muir's *Making of British India, 1756–1858*, is a good selection from the most important documentary material, and P. E. Roberts, *History of British India under the Company and the Crown* (3rd ed. 1952), is the best short history. R. C. Majumdar, H. C. Ray-chaudhuri, and K. Datta, *An Advanced History of India* (1946), is the best general work by Indian historians. *The Legacy of India* (ed. G. T. Garratt, 1937) is a series of essays mainly on Indian culture. E. Stokes, *The English Utilitarians in India* (1959), is an interesting study of the British administration.

T. R. Holmes, *History of the Mutiny* (5th ed. 1904), is the best account of the subject; an older standard work is J. W. Kaye and G. B. Malleson, *History of the Sepoy War in India* (6 vols., 1864–80).

THE CONDITION OF ENGLAND

(i) LOCAL GOVERNMENT AND ADMINISTRATION. The most important account of local government in England is in the series of volumes by S. and B. Webb (Lord and Lady Passfield) under the title *English Local Government from the Revolution to the Municipal Corporations Act*:[1] vol. i, *The Parish and the County* (1906),

---

[1] From vol. iv onwards the general title changes to *English Local Government*.

vols. ii and iii, *The Manor and the Borough* (1908), vol. iv, *Statutory Authorities for Special Purposes* (1922), vol. v, *The Story of the King's Highway* (1913), vol. vi, *English Prisons under Local Government* (1922), vols. vii–ix, *English Poor Law History* (1927–9). *English Poor Law Policy* (1910), by the same authors, covers, in more analytical form, the same ground as these latter volumes, and *The History of Liquor Licensing in England* (1903) is a by-product of the series. These volumes suffer from a certain diffuseness and lack of planning almost inevitable in a pioneer undertaking. They are not altogether free from political bias, particularly against orthodox radicalism, but the authors and their assistants collected and examined an immense quantity of official and other material, and presented the results in original and interesting form. On a much smaller scale, but useful, is J. Redlich, *Local Government in England* (2 vols., ed. with additions, F. W. Hirst, 1903: vol. i, part i, ed. with notes, B. Keith-Lucas (1958)). H. Finer, *English Local Government* (1934), covers the same ground, though from a different angle, *A Century of Municipal Progress, 1835–1935* (ed. H. J. Laski, W. I. Jennings, and W. A. Robson, 1935), has a number of essays, of unequal merits, with shorter bibliographies. Much useful work has been done on the history of the great provincial cities, e.g. A. Redford, *The History of Local Government in Manchester* (3 vols., 1939–40), and C. Gill and A. Briggs, *History of Birmingham, 1865–1938* (2 vols., 1952).

The development of local government and the extension of the authority and range of interference of central and local officials led to a great deal of discussion on the theoretical side, from the literature of Benthamism to the extreme individualism of Herbert Spencer. J. Toulmin Smith, *Government by Commission Illegal and Pernicious* (1849) and *Local Self-Government and Centralization* (1851), are examples of the distrust of central action.

(ii) PUBLIC HEALTH. The reports of the great public inquiries of the 1840's are indispensable. The best summary of developments throughout the period is J. Simon, *English Sanitary Institutions* (2nd ed. 1897). S. E. Finer, *The Life and Times of Sir Edwin Chadwick* (1952), is an excellent study. J. L. and B. Hammond, *Lord Shaftesbury* (rev. ed. 1936), includes Shaftesbury's activities in the field of public health.

(iii) EDUCATION. J. W. Adamson, *English Education, 1789–1902* (1930), contains an excellent bibliography and gives the best general account of the subject. S. J. Curtis, *History of Education in Great Britain* (rev. ed. 1953), is also a good general work. R. L. Archer, *Secondary Education in the Nineteenth Century* (1921), deals with the character and methods of education. Sir J. Kay-Shuttleworth, *Four Periods of Public Education* (1862), is a good account of the early development of elementary education, and should be read with F. Smith, *Life and Work of Sir James Kay-Shuttleworth* (1923). A. P. Stanley, *Life and Correspondence of Thomas Arnold* (12th ed. 1881), and Sir J. Otter, *Nathaniel Woodard, a Memoir of his Life* (1925), illustrate movements for the reform of secondary education. D. Beale, *The Education of Girls* (1869), B. A. Clough, *A Memoir of A. J. Clough* (1897), and E. Davies, *Thoughts on Some Questions relating to Women, 1860–1908* (ed. E. E. C. Jones, 1910), are of importance for the history of women's education. Mark Pattison, *Memoirs* (1883), Sir C. E. Malet, *History of the University of Oxford*, vol. 3 (1927), D. H. W. Winstanley, *Early Victorian Cambridge* (1940), and Sir G. C. Faber, *Jowett* (1957), are the best books on the older universities.

RELIGION

G. S. R. Kitson Clark, *The English Inheritance* (1950), is a most thoughtful essay on the general influence of religion in nineteenth-century England. The standard work on the anglican church is F. W. Cornish's *History of the English Church in the Nineteenth Century*, pts. i and ii (1910); there are short bibliographies at the end of each chapter. Of the earlier works, J. H. Overton, *The English Church in the Nineteenth Century, 1800–33* (1894), is important for the history of the old high church party, and J. Venn, *Annals of a Clerical Family* (1904), is an interesting record of the evangelical party. E. Stock, *History of the Church Missionary Society* (3 vols., 1899), is of value for the missionary work of the evangelicals. R. W. Church, *The Oxford Movement, 1833–45* (rev. ed. 1891), is still the best history of the tractarians; G. C. Faber, *Oxford Apostles* (1933), is a very good analytical account from a modern standpoint. Other important biographies and studies are Isaac Williams, *Autobiography* (ed. Sir G. Prevost, 1893), W. E. Gladstone, *The State in its Relations with the Church* (1838), J. H. Newman, *Essay on the Development of Doctrine* (1845), *Apologia pro Vita Sua* (1864), R. H. Froude, *Remains*, pt. i (1838), G. A. Denison, *Notes of My Life, 1805–78* (1878),

E. Churton, *Memoir of Josiah Watson* (2 vols., 1861), W. Ward, *Life of Cardinal Newman* (2 vols., 1912), Sir J. T. Coleridge, *A Memoir of John Keble* (1869), H. P. Liddon, *Life of E. B. Pusey* (4 vols., 1893–7), A. Blomfield, *Memoir of Bishop Blomfield* (2 vols., 1863), A. R. Ashwell and R. G. Wilberforce, *Life of S. Wilberforce* (3 vols., 1879), R. E. Prothero and G. G. Bradley, *Life of Dean Stanley* (2 vols., 1893), R. T. Davidson and W. Benham, *Life of Archbishop Tait* (2 vols., 1891), and J. W. Burgon, *Lives of Twelve Good Men* (2 vols., 3rd ed. 1889). P. Thureau-Dangin, *La Renaissance catholique en Angleterre* (3 vols., 1906–9). The books of W. Ward, *Life and Times of Cardinal Wiseman* (2 vols., 1897) and *W. G. Ward and the Catholic Revival* (rev. ed. 1912), are the best works on the Roman catholic church in England during the period.

W. Hanna, *Life and Writings of T. Chalmers* (4 vols., 1849–52), is the best account of Chalmers, and R. Buchanan, *The Ten Years Conflict* (2 vols., 1849), a good account of the disruption of the church of Scotland. J. F. Hurst, *History of Methodism* (3 vols., 1901), W. J. Townsend and others, *A New History of Methodism* (1909), A. Peel, *History of the Congregational Union of England and Wales, 1831–1931* (1931), and A. W. W. Dale, *Life of R. W. Dale* (3rd ed. 1899), are the best authorities for the history of nonconformity. R. F. Wearmouth, *Methodism and the Working-class Movement of England, 1800–50* (1937) and R. G. Cowherd, *The Politics of English Dissent* (1959) are interesting studies. A. W. Benn, *History of English Rationalism in the Nineteenth Century* (1906), gives and account of the secularist movement.

AGRICULTURE, COMMERCE, AND INDUSTRY

A London Bibliography of the Social Sciences (B. M. Headicar and C. Fuller, 4 vols., 1931–2; suppl. vols., 1934 and 1937), cover practically all the available material. J. R. McCulloch's *Dictionary, Practical, Theoretical, and Historical, of Commerce and Commercial Navigation* (1832, rev. ed. 1882) and *A Statistical Account of the British Empire* (2 vols., 1837; rev. ed. 1839), are valuable sources of information. The files of the *Economist* (1843–) are also of importance for contemporary facts and opinions about policy. G. R. Porter's *The Progress of the Nation* (1836–51, rev. ed. by F. W. Hirst, 1912) deals with all matters affecting population, taxation, expenditure, trade, production wages, and prices.

Sir J. H. Clapham, *An Economic History of Modern Britain*, vol. i, *The Early Railway Age, 1820–1850* (2nd ed., corrected, 1939), vol. ii, *Free Trade and Steel 1850–1886* (1932) is indispensable, and gives references to most of the material available up to the date of publication. T. S. Ashton, *The Industrial Revolution, 1760–1830* (1948), is a brilliant short survey. W. H. B. Court, *A Concise Economic History of Britain from 1750 to Recent Times* (1954), is also very good. L. C. A. Knowles, *The Industrial and Commercial Revolutions in Great Britain during the Nineteenth Century* (1927), though a little out of date, is still of interest. J. F. Rees, *A Survey of Economic Development, with Special Reference to Great Britain* (1933), has a well-chosen short bibliography. C. R. Fay, *Great Britain from Adam Smith to the Present Day* (5th ed. 1950), is an excellent introductory study to the economic history of the period. Statistical inquiries carried out by British and American scholars during the last twenty years have led to very considerable changes of view in regard to fundamental questions concerning British trade. Three American books are of special importance: A. H. Imlah, *Economic Elements in the Pax Britannica: Studies in British Foreign Trade in the Nineteenth Century* (1958), W. W. Rostow, *British Economy of the Nineteenth Century* (1948), A. D. Gayer, W. W. Rostow, and A. Schwartz, *Growth and Fluctuations of the British Economy, 1750–1850* (1953). An older American book, L. H. Jenks, *The Migration of British Capital to 1875* (new ed. 1938), is an interesting study of the relations between finance and policy, and has much important material, though its political conclusions are often open to question. T. E. Gregory, *British Banking Statutes and Reports, 1832–1928* (2 vols., 1929), is a good selection of contemporary documents, with an introduction. Lord Ernle, *English Farming, Past and Present* (1912; 4th ed. 1927), is the best work on agriculture. W. Smart, *Economic Annals of the Nineteenth Century*, vol. i, *1801–20* (1910), vol. ii, *1821–30* (1917), is as much a history of policy as a chronological record of fact. H. Hamilton, *The Industrial Revolution in Scotland* (1932), and A. H. Dodd, *The Industrial Revolution in N. Wales* (1933), are the best works of the kind. L. Levi, *History of British Commerce and of the Economic Progress of the British Nation, 1763–1878* (2nd ed. 1880), is still of importance. For the history of railways, roads, and canals W. T. Jackman, *The Development of Transportation in Modern England* (2 vols., 1916), is a standard work, with a full bibliography. C. E. S. Sherrington, *A Hundred Years of Inland Transport* (1934), is also useful.

Among other books of importance are: E. L. Hargreaves, *The National Debt* (1930), A. Redford, *Manchester Merchants and Foreign Trade*, vol. i, *1794–1858* (1934), vol. ii, *1850–1939* (1956), G. C. Allen, *The Industrial Development of Birmingham and the Black Country, 1860–1927* (1929), A. H. John, *The Industrial Development of South Wales, 1750–1850* (1950), D. G. Barnes, *A History of the English Corn Laws, 1660–1846* (1930), T. E. Gregory, *The Westminster Bank Through a Century* (2 vols., 1936), Sir J. H. Clapham, *The Bank of England* (1944), and B. C. Hunt, *The Development of the Business Corporation in England, 1800–67* (1936).

WAGES AND CONDITIONS OF LABOUR

The conditions of life between 1815 and 1870 are described in many books, some of them, such as F. Engels, *Condition of the Working Classes in England in 1844* (1845; W. O. Henderson and W. H. Challoner, 1958 Eng. trans.), based almost entirely upon the reports of commissions of inquiry. In addition to the statistical material already mentioned, there are figures dealing with incomes, prices, and wages in Sir W. T. Layton and G. Crowther, *Introduction to the Study of Prices* (1935). C. R. Fay, *Life and Labour in the Nineteenth Century* (1920) and *The Corn Laws and Social England* (1932), give a general account of social conditions; S. and B. Webb, *Industrial Democracy* (1898), is also a standard work, though it is not without some of the defects of the authors' volumes on local government. E. H. Phelps Brown, *The Growth of British Industrial Relations* (1959), is mainly a study of the years 1906–14, but contains valuable comments on earlier developments. I. Pinchbeck, *Women Workers and the Industrial Revolution, 1750–1850* (1930), A. Redford, *Labour Migration in England, 1800–50* (1926), B. L. Hutchins and A. Harrison, *A History of Factory Legislation* (3rd ed. 1936), N. W. Thomas, *The Early Factory Legislation* (1951), and G. J. Holyoake, *History of Co-operation in England* (rev. ed., 2 vols., 1906), cover important subjects. J. L. and B. Hammond, *The Skilled Labourer, 1760–1832* (1919), *The Rise of Modern Industry* (1925) and *The Bleak Age* (rev. ed. 1947) are written with sympathy and distinction, and are more balanced in their treatment of evidence than the earlier books of these two writers.

Sir A. M. Carr-Saunders and A. Wilson, *The Professions* (1933), is outstanding among the very few works dealing with the organization of the middle classes.

SOCIAL LIFE

A good general survey may be found in *Early Victorian England, 1830–65* (ed. G. M. Young) (2 vols., 1934), and in an earlier work, *Social England* (ed. H. D. Traill, vol. vi, 1897). G. M. Young, *Victorian England: Portrait of an Age* (reprinted, with additions, from *Early Victorian England*, 1936), is a brilliant survey of the social life and ideas of the central Victorian period.

LITERATURE AND SCIENCE

There are biographies of all the major and of most of the minor writers of the period, and a great deal of critical literature, reflecting the changing tastes of every decade. For the changes of taste and the appreciation of writers at different periods the files of the quarterly and monthly reviews are the best sources. The standard works on English literature during the period are *The Cambridge History of English Literature* (vol. xii, 1915; vols. xiii and xiv, 1916), with full bibliographies, and O. Elton, *A Survey of English Literature, 1780–1830* (2 vols., 1912), and *A Survey of English Literature, 1830–80* (2 vols., 1920). Among other works, W. J. Courthope, *The Liberal Movement in English Literature* (1885), A. Cruse, *The Englishman and his Books in the Early Nineteenth Century* (1930), V. Scudder, *Social Ideals in English Letters* (1898), Lord David Cecil, *Early Victorian Novelists* (1934), and B. Willey, *Nineteenth Century Studies* (1949) and *More Nineteenth Century Studies* (1956), are of interest. Two essays by G. S. R. Kitson Clark and N. G. Annan in *Studies in Social History*, ed. J. H. Plumb (1955), are also good.

The development of political thought during the earlier part of the period is very well described in E. Halévy, *La Formation du radicalisme philosophique* (3 vols., 1901–4; Eng. trans. 1928), and Sir Leslie Stephen, *The English Utilitarians* (3 vols., 1900). *The Social and Political Ideas of Some Representative Thinkers of the Age of Reaction and Reconstruction* and *The Social and Political Ideas of Some Representative Thinkers of the Victorian Age* (ed. F. J. C. Hearnshaw, 1932–3) contain short essays dealing with English writers, and excellent bibliographies. C. Brinton, *English Political Thought in the Nineteenth Century* (1933), also has a good bibliography. A. V. Dicey, *Law and Public Opinion in England* (2nd ed. 1914), is a classic account of the change in the attitude of public opinion towards *laisser-faire*; like most classics, it is a little out of date.

The best books on the history of the press during the period are A. Aspinall, *Politics and the Press, 1780–1850* (1949), W. H. Wickwar, *The Struggle for the Freedom of the Press, 1819–32* (1928), with a general bibliography, and J. Grant (editor of the *Morning Advertiser*), *The Newspaper Press* (3 vols., 1871–2). Dasent, *Life of J. T. Delane* (2 vols., 1908), and *The History of The Times* (vol. i, *to 1841*, 1935; vol. ii, *1841–1884*, 1952), are important.

The annual reports of the meetings of the British Association are the best summaries, for the layman, of the progress of science during the nineteenth century. Sir W. C. D. Dampier-Whetham, *History of Science* (rev. ed. 1930), C. Singer, *A Short History of Medicine* (1928), and *A Short History of Biology* (1931), give a clear general outline of their respective subjects. Among biographies S. Smiles, *Lives of the Engineers* (3 vols., 1861–2), though written on popular lines, contains a great deal of interesting matter; *The Life and Letters of Charles Darwin* (ed. F. Darwin, 1887) includes an autobiographical chapter. For the more technical accounts of scientific work and its theoretical and practical implications, the *Proceedings* of the Royal Society and the transactions of other learned societies should be studied. C. Singer and others, *A History of Technology*, vol. iv, *1750–1850* (1958), and vol. v, *1850–1900* (1958), covers the whole subject of technical advance, and deals, somewhat unevenly, with the general consequences of technical change. Each chapter has a full bibliography.

ARCHITECTURE AND THE ARTS

T. S. R. Boase, *English Art, 1800–1870* (vol. x in *The Oxford History of English Art*, 1959), contains full bibliographies.

There is no large-scale history of English architecture in the nineteenth century, and there are comparatively few studies or biographies of the leading architects. The period is generally treated in a cursory way at the end of general histories of architectural styles. The *Dictionary of Architecture*, published by the Architectural Publication Society (1853), has useful notices of architects for the first part of the century. M. S. Briggs, *The Architect in History* (1927), has a good chapter on the period, with a short bibliography containing practically all the important monographs. H. M. Colvin, *Biographical Dictionary of English Architects, 1660–1840* (1954) is good. Articles on the architects or architectural styles also appear from time to time in the *Architectual Review*, and in the *Journal* and *Transactions* of the Royal Institute of British Architects. Sir K. Clark, *The Gothic Revival* (2nd ed. 1950), is a good study. Of the older works, J. Fergusson, *A History of Architecture*, vol. iii (1867), is interesting from the point of view of contemporary taste.

Works on painting and sculpture, and lives of painters, are very numerous, but few are written from the point of view of the place of a painter and his work in the general history of the time. Notices in the *Annual Register* record, with some criticism, the exhibitions at the Royal Academy, and A. Graves, *Dictionary of Artists who have exhibited Works in the Principal London Exhibitions from 1760 to 1893* (1895), is a useful work of reference. A. Michel, *Histoire de l'art*, vol. viii, pt. i (1930), is the best general history of the development of painting and sculpture. The literary reviews of the time give a good deal of attention to the fine arts, and are of particular interest for the development of pre-Raphaelitism.

The best short accounts of English music and the theatre during the period are in E. Walker, *History of Music in England*, (2nd ed. 1924), *Early Victorian England*, vol. ii, and *Social England*, vol. vi. Groves, *Dictionary of Music and Musicians* (5th ed. ed. E. Blom, 1954) is essential for reference.

LIST OF CABINETS

1. LIVERPOOL'S CABINET
(at beginning of 1815[1])

Prime minister and first lord of the treasury: Earl of Liverpool.
Lord chancellor: Lord Eldon (cr. earl 1821).
Lord president: Earl of Harrowby.
Lord privy seal: Earl of Westmorland.
Chancellor of the exchequer: N. Vansittart (cr. Lord Bexley 1823).
Home secretary: Viscount Sidmouth.
Foreign secretary: Viscount Castlereagh (marquis of Londonderry 1821).
Secretary for war and colonies: Earl Bathurst.
First lord of the admiralty: Viscount Melville.
Master-general of the ordnance: Earl of Mulgrave.
President of the board of control: Earl of Buckinghamshire.
Master of the mint: W. Wellesley-Pole (cr. Lord Maryborough 1821).
Chancellor of the duchy of Lancaster: C. B. Bathurst.

Changes

June 1816: G. Canning succeeded the earl of Buckinghamshire as president of the board of control. *January 1818*: F. J. Robinson entered the cabinet as president of the board of trade and treasurer of the navy. *January 1819*: the duke of Wellington succeeded the earl of Mulgrave as master-general of the ordnance; the earl of Mulgrave remained in the cabinet until May 1820 as cabinet minister without office. *January 1821*: C. B. Bathurst succeeded Canning as president of the board of control. *January 1822*: R. Peel succeeded Viscount Sidmouth as home secretary; Sidmouth remained in the cabinet until 1824 as cabinet minister without office. *February 1822*: C. W. W. Wynn succeeded C. B. Bathurst as president of the board of control. *September 1822*: Canning rejoined the cabinet as foreign secretary. *January 1823*: F. J. Robinson became chancellor of the exchequer in place of Vansittart, who became chancellor of the duchy of Lancaster. *August 1823*: Lord Maryborough resigned. *October 1823*: W. Huskisson entered the cabinet as president of the board of trade and treasurer of the navy.

2. CANNING'S CABINET
(formed April 1827)

Prime minister and first lord of the treasury⎱ G. Canning.
Chancellor of the exchequer⎰
Lord chancellor: Lord Lyndhurst.
Lord president of the council: Earl of Harrowby.
Lord privy seal: Duke of Portland.

---

[1] The cabinet was formed in 1812.

Home secretary: W. Sturges Bourne.
Foreign secretary: Viscount Dudley and Ward.
Secretary for war and colonies: Viscount Goderich (formerly F. J. Robinson).
Master-general of the ordnance: Marquis of Anglesey.
President of the board of trade and treasurer of the navy: W. Huskisson.
President of the board of control: C. W. W. Wynn.
Chancellor of the duchy of Lancaster: Lord Bexley.
Secretary at war: Viscount Palmerston.

Changes

May *1827*: the earl of Carlisle and G. Tierney entered the cabinet as first commissioner of woods and forests and master of the mint; the marquis of Lansdowne became cabinet minister without office until July, when he succeeded Sturges Bourne as home secretary. Sturges Bourne then became first commissioner of woods and forests, the earl of Carlisle was promoted lord privy seal, and the duke of Portland remained in the cabinet as a minister without office.

3. GODERICH'S CABINET

(formed August 1827)

Prime minister and first lord of the treasury: Viscount Goderich.
Lord chancellor: Lord Lyndhurst.
Lord president of the council: Duke of Portland.
Lord privy seal: Earl of Carlisle.
Chancellor of the exchequer: J. C. Herries.
Home secretary: Marquis of Lansdowne.
Foreign secretary: Viscount Dudley and Ward (earl of Dudley, 1827).
Secretary for war and colonies: W. Huskisson.
Master-general of the ordnance: Marquis of Anglesey.
President of the board of trade and treasurer of the navy: C. Grant.
President of the board of control: C. W. W. Wynn.
Master of the mint: G. Tierney.
Chancellor of the duchy of Lancaster: Lord Bexley.
First commissioner of woods and forests: W. Sturges Bourne.
Secretary at war: Viscount Palmerston.

4. WELLINGTON'S CABINET

(formed January 1828)

Prime minister and first lord of the treasury: Duke of Wellington.
Lord chancellor: Lord Lyndhurst.
Lord president of the council: Earl Bathurst.
Lord privy seal: Lord Ellenborough.
Chancellor of the exchequer: H. Goulburn.
Home secretary: R. Peel (after May 1830 Sir R. Peel).
Foreign secretary: Earl of Dudley.
Secretary for war and colonies: W. Huskisson.

President of the board of trade and treasurer of the navy: C. Grant.
President of the board of control: Viscount Melville.
Master of the mint: J. C. Herries.
Chancellor of the duchy of Lancaster: Earl of Aberdeen.
Secretary at war: Viscount Palmerston.

Changes

May–June 1828: W. Huskisson, Viscount Palmerston, the earl of Dudley, and C. Grant resigned. Sir G. Murray succeeded Huskisson; Viscount Palmerston's successor, Sir H. Hardinge, was not a cabinet minister. The earl of Aberdeen became foreign secretary; his successor at the duchy of Lancaster was not in the cabinet; W. Vesey-Fitzgerald became president of the board of trade and treasurer of the navy. *September 1828*: Viscount Melville became first lord of the admiralty[1] and was succeeded as president of the board of control by Lord Ellenborough. *June 1829*: the earl of Rosslyn entered the cabinet as lord privy seal. *February 1830*: Herries became president of the board of trade.

5. GREY'S CABINET

(*formed November 1830*)

Prime minister and first lord of the treasury: Earl Grey.
Lord chancellor: Lord Brougham.
Lord president of the council: Marquis of Lansdowne.
Lord privy seal: Lord Durham.
Chancellor of the exchequer: Viscount Althorp.
Home secretary: Viscount Melbourne.
Foreign secretary: Viscount Palmerston.
Secretary for war and colonies: Viscount Goderich.
First lord of the admiralty: Sir James Graham.
President of the board of control: C. Grant.
Chancellor of the duchy of Lancaster: Lord Holland.
Postmaster-general: Duke of Richmond.
Cabinet minister without office: Earl of Carlisle.

Changes

June 1831: Lord John Russell and E. G. Stanley (later Lord Stanley and earl of Derby) entered the cabinet as paymaster-general and chief secretary for Ireland. *March 1833*: Stanley became secretary for war and colonies. *April 1833*: the earl of Ripon (formerly Viscount Goderich) succeeded Lord Durham as lord privy seal. *May–June 1834*: the earl of Ripon, Sir J. Graham, the duke of Richmond, and Stanley resigned. T. Spring Rice became secretary of war and colonies and the earl of Carlisle lord privy seal; Lord Auckland, who had been president of the board of trade and master of the mint without a seat in the cabinet, became first lord of the admiralty;

[1] From Apr. 1827 to Sept. 1828 the duke of Clarence (subsequently William IV) was lord high admiral; he did not sit in the cabinet.

J. Abercromby joined the cabinet as president of the board of trade and treasurer of the navy, and master of the mint; E. Ellice, who had been secretary at war since April 1833, was admitted to the cabinet. The duke of Richmond's successor as postmaster-general was not in the cabinet.

6. MELBOURNE'S FIRST CABINET
(*formed July 1834*)

Prime minister and first lord of the treasury: Viscount Melbourne.
Lord chancellor: Lord Brougham.
Lord president of the council: Marquis of Lansdowne.
Lord privy seal: Earl of Mulgrave.
Chancellor of the exchequer: Viscount Althorp.
Home secretary: Viscount Duncannon.
Foreign secretary: Viscount Palmerston.
Secretary for war and colonies: T. Spring Rice.
First lord of the admiralty: Earl of Auckland.
President of the board of trade and treasurer of the navy: C. E. Poulett Thomson.
President of the board of control: C. Grant.
Master of the mint: J. Abercromby.
Chancellor of the duchy of Lancaster: Lord Holland.
Secretary at war: E. Ellice.
First commissioner of woods and forests: Sir J. C. Hobhouse.
Paymaster-general: Lord J. Russell.

After Melbourne's resignation in November 1834, and before the appointment of Peel in December 1834, the duke of Wellington held provisionally the offices of prime minister and first lord of the treasury, home secretary, foreign secretary, and secretary for war and colonies, with Lord Lyndhurst as lord chancellor and Lord Denman as chancellor of the exchequer.

7. PEEL'S FIRST CABINET
(*formed December 1834*)

Prime minister and first lord of the treasury⎫ Sir R. Peel.
Chancellor of the exchequer   ⎭
Lord chancellor: Lord Lyndhurst.
Lord president of the council: Earl of Rosslyn.
Lord privy seal: Lord Wharncliffe.
Home secretary: H. Goulburn.
Foreign secretary: Duke of Wellington.
Secretary for war and colonies: Earl of Aberdeen.
First lord of the admiralty: Earl de Grey.
President of the board of trade⎫ A. Baring.
Master of the mint   ⎭
President of the board of control: Lord Ellenborough.
Secretary at war: J. C. Herries.
Paymaster-general: Sir E. Knatchbull.

8. MELBOURNE'S SECOND CABINET
(*formed April 1835*)

Prime minister and first lord of the treasury: Viscount Melbourne.
Lord chancellor: Lord Cottenham (appointed Jan. 1836; from April 1835 till Jan. 1836 the great seal was in commission).
Lord president of the council: Marquis of Lansdowne.
Lord privy seal ⎫
First commissioner of woods and forests ⎭ Viscount Duncannon.
Chancellor of the exchequer: T. Spring Rice.
Home secretary: Lord J. Russell.
Foreign secretary: Viscount Palmerston.
Secretary for war and colonies: C. Grant (cr. Lord Glenelg, May 1835).
First lord of the admiralty: Lord Auckland.
President of the board of trade: C. E. Poulett Thomson.
President of the board of control: Sir J. C. Hobhouse.
Chancellor of the duchy of Lancaster: Lord Holland.
Secretary at war: Viscount Howick.

Changes

September 1835: the earl of Minto succeeded Lord Auckland as first lord of the admiralty on the latter's appointment as governor-general of India. *February 1839*: Lord Glenelg resigned; the marquis of Normanby entered the cabinet as secretary for war and colonies and Lord Morpeth as chief secretary for Ireland. *August 1839*: Sir F. T. Baring succeeded Spring Rice as chancellor of the exchequer, and H. Labouchere succeeded Poulett Thomson as president of the board of trade. *September 1839*: Lord J. Russell and Lord Normanby exchanged offices; Lord Howick resigned and T. B. Macaulay entered the cabinet as secretary at war. *January 1840*: the earl of Clarendon became lord privy seal, and, in October (temporarily), chancellor of the duchy of Lancaster on Lord Holland's death. Lord Duncannon retained his other office and a seat in the cabinet. *January 1841*: Sir G. Grey entered the cabinet as chancellor of the duchy of Lancaster.

9. PEEL'S SECOND CABINET
(*formed September 1841*)

Prime minister and first lord of the treasury: Sir R. Peel.
Lord chancellor: Lord Lyndhurst.
Lord president of the council: Lord Wharncliffe.
Lord privy seal: Duke of Buckingham.
Chancellor of the exchequer: H. Goulburn.
Home secretary: Sir James Graham.
Foreign secretary: Earl of Aberdeen.
Secretary for war and colonies: Viscount Stanley.
First lord of the admiralty: Earl of Haddington.
President of the board of trade: Earl of Ripon.
President of the board of control: Lord Ellenborough (cr. earl 1844).
Secretary at war: Sir H. Hardinge.

Paymaster-general: Sir E. Knatchbull.
Cabinet minister without office: Duke of Wellington.

Changes

October 1841: Lord Fitzgerald (formerly W. Vesey-Fitzgerald) entered the cabinet as president of the board of control on Lord Ellenborough's appointment as governor-general of India. *January 1842*: the duke of Buckingham resigned and the duke of Buccleuch took his place as lord privy seal. *May 1843*: the earl of Ripon succeeded Lord Fitzgerald as president of the board of control; his successor as president of the board of trade was W. E. Gladstone. *May 1844*: Lord Granville Somerset entered the cabinet as chancellor of the duchy of Lancaster; Sir H. Hardinge was appointed governor-general of India; his successor as secretary at war was not in the cabinet. *January 1845*: W. E. Gladstone and (February) Sir E. Knatchbull resigned; their successors were not in the cabinet; the earl of Lincoln joined the cabinet as first commissioner of woods and forests. *May 1845*: S. Herbert joined the cabinet as secretary at war. *December 1845*: Lord Stanley resigned and W. E. Gladstone succeeded to his office; the earl of Dalhousie, president of the board of trade, joined the cabinet. Lord Wharncliffe died, and in the following month the duke of Buccleuch became lord president of the council; the earl of Haddington succeeded him as lord privy seal. Lord Ellenborough returned to the cabinet as first lord of the admiralty. *February 1846*: Lord Lincoln left the cabinet to become chief secretary for Ireland.

10. RUSSELL'S FIRST CABINET

(*formed July 1846*)

Prime minister and first lord of the treasury: Lord J. Russell.
Lord chancellor: Lord Cottenham.
Lord president of the council: Marquis of Lansdowne.
Lord privy seal: Earl of Minto.
Chancellor of the exchequer: Sir C. Wood.
Home secretary: Sir G. Grey.
Foreign secretary: Viscount Palmerston.
Secretary for war and colonies: Earl Grey.
First lord of the admiralty: Earl of Auckland.
President of the board of trade: Earl of Clarendon.
President of the board of control: Sir J. C. Hobhouse (cr. Lord Broughton 1851).
Chancellor of the duchy of Lancaster: Lord Campbell.
First commissioner of woods and forests: Lord Morpeth (earl of Carlisle 1848).
Chief secretary for Ireland: H. Labouchere.
Postmaster-general: Marquis of Clanricarde.
Paymaster-general: T. B. Macaulay.

Changes

May 1847: H. Labouchere succeeded the earl of Clarendon as president of the board of trade. *August 1847*: T. B. Macaulay resigned; his successor did not sit in the cabinet. *January 1849*: on the death of the earl of Auckland F. T. Baring became first lord of the admiralty. *March 1850*: the earl of Carlisle succeeded Lord Campbell as chancellor of the duchy of Lancaster. *June 1850*: on Lord Cottenham's retirement the great seal remained in commission until the appointment of Lord Truro in July 1850. *February 1851*: Russell resigned, but resumed office a fortnight later. *October 1851*: Lord Seymour, Fox Maule, and Earl Granville entered the cabinet as first commissioner of works, secretary at war, and paymaster-general. *December* 1851: Earl Granville succeeded Viscount Palmerston as foreign secretary. *January 1852*: Fox Maule succeeded Lord Broughton as president of the board of control.

11. DERBY'S FIRST CABINET

(*formed February 1852*)

Prime minister and first lord of the treasury: Earl of Derby.
Lord chancellor: Lord St. Leonards.
Lord president of the council: Earl of Lonsdale.
Lord privy seal: Marquis of Salisbury.
Chancellor of the exchequer: B. Disraeli.
Home secretary: Spencer H. Walpole.
Foreign secretary: Earl of Malmesbury.
Secretary for war and colonies: Sir J. Pakington.
First lord of the admiralty: Duke of Northumberland.
President of the board of trade: J. W. Henley.
President of the board of control: J. C. Herries.
First commissioner of works: Lord John Manners.
Postmaster-general: Earl of Hardwicke.

12. ABERDEEN'S CABINET

(*formed December 1852*)

Prime minister and first lord of the treasury: Earl of Aberdeen.
Lord chancellor: Lord Cranworth.
Lord president of the council: Earl Granville.
Lord privy seal: Duke of Argyll.
Chancellor of the exchequer: W. E. Gladstone.
Home secretary: Viscount Palmerston.
Foreign secretary: Lord J. Russell.
Secretary for war and colonies: Duke of Newcastle.
First lord of the admiralty: Sir James Graham.
President of the board of control: Sir C. Wood.
First commissioner of works: Sir William Molesworth.
Secretary at war: Sidney Herbert.
Cabinet minister without office: Marquis of Lansdowne.

Changes

February 1853: Lord John Russell ceased to be foreign secretary and remained in the cabinet as a minister without office; the earl of Clarendon became foreign secretary. *June 1854*: a new office of secretary of state for the colonies was created in June 1854, and given to Sir G. Grey; the duke of Newcastle remained in the cabinet as secretary for war, and at the end of the year the secretaryship at war was abolished. Earl Granville became chancellor of the duchy of Lancaster without a seat in the cabinet, and Lord John Russell took his place as lord president of the council. *January 1855*: Lord John Russell resigned.

13. PALMERSTON'S FIRST CABINET
(formed February 1855)

Prime minister and first lord of the treasury: Viscount Palmerston.
Lord chancellor: Lord Cranworth.
Lord president of the council: Earl Granville.
Lord privy seal: Duke of Argyll.
Chancellor of the exchequer: W. E. Gladstone.
Home secretary: Sir G. Grey.
Foreign secretary: Earl of Clarendon.
Secretary for war: Lord Panmure (formerly Fox Maule).
Secretary for the colonies: Sidney Herbert.
First lord of the admiralty: Sir James Graham.
President of the board of control: Sir C. Wood.
First commissioner of works: Sir William Molesworth.
Postmaster-general: Viscount Canning.
Cabinet minister without office: Marquis of Lansdowne.

Changes

February 1855: W. E. Gladstone, Sidney Herbert, and Sir James Graham resigned; Sir G. Cornewall Lewis became chancellor of the exchequer, Lord John Russell secretary for the colonies, and Sir C. Wood first lord of the admiralty; R. V. Smith entered the cabinet as president of the board of control. *March 1855*: the earl of Harrowby and Lord Stanley of Alderley entered the cabinet as chancellor of the duchy of Lancaster and president of the board of trade. *July 1855*: Viscount Canning left the cabinet on his appointment as governor-general of India, and Lord John Russell resigned; Sir William Molesworth became secretary for the colonies; his successor as first commissioner of works did not sit in the cabinet. *October 1855*: on Sir William Molesworth's death, H. Labouchere entered the cabinet as secretary for the colonies. *November 1855*: the duke of Argyll took the office of postmaster-general. *December 1855*: the earl of Harrowby became lord privy seal, and M. T. Baines entered the cabinet as chancellor of the duchy of Lancaster. *December 1857*: the earl of Harrowby resigned, and the marquis of Clanricarde joined the cabinet as lord privy seal.

14. DERBY'S SECOND CABINET
(formed February 1858)

Prime minister and first lord of the treasury: Earl of Derby.
Lord chancellor: Lord Chelmsford.
Lord president of the council: Marquis of Salisbury.

Lord privy seal: Earl of Hardwicke.
Chancellor of the exchequer: B. Disraeli.
Home secretary: Spencer H. Walpole.
Foreign secretary: Earl of Malmesbury.
Secretary for war: General Peel.
Secretary for the colonies: Lord Stanley.
First lord of the admiralty: Sir J. Pakington.
President of the board of trade: J. W. Henley.
President of the board of control: Earl of Ellenborough.
First commissioner of works: Lord John Manners.

Changes

May 1858: On the resignation of the earl of Ellenborough, Lord Stanley became president of the board of control, and was succeeded as secretary for the colonies by Sir E. Bulwer-Lytton. *August 1858*: the office of president of the board of control was abolished, and a new secretaryship of state for India took its place. *February 1859*: Spencer Walpole and J. W. Henley resigned, and were succeeded in the cabinet by T. H. Sotheron-Estcourt and the earl of Donoughmore.

15. PALMERSTON'S SECOND CABINET
(*formed June 1859*)

Prime minister and first lord of the treasury: Viscount Palmerston.
Lord chancellor: Lord Campbell.
Lord president of the council: Earl Granville.
Lord privy seal: Duke of Argyll.
Chancellor of the exchequer: W. E. Gladstone.
Home secretary: Sir G. Cornewall Lewis.
Foreign secretary: Lord John Russell (earl Russell 1861).
Secretary for war: Sidney Herbert (cr. Lord Herbert of Lea 1860).
Secretary for the colonies: Duke of Newcastle.
First lord of the admiralty: Duke of Somerset.
Secretary for India: Sir C. Wood (cr. Viscount Halifax 1866).
Chancellor of the duchy of Lancaster: Sir G. Grey.
Chief secretary for Ireland: E. Cardwell.
Postmaster-general: Earl of Elgin.
President of the poor law board: T. Milner-Gibson.

Changes

July 1859: T. Milner-Gibson became president of the board of trade, and was succeeded as president of the poor law board by C. P. Villiers. *March 1860*: the earl of Elgin went on a mission to China, and was succeeded as postmaster-general by Lord Stanley of Alderley. *June 1861*: on the death of Lord Campbell, Lord Westbury became lord chancellor. *July 1861*: Lord Herbert of Lea resigned, and Sir G. Cornewall Lewis took his place as secretary for war; Sir G. Grey became home secretary and E. Cardwell chancellor of the duchy of Lancaster. *April 1863*: on the death of Sir G.

Cornewall Lewis, Earl de Grey became secretary for war. *April 1864*: the duke of Newcastle resigned, and E. Cardwell became secretary for the colonies. *July 1865*: Lord Westbury resigned, and Lord Cranworth entered the cabinet as lord chancellor.

16. RUSSELL'S SECOND CABINET
(formed October 1865)

Earl Russell became prime minister and first lord of the treasury, and the earl of Clarendon succeeded him as foreign secretary; G. J. Goschen entered the cabinet as chancellor of the duchy of Lancaster in January 1866. On the resignation of Sir C. Wood in February 1866 Earl de Grey became secretary for India and the marquis of Hartington joined the cabinet as secretary for war. Otherwise the cabinet remained unchanged after Palmerston's death.

17. DERBY'S THIRD CABINET
(formed June 1866)

Prime minister and first lord of the treasury: Earl of Derby.
Lord chancellor: Lord Chelmsford.
Lord president of the council: Duke of Buckingham.
Lord privy seal: Earl of Malmesbury.
Chancellor of the exchequer: B. Disraeli.
Home secretary: Spencer H. Walpole.
Foreign secretary: Lord Stanley.
Secretary for war: General Peel.
Secretary for the colonies: Earl of Carnarvon.
First lord of the admiralty: Sir J. Pakington.
President of the board of trade: Sir Stafford Northcote.
Secretary for India: Viscount Cranborne.
First commissioner of works: Lord John Manners.
Chief secretary for Ireland: Lord Naas (earl of Mayo 1867).
President of the poor law board: Gathorne Hardy.

Changes

March 1867: the earl of Carnarvon, General Peel, and Viscount Cranborne resigned; the duke of Buckingham became secretary for the colonies, Sir J. Pakington secretary for war, and Sir Stafford Northcote secretary for India. The duke of Marlborough, H. Lowry-Corry, and the duke of Richmond entered the cabinet as lord president of the council, first lord of the admiralty, and president of the board of trade. *May 1867*: Spencer Walpole resigned the home secretaryship and remained in the cabinet as a minister without office; Gathorne Hardy became home secretary.

18. DISRAELI'S FIRST CABINET
(formed February 1868)

B. Disraeli became prime minister and first lord of the treasury, and G. Ward Hunt took his place as chancellor of the exchequer. The earl of

Mayo left the cabinet to become viceroy of India. Otherwise there were no other changes in the cabinet after the earl of Derby's resignation.

19. GLADSTONE'S FIRST CABINET

(to December 1870: formed December 1868)

Prime minister and first lord of the treasury: W. E. Gladstone.
Lord chancellor: Lord Hatherley.
Lord president of the council: Earl de Grey.
Lord privy seal: Earl of Kimberley.
Chancellor of the exchequer: R. Lowe.
Home secretary: H. A. Bruce.
Foreign secretary: Earl of Clarendon.
Secretary for war: E. Cardwell.
Secretary for the colonies: Earl Granville.
First lord of the admiralty: H. C. E. Childers.
President of the board of trade: J. Bright.
Secretary for India: Duke of Argyll.
President of the poor law board: G. J. Goschen.
Postmaster-general: Marquis of Hartington.
Chief secretary for Ireland: C. S. Fortescue.

Changes

June 1870: on the death of the earl of Clarendon, Earl Granville became foreign secretary. *July 1870*: the earl of Kimberley became secretary for the colonies, Viscount Halifax joined the cabinet as lord privy seal, and W. E. Forster as vice-president of the council. *December 1870*: John Bright resigned.

INDEX

Abdul Medjid, sultan of Turkey, 237, 252.

Aberdeen, 4th earl of, 124, 227, 247, 276, 305, 527; biog., 124 n.3; prime minister in coalition (1852), 165–7; *entente* with France, 240–3; eastern policy and the outbreak of the Crimean war, 254, 256–8, 261–4; resigns over Crimean inquiry, 286; negotiations with United States, 305.

Aborigines, committee on treatment of, 390–1.

Abyssinia, 442 n.1.

Academy, Royal, 578, 587, 589.

Acland, Sir H., 521, 619.

— Sir T., 90 n. 4, 268 n. 2.

Acton, Lord, 513, 555, 557.

Adams, C. F., 310–12.

Aden, 236, 431, 414.

Afghan war, first, causes of, 416–17; supported by cabinet, 417–18; occupation of Kabul, 418; retreat from Kabul, 419–20; reoccupation of Kabul, 420–1.

Africa, South, *see* Cape Colony.

— West, 240–1, 267, 374–5.

Agricultural disturbances (1830), 79–80.

Akkerman, convention of, 220.

Alabama case, *see* United States.

Åland Islands, 235, 274, 289.

Albert, Prince, of Saxe-Coburg-Gotha (Prince Consort of England), 104, 178 n. 4, 257, 301–2 n. 1, 500, 589; biog., 106 n. 1; marriage, 106; character and ideas, 106–8; differences with Palmerston, 224, 247–50; modifies note to United States, 308; death of, 314–15.

Alexander I of Russia, 196–8, 218; proposes Holy Alliance, 199; attitude towards European revolutions, 201–4, 208; death of, 217.

— II of Russia, 289.

Allan, W., biog., 157 n. 1.

Allowance system, 1, 9, 449–50.

Almond, H. H., 484 n. 1.

Althorp, Viscount (3rd earl Spencer), 346; biog., 56 n. 5; leader of the whigs in the house of commons (1830), 56; dislike of office, 57 n. 1; supports Canning, 75; supports reform bills, 78, 81, 84; opposes coercion bill, 98, 346; succeeds his father, 101.

American Civil War, *see* United States.

Amherst, Lord, governor-general of

Bengal, 413; *see also* Burmese war (first).

Anderson, J., 494–5.

Animals, Prevention of cruelty to, 470 n. 1.

Anson, General G., 434–5.

Anti-corn law league, 89 n. 2; foundation of, 118; activities, 118–21.

Applegarth, R., 613; biog., 613 n. 1.

Arbuthnot, C., 53 n. 3; biog., 107 n. 1.

Architects, Royal Institute of British, 578.

Army, British, condition of (1815–54), 180 n. 1, 265–71; reforms after Crimean war, 291–3; *see also under* Crimean war.

Arnold, M., 481 n. 1, 531, 533, 623; biog., 499 n. 2; poetry of, 538.

— T., 486–7, 498, 507; biog., 486 n. 1.

Art, Royal Society of, 500.

Arundel Society, 594.

Ashanti, Kingdom of, 375 n. 1.

Ashburton, Lord (A. Baring), 211, 305.

Ashley, Lord, *see* Shaftesbury, 7th earl of.

Ashton, T. S., 11 n. 1.

Aspinall, A., 24 n. 1, 28 n. 1, 56 n. 1, 69 n. 1, 75 n. 1, 78 n. 2, 110 n. 1, 223 n. 1, 466 n. 1.

Attwood, T., 134, 137, 607.

Auckland, 1st earl of, biog., 416 n. 2; governor-general of India, 416, 428; mistaken policy towards Afghanistan, 416–21; *see also* Afghan war.

Austen, Jane, 32.

Australia, early development of, 384–7; transportation abolished, 385–7; discovery of gold, 125, 385, 387; 'systematic colonization', 387–8; grant of responsible government, 388–9.

Austria-Hungary, 195, 197–200, 217–18, 223, 227, 233–5, 237–8, 240–1, 315–16; and Italy, 202–3, 245–8, 298–304; Crimean war, 254, 259, 261–4, 288–91 n. 2; Franco-Austrian war, 301; Schleswig-Holstein question, 319–23; Austro-Prussian war, 323–5.

Bagehot, W., 14 n. 4, 20 n. 2, 110, 552; biog., 552 n. 1.

Bailey, P. J., 534.

Bank Charter Acts (1833), 60, 112; (1844), 112.

Barnard, Sir H., 435.

Barrow, Sir J., 45 n. 2.

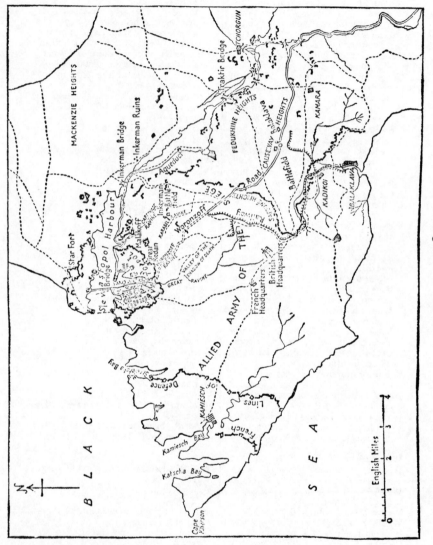

3. CRIMEA, 1855

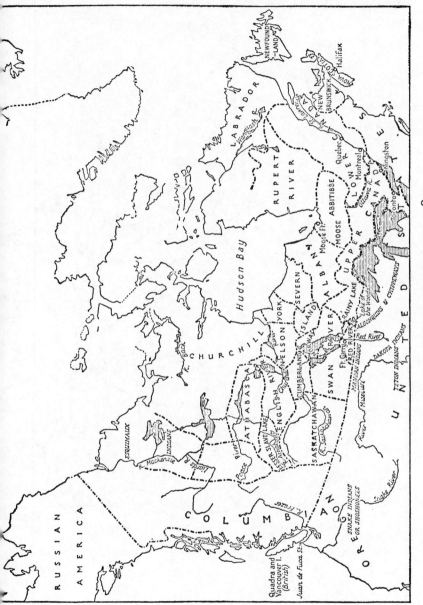

4. BRITISH NORTH AMERICA, 1849

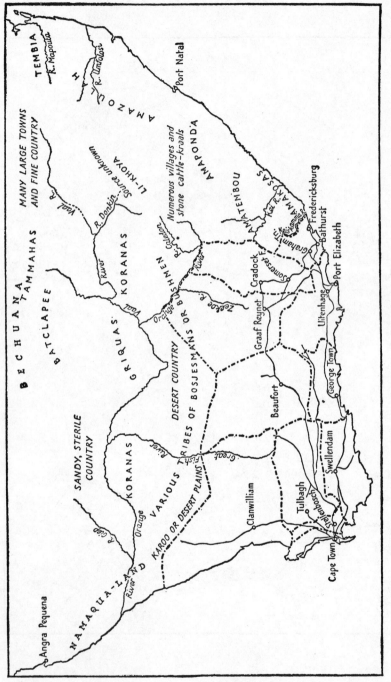

5. SOUTH AFRICA, 1849